WOMEN DURING THE CIVIL WAR

WOMEN DURING THE CIVIL WAR

AN ENCYCLOPEDIA

JUDITH E. HARPER

Routledge
Taylor & Francis Group
New York   London

First published in 2004 by Routledge.

Routledge
Taylor & Francis Group
270 Madison Avenue
New York, NY 10016

Routledge
Taylor & Francis Group
2 Park Square
Milton Park, Abingdon
Oxon OX14 4RN

© 2007 by Taylor & Francis Group, LLC
Routledge is an imprint of Taylor & Francis Group, an Informa business

Printed in the United States of America on acid-free paper
10 9 8 7 6 5 4 3 2 1

International Standard Book Number-10: 0-415-95574-2 (Softcover)
International Standard Book Number-13: 978-0-415-95574-4 (Softcover)

Visit the Taylor & Francis Web site at
http://www.taylorandfrancis.com

and the Routledge Web site at

CONTENTS

Foreword   vii

Introduction   ix

Acknowledgments   xiii

List of Entries   xv

Entries A to Z   1

Glossary   473

Bibliography   477

Index   503

FOREWORD

Back when I entered graduate school at the University of California in the mid-1980s, only a few historians displayed a serious interest in examining the intersection of women and the American Civil War. At the close of the war itself, Frank Moore's *Women of the War* (1866) and Linus P. Brockett and Mary C. Vaughan's *Woman's Work in the Civil War* (1867) had brought to public attention the contributions that numerous individual women of the North had made to the Union war effort, and writers in the vanquished Confederacy had sought to do the same for a host of stalwart female supporters of the white Southern cause. But it was fully a century after Appomattox before Mary Elizabeth Massey's *Bonnet Brigades* (1966) revived for a new age a good chunk of the history of Northern and Southern women's involvement in the Civil War, and also pondered to some degree the impact of the Civil War on American women's lives.

Despite Massey's efforts, it took almost two decades more for a new generation of scholars to fully recognize the depth and breadth of the gap that remained in the historiography of women and the American Civil War, and to commit wholeheartedly to trying to fill that gap with their own thoughtfully composed products of what invariably amounted to very challenging research. Since the mid-1980s, however, the situation has changed dramatically. Nowadays, it is actually possible for a college professor to develop a semester-long seminar entirely devoted to the topic of women and the Civil War, and there is even a surplus of intellectually challenging, analytically sound, and (yes!) reader-friendly resources available for students to consider. Certainly there is a good deal of work left to be done, but we have come a long way from assuming (and proclaiming) that the Civil War was men's work alone, something that Moore, Brockett and Vaughan, and those who actually lived through the war obviously already knew to be incorrect.

Judith Harper's *Women During the Civil War: An Encyclopedia* witnesses to, and also augments, the enormous strides taken in recent years toward understanding the diversity of roles played by women in the Civil War (and in Civil War America generally), and the crucial and sometimes surprising ways in which the war affected

American women's lives, their perspectives, their opportunities, and their futures. Although no encyclopedia ever exhausts the topic it explores, to Harper's great credit she pushes the boundaries of our knowledge to include not only those categories of Civil War women whose stories have by now become relatively familiar (nurses, ladies aid activists, spies, soldiers), but also women in the arts, farm women, business women, nuns, industrial workers, and many from other walks of life. Harper also makes a point of bringing non-white women into the heart of the picture: slave women, freedwomen, Native American women, and Mexican-American women all have a place here, collectively as well as individually. The book contains 128 entries varying in length and scope. A compulsively linear reader such as myself can quite happily read them one after another, in the order in which they appear. Alternatively, one could initially explore a single topic, but beware: rather like Internet links that draw the innocent from one site to another, each individual entry in Harper's encyclopedia entices readers to turn to one or more others. No matter what the approach, an encounter with *Women During the Civil War* offers much new and intriguing food for thought, even to those of us who thought we knew a bit about the subject already.

Elizabeth D. Leonard

INTRODUCTION

Women During the Civil War: An Encyclopedia is the first A to Z reference volume to offer a panoramic presentation of American women during the most turbulent era in U.S. history. Previous works have focused solely on the lives of women who contributed to or were affected by the war itself. This encyclopedia examines the experiences of women from all regions, races, classes, and leading ethnic groups (Irish, German, Norwegian, Jewish, Chinese) during the years 1861 to 1865, including those whose lives were relatively untouched by war. Drawing on a vast collection of sources from the nineteenth century to the present day, from Louisa May Alcott's *Hospital Days* (1863) to Lauren Cook and DeAnne Blanton's *They Fought Like Demons: Women Soldiers in the American Civil War* (2002), this book presents the wartime experiences of white women of the North and South, African-American women born free and in slavery, Native American women, Mexican-American women, frontier women of the West, and immigrant women.

The articles in this book may surprise readers, regardless of their level of familiarity with U.S. history. Persistent popular conceptions of the Civil War and of nineteenth-century American society do not recognize women as having been integral participants. Facts and folklore about men's contributions to the Civil War—sensationalized and romanticized in movies, television, and literature—are well documented and loom large in the nation's collective memory. The generals, soldiers, and battles are well known to most Americans. Yet, despite the contributions of tens of thousands of women, the general public is aware of the war work of only a handful—Clara Barton, Harriet Tubman, Mary Boykin Chesnut, Louisa May Alcott, or Julia Ward Howe. Although relatively little has been reported on the roles of women, many thousands of women nurses and hundreds of female soldiers risked their lives for the United States and the Confederate States of America. Tens of thousands of other women in the North and the South labored within soldiers' aid societies to provide food, clothing, and comfort to the troops. Thousands of women in the North were outspoken about slavery and worked toward emancipation as abolitionists, orators, writers, and artists. In the South, women from all classes actively supported the

Confederacy as novelists, writers, government workers, factory women, and agricultural workers.

The words of the women who endured the Civil War years were vital to the research of the essays in this book. Women's diaries and correspondence, both published and unpublished, bring to light their daily activities, the issues that troubled and captivated them, the values that centered their lives, and the emotions that revealed their hearts. The examination of women's Civil War-era pamphlets, memoirs, newspaper accounts, essays, and fiction makes it apparent that women's viewpoints were a vital part of American letters. The secondary sources consulted for this book include the work of historians and researchers from the mid-nineteenth century to the twenty-first century. The scholarship of the past fifteen years has been particularly illuminating, as it has reexamined women's involvement in the war effort while also revealing the everyday lives of the millions of women of all races, classes, and regions who did not record their experiences.

This volume is designed to be of interest to scholars, students, Civil War buffs and reenactors, and the general public. Ranging in length from 400 to 4,000 words, the 128 entries in this volume are composed of a mix of biographical articles and thematic essays. The biographies examine the Civil War experiences of famous or notable women, and the thematic entries explore the worlds of large groups of women, including women living in the West, industrial workers, doctors, military women, Native American women, Mexican-American women, Catholic nuns, prostitutes, and teachers of the former slaves. Other thematic articles, such as "United States Sanitary Commission" or "Gunboat Societies," concentrate on women's work within the organizations that directed women's war contributions. Numerous articles describe women's involvement in key events during the Civil War: "Bread Rebellions" describes the experiences of Southern working-class poor and women who protested food shortages in the Confederacy; "Gettysburg," "Vicksburg," and "Antietam (Sharpsburg)," portray the experiences of women who endured some of the harshest fighting of the war and tried to save the lives of the wounded. Other articles, such as "Family Life," "Courtship and Marriage," "Girlhood and Adolescence," "Religion," "Education," and "Diaries," examine the personal lives of women of all ages and the impact of the war upon them.

Each essay includes extensive cross-references, directing readers to related articles within the encyclopedia, as well as suggestions for further reading and exploration. The sources mentioned in the Selected Readings section have been chosen because they provide background information on the topic and are most likely to be widely available to readers interested in pursuing the subject. An extensive bibliography, located at the end of the book, will direct scholars researching a topic to the primary and secondary sources of each essay. A glossary is also provided for students and readers who need assistance identifying and defining the personalities, organizations, institutions, and terms specifically related to the Civil War era.

This encyclopedia does not claim to be exhaustive on the subject of women during the Civil War. The aim was not to include an essay on every notable American woman of the period, but to present a selection of individual women and groups of women who significantly contributed to the war effort and to American culture and society during the war years. Many more notable women can be found in the index as they may be discussed in other essays. The work and war-related experiences of Drs. Elizabeth and Emily Blackwell, for example, are presented in "Doctors" and in "Woman's Central Association of Relief," the organization they founded. Similarly, Louisa Lee Schuyler and Abigail "Abby" May, because they were exceptional branch leaders within the United States Sanitary Commission, are discussed thoroughly in the "United States Sanitary Commission" and "Sanitary Fairs" articles. Information about Louisa May Alcott can be found, however, not only in the biographical article about her, but also in the entries "Abolitionist Women," "Literary Women," "Nurses," and "United States Sanitary Commission." The index and the cross-references will help readers find the most comprehensive biographical information on individual women within this work.

If there is one truism that emerges from the study of women during the Civil War era, it is the acknowledgment that an abundance of research remains to be done. Current scholarship has opened doors and laid the groundwork for an examination of women's activities in the war effort and in business, agriculture, literature, education, and industry. Yet only a small fraction of local, state, and federal government records have been analyzed. Troves of letters and diaries, as well as the public writings of women in newspapers and magazines, are as yet untouched. Over the course of the writing of this book, numerous essays had to be revised as new information came to light. Interest in women during the Civil War era remains high as of this writing, and it is likely that the next decade will see a proliferation of books and journal articles uncovering novel aspects of women's war experiences, both public and private, thereby enlarging and enriching our understanding of women in America during the mid-nineteenth century.

Judith E. Harper

ACKNOWLEDGMENTS

Over the course of the five years that I spent researching and writing this book, I was fortunate to have the assistance and goodwill of innumerable librarians, scholars, archivists, and writers. Living close to Boston must be one of the greatest blessings that can befall a historian. My quest for information about women during the Civil War led me to more than a dozen university, college, and public libraries in the Greater Boston area.

My deepest gratitude is reserved for the reference librarians of the Boston Athenaeum, who, despite a massive renovation project, kept the books and journal articles flowing in my direction. What the Athenaeum's collections or my other library haunts could not provide was secured for me via the Athenaeum's inter-library loan program. My thanks to Lisa Starzyk-Weldon, Stephen Nonack, Rebecka Persson, and Jim Woodman. A special debt is also owed to Sally Pierce, Curator of Prints and Photographs at the Boston Athenaeum, who gave liberally of her time and knowledge.

I would also like to extend my thanks to the library staffs at Wellesley College, the Arthur and Elizabeth Schlesinger Library on the History of Women in America at Harvard University, the Boston Public Library, Boston University, Brandeis University, Northeastern University, and the Westwood and Canton Public Libraries. In July 1998, I had the pleasure of investigating manuscript collections at the Museum of the Confederacy and the Virginia Historical Society in Richmond, Virginia, where archivists and other specialists graciously fulfilled all of my research requests.

When books did not yield the answers to my questions, a number of scholars gave freely of their expertise. Many thanks to Herman Hattaway, Michael Chesson, Elizabeth Varon, Catherine Clinton, Jean Fagan Yellin, John Coski at the Museum of the Confederacy, DeAnne Blanton, Jeanie Attie, Judith Giesberg, Matt Gallman, Daniel J. Hoisington, Eileen Conklin, Leah Berkowitz, and Thomas Brown.

When I was first getting my feet wet with this project, I had the good fortune to attend the 1998 Conference on Women in the Civil War at Hood College in Frederick, Maryland, where I met numerous historians and researchers. In the past year, the newly formed Society for Women and the Civil War continues the tradition of nurturing research in this ever-developing area.

Also in 1998, Diana Loski, my tour guide at Gettysburg National Military Park, spent an entire summer afternoon with me, driving me all over the park and to battle-related sites in the town of Gettysburg. Her exuberant enthusiasm and knowledge of the women of Gettysburg afforded me my first vista of the enormity of women's contributions.

For their generous assistance, I'd like to thank Carlin Timmons at the Fort Sumter National Monument, Terrence Winschel at the Vicksburg National Military Park, and Ted Alexander at the Antietam National Battlefield.

A special thank you to my agent Elizabeth Frost-Knappman of New England Publishing Associates for believing unequivocally in this project and for her guidance and patience through the trials that beset me on the path to publication. I am also obliged to Victoria Harlow of NEPA.

A special thank you to fellow writer Barbara Shapiro for her encouragement and innovative ideas on time and task management. And for their support and good cheer, I'm grateful to my writing comrades—Richard Jacobs, Phil Mattera, Stephen Fox, Jan Brogan, Floyd Kemske, Vicki Stiefel, and Thomas Engels.

And, to my husband, Ken Whitney, who never doubted I could do it, I offer my love and deepest appreciation.

Judith E. Harper

LIST OF ENTRIES

A

Abolitionists
African-American Women
Agricultural Women
Alcott, Louisa May
Anthony, Susan B.
Antietam (Sharpsburg), Battle of
Artists

B

Barton, Clara
Battle of the Handkerchiefs
Bickerdyke, Mary Ann
Blalock, Malinda Pritchard
Bowser, Mary Elizabeth
Boyd, Belle
Bread Rebellions
Brown, Clara
Brownell, Kady Southwell
Businesswomen

C

Camp Life
Carroll, Anna Ella
Cary, Mary Ann Shadd
Cashier, Albert D.J. (Jennie Hodgers)
Catholic Nuns
Chesnut, Mary Boykin
Child, Lydia Maria
Contraband Relief Association
Contraband Women
Coppin, Fanny Jackson
Courtship and Marriage
Cumming, Kate
Cushman, Pauline

D

Davis, Rebecca Harding
Davis, Varina Howell
Diaries
Dickey, Sarah
Dickinson, Anna
Dickinson, Emily
Dix, Dorothea
Doctors
Draft Riots

E

Edmonds, Sarah Emma
Edmondson, Belle
Education
Etheridge, Annie
Evans, Augusta Jane

F

Family Life
Fern, Fanny
Fort Sumter
Forten, Charlotte
Frémont, Jessie Benton

G

General Order No. 28
Gettysburg, Battle of
Gibbons, Abby Hopper
Girlhood and Adolescence
Government Girls
Greenhow, Rose O'Neal
Guerrilla War
Gunboat Societies

H

Hale, Sarah Josepha
Hamilton, Gail
Harper, Frances Watkins
Haviland, Laura Smith
Hawks, Esther Hill
Hopkins, Juliet Opie
Hospital Ships
Howe, Julia Ward

I

Immigrant Women
Industrial Women
Invasion and Occupation

J

Jacobs, Harriet

K

Keckley, Elizabeth
Kemble, Fanny

L

Larcom, Lucy
LeConte, Emma
Lewis, Edmonia
Lincoln, Mary Todd
Literary Women
Livermore, Mary Ashton Rice

M

McCord, Louisa Cheves
Mexican-American Women
Military Women
Mitchell, Maria
Morgan, Sarah
Mormon Women
Mountain Charley

N

Native American Women
Nurses

P

Patriotism
Peabody, Elizabeth Palmer
Pember, Phoebe Levy
Phillips, Eugenia Levy
Pleasant, Mary Ellen
Prostitutes

R

Ream, Vinnie
Refugees
Religion
Remond, Sarah Parker
Roswell Women

S

Sanitary Fairs
Secession
Sherman's March to the Sea
Slater, Sarah Gilbert
Slavery and Emancipation
Soldiers' Aid Societies
Spies and Espionage
Stanton, Elizabeth Cady
Stowe, Harriet Beecher
Surratt, Mary
Swisshelm, Jane Grey

T

Taylor, Susie Baker King
Teachers of the Freedpeople
Tompkins, Sally
Treasury Girls
Truth, Sojourner
Tubman, Harriet
Turchin, Nadine Lvova

U

United States Christian Commission
United States Sanitary Commission

V

Van Lew, Elizabeth
Velazquez, Loreta Janeta
Vicksburg

W

Wakeman, Sarah Rosetta
Walker, Mary Edwards
Western Women
Woman's Central Association of Relief
Woman's National Loyal League
Women and Politics
Women's Rights Movement

Z

Zakrzewska, Marie

Abolitionists

I'm opposed to war—to cutting down men like grass—but if ever war was holy, this one, in favor of the most oppressed, most forbearing, most afflicted, down-trodden, insulted part of humanity, is a holy war. But I am hoping that the weak, presumptuous, sickly, clamorous, selfish, traitorous South will be frightened … into subjection.

—Sarah H. Palmer to Abby Hopper Gibbons, May 5, 1861, Philadelphia, Pennsylvania (Gibbons 1897, 292)

Abolitionism, a major political and social reform movement of the early to mid-nineteenth century, was dedicated to the eradication of slavery. Northern women who became active in public and political life during the Civil War owed much to the pioneering efforts of abolitionist women during the antebellum era. Women—black and white—joined other social and political reformers in the quest to remold society into a more just, humane world. Female abolitionists of the 1860s agreed with SUSAN B. ANTHONY that the purpose of the war was "to establish the negro in freedom— against whom the whole nation, North and South, East and West, in one mighty conspiracy, has combined from the beginning" (Stanton et al. 1881, 2: 57).

Although abolitionist activity in the United States had its beginnings in the late eighteenth century, it did not become an established reform movement until 1833 with the birth of the American Anti-Slavery Society (AASS) in Philadelphia. In the 1830s, growing numbers of white and free AFRICAN-AMERICAN WOMEN committed themselves to antislavery work. Throughout the Northeast, the Middle Atlantic seaboard, and the Midwest, women formed female antislavery societies, raising consciousness about the evils of slavery among themselves and throughout their communities. In 1832, black women formed the first women-led abolitionist organization in the United States, the Salem Female Anti-Slavery Society in Massachusetts.

In 1839, the radical element of the AASS's two factions, led by William Lloyd Garrison, seized control of the organization, forcing its more conservative members to establish the American and Foreign Anti-Slavery Society. Those pursuing political solutions to slavery formed the Liberty Party in 1840. Unlike the political faction, followers of Garrison in the AASS supported women's active roles in the movement. Lucretia Coffin Mott, Maria Weston Chapman, and other female Garrisonians served on the executive committees of the AASS and its auxiliaries. Women wrote for and edited the *National Anti-Slavery Standard*, the newspaper of the AASS, lectured widely, influenced decision-making, and pursued the more traditional female duty of fund-raising.

Abolitionist women were never more active than they were during the Civil War years, persuading the public and the federal government to free the slaves and to provide assistance and education to the freedpeople. Northern women wrote and distributed antislavery literature, protested racially discriminatory laws and policies, circulated petitions to legislators to protect fugitive slaves and ban slavery, delivered public lectures, and raised money to support their activism.

The righteousness of the abolitionist cause gave these Northern women the moral sanction they needed to participate fully in the public sphere. Through the WOMAN'S NATIONAL LOYAL LEAGUE (WNLL), organized by Susan B. Anthony and ELIZABETH CADY STANTON, thousands of Northern women became politically active and vocal for the first time.

In October 1859, abolitionists were shocked by the news of the militant abolitionist John Brown's raid on the federal arsenal in Harpers Ferry, Virginia. For many in the movement, Brown's attempt to incite a slave insurrection triggered much soul-searching and confusion followed by a deepening of commitment to the cause. FRANCES ELLEN WATKINS HARPER, LYDIA MARIA CHILD, and other women wrote letters to the imprisoned Brown and his fellow insurgents. They raised funds for Brown's wife and children and for the families of his co-conspirators. A few, including Susan B. Anthony, held memorials to Brown after his execution.

LOUISA MAY ALCOTT, a close friend of one of Brown's collaborators, was inspired by the insurgents' militance. "Glad I have lived to see the Antislavery movement and this last heroic act in it," she wrote in her journal. "Wish I could do my part in it" (Alcott 1989, 3). Yet most white women, including Quakers and pacifists, struggled to reconcile their support of Brown with their history of dedication to nonviolence. The majority of white female reformers stated that although they could not condone Brown's methods, they sympathized with his ideals. As Lydia Maria Child explained, "Certainly honest John Brown, by his direct way of proceeding, has driven us abolitionists into a perplexing corner. We cannot help reverencing the *man* while we disapprove of his *measures*" (quoted in Venet 1991, 100). By contrast, the vast majority of outspoken, prominent African-American abolitionist women unequivocally supported Brown.

During the winter of 1860–1861, as the Southern states seceded from the Union, abolitionists publicly pressed the issue of immediate emancipation. Male and female antislavery leaders shared the podium at lectures all over the Northeast and Midwest. There they confronted the most hostile crowds in the history of their movement. The public's wrath derived from its fears concerning the destructive impact of secession and disunion on government and business. Abolitionists fought for their First Amendment rights to speak and to be heard. At a memorial to John Brown in Boston, antislavery women in the balcony reacted wildly when a combative crowd shouted down Frederick Douglass's attempts to speak. The women hissed and yelled at the mob of Douglass's detractors. When police forcibly removed the women from the hall, a number resisted, taunting the police (Jeffrey 1998, 212).

After Lincoln called for troops following the Confederate attack on Fort Sumter, abolitionist women joined tens of thousands of other Northern women in sewing clothing and preparing supplies for the Union military through the SOLDIERS' AID SOCIETIES, the UNITED STATES SANITARY COMMISSION, and the UNITED STATES CHRISTIAN COMMISSION. Black women assisted black men in the Union military and fugitive slaves in the contraband camps.

In the push for emancipation, women wrote letters to the editors of their community newspapers, to political candidates, and to state and national legislators. Women leaders organized troupes of lecturers and spoke in public. In 1862, Elizabeth Buffum Chace of Rhode Island was so frustrated that President Lincoln had not made the slaves' freedom a national priority that she initiated her own whirlwind of abolitionist agitation. She arranged dozens of protest lectures and circulated petitions all over town, even sending her children door to door gathering signatures. By 1863, such orators as ANNA DICKINSON were famous, admired instead of reviled and abused as they had been in the late 1830s and 1840s. Susan B. Anthony, Elizabeth Cady Stanton, JESSIE BENTON FRÉMONT, and dozens of other women participated in political campaigns.

Although abolitionists were hell-bent on achieving emancipation, only a minority of them believed that enslaved blacks were the equals of whites. The majority was convinced that the slaves were intellectually inferior and fit to work only in menial occupations. The letters and journals of white women involved in the antislavery movement reveal that they had difficulty envisioning the freedpeople fully integrating in Northern society and were disconcerted by their encounters with free-born African Americans in their daily lives.

After the war, abolitionists pressured Congress to pass laws safeguarding the civil and political rights of the freedpeople in the South. Following the ratification of the Fourteenth and Fifteenth Amendments, most white activists no longer concerned themselves with the political or social concerns of African Americans in the North or South. Many white abolitionists became involved in other reform movements, including woman suffrage, temperance, spiritualism, Native American rights, and the international peace movement.

See also **Cary, Mary Ann Shadd; Forten, Charlotte; Haviland, Laura; Swisshelm, Jane Grey; Teachers of the Freedpeople; Truth, Sojourner; Tubman, Harriet**

Selected Readings

Jeffrey, Julie Roy. *The Great Silent Army of Abolitionism: Ordinary Women in the Antislavery Movement.* Chapel Hill: University of North Carolina Press. 1998.
Venet, Wendy Hamand. *Neither Ballots Nor Bullets: Women Abolitionists and the Civil War.* Charlottesville: University Press of Virginia. 1991.

African-American Women

Enslaved or free, living in the North or living in the South, African-American women shared a similar struggle: to gain the freedoms enjoyed by all citizens of the United States. A middle-class free black woman of Philadelphia and an enslaved woman laboring 16 hours a day on an Alabama cotton plantation, despite the vast differences in their circumstances, endured racial hatred, oppression, restrictive laws, and prejudice. Regardless of their class or status, African-American women looked to the Civil War as the climactic, defining era in their people's quest for freedom, and as the single watershed event that held the potential to release them from bondage.

Like white women of the North and South, African-American women, both free and enslaved, faced the exodus of their menfolk once the Civil War began. By the end of the war, nearly 179,000 African-American men had served in the Union army and 29,000 in the Union navy, totaling approximately 10 percent of the African-American male population. 37,000 black enlisted men did not survive the war, nearly 30,000 of them succumbing to disease. Another 200,000 black men worked for the Union military. United States census figures record the population of free African Americans in the United States in 1860 as 488,070 persons—226,152 in the North and 261,918 in the South. Slaves are listed as numbering 3,953,696 persons (Berlin 1974, 136–137).

In general, the absence of husbands, fathers, and male relatives created greater hardships for African-American women than for most Northern and Southern white women. Families of black enlisted men suffered from extreme poverty and starvation as they tried to subsist on a black soldier's pay of $7 per month. Not only were African-American soldiers paid less than their white counterparts, but their wages were also often months late in coming. As a result, the wives and families of black enlisted men were, for months at a time, completely dependent on the pittance that women could earn as laundresses or servants.

Despite the hardships and the federal government's lack of regard for black soldiers' families, free and enslaved African-American women strongly supported the Union war effort. As soon as the United States military began enlisting African-American men, Northern free black women rushed to supply soldier's aid to black troops. They formed independent SOLDIERS' AID SOCIETIES for this purpose, although much of their contributions were raised through preestablished female charities and church benevolent groups. Black women and men were convinced that the military service of African-American men would soon lead to citizenship and a full share of their civil and political rights.

Enslaved and free black women in the South also assisted white and black Union soldiers by volunteering to act as scouts and spies, giving directions and information, and feeding and sheltering those separated from their ranks. In addition to providing support to troops, African-American women nursed the wounded and the sick in military hospitals wherever they were permitted, though more often they were relegated to jobs as laundresses or cooks.

Free African-American Women

By the time of the Civil War, most free African-American families in both the North and the South urgently needed the wages of its female members to survive. Single and married women and girls of all ages contributed to a family's income. In the early nineteenth century, free black men in the North were able to work at skilled trades, and thereby gain wealth and property. By the 1850s, however, only the most menial, unskilled jobs were open to them due to competition from native working-class white men and the influx of immigrant labor. White factory owners and employers in the North and mill owners in the South caved in to political pressures created by white workers to bar African Americans from factory work. In cities where immigrant laborers competed for jobs, black men found it increasingly difficult to claim the more desirable, better-paying unskilled jobs. As they scrambled to find whatever jobs they could, they often had to settle for those that paid the least and were the most dangerous. As this dynamic unfolded, the income of African-American women became critical to the survival of black families.

The most common occupation for free black women in the North was laundress, but they also worked as cooks, domestic servants, and seamstresses. Operating boarding houses was another way that they made ends meet. A few middle-class women owned their own businesses. SARAH PARKER REMOND's sisters Cecilia, Maritcha, and Caroline of Salem, Massachusetts, owned the Ladies Hair Work Salon as well as the largest wig factory in Massachusetts. Other entrepreneurial women owned dressmaker and millinery shops, as well as bakeries and coffee houses. A few earned enough money to purchase real estate.

In the South, most free African Americans lived in rural areas and were extremely impoverished. By the Civil War era, free blacks were increasingly moving from the countryside to the largest Southern cities, all of which had sizable African-American communities. In the South as in the North, black women were often the most steady wage earners of their families.

In general, Southern free blacks found it more difficult to achieve subsistence than Northern blacks. Restrictive laws in every Southern state limited the freedoms of black men and women and made making a living a feat of ingenuity. Yet, unlike Northern black men, a limited number of Southern men managed to remain working as artisans and skilled tradesmen until early in the Civil War. By the end of the war and during Reconstruction, Southern white men had passed laws restricting African-American men and women to agricultural and domestic labor (J. Jones 1998, 222).

A very small number of free African-American women in the South owned property and operated successful businesses and plantations. In 1860, 22 percent of the real estate owned by African Americans in the South belonged to black women. Most of the largest landowners and business owners lived in the Deep South and had acquired their property from white men, many of whom were their relatives. Free mulatto women of the Lower South possessed more status than other free Southern blacks, particularly in Louisiana, which had the largest number of Afri-can-American property-owning women. In the Upper South, African-American women purchased their own properties by painstakingly saving their earnings from their jobs as servants, nurses, waitresses, and other occupations open to women (Schweniger 1990, 18–22).

The Civil War profoundly altered the lives of the largest African-American plantation owners (some of whom were slaveholders) as they lost their plantations to Union INVASION AND OCCUPATION just as their white counterparts did. Unlike white landowners, free black women were prevented from regaining their land and their prosperity by new laws instituted after the Civil War (Schweninger 1990, 26–28).

Despite their work lives and the domestic duties they performed for their families, free black women in the North and the South also found the strength and the time to build and sustain African-American communities. For decades before and after the Civil War, free black women actively supported their churches. African-American churches formed the center of black communities in the North (and in the South, where permitted by law). Northern churches provided information, advice, and a network of support as well as worship and spiritual guidance for the entire African-American community.

Male-dominated religious mutual aid societies raised the funds that kept churches solvent and that fed, housed, and clothed impoverished members. Women organized their own societies to achieve the same goals, establishing female benevolent associations that also raised money for mutual aid, education, and moral uplift. The African-American churches were extraordinarily well connected to one another, not only among churches in their own regions, but also to congregations in other Northern and Southern cities.

Not all of the societies that Northern black women formed were affiliated with churches. They created literary and moral improvement societies to educate themselves and to sharpen their intellects. Since few cities and towns in the North permitted black children to attend public schools, women worked with African-American men to educate their children. Some African-American women were politically involved, especially those who were abolitionists. In 1832, black women formed the first women-led abolitionist organization in the United States, the Salem Female Anti-Slavery Society in Salem Massachusetts. Black women were strong financial supporters of the Underground Railroad. As fugitives fled North in the decades before the Civil War, free black women sheltered them, cooked meals, provided nursing care, and helped them on to the next station. Women also found jobs for female fugitives and helped provide childcare for mothers who worked.

Some Northern free black women were also civil rights activists. In the 1840s and 1850s, women in New England, New York, and Philadelphia joined men in protesting segregation and discriminatory laws and policies. During the Civil War, these challenges continued as women with husbands, brothers, and sons enlisted in the military felt empowered to demand their rights. In July 1864, Ellen Anderson of New York City, whose husband Sergeant Anderson had died while enlisted in the 26th United States Colored Cavalry, took action when a conductor pushed her off a streetcar. She saw to it that the man was arrested for assault. In a similar episode in 1863, Charlotte Brown of San Francisco sued a rail company when a conductor forced her off a train (Forbes 1998, 150). Two other prominent African-American women, SOJOURNER TRUTH and HARRIET TUBMAN, also battled streetcar and railway conductors.

During the Civil War and Reconstruction, free blacks in the North concentrated much of their benevolent activity on providing assistance to the newly freed slaves. Women's organizations raised funds and collected clothing and other supplies to send to the contraband camps.

Beginning in 1862, educated, middle-class black women joined their white male and female counterparts as TEACHERS OF THE FREEDPEOPLE. These "missionaries," as they were often called, were sponsored by both secular and denominational Northern freedmen's aid societies and later by the federally run Freedmen's Bureau.

Although free African-Americans living in the South struggled to build and maintain their communities, in many states this activity had to be informal or covert. In a number of Southern states, African Americans were not permitted by law to worship in their own churches or to form their own mutual aid or benevolent associations, though they had been permitted to do so during the early nineteenth century before these laws were introduced. In these areas, closely knit extended families substituted as the most important community for free blacks.

After the Confederate surrender at Appomattox, and in some Southern cities and towns before this date, black women and men used their new freedoms to institute a variety of religious, benevolent, and political organizations, in a sudden surge of community building. Black church societies devoted to religious endeavors, education, temperance, and poor relief became common (Varon 1998, 173).

Enslaved Women

The major dilemma for historians trying to piece together the nature and quality of the lives of slave women before and during the Civil War is the lack of documents revealing their personal experiences. Although slaveholders and traveling Northerners wrote letters, diaries, and other accounts offering their observations of the lives of enslaved women, there are very few Civil War era documents written by slaves, other than the several written by fugitive slaves after they had become contrabands. The Works Progress Administration (WPA) interviews of former slave men and women, collected in the 1930s, provide a glimpse of enslavement during the Civil War. These records are limited as historical documents, in part because most of the elderly men and women interviewed were recalling the time of their childhoods, 55 to 60 years earlier, and because of the bias of the Southern white interviewers.

It is estimated that four million men and women were living in slavery in 1860. Most of the approximately two million enslaved women lived and worked on plantations and farms. Enslaved women field-workers on the cotton, rice, tobacco, and sugarcane plantations were forced to endure long days of backbreaking labor. Although often organized into women-only work crews, female slaves worked at many of the same tasks as men, including heavy plowing. In the cotton fields, women worked as many as 12 to 16 hours a day, depending on the season, plowing, planting, hoeing, and picking. In winter, they erected fencing, cut down trees and brush, cut wood, and repaired roads (J. Jones 1985, 15–18).

When female slaves left the fields at dusk or later, they returned to the slave quarters to begin what amounted to another day's work, cooking the evening meal for their families, nurturing their children, making and mending clothing, tending their own garden plots, and spinning and weaving their evening quota of cloth for the slaveholder. Although enslaved men had their share of evening duties and home responsibilities—fishing and hunting small animals to supplement their families' meager diets, building furniture, and gathering firewood, for example—their "second-shift tasks" were not as numerous or as time-consuming as women's.

Slave women's domestic chores often gave them the opportunity to visit and form close ties with other women. Spinning and weaving tasks were often performed with other women. On many Southern plantations, slave women gathered together on Saturdays to wash their family's clothing. Time spent on these chores gave women the opportunity to form close bonds and to swap stories, gossip, and medical advice. Strong relationships among enslaved women became even more important during the Civil War as they were left on their own to fend for themselves and their children. As women faced increased workloads in the fields and at home, struggled to nourish their families on a dangerously deficient diet consisting mostly of grains (cornmeal and rice), and suffered increased harassment and abuse from male and female slaveholders and from Union and Confederate troops, powerful female slave communities helped to sustain slave women and their families (White 1985, 122–125).

Before the Civil War, but especially during the conflict, slave women shouldered much of the burden of raising their children. Once the men left the plantations, mothers cared for their families on their own, and with the cooperative assistance of other enslaved women of all ages. Both before and during the war, African-American women were responsible for helping their children adjust to their lives as slaves and for teaching them how to resist and maintain some measure of independence in a culture that was determined to annihilate it. Mothers also directed the religious upbringing of their offspring, and helped to cultivate a strong sense of community spirit in their children (King 1996, 153–154).

Although the slaveholder controlled nearly every aspect of their lives, enslaved women and men managed to create small islands of independence within the confines of slavery. An important part of women's resistance to their bondage before and during the Civil War was their participation in what is commonly referred to as the "domestic slave economy." Throughout the South, some enslaved women and men ran small business operations, bartering, trading, selling, and buying goods from other slaves and from poor whites. The slaveholders' property and goods were the most common sources of the goods traded, including rice, cotton, corn, tobacco, sugar, hogs, cattle, horses, sheep, poultry, eggs, honey, fish, fruits, meats, bread, and other bakery items. By all accounts, slave women were often more active than men as retailers in this clandestine market (Schweninger 1990, 14–15). By surreptitiously tapping into the planters' food and other supplies, slave women were able to acquire the food and the money they needed to survive. Thus they were able to strike a blow at the planter's prosperity while assisting themselves and their families.

As the Confederate and Union governments as well as slaveholders separated fathers from their families and mothers from their children, enslaved women struggled to keep their families together. Many times, when faced with the certainty of separation, mothers made the difficult decision to flee with their children, a peril-fraught choice. By the end of the war, tens of thousands of slave women and their children had fled to Union-occupied areas for freedom and safety. Thousands of others followed their husbands and menfolk to Union army camps. Although these CONTRABAND WOMEN were usually (although not always) secure from their former owners and from reenslavement by Southern whites once they were safely within Union territory, they endured squalid living conditions, extreme poverty, hunger and starvation, epidemic disease, and sexual assault and rape by Union soldiers and officers. Despite these miseries, these women often refused to be separated from their menfolk and children once inside Union lines, even when the government attempted to force them to work on plantations distant from the camps by withholding their food rations.

As soon as the war was over, thousands of freedwomen and men traveled throughout the South searching for lost family members in a massive effort to reunite their families, a task that occupied many slave women for years, even decades. Even though white supremacists, the Black Codes (the laws intended to keep African Americans subservient to white rule), and state court decisions contributed to the impoverishment of African-American families, black women in the Reconstruction era focused on educating themselves and their children, uniting their families, and building strong churches and communities.

See also **Abolitionists; Bowser, Mary Elizabeth; Cary, Mary Ann Shadd; Contraband Relief Association; Coppin, Fanny Jackson; Forten, Charlotte; Harper, Frances Ellen Watkins; Jacobs, Harriet; Keckley, Elizabeth; Lewis, Edmonia; Pleasant, Mary Ellen; Slavery and Emancipation; Taylor, Susie Baker King**

Selected Reading

Forbes, Ella. *African American Women During the Civil War.* New York: Garland. 1998.

Hine, Darlene Clark and Kathleen Thompson. *A Shining Thread of Hope: The History of Black Women in America.* New York: Broadway Books. 1998.

Sterling, Dorothy. *We Are Your Sisters: Black Women in the Nineteenth Century.* New York: W.W. Norton. 1984.

Agricultural Women

The Civil War sharply altered the lives of farm women of the North and South. As their husbands, fathers, brothers, and sons marched off to enlist in the military, agricultural women expanded their traditional farm and domestic duties to include fieldwork, total care of livestock and dairying production, and farm management.

Although the North was more industrialized and urbanized than the South, the North was predominantly a rural, agricultural region during the Civil War. Nearly 75 percent of Northerners lived in rural areas, either on farms or in villages with populations of less than 2,500. The New England states as a whole were 63.4 percent rural, the Middle Atlantic region was 64.4 percent rural, the Midwest east of the Mississippi River was 85.9 percent rural, and Union states west of the Mississippi were over 86.6 percent rural (Paludan 1988, 151). Like the Midwest and West, the South was almost entirely rural, with few cities and large towns.

One truism applied to agriculture throughout the North, South, and West during the mid-nineteenth century: regardless of the class or race of farmers, agriculture was primarily a family enterprise. Husbands, wives, sons, and daughters all labored to keep their family farms productive. Furthermore, the agricultural contributions of women and girls were critically important to their families' subsistence and to the prosperity of their farms.

In the mid-nineteenth century as in previous eras, women on farms labored from before dawn until after sundown alongside their husbands, fathers, and brothers. Although women's farm-related labor varied according to region of the country and the crops and livestock raised, the substance of women's daily lives was remarkably similar during this period.

In the North and in the South, farm women of the middle classes—often referred to as the yeomanry in the South—performed all household tasks (cooking, cleaning, laundering, sewing); cared for children and elderly relatives; planted, tended, and harvested gardens; and canned and preserved food. Male farmworkers plowed the fields, planted the crops, fed most of the livestock, obtained fuel for heat, and maintained all farm buildings, equipment, and machinery. Yet these roles were not rigid. Depending on the family and its members' preferences and customs, men, women, and children assisted each other with tasks on occasion, especially during farm crises and during planting and harvesting (Osterud 1991, 147).

In the 1860s, Lucy Ann Riley helped with the haying for five seasons, even during one season when she was six months pregnant. Her husband, George, occasionally assisted her with the laundry, butter production, and other chores. On at least one occasion he pitched in so that she could help him sow corn in the afternoon. It is possible, however, to overemphasize the extent to which men assisted women with their farm duties. The most critical part of any farm's operation was crop and livestock production, and it was far more common for women to assist men with their farm-related work than for men to assist women with their tasks (Osterud 1991, 162, 186).

The Civil War affected agriculture in the North and South very differently. The Civil War years were boom times for Northern agriculture, despite the heavy loss of male farm labor to enlistment (almost 50 percent of Union soldiers were farmers or agricultural workers). The number of farms, agricultural workers, acres cultivated, and crops harvested increased during the Civil War into the late 1860s.

In the North, women, older children, and men too old to enlist in the military managed farms and performed much of the farm labor themselves. Their work replaced the labor of as many as a million male farmworkers who served in the Union military. Northern women were able to sustain and increase production on their farms, at least partly due to the use of farm machinery. According to Northern farm journals published during the Civil War era, women operated mowers, reapers, rakes (for harvesting hay and other grains), drills, and plows—labor that men typically performed. Women also drove farm wagons loaded with produce and harvested crops to market. When one agricultural journal published a story of a woman and her seven daughters on a New York farm plowing, sowing, and harvesting 100 acres of wheat while also operating a small dairy farm of 22 cows, several readers responded in outrage that women were demeaning themselves by performing farm labor usually reserved for men (Gates 1965, 242).

Emily Hawley Gillespie of Iowa kept a diary of her farm-related activities. From her writings, a clearer picture emerges of the seasonal nature of a woman's farm labor. In addition to the litany of her daily farm and domestic chores, in the spring she planted the garden that grew the family's vegetables and tended nesting poultry. In the summer, she gathered berries, made preserves, and spent countless hours in a hot kitchen canning vegetables. In the fall, she husked corn, cooked three meals a day for the farm laborers hired to help with the harvest, canned vegetable and fruit produce, and helped with the butchering and preserving of meat. The winter months she devoted to sewing the family's clothing (Lensink et al. 1980, 300).

Children of the North and South worked in the fields. Girls as well as boys helped with the planting. In her memoir of three years spent on the Kansas frontier, Adele "Doaty" Orpen recounts the details of farm labor as a child of seven. She refers to the "deadly dogged work" of planting corn, in which seeds were planted in little holes three feet apart in every direction.

> It is quite simple and seems very easy, but nothing is easy when inexorably repeated for five hours at a stretch on a hot prairie field. … At the end of a day's work I began to be unable to drop the seeds steadily. … It was only the direst need that sent me into the field to plant corn, but no one else was to be had. The war had begun to drain men away from the land. (Orpen 1990, 83–84)

The war severely affected Southern agriculture. Southern farms suffered greater losses of male farm labor to the military than Northern farms. White women and male and female slaves struggled to sustain crop yields, while the Union blockade of Southern ports, transportation problems, and Confederate impressment of produce, livestock, and farm equipment caused agricultural production to falter and to be insufficient for both military and civilian needs.

Yeoman farmers of the middle classes owning very few or no slaves predominated in the South. Instead of relying on a single cash crop of cotton, tobacco, rice, or sugarcane as the wealthy planters did, the majority of yeoman farmers owned small farms and grew crops for their subsistence only. The lives of Southern and Northern farm women were remarkably similar, although Southern farm women tended to be more isolated due to the South's smaller population. Although farm women all over the nation worked in the fields, particularly at haying and harvest times, several historians have noted that white Southern farm women, especially the least prosperous, worked in the fields far more than has been commonly recognized. In addition to assisting with the haying and harvesting, they worked in the fields at other times of the growing season as well. Native-born white frontier women in the West, and German and Scandinavian immigrant women in the North and West also worked in the fields and tended livestock more than native-born white farm women in the Northeast and Middle Atlantic states.

White women on the plantation—planters' wives, widows, and single female relatives—were also involved in agricultural production. Only the wealthiest slaveholders, a very small percentage, owned enough slaves to relieve them of most household and outdoor chores. Most planter women supervised the labor of household slaves in the planter's household and gardens. Planter women owning fewer slaves worked alongside slaves while performing the least menial and least difficult tasks. Plantation women planted and tended gardens; supervised all cooking, cleaning, and childcare tasks; and managed all textile production, including the sewing of clothes for the planter's family and the slaves.

As overworked as farm women of the North and South were, managing both domestic and farm duties, they contributed to their respective militaries during the Civil War as best they could. Farm women of the North and South donated hand-sewn and knitted goods to SOLDIERS' AID SOCIETIES. Northern women packaged their fresh fruits and vegetables to improve the limited diets of Union soldiers. Southern women followed the directive of the Confederate government to plant food instead of cash crops, to "plant corn and be free, or plant cotton and be whipped" (quoted in Clinton 1995, 109).

Diaries and letters of Northern and Southern women who managed farms while their husbands were away point to a reality that statistics cannot convey. As competently and as well as many women "managed," they acknowledged in their letters and diaries that their successes were achieved while they were stretched to the limits of their endurance. Women of the North and South acknowledged how difficult the struggle was and how vulnerable they felt in their attempt to shoulder their husband's share of the agricultural enterprise. In Illinois, late in 1864, Louisa Jane Phifer and her children wrote long letters enumerating the farm tasks they accomplished to husband and father George Phifer, who was recuperating from pneumonia in a Union military hospital. In this letter as in others, Louisa begs him to take care so that he might return in good health.

> Now George Do not be taken Prisoner. Rather run than that for you know that I never could never stand to have that News come to me now for all the World. Be careful on mine and your own account George Do. I would rather that you would do any thing than to stand and be taken Prisoner. ... if any thing should happen to you how would I get along. (Phifer 1973, 393)

The mutual interdependence of men and women and their children on their farms was so crucial to their prosperity that any factor that compromised the labor of family members could prove disastrous. For agricultural men and women, health was cherished, guarded, coaxed along, and was the subject of their prayers. George Phifer fully realized that his family's future happiness lay in the health of all its members. In a letter to his wife and children, he writes, "One great satisfaction to me is that I know mother will manage things. ... Only I am afraid she will work too hard or expose herself too much. Don't do that if the things don't do so well for health is better than property." In another letter, he cautions his wife not to overwork their sons. "Only don't work the boys too hard. Steady work wont [sic] hurt them but rushing them might hurt them for life and I don't want that" (Phifer 1973, 400).

Rosella Benton in southwestern New York State effectively managed the family farm in her husband's absence. Accustomed to outdoor work, she chose an unconventional approach to solve her farm labor shortage. She hired a young woman to relieve her of her household chores so that she could be free to manage the farm. Rosella did the dairying herself, planted corn and potatoes, and managed male farmworkers. She relied on relatives to assist her with the haying (Osterud 1990, 374–376).

Southern farm women had overwhelming burdens, according to the letters and the diaries of those who recorded their experiences. Women who had restive slaves to manage encountered especially severe labor difficulties. Unlike Northern women, Southern farm women suffered from a greater scarcity of adult male labor, Confederate impressment or seizure of crops and livestock, the invasion of Union troops, and equipment and supply shortages caused by the Union blockade and transportation disruptions.

Emily Lyles Harris of South Carolina, mother of nine children, coped while her husband was away by driving their slaves herself and by hiring extra farmhands to coax a profitable crop out of their farm. Though she succeeded in achieving a decent crop yield, the emotional cost was more than she could bear. She poured out her depression into her diary.

> I shall never get used to being left as the head of affairs at home. The burden is very heavy, and there is no one to smile on me as I trudge wearily along in the dark with it. I am constituted so as to crave a guide and protector. I am not an independent woman nor ever shall be. (Racine 1980, 390)

The spirits of Northern women also suffered from the strain. In Iowa, when Helen Maria Sharp's husband enlisted in 1861, she was filled with despair, wondering how she would support herself and her children, writing, "It makes me low spirited so that I cant help writeing to you to not for gods sake if you want to save me from getting rid of myself lend your money till you relieve your family." Yet by 1862, she was earning money as a laundress and by stripping sugarcane for molasses. She also plowed and planted a vegetable garden and procured a cow that supplied her children with milk. Despite her ability to manage well, her letters to her husband indicate that she was still overwhelmed. "My back hurts me so that I cant stand it to chop hardly at all ... if I was only out of the way folks would take care of my children but to scatter them while im alive is more trouble than I can bare to think about" (Riley 1981, 120–121).

After the war, white farm women in the North returned to their traditional farm duties and domestic chores as their menfolk returned to the fields. In the South, however, where farms and plantations had been devastated by war and invasion, women worked alongside men to begin the grueling task of returning their lands to productive cultivation.

See also **Immigrant Women; Slavery and Emancipation; Western Women**

Selected Readings

Clinton, Catherine. *Tara Revisited: Women, War, and the Plantation Legend*. New York: Abbeville Press. 1995.

Escott, Paul D. *Many Excellent People: Power and Privilege in North Carolina, 1850–1900*. Chapel Hill: University of North Carolina Press. 1985.

Osterud, Nancy Grey. *Bonds of Community: The Lives of Farm Women in Nineteenth-Century New York*. Ithaca: Cornell University Press. 1991.

Osterud, Nancy Grey. "Rural Women During the Civil War: New York's Nanticoke Valley, 1861–1865." *New York History*. 62 (4) (October 1990): 356–385.

Alcott, Louisa May (1832–1888)

"I want something to do" …
"Write a book," Quoth the author of my being.
"Don't know enough, sir. First live, then write."
"Try teaching again," suggested my mother.
"No thank you, ma'am, ten years of that is enough."
"Take a husband like my Darby, and fulfill your mission," said sister Joan,
"Can't afford expensive luxuries, Mrs. Coobiddy."
"Go nurse the soldiers," said my young brother, Tom …
"I will!"

—Louisa May Alcott, from *Hospital Sketches* (1960, 7)

During the Civil War, Louisa May Alcott worked as a writer, teacher, and nurse as well as serving as a volunteer in SOLDIERS' AID SOCIETIES, abolitionist organizations, and the Boston auxiliary of the UNITED STATES SANITARY COMMISSION. Of all of her wartime activities, her writing most occupied her thoughts, her time, and her dreams. Even while engaged in other business, war-related or not, she was always gathering ideas and organizing material for her next story, novel, play, or poem. Alcott's fledgling professional writing career of the 1850s and early 1860s finally took flight in 1863 with the publication of *Hospital Sketches*, a fictionalized memoir of her experiences as an army nurse in Washington, DC.

Alcott's illustrious family background provided an important impetus and backdrop to her literary efforts and her war work. Aside from her earliest childhood years living in Germantown, Pennsylvania, Alcott was raised in Concord and in Boston, Massachusetts, in an environment steeped in transcendentalism, Unitarianism, and progressive educational reform. The daughter of Transcendental philosopher and writer Amos Bronson Alcott and the social reformer Abigail May Alcott, Louisa grew up in the midst of the most well-known intellectuals, writers, and social reformers of mid-nineteenth-century New England.

As a young woman in the 1850s, Alcott was determined to become the family breadwinner. Though her father was well known, he had never shown much interest in keeping his family out of poverty. At various times, Alcott was a teacher, governess, domestic servant, seamstress, and laundress (Moyle 1985, 225). Although informed by a prominent Boston publisher that she could not write, she vowed that she would succeed as a writer. In 1854, her first book, *Flower Fables*, was published. For the remainder of the decade, she struggled to make time for writing and managed to publish stories and verse in a variety of newspapers and magazines. Her first big break came when the prestigious *Atlantic Monthly* published her story "Love and Self-Love" in March 1860. With the $50 payment in hand, Alcott dared to hope that she might one day support her family by her literary efforts. The *Atlantic Monthly* went on to publish two more of her stories that year.

Alcott's family and all her social connections were strongly antislavery. Her uncle Samuel Joseph May was a leading orator within the American Anti-Slavery Society. Alcott's immediate family all participated as rank-and-file abolitionists. Alcott rejoiced over John Brown's attempt to trigger a slave insurrection in October 1859 and her entire family mourned his execution in early December 1859. She dedicated a poem on the occasion of a memorial service for Brown held in Concord. "With a Rose That Bloomed on the Day of John Brown's Martyrdom" was published in William Lloyd Garrison's abolitionist newspaper *The Liberator* a month later.

From the outset of the war, Alcott yearned to contribute to the war effort. She sewed shirts for the troops during the first weeks of the war in 1861 and attended "Lint Picks" where Concord women and girls scraped and collected lint from cotton fabric to be used for the dressing of battle wounds. Alcott read Florence Nightingale's *Notes on Nursing* and studied the treatment of gunshot wounds, two early clues that she contemplated a future in army nursing. But domestic contributions to the war effort frustrated her. She confided to her journal that she longed to march off to war. Following a difficult and financially unproductive year of teaching and writing, in November 1862, she declared in her journal that she, "Decided to go to Washington as a nurse if I could find a place. Help needed, and I love nursing, and must let out my pent-up energy in some new way.… I want new experiences, and am sure to get 'em if I go" (Alcott 1989, 110).

In December 1862, she arrived at Union Hotel Hospital in Washington, DC, a decaying three-story structure. In January 1863, in letters home and in her diary, she described the details of her life in the wards. Her attention to personal details and her emotions and reactions to events distinguish her writings from other nurses' memoirs.

> Though often home sick, heart sick & worn out, I like it—find real pleasure in comforting tending & cheering these poor souls who seem to love me, to feel my sympathy though unspoken, & acknowledge my hearty good will in spite of the ignorance, awkwardness & bashfulness which I cannot help showing in so new & trying a situation.

Her days were a never-ending series of tasks, providing a glimpse of a Northern nurse's duties.

Up at six, dress by gas light, run through my ward & fling up the windows. … Poke up the fire, add blankets, joke, coax, and command. … Till noon I trot, trot, giving out rations, cutting up food for helpless "boys", washing faces, teaching my attendants how beds are made or floors swept, dressing wounds, taking Dr. Fitz Patrick's orders, (privately wishing all the time that he would be more gentle with my big babies,) dusting tables, sewing bandages, keeping my tray tidy, rushing up & down after pillows, bed linen, sponges, books & directions, till it seems as if I would joyfully pay down all I possess for fifteen minutes rest. (Alcott 1989, 113–114)

After only a few weeks, Louisa fell ill with what doctors believed was typhoid pneumonia. She became more gravely ill as the days passed and as the treatment was administered. She was given calomel, the drug of choice for fevers and pneumonia. Calomel is a mercury compound (mercurous chloride) and Alcott, like most patients to whom it was prescribed, was given huge doses of it. Although commonly administered at the time, it is extremely toxic. In Alcott's case, it appears not only to have precipitated a life-threatening crisis but also to have permanently damaged her health. She returned to Concord to recover but never regained the abundant energy and strength that she had once enjoyed (Saxton 1977, 281, 294–295).

Although Alcott's nursing experience profoundly impacted every aspect of her life, it consumed little of her time during the war years. Prior to her tenure in Washington and afterward, when she was not caring for her parents or sisters, she devoted wholeheartedly to her writing. She did, however, continue to make time for the USSC. In December 1863, Alcott turned her lifelong passion for the theater into a moneymaker for the Boston Sanitary Fair, a fund-raising event for the USSC. A group of amateur actors produced her dramatization "Scenes from Dickens." The six performances yielded $2,500 for the USSC.

Hospital Sketches, her fictionalized narrative of her six weeks as an army nurse, is a strikingly vivid, though sentimentalized portrayal of the relationships between Nurse Tribulation Periwinkle (Alcott) and her wounded patients. Appearing first in newspapers, then reprinted in magazines and journals, it was published as a book in 1863. *Hospital Sketches* was immensely popular, perhaps because it informed readers of the emotional worlds within the army hospital while also providing physical descriptions of life on the wards. Even though *Hospital Sketches* idealizes the wounded and dying soldiers, its understated blend of humor and courage combined with tragedy and loss create a powerful reading experience.

Though the impact of Alcott's nursing experience was profound and longlasting, it was merely one episode in a long chain of experiences in the 1860s that advanced her career as a writer. The Civil War's effect on society, marked by profound sweeping social upheaval and gender role reversals in the North and South, deeply affected Alcott's literary life. During the 1860s, she vigorously pursued the role of family provider, author, and businesswoman at the time when women throughout the North and South were taking a more active role in the public sphere.

She achieved her financial goals through the production of literary works that she knew her parents and the people of Concord would approve and those that she knew they would not.

In addition to her socially acceptable fiction, Alcott secretly became a popular writer of what she dubbed "lurid tales." Writing either anonymously or under several pseudonyms, she wrote many sensational stories of revenge and jealousy, including such thrillers as "Pauline's Passion and Punishment," "A Whisper in the Dark," and "A Marble Woman" for the Boston-based *The Flag of Our Union* and for several of newspaper mogul Frank Leslie's publications. Following disappointing reviews of her adult novel, *Moods*, published in 1864, she acknowledged in her journal, that she "… fell back on rubbishy tales, for they pay best, and I can't afford to starve on praise, when sensation stories are written in half the time and keep the family cosy" (quoted in Stern 1998, 98). By 1866, Frank Leslie was paying her $100 for each story, making her a highly paid newspaper writer.

In addition to publishing several war stories, she wrote tales in which she grappled with the paradoxes of interracial relations in a new society without slavery, based on issues that emerged in her awareness while working among the freedpeople or "contrabands" at Union Hotel Hospital in Washington. These "abolitionist stories," as she called them—"M.L." (written in 1859 but not published until 1863), "Brothers" (renamed in 1869 to "My Contraband)," and "An Hour"—were all examples of her literary fiction.

After the war, Alcott continued writing in two opposing veins. Her sensational novel *Behind a Mask: or A Woman's Power* was published in 1866. To Alcott's surprise, *Little Women*, her novel for girls based loosely on her own experiences growing up in Concord, was published in 1868 and became an immediate, enduring best-seller. When the book's publisher asked her to write a book for children in 1867, she had only consented because of her shaky family finances. *Little Men*, *Jo's Boys*, and five other books for children followed, proving the popularity of books displaying strong, creative girls who grow up to have interests aside from securing a husband. Alcott also published two novels for adults in the 1870s, *Work: A Story of Experience* and *A Modern Mephistopheles*.

With the publication of *Little Women*, Alcott was a wealthy woman. Yet she needed to keep publishing to maintain her entire family in comfort. In addition to her parents, she supported her older, widowed sister and two nephews, and after 1879, the niece of her deceased youngest sister. Despite increasing weakness and ill health, Alcott drove herself unmercifully, often working in the face of debilitating pain and exhaustion. She confided the inner conflict in a journal entry.

> Very poorly. Feel quite used up. Don't care much for myself, as rest is heavenly even with pain; but the family seem so panic-stricken and helpless when I break down, that I try to keep the mill going. (quoted in Moyle 1985, 278)

Alcott continued writing until her death, despite her ill health. Two days after the death of her father in March 1888, Alcott died at the age of 55. Her illness was never named or officially diagnosed, though her biographer and other researchers believe that the long-term effects of mercury poisoning had taken their toll on her system.

See also **Literary Women; Nurses**

Selected Readings

Alcott, Louisa May. *The Journals of Louisa May Alcott*. Edited by Joel Myerson and Daniel Sheahy. Boston: Little Brown. 1989.
Saxton, Martha. *Louisa May: A Modern Biography of Louisa May Alcott*. Boston: Houghton Mifflin. 1977.

Anthony, Susan B. (1820–1906)

What is American Slavery? It is the Legalized Systematized robbery of the bodies and souls of nearly four millions of men, women and children…. Its [sic] the legalized prostitution of nearly two millions of the daughters of this proud republic…. It is theft, robbery, piracy, murder. It is avarice, covetousness, lust, licentiousness, concubinage, polygamy; it is atheism, blasphemy, and sin against the Holy Ghost.

—Susan B. Anthony, "What Is American Slavery?" Speech, 1857, SBA Papers, Library of Congress Manuscript Division in *The Papers of Elizabeth Cady Stanton and Susan B. Anthony*. Edited by Holland and Gordon, 1991

During the early months of the Civil War, the women's rights leader and abolitionist Susan B. Anthony was hard at work on her family's farm in Rochester, New York.

Although farm chores were a welcome respite from the ceaseless labor of social and political reform, she grew increasingly restless and discouraged as the national conflict heightened.

The enforced "vacation" made no sense to her. She strongly disagreed with her women's rights and antislavery colleagues who concurred that all reform agitation—speeches, rallies, and persuasive writings—must cease for the duration of the war as a means of encouraging Northerners to unite. She tried to convince her fellow activists that abolitionists must keep the pressure on President Abraham Lincoln and Congress to emancipate the slaves, just as women must not slacken their efforts to achieve their legal and political rights. Her protests were ignored. On her own, and in her partnership with ELIZABETH CADY STANTON, Anthony refused to sit back and wait for the national crisis to take its course.

For Anthony, the years immediately prior to the war had been filled with struggle and victories. The daughter of a Quaker businessman and reformer, she began her reform career in 1848 when she left teaching to become a temperance activist. By 1854, the women's rights movement and abolition were her primary causes. In collaboration with Cady Stanton, Anthony conducted a six-year campaign to expand the Married Women's Property Law in New York State. This massive effort was her most significant contribution to the antebellum women's rights movement. The new law, passed by the New York legislature in 1860, made it legal for married women to own property separately from their husbands, to conduct business transactions, to manage their wages and other income, to sue and be sued, and to share custody of their children with their husbands.

Since 1856, Anthony had been working as general agent for the American Anti-Slavery Society (AASS) in New York State. In this capacity, she organized groups of abolitionist orators to lecture throughout the state. In addition to being the leader and organizer, Anthony frequently delivered speeches herself, acquiring the fiery oratory characteristic of William Lloyd Garrison's followers.

Garrisonian abolitionists had confronted angry mobs in their audiences since the 1840s, but the hostile crowds that Anthony's troupe of lecturers encountered during January and February 1861, on the eve of the Civil War, surpassed any she had previously experienced. During what she referred to as "the winter of mobs," she, Wendell Phillips, Stephen Symonds Foster, Elizabeth Cady Stanton, Samuel Joseph May, and other AASS orators urged the public to demand that the federal government accept "No Compromise with Slaveholders" and institute "Immediate and Unconditional Emancipation" (I. Harper 1899, 1:208).

The violence Anthony faced did not deter her nor did it appear to rattle her, even when others were convinced their lives were in danger. Frequently she was the only woman on the platform. The more difficult the mob, the more righteous she believed was their cause. She was infuriated that the male "rowdies" refused to allow AASS lecturers to speak. With each explosive encounter, her oratory became more vituperative and unyielding. A week after she and Samuel Joseph May were burned in effigy following their unsuccessful attempt to speak to a crowd in Syracuse, New York, Anthony stood up and taunted a group of men in Auburn, New York. "Why, boys, you're nothing but a *baby mob*. You ought to go to Syracuse, and learn how to do it, and also learn how to get before the Grand Jury" (quoted in Venet 1991, 30).

A year later in the spring of 1862, following her difficult period of idleness in Rochester, Anthony decided to agitate for abolition on her own by conducting a one-woman lecture tour of western New York State. She not only stirred her audiences to press the government for immediate emancipation, she also insisted that they confront their racial prejudice and discrimination, particularly their fears that an influx of freed African Americans would displace white workers and upset the precarious balance of the social class structure. To questions concerning what shall be done with the freedpeople, Anthony replied, "Do with the Negroes? What arrogance in *us* to put the question, what shall *we* do with a race of men and women who have fed, clothed and supported both themselves and their oppressors for centuries" (quoted in J. Harper 1998, 70). During the late winter of 1863, Anthony met with Cady Stanton at her home in Brooklyn, New York, to discuss plans to establish a national women's political organization dedicated to promoting the freedom of African Americans. From these conversations the WOMAN'S NATIONAL LOYAL LEAGUE (WNLL) was born, a cause that would address the issues of freedom for African Americans and women's rights. Anthony's official position was secretary of the WNLL, but in reality she was the principal organizer and publicist, and was in charge of all political strategy and finances (Venet 1991, 110).

Despite the constant attention that the WNLL required, Anthony made the time to become involved in the 1864 presidential campaign of John Charles Frémont, the third-party candidate of the Radical Democratic Party. Although Cady Stanton was familiar with presidential campaign politicking based on her husband's involvement in the Republican Party's campaigns in 1856 and 1860, this was Anthony's first full immersion in the process, an involvement that would become a prominent feature of her suffrage activism.

Following Congress's approval of the Thirteenth Amendment abolishing slavery in January 1865, the work of the WNLL was complete. During the final months of the war, Anthony traveled to Kansas, to the home of her brother Daniel Read Anthony, the mayor of Leavenworth. For a time she helped supervise her brother's newspaper, with his strict orders "not to have it all woman's rights and suffrage" (I. Harper 1899, 1:242). As she witnessed the thousands of starving African Americans pouring into the city, searching for food and shelter, she was moved to act. She helped organize relief for the freedpeople and helped them locate employment and organize educational opportunities. As the weeks passed, and as increasing numbers of African Americans faced the barriers of racial prejudice and oppression, she helped a group form an equal rights league. She also lectured white citizens of Kansas on the urgency of suffrage for the former slaves.

These efforts kept her busy throughout the spring and summer of 1865. In August, she read newspaper reports that Republican members of Congress, in the midst of discussing their plans for the Fourteenth Amendment (designed to protect the civil freedoms of African Americans), were planning to use the word "male" in the amendment's second section. Anthony was alarmed because the gender of citizens had never been established in the Constitution before. She was extremely concerned that the addition of the qualifier "male" would weaken women's claims to their rights as citizens and eliminate the possibility of any discussion or movement on the issue of women's right to vote.

Anthony hastened to New York to confer with Cady Stanton and her women's rights colleagues. Thus began the most contentious struggle of the two suffragists' careers. All through the Civil War, both women had been certain that women would gain the suffrage after the war. By 1869, women's rights activists had lost their battle to gain the suffrage through both the Fourteenth and Fifteenth Amendments. In May 1869, Cady Stanton and Anthony established the National Woman Suffrage Association, an organization dedicated to securing a federal woman suffrage amendment.

After a lifetime leading the National Woman Suffrage Association and the National American Woman Suffrage Association (established in 1890), Anthony died of pneumonia and heart failure in 1906 at the age of 86, the ballot still beyond the reach of most American women. Not until 1920 did the Nineteenth Amendment grant the right to vote to all women citizens in the United States.

See also **Abolitionists; Dickinson, Anna; Women's Rights Movement**

Selected Readings

Harper, Judith E. *Susan B. Anthony: A Biographical Companion*. Santa Barbara, CA: ABC-CLIO. 1998.

Venet, Wendy Hamand. *Neither Ballots Nor Bullets: Women Abolitionists and the Civil War*. Charlottesville: University Press of Virginia. 1991.

Antietam (Sharpsburg), Battle of

In early September 1862, as Confederate General Robert E. Lee's Army of Northern Virginia invaded western Maryland, the fields and pastures of the surrounding countryside were bursting with ripe corn, apples, grains, and potatoes ready for the upcoming harvest. By leading his army northward out of battle-scarred northern Virginia, Lee hoped to give civilians in Virginia a chance to harvest their crops while nourishing his starving troops upon Maryland's land of plenty. After winning two minor battles in the North in early September, Lee wanted to win another battle, possibly a decisive one, before heading back to the South. Near the village of Sharpsburg, a farming hamlet of 1,300 men, women, and children, Lee's army collided with Union troops. In the village and on the surrounding farms of Sharpsburg near Antietam Creek on September 17, 1862, the Battle of Antietam (known in the Confederacy as the Battle of Sharpsburg) began at dawn. Union Major General George McClellan commanded the Army of the Potomac's 75,000 men. Although Union forces did not know it, Lee's army had only 40,000 soldiers, setting the stage for a critical Union victory. What ensued has commonly been acknowledged as the bloodiest day of the Civil War. When the one-day battle ended, over 6,000 men were dead—the most American soldiers killed in one day in United States history—and many more were wounded or missing.

Very little has been written about the civilians of Sharpsburg before, during, and after the battle, although they played a major role, particularly after the fighting when thousands of the wounded needed water, food, and medical attention. Despite the trauma and the overwhelming property losses they suffered, the women, men, and children of Sharpsburg pitched in to assist the wounded during the days and weeks after the battle. Women throughout the region volunteered as nurses, donated food and clothing, and raised money to help the survivors.

In the two weeks before the battle, during Lee's Maryland Campaign, men and women were shocked by the spectacle of the ragged, skeletal bodies of the Confederate soldiers marching through their villages. Although Lee's soldiers foraged off the countryside, seizing ripe produce straight from the fields, women—some of whom held Unionist sympathies—offered the Confederates food or sold it to them. Confederate sympathizers, of whom there were many in Maryland, offered whatever food and clothing their families could spare.

The Confederate soldiers tried to persuade Sharpsburg residents to leave their homes, warning them of the impending battle. A number of farmers, such as William and Margaret Roulette, refused to leave their homes, hoping to protect them from looters and their crops from ravenous soldiers. Yet their presence did not safeguard their property. Before the battle, the Roulettes watched helplessly as soldiers took all the meat from their meat house, the corn from their corn crib, and the hay from their barn. Even the fencing on their property was not spared (Ernst 1999, 121–122).

The battle itself caused the most damage to homes, farm buildings, crops, and the land. While civilians huddled in their houses and cellars, the artillery and cannon fire shook the earth with deafening blasts. The bombardment was so intense that it caused some terror-stricken residents to run from their shelters. After a particularly overwhelming sequence of cannon fire, a group of women raced from their refuge "like a flock of birds," one Southern cavalryman reported. With their children tagging along behind them, they attempted to run across a recently plowed field, tripping and nearly falling as they did so. As a soldier on horseback rushed forward to rescue them and herd them away from the attack, both Union and Confederate soldiers halted their firing until the women and children were safely out of harm's way. In another instance, when a shell exploded and caused one house to ignite in flames, four courageous young women abandoned safety to seize buckets and basins of water to douse the fire. The fire reignited a short time later, but the women returned and were successful in saving the house from destruction (Ernst 1999, 139).

For the first time since CLARA BARTON had been transporting food and medical supplies to the battlefields, she arrived at a battle before it began as she had been determined to do. She believed that to accomplish the most good she needed to be on hand to assist the surgeons and the wounded as soon as the casualties occurred. In August 1862, she had been frustrated at the Battle of Cedar Mountain and at the Second Battle of Bull Run (known in the Confederacy as the Second Battle of Manassas) because she could not arrange for her transportation to arrive until after the battle was long over.

With a wagon, a driver, and her assistant, Cornelius Welles, Barton arrived with alcoholic beverages (to be used as stimulants), pickled and canned goods, numerous candle lanterns, bandages, salves, and dressings. In the dark early morning hours before the battle, she had her driver move as close to the army as was possible. By 9 AM, the battle having raged for several hours, Barton located a barn surrounded by a cornfield where she discovered 300 wounded soldiers. She immediately set to work, offering drinks and food to sustain them until surgeons arrived. She then set out on foot to locate a surgeon, finding one in a stone house not distant from the barn, which was also full of wounded men. The surgeon reported that his medical group had no supplies except for their instruments and a bit of chloroform to anesthetize patients. As Barton examined the floors covered with bleeding soldiers, she noticed that their wounds were bound only with corn leaves (Oates 1994, 79, 85).

Until the battle was over and for hours afterward, Barton tended the wounded and the dying in the barn and the farmhouse. When her food supplies were exhausted, she concocted a gruel out of sifted cornmeal and water. With the discovery of three barrels of Indian meal (a whole-grain cornmeal), marked as Confederate issue, she continued to eke out a barely palatable gruel. At one point, as she was moving between the house and the barn, she leaned down to give a drink to a soldier begging for water. When she raised his head to allow him to swallow, a bullet passed through the sleeve of her blouse, hitting and immediately killing the man she held in her arms (Oates 1994, 85, 87).

As the din of the battle ceased and the smoke cleared, a scene of total devastation overwhelmed the civilians who emerged from their shelters. The pastures, roadsides, and fields were covered with thousands of the wounded and the dead. Sharpsburg residents returned to their homes to find their livestock gone, their fields and crops destroyed, and their land ruined by the cannon and artillery barrages. Buildings in the village were so riddled with bullet holes that onlookers declared that the walls resembled honeycomb. Despite their personal losses, the women and men of Sharpsburg did what they could to assist the wounded. Women dispensed tea and bits of food that they scavenged from what was left of the soldiers' foraging and the destruction. They also comforted the dying, sang hymns, and bandaged wounds. Every house and farm dwelling was utilized as a hospital, displacing the owners, who were forced to go without shelter.

As the days passed, relatives of the soldiers and volunteers from the surrounding villages arrived. The women prepared meals for the 4,000 wounded and ill soldiers billeted in Sharpsburg. The women of Funkstown, Maryland, worked into the night cooking chicken, mashed potatoes, and fried ham sandwiches to feed the men. Other female volunteers bathed the soldiers, laundered soiled clothing and bandages, and wrote letters for the wounded who could not do so themselves (Ernst 1999, 158–169). The menfolk of Sharpsburg and the neighboring region worked alongside the women, especially in the hours after the battle. Later, they were pressed into service to bury the dead.

The day after the battle, the UNITED STATES SANITARY COMMISSION (USSC) began delivering food, bedding, clothing, and medical supplies that women from all over the North had produced, donated, or collected. In a letter to a colleague on September 23, 1862, Frederick Law Olmsted, the general secretary of the USSC, listed the items sent, making clear the enormity of Northern women's contributions to the war effort.

> We have sent … 28,763 pieces of dry goods, shirts, towels, bedticks, pillows, & c.; 30 barrels old linen, bandages, and lint; 3188 pounds of farina; 2620 pounds

condensed milk; 5000 pound beef-stock and canned meats; 3000 bottles of wine and cordials, and several tons of lemons and other fruit. (Wormeley 1863, 99–100)

Weeks after the battle, the wounded still filled the homes and barns of Sharpsburg residents as epidemics of typhoid fever and smallpox plagued soldiers and civilians alike. Many months passed before the civilians of Sharpsburg resumed a semblance of their prebattle routines, and it took years for the land to heal its scars.

Selected Readings

Ernst, Kathleen A. *Too Afraid to Cry: Maryland Civilians in the Antietam Campaign.* Mechanicsburg, PA: Stackpole Books. 1999.
Oates, Stephen B. *A Woman of Valor: Clara Barton and the Civil War.* New York: The Free Press. 1994.

Artists

I honor every woman who has strength enough to step out of the beaten path when she feels that her walk lies in another; strength enough to stand up and be laughed at if necessary. That is a bitter pill we must all swallow at the beginning; but I regard those pills as tonics quite essential to one's mental salvation.

—Harriet Hosmer, sculptor (quoted in Rubinstein 1990, 44)

Women artists in the North began to achieve increasing public recognition and acceptance of their work during the Civil War era. Although lingering prejudices produced obstacles that women struggled to overcome, they were managing to acquire the education and training necessary to make them competitive with men as professionals. By this time, women artists were also showing their work alongside their male colleagues in exhibitions in the large cities of the North. In the South, women did not become professional artists by and large, though they created art at home and in the female colleges, seminaries, and academies.

In the early decades of the nineteenth century, the majority of professional women artists were miniaturists, producing the small portraits that were so popular at the time. A number of women worked as portrait painters, traveling from one village to the next, barely making a living wage like many of their male counterparts. Most women artists of this era received no formal art education. In general, they learned all they knew from their male relatives or private tutors.

In the 1840s, the first art schools began accepting women students. Only a slight minority of female art students intended to make a living from their work, but by this decade, a formal education in an art school was necessary for any artist who wished to become professional (Prieto 2001, 31).The academies and seminaries offered instruction in drawing and painting as these skills came to be viewed as the proper accoutrements of a middle- and upper-class lady.

Two of the nineteenth century's finest art schools, the Pennsylvania Academy of Fine Arts in Philadelphia and the National Academy of Design in New York City, opened their doors to women in 1844 and 1846, respectively. In 1860, the young Mary Cassatt, a leading late-nineteenth-century American impressionist painter, decided to pursue art seriously. In the fall of 1861, when she was 17 years old, she enrolled at the Pennsylvania Academy of Fine Arts, taking instruction in the junior group. Her early education consisted of making drawings from plaster casts of heads, hands, and feet. Once proficient at this level, she joined her fellow students in composing studies from casts of classical antique sculptures of the human figure. In the early 1860s, women did not work from nude models as male students did. When women were first permitted to work from life in 1868, the models were female and men were excluded from the classes. The first opportunity women had to study the male nude figure came in 1877, in all-female classes (Rubinstein 1982, 40).

Mary Cassatt attended the academy for four years. Following her graduation in 1865, she persuaded her father to fund further art study in Europe, a common destination for women artists of the mid- to late nineteenth century. Women painters and sculptors flocked to Italy, France, and Germany, not to attend school, but to study, learn, and copy from the works of the "Great Masters." Women spent hours in museums and galleries, trying to reproduce paintings and drawings as precisely as possible. Many women paid for the journey with money saved from years of teaching. Others had supportive families to finance their time abroad. Elizabeth Gardner and Imogene Robinson operated a School of Design in Worcester, Massachusetts, in the early 1860s. In 1864, they departed for France with the money earned from their business.

In Rome, a group of American women sculptors formed their own supportive peer network with the help of Charlotte Cushman, a former American actress. The best women sculptors of the day—Harriet Hosmer, Emma Stebbins, the African-American EDMONIA LEWIS, Anne Whitney (after 1865), and a few others—gathered, inspiring and encouraging each other. Though living and working in Rome, they were successful in acquiring sculpture commissions from American city and state governments. In 1861, Harriet Hosmer completed a sculpture of Missouri Senator Thomas Hart Benton, the father of JESSIE BENTON FRÉMONT, for the state of Missouri. Stebbins sculpted a statue of Horace Mann, the leader of the movement for public education, in 1864, for the state of Massachusetts. Her most famous work, *Angel of the Waters or Bethesda Fountain*, was commissioned by the City of New York. Completed in 1862, it was not erected in Central Park until 1873.

Despite the gains women artists were making during the Civil War, many Americans and Europeans continued to believe that women could not create great works of art on a par with men. During the Civil War, Hosmer, considered one of the great sculptors of the nineteenth century, suffered from accusations that her male assistants produced one of her finest works. Despite the rumors, her statue *Zenobia* drew tens of thousands of viewers when it toured Boston, New York City, and Chicago. The New England poet John Greenleaf Whittier commented, "In looking at it, I felt that the artist had been as truly serving her country, while working out her magnificent design abroad, as our soldiers in the field … in their departments." (quoted in Rubinstein 1990, 40). Hosmer fought the charge made against her work. By suing for libel, she forced two British publications to publish retractions of their false claim that others had sculpted *Zenobia*.

Anne Whitney, working in Massachusetts during the Civil War, crafted two sculptures that captured the attention of war-weary Northerners. Her rendering of *Lady Godiva*, completed in 1862, portrays the fully clothed woman of legend as she prepares to disrobe in order to help relieve her fellow citizens of the burdens of heavy taxation. For the Northern public, the sculpture evoked a woman's sacrifice to help her country, an inspiring theme for women and men during wartime. Whitney, an ardent abolitionist, expressed her longing for the emancipation of African Americans in her statue *Africa*, completed in 1864. The sculpture depicts a black woman rising from sleep to greet her newfound freedom.

Sarah Miriam Peale, born in 1800, has been frequently acknowledged as the first professional woman artist. She was a highly successful portrait painter in Baltimore and St. Louis for decades before the Civil War. The niece of the prominent painter Charles Willson Peale and the daughter of the painter James Peale, by the late 1850s, she had immersed herself in the painting of still-lifes. In 1859, 1861, 1862, 1866, and 1867, her still-lifes earned prizes at art fairs in St. Louis.

Lilly Martin Spencer, a genre painter living in New York City, reached the height of her fame during the Civil War. She commanded fees as high as the period's most well-known genre painter, George Caleb Bingham. Martin Spencer was the mother of 13 children and the sole breadwinner for her family. (Her business manager was her husband who also cooked, cleaned, and cared for their children.) Martin Spencer's domestic themes were extremely popular and were frequently reproduced as engravings and lithographs. Her painting *The War Spirit at Home, Celebrating the Victory at Vicksburg* re-creates a homey scene in which a mother reads about the famous battle in a newspaper, her baby in her arms, while three children march around the family sitting room honoring the victory.

Fanny Palmer (Frances Flora Bond Palmer) is regarded as one of the most significant graphic artists of the nineteenth century. One of the busiest lithographers working for Currier and Ives, she specialized in creating romanticized images of agricultural and frontier life. During the Civil War, her work focused on still-lifes of fruits and flowers.

After the war, opportunities for women in the art world rapidly expanded. Women and girls entered the art schools in the United States in ever-increasing numbers. Excluded from all men's art groups for decades, women flocked to form art clubs of their own. In 1866, the first women's art club, the Ladies' Art Association, was established. These groups supported and inspired women in the creation of art and art collecting while also providing art education.

See also **Ream, Vinnie**

Selected Readings

Prieto, Laura. At Home in the Studio: The Professionalization of Women Artists in America. Cambridge, MA: Harvard University Press. 2001.
Rubinstein, Charlotte Streifer. American Women Artists from Early Indian Times to the Present. New York: Avon Books. 1982.

B

Barton, Clara (1821–1912)

Though best known for founding and leading the American Red Cross in the late nineteenth century, Clara Barton contributed all of her energies to helping the Union soldiers during the Civil War—from the arrival of the first soldiers in Washington, DC, in April 1861, through the war's aftermath and the grim task of identifying the unknown war dead.

Clarissa Harlowe Barton was born and raised in North Oxford, a small rural community in central Massachusetts. An active, spirited girl who loved the outdoors, she was an accomplished equestrian and sharpshooter. She spent her young adulthood teaching in Massachusetts and in Bordentown, New Jersey, where she created one of New Jersey's first public schools. In the mid-1850s, she became the first female clerk in the U.S. Patent Office and was one of the first women civil servants in the United States.

In September 1857, she returned home to Massachusetts when she found it difficult to maintain her post in the Patent Office following a change in presidential administration. Although she busied herself with courses in French and drawing, she felt a lack of purpose in her life. Caring for a succession of ailing relatives did nothing to alleviate her sense that her life held no meaning. As a single woman with no husband or children to care for, she fulfilled her family's expectation that she devote herself to nursing her sick relations. She discovered that the longer she dedicated herself to these duties the more depressed she became. The confinement whittled away at the self-confidence and inner strength that she had gained from teaching and working as a clerk. In a letter to a nephew, she wrote, "I must not rust much longer … [but]push out and do *something somewhere*, or *anything, anywhere*" (quoted in Pryor 1987, 70).

Following the election of President Abraham Lincoln in November 1860, Barton regained her Patent Office clerkship. Shortly thereafter, after the fall of Fort Sumter and following Lincoln's call for the enlistment of 75,000 male volunteers in April 1861, the 6th Massachusetts Regiment was attacked in Baltimore as they made their way to Washington, DC. The entire regiment was transported by rail to Washington where there were no army hospitals or medical corps to receive them. Upon hearing the news, Barton immediately responded and met the transport at the station. She assisted the wounded and transported a number of the most critically injured to her sister Sally Barton Vassall's house in Washington. As she provided nursing care to the wounded, she became concerned about the fate of the rest of the regiment that was stationed in Washington with no provisions. Acting on her own initiative, Barton rushed to grocers, shopkeepers, and neighbors to ask for contributions of food and supplies for the soldiers. With her food and medical supplies in tow, she promptly advanced to the location where the soldiers' needs were greatest, thereby establishing a pattern of service that would be her stock and trade throughout the war.

As the weeks passed, women from SOLDIERS' AID SOCIETIES in central Massachusetts sent her supplies. Soon she was writing letter after letter soliciting relief from women's groups. Her medical supplies and foodstuffs multiplied rapidly, forcing her to move to larger quarters, and six months later, to pack three warehouses with goods.

Beginning in August 1862, as Barton became closely attuned to the needs of a burgeoning, grossly undersupplied army, she took her crusade directly to the battlefields. At the Battles of Culpeper, Second Bull Run, Antietam, Fredericksburg, and elsewhere, she arrived with her medical and food supplies, delivering them directly to the soldiers and medical corps. By this time, the army had acknowledged its need of her assistance by informing her of the locations of upcoming battles. During the hours and days following these engagements, when thousands of casualties covered acre upon acre, she cared for the most immediate needs of the wounded, supplying them with fresh water and a bit of sustenance so that they could survive until they were transported to the army hospitals. When her cornmeal mush ran out, she improvised a mixture of "crushed army biscuits, wine, water, and brown sugar" (quoted in Pryor 1987, 93). She bandaged wounds, assisted the surgeons, and enlisted whomever she could find to help her clean the blood-drenched and filthy makeshift battlefield hospitals.

By 1863, the Union army's management of its casualties on the battlefield and in the hospitals had improved and had settled into a bureaucratized semblance of organization. The success of the UNITED STATES SANITARY COMMISSION's (USSC) distribution of food and medical supplies, the reliance on Union army nurses in the army hospitals, and the vast improvements in the ambulance corps all served to diminish the need for the efforts of private individuals, including Barton. With these changes, Barton experienced difficulties in accessing supplies that had once flowed freely, and her work halted.

In June 1863, Barton resumed her customary battlefield role following the Union army's attack on Battery Wagner on Morris Island in South Carolina. Yet, by September, General Quincy A. Gillmore informed her that her "services will be no longer required in connection with the hospital in the field" (quoted in Pryor 1987, 118). Distressed and downcast, Barton retreated. With the encouragement of the midwestern abolitionist Frances Dana Gage, she became immersed in assisting the freedpeople.

By May of 1864, the federal government again called on her, when the army underestimated the enormity of the casualties General Ulysses S. Grant's Spotsylvania Court House Campaign (VA) entailed. For six months beginning in June 1864, Barton served as supervisor of nurses at a field hospital for the Army of the James in Virginia.

Immediately after the war, Barton was consumed by the herculean task of identifying the tens of thousands of unknown war dead. More than 50 percent of the fallen Union soldiers had never been identified. Once again, working most often alone, she submitted names of missing soldiers to newspapers, post offices, and veterans organizations. Family members and friends of the missing soldiers gave her the names to be published, in the hopes that returning veterans would inform Barton about any soldier about whom they had knowledge. As she heard from veterans, she then passed on the information to those who made the initial inquiries. Although there was clearly a large public demand for this service, Barton did not succeed in mustering the political or public support she needed to adequately fund The Office of Correspondence with Friends of the Missing Men of the U.S. Army.

Around this time, Barton was invited to accompany administration officials to the site of the Confederate prison at Andersonville, Georgia. The tour was intended to establish a national cemetery for the thousands of Union prisoners of war who had died at the prison. Even Barton, who had experienced more firsthand battlefield gore than most of the other tour members, was horrorstruck by the dreadful remnants of Andersonville. Approximately 33,000 Union soldiers had been imprisoned in a 26-acre enclosure designed for no more than 10,000 prisoners. Suffering from rampant dysentery, scurvy, hospital gangrene, typhoid, and massive starvation, soldiers had died by the hundreds each week. Conditions were so unrelentingly filthy that the merest insect bite or splinter became infected with gangrene, necessitating an amputation that guaranteed a soldier's death (Oates 1994, 322–328; Pryor 1987, 139–140).

With Frances Gage's encouragement, in 1866, Barton petitioned Congress for funds that would enable her to continue her work for The Office of Correspondence. They awarded her $15,000. In 1868, she officially closed the office. In all, she and her clerks had responded to 63,182 letters of inquiry. They identified 22,000 missing war dead (Pryor 1987, 154).

Beginning in the fall of 1866, Barton embarked on a nationwide lecture tour, speaking primarily on "Work and Incidents of Army Life." Through her speeches, she received enormous public exposure, gained celebrity and wealth, and became one of the most well-known women to serve the nation during the Civil War.

In the late 1860s, Barton traveled to Europe to regain her health and strength following two years of public speaking. While recuperating, she learned of the work of the International Red Cross. When the Franco-Prussian War erupted, she assisted wounded soldiers and civilian refugees as a Red Cross worker. Upon her return to the United States following the Franco-Prussian War in 1873, she embarked on an arduous campaign to convince the U.S. government to sign the Geneva Treaty (an international agreement dictating the humanitarian treatment of the wounded in wartime). Finally, in 1882, the U.S. Senate formally agreed to the terms of the Geneva Convention.

In 1881, Barton established the American Red Cross. For the next two decades, she directed the organization, supervising its efforts to aid the victims of natural disasters. In the Spanish-American War of 1898, she was at the helm when the American Red Cross tended to sick and wounded U.S troops as well as prisoners of war.

Barton served as the organization's president until 1904, when at the age of 83 she reluctantly resigned. For years, her fellow managers had criticized her management and questioned her ability to govern. Barton spent her remaining years at her home in Glen Echo, Maryland. She contracted double pneumonia and died in April 1912, at the age of 90.

See also **Nurses**

Selected Readings

Oates, Stephen B. *A Woman of Valor: Clara Barton and the Civil War.* New York: The Free Press. 1994.

Pryor, Elizabeth Brown. *Clara Barton: Professional Angel.* Philadelphia: University of Pennsylvania Press. 1987.

Battle of the Handkerchiefs

On February 20, 1863, thousands of citizens of New Orleans, most of them white women, engaged in the legendary Battle of the Handkerchiefs. This effusive public display of Confederate patriotism came just two months after Union Major General Benjamin "Beast" Butler's iron rule of Louisiana—a time when few women dared to voice their support of the Confederacy.

Under Union General Nathaniel Banks's command in December 1862, the residents of New Orleans were not as threatened as they had been during the command of Butler. Although Banks was fastidious about tracking down and punishing perpetrators of treasonous acts in the public schools, most of them schoolmistresses and female teachers, he did not share Butler's zeal or highly controversial methods for silencing the entire female population. Butler's infamous GENERAL ORDER NO. 28, while effective, had enraged men and women throughout the Confederacy. Under Banks's rule, women once again felt free to sing Confederate songs and act defiantly toward Union soldiers without fear of retribution.

Around noon on February 20, an enormous crowd, composed mostly of women, assembled at the New Orleans Levee on the Mississippi River to witness and cheer a gathering of Confederate soldiers. As Julia Le Grand noted in her diary, citizens were desperate for a glimpse of the rare but cherished "dear gray uniform" (Le Grand 1911, 137). As approximately 400 Confederate prisoners boarded a steamboat to travel upriver for a prisoner exchange with captured Union soldiers, women, children, and old men waved Confederate flags, handkerchiefs, and parasols while shouting their loyalty to the Confederacy and President Jefferson Davis.

When Union troops guarding the prisoners decided that they had endured enough of the din and chaos, they ordered the mob to move back and to stop waving their handkerchiefs (Huber 1962, 50). Not only did the women refuse to budge, the command seemed to encourage even more resistance. Women mocked and insulted Union soldiers as powerfully as they had before the order was given.

Not until Brigadier General James Bowen called in reinforcements did the crowd begin to disperse. Union soldiers moved toward the mob armed with bayonets. A number of women later reported that they felt the tips of the bayonets through the backs of their outer clothing. Then, as the soldiers poised the cannon to fire on the mob, the women scattered and headed home, though they did not go quietly.

As in New Orleans, despite the efforts of Union forces to control and silence hostile civilians, women throughout the Confederacy sometimes found that soldiers' deference to their gender permitted them to voice and demonstrate their resistance.

See also **Invasion and Occupation**

Selected Reading

Huber, Leonard V. "The Battle of the Handkerchiefs." *Civil War History.* 8 (1) (1962): 48–53.

Bickerdyke, Mary Ann (1817–1901)

By the latter half of the Civil War and throughout the late nineteenth century, Mary Ann "Mother" Bickerdyke was one of the most widely known of all Northern women who had nursed Union soldiers. Her gutsy, no-nonsense approach to hospital work, her disregard of military protocol and social convention, and her contact and connections with several Union generals including Ulysses S. Grant and William Tecumseh Sherman made her a Civil War legend. The dilemma for modern historians lies in sifting her real-life accomplishments from the unconfirmed, often exaggerated stories that have been told about her.

Mary Ann Ball was born in Knox County, Ohio, the daughter of farmers. While it is known that she lived with her grandparents after her mother's death and received some education, it is difficult to confirm much else about her early life, as recent research has cast doubt on several stories that have been reported. Evidently she did not attend Oberlin College nor was she integral to the Underground Railroad in Ohio. She did marry Robert Bickerdyke in 1847, lived in Cincinnati, and gave birth to two sons. After Robert died in 1859, while the family was living in Galesburg, Illinois, she struggled to support her children by laboring as a laundress, domestic servant, and nurse.

At the beginning of the Civil War, Bickerdyke eagerly accepted her church's mission to transport food and other supplies to a regimental hospital in Cairo, Illinois. Once she arrived there and surveyed the wretched condition of the hospital and its patients, she decided to volunteer her services. One of her first self-appointed tasks was to wash the dirt-encrusted bodies of every patient in the hospital. She removed the convalescent soldier-nurses from duty, most of whom were diseased and verminous, and replaced them with healthy soldiers who were idling in jail while incarcerated for minor infractions. When the surgeons discovered that their orders and the standards of military protocol meant nothing to Bickerdyke, they complained to Brigadier General Benjamin Prentiss, in the hopes that he would remove her. In a scenario that was to be repeated many times in Bickerdyke's Civil War career, she met with the general and persuaded him to act in support of her nursing priorities.

In November 1861, when the first general military hospital in Cairo was established, the head surgeon refused to accept her services. Bickerdyke appealed directly to General Grant who then appointed her matron of the hospital. In this role, she was instructed to receive and dispense supplies sent from the Chicago Sanitary Commission. As matron, Bickerdyke focused on preparing meals for patients, rather than on nursing.

Following the Battle of Fort Donelson in February 1862, Bickerdyke worked night and day as a nurse on the hospital steamer *City of Memphis*. She made a total of five round trips from the hospitals to the battlefields. On her last trip, she was informed at midnight that all soldiers had been removed from the battlefield. She left the ship and insisted on making one final tour of the area herself, to ensure that no soldier was being abandoned on the mud- and ice-covered battlefield—a mission that earned her widespread press coverage and instant celebrity. From that point on, Bickerdyke chose to work in the field or "tent" hospitals close to the front. Her next stint on the battlefields were the days and weeks following the Battle of Shiloh in Tennessee in April 1862.

Bickerdyke developed a reputation for seizing supplies "for her boys" from USSC and NSC stores without any requisition. To handle this problem, the NSC made her a sanitary agent, which gave her legitimate access to all supplies.

In late 1862, Grant suggested that she work in the military hospitals in Memphis, Tennessee. In January 1863, the medical director in Memphis, perhaps hoping to get rid of her once and for all, sent her to work at the army pesthouse for smallpox victims at Fort Pickering. When she arrived, she found there was no medical or nursing staff. The patients were alone, lying in agony, helping each other to the limited extent that they were able. Bickerdyke located a number of African-American men, all smallpox survivors, and supervised them in the cleaning of the building. She cleaned the patients, fed them plenty of vegetables and milk products, and dosed them with herbs. Once the hospital was efficiently established, she moved on to Gayeso military hospital in Memphis where she superintended the laundry and meal preparation. As food supplies became scantier and more difficult to procure, she traveled to Illinois to encourage farmers to donate live cows and chickens so that soldiers in the Memphis hospitals would have fresh eggs and milk. With the help of the NSC, she shipped the livestock to Memphis.

In late spring 1863, Bickerdyke nursed the men in Grant's army during the siege of Vicksburg in Mississippi. Then, in late summer, she joined General William Tecumseh Sherman's army on its march to Chattanooga, Tennessee. During the Battles of Lookout Mountain and Missionary Ridge, she was the only woman on the frontlines. For months, she and Eliza Porter nursed the wounded in Tennessee and Alabama. The two women then accompanied Sherman's army as it fought its way to Atlanta, Georgia. After the fall of Atlanta in September 1864, Bickerdyke pleaded with Sherman to allow her to continue with the army on its way to Savannah, but he refused. Not long after her release, she lectured for the USSC and traveled to Wilmington, North Carolina, to tend to Union prisoners returning from the Confederate prison at Andersonville.

Immediately after the war, Bickerdyke assisted with the demobilization of Illinois regiments. She then worked for a year as a cook and housekeeper at the Home for the Friendless in Chicago. Not satisfied with that position, she assisted veterans who wished to claim land in Kansas under the Homestead Act of 1862. She moved to Kansas with her two sons and remained for a time in Salina, where the Bickerdykes operated a hotel. After she suffered a long illness, her sons sent her to recuperate in San Francisco in 1876 where she worked for a time in the San Francisco Mint. While in California, she also volunteered her time helping soldiers claim their pensions and eventually worked as a pension attorney, traveling to Washington, DC.

In her later years, Bickerdyke left California to live with her son in Bunker Hill, Kansas, where she died at the age of 84.

See also **Nurses**

Selected Readings

Adams, George W. "Bickerdyke, Mary Ann Ball." In *Notable American Women, 1607–1750: A Biographical Dictionary*. Edited by Edward T. James. Cambridge, MA: Belknap Press of Harvard University Press. 1971. Vol. 1: 144– 146.

Baker, Nina Brown. *Cyclone in Calico: The Story of Mary Ann Bickerdyke*. Boston: Little, Brown. 1952.

Blalock, Malinda Pritchard (1842–1903)

Although a small number of women were known to have participated in the GUER-RILLA WAR in the mountains of western North Carolina, few of their stories have been preserved. Unionist Malinda Pritchard Blalock is one exception. Pritchard Blalock fought for three years for the Union alongside her husband in the mountains. Early in the war, she wore a Confederate uniform, having enlisted with her husband in the 26th North Carolina Infantry. She is the only known woman to have fought for both the Confederacy and the Union. In fact, she and husband William McKesson "Keith" Blalock are the only known husband and wife to have served together for both armies (Stevens 2000, vii).

Although the Blalocks' guerrilla activities are well known, Pritchard Blalock's motivations for going to war are less clear as there is no surviving correspondence or other personal papers that reveal her sentiments. The folklore suggests that she was deeply in love with her husband, took his cause as her own, and could not bear to be separated from him. Other legends indicate that it was Blalock's desire that his wife accompany him. Given the trials and hardships she endured as a guerrilla fighter, however, and the missions she undertook on her own without her husband's aid or presence, it is likely that she harbored powerful convictions about her military actions, aside from her love for her husband. Like many Unionists in the mountains of North Carolina, it is likely that she abhorred her neighbors' secessionism as strongly as her husband and believed wholeheartedly in the Union cause.

In western North Carolina, pro-Union and pro-Confederate families spent the entire war feuding with one another, drawing neutral families into their conflicts. Small groups of men on horseback terrorized entire families by attacking farmhouses. These marauders burned houses, stole livestock, plundered grain from food storage bins, and often wounded or killed the menfolk of the household. Women and children were not exempt from the violence as they were often forced to feed the raiders and reveal the hiding places of their relatives and neighbors. Personal grudges predating the war years sometimes fueled the violence that neighbors inflicted on one another.

As a girl, Malinda Pritchard wandered the mountain trails with her brothers near their home in Caldwell County, North Carolina. At an early age she learned to handle guns and to hunt. Although she preferred the outdoors, her domestic training was not neglected. By the time she was a teenager, she was assisting with all the domestic chores at home—housekeeping, cooking, baking, sewing, and quilting. She likely learned to read, write, and do simple arithmetic, though her education probably did not extend beyond the basics.

In April 1861, Pritchard married Keith Blalock, a Lincoln Republican who did not hide the fact that he wanted nothing to do with defending slaveholders. Despite his Unionist sympathies, his pro-Confederate neighbors exerted enough pressure to cause him to enlist in the Confederate military. Although he was tempted to defy the mandate that he join up, he did not, realizing that his rebel neighbors would threaten his wife's safety and perhaps her life in his absence.

Pritchard Blalock refused to remain at home when Keith marched off to enlist in the 26th North Carolina Infantry. She cut her hair short, dressed herself in her husband's clothing, grabbed his hunting rifle, and accompanied him. When the time came to join the army in November 1861, she enlisted as Sam Blalock, claiming to be Keith's brother. While at Camp Carolina, "Sam" drilled and marched, practiced shooting firearms, and learned how to use a bayonet. Her comrades selected her to take the role of "Mess-Wife," whereby she took charge of cooking the rations for a group of soldiers. During her time in the 26th North Carolina, she spent grueling hours building fortifications. She also fought in combat, eventually wounding her shoulder in a skirmish. When a surgeon tended to her wounds, her gender was discovered. Her husband convinced the surgeon to say nothing for several days. While Pritchard Blalock recuperated, Blalock worked on a plan to secure a medical discharge for himself. He rolled in poison oak until his skin was a mass of red eruptions. The surgeons, believing that he had smallpox or swamp fever, agreed to discharge him. Pritchard Blalock received her discharge when she revealed to her commanding officers that she was a woman.

In April 1862, the Blalocks walked home to Watauga County, North Carolina, relieved to be free of the Confederate army. As the summer months passed, local Confederates ordered Blalock to reenlist. After he consented to return to the Confederate military, the Blalocks disappeared high into the mountains. During the ensuing weeks, Blalock was captured and escaped several times. In November 1862, they escaped to East Tennessee, with the intention of joining the Union army then occupying the region.

In East Tennessee, the Blalocks encountered several pro-Union supporters who encouraged them to return to North Carolina to guide Unionist mountain men to Tennessee and to enlist in a new regiment being formed, the 10th Michigan Cavalry. Pritchard Blalock and her husband donned Union uniforms when he agreed to become a recruiting officer for this regiment. In the course of piloting men back and forth to Tennessee, the Blalocks met up with Union officer George W. Kirk, whose mission it was to establish a transportation network to convey pro-Union North Carolina mountain men, Confederate deserters, and escaped Union prisoners of war from the Confederate prison camp in Salisbury, North Carolina, to the Union army in Tennessee. Kirk enlisted the Blalocks to work in western North Carolina, to organize escape routes and safe houses, and to gather food supplies so that they could guide recruits through the mountains to Tennessee and the Union army.

Pritchard Blalock did not always act in concert with her husband. At times she guided potential Union recruits through the mountains on her own. She was well armed, carrying her Union-issue Spencer repeating rifle, far superior to any she had handled before.

During 1863, the Blalocks discharged their assigned duties, while also attacking their pro-Confederate and neutral neighbors in North Carolina. As marauders, they rounded up livestock, stole food supplies, and settled some of Blalock's personal grudges against his longtime enemies, gaining reputations for being ruthless murderers in the process.

In September 1863, Pritchard Blalock discovered that she was pregnant, which abruptly interrupted her military activities. She traveled to Knoxville, Tennessee, to live with a woman whose husband was part of the Blalocks' guerrilla band. On April 8, 1864, she gave birth to a baby boy. For a brief time, she stayed with relatives in Carter County, East Tennessee. Two weeks after the baby's birth, she returned to her husband and the guerrilla network to fight once more, leaving her baby with her relatives.

For the remainder of the war, the Blalocks and their comrades continued gathering and guiding recruits to Union outposts in Tennessee while also launching raids on pro-Confederate households in the western North Carolina region. In January 1865, in the midst of a murderous raid to settle an old score in their home community, Blalock was critically wounded and lost an eye. Pritchard Blalock followed the advice of a doctor they consulted and nursed her husband back to health. In the final weeks of the war, he was once again in action, and, with his wife, managed to destroy miles of railroad track and bridges to hasten the Confederate defeat.

As soon as the war was over, Pritchard Blalock resumed wearing female attire and returned to her relatives in Tennessee to become reacquainted with her son. In August 1865, she traveled to Memphis to join her husband, and two months later, when he was discharged from his regiment, the family returned home to North Carolina. The Blalocks spent the postwar years farming and storekeeping. They maintained their interest and involvement in Republican politics.

See also **Military Women**

Selected Reading

Stevens, Peter F. *Rebels in Blue: The Story of Keith and Malinda Blalock*. Dallas, TX: Taylor Publishing. 2000.

Bowser, Mary Elizabeth (1839–?)

The most highly situated spy of ELIZABETH VAN LEW'S Union espionage ring was the African-American Mary Elizabeth Bowser. Bowser spent a number of months, from sometime in 1863 until January 1864, posing as an illiterate, feeble-minded slave servant in Confederate President Jefferson Davis's White House in Richmond, Virginia. Bowser's extraordinary abilities perfectly matched her spying tasks. As she carried out her housekeeping and childcare duties, her impeccable photographic memory enabled her to remember details of the most sensitive Confederate military and government documents that she found within the household. As she served meals to Davis, and to his Cabinet members, politicians, and military officials, she committed to memory the contents of entire conversations that she then relayed to Union spies in the area.

Bowser was born a slave and was owned by John Van Lew, Elizabeth Van Lew's father. She first lived on the Van Lew family farm outside of Richmond. She was freed after Elizabeth's father died, probably in 1851. Elizabeth, no doubt impressed by Bowser's intellectual abilities, paid for her servant's education at the Quaker Negro College in Philadelphia.

When the Civil War began, Bowser returned to the Van Lew household at Elizabeth's request to assist her in her work for the Union. It was not until 1863 that Van Lew was able to secure a position for Bowser in the Confederate White House. As Bowser gathered information, she relayed it either to Van Lew or to bakery owner Thomas McNiven, a leading Union spy in Richmond, who regularly delivered baked goods to the White House. According to one historian, Bowser fled north after an attempt to burn the Confederate White House in January 1864 (Forbes 1998, 48).

Bowser's postwar activities have not been uncovered, nor is the place or the date of her death known.

See also **Spies and Espionage**

Selected Readings

Peterson, Harriette A. "Mary Elizabeth Bowser." *Notable Black American Women*. Edited by Jessie Carney Smith. Detroit, MI: Gale Research. 1992. (1): 100.

Van Lew, Elizabeth. *A Yankee Spy in Richmond: The Civil War Diary of "Crazy Bet" Van Lew*. Edited by David D. Ryan. Mechanicsburg, PA: Stackpole Books. 1996.

Boyd, Belle (1843–1900)

… (T)he rifle balls flew thick and fast about me, and more than one struck the ground so near my feet as to throw the dust in my eyes …. I shall never again run as I ran on that day. Hope, fear, the love of life, and the determination to serve my country to the last, conspired to fill my heart with more than feminine courage.

—Belle Boyd, from *Belle Boyd in Camp and Prison* (Boyd 1968, 167–168)

Of all the women who gained renown for their service to the Confederate cause, Belle Boyd is one of the most popular. Working at different times as a nurse, courier, spy, mail carrier, smuggler of medical supplies, and informant, the "Amazon of Secessia," as she was sometimes called, plunged into each job with enormous gusto. She was always on the lookout for opportunities to exhibit greater heroism and gain wider celebrity. Despite the difficulties of authenticating the factual details of her 1865 best-selling memoir, *Belle Boyd in Camp and Prison*, most modern scholars agree that this tale of her exploits is based on actual events (Boyd 1968, 8; D. Faust 1997, 214).

Maria Isabella Boyd was born in the village of Bunker Hill near Martinsburg in the Shenandoah Valley of Virginia, in 1843 (historians contest her claim that she was born in 1844). As a child, she was spirited, willful, and daring. Once when barred from attending one of her parents' parties, she protested by riding her horse into the house in the midst of the gathering (D. Faust 1997, 215). At age 11, a classmate observed that she was "a perfect scalawag, never would obey a rule." One day, when her teacher had had enough, she expelled Boyd and carried the girl's desk from school to deposit it on her doorstep (Davis 1975, 36). Her education did not end there, however. From 1856 to 1860, she continued her studies at a female seminary in Baltimore, Maryland.

Once the war began, the teenaged Boyd only had time for the Confederate cause. In the early months of the war, she nursed wounded and sick soldiers in Martinsburg. On July 4, 1861, after the Union army invaded western Virginia, she launched her career as a celebrated heroine when she shot a Union officer who cursed and swore at her mother. Boyd claims in her memoir that she killed the man, but it is more likely she only wounded him (C. Davis 1975, 36).

In late 1861 and early 1862, Boyd operated as a courier for Confederate Major General Thomas J. "Stonewall" Jackson and Brigadier General P. G. T. Beauregard. While Boyd was living at a relative's house in Front Royal, Virginia, in 1862, Union Brigadier General James Shields requisitioned the house. One night, while he and his officers discussed military strategy, Boyd eavesdropped, recording everything she heard. She carried the information on horseback to Confederate forces stationed 15 miles away, returning to Front Royal by daybreak.

In May 1862, as Boyd gathered intelligence on Union activity in Front Royal, she perceived that the ideal time had arrived for Confederate troops to drive the Union occupiers from the town. She ran from Front Royal to the Confederate frontlines to urge Jackson to advance on the town. As she carried out this mission, she crossed fields full of gunfire from Union soldiers. Since her data substantiated Jackson's other reports, his troops advanced and succeeded in ousting Union forces from Front Royal. Of all Boyd's daring maneuvers, this single act became the most famous.

In the ensuing months of her espionage work, Boyd was twice arrested and imprisoned in Old Capitol Prison in Washington, DC. After her first incarceration, while she was in Richmond, Virginia, during the winter of 1862 to 1863, Jackson selected her to be an honorary aide-de-camp, assigning her the rank of captain.

Following her second imprisonment, during which time she fell ill with typhoid fever, Boyd was deported to the South. Not one to be idle long, she succeeded in persuading Confederate President Jefferson Davis to allow her to transport documents to Confederate representatives in Europe. Not long after the *Greyhound*, a Confederate blockade runner, disembarked, it was seized by the USS *Connecticut*. During the time of the ship's capture and its sequestered journey to Fortress Monroe in Virginia, Boyd developed a close personal relationship with Union Naval Lieutenant Samuel Harding, acting ensign of the *Connecticut*.

Although several versions of events account for the next 18 months of Boyd's life, it is known that Harding left the U.S. Navy and followed her to London where the couple married in August 1864. Following his brief trip to Virginia to fulfill Boyd's wish that he defend the Confederate cause, Harding was briefly imprisoned by federal authorities. He returned to London where the couple's first child was born sometime in mid-1865. To support herself, Boyd wrote and published her memoir *Belle Boyd in Camp and Prison* in 1865. Although some historians indicate that Harding died in

1865 or 1866, it appears that the couple may have separated for reasons other than an untimely death. According to researcher Curtis Carroll Davis, Harding returned to the United States, surviving until 1879.

In 1866, Boyd was on her own once more. She became an actress in London, and months later, pursued a career on the stage in the United States. During the postwar decades, Boyd married two more times and had three additional children. She earned a meager living reprising her deeds of Confederate heroism for audiences throughout the East, the Midwest, and Texas. She died while on tour in Kilbourne (Wisconsin Dells), Wisconsin, in 1900 of a heart attack.

See also **Spies and Espionage**

Selected Readings

Boyd, Belle. *Belle Boyd in Camp and Prison*. Edited, with an introduction, by Curtis Carroll Davis. Cranbury, NJ: Thomas Yoseloff. 1968.

Faust, Drew Gilpin. *Mothers of Invention: Women of the Slaveholding South in the American Civil War*. New York: Vintage Books. 1997. 214–219.

Leonard, Elizabeth. *All the Daring of the Soldier: Women of the Civil War Armies*. New York: Penguin Books. 2001.

Bread Rebellions

[N]ecessity has no law & poverty is the mother of invention. These shall be the principles on which we will stand. If fair words will not do, we will try to see what virtue there is in stones.

—Inscription printed on cards distributed by a female rioter in Savannah, Georgia (quoted in D. Faust, in Clinton and Silber 1992, 197)

On the morning of April 2, 1863, several hundred working-class women of Richmond, Virginia, and its surrounding communities armed themselves with axes and homemade knives, horse pistols, and hatchets. Having made their demands for food known to Virginia governor John Letcher at the State Capitol and having been denied a satisfactory response, they marched past a crowd of shocked men and descended upon the heart of the city's commercial center to seize by force what they believed the government was refusing to provide—bread and meat. Vowing to have "Bread or Blood," the women gathered hundreds more men, women, girls, and boys as they advanced. As the mob entered the business district, a wildly chaotic morning of rioting and looting ensued. Not until at least a dozen stores and warehouses had been ransacked was Virginia's heavily armed Police Guard able to quell the mob. Only 44 women and 29 men were arrested out of a crowd that was estimated to include over one thousand rioters. Most of the women looters were successful in carrying off the food, shoes, fabric, and other goods they had plundered.

News of a riot in Atlanta and a flour rebellion in Salisbury, North Carolina, two weeks prior to the Richmond rebellion, probably influenced several Richmond women to organize a rebellion of their own. Mary Jackson, a 37-year-old market huckster and mother of four children, and Minerva Meredith, a 40-year-old butcher's apprentice, are believed to have been the leaders most responsible for the organizational meeting on the evening of April 1 that led to the rebellion. Neither Jackson nor Meredith were among the desperately poor. Though they were working class, they each possessed some means and a livelihood. As Michael Chesson, scholar of the Richmond Bread Rebellion has pointed out, both women appear to have been inspired more from their political convictions than from hunger (Chesson 1984, 154). Like many citizens of Richmond, they held the government responsible for the increased suffering and famine among the poor.

As noted, Richmond was not the only Southern city or town to experience a food riot. From 1863 until the end of the war, women planned and executed similar rebellions throughout the Confederacy. Savannah, Atlanta, Milledgeville, Macon, and Columbus in Georgia were affected, as were Mobile, Alabama, and Petersburg, Virginia. Scattered groups of poor and yeoman farm women throughout much of North Carolina stormed food storage sites from 1863 through the end of the war.

Only a handful of historians have brought to light the depth of misery of the poor white men and women of the Confederacy. Jobs and food were rarities for all social classes in the overcrowded cities that were teeming with refugees, but the poor—both whites and free blacks with little or no resources to buffer them—suffered most. The number of women-led households trying to survive on a Confederate soldier's pay increased, causing many among the middle classes and yeomanry to face hunger. The Northern blockade of Southern ports, the Confederacy's inability to control speculators and extortioners, and its failure to prevent out-of-control inflation severely impacted the availability and price of food. To further exacerbate the food crisis, the Confederate military impressed wagons and other vehicles normally used to transport food. By 1863 to 1864, Union invasion and destruction of bridges and rail lines halted the delivery of food supplies to many regions throughout the South.

From 1863 on, yeoman farm women in North Carolina repeatedly petitioned state and local government officials to provide relief. When the government's response was late in coming, or insufficient to meet their needs, the women participated in raids on government and privately owned warehouses. They also stole food from merchants, grain mills, and their wealthier neighbors. A careful study of these protests reveals that the raiders felt justified in seizing the goods they needed. From their letters and petitions to the government, it is apparent that many women believed that their families, by contributing their menfolk and the food, livestock, and goods the Confederate army impressed from them, had already given more than they could withstand. The women also expressed the conviction that the government was not meeting its basic obligations to its citizens.

Throughout the South, the upper and prosperous middle classes were appalled at reports of armed women forcibly seizing food and other goods. In Richmond, the press and well-to-do citizens deplored the riot and denigrated the rioters. They were eager to assert that the rebellion had been fomented by greed rather than a need for food. Newspaper accounts focused attention on the luxury items that were stolen and neglected to report the huge amounts of food, especially meat, that had been looted, thereby denying that hunger had been the women's primary motivation. The press exaggerated the immigrant element among the rioters and portrayed the female participants as subhuman, unsexed viragoes. The Richmond *Examiner* described the mob as "a handful of prostitutes, professional thieves, Irish and Yankee hags, [and] gallows-birds from all lands but our own" (quoted in Chesson 1984, 132). Newspaper editors also argued that the women could not have been driven by hunger because public and private charities were distributing free food. Although a number of organizations were donating food, the need far outweighed the help that was available. Furthermore, most charities did not go forth and distribute the food. Most relied on the needy to come to them, which necessitated that the hungry realize that the charity existed. Historians have surmised that many among Richmond's poor were unaware of the assistance.

The middle and upper classes echoed the arguments they read in the press and seem to have been unaware that the poor were starving—a fact that highlights the sharp divisions between the city's lower and upper classes. In her memoir, Sallie Brock of Richmond parroted arguments that were in common currency among the city's elite. Her statements about the rebellion indicate how out of touch most well-to-do Richmond citizens were and reveal the extent of their misinformation and denial about the realities of life for the poor. "Starvation to them [the Richmond poor] was not imminent," Brock asserts, "and the pauper class were indeed in more comfortable circumstances than persons who lived on salaries, or depended upon a moderate income for support" (Putnam 1996, 343). She agreed with the opinions of a number of Richmond's leading editors that, "This demonstration was made use of by the disaffected in our midst, and by our enemies abroad, for the misrepresentation and exaggeration of our real condition" (Putnam 1996, 210).

The wealthy neglected to consider that by April 1863, basic staples of the diet cost more than ten times their 1860 prices. Bacon had increased from $.12.5 to $1.50 per pound, butter from $.23 to $3, and coffee from $.12.5 to $5 a pound. In 1863, a bushel of potatoes soared to $12 and flour to $40 a barrel (Furgurson 1996, 180, 188). When these prices are compared with the $11 monthly pay of privates in the Confederate army, it becomes clear that the families of soldiers and those in working-class occupations found it nearly impossible to meet their most basic needs.

Unlike some Southern communities, Richmond did not experience any additional food riots after the April 2 rebellion. Following the riot, the state police guard placed cannons at strategic sites in the business district. City officials responded by immediately stepping up relief efforts to ease the suffering.

Yet, in other parts of the Confederacy, as both poor and yeoman farm women struggled to keep their children and elderly relatives from starvation, their continued participation in food rebellions suggests that few states and local governments were effective in meeting citizens' needs. In these circumstances, women were unaffected by threats of criminal prosecution or by social pressure to conform to upper- and middle-class notions of a woman's proper behavior. The women-led food rebellions of the Civil War underscore the alienation of poor white women from the affluent middle and upper classes and from the mainstream of Southern society and culture.

See also **Industrial Women**

Selected Readings

Bynum, Victoria E. *Unruly Women: The Politics of Social and Sexual Control in the Old South.* Chapel Hill: University of North Carolina Press. 1992.

Chesson, Michael. "Harlots or Heroines? A New Look at the Richmond Bread Riot." *The Virginia Magazine of History and Biography.* 92 (April 1984): 131–175.

Tice, Douglas O. " `Bread or Blood!' The Richmond Bread Riot." *Civil War Times Illustrated.* 12(10)(1974): 12–19.

Brown, Clara
(1803 or 1806–1885)

Colorado pioneer, humanitarian, and African-American entrepreneur, Clara Brown created a refuge for poverty-stricken men and women of all races during the Civil War. As with African-American businesswoman MARY ELLEN PLEASANT, there are many conflicting stories and legends about Brown's life that historians have not been able to authenticate.

Born a slave in Spotsylvania County, Virginia, Clara was sold at age three to Ambrose Smith in Kentucky. She married at age 18 and had four children, one son and three daughters; one of her daughters drowned in childhood. When Smith died in 1835, Clara, her husband, and their children were sold and separated from one another. The ultimate destinations of her husband and son are unknown, although it is known that they had been bound for cotton plantations in the Deep South. Clara's two daughters were sold to separate Kentucky slaveholders. Clara was purchased by George Brown of Russellville, Kentucky, a friend of Smith's. It is from this owner that Clara received the surname of Brown.

During the approximately 20 years that Clara labored for George Brown, she tried repeatedly to ascertain the whereabouts of her husband and children, often with the cooperation and help of George Brown. The mission to find her family would continue for nearly her entire life. She located her two surviving daughters, Margaret and Eliza Jane, although the latter disappeared again when she was sold in 1852.

After George Brown died in 1856, his daughters freed Clara. As much as she wanted to remain in Kentucky to search for her family, a state law prohibited free African Americans from living there. If she neglected to leave, her slave status would be reinstated after one year. In the spring of 1857, she traveled by flatboat to St. Louis, Missouri, to seek employment as a domestic servant. While working as a cook for the Jacob Brunner family, she was intrigued by the idea of migrating to the West. When the Brunners moved to Leavenworth, Kansas, Brown accompanied them. In the pioneer environment, she became even more entranced by the prospect of venturing westward. A devout Christian, Brown was an active member of the First Baptist

Church in Leavenworth, an all-black congregation, and was involved in the town's sizable African-American community.

When the Brunners prepared to journey to California, Brown decided to remain in Leavenworth where she worked independently as a laundress. News of the discovery of gold in the Colorado Rockies motivated her to search for a means to travel there. She soon discovered a wagon train of would-be prospectors preparing to leave for Pike's Peak, Colorado. In 1859, she convinced the train's agents to take her along as a cook, laundress, and nurse for the 26 male travelers.

Brown decided to settle in Cherry Creek, the small pioneer hamlet that would soon become the city of Denver. After a brief period working in a bakery, she was able to buy a small one-room cabin where she operated a laundry. With the profits from her business, she cooked large soups and stews to feed the impoverished. With no laws to bar African Americans from purchasing and owning property, she invested in real estate. Brown became deeply involved in the religious life in Cherry Creek. While she and her friends were involved in the lengthy process of raising funds to build a church, she offered her cabin as a site for prayer meetings and for church services.

Not long after settling in Cherry Creek, Brown followed the mining boom up into the Rocky Mountains. In the mining camp named Mountain City (later absorbed into the town of Central City), she acquired a two-room cabin and once again established a laundry business. Unlike her experience in Cherry Creek—living in a community that had an almost entirely white population—Brown was able to befriend a number of African-American prospectors in Mountain City. She quickly became involved in the religious community and donated large sums toward the construction of a Methodist Church.

By 1863, the initial gold mining boom in Colorado Territory was rapidly dissipating and miners began abandoning Central City. The families of prospectors who remained faced poverty. Brown assisted them as best she could, offering food and housing to the neediest. Despite the hard times, Central City continued to be Brown's home. As time passed, advances in mining technology enabled miners to find new ways to extract gold and other minerals from the earth, causing Central City to prosper once again.

In the spring of 1864, a devastating flood in Denver caused Brown to lose her property there when all the deeds to her buildings and lands were swept away. The disaster was not a total loss for her as she still had her property in Central City, Boulder, and in several other Colorado communities.

By the end of the Civil War, Brown had enough money invested to be considered a relatively wealthy woman, though she continued to donate most of her profits to the poor. With slavery abolished, no law prohibited her from going to Kentucky. In 1866, she traveled east to search for her daughter Eliza Jane in Kentucky. (Brown's other daughter Margaret had died before Brown attained her freedom.)

Although she failed to locate Eliza Jane, she did find 16 former slaves who wanted to start new lives in Colorado. With the proceeds from her investments, she paid for their travel and supported them in Central City until she obtained a home and a job for each adult. At some point on this trip, probably while she was purchasing supplies for the journey west, she was cheated out of $4,000, a sum large enough to deplete her savings.

In 1873, another calamity befell Brown when a fire destroyed three of her buildings. Although she still had some money saved and a few mining claims co-owned with other investors, she was no longer a woman of means. A friend and fellow real estate investor offered her a home in one of his cottages where she lived through the late 1870s. As she aged, Brown continued to provide for the poor with the profits from her laundry business. In 1880, suffering from a heart ailment, she moved to Denver.

In 1881, Brown was honored with membership in the Society of Colorado Pioneers when the organization's bylaws were relaxed to admit both men and women who had arrived in the region before 1861. Months later in 1882, Brown, then in her late seventies, discovered that her widowed daughter Eliza Jane Brewer was alive and working as a laundress in Council Bluffs, Iowa. According to newspaper reports in 1882, Brown traveled east to Iowa to be reunited with Eliza Jane. Historians have not uncovered the details of Brown's final years in Denver, though it is known that she died there in 1885.

See also **African-American Women; Businesswomen; Slavery and Emancipation; Western Women**

Selected Readings

Bruyn, Kathleen. *"Aunt" Clara Brown: Story of a Black Pioneer*. Boulder: Pruett Publishing. 1970.

Ravage, John W. *Black Pioneers: Images of the Black Experience on the North American Frontier*. Salt Lake City: University of Utah Press. 1997.

Brownell, Kady Southwell (1842–1915)

Like scores of Northern and Southern women during the Civil War, Kady Southwell Brownell accompanied her husband when he enlisted in the 1st Rhode Island Volunteer Infantry in the spring of 1861. She did not try to pass as a man as some women did when they enlisted with their husbands, although she became as actively involved in the CAMP LIFE of her regiment as any woman soldier. As the designated "daughter of the regiment" of the 1st Rhode Island, she encouraged and provided moral support to her male comrades in military exercises, in camp, and in battle. In addition to her traditional role as female mascot, she participated in rifle and saber practice alongside the men and by all accounts was militarily adept. Her self-designed "uniform" consisted of a combination of male and female dress—a blouse, a knee-length skirt, and long pants. Her rifle and sword were attached to the belt around her waist (Leonard 2001, 114). She also carried the regimental flag, another duty commonly associated with daughters of the regiment. Yet she took charge of this responsibility in a way that set her apart from other daughters—she also bore the colors into battle.

The daughter of a Scottish soldier and a French mother, Kady Southwell was born at a military camp in Africa in 1842. After her mother died when Southwell was a young child, she immigrated to the United States to be raised by friends of her family. In March 1861, she was working as a weaver in Providence, Rhode Island, when she wed Robert Brownell, a millwright (Leonard 2001, 114).

When the 1st Rhode Island arrived in Washington, DC, during the spring of 1861, Southwell Brownell was adamant about serving alongside her husband. After Colonel Ambrose Burnside refused to let her stay, she sought the aid of Rhode Island Governor William Sprague. He made it possible for her to return to her regiment.

During the First Battle of Bull Run (known in the South as the First Battle of Manassas), Southwell Brownell stood by her regiment's flag so that the soldiers of her regiment could rally around it. As the thick, blinding smoke of shell and cannon fire threatened to separate the soldiers from each other, she held the flag high so that they could regain and hold their positions. As Union forces fled to the rear after hours of fighting, she continued to hold the colors until she was alerted that she must retreat to avoid being overcome by a Confederate advance.

After the 1861 campaign in northern Virginia was over, the 1st Rhode Island was sent back to Providence in August 1861, and disbanded. In October 1861, the Brownells reenlisted, this time in the 5th Rhode Island Infantry. In this regiment, Southwell Brownell served as a nurse and color bearer. When the 5th Rhode Island moved into North Carolina, she and her husband participated in the Union seizure of Roanoke Island, situated off the North Carolina coast. The regiment then proceeded to New Bern, North Carolina, where her orders were to carry the flag only until her company initiated the attack on the Confederate breastworks in that city. Just as the barrage was about to begin, she noticed that her company's arrival and unusual position might confuse other nearby Union military units into thinking that it was a Confederate company disguised in Union blue. Before the neighboring Union soldiers could fire on her compatriots, she sprinted forward waving the regimental flag high above her head, rescuing them from attack.

After Brownell was badly wounded in the Union capture of New Bern, Southwell Brownell nursed him as well as wounded Union and Confederate prisoners. Because of the disabling injury, the Brownells returned to Rhode Island and then proceeded to New York City where Southwell Brownell carefully nursed her husband back to health at the Soldier's Relief Hospital. After their discharge from the army in 1863, Brownell found work in the city, and it was there that the couple resided until their final years. Southwell Brownell died in January 1915, and her husband followed her eight months later.

Selected Readings

Larson, C. Kay. "Bonny Yank and Ginny Reb." *Minerva: Quarterly Report on Women and the Military.* 8 (Spring 1990): 33–48.

Leonard, Elizabeth D. *All the Daring of the Soldier: Women of the Civil War Armies.* New York: Penguin Books. 2001.

Businesswomen

During the mid-nineteenth century, throughout every state and territory in the United States, thousands of single, married, and widowed white, African-American, and Hispanic women of the middle and working classes owned their own businesses or managed family-owned concerns. Some Native American women in the West also participated in the business arena. The vast majority of women entrepreneurs operated businesses that related to the domestic arts. The dressmaking and millinery industry attracted the greatest number of business-oriented women, and according to the 1870 United States census, dressmaking was the fourth most frequently reported female occupation. [Domestic servants, agricultural workers, and seamstresses formed the top three groups of workers (Gamber 1997, 7). Although seamstresses sewed women's clothing, they are differentiated from dressmakers because they were wage workers. Dressmakers were self-employed.] Food-related enterprises were also popular businesses for women, with bakeries, coffee shops, and confectioneries being among the most commonly owned. Boardinghouse management employed large numbers of women, as did hotel-keeping, though to a lesser extent. At mid-century, women were establishing schools, academies, and female seminaries; fiction writers, journalists, essayists, and other LITERARY WOMEN were making a good living in the world of publishing; women DOCTORS and midwives were managing their own medical practices; and some actresses were venturing into theater management.

The Civil War expanded women's sphere beyond the domestic realm and created many new business opportunities for women. The enlistment of husbands, brothers, fathers, and sons gave married and single women the chance to direct family businesses or to start new firms. In many cases, these new entrepreneurs used the knowledge and skills they had acquired in their years as key workers in family businesses.

In Barry, Illinois, Agnes Watson took over her husband's shoemaking shop when he went to war. Economic necessity also prompted Elizabeth Jones of Bloomington, Illinois, to create a fabric dyeing and cleaning business after her husband enlisted. When he returned in 1864, her husband worked with Elizabeth in her business rather than resume his job as a laborer. Other Illinois veterans came home to work in their wives' millinery, fancy-goods, and hair jewelry shops (Murphy 1991, 74).

When Michael O'Sullivan of Albany, New York, was mustered in as a boat inspector, his wife and daughters—all teachers—kept his Catholic bookstore going in his absence (Lewis 1992, 68). Financial need did not spur Catherine Snyder of Peoria, Illinois, to become a sewing-machine agent and cloakmaker. In 1860, before her husband left to enlist, census figures listed the family's wealth as $3,200, an economic cushion that would have kept Catherine and her children comfortable all through the war. Perhaps a sense of adventure or desire for a challenge encouraged her to become an entrepreneur (Murphy 1991, 75). In the North, wartime inflation and tax increases did not deter some single women from entering into business. Mary Hickey, a shop clerk, started a fancy-goods shop in 1863 (Lewis 1992, 70). Her father, a carpenter, and her brothers likely helped her with the initial investment. Matilda and Eliza Oliver of Boston, Massachusetts, left teaching during the war years to devote all their time to their knitting and sewing business.

It is impossible to make broad generalizations about the prevalence or extent to which women engaged in entrepreneurial activity because only certain regions of the United States have been thoroughly investigated. Historians have documented that some women in the Northeast, the Middle Atlantic states, and the Midwest undertook their own business ventures. There is also significant anecdotal evidence to indicate that women were successful entrepreneurs in the West, and that they engaged in business in the South, though to a lesser extent than in all other regions of the country.

Census figures from this era do not accurately reveal the total number of women involved in business. Entrepreneurial women were sometimes invisible to census workers. Many of these women were workers and managers of businesses owned, sometimes in name only, by male family members. John Reed, also of Albany, was a manufacturer of fringes and dress trimmings as well as the owner of a fancy-goods shop. Though the store was in his name, it was his wife who managed it from the late 1850s through the 1860s, a fact that census takers sometimes ignored or did not consider significant enough to report (Lewis 1992, 69).

The seasonal nature of the dressmaking and millinery trades was another factor influencing the underreporting of women in business, as these artisans appeared employed only during the months their businesses were busiest. In Albany, Mary T. Carroll, an Irish immigrant, owned a millinery shop from 1860 to 1864. In 1860, as she was struggling to establish her business, census workers recorded her total property value as $40. If the census had been taken in January or February, one of the two quiet periods in the trade, recorders might easily have overlooked or dismissed her occupational status (Lewis 1995, 100). In addition, some women operating very small businesses were overlooked because their work situations were not large or visible enough to attract the attention of male census takers.

Women's businesses at mid-century were typically small concerns. Most employed no more than five workers. Women's firms did not endure as long as men's, nor did they grow and expand as rapidly or to the extent that men's did, in part because credit was extremely difficult for women to obtain. Many female entrepreneurs' initial investments were also small. Women broke free of these economic constraints only when they had male benefactors or patrons who could help them acquire the capital and credit they needed to expand.

Prostitution and brothel-keeping, other common businesses for women, were particularly lucrative trades for some white women. Although fraught with health-related perils, a number of PROSTITUTES earned enough after a few years to own their own brothels, or to co-own them with their husbands. Others invested their earnings in real estate or started new businesses unrelated to prostitution.

Throughout the country, especially in the North, Midwest, and West, a number of women were making inroads in the field of photography by the 1860s. Although a few became successful independent photographers, many others worked as gallery managers and owners, photo-finishers and card-mounters, retouchers and colorists, and sales directors.

In Minnesota during the 1860s, half of all the photographers featured in the business directories for the larger cities in the eastern part of the state were women (Baker 1989, 18). Not all women engaged in the photography trade were independent entrepreneurs, however. Many were integral to businesses owned by their families or by their husbands. In California, women were engaged in daguerrotypy, an early photographic process, by 1850. Julia Shannon of San Francisco advertised her midwifery and photography services in a San Francisco business directory. By the 1860s, many more women were working as photographers in the larger towns of the San Francisco-Sacramento region of California (Palmquist 1992, 115).

Photography was sometimes a dangerous profession. Olive E. Goodwin of Minneapolis advertised herself as a "daguerrian artist." In 1860, by all accounts, her photography business was a thriving enterprise. According to a St. Paul newspaper, her career ended when she committed suicide in September, three days after "inhaling the poison from some of her chemicals" (Baker 1989, 17). Although bulky photographic equipment, inadequate ventilation, and toxic chemicals injured the health of some pioneering women photographers, others endured in long-prospering businesses.

Not all women's businesses remained small. Ellen Curtis Demorest of New York City, in partnership with her husband, William, created an enterprise based on the mass production of tissue-paper patterns suitable for women sewing dresses at home. Before her marriage in 1858, she had managed a successful millinery shop in the city. Always keenly interested in dress design, at some point in the late 1850s, she developed the idea for the dress-pattern business after watching her African-American maid employ a not uncommon dressmaking technique of the time, using a paper pattern to cut out a dress.

Late in 1860, Curtis Demorest and her husband initiated publication of their quarterly *Madame Demorest's Mirror of Fashions.* A colored plate and a dress pattern of one of her designs were featured within each issue. She also managed her dress design and millinery shop, Emporium of Fashions, in New York City. Throughout the Civil War, the magazine and the dress shop thrived, and years later, the entire operation became a million-dollar business with 1,500 franchise agencies, employing mostly women. In 1864, the magazine had a circulation of 60,000 and was so successful that she and her husband expanded it, adding more articles and commentary written for and by women (Kwolek-Folland 1998, 60; E. James 1971, 3: 459–460).

Margaret Haughery was a prosperous entrepreneur who devoted as much of her time and energy to philanthropy as she lavished on her businesses. Haughery, an Irish immigrant living in New Orleans, first earned her living as a laundress following the death of her husband and daughter. During the late 1830s, she started a dairy. Donating much of her profits to Catholic charities, she continued to expand her business in the 1840s and 1850s. In 1858, she obtained a bakery and, in short order, transformed it into New Orleans's most successful export business. She funded a total of 11 charitable institutions, including orphanages, an asylum for infants, and homes for widows and the elderly. During the Civil War years, she led sewing and knitting associations and assisted the poor families of Confederate soldiers (E. James 1971, 2: 153–154).

Even though mid-nineteenth-century society dictated that white women should remain confined to the domestic sphere and avoid the public sphere of business and politics, some white female entrepreneurs ventured forth regardless. The evidence indicates that women may have found it easier and more socially acceptable to engage in business in the Midwest and West than in the Northeast and South. But regional variations aside, recent research into the lives of mid-nineteenth-century businesswomen suggests that large numbers of women did not strictly confine themselves to domestic duties and childrearing. Women of business, whether they were working in family-owned enterprises or running businesses of their own, appear to have been respected, well-accepted members of communities that supported the propriety of some women making their own way.

See also **Agricultural Women; Artists; Brown, Clara; Keckley, Elizabeth; Pleasant, Mary Ellen**

Selected Reading

Kwolek-Folland, Angel. *Incorporating Women: A History of Women and Business in the United States.* New York: Twayne Publishers. 1998.

C

Camp Life

Thousands of white and African-American women populated the Union and Confederate military encampments during the Civil War. Although most military histories never mention the contributions of women attached to the Civil War armies, women performed dozens of essential services for the troops. Laundresses; cooks; NURSES; MILITARY WOMEN (soldiers); female sutlers or vivandières selling spirits, food, tobacco, and dry goods; daughters of the regiment; soldiers' and officers' wives; and PROSTITUTES worked in or near the camps. When regiments went on the march, the womenfolk packed up their household belongings and accompanied them, usually walking or riding on wagons and carts at the rear of the troops.

The phenomenon of women laboring within the military camps was not a new development of the Civil War. The European continental armies of the eighteenth century welcomed women into their midst. In the American Revolutionary War, women worked in an unofficial capacity among the rank-and-file: washing clothing, cooking, sewing and repairing uniforms, nursing and cleaning. Revolutionary War soldiers depended on the services women provided for their well-being. Women were recompensed, in most cases, with half a soldier's food ration, and, occasionally, a small wage.

During the Civil War, the main priority of most camp women was to be near their husbands, male relatives, lovers, or friends. When women could spare the time, they helped other men in the regiment in other capacities. They nursed soldiers during epidemics, lugged water to the campsites, cleaned weaponry, prepared ammunition, entertained the troops with storytelling and songs, or sang hymns to inspire the men. During battles, women distributed water and sustenance, nursed fallen soldiers, and sometimes carried ammunition.

A role that a small number of young soldiers' wives and other camp women assumed was the position of daughter of the regiment. Although not officially acknowledged by the Union or the Confederate militaries, daughters were an important source of inspiration and assistance to the men in the regiments they represented. In many ways, the daughters were female mascots, although their contributions to their regiments went beyond their symbolic role. Usually stylishly dressed in a jacket or blouse, a knee-length skirt worn over pants, and a hat, the ideal daughter of the regiment was a pure, courageous young woman who marched and rode with the soldiers on campaigns, tolerated the discomforts of life in camp and on the march, and encouraged and supported the troops in military drills as well as on the battlefield. Many, if not most, daughters of the regiment spent much of their time nursing soldiers during battle engagements in the field hospitals and in camps. ANNIE ETHERIDGE was perhaps the most famous daughter of the Civil War; her regimental activities focused on nursing soldiers on the active battlefields and in the tent hospitals. Another Union daughter, KADY SOUTHWELL BROWNELL, was committed to her nursing duties, although she is better known for carrying the regimental flag into battle.

An Irish immigrant, Bridget Divers (Deaver, Devens) went with her husband to war and became the daughter of the 1st Michigan Cavalry. "Irish Biddy" or "Michigan Bridget," as she was sometimes called, was so adept on horseback that she accompanied the soldiers on raiding sorties. Like Annie Etheridge and Kady Brownell, she, too, cared for the men's wounds and illnesses. After her husband enlisted, the Confederate Lucy Ann Cox became the daughter of the 13th Virginia Infantry. She remained with this regiment until the end of the war. Arabella "Belle" Macomber Reynolds resisted the attempts of her relations and friends to keep her at home when her husband signed up with the 17th Illinois Infantry. Although she, too, was designated a daughter by her husband's regiment, she seemed to have shunned the more military aspects of the role and never accompanied the men into battle. She was, however, a caring, devoted nurse in the field hospitals who frequently marched with the soldiers, her musket by her side (Leonard 2001, 121–131). From the pen of Belle Reynolds, a realistic portrayal of life in a military camp unfolds.

No floors, no chairs, the narrow cot my seat, my feet imbedded in the hot sand, the confusion of camp close around me, with but the thickness of cloth between me and the eyes of all, the scorching August sun streaming through the low-roofed covering—it seemed almost too much to endure; but I resolved to make the trial. (quoted in Leonard 2001, 126)

Many a woman within the army camps performed some of the duties of daughters of the regiment, though the regiment never appointed them to fill that role. Marie "French Mary" Tepe (Tebe), a French immigrant, has most often been referred to as a *vivandière*. She entered the army with her husband, joining the 27th Pennsylvania Infantry. At the outbreak of war, so the story goes, Tepe's husband insisted that she remain in Philadelphia and run his tailoring business in his absence. He was not at all pleased when she accompanied him to camp. She soon found work as a sutler, selling whisky and other goods to the soldiers.

At some time during 1862, Tepe's husband and several collaborators stole the money she had earned. She promptly left the 27th Pennsylvania and her husband and entered the camp of the 114th Pennsylvania, a Zouave regiment. Tepe's Zouave uniform resembled that of most daughters of the regiment. She sported a blue jacket similar to the one worn by the Zouaves in her regiment, a skirt with a red braided trim, and red pants. She is said to have worn a men's sailor's cap with the brim turned down (Conklin 1993, 105). She cooked, washed clothes, and sewed for the soldiers and nursed them when they fell in battle. Remarkably courageous under fire, like Etheridge, she received the Kearny Cross following the Battle of Chancellorsville (Virginia) in May 1863 (Conklin 1993, 105–110; Leonard 2001, 150–151).

Many large Union encampments, particularly those of the Army of the Potomac, had more African-American women than white women (Schultz 1988, 225). Most were CONTRABAND WOMEN—fugitives from slavery—who flocked to the Union camps for protection from reenslavement. Black women attached themselves to Union camps with their children and elderly relatives. They labored as laundresses and cooks for the most part, receiving barely enough food to keep their families from starvation. At the age of 14, the African-American SUSIE BAKER KING TAYLOR became a laundress for the 1st South Carolina Volunteers (later renamed the 33rd U.S. Colored Troops). She later served as a cook and nurse for the regiment. In the evenings, she taught the soldiers to read and write. She enjoyed cleaning and firing the soldiers' muskets. Black women were prevalent in the Confederate camps as well, although most were slave women. As in the Union camps, black women performed the most menial chores.

When all-black Union regiments entered the military service, soldiers' wives and female family members occasionally accompanied them. Martha Gray attached herself to the 54th Massachusetts Infantry, an all-black regiment. After the war, she described her role: "I consider myself a worn out soldier of the U.S.

I was all around the South with the regiment administering to the wants of the sick and wounded and did have the name of Mother of the Regiment" (quoted in De Pauw 1998, 163).

Whether women were black or white, the wives of soldiers who took up residence within or near the military camps were primarily poor and from the working classes. Middle-class women followed their menfolk to camp, but in smaller numbers. Poor women who were accustomed to harsh or primitive living conditions in city slums and rural areas probably adjusted more easily to the challenges of camp life than more affluent women, taking in stride the necessity of living in bug-infested, damp, and drafty tents; cooking over an open fire; and eating a limited diet.

Women were tolerated in the camps by Union and Confederate military authorities, especially early in the war, when the medical departments were not established and nursing assistance was needed. Women were also accepted in the armies' winter camps, when foul and frigid weather kept soldiers off the battlefields. Some officers viewed women as a civilizing, calming influence on enlisted men, believing that the "fairer sex" tempered men's indulgence in alcohol and made them less inclined to indulge in rowdy behavior and dangerous pranks and pastimes—common hazards of soldiers idle for long periods of time.

During long military campaigns, while regiments were on the march, military officials considered women a liability and complained that they hampered the progress of troops hurrying to their next destination. This attitude was especially evident among Union commanders in their dealings with contraband women and their families whose vast numbers sometimes overwhelmed military authorities.

Officers' wives, predominantly middle- and upper-class white women, were no strangers to the Confederate and Union army camps, especially when the camps were located near a town or city. The wives, and sometimes their children, resided in boarding houses, or in rented apartments or houses near the encampments. Like NADINE LVOVA TURCHIN, the few officers' wives who accompanied their husbands on military campaigns lived in tents as they traveled from campsite to campsite. Most officers' wives were separated from their husbands while their troops were on the move, returning to live at home or with relatives. When their husbands settled once again in one location, wives who were eager for a reunion joined them for a brief visit or for a lengthy stay that might last until the army left camp once more.

Julia Dent Grant, wife of Union General Ulysses S. Grant, repeatedly visited her husband in camp. As was the case for most military wives, she worked at making his quarters more comfortable and homelike. During the early part of the war, she stayed by her husband's side while he suffered from crippling migraine headaches. After the siege of VICKSBURG (Mississippi) in 1863, she and Grant lived in a mansion in the area. From time to time, she would visit him in camp, sleeping in a tent, while his troops were on the move (Bleser and Gordon 2001, 127).

LaSalle Corbell Pickett, the young wife of Confederate Major General George E. Pickett, stayed with her husband close to his Petersburg, Virginia, headquarters. They shared a tent at times, and also spent weeks living in a log cabin. She spent her days visiting with the wives of her husband's fellow officers and her evenings hosting dances and musical events (Bleser and Gordon 2001, 78, 127).

Not all officers wanted their wives to live near their quarters. Ellen Ewing Sherman, wife of Union General William Tecumseh Sherman, remained at her father's Lancaster, Ohio, home, largely because her husband preferred not to combine his public and domestic lives. When the general's troops occupied Vicksburg, however, she joined him in camp, bringing their children with her, as so many other officer's wives were doing. In August 1863, the family took a long holiday living in tents near Sherman's quarters. On the way home, tragedy struck when the Shermans' son Willy died of dysentery and malaria, common but deadly illnesses for children in the Southern summers of the mid-nineteenth century (Bleser and Gordon 2001, 149).

During the winter of 1863 to 1864, Elizabeth "Lizinka" Brown Ewell, wife of Confederate Lieutenant General Richard S. Ewell, resided with her husband while he was stationed at Second Corps headquarters in Virginia. At that time, public sentiment in the South agreed with the conventional view that women should remain at home, not flock to the army camps. Brown Ewell, in particular, was not welcome at her husband's headquarters. Like JESSIE BENTON FRéMONT, wife of Union General John C. Frémont, the men in General Ewell's command accused her of controlling "everything from the general's affairs down to the courier's who carries his dispatches. All say they are under petticoat government" (Bleser and Gordon 2001, 98). In 1864, both Confederate General Robert E. Lee and Union General Grant ordered their officers to ensure that women depart from the encampments and the front.

Selected Readings

Bleser, Carol K. and Lesley J. Gordon, eds. *Intimate Strategies of the Civil War: Military Commanders and Their Wives.* New York: Oxford University Press. 2001.

Leonard, Elizabeth D. *All the Daring of the Soldier: Women of the Civil War Armies.* New York: Penguin Books. 2001.

Carroll, Anna Ella (1815–1894)

> Now, an atrociously wicked war is waged against the Government, and its formidable armies have overwhelmed every civil right from the Potomac to the Rio Grande, and threatens the annihilation of the Government and the nation itself. By virtue of the express and implied powers of the Constitution … it is impossible to question the duty of the President to use every belligerent right, every instrument known to the law of war:—To annoy, to waken, to destroy the enemy, until its armies are overthrown and the civil authority is re-established.
>
> —Anna Ella Carroll, Reply to the Speech of the Honorable John C. Breckinridge, August 1861 (Carroll 1992, 145)

Although Anna Ella Carroll is best known for her claim that she was the mastermind of the "Tennessee Plan," the strategy that Union forces used in their conquest of the war's Western Theater, her greatest contribution to the Union cause was her political writings. During the early months of the Civil War, Carroll's influential political pamphlets, buttressing and promoting President Abraham Lincoln's war policies, were of enormous benefit to the Lincoln administration as it confronted a hostile Congress and reluctant Northern public.

Anna Ella Carroll grew up in Maryland, the daughter of Thomas King Carroll, politician, governor of Maryland, and plantation owner and slaveholder. Thomas Carroll directed his daughter's education, seeing that she received a thorough background in law, politics, history, and philosophy. In the late 1830s, her father's improvidence necessitated that she support her family. She established a school and operated it until 1843. By 1845, she had shifted course and was earning money as a writer for railroad promoters, work that eventually gave her the contacts and the background to devote herself to full-time political writing and lobbying for various special interests.

By 1855, she was a writer for the Know-Nothing Party, also known as the American Party, which had a large following in Maryland. She quickly made a name for herself, writing pamphlets espousing the Know-Nothing platform of nativism and anti-Catholicism. She also wrote a book *The Great American Battle; or, The Contest Between Christianity and Political Romanism*, published in 1856.

Following the demise of the Know-Nothing Party in 1856, Carroll continued to pursue a political career. A relentless influence-seeker, she cultivated her political connections and asked for political favors and appointments for her family and friends.

As the Southern states seceded, Carroll, a determined Unionist and nationalist, started to formulate her theories concerning the constitutionality of President Abraham Lincoln's responses to the challenges posed by the Confederacy's defection. During the first year of the war, she wrote four pamphlets advocating the president's actions, including his mustering of troops, the establishment of a naval blockade of Southern ports, and his suspension of the writ of habeas corpus. To Carroll's mind, the president was justified in executing all of these actions because the preservation of the Union transcended all other concerns. She believed that Lincoln was obligated to use all of his powers to enforce the leaders of the seceded states to return to the Union.

When Kentucky Democratic Senator John C. Breckinridge accused Lincoln of illegally exercising the powers that the Constitution reserved for Congress, Carroll authored her first and perhaps her most influential pamphlet, *Reply to the Speech of Honorable John C. Breckinridge*, in August 1861. This and her subsequent tracts were eagerly embraced and her arguments broadly disseminated by the Lincoln administration.

Carroll, however, did not concur with all of Lincoln's policies. She authored pamphlets opposing the Confiscation Acts, arguing that the Constitution does not give the federal government the authority to interfere with the property rights of slaveholders. According to Carroll, even though most slaveholders were either perpetrators or participants in the rebellion, they had never ceased being U.S. citizens. Carroll may have defended the property rights of slaveholders, but she personally could not abide slavery and had freed her family's slaves in 1855.

Like many residents of the border states, Carroll was a champion of colonization as a solution to the problems resulting from emancipation. During the first years of the war she helped promote New York businessman Aaron Columbus Burr's scheme to establish a colony for the freedpeople in British Honduras in Central America. Despite her and Burr's considerable lobbying, Lincoln not only decided against British Honduras, but also rejected colonization as a viable solution to emancipation.

In the final months of 1861, Carroll traveled to Missouri where she planned to continue researching and writing pamphlets for the federal government. While in St. Louis, she concerned herself with the immense risks that an invasion of the Confederacy via the Mississippi River posed to Union forces. Discussions with a riverboat captain, friends, and acquaintances in Missouri contributed to her conclusion that a Union invasion via the less well-fortified Tennessee and Cumberland Rivers would be a less hazardous invasion route into the Confederacy.

Thrilled by the possibilities of the plan, in late November 1861, she sent letters to Attorney General Edward Bates, Assistant Secretary of War Thomas A. Scott, and President Lincoln. According to Carroll, on November 30, she presented the details of the plan to Scott in Washington. In February 1862, when the Union army captured

Fort Henry and Fort Donelson in Tennessee, Carroll assumed that her documents had been instrumental to the Union's execution of the Tennessee Campaign. Unbeknownst to Carroll, General Ulysses S. Grant and other Union military leaders had been considering such a move for months prior to her delivery of the strategy. They had been prevented from initiating the Tennessee campaign due to many factors, particularly a lack of gunboats and other supplies.

For the rest of her life, Carroll persisted in the conviction that she was the originator of the Tennessee Plan. She refused to give up her claim, even when presented with evidence refuting that she was the military's source. Despite her political savvy and intellect, she could not imagine that the Union's top military leaders and strategists might also have considered these two rivers as an invasion route.

During the rest of the war and for decades after, she demanded payment for her services to the Union, not only for her pamphlet writing but also for her role in the development of the Tennessee Plan. Aside from the $750 she was paid for her pamphlets in 1862 (in addition to the $1,250 Scott paid her out of his own pocket), the federal government never compensated her further. Although Carroll was never a suffragist, suffrage leaders publicized her claims and her demand for recognition. Suffragists viewed Carroll as a perfect example of the many women whose accomplishments and contributions were never recognized or compensated during the Civil War.

See also **Women and Politics**

Selected Readings

Carroll, Anna Ella. *Anna Ella Carroll (1815–1893) American Political Writer of Maryland*. Edited by James Biser Whisker. Lewiston, NY: The Edwin Mellen Press. 1992.

Coryell, Janet L. *Neither Heroine Nor Fool: Anna Ella Carroll of Maryland*. Kent, OH: Kent State University Press. 1990.

Cary, Mary Ann Shadd (1823–1893)

Mary Ann Shadd Cary is one of the most frequently overlooked of all the prominent African-American women activists of the mid-nineteenth century. A vigorous abolitionist, emigrationist, and integrationist, Shadd Cary was the first black woman to publish and edit a newspaper and the second to become a lawyer. Her lifelong radical activism, regardless of the forms it took, focused on helping African Americans and Afro-Canadians to achieve self-reliance, control of their own futures, and equality with whites. During the Civil War, these aims eventually led her to become a Union army recruiter of African-American men. Like other free African Americans, Shadd Cary was convinced that by fighting for the Union, African-American men would prove that they were the equals of white Americans.

Among nineteenth-century female reformers, Shadd Cary was unique in her determination to express her political opinions publicly and forcefully, without deferring to black or white male authority or abiding by the conventions of appropriate language for women abolitionists. In print and on the podium, she spoke her mind, sparing no delicacies of speech. Though she made enemies at times, the ideas of this intellectual, well-read woman commanded attention.

A daughter of the prosperous Delaware abolitionist Abraham Shadd, Mary Ann Shadd was raised in a household where antislavery activism was a central part of daily life. When her education was completed at age 16, she became a teacher—a role that she returned to throughout her life. In 1851, following the passage of the 1850 Fugitive Slave Act, Shadd and her brother Isaac immigrated to Canada with other free and fugitive African Americans. In Canada, African Americans established new communities with the hope that they would eventually achieve equality with whites. A staunch believer in emigration to Canada, Shadd published literature urging African Americans to relocate there.

In 1853, Shadd and her brother established the *Provincial Freeman*, a newspaper dedicated to informing Afro-Canadians and African Americans about politics, abolitionism, emigration, and racism in Canada. For the next six years, Shadd, the driving force of the paper, struggled to keep the paper solvent with help from her brother and other family members. With its 3,000 subscribers, the *Provincial Freeman* was a major black abolitionist newspaper of the antebellum era. Besides being the sole editor and the principal writer, Shadd also had to travel to raise funds to continue publication.

After Shadd's marriage to Thomas Cary in 1856, she continued to be immersed in her newspaper work. Lingering aftereffects of the 1857 depression resulted in the financial collapse of the *Provincial Freeman* in 1859. By this time, blacks in Canada were nervously watching the civil conflict intensifying in the United States. When John Brown toured Canada West (a region that is now part of western Ontario) in both 1858 and 1859 to gain support for the slave insurrection he was planning, Shadd Cary and several other black women strongly supported him, though there is evidence that financial help was the only aid they were permitted to give. It was not until 1861 that Shadd Cary finally had her opportunity to commemorate Brown's sacrifice for enslaved African Americans when she edited her friend and neighbor Osborne Perry Anderson's memoir, *A Voice from Harpers Ferry*. Published in Boston in 1861, the volume describes Anderson's experiences as a participant in the raid on the federal arsenal in Harpers Ferry, Virginia, in October 1859.

At the beginning of the war in 1861, Shadd Cary was consumed by problems at home. Her husband died in November 1860 at the age of 35, leaving her with a baby, a young child, and three stepchildren. With help from her extended family, she managed to continue teaching at the school she operated with her sister-in-law Amelia Freeman Shadd. In addition to teaching, Shadd Cary was the primary fund-raiser for the integrated school, supported in part by the American Missionary Association. Since most of the students were the sons and daughters of fugitive slaves who could not afford to pay tuition, financing the school was a never-ending problem.

Despite an increase in discrimination and segregation in Canada, Shadd Cary remained committed to living in Canada during the early years of the Civil War. She became a Canadian citizen in 1862 just as many African-American émigrés were returning to the United States.

In 1863, Martin Delany, the black nationalist leader, emigrationist, and long-time resident of Canada, began serving the Union army as a recruiter. Already well acquainted with Shadd Cary's strengths, he asked her to return to the United States to recruit African-American soldiers for the 29th Connecticut Volunteer Infantry. She eagerly accepted the position and became the only African-American woman to be an official recruiter of black soldiers for the Union army. (Other black women, including HARRIET JACOBS and Josephine St. Pierre Ruffin, were recruiters on a volunteer basis.)

Earning $5 for every free African American and $15 for every enslaved man she signed up, Shadd Cary traversed the midwestern states—through Pennsylvania, Ohio, Michigan, Wisconsin, Illinois, and Indiana—convincing every black male she could find that serving the Union would lead African Americans to complete equality with whites.

Recruiting black soldiers was a formidable task for any person—whether black or white, male or female—but was especially so for an African-American woman who not only had to bear the intense racial discrimination of the Midwest but also had to rise above the taboos restricting women from taking any active role in public life (Rhodes 1998, 153–155). As she journeyed from one town to the next, she relied on the recruiter's stock-and-trade. She gave speeches on church and courthouse steps, wrote and submitted notices to newspapers, distributed literature, and found potential recruits at their own doorsteps. In 1864, while immersed in these recruiting tasks, she agreed to be a fund-raising agent for the Colored Ladies Freedmen's Aid Society of Chicago.

Late in 1864, Shadd Cary returned briefly to Canada West. She soon moved to Detroit, Michigan, where she lived for a brief time before settling in Washington, DC, in the late 1860s. Although she felt torn about leaving Canada (she never lost hope in a fully integrated Canada), she decided that educating the newly freed men and women in the United States was the most critical task facing her race (Silverman 1988, 97). Besides education, the causes that occupied her in the United States included African-American civil rights, woman suffrage, and women's legal rights. Beginning in 1869, she enrolled in evening law courses at Howard University, eventually earning her degree in 1883 at the age of 60.

See also **Abolitionists; African-American Women**

Selected Readings

Calloway-Thomas, Carolyn. "Cary, Mary Ann Shadd." In *Black Women in America: An Historical Encyclopedia*. Edited by Darlene Clark Hine, Elsa Barkley Brown, and Rosalyn Terborg-Penn. New York: Carlson Publishing. 1993.

Rhodes, Jane. *Mary Ann Shadd Cary: The Black Press and Protest in the Nineteenth Century*, Bloomington: Indiana University Press. 1998.

Silverman, Jason H. "Mary Ann Shadd and the Search for Equality." In *Black Leaders of the Nineteenth Century*. Edited by Leon Litwack and August Meier. Urbana: University of Illinois Press. 1988.

Cashier, Albert D. J. (Jennie Hodgers) (1844–1915)

I never suspected anything of that kind [that Cashier was a woman]. I know that Cashier was the shortest person in the Co. I think he did not have to shave …. Albert D. J. Cashier was very quiet in her manner and she was not easy to get acquianted [sic] with. I rather think she did not take part in any of the sports and games of the members of the Co. When I was examined for enlistment, I was not stripped and a woman would not have had any trouble in passing the examination.

—Robert D. Hannah of Huron, South Dakota, a Civil War veteran who served with Albert Cashier in the 95th Illinois Infantry, January 1915 (Blanton 1993, 30)

Union Private Albert D. J. Cashier was not only one of the best documented cases of women serving as soldiers in the Civil War, but she was also one of the few women soldiers known to have served more than three continuous, uninterrupted years in the Confederate or the Union military. Born as Jennie Hodgers in Belfast, Ireland, she immigrated to the United States during the 1850s, perhaps having crossed the Atlantic as a stowaway. As a girl in Ireland, she herded sheep on her family's farm. In the United States, she may have worked in a shoe factory in an occupation that necessitated her assuming a boy's identity (Leonard 2001, 185). When the Civil War began, she was living in Belvidere, Illinois. On August 6, 1862, at the age of 18, she enlisted in the 95th Illinois Volunteer Infantry as Albert D. J. Cashier.

As part of the 95th Illinois Infantry, Cashier and her comrades were attached to the Army of the Tennessee. She participated in the Vicksburg Campaign in Mississippi in mid-1863, the Red River Campaign in Louisiana during the spring of 1864, the Battle of Nashville in December 1864, and the invasion of Mobile, Alabama, on April 12, 1865, the same day that the Confederacy formally surrendered to the Union. All in all, Cashier was engaged in at least 40 battles and skirmishes. She did not receive any wounds or injuries throughout her long and hazardous service.

After the war, Cashier returned to Illinois. She retained her male identity and worked as a farm laborer, handyman, janitor, and caretaker. In 1911, while she was employed by former Illinois state senator Ira Lish, Cashier's upper leg was broken when Lish accidentally ran over her with his car. When a doctor discovered that she was a woman, Cashier begged him, Lish, and the others assisting her not to reveal her secret. They complied, and as she was permanently disabled, it was arranged for her to reside at the Illinois Soldiers' and Sailors' Home in Quincy, Illinois. In 1914, Cashier's failing memory and deteriorating mental abilities caused her to be admitted to the Watertown State Hospital for the Insane.

Cashier's secret was revealed once she was admitted to the state hospital. The press jumped on the story and widely publicized it, causing a number of her former comrades from the 95th Illinois to come forward. They attested to her skill with a musket, her courage under fire, and her willingness to help others in all the work of the regiment. No veteran admitted that he had suspected she was a woman at any time during the war. In the state hospital, Cashier was forced to wear long skirts, a change that disturbed the final months of her life. She died in October 1915 and received a full military burial in Saunemin, Illinois.

See also **Military Women**

Selected Readings

Blanton, DeAnne and Lauren M. Cook. *They Fought Like Demons: Women Soldiers in the American Civil War.* Baton Rouge: Louisiana State University Press. 2002.
Clausius, Gerhard P. "The Little Soldier of the 95th: Albert D.J. Cashier." *Journal of the Illinois State Historical Society.* 51 (Winter 1958): 380–387.
Leonard, Elizabeth D. *All the Daring of the Soldier: Women of the Civil War Armies.* New York: Penguin Books. 2001.

Catholic Nuns

During the nineteenth century, the religious orders or communities of Catholic sisters grew rapidly and became firmly established in the United States. From 1790 to

1920, 38 new American orders were founded and 119 European orders formed houses in the United States. In 1822, there were only 200 Catholic sisters in the United States; by 1870, their numbers had swelled to 9,513 (Brewer 1987, 13, 14). At the beginning of the Civil War, most Americans in rural areas and in the South had little or no knowledge of the Catholic sisterhood. By the end of the Civil War, Americans throughout the North and South had gained an awareness, as nursing nuns cared for sick and wounded Union and Confederate soldiers in the military hospitals.

The Catholic sister orders provided a way of life that attracted many nineteenth-century native-born and immigrant Catholic women. Life in the convent offered women a release from some of the biggest dilemmas facing women in nineteenth-century society, advantages that especially appealed to poor and working-class women. The religious life offered women a powerful group identity, meaningful work, an alternative to the economic necessity of marriage, a refuge from the dangers and trials of incessant childbirth and childrearing, and protection from destitution and starvation.

Although protected from some of society's tribulations, the life of a mid-nineteenth-century nun was difficult in many respects. The trials imposed upon a nun-in-training (as a postulant and as a novice) were designed to instill obedience to God, to her superior, and to the rules of the order. A nun's day was strictly regulated. She was to observe the rule of silence at all times except during the one brief recreation period set aside each day. In addition to her daily labor for the order, she spent the rest of the day and the evening hours reciting prayers, meditating, saying the rosary, attending mass, listening to spiritual readings during meals, and examining her conscience. She was not permitted to develop a friendship or special fondness for any particular sister or to enjoy close family relationships. If a young nun survived the difficult entry period, she took her vows of poverty, chastity, and obedience and became an official member of the order.

Many American Catholic nuns of the mid-nineteenth century were teachers and nurses; others cared for orphans and the elderly indigent. During the Revolutionary War, the War of 1812, and cholera epidemics from 1830 to 1860, nuns nursed the wounded and the sick. During the Civil War, a minimum of 617 nuns representing 12 religious orders nursed Confederate and Union soldiers throughout the North, South, and parts of the West. These nursing sisters formed approximately 20 percent of all nuns living in the United States during the Civil War era (Maher 1989, 70). The Catholic sister nurses served on the battlefields, on HOSPITAL SHIPS, in field hospitals, in general military hospitals, and in private hospitals of the religious orders.

Federal and Confederate government officials at the national, state, and local levels entreated the Catholic sister orders to nurse and provide other care to soldiers. As the war progressed, Confederate and Union surgeons requested that their hospitals be staffed with nuns. Surgeons stated that they preferred Catholic sister nurses over white Protestant nurses because the former worked quietly, solved problems with their fellow sister nurses without disturbing the medical staff, obeyed surgeons' orders without discussion or debate, did not complain about the food or the accommodations, and did not waste time consorting with the soldiers.

Catholic sister nurses performed the same duties as other female Civil War nurses. They did housekeeping chores, distributed supplies, cooked and served meals, dressed wounds, dispensed medication, and occasionally assisted surgeons with amputations and other surgical procedures (Maher 1989, 109). The nuns also assumed other, more religious duties. They provided religious comfort to soldiers, encouraged the dying to seek God's forgiveness, baptized soldiers who wished it, and prepared the dead for religious burial.

Not everyone approved of the Catholic sisters' nursing. Besides the virulent anti-Catholic feeling in many parts of the country, the sisters, more than half of whom were Irish-born or of Irish descent, encountered a rigid anti-Irish discrimination. From time to time, the nuns encountered soldiers who refused to be tended by them. The sisters overcame these prejudices by quietly continuing to perform their nursing duties. Over time, in most cases, they won the respect of the men they served.

Although a number of white female Protestant nurses recorded their admiration of the nuns' skill and single-minded devotion to their duties, others harshly criticized them. ABBY HOPPER GIBBONS, a Quaker humanitarian and abolitionist who nursed in several large military hospitals, scorned the nuns for what she perceived as their lack of compassion. "Sisters don't ever enter into conversation with soldiers," she complained (Gibbons 1897, 2: 32). The nuns' vow of chastity and the rules of their orders prohibited them from conversing with men unless the talk was religion-based. Because of this restriction (which Gibbons may not have realized or understood), the nuns did not dispense words of encouragement and sympathy or engage in the light-hearted banter that lay nurses used to cheer the wounded and the sick.

Journalist JANE GREY SWISSHELM, who spent months nursing in a military hospital near Washington, DC, chided the nuns for absenting themselves from the "dangerous," onerous chore of dressing wounds. Although there were Catholic sister nurses who dressed wounds during the war, the chastity vow may have prevented other nuns from doing so. Like many white Protestant nurses, Gibbons felt the sting of the surgeons' rejection of mature, capable lay women.

> The presence of Protestant women, with ability to regard the need of the sick, and to sympathize with suffering humanity is a treasure beyond price. And here I must be allowed to contrast such with the cold intercourse of Catholic nurses, who are the machinery of an Institution and do not minister to the broken-down in spirit. (Gibbons 1897, 1: 347–348)

Historians have often noted DOROTHEA DIX's disdain for the Catholic sister nurses, charging that her anti-Irish and anti-Catholic sentiments fueled her passion against them. These prejudices were not confined to Dix but were rampant among Northern white Protestants of the mid-nineteenth century. Dix's crusade as the Union army's Superintendent of Female Nurses was to establish a white, largely

Protestant nursing corps. Part of this job, as she saw it, was to fight back against what she believed was the Surgeon General's and army surgeons' prejudices against lay nurses. As Gibbons explains,

> Miss Dix deserves much credit for the manner in which she resisted the Catholic invasion. She was insulted at every turn, and, but for her persistence, every Protestant would have been sent off the Point [Union army hospital at Point Lookout, Maryland] at once. She said it was a point she would never yield and entreated us to do our best, as it depended entirely upon us whether Protestants should have a hold here or not. From the day of our arrival, obstacles have been thrown in our way and everything done ... to remove us. (Gibbons 1897, 1: 355)

Gibbons laid much of the blame at the feet of the Surgeon General. "The truth is," she explained, "he is at war with Protestant nurses, and is using his best endeavors to introduce the 'Sisters,' who are mere machines in a hospital, and not allowed to extend sympathy to the poor men. It is a disgrace that such impositions are practiced" (Gibbons 1897, 1: 389).

The Catholic sisters, for their part, did not engage in the battle between the lay nurses and the army surgeons. Throughout the debate, the sisters continued to serve wherever asked to do so. From the point of view of the Catholic leadership in the United States, the Civil War nursing efforts of the Catholic sisters was a resounding success. Their humanitarian contributions not only increased the American public's positive perception of the Catholic sisterhood, they also served to improve the public's image of the Catholic Church, an institution that had suffered greatly from ignorance, prejudice, and discrimination.

See also **Hospital Ships; Nurses**

Selected Readings

Brewer, Eileen Mary. *Nuns and the Education of American Catholic Women, 1860–1920*. Chicago: Loyola University Press. 1987.

Maher, Sister Mary Denis. *To Bind Up the Wounds: Catholic Sister Nurses in the U.S. Civil War*. New York: Greenwood Press. 1989.

Chesnut, Mary Boykin (1823–1886)

Mary Boykin Chesnut's published diary of her Civil War experiences, crafted from her wartime journals and her memories, is one of the most critically acclaimed literary works to emerge from the Civil War era. Edmund Wilson, the celebrated twentieth-century American literary critic, declared the diary "an extraordinary document—in its informal department, a masterpiece." Wilson also observed that the diary is "much more imaginative and revealing than most of the fiction inspired by the [Civil] war" (Wilson 1962, ix, 279).

First published in 1905, nearly 19 years after her death, Boykin Chesnut's diary has proven invaluable to historians because it is one of the most comprehensive, perceptive records portraying the people and the events that dominated the leadership of the Confederacy and the world of the South's ruling class from 1861 to 1865. As historian C. Vann Woodward explains in the introduction to his Pulitzer Prize–winning edition of the diary, *Mary Chesnut's Civil War*, the significance of Boykin Chesnut's achievement transcends its usefulness to historians. Woodward states that "the enduring value of the work … lies in the life and reality with which it endows people and events and with which it evokes the chaos and complexity of a society at war.… . She brings to life the historic crisis of her age" (Chesnut 1981, xxvii).

The published versions of Boykin Chesnut's diary are not the same document as the journals that she produced during the Civil War, prompting some critics to doubt the published diary's accuracy and authenticity. She revised and restructured her Civil War journals from 1881 to 1884, 20 years after she wrote them. In the years immediately following the war, she was determined to re-create her war experiences and observations in a literary format, and she experimented with writing in several genres. By 1881, she had focused on the literary form that enabled her to convey the immediacy and impact of her experiences while allowing her to sustain a role as both witness and commentator. Woodward, who is also co-editor of the published volume of her war journals, asserts that she thoroughly maintained the integrity of the original war journals when she produced the diary.

Mary Boykin Miller was born in Statesburg, South Carolina, the daughter of Mary Boykin, a member of South Carolina's planter aristocracy, and Stephen Decatur Miller, a lawyer and politician. During Mary's childhood, her father became prominent in both South Carolina and national politics. He served a term in the U.S. House of Representatives, was governor of South Carolina, and eventually became a U.S. Senator. He was also a leader of the group that formulated South Carolina's states' rights and nullification theories. His daughter grew up with a fascination for politics, a direct result of her upbringing in the midst of South Carolina's highly charged political atmosphere.

During her teenage years, she attended an academy in Charleston, South Carolina, where she received an outstanding education for a young woman of her era, including instruction in French, German, history, rhetoric, and the natural sciences. Well read and possessed of a highly developed intellect, she continued her education throughout her life, reading voluminously in history and literature.

In 1840, a few weeks after Mary's seventeenth birthday, she wed attorney James Chesnut, Jr. (1815–1885), the son of the wealthiest plantation owner in South Carolina. At this time, she stopped using her father's surname, preferring to use her mother's more prestigious birth name as her middle name. Her husband initiated his career in politics during the same year as their marriage. He served in both houses of the South Carolina legislature during the 1840s and 1850s, and in 1858 was elected to the U.S. Senate. Boykin Chesnut was deeply involved in her husband's political activities. As his career progressed, she eventually became his personal secretary, and as such, was intimately familiar with all aspects of his political life. In 1859 to 1860, she thrived on the political and social life in Washington. A brilliant hostess, she developed a reputation as an astute, outspoken observer of the national political scene. During the chaotic political frenzy in Washington on the eve of the Civil War, Boykin Chesnut became acquainted with Varina Howell Davis, the wife of Mississippi Senator Jefferson Davis. The two women developed a close friendship that endured the rest of Boykin Chesnut's life.

In November 1860, James Chestnut became the first Southerner to resign from the Senate in defiant opposition to the election of President Abraham Lincoln. He immediately turned his energies to South Carolina's secession convention and helped write its Ordinance of Secession. In February 1861, he helped launch the new government of the Confederacy in Montgomery, Alabama, and throughout the war served Confederate President Jefferson Davis in several leading capacities. Consequently, Boykin Chesnut had a close, inside view of the workings of the Confederate government and the personalities and battles of its leaders. Her vantage point allowed her to observe and document the infighting, petty jealousies, and rivalries that impeded the efficiency of the Confederate Cabinet and weakened the government.

For much of the war, and especially while the Chesnuts resided in the Confederate capital of Richmond, Virginia, she was fully occupied acting as her husband's secretary and hostess. She also visited the soldiers in Richmond hospitals, but soon found that she was much better suited to the task of collecting and delivering supplies to the hospitals than sitting at soldiers' bedsides. She persisted at hospital work, even after suffering throughout most of 1862 from a so-called "hospital fever" she contracted in the course of her duties. She also contributed to the war effort by knitting and sewing garments for the troops, as did most of the upper-class ladies of Richmond. She also helped to construct sandbags for the defense of Richmond along the James River.

The antislavery statements that Boykin Chesnut made in her diary have stimulated enormous debate among twentieth-century historians. Her comment, "I wonder if it be a sin to think slavery a curse to any land. Sumner [the radical abolitionist Massachusetts Senator Charles Sumner] said not one word of this institution which is not true … god forgive us, but ours is a *monstrous* system & wrong & iniquity," is often credited as the most strongly worded antislavery statement written by a Southerner (Chesnut 1984, 42).

When discussing slavery, she revealed her disdain and revulsion for the institution, occasionally citing examples of incidents between slave and slaveowner that she considered cruel or brutal. In doing so, she frequently linked the injustices and inhumanity of slavery to the despicable conduct of "bad masters" and to slavery's domination by Southern white men. In her view, the elite women of her class were powerless to change or to terminate the slave system because of the political and economic domination of white men. Southern white women were, in effect, impotent witnesses to an institution that they did not create, want, or wish to continue. Although slavery was indeed the linchpin of the South's patriarchal society, Chesnut appears to overlook the fact that the wives, mothers, and daughters of male slaveholders perpetrated cruelties on slaves as did the 10 percent of slaveholders who were women.

How typical were Boykin Chesnut's antislavery views among women of the Southern elite? Although other upper-class women recorded their protests against slavery in their diaries and letters, most historians who have reviewed these manuscripts assert that though Boykin Chesnut's antislavery sentiments were not unique, they were not at all common or as widespread as she suggested. Studies of Southern white women of the planter elite, for all the challenges and troubles that slaveholding created for them in their daily lives, for the most part supported the institution and viewed slave labor as crucial to the continuation of their way of life.

As many writers have pointed out, as much as Boykin Chesnut abhorred slavery, her entire existence depended on slave labor. At no time does it appear that she took direct action to alter slaveholding in her own home. Nor is it apparent that she ever considered freeing one or more of her slaves or persuading her husband to do so. Her privileged, comfortable lifestyle—one which she acknowledged enjoying to the fullest—seems to have been unaffected by her abolitionist sentiments. While some have found this discrepancy a contradiction, it is unlikely that she would have found it so since she perceived women as powerless to change or to put an end to slavery. In any event, she was convinced that the war (in her view another male-dominated activity over which women had no control) would finish slavery whether the South won the war or not (Chesnut 1981, xlvi).

The enormous chasm between Boykin Chesnut's world and that of her slaves is evident throughout the diary. Despite her enlightened antislavery views, her perceptions and attitudes toward her slaves mesh with those of her fellow Southerners and most Northerners. To Boykin Chesnut, African Americans were an inferior, infathomable race. "Now if slavery is as disagreeable as we think it, why don't they [the slaves] all march over the border where they would be received with open arms?" she asked. "It amazes me. I am always studying these creatures. They are to me inscrutable in their ways and past finding out." Since her slaves appeared docile and uncomplaining, she concluded that they must be satisfied with their existence (Chesnut 1981, 113–114).

In the early months of 1865, as Union General William Sherman's troops invaded South Carolina, Boykin Chesnut recorded the chaotic, fearsome turmoil of her flight from Columbia, South Carolina, to Lincolnton, North Carolina. Weeks later, in the days following Lee's surrender at Appomattox, she again fled, this time to Chester, South Carolina, where she and James were soon reunited.

When the war ended, the Chesnuts began the grim journey back home to Mulberry, the Chesnut family's plantation in Camden, South Carolina. They found their home, the mills, the cotton gins, and much of their lands ravaged by Sherman's troops. As the Chesnuts had no way of paying off their enormous debts or of earning much money, they faced a future that was in stark contrast to their privileged past. July 26, 1865, marks the last entry in Boykin Chesnut's diary. It reads, "I do not write often now—not for want of something to say, but from a loathing of all I see and hear. Why dwell upon it?" (Chestnut 1981, 834).

As they struggled to survive during the early months of Reconstruction, Boykin Chesnut found herself haunted and tormented by her grief and her memories of a lost past. In April 1866, she wrote to her old friend Virgina Tunstall Clay, "There are nights here with the moonlight, cold & ghastly, & the whippoorwhills, & the screech owls alone disturbing the silence when I could tear my hair & cry aloud for all that is past & gone" (Chesnut 1984, xxiii).

By 1868, Chesnut was once again fully occupied by politics and public service. Boykin Chesnut continued to manage and operate the small dairy business that she started after the war, a concern that was the primary source of the couple's income. She also dedicated herself to her writing. She was still in the process of revising her war journals when her husband became severely ill in late 1884. After his death in February 1885, her health, which had never been strong, deteriorated and she died in November 1886, with the 2,500-page revision of her wartime journals still incomplete. Before her death, she entrusted her journals and the reconstructed diary manuscript to her young friend Isabella Martin. Martin held on to the manuscript until 1904, when she met a New York journalist who helped find a publisher for the diary. In 1905, the first edition of Boykin Chesnut's diary, *A Diary from Dixie*, was published.

See also **Diaries; Fort Sumter**

Selected Readings

Chesnut, Mary Boykin Miller. *The Private Mary Chesnut: The Unpublished Civil War Diaries*. Edited by C. Vann Woodward and Elisabeth Muhlenfeld. New York: Oxford University Press. 1984.

Chesnut, Mary Boykin Miller. *Mary Chesnut's Civil War*. Edited by C. Vann Woodward. New Haven: Yale University Press. 1981.

DeCredico, Mary A. *Mary Boykin Chesnut: A Confederate Woman's Life*. Madison, WI: Madison House. 1996.

Muhlenfeld, Elisabeth. *Mary Boykin Chesnut: A Biography*. Baton Rouge: Louisiana State University Press. 1981.

Child, Lydia Maria (1802–1880)

The most influential female antislavery writer of the North, Lydia Maria Child passed the Civil War years engaged in abolitionist activism, soldiers' aid, and freedmen's relief and education. Her controversial writings, especially those during the "John Brown Year," from the autumn of 1859 through the election of 1860, further polarized the North and South, and played a pivotal role in delineating the sectional arguments concerning the future of slavery in the United States.

Lydia Maria Francis launched her literary career in her early twenties. Her novels, domestic advice books, and juvenile writings made her a celebrity. Following her marriage to David Lee Child in 1828, the couple was deeply involved in the fledgling abolitionist movement of the early 1830s, and became adherents of William Lloyd Garrison's views. With the publication of one of her most controversial writings, an 1833 volume titled *An Appeal in Favor of That Class of Americans Called Africans*, she lost her devoted fans, her literary stature, and her financial security. Yet she did not turn away from her antislavery activism or her literary efforts to expose the evils of slavery. The book, though not immediately embraced by reformers, influenced a number of New Englanders to become abolitionists, including the American Anti-Slavery Society (AASS) leader Wendell Phillips, Massachusetts Republican Senator Charles Sumner, and Unitarian founder William Ellery Channing.

In 1840, Francis Child was a member of the executive committee of the AASS. She and several other women pioneered women's leadership roles in the AASS wing of the abolitionist movement. During the early 1840s, she edited the AASS newspaper, the *National Anti-Slavery Standard*. For most of her antislavery career, however, she was not politically involved in any organization's leadership. She much preferred close associations with her reform colleagues while she pursued the expression of her individual voice as an abolitionist writer.

Through her writings, Francis Child remained politically active throughout the Civil War. But she was never more centrally involved in the nation's sectional crisis than she was during what she called the "John Brown Year," the 12 months following the militant abolitionist's failed raid on the federal arsenal at Harpers Ferry, Virginia, in October 1859. Brown had hoped that this attack would ignite a massive slave insurrection across the South.

The intensity of the "John Brown Year" began for Francis Child when she mailed to Governor Henry A. Wise of Virginia her personal request to nurse the imprisoned Brown. Wise sent her letter and his response to several newspapers in the hopes of exposing Northern abolitionists' apparent disregard for the safety of white Southerners. Her incisive response to Wise's letter created an explosion of counterblasts from irate Southerners, male and female.

In her response to Wise's epistle, she found herself, an avowed pacifist, defending Brown's motives for staging a slave revolt against white slaveholders. "I believe that old hero to be no criminal," she argued in her retort to Wise, "but a martyr to righteous principles which he sought to advance by methods sanctioned by his own religious views, though not by mine" (Child 1860, 7). Margaretta Mason, the wife of Virginia Senator James Mason, wrote a letter blasting Francis Child for her hypocrisy. Mason found Francis Child's attacks on Southerners for their cruelties to slaves especially egregious, considering that the abolitionist condoned the brutality of Brown's mission.

> A man whose aim and intention was to incite the horrors of a servile war—to condemn women of your own race, ere death closed their eyes on their sufferings from violence and outrage, to see their husbands and fathers murdered, their children butchered, the ground strewn with the brains of their babes. (AASS 1860, 16)

Mason enumerates the kindnesses and care she devotes to her slaves, then chastises Northern women for their disinterest in the needs of the Northern poor. In response to Mason's recital of biblical verses supporting Southern attitudes and positions, Francis Child wrote back, bombarding Mason with 18 biblical verses in opposition to slavery and oppression.

The published correspondence, as it unfolded in the pages of the *New York Tribune* and the Richmond (Virginia) *Examiner*, riveted both Northerners and Southerners. In 1860, the AASS published the correspondence as a tract, selling and distributing 300,000 copies, making it the best-selling publication of Francis Child's career.

The enormous public reaction prompted her to write three more pamphlets during that year. She published *The Right Way, the Safe Way, Proved by Emancipation in the British West Indies, and Elsewhere* to convince white slaveholders that the key to their future prosperity lay in following the example of the West Indies, which had abolished slavery. The pamphlet's power, she believed, lay in the fact that it was not a political document and did not cast blame on the South, but approached the entire issue from an economic point of view (Karcher 1994, 430).

Her tract *The Patriarchal Institution, as Described by Members of Its Own Family* was a political document targeted at Northern white laborers vulnerable to Northern pro-slavery arguments. And, in *The Duty of Disobedience to the Fugitive Slave Act: An Appeal to the Legislators of Massachusetts*, she condemned the state's lawmakers and its citizens for acquiescing to the demands of the federal Fugitive Slave Act.

> Shame on my native State! Everlasting shame! Blot out the escutcheon of the brave old Commonwealth! Instead of the sword uplifted to protect liberty, let the slave driver's whip be suspended over a bloodhound, and take for your motto, "Obedience to tyrants is the highest law." (Child 1860, 5)

She hoped that the tract would persuade Massachusetts lawmakers to revise the state's Personal Liberty Law to imitate Vermont's bill nullifying the Fugitive Slave Act.

Also during this prewar year, she edited the autobiography of HARRIET JACOBS, *Incidents in the Life of a Slave Girl, Written by Herself.* Jacobs came to Francis Child via the African-American abolitionist William C. Nell. Francis Child agreed to read and lend a critical eye to the volume. Despite her assertion in the book's preface that her editing had been minimal, twentieth-century critics gave birth to the notion that she was the author of *Incidents*, a view commonly held until 1981 when historian Jean Fagan Yellin's research firmly established Jacobs as the author.

In an overwhelmingly busy year, Francis Child sacrificed the time to edit *Incidents* because of the book's potential to garner support for immediate emancipation. As she stated in a letter to Jacobs on August 13, 1860, "I should not take so much pains, if I did not consider the book unusually interesting, and likely to do much service to the Anti-Slavery cause.... You know I would go through fire and water to help give a blow to Slavery" (quoted in Jacobs 1987, 244).

Once the Civil War began in April 1861, she stepped back from the heart of the fray. She was no less emotionally involved in the effort to emancipate the slaves and no less interested in thinking and writing about the nation's political affairs. But the ceaseless activity of the "John Brown Year" had exhausted her. As she put it, "I have never done so much anti-slavery work in any year of my life" (quoted in Karcher 1994, 416). In 1861, she was nearly 60, and her husband's health was failing. She involved herself in the war effort from a distance, remaining close to home in a rural community outside of Boston.

Even at this slackened pace, Francis Child accomplished more than most women. Her articles and letters continued to appear in *The Liberator* and the *National Anti-Slavery Standard*. She also produced a steady stream of propaganda urging the public to demand emancipation. Most of these essays and letters, published in the *New York Tribune* and other leading newspapers, she contributed anonymously. Occasionally she used a pseudonym. She hoped that by omitting her name (the sight of which might inflame anyone who was not a committed abolitionist), her message would attain a broader readership.

Francis Child delved into soldiers' aid work, assisting only confirmed Kansas "abolitionist regiments," led by abolitionist officers. She knitted dozens of pairs of socks and rolled bandages. She also made clothing for the freedpeople living in the contraband camps, and raised money to sustain the activities of the AASS. She compiled and published *The Freedmen's Book* in 1865, a compendium of writings— biography, poetry, speeches, and memoir—primarily written by African Americans for the newly emancipated slaves.

After the war, Child continued to write for the *National Anti-Slavery Standard*. In 1868, she turned her attention toward advocacy for the civil and political rights of Native Americans.

See also **Abolitionists**

Selected Readings

Clifford, Deborah Pickman. *Crusader for Freedom: A Life of Lydia Maria Child*. Boston: Beacon Press. 1992.

Karcher, Carolyn. *The First Woman in the Republic: A Cultural Biography of Lydia Maria Child*. Durham, NC: Duke University Press. 1994.

Meltzer, Milton. *Tongue of Flame: The Life of Lydia Maria Child*. New York: Thomas Y. Crowell. 1965

Contraband Relief Association (CRA)

If the white people can give festivals to raise funds for the relief of suffering soldiers, why should not the well-to-do colored people go to work to do something for the benefit of the suffering blacks[?]

—Elizabeth Keckley, *Christian Recorder*, March 14, 1863 (Forbes 1998, 69)

Beginning in the early weeks of the Civil War, thousands of fugitive slaves or "contrabands" fled to Washington, DC. The federal government responded by crowding the African-American men, women, and children into hastily prepared contraband camps that supplied insufficient food and clothing, had little or no sanitation, and were breeding grounds for infectious diseases. As white charitable organizations struggled to organize themselves to assist the freedpeople, ELIZABETH KECKLEY, the dressmaker of the First Lady MARY TODD LINCOLN, established a relief society run by the free African-American women of Washington.

Keckley was eager for the prosperous middle-class African-American community to support the newly freed men and women. As a former slave who had worked hard to build a successful dressmaking business, she was concerned that white philanthropists and charity workers who underestimated the abilities and the potential of the formerly enslaved would undermine their efforts to elevate themselves. She knew from her own experience that it was possible for former slaves to care for themselves, find employment, and direct their own lives.

With forty African-American women from her church, Keckley established the Contraband Relief Association (CRA) "for the purpose, not only of relieving the wants of those destitute people, but also to sympathize with, and advise them" (quoted in Forbes 1998, 69). The CRA was by no means the first African-American relief society. Free African Americans in the North, and, to a much lesser extent, in the South, had been volunteers in charitable relief for the poor, the sick, and the elderly for decades through their churches, and, in the North, through the antislavery societies as well.

Mary Todd Lincoln contributed the first $200 to the fledgling organization and strongly supported Keckley in her fund-raising activities. While accompanying the First Lady on a trip to New York and New England, Keckley sought the assistance of the free black community in Boston. There she encouraged Octavia Grimes to establish the Colored Ladies' Relief Association and Sarah Martin the Fugitive Aid Society of Boston. Both organizations were attached to all-black Boston churches and became auxiliaries of the CRA.

Keckley sought and received large donations from Frederick Douglass, President Abraham Lincoln, Northern abolitionists, and antislavery societies in Scotland and England. She also enlisted abolitionist speakers to raise money for the CRA during their lectures. Wendell Phillips of the American Anti-Slavery Society, Frederick Douglass, and Henry Highland Garnet were among those who assisted the CRA in this way.

During 1863, the CRA expanded its focus and changed its name to the Ladies' Freedmen and Soldiers' Relief Association. As thousands of contraband men enlisted in all-black Union regiments in 1863, the CRA helped outfit the African-American soldiers just as white women had supplied white soldiers through the soldiers' aid societies early in the war.

See also **Contraband Women; Slavery and Emancipation**

Selected Readings

Forbes, Ella. African American Women During the Civil War. New York: Garland. 1998.

Keckley, Elizabeth. Behind the Scenes, Or, Thirty Years a Slave, and Four Years in the White House. New York: G.W. Carleton. 1868. Reprinted. New York: Oxford University Press. 1988.

Sterling, Dorothy. We Are Your Sisters: Black Women in the Nineteenth Century. New York: W.W. Norton. 1984.

Contraband Women

There were approximately two million enslaved women on the eve of the Civil War, and an estimated half-million refused to wait for the war's end to release themselves from bondage. As soon as Southern white men left their homes and plantations in 1861 to enlist in the Confederate military, male and female slaves began to flee, despite the dangers. Tens of thousands flocked to Washington, DC, and to the Sea Islands off the coast of South Carolina, which came under the control of the Union army late in 1861. As the war proceeded and as the Union confiscated more Confederate territory, thousands more fugitives attached themselves to the Union army encampments for protection. Women were just as likely to escape from their owners as men, a fact that shatters the myth of the female slaves' passivity. By claiming their freedom and resolutely resisting Confederate and federal efforts to return them to slavery, women shared an equal role with African-American men in bringing about the eradication of slavery.

The African-American refugees who crowded into Washington, DC, flummoxed the federal government. Hamstrung by its noninterventionist policy on slavery, President Abraham Lincoln, government officials, and Congress debated the future of the fugitives. Ambitious Massachusetts politician and Union Brigadier General Benjamin F. Butler created a plan that he believed would promote his political career and placate all Northern interests involved in the crisis—irate abolitionists in his home state, federal officials, and the Union army leadership. He welcomed fugitive slaves into his camp at Fort Monroe, Virginia, and declared them "contrabands of war." Slaves were contraband, he argued, because the Confederacy intended to use their labor against the Union. And, as seized property, the Union could utilize fugitive men as laborers and soldiers against the Confederacy.

There was one huge flaw in his plan, however. Fugitive men did not travel alone but in family groups. Once Butler opened the floodgates, he soon discovered that contraband women and children were an enormous liability to the Union army. In a statement that would come to identify the federal government's position, he admitted, "I am in the utmost doubt what to do with this species of property" (quoted in Glymph 1996, 58).

Regardless of the federal government's indecision and the Union army's hostility toward contrabands, African-American men, women, and children continued to pour into army encampments. The army immediately pressed fugitive African-American men into building encampments and fortifications, digging canals and trenches, and cultivating crops on Northern-seized plantations. And beginning in 1863, it urged and sometimes forced them to enlist in all-black Union regiments, though most African-American men were eager to join up.

Contraband women and children struggled to remain close to their menfolk in the military. They spent their days scrounging for food, constructing makeshift huts and shanties adjoining the army camps and plantations, and planting small gardens of corn and sweet potatoes. They, too, served the army—washing soldiers' uniforms, cooking, nursing, and working as servants to officers and soldiers—an arrangement they willingly accepted in exchange for meager wages and protection from Confederate reenslavement. Contraband women and their families, especially those who were trying to survive on their own or on only a black soldier's paltry pay ($7 per month in 1863, not including the clothing allowance), found that their income was inadequate to feed and clothe their families. The federal government was frequently late in compensating contraband workers and black soldiers. Women in the contraband camps sometimes had to steal or prostitute themselves to keep their families from starvation.

Fugitive African-American men were welcomed in Union encampments because of the cheap labor they represented. Contraband women and their children, on the other hand, were perceived as an overwhelming encumbrance and a danger. Unlike their male counterparts, they were resented and often hated by Union troops, who often treated them with neglect, disdain, and physical and sexual abuse. White officers and soldiers complained that refugee women and children made it impossible for soldiers to react quickly in the event of Confederate attack. Army commanders also accused the women of turning the camps into brothels and stealing soldiers' rations and supplies. When black soldiers and military workers demanded access to their wives, some officers denied them, refusing to acknowledge that the contraband women and children were family members. Yet black soldiers insisted on their right to have their families live nearby as white soldiers did. In Memphis, Tennessee, in January 1865, black Union soldiers joined their wives and children in the contraband shantytown adjoining their encampment. The soldiers then threatened to fire their weapons on any of their fellow Union soldiers who attempted to carry out the order to relocate their families (Berlin and Rowland 1997, 76).

The policies of the federal government concerning the contraband camps worked against the desperate plight of African-American women and children throughout the war. Although the Second Confiscation Act and the Militia Act, both passed by Congress in 1862, legislated that African-American wives and children of military men must have their safety and freedom protected, the laws did not prevent massive malnutrition and starvation, abandonment by Union forces, or abuse by Union troops. Furthermore, the acts did not protect all contraband women and their families. Single women, widows, and unmarried heads of households who did not have enlisted husbands could not claim the benefits provided by the acts.

All too often army commanders ignored the laws. Desperate to shake their regiments free of the contrabands, they sometimes turned African-American women and children over to Southerners to be reenslaved. During the final months of 1864, in a scenario that had been repeated elsewhere in the Union-occupied South, Union soldiers destroyed the huts of approximately 400 African-American women and children attached to Camp Nelson, Kentucky. Acting on orders from their commanding officer, the soldiers herded the fugitives onto wagons and moved them to a site behind Union lines, abandoning them without food, clothing, shelter, or water. The women's husbands were many miles away, fighting in Union regiments. Alone and without any means to defend themselves, they were vulnerable to attack, rape, and seizure by roving bands of Confederate soldiers. Days later, Lincoln's Secretary of War Edwin Stanton intervened, forcing the commander of Camp Nelson to provide the women with the protection the law promised. For women turned out of other encampments, their only hope was to locate another contraband camp or to wander until they connected with other groups of women and children heading north.

African-American women who received a Union refuge from Confederate reenslavement were not always safe. Some Union officers and soldiers sexually assaulted and raped African-American women with impunity. When other women or their family members resisted these violations, they, too, were sometimes attacked. In 1862, ESTHER HILL HAWKS, a white Northern missionary teacher in the South Carolina Sea Islands, protested the rampant sexual abuse of African-American women that she found there.

> No colored woman or girl was safe from the brutal lusts of the [white] soldiers—and by soldiers I mean both officers and men …. Mothers were brutally treated for trying to protect their daughters, and there are not several women in our little hospital who have been shot by soldiers for resisting their vile demands. (quoted in Schwalm 1997, 102)

Although some Union commanders refused to tolerate these assaults, others turned a blind eye. On the Sea Islands, General Rufus Saxton expressed a common Union military viewpoint when he asserted that contraband women were the cause of their own sexual abuse. Like many white Northerners and Southerners, Saxton was convinced that slavery had sexually debased African-American women, turning them into wild seductresses with uncontrollable "animal urges." According to this logic, his men could not be held responsible if they responded to women whom he believed wantonly threw themselves at soldiers.

On the Union-confiscated Sea Island cotton plantations in South Carolina and elsewhere in the South as the war progressed, Northern expectations of the future of the freed slaves clashed with what African-American men and women wanted for themselves. While the freedmen and women wanted their own land and the freedom to live and make a living on it, the federal government and the Northern businessmen who owned and managed the plantations insisted that African Americans labor for wages. Most Northerners claimed that the former slaves were not yet competent to manage their own lives.

One crack in the foundation of the Northern industrial model of plantation production, however, was the practice of some Northern plantation owners to withhold wages or to pay their female field hands less than they first promised. African-American women refused to accept these conditions. In fact, delays in payment and wage disputes topped the list of freedwomen's protests to the federal government's Freedmen's Bureau. On the cotton plantation that Edward S. Philbrick was managing on the island of St. Helena, a woman named Grace, on two separate occasions, presided over a group of female field hands in protesting unpaid wages. They also demonstrated against the price-gouging of the white storeowner on whom they depended for food and other goods (White 1985, 15; Forbes 1998, 138). On a Northern-owned sugar plantation in Union-occupied Louisiana in the fall of 1862, freedwomen banded together to rebel against the planter's refusal to meet his fiscal obligations to them. At first they slowed their production, and when that proved ineffective, they went on strike. A week later, the freedmen on the plantation also stopped work. The planter, in danger of losing his entire crop, finally paid them what he owed them (J. Jones 1985, 56).

During the first year of the war, when Northern African-American and white abolitionists and leaders of religious organizations learned of the desperate needs of the contrabands in Washington, DC, and on the Sea Islands of South Carolina, they raised money, and sent teachers, nurses, clothing, food, and medical supplies. White and free African-American men and women from the North, many of them volunteers, traveled south to teach in the contraband camps. They believed that their educational program must be geared toward preparing African Americans for life in the North. Beyond teaching basic literacy skills, they tried to instill "Northern" values—the necessity of working for a wage, the value of hard work, and the character-building qualities of industriousness, self-sufficiency, and tidiness—an educational program that often baffled their students.

Most Northern missionaries viewed their African-American students as intellectually limited, morally deficient, and in need of constant supervision and control. Lucy Chase, a young white Quaker woman teaching on Craney Island, Virginia, made a typical observation. "There are now eighteen hundred negroes here; and they continue to arrive," she wrote in a letter to her family in Massachusetts. "They come almost wholly destitute of clothing, covered with vermin, and extremely ignorant, and incompetent for noble, self-originating action of mind or body" (Swint 1966, 24).

Northerners were not the only teachers in the contraband camps. SUSIE BAKER KING TAYLOR, herself a fugitive slave from Georgia, spent the war years teaching and nursing the men in her husband's regiment, among her other duties. Former slave HARRIET JACOBS, author of the autobiographical slave narrative *Incidents in the Life of a Slave Girl, Written by Herself,* spent years in Washington working with the freedpeople. She was alarmed at the condescending attitudes of Northern missionaries toward African-American refugees and chastised them in a letter published in *The Liberator,* the most influential abolitionist newspaper. "Some of them [ex-slaves] have been so degraded by slavery that … they know little else than the handle of the hoe, the plough, the cotton-pod and the overseer's lash. Have patience with them. You have helped to make them what they are" (quoted in Sterling 1984, 246–247).

Immediately after the war, freedwomen searched for their husbands, sons, and brothers; many devoted decades to the struggle to reunite their families. But for most women, freedom and safety would continue to elude them. "Freedom ain't give us notin' but pickled hoss meat an' dirty crackers an' not half enough of dat," declared Mattie Curtis, a former contraband (quoted in Sterling 1984, 323). But no matter how difficult their lives after slavery, African-American men and women now had the option to turn their backs on abusive employers and working conditions to seek new opportunities.

See also **Abolitionists; African-American Women; Forten, Charlotte; Slavery and Emancipation; Teachers of the Freedpeople**

Selected Readings

Berlin, Ira and Barbara J. Fields, Seven F. Miller, Joseph P. Reidy, and Leslie S. Rowland, eds. *Free at Last: A Documentary History of Slavery, Freedom, and the Civil War.* New York: The New Press. 1992.

Glymph, Thavolia. " `This Species of Property': Female Slave Contrabands in the Civil War." In *A Woman's War: Southern Women, Civil War, and the Confederate Legacy.* Edited by Edward D. C. Campbell, Jr. and Kym S. Rice. Richmond and Charlottesville, VA: The Museum of the Confederacy and the University Press of Virginia. 1996.

Sterling, Dorothy. *We Are Your Sisters: Black Women in the Nineteenth Century.* New York: W.W. Norton. 1984.

Coppin, Fanny Jackson (1837–1913)

A leading educator of the nineteenth century, Fanny Jackson Coppin was one of the first black women to receive a full-fledged collegiate education. At a time when the vast majority of African Americans were illiterate, and when most free blacks in the North were struggling to obtain an elementary education, Jackson, a former slave, was excelling in the most challenging courses at Oberlin College in Oberlin, Ohio. In the years following her graduation from Oberlin, Jackson became the first African-American woman to serve as head principal of a school of higher education in the United States (Perkins 1987, 90). She was renowned for her innovative teaching methods, her preparation of future teachers, and her crusade to establish industrial and vocational education for African-American men and women in Philadelphia.

Not much is known of Fanny Jackson's early life, though it is known that she was born a slave in Washington, DC, in 1837. An aunt purchased her freedom when Jackson was a girl, probably when she was between ten and twelve years of age. Not long afterward, she lived with another aunt in New Bedford, Massachusetts, working as a domestic servant. Her work prevented her from attending school on a daily basis. As she explained in her memoir, "I could not go on wash day, nor ironing day, nor cleaning day, and this interfered with my progress" (Coppin 1995, 11). She felt her lack of education keenly, and it awakened a hunger for knowledge that remained with her throughout her life.

In 1851, when Jackson moved with her relatives to Newport, Rhode Island, she again worked as a domestic servant, this time for a wealthy, highly educated couple from whom she learned much about literature and the arts. At 14 years of age she was determined to obtain the education she had been craving throughout her childhood. With her wages of $7 per month, she engaged a tutor to teach her one hour a day, three days a week. During the six years she was employed in this household, she received enough education to prepare her for a teaching career. She attended a public school for African Americans in Newport (a rarity in a nation that largely excluded blacks from the public schools) so that she could study for the entrance exams at the Rhode Island State Normal School, an institution of higher education specializing in teacher training. It was then that Jackson vowed to dedicate her life to teaching other African Americans.

When Jackson started attending the Rhode Island State Normal School, most likely in 1859, she hired a tutor to teach her French, a subject that was not part of her teacher preparation courses. After she graduated, she realized that her normal school training had only given her a partial education, and she began to investigate options for broadening her knowledge. She decided to apply to Oberlin College, because it bestowed degrees on both African Americans and women. In 1860, Oberlin was the only college or university to permit black women to work toward a baccalaureate, or bachelor's degree. Although black male and female students had attended Oberlin for decades, they were a small minority. In 1859, only 32 students out of a total enrollment of 1,200 were African American (Perkins 1987, 23). In 1860, Jackson entered the Preparatory or "Ladies' Department" at Oberlin, with the firm intention of entering the more challenging Collegiate Department as soon as she was ready to take on the more advanced coursework. In the fall of 1861, having passed the entrance examination for the Collegiate Department, she began the four-year Collegiate course.

Jackson studied with a fierce determination while at Oberlin, convinced that it was her duty to prove that African Americans were the intellectual equals of whites. "I felt that I had the honor of the whole African race upon my shoulders," she explained. "I felt that, should I fail, it would be ascribed to the fact that I was colored" (quoted in Perkins 1987, 25). In addition to her Oberlin classes, she continued her private French lessons.

When newly emancipated African Americans began arriving in the town of Oberlin in 1863, Jackson organized an evening school four nights a week for the formerly enslaved men and women who worked by day. Despite her own busy course of study, she was able to teach them reading, writing, spelling, and grammar. It was deeply satisfying work, primarily because it was her first opportunity to fulfill her goal, as she expressed it, to teach "my people" (quoted in Perkins 1987, 18). Realizing that she also needed to educate the white citizens of Oberlin about the intellectual capacity of African Americans, she held public exhibitions of her students' work and permitted townspeople and other visitors to sit in on her classes.

Due to the well-publicized success of her evening school, the Oberlin administration appointed Jackson to teach grammar in its Preparatory Department, making her the first African American to be chosen for this position. As a condition of her teaching, the class officials informed her that if any white students objected to her instructing them she would have to step down. Her class was so popular that it soon had to be divided into two sections. Thus, she performed the unusual distinction of teaching two classes in the Preparatory Department in addition to keeping up with her own studies. Unlike other Oberlin students who taught in the department, she was not invited to assume a permanent position at Oberlin after graduation. Not until 1948 would Oberlin College hire an African American to teach full time.

Despite this incident of racism, Jackson always maintained that she was not hindered by racial discrimination or prejudice while at Oberlin. She later stated that, "Prejudice in Oberlin is preached against, prayed against, sung against, and lived against" (quoted in Perkins 1987, 39). She also maintained that any ill feeling she experienced on account of her race was minor. When she graduated in 1865, she became the second African-American woman to receive a bachelor's degree from Oberlin. The first, Mary Jane Patterson, had graduated in 1862.

In August 1865, Jackson traveled to Philadelphia to take a job as principal of the Female Department at the Institute for Colored Youth, a Quaker-funded high school and teacher-training school for African Americans. After having experienced racial tolerance at Oberlin, her confrontation with rampant race prejudice in Philadelphia came as a shock. In her memoir, she described her first encounter with discrimination.

> I had been so long in Oberlin that I had forgotten about my color, but I was sharply reminded of it when, in a storm of rain, a Philadelphia street car conductor forbid my entering a car that did not have on it for colored people, so I had to wait in the storm until one came in which colored people could ride. (Coppin 1995, 14)

Jackson, however, was soon recognized as an outstanding teacher at the Institute, and in 1869, was appointed principal of the entire school.

During her residence in Philadelphia, Jackson grew increasingly concerned about the poverty of African Americans and their lack of employment opportunities. Because most black workers were unskilled, they earned a pittance and had no job stability. With skills, Jackson maintained, African-American men and women could command higher wages and more secure positions and thereby eliminate the poverty that plagued the African-American community. With this goal in mind, Jackson became a leading proponent of industrial and vocational education. Although her efforts met with resistance at every turn, by 1889, she succeeded in bringing an industrial education program to the Institute for Colored Youth. Evening classes in carpentry, bricklaying, shoemaking, printing, plastering, and tailoring were offered for men, and training in millinery and dressmaking were open to women. Instruction in typewriting, stenography, and cooking were available to both men and women.

During the 1880s, while immersed in her mission for industrial education, religion became more important. She was deeply involved in the African Methodist Episcopal Church, and married an A.M.E. minister in 1881, the Reverend Levi J. Coppin. She became a leader in the Home and Foreign Missionary Society, and served a number of terms as its president. Following her retirement from teaching in 1902, she became a missionary, traveling with her husband to South Africa. She died in Philadelphia in 1913.

See also **African-American Women; Education; Teachers of the Freedpeople**

Selected Readings

Coppin, Fanny Jackson. *Reminiscences of School Life, and Hints on Teaching.* New York: G.K. Hall. 1995.

Perkins, Linda M. *Fanny Jackson Coppin and the Institute for Colored Youth, 1865–1902.* New York: Garland. 1987.

Courtship and Marriage

I write so often to you my dear Will, that really sometimes, I scarcely know what to say, I am afraid you will get tired of reading over the selfsame words, "how much I love you" … I expect you will think me too foolish and sentimental, I can't help it, I do love you devotedly, and can't help telling you so.

   Write as often as you can

   Ten thousand kisses from your devoted wife, Annie

—Grand Rapids [Michigan] August 23, 1863 (JEB Stuart Captured Mail File, Southern Women's History Collection, Museum of the Confederacy)

Just as the Civil War wrought changes in many aspects of civilian life, so, too, did the conflict disrupt and alter courting and marital relationships. The clearest evidence of the war's impact on the intimate lives of courting and married couples can be found within the correspondence and DIARIES of white middle- and upper-class men and women of the North and South. For many couples separated by war and invasion, writing letters was the only vehicle of communication during the war. Men as well as women used letters to keep their bonds intact when faced with lengthy separations that sometimes went on for years. Although there is very little surviving correspondence that reveals how the war affected the ties of poor white and African-American couples, the war had just as powerful an impact on their relationships as on those of the middle and upper classes.

   Whether wealthy or poor, the prolonged separations of wartime altered the traditional roles of husbands and wives. Before and after the war, mid-nineteenth-century husbands held a great deal of the power in the marital relationship. Men were the leaders of their families and the ultimate decision-makers although women were in control of all housekeeping arrangements and were responsible for almost all aspects of childcare and early childhood education. Mid-nineteenth-century society also gave women the most power in directing the spiritual, moral, and religious concerns of the family. While men were active in the sphere of business and work outside the home, women were expected to rule the domestic sphere. With the onset of war and the departure of husbands, the power shifted in many marital relationships. Women saw their roles expanded as they were forced to take charge of their families and assume the decision-making powers of their husbands. Men saw their responsibility as the decision-makers decrease and discovered that their perils away from home made them more emotionally reliant on their wives.

The nineteenth-century ideal of romantic love, with its characteristic language of intimacy and devotion, infuses Civil War era love letters. Romantic modes of expression provided the universal language by which couples kept their love alive. The romantic ideal also required that men and women reveal their innermost selves to one another. The candid, open discussion of feelings was frequently the subject of letters. By sharing intimate thoughts and passions, nineteenth-century lovers believed that they could more easily unite as a couple and become one sacred unit. The rigors and hazards of military campaigns heightened the intensity of these sentiments.

For some partners it was easier to reveal one's deepest emotions in a letter than to share them in person. After shipping out with the 2nd Vermont Infantry, James E. Hart wrote to his sweetheart in June 1861, "Nellie you don't know how bad I felt that Night I left you I tried to conceal it from you but I thought my heart would break to think of leaving for so long a time" (quoted in Marshall 1999, 32).

During the long stretches of time apart, both women and men—whether in courting or marital relationships—viewed letters as a physical extension of their loved ones. Men and women admitted to kissing letters, speaking fondly to them, and even sleeping with them. When Fannie Gordon received a letter from her husband Confederate Major General John Gordon, she confided to him, "I pressed to my lips over and over the spot that yours had touched and tried to imagine I could feel your own precious lips & that dear moustache that I love so much" (quoted in D. Faust 1997, 117). Men were just as demonstrative with the mail they received from their sweethearts. When a Union attack was imminent, Eldred Simkins, also a Confederate officer, burned all of his correspondence except for the letters from his fiancée. He later explained to her, "I hadn't the heart to burn yours, but put them very poetically in my breast pocket till all the row was over. It looked like sending you away to part with them, so I kept them with me" (quoted in Lystra 1989, 24). Adelaide Case noted in a letter to her beau, Charles Tenney, that his letter conjured up his presence, which made the burden of separation easier to bear: "Dearest, while reading your noble and true thoughts I can hardly realize that hundreds and hundreds of miles separate us. I seem to see you and listen to your darling words. your [sic] presence seems ever near me strengthening me to bear this ordeal through which I am passing" (E-Text collection. University of Virginia Library, Nettleton Collection. http://etext.virginia.edu/civilwar/nettleton/Letters.html).

Although married men and women expressed love in their letters prior to the war, there was typically less emotional fervor and anguish avowed in prewar correspondence. The bulk of most mid-century married couples' letters focus primarily on their children, health concerns, household details, and news about neighbors and friends as opposed to exchanges about the marital bond. The correspondence of husbands and wives separated by war also dwelled on their children and affairs at home, but wartime letters often matched the intensity and passion of those written during courtship. The greater the threat of danger, the more intense were the expressions of love. Harriet and Theophilus Perry, a young married couple in east Texas, habitually wrote of their devotion for each other while Theophilus served in the Confederate army. In the days leading up to the Red River Campaign in the spring of 1864, their words became more desperate as a prolonged battle appeared imminent. On March 27, Harriet wrote Theophilus,

> My mind does not rest during the hours of sleep. I dream of you all the time. I never was so anxious to see you—I know you are suffering mentally and physically. I sympathise with you with all my heart, and would willingly share your privations and troubles, if it would lessen them and relieve you—My love for you was never so fond or intense as in these hours of danger and trial. (Perry 2000, 235–236)

Separation and anxiety altered married couples' wartime letters in other ways as well. Women and men verbalized their insecurities and uncertainties about the steadfastness of their mates, their anxieties resembling the types of concerns that more normally afflicted courting couples. Women's war letters articulated worries that the war and the pernicious influences of military camp life would dramatically change their husbands. Harriet Perry scolded Theophilus because his letters had contained no thank-yous or mention of any of the clothes she had sent him. She made it clear that if he did not thank her, "I shall think Husband is not himself, not like he used to be, that Camp life has made an awful change in him—I cant bear to be treated with indifference & especially by you" (Perry 2000, 85).

Men and women also voiced fears that their spouses might become involved with other partners. From his camp in Virginia, Union Private Tabor Parcher of Waterbury, Vermont, poked fun at his wife Sarah's fears about his fidelity by jesting about his roving eye.

> ... you wanted to know why I doant say who goin to have baby wall there is three girls that is goin to have babies that I know *Hon* John Minor Bottss Girl is a goin to have one she is a nice pretty girl of about 20 years of age the safe guard knock[ed] her up I wish it had been me .... I wish I was at home now I believe I would go up the brook & see what them nebraskey women wer made of ... (quoted in Marshall 1999, 226)

For the most part, sexuality was not a topic commonly addressed in mid-nineteenth-century spousal correspondence. Married couples, when they did broach the subject, often linked mention of their sexual needs and practices to their concerns about fertility, reproduction, and FAMILY LIFE. As far as adultery was concerned, a double standard existed in nineteenth-century marriages. A man could expect to be forgiven for an adulterous transgression, whereas a woman was far more likely to suffer disastrous consequences, including a loss of reputation and divorce. Men were much more likely to begin divorce proceedings and seize custody of the children when their wives were discovered to be engaging in adultery.

In the North and South, the war affected courtship behavior and rituals. For a young woman of the nineteenth century, the years of courtship and the ultimate selection of a marriage partner were critical to her future well-being. Women focused time and energy on courtship, the choice of a husband, and preparations for marriage. The dislocations of war made this period in a young woman's life more stressful and difficult. In some areas of the North and in most of the South, single women were anxious about the lack of eligible young men and wondered what the situation portended for their matrimonial prospects. As Alice Ready of Tennessee commented, "… *beaux* are a very scarce article" (quoted in D. Faust 1997, 146). For women already courting a steady partner or fiancé, the uncertainty of their sweethearts' futures created enormous discomfort. In the South, the death of approximately a quarter million men during the war permanently affected women's prospects of courtship. Some women declared that the lack of men made the possibility of becoming a spinster less onerous and less of a social stigma than was the case before the war. The dwindling numbers of available men caused elite young women to be less concerned about the necessity of courting men only within their social class. Differences in age also became less important as some women courted and became engaged to younger men (D. Faust 1997, 147–148).

Not all changes in courtship rituals at mid-century were a direct result of the Civil War. Unlike courting couples of the eighteenth and early nineteenth centuries, mid-nineteenth-century men and women expected to fall in love with a special man or woman as a normal part of courtship. In fact, "falling in love" was considered an essential prerequisite to engagement. Another change not related to the war was that by mid-century, it was no longer necessary for young couples to have their parents' permission to wed. Although men did ask the fathers of their fiancées for their daughters' hand in marriage, by 1860, the ritual had become a formality. Parents might object to a son's or a daughter's proposed union but were powerless to prevent it.

Prior to the war, elite young women in the South were accustomed to having their visits with men chaperoned by some member of their family. By 1860, chaperonage was becoming less common, and during the war, there is evidence to suggest that many young Southern men and women were released from their relatives' watchful eyes.

Although celibacy was what society expected of unmarried couples, more freedom in courtship may have encouraged a more open expression of physical intimacy and sexuality between some young men and women. In his diary, Lester Ward, living in Pennsylvania, wrote in the spring of 1861 about a happy night he spent with his beloved Lizzie.

> Closely held in loving arms we lay, embraced, and kissed all night (not going to bed until five in the morning). We have never acted in such a way before. All that we did I shall not tell here, but it was all very sweet and loving and nothing infamous. (quoted in Rothman 1984, 129)

Although the language suggests that they did not engage in sexual intercourse on this night, in the fall of 1861, Lester writes that they "tasted the joys of love and happiness which only belong to a married life" (Rothman 1984, 129). Two days after enlisting in the Union army in August 1862, Lester and Lizzie wed. Augusta Hallock's teasing letter to her lover James Bell in December of 1861 displays a frankness about the physical intimacy they shared in the past.

> Well I'm naughty enough to say that I *mean* to bite you the first chance I get, Now depend on it. I havent forgotten what a delight it was for me years ago and what a powerful effect this biting had on you. It makes me laugh even now to think of it. (quoted in Lystra 1989, 65)

Courtship was an equally important time in the lives of African-American young people. Slave girls and women waited anxiously for young men to notice them and steal a moment of time to be with them in the evenings and on the way to and from the fields. Saturday night dances provided moments to be together and to get to know one another more intimately. After a time, a courting couple might engage in sexual relations or marry. In most slave communities, having a child before marriage was a socially acceptable practice. Once a man and woman wed, however, the community expected the couple to be faithful to each other (J. Jones 1985, 33–34). Slave women and men were not always free to choose their spouses. Slaveowners sometimes controlled slave marriages, preventing matches that they did not favor by selling either the man or woman, by sending one partner away, or by arranging another marriage for one or both partners.

The war profoundly influenced the traditional roles of husbands and wives of all races and social classes. When their husbands enlisted in the military, women's roles at home were expanded and transformed. This was especially true of AGRICULTURAL WOMEN and BUSINESSWOMEN. After a brief period of adjustment, most married military men accepted that they would have to give up some of the control over their homes, farms, and businesses while their wives assumed the duties and the power that the husbands had exercised. As the war progressed, women in the South and North increasingly made the decisions on their farms and plantations. Even when a husband did not willingly relinquish his authority, as was the case with

William and Kate McLure of South Carolina, the wife often had to take the reins and assume management if the farm and the family were to survive. As far as the McLures were concerned, William insisted that white overseers remain in charge of their plantation. Even when Kate pointed out the overseers' failures and proved her ability to manage on her own with only their slaves to assist her, William never quite caught on that it was Kate who superintended plantation affairs (Cashin 1992, 150).

Two prestigious elite couples of the South experienced a complete reversal of roles when both husbands, distressed by the Confederacy's losses, became emotionally dependent on their wives. Virginia Clay, the self-acknowledged flighty "belle of the fifties," emerged as the stronger, more assertive partner after the destruction of the Confederacy and the economic collapse of the South. She undertook a letter-writing campaign to release her husband Clement from prison, and coaxed him and their farm along, as he drank to excess, experienced poor health, and gave in to defeatism. As she told a friend, "… it is not my style to die in advance of death's summons" (quoted in Bleser and Heath 1991, 150).

At the beginning of the war, Henry Clayton became an officer in the Confederate army and left his wife, Virginia, to care for their plantation. Virginia consented, although she wished to manage without following the detailed orders of Henry and her father-in-law. In 1863, following the death of Henry's brother, Henry's and Virginia's roles shifted. Henry, no longer confident and self-assured, depended on Virginia for emotional support. At the front, as he confronted his fears of dying in battle, Henry abandoned his role of absentee manager and allowed his wife to share equally in the operation of their plantation (Walker 2000, 175–191).

During slavery, slave marriages came into existence and endured according to the will of the slaveholder. Sometimes a slaveholder approved of a match, and provided ceremonies and parties for couples to mark the occasion. Other couples had no celebration aside from observing the ritual "jumping over the broom," a slave custom of unknown origin that traditionally united a bride and groom. No matter what the wedding day was like, slave marriages were not legal unions. Regardless of the attitude of the slaveholder, married couples knew that the slaveholder could separate them at any time (Degler 1980, 114).

The prospect of separation by the sale of one or both partners threatened the bond that slave couples worked to build. Long-distance marriages were sometimes a possibility for separated couples, with messages carried back and forth over the slaves' informal communication network that linked some plantations together. Nevertheless, devoted yet separated couples longed for the day when they would be reunited. In 1859, the enslaved Harriet Newby wrote to her recently freed husband Dangerfield Newby:

> I want you to buy me as soon as possible, for if you do not get me somebody else will …. I know not what time he may sell me, and then all my bright hopes of the futer are blasted, for there has ben one bright hope to cheer me in all my troubles,

that is to be with you, for if I thought I shoul never see you this earth would have no charms for me. (Degler 1980, 121)

Harriet had reason for anxiety as Dangerfield was one of the abolitionist co-conspirators in John Brown's raid on the federal arsenal at Harpers Ferry, Virginia, in October 1859. Unfortunately, Dangerfield died in this attempt to incite a massive slave uprising, leaving Harriet to grieve and suffer her enslavement alone.

As soon as slaves freed themselves or were decreed emancipated, many former slave couples rushed to marry so that no legal power could forcibly separate them again. Within Union army encampments, white army chaplains performed the ceremonies. In the South and North, newly freedmen and women struggled to raise the money to be formally married. Yet just as many couples whose marriages were formed in slavery did not have their unions legalized. The expense was more than many freedmen and women could spare. Furthermore, leaving or "quitting" the marital relationship was often preferable to making a permanent bond. Still other couples were convinced that legalizing their marriages was redundant and unnecessary and that their original marriages made in slavery were all that they and their community required (Shaffer 2000, 60–61).

See also **Family Life**

Selected Readings

Degler, Carl N. At Odds: Women and the Family in America from the Revolution to the Present. New York: Oxford University Press. 1980.

Lystra, Karen. Searching the Heart: Women, Men, and Romantic Love in Nineteenth-Century America. New York: Oxford University Press. 1989.

Rothman, Ellen K. Hands and Hearts: A History of Courtship in America. New York: Basic Books. 1984.

Cumming, Kate
(1828 or 1835–1909)

Gray-haired men—men in the pride of manhood—beardless boys ... mutilated in every imaginable way, lying on the floor ... so close together that it was almost impossible to walk without stepping on them .... O, if the authors of this cruel and unnatural war could but see what I saw there, they would try and put a stop to it!

—Kate Cumming (Cumming 1998, 14)

Historians consider Kate Cumming's Civil War diary to be one of the best and most thorough personal accounts of work within the Confederate hospital service. Cumming, a young, middle-class white woman from Mobile, Alabama, began her diary in April 1862, when she first volunteered to nurse the wounded and sick soldiers of the Confederate army of Tennessee. She completed it more than three years later in May 1865, weeks after the Confederate surrender. Her journal contains a wealth of detail concerning the day-to-day operation of Confederate military hospitals. As a hospital matron from the fall of 1862, Cumming directed all hospital domestic affairs and closely attended to the physical and emotional needs of individual soldiers. Unlike many Northern and Southern women NURSES, she declared that her relationships with the male hospital staff were positive. Although she encountered surgeons who believed women had no place in the military hospital, she worked with many who valued the hard work she and her female colleagues performed.

The precise year of Kate Cumming's birth in Edinburgh, Scotland, is not known. When she was a young child, her parents emigrated with their four children to Montreal, Canada, before making their permanent home in Mobile, Alabama. Cumming was raised in a prosperous, middle-class environment, though not much is known of the details of her schooling and upbringing.

In the early spring of 1862, Cumming learned that a local minister was urging women to leave their homes to nurse wounded Confederate soldiers. When she broached the subject with her family, her father and brothers-in-law concurred that nursing was not a respectable undertaking for a woman and she must remain at home. Cumming, inspired by Florence Nightingale's nursing exploits in the Crimean

War, was convinced that tending the soldiers was exactly the sort of work Southern women should undertake for their country. The departure of a local regiment provoked her to action. Acquainted as she was with many of the men in this regiment, she explained,

> I resolved then and there that if Mr. Miller [the minister] would take me, I would go with him and do my best. I had never been inside of a hospital, and was wholly ignorant of what I should be called upon to do, but I knew that what one woman [Florence Nightingale] had done another could. (Cumming 1998, xii)

Cumming and a troupe of approximately forty women left Mobile on April 7, 1862. Days later, they had traveled as far north and west as Corinth, Mississippi, and prepared to treat those who had been wounded at the Battle of Shiloh in Tennessee. Cumming's initiation to nursing was harrowing, yet unlike many of the female volunteers who soon retreated to the safety and calm of Mobile, she weathered the hardships. Abandoning sleep, Cumming worked into the night washing the soldiers' wounds and dispensing water. Despite the pressing nature of her duties, she also took the time to record what she experienced.

> The men are lying all over the house, on their blankets, just as they were brought from the battle-field. They are in the hall, on the gallery, and crowded into very small rooms. The foul air from this mass of human beings at first made me giddy and sick, but I soon got over it. We have to walk, and when we give the men any thing kneel in blood and water; but we think nothing of it at all. (Cumming 1998, 15)

Over the next two months, Cumming nursed the wounded in Corinth and in Okolona, Mississippi. After spending the summer of 1862 in Mobile, she traveled to Chattanooga, Tennessee, where she worked at Newsom Hospital for nearly a year. In the fall of 1862, while nursing in Chattanooga, the Confederate Congress passed a law authorizing and formalizing the work of women in the military hospitals of the South. Now designated as a hospital matron, Cumming was officially charged with supervising "the entire domestic economy of the hospital," which included the preparation, cooking, and service of food; the administration of medicines; and the laundering and distribution of bedding and clothing. Unofficially, Cumming and her female volunteers also wrote letters to soldiers' loved ones, offered spiritual solace in the form of prayer and Bible readings, and gave whatever comfort they could. In her role as hospital matron, Cumming guided the female assistant matrons and ward matrons who worked closely with the patients. Men performed the hands-on nursing care and were not under her jurisdiction.

Although Cumming claimed that her experiences with surgeons and male nurses were good ones, at times she pitied the male nurses, most of whom were recuperating patients.

> And as for the nurses in the hospitals, how can I say enough in their praise ... patient, kind; as good nurses as it is in the power of men to be; for they were never

designed to nurse. Not one where I have been is able for field service .... Many a time have I felt indignant, when I have heard these brave men and patriots, who have lost health and been maimed in the service of their country, called by the ignominious name of "hospital rats". (Cumming 1998, 134).

From 1863 until several weeks after the Confederate surrender in April 1865, Cumming served in a succession of military hospitals in Georgia as the medical service followed the Confederate army retreating from Union General William Tecumseh Sherman's advancing troops. Much of the time medical workers were forced to organize the hospitals in tents and hastily erected sheds. Cumming, her assistant matrons, and ward matrons discovered that even though it was difficult to keep the tent hospitals clean, the soldiers appeared to heal much more quickly in the open air of canvas dwellings.

Throughout her diary Cumming expressed her disappointment and anger at the women of the South who did not do more to assist the sick and wounded. In January 1864, she again bemoaned the fact that the women of her social class had not volunteered their services. In this instance, she wished that more ladies would come forward to sew and mend soldiers' clothing.

I often think of how much good the ladies of this place could accomplish .... Many a man goes back to the front as ragged as he came from it. I had determined to let this subject drop, but somehow I always get back to it. I can not help losing my temper when I see so many idle women unwilling to do any little thing for these heroes, who have suffered so much. (Cumming 1998, 186)

On May 14, 1865, Cumming reflected on the Confederate defeat, stating her conviction that, "Had we been true to our God and country .... I believe we could have kept the North, with all her power at bay for twenty years" (Cumming 1998, 292). She listed numerous groups whom she claimed had shirked their duty to the Confederacy, thereby hastening the Southern defeat. She particularly denigrated the "speculators," the businessmen who had cheated the government of money and food for their self-aggrandizement. And she once more faulted the women who had not stepped forward to offer their services in the chronically understaffed hospitals.

Cumming's patriotism did not cool with news of defeat. She maintained her optimism and faith in the Confederacy until the end of the war. In February 1865, upon news of the Confederate armies' failures, she described the suffering of the troops but concluded, "Well, though every thing looks dark at present, that is nothing. The sun is often obscured with clouds, only to shine out more resplendent than ever" (Cumming 1998, 254).

Following her final diary entry of May 29, 1865, Cumming returned home to Mobile and immediately prepared her diary for publication. *A Journal of Hospital Life in the Confederate Army of Tennessee* was published in 1866, though it received scant notice. In 1895, she revised and republished the diary as *Gleanings from Southland*.

The diary did not rouse much interest until its 1959 revision appeared, at which time it came to the attention of medical and social historians.

In the postwar years, Cumming was a schoolteacher and instructor of music. She became deeply involved in her local Episcopal Church and was active in the United Daughters of the Confederacy and the United Confederate Veterans. She died in Rosedale, Alabama, in 1909.

See also **Diaries**

Selected Reading

Cumming, Kate. *The Journal of a Confederate Nurse.* Edited by Richard Barksdale Harwell. Baton Rouge: Louisiana State University Press. 1998.

Cushman, Pauline (1833–1893)

Although no two accounts relating the Civil War experiences of the renowned Union spy Pauline Cushman agree, historians and writers concur that she aided Union forces in Tennessee in 1863. Like many male and female spies, she aggrandized her exploits in her memoirs. Her volume of recollections, published in 1864 as *The Romance of the Great Rebellion* and as *The Thrilling Adventures of Pauline Cushman*, gave the reading public precisely what it craved—romanticized, spine-tingling adventure and melodrama.

Cushman was born Harriet Wood in New Orleans, Louisiana. During her childhood, her family moved to Grand Rapids, Michigan. From this frontier town she fled to New York City to become an actress when she was 18 years old. Years later, after returning to New Orleans, she married a fellow performer and musician, Charles Dickenson. After he died of dysentery in 1862 while serving in the Union army, Cushman continued to work as an actress, and in 1863, she was performing in Louisville, Kentucky.

Although some writers claim that Cushman was working as a Union spy early in the war, others state that she began her brief espionage career in Louisville in 1863 when several Confederate officers challenged her to make an onstage toast to Confederate President Jefferson Davis. Cushman, an ardent Unionist, accepted their proposition, foreseeing the possibility of spying and gaining closer access to Confederate officers and soldiers. Before giving the toast, she met with the Union army's local provost marshal who accepted her offer to use the opportunity to go undercover as a spy for the Union.

As Cushman must have expected, shortly after her toast the Unionist theater management fired her. She then traveled to Union-occupied Nashville, Tennessee, and met with the local chief of army police Colonel William Truesdail who assigned her to go undercover. Cushman claims that she donned a number of disguises, including men's clothing, in the course of her espionage. She spied on the Confederate military and gathered information about Confederate spies in Tennessee, Kentucky, Alabama, Mississippi, and northern Georgia. She then relayed the information to Union officers (Leonard 2001, 58–59).

Cushman's success as a spy did not last long. In late 1863, she was arrested not far from Shelbyville, Tennessee, by Confederate Brigadier General John Hunt Morgan. He handed her over to Confederate Brigadier General Nathan Bedford Forrest who, after questioning her at length, ordered her execution. According to several accounts, as Cushman awaited her death in Shelbyville, a raid of Union soldiers burst into the encampment where she was incarcerated and forced the Confederates to hastily retreat. Cushman was rescued by Union soldiers shortly thereafter. She became an instant heroine and press attraction.

Cushman was then much too famous to return to spying. The Union tapped her considerable knowledge of the topographical terrain of Tennessee, Alabama, and Mississippi and enlisted her to advise mapmakers. After receiving the honorary title of "Major," she embarked on a stage tour, dramatically relating her adventures to her audiences. After the war, she returned to acting for a while, married twice, and eventually worked in San Francisco as a seamstress. She died of an overdose of morphine during a long illness in 1893.

See also **Spies and Espionage**

Selected Readings

Leonard, Elizabeth D. *All the Daring of the Soldier: Women of the Civil War Armies.* New York: Penguin Books. 2001.

Massey, Mary Elizabeth. *Women in the Civil War.* 1966, 1994 reprint. Lincoln: University of Nebraska Press. 1994.

D

Davis, Rebecca Harding (1831–1910)

During the early years of the Civil War, Rebecca Harding Davis produced several of her most critically acclaimed short stories and novels just as her writing career was beginning. Several weeks before the firing on Fort Sumter, her first published short story, "Life in the Iron Mills," appeared in the April 1861 edition of the *Atlantic Monthly*. It met with immediate critical success and has since been heralded as a pioneering work of American realism. Though this story focuses on the evils of industrialization rather than on the brewing national conflict, several of her later stories depicted the brutality of war and addressed the issue of race relations. By the end of the Civil War, Harding Davis was a nationally recognized writer, and one who continued to produce throughout the rest of the nineteenth century.

Born in Washington, Pennsylvania, Rebecca Blaine Harding spent her early childhood years in Alabama. When she was five years old, the Harding family moved to Wheeling, Virginia, on the Ohio River. Her father held several civic positions in Wheeling, including city treasurer. Her mother, an exceptionally well-educated woman, tutored Rebecca during her girlhood. At age 14, she enrolled at Washington Female Seminary, located in the town of her birth. In 1848, she graduated at the top of her class and returned home to help her mother manage the family household. Although her parents employed servants, Rebecca was needed to assist her mother with the cooking, the sewing, and the care of several of her youngest siblings. She also helped to educate them. In the early 1850s, she continued her education by studying with her younger brother, a college student.

Late in the 1850s, Harding began writing reviews, editorials, and poetry for the *Intelligencer*, the largest daily newspaper in western Virginia. By this time, she had dedicated herself to her writing, spending long hours perfecting her prose. When the *Atlantic Monthly* published "Life in the Iron Mills," Harding was 29 years old. The story, a radical departure for the magazine and for its time, was published when women writers were primarily creating domestic fiction—stories dealing with issues of concern to women's domestic lives. Harding's tale, exposing the grim realities of industrial life for mill workers, was unprecedented in magazine fiction. She demanded that her middle-class readers confront the grinding poverty and ugliness of a factory worker's life. At the beginning of the story, Harding has her middle-class narrator address readers directly, beckoning them to enter the slum and the factory.

> Stop a moment. I am going to be honest. This is what I want you to do. I want you to hide your disgust, take no heed to your clean clothes, and come right down with me—here, into the thickest of the fog and mud and foul effluvia. (Davis 1995, 4)

By describing the trials of Deborah, a cotton mill picker, and Hugh, an iron worker, Harding recounts the ways in which industrial labor debases the lives and minds of its workers.

> Their lives were like those of their class: incessant labor, sleeping in kennel-like rooms, eating rank pork and molasses, drinking—God and the distillers only know what; with an occasional night in jail, to atone for some drunken excess. Is that all of their lives?—of the portion given to them and these their duplicates swarming the streets to-day? (Davis 1995, 5)

Harding received $50 for the story and was encouraged when she learned that the *Atlantic Monthly* editor wanted her to submit more. She went on to write "The Story of To-Day," a serialized piece of fiction that was later published as the novel *Margret Howth* in 1862. As was the case with "Life in the Iron Mills," *Margret Howth* concentrated on the lives and struggles of factory workers.

As Harding was writing for the *Atlantic Monthly*, the war was heating up, and the region around Wheeling was in an uproar. Situated as it was on the southern side of the Ohio River, Wheeling had long suffered the turbulence of a border region straddling the North and South. (In 1863, Wheeling was incorporated into the new state of West Virginia.) Prior to the war, Wheeling was active in the slave trade, while also serving as an important nexus on the Underground Railroad, both of which pushed Harding to embrace abolitionism. During the war, she wrote three stories for the *Atlantic Monthly* that dealt with the cruelties of slavery and the trauma of race relations. In "John Lamar," "Blind Tom," and "David Gaunt," she portrayed her African-American characters as autonomous individuals rather than the stereotypes white Americans were accustomed to seeing in the Northern press. Through her fiction, Harding insisted that her audience realize that the eradication of slavery was the main purpose of the Civil War (Davis 1995, xxvii).

"David Gaunt" describes the experiences of ordinary men and women encountering the horrors of war in a village in western Virginia. The story's background bore some resemblance to Harding's experience. While living in Wheeling in 1861 to 1862, she observed the impact of the war on soldiers and civilians. Toward the end of her life, in her memoir *Bits of Gossip*, she reflected on the upheaval of the war years as she experienced them in Wheeling.

> The histories which we have of the great tragedy give no idea of the general wretchedness, the squalid misery, which entered into every individual life in the region given up to the war. Where the armies camped the destruction was absolute. Even on the border, your farm was a waste, all your horses or cows were seized by one army or the other, or your shop or manufactory was closed, your trade ruined .... Below all the squalor and discomfort was the agony of suspense and the certainty of death. (Davis 1904, 116–117)

A bright spot in the midst of the devastation of war was Harding's marriage to the attorney Lemuel Clarke Davis in March 1863. Davis, a fan of Harding's writing, had initiated a correspondence with her following publication of "Life in the Iron Mills." Davis later visited Harding in Wheeling and the two became engaged. Once married, the couple settled in Philadelphia.

Following her marriage, Harding Davis wrote much less for a time. She continued submitting popular fiction to *Peterson's Magazine*, a magazine for women, a connection that her husband provided for her. She wrote for Peterson's strictly for the income, which she needed just as much after her marriage as before. The *Atlantic Monthly*, for all its literary prestige, paid far less than the popular press. As an independent woman of business, she did not accept the *Atlantic Monthly*'s low payments without question. In November 1862, she convinced the magazine's editor to pay her $8 a page, and thus became one of the magazine's most highly paid writers (Harris 1991, 99). Years later, when her husband's editorial career solidified, there was less pressure on her to be the family breadwinner.

In April 1864, when Harding Davis gave birth to a son, the first of the couple's three children, she found it difficult to manage both her career and her family. She opted to spend more time with her family and write when she could find the time. In 1864, she completed a piece of short fiction, "The Wife's Story," and throughout the 1860s and 1870s, she returned to the theme of the problems of married women, particularly focusing on the restrictions that marriage posed for women. She believed that a married woman's first responsibility was to her husband and children, and that a woman's career must not come at the expense of either. She strove to maintain this principle in her own life, though in the pages of her fiction, her female characters bear witness to the suffering and loss of creative experience that this sacrifice entails.

After the war in 1867, Harding Davis wrote *Waiting for the Verdict*, a novel concerning the problems of African Americans in the North. She became a contributing editor to the *New York Tribune* in 1869, a position she held for 20 years. Throughout the rest of the nineteenth century, she authored stories and articles for numerous literary and popular publications, children's magazines, and religious periodicals. Harding Davis died at the age of 79, while visiting her son in Mount Kisco, New York.

See also **Literary Women**

Selected Readings

Davis, Rebecca Harding. *A Rebecca Harding Davis Reader.* Edited with an introduction by Jean Pfaelzer. Pittsburgh: University of Pittsburgh Press, 1995.
Harris, Sharon M. *Rebecca Harding Davis and American Realism.* Philadelphia: University of Pennsylvania Press, 1991.

Davis, Varina Howell (1826–1906)

As the wife of Jefferson Davis, the president of the Confederacy, Varina Howell Davis spent the Civil War years living in the midst of the military, political, and social turmoil that characterized the seat of the Confederate government. Although she was privately convinced that secession and war would irreparably harm the South, she supported her husband and did all she could in her position to help the people of the Confederacy.

Varina Anne Banks Howell grew up in Natchez, Mississippi, where her father, a member of the planter elite, owned a modest plantation. William Howell was not a Southerner by birth, but a New Jersey native who saw to it that his daughter had the best education the North could provide. After Varina attended a private academy in Philadelphia for two terms, her father employed a Harvard-educated scholar from Massachusetts to tutor her at home. As his student for 12 years, her education far surpassed that of her peers.

At age 17, she met Jefferson Davis, a widower 18 years her senior, whom she married in 1845. Later that year, Davis was elected to Congress, and in 1846, he left the House of Representatives to serve in the Mexican-American War. Following his acclaimed military leadership in that conflict, his political career soared.

Howell Davis did not begin her role as an active political wife until late in 1849, when her husband returned to Washington to sit in the U.S. Senate, a position to which he had been appointed in 1847. During the 1850s, while Davis served as Secretary of War in President Franklin Pierce's administration, and later, once more as a U.S. Senator, Howell Davis was a leading Washington hostess. She became known for her lively repartee, her acute knowledge of political affairs, her outspoken opinions, and fierce convictions—all qualities in conflict with the ideal role of the deferential Southern lady. An articulate, intelligent, energetic woman, Howell Davis felt constrained throughout her life by the societal pressure and expectation that she conform to the role of a Southern lady of the elite plantation class (Cashin 1991, 260–261).

As the secession crisis drew near in 1859 to 1860, Howell Davis frequently observed the often volcanic debates on the Senate floor. She was torn between her anti-secessionist sentiments and the need to support her husband as he advanced the Southern states' constitutional right to form an independent government.

When Davis was selected to serve as president of the Confederacy, Howell Davis and their children followed him to Montgomery, Alabama. They lived there briefly until the Confederate capital was moved to Richmond, Virginia, in mid-1861. Throughout the Civil War, Howell Davis's time and energies were largely consumed by the care of her husband and children. Davis's health was extremely fragile. Frequently overwhelmed by the stresses of leading the Confederacy and managing warring factions within the Confederate leadership, he demanded her constant support and nurturance. Howell Davis's correspondence with her husband reveals that he regularly shared information about military and political affairs with her and that she freely offered her opinions and advice, although it is unclear whether Davis ever acted according to her counsel.

Howell Davis gave birth to two additional children during the war (she bore four children in the 1850s). She faced the near-fatal illness of her son Billy in 1862 and the death of her five-year-old son Joseph in 1864 following a fall from a Confederate White House balcony. For much of the war, she was busy rearing five children, and although she had plenty of servants, both free and enslaved, domestic concerns dominated her days.

Because Howell Davis did not keep a diary during the Civil War, and because very few of her letters from this period survive, there is little personal documentation of her wartime activities. Yet plenty of evidence confirms that she made regular visits to the wounded and sick soldiers in Richmond hospitals. She delivered supplies to the hospitals and talked with the wounded and ill. Before sugar became scarce, she acquired and dispensed candy and other confections to the soldiers. According to Howell Davis's memoir, her husband prevented her from nursing the wounded. As much as she chafed against conforming to the role and duties of a Southern lady, she dutifully abided by her husband's wishes, even when it pained her to do so.

Perhaps Howell Davis's most pressing public activity was her task of processing the huge volume of requests sent to her from citizens living throughout the Confederacy. Women urged her to request furloughs, pardons, prisoner exchanges, and military discharges for their menfolk. Women also petitioned her for relief from their desperate financial circumstances and other problems resulting from their experiences as refugees. She was powerless to address many of the hardships and tragedies presented to her. Those citizens she could help, she did; those she could not received a thoughtful reply.

For most of the war, Howell Davis did not have the opportunity to entertain as much as she had during her years in Washington and in the early months of the Confederacy. She looked toward social events as strategic occasions to improve political relationships between the reticent Davis and his disgruntled and disaffected officials, political and military leaders, and staff. Yet Davis was so exhausted by his presidential duties that for most of the war, he swore off hosting large receptions and parties.

Like MARY TODD LINCOLN, Howell Davis was severely criticized by the press. Many, though not all, of the attacks were completely unfounded, including the accusation that she hid Union spies in the Confederate White House. When it appeared that the Union army would attack Richmond in May 1862, she was berated for fleeing the city, something she agreed to reluctantly and only at her husband's demand that she do so. The Richmond upper crust dismissed her as an unrefined Mississippi frontier woman while others condemned her for her Northern education, heritage, and superior airs. The press blasted her for her extravagant entertaining while Richmond's elite criticized her for her too infrequent hostessing of social occasions. And she was universally condemned for her outspokenness about politics and for her supposed efforts to influence her husband's decision-making. Little wonder, then, that she wrote to her dear friend MARY BOYKIN CHESNUT, "How I wish I were the wife of a dry goods clerk" (quoted in Ross 1958, 142). As much as Howell Davis was vexed by the criticism, she refused to tolerate verbal attacks on her husband. Condemnations of Davis enraged her, provoking her to release equally acrimonious public retorts, for which she was heartily criticized.

The Davises fled Richmond separately during the final days of the war, reuniting in Georgia. On May 10, 1865, the entire family was captured by federal troops. Howell Davis and her children were sent to Savannah, Georgia, while Davis was incarcerated at Fort Monroe, Virginia, where he was initially accused of being an accessory to the assassination of President Abraham Lincoln (the charge was soon reduced to treason). When she learned that Davis was manacled and chained in his prison cell, she launched a one-woman campaign to secure more humane treatment for her husband and the termination of his sentence. She repeatedly petitioned President Andrew Johnson and other influential politicians in Washington. In 1866, she received permission to reside at Fort Monroe where she was able to supervise Davis's physical condition and support him emotionally. In 1867, Davis was released to his family.

Following Davis's death in 1889, Howell Davis, at age 63, spared no effort in reversing what she perceived as the disintegration of her husband's memory. She wrote an immense two-volume work *Jefferson Davis: A Memoir by His Wife*, but its publication in 1890 fell far short of her expectations. The 1,638-page memoir was considered poorly written, too long, and too laudatory to be regarded seriously. It sold very few copies and did not reach the mass audience she craved.

Howell Davis then devoted herself to supporting efforts to create monuments to her husband. She also prodded public speakers to praise Davis in their lectures and speeches. After the publication of her memoir, she moved to New York City where she became a correspondent for the *New York Sunday World*. Nostalgic essays about the Confederacy and articles relating to women's domestic concerns were her mainstay. She died of pneumonia and heart disease in 1906, at the age of 80.

See also **Secession**

Selected Readings

Bleser, Carol K. "The Marriage of Varina Howell and Jefferson Davis: A Portrait of the President and the First Lady of the Confederacy." In *Intimate Strategies of the Civil War: Military Commanders and Their Wives*. Edited by Carol K. Bleser and Lesley J. Gordon. New York: Oxford University Press. 2001.

Cashin, Joan. "Varina Howell Davis (1826–1906)." In *Portraits of American Women: From Settlement to the Present*. Edited by G. J. Barker-Benfield and Catherine Clinton. New York: St. Martin's Press. 1991. 259–277.

Ross, Ishbel. *First Lady of the South: The Life of Mrs. Jefferson Davis*. New York: Harper and Bros. 1958.

Diaries

I think I shall write … telling all the events of the day, my thoughts, feelings … It will be good employment these war times, when we have no visitors to receive and no visits to pay, no materials to work upon and no inclination to read anything but the Bible and the newspapers …. [W]hat sort of friend shall I choose? It is a hard question to decide. Upon reflection, I think I shall select a female … whose deep and loving interest in my family shall induce me to write anything which concerns them. I never had such a friend and I shall love her so much.

—From the first diary entry of Lucy Breckinridge of Grove Hill, Virginia, August 11, 1862 (Breckinridge 1979, 17)

The Civil War stimulated more women and men to keep diaries than any other single event in American history. Unlike diarists writing since the late nineteenth century, most early- and mid-nineteenth-century women did not view their journals as a means to commune with their innermost thoughts. Their diaries were primarily a record of their activities that they later shared with family and close friends. But as the Civil War progressed, some women discovered that their diaries evolved into a form that transcended a mere accounting of their days; they became anchors in crisis, receptacles for overpowering emotions, and helpful reminders that they had survived devastating losses and could endure additional pain and suffering. For other women, their diaries were a means of preserving a historical record of the national conflict for themselves and for future generations.

For the most part, only well-educated, white, elite and middle-class women and men kept diaries, and as historical documents, they reveal the experiences and perceptions of only one segment of the population. Very few Civil War diaries of African-American and immigrant women endure, and among Native American and Mexican-American women, they are nonexistent. Shortages of ink and paper prevented many Southern women from writing after 1863, although those wealthy enough to own private libraries managed to squeeze their journal entries between the lines of pages of books. When forced to flee from invasion or occupation, they tore the pages from their bindings and carried them in their skirts. In April 1865, Catherine Devereux Edmondston of North Carolina feared that the impending Union occupation would cause her journal to fall into Yankee hands.

> And now, old friend, you my Journal, for a time good bye! You are too bulky to be kept out, exposed to prying Yankee eyes and theivish [sic] Yankee fingers. You go for a season to darkness & solitude & my record must henceforth be kept on scraps of paper, backs of letters, or old memorandum books which I can secrete .... So once more, Good bye! (Edmondston 1979, 692)

Miraculously, hundreds of women's Civil War diaries survive, published by the diarists themselves, by their families, or by twentieth- and twenty-first-century scholars and editors. State and national archives, state and local historical societies, and various private collections house many hundreds more unpublished diary manuscripts. More Southern women's diaries are in print than Northern women's, largely due to the recent scholarly interest in documenting the dramatic history of Confederate women during the Civil War.

Women's motivations for keeping a diary during the war were as uniquely varied as the individual women themselves, yet most spoke to the conviction that they were living through a remarkable period of time. As a result, they desired to keep a record of events, their experiences, and perceptions during this crucible of history. In June 1864, Maria Lydig Daly of New York City wrote that she regretted each day that she neglected to write a diary entry: "I have so much to do and think of that I forget my diary, which, in such momentous times, is a *crime* against myself. Should I live to be an old lady, I shall deeply regret this" (Daly 2000, 298).

Cornelia Peake McDonald of Winchester, Virginia, started her journal at her husband's urging, after he marched off to join the Confederate army. He hoped that she would chronicle the Yankee's occupation of northern Virginia. In the midst of caring for their seven children, she faithfully fulfilled her promise to him. In the process, she discovered that the journal documented her personal struggle to retain her emotional and physical strength in the face of repeated Union invasions, loneliness, and severe hunger.

In the final weeks of the war and immediately after the Confederate defeat, Eliza Frances Andrew of Georgia used her diary, as many Southern women did, to help her come to terms with the devastating loss of her country.

> ... while out I heard fresh rumors of Lee's surrender. No one seems to doubt it, and everybody feels ready to give up hope. "It is useless to struggle longer," seems to be the common cry, and the poor wounded men go hobbling about the streets with despair on their faces. There is a new pathos in a crutch or an empty sleeve, now, that we know it was all for nothing (quoted in Culley 1985, 136).

As the vessel of intensely private emotions, women and girls often experienced a profound attachment to their diaries. Sixteen-year-old Clara Solomon of New Orleans, Louisiana, wrote of her adoration for her diary.

> Need I say how dear you are to my heart, how essential to my existence? ... I will tell you how I love you, how in the tumultuous past time the thought of being separated from you was madness, & the joy when I again communed with you was overwhelming ... each succeeding month has strengthened the ties which bind me to you & like wedded love, I find that I love you more each day. (Solomon 1995, 357–358)

Women of the Civil War era also focused their gaze on the outer world where they observed the disturbing and sometimes violent transformations in their environments. Southern diaries starkly portray the horror of modern warfare, the impact of battles on civilians, the terror of invasion and occupation. By contrast, because the war was fought in the South, Northern women's diaries focus on the more mundane details of life on the homefront. For many Northern women, the war was a distant storm that rarely touched them directly. But, there was one commonality that Northern and Southern women shared: the internal shock wave resulting from the news of the death of a loved one, which Virginia diarist MARY BOYKIN CHESNUT illustrates in her diary.

> I know how it feels to die ... For instance, some one calls out, "Albert Sydney Johnston is killed." My heart stands still. I feel no more. I am ... without sensation of any kind—dead; and then, there is that great throb, that keen agony of physical pain. ... The ticking of the clock begins, and I take up the burden of life once more (quoted in Sullivan 1995, 34).

Nineteenth-century literary critics did not consider diaries a form of literature. Yet Civil War women's journals reveal that their writers were self-consciously aware that they were creating art. EMMA LECONTE was one diarist who deliberately crafted unforgettable images of war. After witnessing General William Sherman's destruction of Columbia, South Carolina, she wrote,

> Imagine night turned into noonday, only with a blazing, scorching glare that was horrible—a copper colored sky across which swept columns of black, rolling smoke glittered with sparks and flying embers ... while every instant came the crashing of timbers and the thunder of falling buildings. (LeConte 1957, 45–46).

Like LeConte, women edited, embellished, and completely reworked their diaries after the war. Most prominent among this group is Mary Boykin Chesnut's critically acclaimed masterpiece *A Diary from Dixie*, reedited and republished in 1981 as C. Vann Woodward's Pulitzer Prize–winning edition *Mary Chesnut's Civil War*. When first published, readers were stunned to discover that Chesnut wrote this "diary" nearly 20 years after the war from notes recorded in her Civil War journal. Yet the authors of most published Civil War diaries did not consider that their postwar revisions made their work any less authentic.

For historians, women's war diaries sometimes describe events for which there are no other surviving records. Military historians have analyzed the journals of Pennsylvania women living in the communities surrounding Gettysburg to reconstruct the details of the staging for the July 1863 battle. Rachel Cormany, a young mother living on her own with a young child in neighboring Chambersburg, not only records Confederate troop movements advancing on Gettysburg, but also her disdain and pity for the barefoot, ragged Confederate "Greybacks" who were so ecstatic to be fighting on Northern soil. On June 27, 1863, a week before the Battle of Gettysburg, she declares that she wished she "dared spit at their old flag," while the next day she reveals that she "felt real badly to see these poor men going through as they did; likely many of them will be killed" (Mohr 1982, 337–338).

No group of women witnessed the brutality of war as the army nurses and doctors did, and it was to their diaries that they poured out their anguish and revulsion. Though they hardened to the sight of mutilated bodies, even the most seasoned nurse could be rocked off her feet. "I had a terable fright this morning," Confederate nurse Ada Bacot recalled,

> [M]y eye fell on a man who had been put there … without my knowledge. Such an object I never before beheld, he is shot in the face, his eyes are blood shoten & his face all bandaged up, face very much swolen & the blood trickling from his noze …
> I almost droped on the floor. (Bacot 1994, 134)

Missing from women's war diaries are emotions that might be expected from women who braved new worlds and achieved success—pride, self-confidence, a joy in personal growth. Ever faithful to the nineteenth-century cultural ideal of "True Womanhood," female diarists conscientiously avoided self-congratulation. But buried in their expressions of pious humility and their effusive joy in serving others are clues that they gained personal satisfaction from mastering new skills and weathering hardship.

LOUISA MAY ALCOTT, who served six weeks as a nurse in a Union army hospital during the winter of 1862 to 1863, observed in her journal, "Though often home sick, heart sick & worn out, I like it—find real pleasure in comforting tending & cheering these pour souls who seem to love me" (Alcott 1989, 113). In Alcott's case, admitting that she received love from her patients is the only way that she acknowledges that she is a competent nurse.

Although women did not emote about their achievements in their diaries, their day-in-and-day-out description of the minutiae of their tasks and the obstacles they surmounted are confirmation that they experienced self-fulfillment from their wartime contributions. Months after the surrender of the Confederacy, as Cornelia Peake McDonald reflected on her years of hardship and sacrifice to ensure the well-being of her family, she permitted a speck of self-admiration to peek through the blandest of understatements—a solid recognition of her remarkable achievement.

> And here ends my account of my trials, and though they were not at an end entirely, I was able in various ways to take care of my family till they were fitted to be of use to themselves; and when they were able to bear the burden they took it up manfully and acquitted themselves well. (McDonald 1992, 291)

See also **Cumming, Kate; Forten, Charlotte; Kemble, Fanny; Morgan, Sarah; Nurses**

Selected Readings

Breckinridge, Lucy. *Lucy Breckinridge of Grove Hill: The Journal of a Virgina Girl, 1862–1864.* Edited by Mary D. Robertson. Kent, OH: Kent State University Press. 1979.

Edmondston, Catherine Ann Devereux. *"Journal of a Secesh Lady": The Diary of Catherine Ann Devereux Edmondston.* Edited by Beth G. Crabtree and James W. Patton. Raleigh, NC: North Carolina Division of Archives and History. 1979.

Mohr, James C., ed. *The Cormany Diaries: A Northern Family in the Civil War.* Pittsburgh, PA: University of Pittsburgh Press. 1982.

Solomon Clara. *The Civil War Diary of Clara Solomon: Growing Up in New Orleans, 1861–1862.* Edited by Elliott Ashkenazi. Baton Rouge, LA: Louisiana State University Press. 1995.

Dickey, Sarah (1838–1904)

From a young age, Sarah Dickey was driven by the desire to help African Americans learn to read and write. What made this ambition so unusual was that it was held by a poor white illiterate farm girl living in pro-slavery southwestern Ohio. She aspired to attain the best education available for a woman of the 1860s, become a teacher, instruct the freedpeople, and finally establish a school of higher education for African-American women in Mississippi. Her achievement of these goals exemplifies the ways in which religious faith and the desire to improve the lives of those less fortunate—two nearly universal inspirations influencing women's lives during the mid-nineteenth century—dominated the life of one young woman from rural America.

Sarah was born in a farming community not far from Dayton, Ohio. After her mother's death in 1846, Sarah's father arranged for her to live with an aunt on her farm, with the understanding that Sarah would be permitted to attend school. She did not see her father again until 1851, five years later, when he arrived following her aunt's death. He then made the discovery that Sarah was completely illiterate and had not received a day's schooling. The next lodging her father found for her was not much better. Over a two-year period, Sarah went to school less than four weeks, a total of ten to fifteen days during each of the two winters. By the time she was 16, she was able to read a bit but had not learned to write.

It was at this time that Sarah was inspired to take charge of her own destiny. She announced her intention to become a teacher, arousing skepticism and dismay among those who believed she did not have the intellectual capacity, the drive, or the means to fulfill her goal. Convinced that she was carrying out God's will, she resolved to make changes in her life so that she could acquire an education. She searched for and located a farm family that agreed to give her room and board in exchange for work she would perform only during the hours before and after school. Following this plan, she received her teacher's certificate three years later at age 19. In the autumn of 1857, she began her first teaching job in Lewisburg, Ohio.

In 1858, Dickey's deepening faith in God led her to become a member of the Church of the United Brethren in Christ, a denomination that adamantly opposed slavery. She hoped that she would receive an assignment to teach Africans in the United Brethren mission in Sierra Leone but was rejected for that post. In 1863, she was selected for another mission, in Union-occupied Vicksburg, Mississippi, where the United Brethren were planning to dispense aid to the newly freed slaves and impoverished whites.

In 1863, Vicksburg was inundated with thousands of African-American refugees. They lived miserably, crowded into hastily constructed shacks made of the shoddiest of materials. The vast numbers of freedpeople completely overwhelmed the federal government's attempts to provide aid. Beginning in December 1863, Dickey and two other female mission teachers taught 300 emancipated men, women, and children. Despite arduous conditions—the constant threat of Confederate attack, a scarcity of supplies, and the poorest of accommodations—an 1865 United Brethren Church report stated that the mission had provided schooling for 700 people in the previous year. The staff also built a church and operated a Sunday school, which kept Dickey and her fellow teachers busy all day Sunday, in addition to their regular six-day work week.

In the weeks following the Confederate surrender, Dickey confronted another difficult decision: whether to continue to teach in the South or to pursue higher education. As with other critical life choices in her past, Dickey asked for divine direction. In the early fall of 1865, she was inspired to travel north to Mount Holyoke Female Seminary in South Hadley, Massachusetts, carrying only a portion of the funds she needed to complete her trip. Perhaps she convinced railway authorities to help her on her way once her money ran out. In any event, she arrived at Mount Holyoke, passed the entrance examinations, and received the opportunity to work her way through the four-year program.

In 1869, Dickey graduated from Mount Holyoke and returned to Mississippi to teach the freedpeople, first at an American Missionary Association school in Raymond, and a year later in a public school in Clinton. By 1872, she was pursuing her goal to create "a Mt. Holyoke seminary for the colored girls" in Mississippi, a herculean task in a state so firmly opposed to education for African Americans. In a letter to a friend, she wrote, "I also fully anticipate the difficulties which I shall have to encounter, yet when God calls I have no right to plead difficulties as a reason why I should not cheerfully and heartily respond" (quoted in Robenstine 1994, 197). By the fall of 1875, she had obtained the acreage and buildings for the Mount Hermon Female Seminary and had begun leading and teaching her students as she continued to do until her death in 1904.

See also **Education; Teachers of the Freedpeople**

Selected Readings

Griffith, Helen. *Dauntless in Mississippi: The Life of Sarah A. Dickey 1838–1904.* South Hadley, MA: Dinosaur Press. 1965.

Robenstine, Clark. "Sarah Ann Dickey." In *Women Educators in the United States 1820–1993: A Bio-bibliographical Sourcebook.* Edited by Maxine Schwartz Seller. Westport, CT: Greenwood Press. 1994. 193–202.

Dickinson, Anna (1842–1932)

Here stands the North and liberty; yonder stands the South and slavery; and one straight line of gore that reaches from one to the other is the only pathway we dare to tread until the Union and Freedom are triumphant!

—Anna Dickinson, speaking at Cooper Union, New York City, April 1863 (quoted in Chester 1951, 60)

Abolitionist and women's rights orator Anna Dickinson was barely out of her teens when her pro-war political speeches catapulted her into celebrity. During the Civil War, she lectured to huge audiences on antislavery issues, the progress of the war, the foibles of national political leaders, and the deficiencies of President Abraham Lincoln's reconstruction policies. In 1863, she entered the male-dominated world of party politics when the Republican Party recruited her to campaign for its politicians. In January 1864, she became the first woman to speak within the U.S. House of Representatives in Washington, DC. Dickinson electrified audiences with her acute understanding of political issues and her dramatic presentation, prompting the press to herald her as the Joan of Arc of the Union cause.

Anna Dickinson was raised a Quaker in Philadelphia, Pennsylvania. Her abolitionist father died when she was two years of age. To support the family, her mother became a schoolteacher and rented out rooms to boarders. Dickinson attended Quaker-sponsored schools until she was 15 years old, at which time she entered the labor force as a copyist, first in a publishing house, then in a law office. A year later, she became a teacher.

Dickinson began her career as an orator in April 1860 when, at the age of 17, she stood up at a Quaker "Friends of Progress" meeting in Philadelphia and criticized the views of a male speaker who had chastised women for stepping outside of their domestic sphere. Encouraged by the enthusiastic response of her audience, days later, she gave a lengthy speech on "The Rights and Wrongs of Women" at the same forum. She was soon invited to speak at abolitionist and women's rights meetings in the Philadelphia area, gaining the respect of prominent male and female reformers.

As the Civil War began in April 1861, Dickinson obtained a job working as an adjuster at the U.S. Mint in Philadelphia. The work itself was not difficult, but the hours were long and the pay, although better than teaching, was still low. She worked six days a week from 7 AM until 6 PM for $28 a month. As all-consuming as the job was, Dickinson was determined to help support her family who were living in poverty. Although she was the youngest of five children, her mother, older sister, and an ill brother depended on the money Dickinson earned.

Following the Union defeat at the Battle of Ball's Bluff (Virginia) in October 1861, Dickinson lectured at the annual meeting of the Pennsylvania Anti-Slavery Society where leading abolitionists from all over the Northeast had gathered. She offered a critical analysis of the battles waged up to that point in the war and attacked Union Major General George McClellan for what she perceived was his traitorous mishandling of the Battle of Ball's Bluff. It was a risky move, given that McClellan was one of Philadelphia's favorite native sons. When the speech, reported in the Philadelphia newspapers, came to the attention of administrators at the U.S. Mint, Dickinson was fired.

Although she was out of a job, she had attracted the attention of several prominent abolitionist leaders. William Lloyd Garrison, editor of the radical antislavery newspaper *The Liberator*, immediately offered to mentor her. He invited her to Massachusetts, arranged speaking engagements for her, and instructed her in abolition and other political issues.

Throughout 1862, Dickinson lectured in New England and elsewhere in the Northeast, making a name for herself while honing her oratorical powers. Despite her success, she was discouraged. Although she was in high demand as a speaker, she was still earning only $20 or so from most of her engagements at antislavery meetings and small forums. Occasional lectures at larger venues paid more but were not enough to satisfy her family's needs. Her older sister, in particular, was becoming impatient. The family needed more income. In December 1862, she urged Dickinson to return home and resume teaching.

Dickinson did not heed her sister's request. In the early months of 1863, the tide turned when the Republican Party in New Hampshire invited her to engage in party politics. The party, sensing it was destined to lose many of its key races in the upcoming state elections, hired Dickinson to campaign throughout New Hampshire. In a matter of a few weeks, she spoke in 20 different communities. When the elections were held, Republicans won most of the seats contested. From there, Dickinson's success on the campaign trail brought her first to Maine, and then to Connecticut to stump for candidates in those states. Wherever she traveled, she lectured on the military status of the war, the need for immediate emancipation, and the heresy of President Lincoln's liberal treatment of Confederate sympathizers. She also strongly supported the enlistment of African Americans into the Union military. Republican victories in both states further boosted her stature and fame.

Dickinson created excitement wherever she spoke. Men and women packed into lecture halls to hear the female dynamo whip the crowds into a passion. A Connecticut reporter recorded his impression of her oratorical style:

She reminded me of a lioness or tigress pacing back and forth in her cage, as she herself paced back and forth on the stage; if anything, her look was more fierce, her bearing more majestic, and her wrath more terrific …. she roused herself like a tigress about to spring upon her prey—her whole manner fierce and imposing—her eyes almost literally flashing coals of fire.

Her audiences responded with equal ardor. In Connecticut, one speech was reported to have been interrupted by "storms of applause that fairly shook the hall," preventing Dickinson "from being heard for five minutes at a time" (quoted in Chester 1951, 57).

At the Cooper Union in New York City in April 1863, 5,000 people crowded into the lecture hall to catch a glimpse of Dickinson and to hear her blast the Confederacy and Union General McClellan. According to one report, the audience "went crazy." As one observer recalled, "Applause came often and in long-continued storms, hats were swung, handkerchiefs waved, and at times the whole house was like a moving, tumultuous sea, flecked with white caps" (quoted in Chester 1951, 61).

Audiences were not always so positive. In the fall of 1863, in the coal-mining regions of Pennsylvania, where pro-Democratic miners detested the federal government's draft law and opposed the war, Dickinson confronted hostile crowds. While trying to speak to one group that heckled her unmercifully, a man raised a pistol and shot off a lock of her hair. Dickinson glowered but did not budge from the staging. Eventually the crowd quieted so that she could speak.

Although Dickinson was not always paid what she was promised, she was now a wealthy woman. By this time, her family had moved into expensive lodgings. Dickinson lavished money on them, on her own clothing, and gave generously to charity, saving nothing.

On the evening of January 16, 1864, at the age of 21, Dickinson reached the pinnacle of her political career when she gave an address before the nation's senators, congressmen, and Vice President Hannibal Hamlin. As in her previous speeches, she demanded emancipation for all the slaves. She vilified the South and all Northern Democrats who were campaigning against the war. She condemned President Lincoln for bestowing amnesty on Confederate soldiers who agreed to swear an oath of allegiance to the U.S. government. She also harshly criticized the president for proposing lenient treatment of Confederates in his plans for reconstruction after the war. Like most Northern abolitionists, Dickinson was convinced that the South should suffer for its crimes and be so severely punished that slaveholders could never return to slavery or hold power in Southern society.

Just as Dickinson was castigating Lincoln, the president and his wife, MARY TODD LINCOLN, arrived and took their seats. Seemingly nonplussed, Dickinson continued her attack, but as her speech drew toward its conclusion, she surprised the audience by supporting Lincoln's bid for re-election. In the days following the address, the Republican and Democratic press condemned her for her about-face. She did not speak out in favor of Lincoln in subsequent speeches. Yet by the summer of 1864, she had endorsed Lincoln in his campaign against the Democratic candidate George McClellan and the Radical Democratic candidate John C. Frémont.

Once the war was over, Dickinson's fame soared as she became an immensely popular speaker on the lyceum circuit, lecturing throughout the East and Midwest. During the late 1860s and early 1870s, she was able to earn approximately $20 thousand a year, money that she spent as quickly as she earned it. After stumping in 1872 for the Democratic Party's presidential candidate, the *New York Tribune* editor Horace Greeley, Dickinson's credibility and popularity diminished and she experienced difficulty securing an adequate number of lecturing engagements.

In the mid-1870s, Dickinson turned to the theater as a playwright and occasional actress. In 1876, she took the leading role in her play *A Crown of Thorns, or Anne Boleyn.* Her second drama, *Aurelian,* was produced in 1878, and her most successful venture, *An American Girl,* appeared in 1880. Her theatrical career faltered when she assumed the role of Hamlet. She then retired from public life to live with her mother and sister.

Aside from a brief campaign tour on behalf of Republican candidate Benjamin Harrison in the 1888 presidential campaign, Dickinson lived a quiet life until 1891 when her sister committed her to the State Hospital for the Insane in Danville, Pennsylvania. Although Dickinson had been suffering from depression, she managed to obtain her freedom and sue the doctors responsible. Once released, she spent the rest of her life living with a couple who opened their home to her after she left the hospital. She died at the age of 89 in 1932.

See also **Abolitionists; Women and Politics**

Selected Readings

Chester, Giraud. *Embattled Maiden: The Life of Anna Dickinson.* New York: Putnam. 1951.

Gallman, J. Matthew. "Anna Dickinson: Abolitionist Orator." In *The Human Tradition in the Civil War and Reconstruction.* Edited by Steven E. Woodworth. Wilmington, DE: Scholarly Resources. 2000. 93–110.

Dickinson, Emily (1830–1886)

It feels a shame to be alive
When men so brave are dead.

—Emily Dickinson (Dickinson 1931, 322)

Although unrecognized during her lifetime, Emily Dickinson is now acknowledged as one of the greatest American poets. An intensely private person, Dickinson lived a quiet, unassuming life in Amherst, Massachusetts. Decades of research and professional scrutiny have not revealed the details of the crises and passions that informed her poetry, leaving her biographers to rely on speculation and conjecture to shape her personal history. Dickinson did not contribute to the war effort as many New England women did, yet the war powerfully influenced her work. The height of her artistic production encompassed the years 1858 to 1865. In fact, more than half of her entire body of work was written during the Civil War, from 1861 to 1865.

Emily Dickinson was born in Amherst, a town situated in the Connecticut River valley. Her father, Edward Dickinson, an attorney, was active in local politics and government. A member of the Whig Party, he served one term in the U.S. House of Representatives from 1853 to 1855. Her mother, Emily Norcross Dickinson, was a passive, though dutiful wife and mother. Her daughter Emily, the second of three children, received an excellent education at Amherst Academy. After graduating in 1847, she attended Mount Holyoke Female Seminary in South Hadley, Massachusetts, for one year. As much as she enjoyed the school, her father decided to terminate her education for reasons that are unknown. His decision may have been related to his belief that women do not possess the intellectual capacity of men.

During the late 1840s and early 1850s, following her two terms at Mount Holyoke, Dickinson enjoyed close friendships with both young women and young men. She and her younger sister Lavinia participated in an active social life in Amherst. Although their time was consumed with social calls and parties, Dickinson was writing poetry regularly by this time. As her women friends married and moved away, she began to curtail her social life. Following her mother's severe illness in 1855, Dickinson stayed close to home to look after her. Despite her family responsibilities, by 1858, the writing of poetry had become the focus of her life.

No literary historian or biographer questions the fact that Dickinson suffered the loss of a beloved individual in the early 1860s. Although the identity of the person and the details of the relationship are unknown, it is clear that she experienced a profound personal crisis, the emotions of which she detailed in the hundreds of verses she produced during the Civil War years.

Scholars have attempted to uncover the reasons why Dickinson did not publish her work. Although she shared her poems with her family and close friends, only ten poems appeared in print during her lifetime, almost all of them anonymously (Habegger 2001, 389 n.12). It is in doubt whether she submitted the published verses herself or if a relative or friend arranged publication without her knowledge or consent. Unlike many aspiring women poets of her era, Dickinson had the connections she needed to be published. Her friend Samuel Bowles, the prominent editor-in-chief and owner of the newspaper the *Springfield Republican* (Massachusetts), actively endorsed and published the work of women writers. He was also well known among Boston's literary elite and could have arranged for her to meet the most respected writers in New England. Despite the possibilities available to her, Dickinson seems to have deliberately resisted opportunities to publish her work.

Yet during the early years of the Civil War, she sought out the literary advice of the Massachusetts writer Thomas Wentworth Higginson. A former minister and militant abolitionist, Higginson had just written "Letter to a Young Contributor," an article published in the April 1862 issue of the *Atlantic Monthly*. After reading Higginson's advice to young writers, she sent him four poems and asked, "Are you too deeply occupied to say if my Verse is alive? …Should you think it breathed—and had you the leisure to tell me, I should feel quick gratitude" (Sewall 1974, 2: 541). Thus began a correspondence and friendship that would endure for the rest of her life. In Higginson's initial response to her, he evidently performed what she described as "surgery" on her poems. In subsequent letters, he was mildly encouraging about her work, but recommended that she not attempt to publish. For all his radical political views, Higginson was conservative in his literary tastes and not in a position to appreciate the artistry or the marketability of Dickinson's innovative style.

As far as is known, Dickinson did not reach out to any other writer to ask for mentoring, nor did she approach any publisher. If she had been truly determined to publish, it is likely that she would have submitted her work to multiple editors as so many LITERARY WOMEN were doing. It is also likely, given the number of women being published and the high demand for women's writing, that her work would have appeared somewhere. Although the reasons for her failure to publish will probably never be known, it does appear that she was ambivalent about being a published poet.

Although Dickinson may have lacked literary colleagues and contacts, she was not completely isolated. She read extensively—contemporary literature as well as the classics. Her household subscribed to numerous leading newspapers and periodicals so that she kept abreast of both popular and literary poetry and prose. She had many friends with whom she corresponded regularly. By the time of the Civil War, Dickinson had become so tied to her home that letters were the primary vehicle for her friendships. She visited with members of her family but rarely received calls from neighbors or friends as she had in the past.

Dickinson's poetry does not directly address the war, slavery, or other issues related to the national conflict. Her body of work does not include any patriotic verse. Yet a number of her poems created during the war years incorporate battle-related imagery to illustrate her recurring themes of suffering, pain, and loss. A number of her poems refer to guns, blood, cannons, drums, bullets, and balls (minié balls). As one of her biographers has noted, the Civil War provided her with a "stark symbolic theater" that she used to convey the intensity of the emotions she was expressing (Habegger 2001, 403). Several of her poems were inspired by the deaths of young men from her hometown. The following is an excerpt from one verse written in 1861 in honor of the first Amherst soldier to die in battle.

> When I was small, a woman died.
> To-day her only boy
> Went up from the Potomac,
> His face all victory,
>
> To look at her; how slowly
> The seasons must have turned
> Till bullets clipt an angle,
> And he passed quickly round! (Dickinson 1931, 171)

"It feels a shame to be alive" and "They dropped like flakes" are two other poems that convey the horror and the helplessness of the noncombatant watching and waiting on the homefront.

Dickinson suffered from a severe eye disorder during the latter half of the Civil War. Although the name and nature of the illness are not known, the problem was severe enough to warrant a lengthy series of treatments from Boston's leading ophthalmologist. Dickinson traveled to Boston in April 1864, for her first round of therapy and remained until November of that year, staying with relatives in Cambridge. The second set of treatments lasted from April until October of 1865. The treatment sessions were "painful," but were not the worst of the agony of the experience. Far more difficult for Dickinson was the doctor's order that she abstain from reading and writing during these months. Deprived of books, her most cherished companions, as well as her ability to practice her craft, the months spent in Cambridge were torturous ones (Wolff 1986, 166).

Dickinson may not have wrapped bandages or scraped lint as so many Massachusetts women were doing for the war effort, but she did contribute to the cause. In February and March 1864, three of her poems appeared in the *Drum Beat*, a newspaper published daily during the Brooklyn and Long Island Sanitary Fair (New York). The publication was compiled as a fund-raiser for the UNITED STATES SANITARY COMMISSION and writers, some of them well known, donated their work.

The three Dickinson poems appeared anonymously and were later reprinted in other newspapers, including the *Springfield Republican* (Dandurand 1984, 17). While some literary historians claim that Dickinson agreed to their submissions, others argue that they may have been published without her awareness, perhaps forwarded by a family member or friend. A supporter of this theory points out that in December 1864, Dickinson refused to contribute her work to another, similar publication, the *Springfield Musket*, which was published to raise money for the Soldiers' Rest in Springfield, Massachusetts, a wayside station for sick and wounded soldiers passing through the city on their way to hospitals or to their homes (Habegger 2001, 403).

Despite the continuing difficulties with her eyes in 1865, Dickinson managed to write more than 200 poems during the final year of the war. Beginning in 1866, however, her output dropped dramatically. She wrote only 70 poems in the entire five-year period following the war. The decrease was probably related to the Dickinson household's dearth of domestic help. For four of those years, there was no full-time servant, which left Dickinson and her sister Lavinia to cope with the cooking, baking, and cleaning as well as the care of their ill mother. Finally, in 1869, the Dickinsons hired full-time domestic help (Habegger 2001, 498). While the assistance undoubtedly freed up Dickinson's time, she never returned to her level of wartime productivity.

In the 1870s, Dickinson continued to write verse, though she produced fewer and fewer poems as the years passed. Her father's death in 1874 and her mother's stroke and resultant paralysis in 1875 were severe blows that taxed her energies. In the late 1870s and early 1880s, she experienced a love relationship with an older man, a retired judge who was a friend of her father's. The couple communed primarily through their passionate correspondence. Following his death in 1884, Dickinson's health became precarious. By the fall of 1885, she was seriously ill, suffering from kidney disease, which was the cause of her death in 1886.

After her death, her sister Lavinia discovered Dickinson's body of work in her bedroom bureau. Although Lavinia destroyed her sister's correspondence as she had requested, Lavinia was seized with the desire to see her sister's work published. With Higginson's and editor Mabel Loomis Todd's help, the poems were edited, organized, and published in 1890. Since that time, numerous scholars have studied and produced variant editions of her poems. By the mid-twentieth century, Dickinson was recognized not only as a leading American poet, but as one of the most brilliant to have written in the English language.

Selected Readings

Habegger, Alfred. *My Wars Are Laid Away in Books: The Life of Emily Dickinson.* New York: Random House. 2001.

Wolff, Cynthia Griffin. *Emily Dickinson.* New York: Knopf. 1986.

Dix, Dorothea (1802–1887)

At the outset of the Civil War, Dorothea Dix was already well known to most Americans for her one-woman crusade to revolutionize the care of the mentally ill in the United States. During the 1840s and 1850s, she inspected almshouses, workhouses, prisons, and jails, and compiled graphic treatises documenting the horrors she witnessed. She presented them to state legislators and pressed them to institute reforms. As a self-acknowledged expert on hospital administration, in April 1861, hours after hearing the news that President Abraham Lincoln was mustering soldiers, she rushed to Washington, DC, to launch her mission to establish an army nursing corps of white female volunteers.

Dix was born in the town of Hampden in the Maine wilderness, the daughter of an itinerant Methodist minister. She received her education in Boston and established her first school for young children at the age of 14. Over the next 20 years, she taught and was headmistress of several of her own schools. Long spells of respiratory illness disturbed her work beginning in 1824. By the early 1830s, she was diagnosed with tuberculosis. Still frail and unwell at the age of 40 in 1841, Dix's life was transformed when she taught a class for women in a local jail. She became outraged by the inhumane living conditions when she discovered that "lunacy" was the only crime of many prisoners. From that moment on, she devoted herself to reforming the care of the mentally ill.

In April 1861, with two decades of successful reform behind her, Dix used her political connections in Congress and in the president's Cabinet to secure the volunteer position she wanted. On April 23, Secretary of War Simon Cameron appointed Dix to enlist female nurses, and to help supervise the organization of military hospitals and the requisition of supplies from the homefront. She received her official commission as Superintendent of Female Nurses on June 10. In delineating her powers and jurisdiction, Cameron helped set the stage for the series of misunderstandings and battles that ensued between Dix and the surgeons and officers of the Army Medical Bureau.

Cameron ordered her to maintain "diligent oversight" of her nurses, yet added that "all women nurses are under the direction of the Surgeons . . ." He gave her "the right and duty of visitor and inspector" in the military hospitals, yet ordered the

Medical Corps to respect "her suggestions, wishes and counsels ...[only] as far as is compatible with the order of the Medical Bureau" (quoted in Brown 1998, 290). By giving neither the surgeons nor Dix the ultimate authority concerning the work of women nurses, he doomed Dix's mission to failure. Both the surgeons and Dix interpreted Cameron's directives to suit their own imperatives.

Dix's conflicts with the surgeons and medical officers began immediately. The physicians wanted total control of the hospitals, the nurses, and all aspects of patient care. Dix supported her female nurses' prerogative to provide the type of care as outlined by British nursing pioneer Florence Nightingale in the 1860 best-seller *Notes on Nursing: What It Is and What It Is Not*. In 1855 to 1856, Dix had traveled to the Crimea to visit the hospital that Nightingale had resurrected from disease and neglect. Like Nightingale, Dix wanted to transform the care in military hospitals by supplying a nutritious diet, cleanliness, fresh air, light, and compassion, emphasizing these elements as the most critical aspects of patient care.

Dix also appears to have accepted Nightingale's attitudes toward nurses' relationships with male surgeons. Another of Nightingale's books, *Notes on Hospitals*, claims, "...a patient is much better cared for in an institution where there is the perpetual rub between doctors and nurses" (quoted in Brown 1998, 288). When Dix's nurses' care conflicted with the surgeons' instructions and authority, she attempted to intercede on the nurses' (and the patients') behalf, a situation that left surgeons clamoring for her removal.

Dix did not weather these hostilities with her authority intact, partly because she failed to solidify her own political position. Accustomed to working as a lone reformer, she cultivated relationships with a few politically powerful men in Washington while backing away from cooperative ventures with civilian organizations, women's groups, the Army Medical Bureau, and influential women reformers. She eventually accepted but did not champion Drs. Elizabeth and Emily Blackwell's nurses' training initiative in the spring of 1861, thereby antagonizing their WOMAN'S CENTRAL ASSOCIATION OF RELIEF (WCAR), which was to become the largest, most productive auxiliary of the UNITED STATES SANITARY COMMISSION (USSC). Then, when Dix used her influence to help raise thousands of dollars among New Englanders for the Western Sanitary Commission's relief efforts, funds that might otherwise have gone into the coffers of the USSC, she forever alienated USSC leaders (Gollaher 1995, 409–410).

Dix's isolated position left her vulnerable to a whirlwind of negative publicity. Though some of the charges were untrue and others misinterpreted her actions and motivations, Dix compounded the damage by never setting the record straight.

When the newly appointed Surgeon General William A. Hammond reconfirmed Dix's role as director of recruitment and assignment of women nurses in July 1862, he appeared to reinforce Dix's authority over her nursing corps. At this politically crucial moment, Dix neglected to place more female nurses in the military hospitals. By this time, however, her faltering reputation was limiting her recruitment opportunities (Brown 1998, 308).

In October 1863, while Hammond was in the West, a new War Department order clarified the roles of Dix and the Medical Bureau regarding female army nurses. The new directive gave the army surgeons the ultimate authority to select, hire, discipline, and direct their own nurses (Brown 1998, 314).

Stripped of most of her powers, Dix continued to screen nurses and visit the military hospitals as if nothing had happened. Despite her difficulties, she had appointed at least 3,200 nurses to the military hospitals. At the end of the war and immediately after, she assisted returning Union prisoners of war. She helped veterans petition the government for their back pay, found homes for war orphans, and raised eight thousand dollars toward the building of a monument to the Union war dead—a 45-foot granite obelisk in a cemetery at Fortress Monroe, Virginia, where 6,000 Union soldiers were buried. She did not become involved in the movement to professionalize nursing, though she did, for a time, reengage in asylum reform.

See also **Nurses**

Selected Readings

Brown, Thomas J. *Dorothea Dix: New England Reformer*. Cambridge: Harvard University Press. 1998.

Gollaher, David. *Voice for the Mad: The Life of Dorothea Dix*. New York: Free Press. 1995.

Doctors

During the Civil War, the first generation of women physicians in the United States continued the struggle to open the medical profession to women. Pioneers Elizabeth and Emily Blackwell, MARIE ZAKRZEWSKA, Ann Preston, Clemence Sophia Lozier, and several other women graduated from the few medical colleges that were accepting women students from the late 1840s through the 1850s and 1860s. Once this first generation of female medical students graduated, they searched, often in vain, for hospitals that would permit them to enter clinical training programs. During these early years, most of those who received training had to travel to Europe.

The first women physicians recognized that women medical graduates' lack of on-the-job hospital training prevented them from being accepted as professionals by the male medical community. To compensate for this deficiency, they chose to create clinical training programs themselves. This mission was the focus of much of their activism during the Civil War era.

The Quaker Ann Preston, an 1851 graduate of the Female Medical College of Pennsylvania (soon renamed the Women's Medical College of Pennsylvania), presented lectures at the medical school the year after her graduation. In 1853, she became a professor of hygiene and physiology. When male doctors in the Philadelphia hospitals refused to allow the college's female graduates to receive hospital training, Preston determined that the Women's Medical College should add a hospital where students could practice medicine. Quaker abolitionist and women's rights reformer Lucretia Coffin Mott and her fellow activists successfully collaborated to raise the funds and the new Woman's Hospital was established in 1861. Preston became the first woman dean of a medical college in 1866 when the Women's Medical College appointed her to that post (Ogilvie and Harvey 2000, 2: 1051).

Elizabeth Blackwell, the first woman to receive a medical degree in the United States, graduated from Geneva Medical College in Geneva, New York, in 1849. When the Civil War began in April 1861, Elizabeth and her physician sister Emily hoped that the Union army's need for skilled doctors would speed up the process of the professionalization of women in medicine—both as physicians and as nurses. In late April, the Blackwells called a meeting of New York male and female reformers to propose the training of women nurses for the Union military. Through the new organization they established, the WOMAN'S CENTRAL ASSOCIATION OF RELIEF (WCAR), the Blackwells superintended the selection and training of up to 100 nurses during the war years.

A number of women physicians offered their professional services to the U.S. military at the outset of the Civil War. Soon after the war began, Boston-trained physician ESTHER HILL HAWKS of New Hampshire traveled to Washington, DC, to volunteer her expertise. Not only was she rejected as a physician, but she also was refused an appointment as a nurse. Several years later, when traveling with her husband, a surgeon in the United States army, she had the opportunity to work as a surgeon on the frontlines in an unofficial capacity. Dr. MARY EDWARDS WALKER of New York State rushed to Washington in the first days of the war. She, too, was turned away, though rejection did not diminish her determination to serve the Union as a doctor. In the midst of working as a volunteer on the frontlines, she spent nearly the entire war struggling to obtain a commission as a Union army surgeon.

Away from the center of the national conflict, German immigrant Dr. Marie Zakrzewska, an 1856 graduate of Cleveland Medical College, opened the New England

Hospital for Women and Children in Boston in 1862. As Zakrzewska envisioned it, this new facility would give women, especially poor women of all ethnic groups, the opportunity to receive medical care from women doctors while also providing clinical training for women medical school graduates. Zakrzewska also planned that the New England Hospital would offer training to female nurses. Like the Blackwells, Zakrzewska prepared women nurses specifically for the Union military hospitals.

A close-knit network of female and male women's rights activists supported the New England Hospital for Women and Children from its earliest days. Boston reformers Abigail (Abby) Williams May, regional leader within the UNITED STATES SANITARY COMMISSION; Caroline Severance; Ednah Dow Cheney; Henry Browne Blackwell (Elizabeth and Emily's brother) and his wife, Lucy Stone; and Samuel Edmond Sewall gave freely of their money and time, and launched zealous fund-raising campaigns among reform-minded Bostonians. Collecting donations was a challenge during the Civil War. Many women who wished to contribute wrote that they wished to support the hospital but could not because they were supporting the Union cause or were suffering from the effects of wartime inflation.

Zakrzewska boosted the hospital's prestige and reputation in the Boston medical community by enlisting respected male doctors to serve as consulting physicians. Though they were sympathetic to the hospital's mission, this small minority of the Boston medical community did not endorse all of Zakrzewska's goals, particularly her objective that women gain entry to the medical profession on an equal footing with men. Most of the consulting physicians accepted the presence of women in medicine, but only with the understanding that they do so in institutions separate from men's (Drachman 1984, 54).

Several graduates of the New England Hospital became pioneers themselves. When Rebecca Lee graduated in 1864, she became the first African-American woman to receive a medical degree. After the war, she established a practice in Richmond, Virginia. A white 1863 graduate, Mary Harris Thompson, founded the first hospital for women and children in the West when she formed the Chicago Hospital for Women and Children in 1865.

In the mid-nineteenth century, women who aspired to be doctors found it easier to be admitted to institutions specializing in alternative medicine, in medical schools that were then labeled "irregular," "sectarian," or "eclectic." In 1863, Sophia Clemence Lozier founded the first medical school for women in New York when she established the New York Medical College and Hospital for Women. Lozier's medical school and hospital specialized in training women to become homeopathic physicians. Zakrzewska and the Blackwells scorned these schools and hospitals, declaring that women would never be fully accepted by the mainstream medical community unless they received rigorous, superior training in "regular" medicine.

See also **Nurses**

Selected Readings

More, Ellen S. Restoring the Balance: Women Physicians and the Profession of Medicine, 1850–1995. Cambridge: Harvard University Press. 1999.

Ruth Abram, ed. "Send Us a Lady Physician": Women Doctors in America, 1835–1920. New York: Norton. 1985.

Walsh, Mary Roth. "Doctors Wanted: No Women Need Apply": Sexual Barriers in the Medical Profession, 1835–1970. New Haven: Yale University Press. 1977.

Draft Riots

The draft began on Saturday, the twelfth, very foolishly ordered by the government, who supposed that these Union victories would make the people willing to submit …. All day yesterday there were dreadful scenes enacted in the city. The police were successfully opposed; many were killed, many houses were gutted and burned: the colored asylum was burned and all the furniture was carried off by *women*: Negroes were hung in the streets! All last night the fire-bells rang …. I did not wonder at the spirit in which the poor resented the three-hundred-dollar clause.

—Maria Lydig Daly, July 14, 1863 (Daly 2000, 246)

From July 13 to July 17, 1863, a little more than a week following the Union victory at GETTYSBURG, enraged mobs of working-class immigrant and native-born white men, women, and children filled the streets and alleys of New York City, wreaking death and destruction wherever they roamed. By the time the Union army wrested control of the streets, at least 105 people were dead, thousands were injured, and over a million dollars' worth of property had been damaged or destroyed. It remains to this day the most severe case of civil disorder in U.S. history.

The outpouring of violence and hatred was a direct response to the first federal draft law, the Conscription Act of 1863. According to its provisions, all white men between the ages of 20 and 35, and all unmarried men between the ages of 35 and 45, were eligible for the draft. Any man who could provide a substitute to serve in his place or who paid $300 was exempted and did not have to serve. For the masses of unskilled laborers and artisans in the city—many of whom were poor Irish immigrants earning less than $500 per year—exemption was beyond their reach. For them and for their families, the draft created an overwhelming economic hardship as it removed the most highly paid wage earners from their households.

In the best of times, the city's poor lived on the brink of destitution and starvation. The new draft law could not have come at a worse time. In 1863, wartime inflation was hitting the city's poor hard. By the time of the riot, prices had increased 43 percent since 1860 while wages had risen no more than 12 percent (Cook 1974, 50). Factory workers throughout the city were restive and had been participating in strikes on their employers.

At the beginning of the disorder, rioters vented their rage against federal and city officials and offices, including the police. Many of the mobs, composed largely of young men and boys, shut down factories and looted and destroyed stores. Men, women, and children demolished the office of the Provost Marshal, the federal official in charge of the conscription effort. Groups of women, undoubtedly frustrated and overwhelmed by the prospect of being thrust deeper into poverty by the enlistment of their menfolk, vented their fury by wielding crowbars to destroy railroad and streetcar tracks. With their children in tow and babies in their arms, they attacked police officers, soldiers, and federal officials. When a Colonel Henry O'Brien fired a howitzer into a crowd of rioters and killed a woman and her child, a mob composed mostly of women attacked him and chased him through the streets, eventually bludgeoning him to death (Bernstein 1990, 36–37).

Ellen Leonard, a white middle-class observer described the mayhem she witnessed. She observed that First Avenue was jammed,

> with thousands of infuriated creatures, yelling, screaming and swearing in the most frantic manner; while crowds of women, equally ferocious, were leaning from every door and window, swinging aprons and handkerchiefs, and cheering and urging them onward. The rush and roar grew every moment more terrific. Up came fresh hordes faster and more furious; bareheaded men, with red, swollen faces, brandishing sticks and clubs, or carrying heavy poles and beams; and boys, women and children hurrying on and joining with them in this mad chase up the avenue like a company of raging fiends. (quoted in Cook 1974, 69)

On the second day of the riot, the mobs turned their hatred toward African Americans, harassing, attacking, lynching, and murdering them and destroying their homes and property. The crowds also attacked the city's wealthier classes and well-known abolitionists.

Under constant attack, the police could do little to protect the city's black population. The Colored Orphan Infant Asylum was burned to the ground, the children hustled at the last minute to a secure shelter before any harm could come to them. Eight black women banded together and vowed they would not become victims. They prepared a concoction of water, soap, and ashes, heated it in a number of large boilers, and made ready to pour it on anyone who dared to break into their room (Forbes 1998, 157).

Historians have debated the mob's motivation for targeting African Americans. All point to the intense racial prejudice of white working-class New Yorkers. But what remains unclear is why this hatred was linked to the draft riots. African Americans were exempt from the Conscription Act, a fact that may have antagonized whites. Some scholars have noted that white workers feared that they and black laborers were competing for the same jobs. This perception was completely unfounded, although it aroused the animosity of white workers. In the 1850s and 1860s, African Americans in New York City were being pushed out of their traditional work by whites, not the other way around (Cook 1974, 204–205). Despite the reality, the white working class, frenzied by Democratic Party rhetoric, was convinced that their livelihoods were threatened.

White middle- and upper-class New Yorkers observed the rioting with fear and horror, yet there was nothing they could do to protect themselves or their property. Some, like women's rights activist and abolitionist ELIZABETH CADY STANTON, fled the city, leaving her to observe,

> Last Thursday I escaped from the horrors of the most brutal mob I ever witnessed, and brought my children here for safety [Johnstown, NY]. The riot raged in our neighborhood through the first two days of the trouble largely because the colored orphan asylum on Fifth Avenue was only two blocks away from us. I saw all those little children marched off two by two. A double portion of martyrdom has been meted out to our poor blacks, and I am led to ask if there is no justice in heaven or on earth that this should be permitted through the centuries. (Stanton and Blatch 1922, 2: 94)

Abolitionists had much to fear, as the family of ABBY HOPPER GIBBONS discovered. While Hopper Gibbons was away nursing soldiers, her daughter Julia was at home in the city. On July 15, she reported,

> The rioters yesterday gutted our house completely. We had time to save most of our valuable clothing, the pictures and bust of Willie, and a few other valuables, but the furniture is all gone and most of the pictures, *all* the books & c …. We had scarcely been out of the house fifteen minutes when the rabble came. (Gibbons 1897, 2: 43–44)

Daughter Lucy Gibbons wrote her mother about the bravery of their neighbors during the ordeal:

> Another, Mr. Horn, stood in the parlor and threatened the mob with a pistol. He drove off the women (!!!) who were trying to set fire to the house with torches, but was finally obliged to retreat through the back window …. They destroyed and carried off everything, throwing bureaus and other pieces of furniture from the windows; setting fire to the house in many places; and leaving it completely stripped. (Gibbons 1897, 2: 49–50)

New York City was not the only scene of civil disorder following implementation of the Conscription Act. Violence erupted in Holmes County, Ohio, in several counties in

Indiana, in mining communities in Pennsylvania, and in parts of Missouri, Maryland, Delaware, and Kentucky. Boston was another of several Northern cities that experienced a draft riot. Unlike the New York disturbance, Boston rioters—almost exclusively Irish—did not lash out against African Americans but focused their fury on the group they held responsible for the draft and their oppression, the native-born "Yankee" Protestants.

On July 14, a draft official delivered a draft notice at a tenement in the principal Irish neighborhood of Boston. In the course of doing so, he argued with a woman who swore at him and hit him. When the draft official shouted that he planned to have her arrested, a large group of women, children, and men immediately gathered and attacked him and the police officer trying to protect him. Using stones and pieces of rock pulled up from the street and sidewalks, the group, gathering onlookers into its ranks, pelted the officers who arrived at the scene. Hours later, the mob, still composed of a mixed group of men, women, and children, stormed the armory located in the heart of the Irish enclave. After breaking the windows and battering the doors in their search for the weapons stored inside, the state militia shot a cannon into the crowd, killing and wounding an unknown number of rioters, including at least four children. This police action did not quell the revolt. While militia units kept trying to gain control of the streets, the crowds continued to throw stones and battle with soldiers. More militia units were called in, and by the end of the evening, they managed to quiet the streets.

As far as New York City's rebellion is concerned, the draft riots successfully interrupted conscription until mid-August of 1863. In the wake of the riot, the city's Democratic Party leadership announced its plan to raise $2.5 million to pay the $300 exemption fee for each draftee. Several months later, white elite New York City reformers focused on assisting the poor of the city by attempting to upgrade the miserable, overcrowded living conditions in the tenement districts and to improve the health of their inhabitants. The reformers also favored launching a moral education campaign in the wake of the rebellion. In Boston, the initial quota for the draft—3,300 men—was never met. Only 713 of the city's men were drafted after the riot (Tager 2001, 138).

See also **Immigrant Women; Industrial Women**

Selected Readings

Bernstein, Iver. *The New York City Draft Riots: Their Significance for American Society and Politics in the Age of the Civil War.* New York: Oxford University Press. 1990.

Cook, Adrian. *The Armies of the Streets: The New York City Draft Riots of 1863.* Lexington, KY: University of Kentucky Press. 1974.

Tager, Jack. *Boston Riots: Three Centuries of Social Violence.* Boston: Northeastern University Press. 2001.

E

Edmonds, Sarah Emma (1841–1898)

Sarah Emma Edmonds's record of service in the Union army during the Civil War is one of the most thoroughly researched cases of a woman soldier enlisted in the Union or Confederate military. Although her memoir of her exploits contains exaggerated and fictionalized events and elements, her service as a soldier and nurse has been amply authenticated.

Born Sarah Emma Evelyn Edmonson (her name later appears as Edmonds) in New Brunswick, Canada, she grew up on a farm, the youngest of her parents' six children. With only one frail son in the family, her father needed the labor of all of his daughters to sustain the farm. Sarah grew strong performing agricultural labor and she enjoyed a rugged, outdoor lifestyle, hunting, fishing, and boating.

When Edmonds's father promised her in marriage to an aging farmer, she ran away from home to work as a milliner in a town in New Brunswick. As soon as she learned that her father had discovered her whereabouts, she disguised herself as a man and assumed the alias of Franklin Thompson. She soon made a success of selling bibles door to door, based largely on her ability to establish a strong rapport with her customers. Edmonds was enthusiastic about the freedom she found in her new life as she traveled from town to town in New Brunswick and Nova Scotia.

Yearning for a more adventurous life in the West, Edmonds, still disguised as Thompson, migrated to Flint, Michigan, in 1860. A month after war was declared, on May 17, 1861, she and a male friend enlisted in a unit that soon became part of the 2nd Michigan Voluntary Infantry. By mid-1861, Private Franklin Thompson's regiment was attached to the enormous Army of the Potomac. In a newspaper interview printed years after the war, Edmonds said that she had determined that she "could best serve the interest of the Union cause in male attire—could better perform the … duties for sick and wounded men, and with less embarrassment to them and to myself as a man than as a woman" (quoted in Hall 1993, 80–81).

As part of the Army of the Potomac during the first two years of the war, Edmonds experienced combat at its most harrowing. She cared for the wounded after the disastrous Union defeat at the First Battle of Bull Run (known in the South as the First Battle of Manassas) on July 21, 1861, in northern Virginia. In addition to her camp and drill duties, she worked as a male nurse in the regimental hospital and at a general military hospital in Georgetown, on the outskirts of Washington, DC. In April 1862, she was pressed into service as a postmaster and mail carrier for her regiment. Both duties occupied her throughout much of the Army of the Potomac's Peninsula Campaign (Virginia), from March through August 1862.

With the greater freedom and mobility that her mail carrying offered, Edmonds discovered that she could escape detection more easily. During the Peninsula Campaign, she ceased her mail duties temporarily to fight in the Battle of Williamsburg on May 5, 1862, and in the Seven Days' Battle in late June. During the Battle of Seven Pines on May 31 to June 1, she nursed in the field hospital and helped bury the dead (Blanton and Cook 2002, 12). Zealous in the performance of her duties, she was well liked by both officers and enlisted men. According to her memoir, she was selected to serve as an espionage agent in 1862. As a spy, she wrote that she created unique disguises and personae so that she could convincingly impersonate a male slave, an Irish peddler woman, a female fugitive slave, and a Kentucky male civilian. In fact, it has not been definitively determined whether Edmonds served as an espionage agent as her memoir claimed. Although some historians assert that the evidence supports the fact that she engaged in espionage, others point out that as an older woman, she made statements that appear to be denials that she acted as a spy. She may have included tales of her spy activities to add excitement to her war record and increase the sales of her book (Leonard 2001, 182–183).

While delivering mail and military communications to Union Major General George McClellan's forces in Maryland in September 1862, Edmonds was caught up in the Battle of Antietam on September 17. Throughout this horrific battle, she cared for the wounded. During the first Battle of Fredericksburg (Virginia), in December 1862, she had the distinguished honor of being chosen to serve as Brigadier General Orlando M. Poe's orderly. In this role, she raced on horseback from the general's headquarters to the front and back, dodging bullets while carrying messages and orders to the commanders on the frontlines (Blanton and Cook 2002, 14–15).

Several months after the 2nd Michigan Infantry was transferred to the Western Theater, Edmonds contracted a severe case of malaria, which landed her in a hospital in Lebanon, Kentucky. Though severely ill, she claims that she was more concerned that her sexual identity would be revealed. Out of her fear of discovery, she fled the hospital and deserted the army, traveling north as far as Oberlin, Ohio, where she spent weeks recovering her strength. As she explained decades later, "I never for a moment considered myself a deserter. I simply left because I could hold out no longer, and to ... become a helpless patient in a hospital was sure discovery, which to me was far worse than death" (quoted in Hall 1993, 92).

Two diaries of men serving in Edmonds's regiment, now archived in the Michigan Historical Collections at the University of Michigan, suggest that her romantic relationship with an officer may have precipitated her abrupt departure from her regiment. Although both men's diaries do not solidly identify the reason for her decision to desert the army, they do confirm that Edmonds's gender was known by at least two men in her regiment (Fladeland 1963, 357–362).

While Edmonds regained her health in Ohio, she resumed dressing in women's attire. She soon began writing her memoir while living in Hartford, Connecticut. At some point after finishing her book, she volunteered as a female nurse under the auspices of the UNITED STATES CHRISTIAN COMMISSION (USCC). In 1864, one of her former employers published her memoir, then titled *Unsexed; or, The Female Soldier*. From the first, the book was a best-seller, selling 175,000 copies. In the memoir, which in 1865 was renamed *Nurse and Spy in the Union Army*, she does not reveal that she hid her femaleness and lived as a man. Instead, she portrays herself as a woman who only occasionally wore a male disguise to achieve a military objective.

Though Edmonds desperately needed money, she donated the proceeds from the sales of her book to a number of organizations supplying aid to Union soldiers, including the UNITED STATES SANITARY COMMISSION and the USCC. During the latter part of the war, she volunteered as a nurse for the USCC at Harpers Ferry, West Virginia.

In 1867, Edmonds married a carpenter from New Brunswick, Linus H. Seelye, with whom she eventually adopted two sons (their three natural children did not survive). One source indicates that the couple worked in the Midwest to assist the freed slaves, and in 1875, established an orphan's home for African-American children in

Kansas. Sarah tried to obtain a soldier's pension when she and her husband faced poverty in the 1880s. With her efforts and the glowing testimonials of ten former comrades from the 2nd Michigan, she was awarded a pension and a bounty in 1886, though the money did little to relieve the couple's financial situation. She died in Fort Scott, Kansas, in 1898 at the age of 56.

See also **Military Women; Nurses**

Selected Readings

Blanton, DeAnne and Lauren M. Cook. *They Fought Like Demons: Women Soldiers in the American Civil War.* Baton Rouge: Louisiana State University Press. 2002.

Fladeland, Betty. "New Light on Sarah Emma Edmonds Alias Franklin Thompson." *Michigan History.* 47 (4) (1963): 357–362.

Leonard, Elizabeth D. *All the Daring of the Soldier: Women of the Civil War Armies.* New York: Penguin Books. 2001.

Edmondson, Belle (1840–1873)

At one o'clock Mrs. Fackler, Mrs. Kirk & I began to fix my articles for smugling. We made a balmoral [petticoat] of the Gray cloth for [Confederate] uniforms, pin'd the Hats to the inside of my hoops, tied the boots with a strong list, letting them fall directly in front.... All my buttons, brass buttons, Money & c in my bosom.... Left at 2 o'clock ... started to walk, impossible that, hailed a hack.... Arrived at Pickets [Union guards who searched civilians leaving and entering Memphis], no trouble at all—although I suffered horibly in anticipation of trouble.

—Belle Edmondson, March 16, 1864, Memphis, Tennessee (Edmondson 1990, 97)

Belle Edmondson's Civil War diary is one of the few women's war journals that detail the daily life of a female Confederate smuggler and informant. Most espionage agents of the North and South left no personal documents of any kind, in the event that letters or diaries might one day incriminate them. Edmondson's war diary reveals her mundane, uneventful domestic existence that was intermittently punctuated by the excitement and danger of her forays as a scout and smuggler.

Born Isabella Buchanan Edmondson in Pontotoc, a town on the Mississippi frontier, she was the daughter of a comfortably well-off farmer, slaveholder, and former government land agent. Immediately prior to the war, Edmondson's father moved his family to a farm eight miles south of the booming commercial center of Memphis, Tennessee, the sixth largest city in the South. Its location on the Mississippi River and its importance as a rail terminus for the only east–west railroad available to Confederate troops made Memphis a strategic location and persistent site of conflict between Union and Confederate forces.

After the Battle of Shiloh on April 6 to April 7, 1862, Edmondson, a zealous Confederate patriot, nursed the wounded at a Memphis hospital. Two months later on June 6, 1862, Memphis surrendered to Union forces and was occupied. With the Union in control of much of the Mississippi River, Confederate troops continued to roam the backcountry—the lands leading east and west from the river. After the surrender of Memphis, city residents, including Belle Edmondson, established vital pathways of communication with these Confederate regiments, relaying information about Union troop movements and smuggling supplies.

High spirited, daring, and adventurous, Edmondson eagerly signed on as a scout for Confederate Captain Thomas H. Henderson's company of agents. Throughout 1863 and in the early months of 1864, she carried documents and letters to and from western Tennessee and Memphis, smuggled medical and other essential supplies to Confederate troops, and acted as an informant. From Henderson's letters to Edmondson, it is apparent that he valued and relied on her expertise.

In 1864, Edmondson was arrested, as she described it, "for carrying letters through the lines and smuggling, and aiding the Rebellion in every way in my power" (Edmondson 1990, 117). Although she was released, thanks to the intervention of a Union officer "friend," by late spring she realized that she had to flee south to Mississippi, where she remained until the end of the war. Piecing together her postwar existence has proven difficult. She continued living in Mississippi and is briefly mentioned in the correspondence of family and friends. In 1873, at the age of 33, she died of diphtheria shortly after becoming engaged to marry.

See also **Spies and Espionage**

Selected Readings

Edmondson, Belle. *A Lost Heroine of the Confederacy: The Diaries and Letters of Belle Edmondson*. Edited by Loretta and William Galbraith. Jackson: University Press of Mississippi. 1990.

Markle, Donald E. *Spies and Spymasters of the Civil War*. New York: Hippocrene Books. 1994.

Education

The Civil War interrupted a long period of change and innovation in education for men and women in the United States. The years 1830 to 1860 saw many new developments in elementary, secondary, and collegiate instruction and institutions that had broad implications for the advancement of education for women. Despite the progress and the evidence that girls and women could master academic disciplines once reserved for males only, the belief that women's intellects were inferior to men's persisted. By the 1870s, the new women's colleges and women's increased presence in coeducational colleges eventually began to shift public opinion.

Despite the turmoil of the Civil War, education continued to flourish in many regions of the country. Even in the South, where most of the fighting took place, school administrators and teachers struggled to keep schools open for much of the war, though they were not always successful. When male teachers in the South vacated the classrooms to enlist, women did not step up to fill the teaching ranks in the numbers that they did in the North. Part of the difficulty was that few Southern women had sufficient education to teach beyond the lower elementary grades (Stillman 1972, 273). Southern schools closed for other reasons besides a lack of teachers. When inflation of Confederate currency and economic hard times ensued, parents could not afford to send their children to school, leaving administrators without the funds to keep schools open. In regions of active warfare, schools were sometimes closed so that they could be turned into hospitals, military headquarters, or barracks.

In the North, the enlistment of thousands of male teachers accelerated the entrance of Northern women into the teaching profession, a development that had its origins in the 1830s and 1840s. In the New England states, women filled 40 percent of all teaching posts before the Civil War. By 1880, that figure had increased to 80 percent (Eisenmann 1998, 151). The growth of women's teaching opportunities in Iowa exemplifies the war's impact on the numbers of women entering the profession. In 1848, 23 teachers out of 124 were women. In 1865, 65 percent of all Iowa teachers were women (Kaufman 1984, xxi).

The most important educational development during the decades before the war was the movement to create common schools, or public schools, throughout the nation. Before 1830, only private schools were available, their fees prohibiting the enrollment of children from the poorest classes. Educational reformers in the North convinced the American public that the benefits of public education—creating literate, responsible, moral, and loyal citizens—would far outweigh the costs to local communities and the states. The Southern states were slow to develop common schools and did not achieve widespread public education until after the Civil War.

Girls, whose educational needs had been ignored in the past, were included in the North's mass education plan. By the mid-nineteenth century, most people no longer quarreled with the idea that all girls needed grounding in the basics of education to become good mothers capable of guiding the next generation of citizens into adulthood.

The expansion of the common schools in the North and West boosted female literacy rates. By 1860, only six percent of all Northern women were illiterate. In the South, where communities were slower to install common schools, 15 percent of women were illiterate. Among free African Americans, who were excluded from most public education, only 50 percent were literate by 1860. Some free African-American children living in urban areas were educated in private schools organized by black communities. Laws in most Southern states prohibited the education of slaves, though a small number managed to learn to read and write. Historians approximate that literacy rates for slaves ranged from five to ten percent (Hobbs 1995, 11).

The rise of the common schools in the North, Midwest, and West had another positive outcome that advanced women's education. As the number of public grammar schools proliferated, the demand for teachers exploded. It was not uncommon for communities to build schoolhouses and then discover that there were no men available to teach. Because teaching was not a respected male profession, most men taught for a brief time and as soon as possible moved on to other occupations. To fill the void, many communities experimented with the hiring of educated women to teach their children. As the common schools multiplied, more and more women took the helm in the classrooms, so much so that by the 1850s, more women than men were teaching in the elementary grades. Although the feminization of the teaching force was not without controversy, most communities accepted women teachers because they could be paid a fraction of a male teacher's salary, the rationale being that women, unlike men, had only themselves to support. Educational reformers also argued that women were better suited to teach young children because of their gentler, kinder, more patient natures. Another common viewpoint held that teaching helped to ready a young woman for marriage and motherhood (Woody 1929, 1: 464,490).

By the time of the Civil War, many Americans believed that women were "born teachers" and were naturally superior to men as instructors of the young. Before the war, female teachers were restricted to teaching the youngest pupils in the elementary grades. As male teachers left the classroom during the Civil War, however, women successfully taught older children, adding to their credibility as excellent educators of all common school students. HARRIET BEECHER STOWE, popular author and sister of the pioneering educator Catherine Beecher, voiced the opinion of many educated women when she declared, "We have come to the conclusion that the work of teaching will never be rightly done till it passes into female hands" (Woody 1929, 1: 464).

Most female teachers were forced to be satisfied with paltry wages, the vast majority earning less than half of a male teacher's salary at the time of the Civil War. Many women did not remain in the profession, most teaching only a few years while young and single, then resigning as soon as they married. From 1852 to 1862, women's rights leader SUSAN B. ANTHONY, a former teacher, attended state teachers' conventions in her home state of New York to urge women teachers to struggle for equal wages and equal opportunities in education. Progress in this area remained slow throughout the nineteenth century and into the twentieth. When wartime journalist GAIL HAMILTON was a teacher before the war, she voiced the sentiments of many mid-nineteenth-century women who left the profession, explaining, "As for wearing out my life, and soul, and brain, and lungs, in teaching and getting just enough to keep body and soul together, I won't do it any longer" (Woody 1929, 1: 490).

For other women, the rewards of teaching could not be measured monetarily. Many expressed their missionary zeal for the profession, believing that educating the young was doing God's work. The thousands of white and African-American women and men who were TEACHERS OF THE FREEDPEOPLE in the South and border states echoed this viewpoint.

A debate in the common school movement from its earliest years focused on the issue of the preparation of female teachers. Most agreed that women needed education beyond the elementary grades. During the Civil War, secondary education, with few exceptions, was not public. By 1860, there were only 40 public high schools offering secondary level coursework in the country. During the 1860s and 1870s, more urban communities struggled to establish high schools. By 1870, there were 160, and by 1880, approximately 800 nationwide (Woody 1929, 1: 545).

From 1830 through the 1870s, the most common secondary and higher education for girls and young women were private schools known as female seminaries. In the North, many seminary graduates became teachers. For the most part, only white middle-class girls in the North and elite and well-to-do middle-class students in the

South attended these schools. As far as upper-class students in the North and South were concerned, many continued to be tutored at home. Pioneering Northern educators Emma Hart Willard, Catherine Beecher, and Mary Lyon all founded female seminaries in the early to mid-nineteenth century. The success of their three institutions in the Northeast influenced educators across the nation to found similar private schools as well as public high schools.

Yet the female seminaries did more than train teachers. For the first time, they offered female students from ages 12 through 20 the opportunity to study subjects previously off limits to women, such as higher mathematics (geometry, trigonometry, algebra), the sciences, and Latin, subjects previously assumed to be too demanding of the less capable female mind and too taxing for the fragile female body. In addition to teaching the subjects taught to boys and young men in the academies and colleges, the seminaries continued to teach the disciplines formerly deemed appropriate for girls and young women: English grammar and composition, French and several other modern European languages, religion, history, the arts, health education, and domestic science (home economics).

In the South, female academies and seminaries were staffed largely by graduates of their Northern counterparts. Unlike Northern private schools, only the daughters of the most prosperous planters, farmers, merchants, and professionals could afford to attend. In the 1850s, numerous "female colleges" were founded in the South. These schools were either new institutions or were upgraded from the female academies and seminaries. Although the female colleges intended to provide collegiate instruction equal to the coursework in men's colleges, the Southern female colleges' curricula more closely resembled the education provided in Northern seminaries, with a few exceptions. Southern schools were unique in that they offered mandatory instruction in both Latin and Greek. In Southern society, knowledge of the classics was considered necessary to distinguish an elite man or woman. Southern educators believed that young men and women should study the Bible in the original Latin and Greek and that familiarity with the classical languages was critical to understanding the history of Western civilization (Farnham 1994, 2, 73).

Southern female colleges also required that students study rhetoric. Although women did not engage in debates and other forms of public oratory as male students did, girls and young women learned the principles of rhetoric and applied them to the writing of essays and compositions. Female students in the Southern schools were also permitted to give recitations at graduation ceremonies, whereas in the North, any form of public speaking for girls and women was considered taboo.

Unlike the Northern female seminaries, Southern schools did not prepare students for the teaching profession. For the most part, Southern women did not enter the teaching force in any sizable numbers until well after the Civil War. Without a career to prepare for, Southern students had little incentive to study or to graduate. Many girls attended only for a year or two and then left to marry. The goal of a

Southern girl's education, as one Alabama father explained to his daughter in 1858, was "the development of the girl into a *lady*, healthy in person, refined in feeling, pure in morals & humble in religion" (quoted in Farnham 1994, 120).

By the 1850s, Northern critics of the female seminaries in the North argued that their students, although taught most of the same subjects as young men, did not receive the same depth of instruction as provided in the men's colleges. As these voices became louder, a few new, more rigorous women's colleges emerged in the North and South, and the demand for coeducation became more insistent. The female seminaries, though popular through the 1870s, began to decline in importance in the 1860s as educational reformers struggled to found institutions that would provide the same level of instruction to women as men received in the best male colleges and universities. Although the female seminaries did not endure, they were immeasurably important to women's education as they proved to a dubious public that girls possessed the ability to succeed academically.

Many women's rights advocates of the 1850s, including ELIZABETH CADY STANTON and Susan B. Anthony, argued that women would never be educated as thoroughly as men until they were permitted to attend the same institutions. Oberlin College in Ohio, which admitted women students in 1837, was the first coeducational college. Others included Antioch College, also in Ohio, Knox College in Illinois, and Bates College in Maine, to name a few. Swarthmore College in Pennsylvania, founded by the liberal Hicksite Quakers in 1864, was committed to the principles of coeducation. At Swarthmore, men and women were equally represented on the board of managers (trustees) (Solomon 1985, 50–51). Yet in many of these institutions, women were not permitted to take the same courses as male students. They either attended separate classes or, if they were allowed to receive instruction sitting side by side with men, they were enrolled in separate "ladies" departments holding different, lower standards than those held by men. As a result, a woman's diploma frequently did not represent the same level of educational achievement as a man's.

The founding of state-funded universities in the 1850s opened up many more coeducational opportunities for women in higher education. Although a few state universities vowed to accept women during the years before the Civil War, only the University of Iowa made good on the promise, accepting both men and women when it opened its doors in 1855. In 1858, a new board of managers embraced a resolution to ban women, but in the end, despite the controversy, women were not excluded. In 1860, 30 women and 29 men attended lectures in the Normal Department (teacher-training program) at the University of Wisconsin. For the most part, women were relegated to the normal departments at the state universities during this era.

The Civil War expedited women's entrance into the state universities. As men left the classrooms to enlist, a number of universities, especially those located in the Midwest, accepted female students in ever-increasing numbers to fill the vacancies. The Morrill Land Grant Act of 1862 was another boon for women desiring higher education as the new law mandated the sale of public lands to provide each state with the means to support at least one college. (During the Civil War, the new law was only in effect in the Northern states.) Although the law was enacted so that instruction in agriculture and the industrial arts would be offered, the land-grant colleges and universities provided instruction in teacher-training and many other subjects as well. The law did not mention women, though the founding of additional publicly funded universities in every state resulted in more low-cost educational opportunities for women.

Women did not enter the state universities without male protest. At the University of Wisconsin, as at other coed institutions, women were tolerated as long as they were enrolled in separate departments. During the Civil War, men objected when women were permitted to take courses outside of the normal departments, a common policy while male enrollment was slight. They argued that women would "bring down the culture," diminishing the rigorous nature of the traditional male curriculum (Olin 1909, 32). In particular, men protested when women enrolled in the ancient Greek language course, a traditionally male discipline in the North.

The female seminaries did not provide all the teachers needed by the common schools, causing teacher shortages to continue. Beginning in the early to mid-nineteenth century, a few states established normal schools, public institutions devoted to teacher training. These schools of higher education offered collegiate instruction and teacher-training courses at a low cost, opening higher education to the less affluent. By the time of the Civil War, state normal schools were popular in the Northeast, Midwest, and West. In most of the schools, women formed two-thirds of the student body (Eisenmann 1998, 307). As mentioned previously, state universities and other colleges also opened normal departments in which women enrolled to train as teachers.

Immediately before and during the Civil War, public debate on women and higher education focused on the question of the desirability of women enrolling in the colleges. As this debate filled women's magazines and the rest of the popular press, Vassar College was in its initial stages of development. In January 1861, the New York State legislature issued a charter establishing Vassar Female College (the word female was dropped in 1866). Although the school would not be ready for students until the fall of 1865, the war years were spent preparing the institution to be the first of its kind—that is, the first women's college to offer a collegiate course truly equal to that given at the best men's colleges. As founder Matthew Vassar declared, Vassar was to be "an institution which should be to young women what Yale and Harvard are to young men" (D. Herman 1982, 8). As the first women's college to have an endowment, Vassar had the potential to live up to its promise. Female seminaries suffered from a chronic lack of funding, which resulted in their inability to expand and maintain their buildings and to provide the books and equipment that the wealthier boys' and men's schools took for granted.

John Howard Raymond, president of Vassar when its doors finally opened in September 1865, was fully aware of all that was at stake in this new collegiate experiment.

The college's opening received unprecedented attention in the press; all eyes were focused on the school located on 200 acres of farmland two miles east of Poughkeepsie, New York. In its first few days, Vassar, Raymond, and the faculty welcomed 353 students, ranging in age from 14 to 24 years. Raymond dealt with the public exposure by ruling Vassar with extra caution. Strict rules structured every waking moment of each student's day, as was the practice in the female seminaries. Rest periods, exercise schedules, and study hours were rigidly adhered to so that no student would overtax herself and become ill from the workload, thereby drawing attention from critics.

Raymond and his corps of professors and instructors encountered their first serious obstacle within weeks of the college's opening. The results of entrance examinations demonstrated that two-thirds to three-quarters of the student body were not prepared for the level of collegiate instruction that Raymond and his faculty were ready to administer. Because the college could not afford to turn students away, a preparatory department was established. As the years passed, and as the secondary schools better prepared students for college, the numbers of students requiring preparatory instruction decreased.

The earliest students at Vassar fully realized that they were at the center of a highly publicized experiment. President Raymond and the faculty repeatedly told them that their actions—their success or failure—would decide "the educational fate of future generations of women." As Raymond told them, "the honor of the college was in their hands." Mary Norris, a member of the second class to enter Vassar, remembered that her fellow students wished "to accomplish something for humanity which would prove how good a thing it was to give a college education to women" (D. Herman 1982, 52).

Vassar Female College and its student body did not fail. Vassar and most of the endowed women's colleges founded in the years to follow proved that women could master an education as challenging as that offered at the best men's colleges. These successes led to the establishment of additional women's colleges and increased the enrollment of women in all coeducational institutions.

See also **Coppin, Fanny Jackson; Dickey, Sarah; Forten, Charlotte; Girlhood and Adolescence; Mitchell, Maria**

Selected Readings

Eisenmann, Linda, ed. *Historical Dictionary of Women's Education in the United States*. Westport, CT: Greenwood Press. 1998

Farnham, Christie Anne. *The Education of the Southern Belle: Higher Education and Student Socialization in the Antebellum South*. New York: New York University Press. 1994.

Solomon, Barbara Miller. *In the Company of Educated Women: A History of Women and Higher Education in America*. New Haven: Yale University Press. 1985.

Etheridge, Annie (c. 1839–1913)

During the Civil War and throughout the rest of the nineteenth century, Annie Blair Etheridge was the best-known and most celebrated woman attached to the Union army. For four years, she worked as a nurse and as a daughter of the regiment for several regiments of Michigan infantry. Soldiers and officers of all ranks venerated her and praised her courage, humility, endurance, gentleness, and kindness. Blair Etheridge spent much of the war on the frontlines by nursing on the battlefields and in the field hospitals. Despite her gentle demeanor, she could be tough when the occasion warranted. In the midst of battle, she rode through the ranks, her skirts pockmarked by bullet holes, exhorting the soldiers to fight on against the enemy at times when their strength was flagging. Blair Etheridge's record of military service is particularly striking because she was on the frontlines during many of the bloodiest, most brutal battles of the war. According to officers' and soldiers' accounts, regardless of the intensity of the shellfire and cannon bombardment, she steadfastly prevailed, bringing bandages and nourishment to fallen soldiers on the battlefields. Her extraordinary bravery in the heat of battle was officially acknowledged when she was awarded the Kearny Cross in May 1863, a medal named for Union Major General Philip Kearny, who was killed at the Battle of Chantilly (Virginia) in September 1862.

The details of Blair Etheridge's childhood are not clear. The evidence suggests that Lorinda Anna "Annie" Blair was born in Detroit, Michigan, between the years 1832 to 1844. Considering that Annie's age was recorded as 11 years in the 1850 census, it seems likely that she was born in 1838 or 1839. Some sources indicate that her father provided a comfortable lifestyle for his family while Blair was a child, though his occupation is not identified. According to these writers, her father suffered a financial reversal at about the time she entered adolescence. Another source maintains that he earned a living as a blacksmith. In any event, it seems clear that Blair spent her childhood living in Michigan, Wisconsin, and perhaps Minnesota.

Although the date and length of Blair's first marriage to David Kellogg has not been uncovered, in 1860 she was married a second time to James Etheridge. In the spring of 1861, when her husband joined the 2nd Michigan Infantry, Blair Etheridge enlisted with him, although not as a soldier. Unlike many MILITARY WOMEN, she never attempted to conceal her female identity. According to a postwar volume memorializing the contributions of women to the Union war effort, 19 women signed on as regimental nurses with the 2nd Michigan when it was first mustered. At the end of a few months, only Blair Etheridge remained, the rest having returned home because of illness, exhaustion, or from the realization that they were unsuited for the labor expected of them (Moore 1866, 514). At some point during the ensuing months, her husband deserted the regiment. This time she did not follow him. She left the 2nd Michigan, and became attached to the 3rd Michigan Infantry, where she was named its daughter of the regiment. She served with the soldiers and officers of the 3rd Michigan for three years.

Blair Etheridge's first engagement was the skirmish at Blackburn's Ford, on July 18, 1861, near Centreville, Virginia. During the First Battle of Bull Run (known in the South as the First Battle of Manassas) on July 21, her regiment was ordered to wait in the rear of the units who were actively fighting. She weathered combat on the frontlines in the Battle of Williamsburg in May 1862, and in the Second Battle of Bull Run (Second Battle of Manassas) in late August 1862, both in Virginia.

At some point in 1862, perhaps due to a commanding general's directive prohibiting women from the frontlines, Blair Etheridge joined UNITED STATES SANITARY COMMISSION (USSC) nurses on the HOSPITAL SHIPS operating during the Union offensive known as the Peninsula Campaign (Virginia). While a member of the USSC's Hospital Transport Service, she is reported to have nursed wounded and ill soldiers on such steamships as the *Knickerbocker*, the *Louisiana*, and the *Daniel Webster*.

After several months working on the "floating hospitals," Blair Etheridge was permitted to return to the 3rd Michigan. Following the Second Battle of Bull Run, she cared for the wounded at the Battle of Antietam (known in the South as the Battle of Sharpsburg) in Maryland on September 17, 1862, and in December during and after the Battle of Fredericksburg (Virginia). While in camp between battles, Blair Etheridge is known to have cooked for her regiment, in addition to attending to her nursing duties.

In May 1863, at the Battle of Chancellorsville (Virginia), she is remembered by one soldier as having distributed coffee and hard tack to famished troops braving a barrage of shellfire. Although officers demanded that she report to the rear and take cover, she finished her self-appointed task, her facial expression and composure showing no recognition of the danger she was in, as was characteristic of her (Conklin 1993, 96). She worked tirelessly while under fire throughout the length of that battle despite being shot in the hand, the only time she was wounded throughout the war. At the end of May, in recognition of her valor at Chancellorsville and other battles, Union Brigadier General David B. Birney honored her with the Kearny Cross.

Blair Etheridge was with her regiment all through the BATTLE OF GETTYS-BURG (Pennsylvania) in 1863. Two weeks later, she traveled alongside the troops to

New York City when the 3rd Michigan assisted in the army's effort to extinguish the citizens' rebellion known as the New York DRAFT RIOTS.

In Virginia in May 1864, she endured the most vicious combat of the war during the Battle of the Wilderness, the two-week-long Battle of Spotsylvania Court House, and, in early June, the Battle of Cold Harbor. In July 1864, following Union Lieutenant General Ulysses S. Grant's order that officers exclude women from the frontlines, Blair Etheridge left the 3rd Michigan to nurse at a Union military hospital in City Point, Virginia. When the 3rd Michigan disbanded during the latter half of 1864, she eventually transferred her services to the 5th Michigan Infantry. Precisely when she joined the 5th Michigan after serving at City Point is not clear, although it is known that she remained with this regiment until it was mustered out in July 1865.

After the war, Blair Etheridge was awarded a coveted position as a clerk in the U.S. Pension Office in Washington, DC. In 1870, she wed a fellow war veteran, Charles E. Hooks. Congress authorized a $25 per month pension for her in 1886, acknowledging her service as a "daughter of the regiment." When she died in 1913, she was buried in Arlington National Cemetery.

See also **Camp Life**

Selected Readings

Conklin, E. F. *Women at Gettysburg 1863*. Gettysburg, PA: Thomas Publications. 1993.

Leonard, Elizabeth D. *All the Daring of the Soldier: Women of the Civil War Armies*. New York: Penguin Books. 2001.

Evans, Augusta Jane (1835–1909)

Augusta Jane Evans, novelist and ardent Southern nationalist, was the celebrated author of *Macaria, or Altars of Sacrifice*, the novel that became the literary sensation of the Confederacy. Throughout the Civil War, Evans struggled to make an invaluable contribution to the Confederate cause. Of all her efforts, her runaway best-seller *Macaria* came closest to fulfilling her goal as this novel succeeded in broadcasting to a mass audience her nationalistic vision of a woman's role in the fight for Southern independence.

Evans was born in 1835 in Columbus, Georgia, the daughter of a prosperous businessman. She and her family migrated to Texas in 1845, several years after her father's bankruptcy. Traveling by covered wagon, the family eventually settled in San Antonio. Her family's trials on the frontier and their experiences living in the midst of the Mexican-American War contributed to her inspiration to write her first novel, a project she began when she was 15 years old. By this time, her family had moved to Mobile, Alabama. *Inez: A Tale of the Alamo* was published five years later in 1855. With the publication of her second novel, *Beulah*, in 1859, Evans became a wealthy celebrity.

In 1860, in the midst of the emerging drama of secession, Evans backed out of her engagement to a New York journalist. She had met her fiancé while in New York visiting her publisher. As the secession crisis and her allegiance to the cause of Southern nationalism deepened, she found the prospect of marriage to a pro-Union Lincoln supporter untenable.

Upon hearing the news of Alabama's secession on January 11, 1861, she rushed to Montgomery, the state capital, to join in the gala celebrations. Days later, back in Mobile, Evans threw herself into local war work. She organized a group of women to construct sandbags for the defense of the city's Gulf coastline, gave patriotic speeches to mustering regiments, established a hospital for the wounded, and worked tirelessly as a nurse, in spite of the protests of her brothers. All through the war she penned articles of rousing Confederate propaganda for newspapers and magazines and sent stirring letters to the editor, many of them signed anonymously.

Despite her heroic contributions, she was plagued by a persistent sense of her own uselessness. She was frustrated that all her war work could never match the sacrifices of the Confederate soldiers. Yet, unlike the vast majority of her Northern and Southern female contemporaries who undervalued their war work, Evans recognized that her contributions had political value. Even though she perceived herself as being isolated on the periphery of the Confederacy, she voiced her opinions in her articles with aplomb and verve, and she confidently embarked on a regular correspondence with Confederate General P. G. T. Beauregard and other prominent officials.

Although Evans had only disdain for Northern advocates of the women's rights movement, in reality what she rejected was the stereotyped image of Northern feminists popularized in the Southern press. Although she always upheld traditional roles for women, Evans had more in common with active, patriotic Northern women than she would have tolerated admitting. For one thing, Evans saw no reason why women's domestic lives could not be expanded so that women could give their country the labor and the support it so desperately needed.

In the midst of her frustrated quest, Evans began work on a new novel *Macaria, or Altars of Sacrifice.* Just as Macaria, the daughter of Heracles in Greek mythology, rescued war-ravaged Athens by offering her life as a sacrifice to the gods, so the heroines of Evans's novel devoted themselves to war work for the Confederacy, finding spiritual and personal fulfillment on the way. Evans spared no effort in the research of *Macaria.* She wrote to General Beauregard in March of 1863 to confirm the details of the First Battle of Manassas (First Battle of Bull Run). Overcome by artistic and political inspiration, she wrote the novel, often while sitting by the bedsides of wounded soldiers.

Macaria, Evans's tribute to Confederate nationalism, was published in Richmond in 1864. Her political agenda to revitalize Southerners' dwindling patriotism uppermost in her mind, Evans dedicated the novel to "The Army of the Southern Confederacy, who have delivered the South from despotism, and who have won for generations yet unborn the precious guerdon of constitutional republican liberty." She concluded the lengthy dedication, writing,

> These pages are gratefully and reverently dedicated by one who, although debarred from the dangers and deathless glory of the "tented field," would fain offer a woman's inadequate tribute to the noble patriotism and sublime self-abnegation of her dear and devoted countrymen. (Evans 1992, frontispiece)

Although no more than a half-dozen books were published in the Confederacy during the war, *Macaria* became the leader among them, selling over 20,000 copies. A copy of the book was smuggled into New York City via a blockade runner and soon became a best-seller. When a Union general banned *Macaria* among his troops, it spurred the determination of his soldiers to read it, a feat many of them managed, despite the order.

After the war, Evans burned with the desire to write the consummate history of the Confederacy, a work that she hoped would immortalize the Confederate cause for all time. She dropped the project when she learned that the former vice president of the Confederacy, Alexander Stephens, planned a similar volume. Although she yielded to his greater claim to authorship of a Confederate history, to her mind, it was not only his superior political authority that disqualified her. In a letter to Beauregard, Evans admitted that her gender was a major obstacle.

> I humbly put my fingers on the throat of my ambitious daring design of becoming the Confederate Xenophon and strangled it …. I confess it cost me a severe struggle to relinquish the fond dream … but abler hands snatched it from my weak womanly fingers and waved me to humbler paths of labor. (Evans 1992, xxvi)

Evans willingly bowed down to the edicts of "women's sphere" and returned to the sanctioned female activity of writing domestic fiction, but it is unlikely that she considered her fingers or her abilities weak. Her comments to Beauregard contained more hyperbole than an accurate reflection of her self-opinion. *St. Elmo* was published in 1867, which, of all her books, sold the most copies. In 1868, she married Colonel Lorenzo Madison Wilson, a man 27 years older. Over the course of the next 35 years, she wrote five additional novels and volunteered her time to numerous charities and to memorializing the Confederate dead. She died at the age of 74 in May 1909.

See also **Literary Women; Patriotism; Secession**

Selected Readings

Evans, Augusta Jane. *Macaria, or Altars of Sacrifice.* Edited by Drew Gilpin Faust. 1864. Reprinted. Baton Rouge: Louisiana State University Press. 1992.

Faust, Drew Gilpin. *Mothers of Invention: Women of the Slaveholding South in the American Civil War.* New York: Vintage Books. 1997.

Fox-Genovese, Elizabeth. "Evans, Augusta Jane." In *Encyclopedia of the Confederacy.* Vol. 1. Edited by Richard N. Current. New York: Simon & Schuster. 1993.

F

Family Life

Family life was of supreme importance to nineteenth-century Americans of all races and social classes. Husbands and wives, and parents and children, looked to the family for nurturance and support in a world that was often perceived as cold and hostile. For white and African-American families of the North and South, children were the focus of family life, and couples were eager to start their families soon after marriage. Fathers and mothers were equally invested in the upbringing of their children, although mothers shouldered most of the burdens of daily childcare.

Nineteenth-century white middle-class Americans looked upon the home as a refuge, a place where parents and children could reside together in safety and harmony, away from the pressing problems of the society at large. It was the role of the women of the family to cultivate the home so that it was a restful and pleasing place. It was the duty of the menfolk to brave the harsh, competitive environment of the work world and to earn the income necessary to maintain the home and provide for the family. Children were instructed to obey their parents, learn their lessons, and mature into responsible, moral adults. In spite of the challenges of each family member's role, families expected to enjoy being together at home. Evenings were a particularly cherished time for the entire family to come together. Parents and children took pleasure in reading aloud from newspapers, magazines, and books; playing games; playing music and singing hymns and popular songs; and sharing hobbies. Many families—both Protestant and Catholic—spent part of this evening time reciting prayers. Protestant fathers often read passages from the Bible. In their letters home, fathers in the Union and Confederate militaries frequently reminisced about the time spent at home with their families. They wrote of their longing to be at home with their loved ones and their desire to spend time by the fireside in the evenings talking, reading, and playing with their children (Marten 1998, 69).

The Civil War tore at the tightly woven fabric of mid-nineteenth-century families as husbands and fathers enlisted in the Union and Confederate militaries, abandoning their loved ones, sometimes for years at a time. The lengthy separations deeply affected children's relationships with their mothers and fathers. By necessity, mothers assumed command of all childrearing and, for the most part, made all the decisions concerning children's daily care, discipline, and education. Fathers of the North and South struggled to maintain their relationships with their children by mail, devoting hours to the responsibility of long-distance parenting. White and African-American families in the South suffered from threats that did not affect Northern families. Southern children not only lost their fathers to the army, but also suffered from INVASION AND OCCUPATION, homelessness, and unsettled lives as REFUGEES.

Reproduction and Birth Control

For mid-nineteenth-century husbands and wives, sexuality was interwoven with concerns about reproduction. Birth control and contraceptive methods, although known and practiced by many married couples of this period, were far from reliable. Although both men and women involved themselves with family planning, women especially found the prospect of pregnancy a never-ending source of concern. As ardent as some mid-nineteenth-century husbands and wives were about expressing their love sexually, no couple could evade the ever-present possibility of pregnancy.

Over the course of the nineteenth century, families decreased in size. The fertility of white American women dropped 50 percent from 1800 to 1900, a huge decrease. The total fertility rate (the average number of children born to a woman) dropped from 7.04 in 1800 to 3.56 in 1900 (Degler 1980, 181). Raising fewer children meant that parents could invest more time and resources on each child. Most historians agree that this decline, which began very early in the century, was a result of the decrease in the availability of land suitable for agriculture. With fewer acres of arable land to leave to one's children, men and women tended to marry later than they had in the eighteenth century, thereby limiting the number of years a married woman could bear children. Women, however, also stopped giving birth to children at an earlier age than in years past, which also served to limit family size. To bring about this change, married couples had to use some form of birth control (Degler 1980, 182, 184).

Although no one knows for certain how mid-nineteenth-century white middle-class and upper-class couples limited the size of their families, numerous methods of birth control were available. Abstinence was a common practice, and one that was well accepted throughout the North and South. Women nursed their children for as long as possible in an attempt to delay additional pregnancies. Contraceptives were another form of birth control that was becoming increasingly popular by mid-century. A wide array of marriage advice manuals provided instructions on the uses of a variety of contraceptives. Condoms, though expensive, were readily available during the Civil War. Diaphragms, though not widespread, were available at mid-century as were vaginal sponges and vaginal syringes. The birth control manuals, many written by doctors, also explained how women could restrict sexual intercourse to the so-called "safe period" in their menstrual cycles to avoid pregnancy. Perhaps the most popular form of birth control at the time of the Civil War was coitus interruptus, in which the man removes his penis from the woman's vagina prior to ejaculation (D'Emilio and Freedman 1988, 59). Although these methods may have worked well for some couples, none were so reliable that they guaranteed a woman's freedom from pregnancy.

Why did husbands and wives seek to limit the size of their families? By mid-century, women and men were recognizing that women had a right to be released from the exhausting burden of bearing children year after year if she so chose. Yet women were not alone in wanting smaller families. Both fathers and mothers wished to devote their love and resources to fewer children. Because many forms of birth control relied on male cooperation (condom, coitus interruptus, and the "safe period"), it appears that husbands were as willing as women to curtail the number of their offspring (Degler 1980, 208). For many middle-class parents, educating their children and giving them a proper start in life was the family's top priority.

Northern middle- and upper-class white men and women were the groups most concerned with restricting the size of their families. In the South and in frontier regions of the West, the fertility of white women was much higher than in the North. Southern elite and middle-class white couples appear to have resorted to abstinence as their primary form of birth control. Contraceptives were not widely used at mid-century in the South and it is unclear to what extent contraceptive information and devices were available to Southern men and women (D. Faust 1997, 124). In the North and South, immigrant women and poor white women had higher fertility rates than native-born and middle-class women respectively.

During the Civil War, many soldiers' wives tried to avoid pregnancy. The evidence also suggests that women's fear of childbearing (always an issue in an era when it was not uncommon to die as a result of childbirth) increased during the war years, particularly for women whose husbands were far from home. For these wives, a husband's furlough produced a mixture of joyous and anxious moments. Lizzie Neblett of Texas explained the dilemma to her husband, Will, in this way: "This constant & never ceasing horror I have of childbearing constantly obtrudes itself between me & my desire . . . & thus my longing wears a curb" (quoted in D. Faust 1997, 124). Lizzie insisted that Will bring plenty of "preventives" with him when he returned home if he hoped to have any intimate moments with her. Equally perplexing for some military wives was a husband's request to visit him in camp. Confederate General William Dorsey Pender understood his wife's reluctance. He wrote to her, "if you do not want children you will have to remain away from me, and hereafter when you come to me I shall know that you want another baby" (quoted in Degler 1980, 223).

For women who did give birth while their husbands were away, the stress, fear, and loneliness could be overwhelming. Harriet Perry of east Texas wrote her husband, Theophilus, an officer in the Confederate army, of her terror as the birth of her second child drew near.

> I feel very anxious and concerned about myself being here alone at this time. I cannot sleep at night—I experience daily & nightly all the horrors of giving birth to an infant in mind .... I dread it much more, for I know now how bad it is—my being alone is worst still .... Heaven only knows what will become of me. I pray its deliverance & protection. Oh if you were with me, this trying time would be robbed of half its fears & terrors.

About four weeks later she added, "I do hope & pray I never shall be in this condition again. Death is nearly preferable" (Perry 2000, 51, 67).

Southern white women were accustomed to having their husbands by their sides while they endured the trials of childbirth and was another key reason why they may have wished to avoid pregnancy during wartime. (D. Faust 1997, 128). For mothers of small children struggling to manage their households and farms or businesses alone, the possibility of another child to care for was most unwelcome and for some, a frightening prospect. Some Southern women worried about giving birth to additional children while food was so scarce in the Confederacy. And in both the North and South, soldiers' wives were concerned about bringing a fatherless child into the world while others fretted that their deaths in childbirth might orphan their children.

In the mid-nineteenth century, abortion was becoming an increasingly common form of birth control for married couples. White, African-American, and Native American women of all social classes, both single and married, resorted to abortion, using a wide variety of techniques, not all of which were effective. Drugs and mild poisons were especially common methods by which women tried to abort their pregnancies. By the time of the Civil War, segments of the population were becoming so concerned about abortion that there was more and more of an outcry against it. By the early 1860s, a number of states had passed anti-abortion legislation, which did not halt the practice. Many doctors deplored it, though others readily performed abortions. In 1867, writing for an audience of doctors in the *Detroit Review of Medicine and Pharmacy*, an outspoken abortion critic declared, "Among married persons ... so extensive has this practice become, that people of high repute not only commit this crime, but do not even shun to speak boastingly among their intimates, of the deed and the means of accomplishing it" (quoted in Degler 1980, 229).

Childrearing

In the nineteenth century, both fathers and mothers devoted loving and nurturing attention toward their children as families became more child-centered than in the past. With most fathers working outside the home, mothers performed the bulk of the actual labor of childrearing and childcare. Even though men were absent for much of the time, they were involved in making decisions about their children's upbringing and education. In fact, many nineteenth-century fathers were the ultimate authority on their children's academic and moral educations. Children's religious instruction, however, was primarily the mother's concern.

Well-educated middle-class mothers taught their children and assisted them with their studies, but fathers performed this role as well, as their time permitted. Early in the nineteenth century, women were unable to help their children to learn much more than the basics in reading, writing, and arithmetic due to women's lack of educational opportunities. By mid-century, many white middle-class women of the North and South had received sufficient education to enable them to teach their children a broader array of subject matter.

Mid-nineteenth-century white parents regularly consulted the popular parental advice literature of the day. Most of these manuals were written primarily for mothers, though fathers consulted them, too (Rose 1992, 172). As far as discipline was concerned, the nineteenth century heralded an era when corporal punishment, including whippings and beatings, was no longer the preferred method of discipline. Parents still resorted to physical punishment, but, in general, it was viewed as a method to employ when all other means had failed. Nineteenth-century mothers were more likely to use shame to control their children. Parents also tried to instill guilt in their children to eliminate undesirable behaviors. Withholding food was another common method of punishment. According to British observers and other European travelers to the United States, American parents were noteworthy for their indulgence of their children, in contrast to the stricter, harsher methods of raising children in Europe (Degler 1980, 89–95).

The Civil War had a profound impact on childrearing as fathers enlisted in the military were not available to assist their wives or to guide their children. The full load of responsibility for children rested on the mothers' shoulders. In addition to their regular domestic duties and their new role as farm or business managers, women now had to be both father and mother. They had to make all the decisions concerning their children and superintend all discipline. For many women in the South and North, the responsibilities were a crushing burden.

Fathers in both the Union and Confederate militaries kept their parental bonds strong through the letters they wrote to their children. Fathers gave advice by mail and insisted that their children be well behaved, obey and assist their mothers, and study their lessons well. Husbands did not hesitate to direct their wives on the use of discipline methods, providing instructions that were sometimes difficult for women to carry out. Some women found they managed best when following their own instincts and devising their own discipline strategies. Fathers' letters were also full of love and affection and included stories about military life and battles won and lost. They also imparted wisdom about moral and political issues (Marten 1998, 70, 94).

Wives likewise kept their husbands fully informed about their children's growth and progress, describing in detail their children's antics and sayings. M. E. King of Danville, Texas, wrote her Confederate soldier husband, "Oh Adam I would give the world for you to see you baby this morning Adam he is the sweetest child you ever seen he says tell his papa to come home and bring him that yankee gun" (Soldiers'

Letters Collection, Texas Women Folder, Museum of the Confederacy). Esther Thayer of Warren, Vermont, reported to her husband about their children's doings.

> i am agoin to git Sister a litle Chare I don't know but you will think it is folish but she takes so much confort when she is to Reubins that i thout that i would git one . Sister fedes her self to the table Wille and Libby are runing and holring as loud as tha Can Burty is at scool Willy ses tell Father to send a leter and a Kiss to him he kiss this for Father so good by for this time. (quoted in Marshall 1999, 131–132)

Mothers struggled to keep the home a tranquil sanctuary from the world despite their additional responsibilities and anxieties. They tried to maintain rituals and routines, gathering their children together in the evening for prayers and Bible readings and for letter-writing sessions to Father. Children helped mothers with their work for the war effort, knitting socks, scraping lint, and collecting food and other items for soldiers. Especially in the South, in regions that endured Union invasions, women found that maintaining a semblance of family life was sometimes more than they could accomplish. Children in these situations suffered, taking on their mothers' anxieties and fears for the future.

Eliza Fain of East Tennessee confided to her diary that her efforts to juggle all of her husband's roles and her regular domestic duties left her feeling she was failing at all of them: "I often feel so cast down, my family large, my anxiety for their worldly comfort often causes me to feel so depressed feeling ever my great lack as a managing housewife." As sorely as the extra workload taxed her, Fain did not beg her husband to leave the army and return home as some wives of Confederate soldiers believed was necessary. She makes her sacrifice clear, however, and reveals that her religious faith is the force that enables her to stand firm.

> I do not want him to resign if he is useful to his country as I hope and believe he is. I feel it is important for everyone to stand firm and unshaken at his post. I do trust that wisdom may be given from God my Heavenly Father to him who is my earthly stay to enable him to do that which is best for him to do. (quoted in Stowell 2000, 158)

Many women reported that their children were a comfort to them while their husbands were away, despite the extra workload (D. Faust 1997, 129). Children, with their ever-present needs, provided a distraction from the loneliness and the uncertainties that went along with having a husband away at war.

The letters of mothers of enlisted sons make clear the extent of women's motherly influence on their children, even when their sons were no longer under their roofs. Mothers of Union and Confederate soldiers worried that military life would corrupt their sons and undo the moral and religious instruction that they (the mothers) had so painstakingly instilled. Women knew they were powerless to keep their families intact when a war was at hand, but they could use the mail to bring their homes closer to their loved ones. Jerusha H. Hubbard of Whiting, Vermont, lectured her son Franklin in a lengthy letter written in February 1862.

Do not I beg of you seek the company of the rough, the profane, the intemperate the gambler or any other immoral person, but seek the society of those who will exert a good influence over you Oh Frank I have many fears for you. I dread the influence of a camp life over you … remember that it is very important you keep yourself your body and clothes as clean as possible. change your shirts often be particular about this if you wish to keep well. Wash your body often… . (Marshall 1999, 62)

During the Civil War, slave families were embroiled in a constant struggle to survive. As the war brought the hope of freedom closer to home, it also carried disruption, chaos, separation, and tragedy to families. Whether on the plantations, in the cities, or on the road and in camps as CONTRABAND WOMEN, slave women's days were focused on finding food, clothing, and shelter for their children while they also endeavored to keep their families intact.

Although slave families on plantations were insulated from the war's ravages for a time, they were eventually vulnerable to the hardships wrought by Union invasion. As the prospect of invasion drew closer, white slaveholders fled to the interior—southward and westward—separating slave families by taking only their most valued slaves with them. The remainder, usually women and children, were left behind or were abandoned en route to fend for themselves. These fatherless families then attempted to escape to the North or to Union encampments while trying to evade Confederate soldiers and white men eager to reenslave or abuse them.

Like white women of the North and South, many slave women were left to raise their children on their own when their husbands went to war or when white planters drove their menfolk to more secure locations. The Confederate military separated families when it impressed slave men to build fortifications and bridges. Families were torn apart when slaveholders ordered slave men to join them when they enlisted in the Confederate military. Other male slaves ran away to enlist in the Union military, while still others were coerced into the Union army in the wake of Union invasion (Krowl 2000, 37). With their children in tow, slave women whose husbands joined the Union military, hastened to rejoin them in shantytowns outside of the military camps. Those who remained in the Confederacy and did not follow their husbands were subject to the brutal treatment of whites, who punished the families for the "disloyalty" of their menfolk. White planters pushed them off the plantations, refused to give them food and clothing, and physically abused them (Bardaglio 1992, 225). Wherever white Union officers were reluctant to permit contraband family encampments, African-American soldiers pressed their commanders to allow them to exist, thereby securing their families' safety. Free black families of the South suffered many of the same trials and dangers as slave families as the Confederate military and unscrupulous white slave traders did not always discriminate between slave and free men during roundups.

During the later years of the war and after, former slave women traveled enormous distances to try to reunite their families. Husbands and wives legalized their marriages so that no governmental authority could separate them again. Immediately after the war, former slave men and women fought to retain custody of their children, often unsuccessfully, when the so-called "apprentice laws" in some Southern states permitted former slaveholders to force the young sons and daughters of former slaves to work the plantations.

Like white families of the North and South, African-American families looked forward to the postwar years as a time to strengthen family relationships and connections. For black families especially, the family was to become the solid, unshakable institution that helped African-American men, women, and children brave the harshness and cruelties of the postwar South and North.

See also **Courtship and Marriage; Girlhood and Adolescence; Slavery and Emancipation**

Selected Readings

Degler, Carl N. At Odds: *Women and the Family in America from the Revolution to the Present*. New York: Oxford University Press. 1980.
D'Emilio, John and Estelle B. Freedman. *Intimate Matters: A History of Sexuality in America*. New York: Harper. 1988.

Fern, Fanny (1811–1872)

From the mid-1850s until 1872, Fanny Fern was one of the most popular newspaper writers in the United States. When Fern agreed to write a weekly column for the *New York Ledger* in 1855, she gained national celebrity and became the first salaried female newspaper columnist to write a regularly published newspaper opinion piece in the United States. Focusing primarily on women's rights, the institution of marriage, and myriad social issues of interest to both genders, Fern had a writing style that was fresh, bold, candid, and sharply satirical, so much so that her critics frequently lambasted her for being unsexed and devoid of the feminine graces. No matter how much she was criticized, Fern unequivocally spoke her mind and acquired a huge following in the process. Above all, she wanted women to be independent and to rebel against the constraints that society placed on them. Although the *New York Ledger* was firmly apolitical, during the Civil War, Fern's columns grappled with issues relating to the conflict. She particularly championed women who were struggling to survive on the home front.

Fanny Fern was born Sara Payson Willis in Portland, Maine. Her father, Nathaniel Willis, moved his family to Boston shortly after her birth to engage in the printing trade. In 1816, he established the *Recorder*, one of the first religious newspapers in the United States. In 1827, he launched the *Youth's Companion*, the first periodical published expressly for children. As an older child and as a young woman, Sara assisted her father by proofreading and writing for his publications. Spirited, intelligent, and acknowledged by her elders to be incorrigibly irrepressible, she attended noted educator Catharine Beecher's Hartford Female Seminary in Hartford, Connecticut. After completing her education, she returned home to Boston to help her mother manage the family household and to work for her father.

Sara married Charles H. Eldredge in 1837, and bore three daughters in the late 1830s and early 1840s. When Eldredge died in 1846, she was left in dire financial circumstances. When her father and her husband's parents assisted her only partially, she felt obligated to marry again to relieve her economic distress. Her marriage to Samuel P. Farrington in 1849 proved to be a disaster. When she left him in 1851, her family was horrified at the scandal she brought on herself and the Willis family. Consequently, she received no assistance from her relations and, with two daughters (her firstborn had died in 1845), was forced to become self-supporting. As soon as she found inexpensive lodging in Boston, she peddled her essays from one newspaper editor to the next. Within a year, she was writing between five to ten opinion pieces for two small Boston papers and earning $6 a week. During this time, she began using the byline "Fanny Fern."

In 1853, Fern's earnings more than doubled when she was hired to write for the *Musical World and Times* in New York City. Her income increased when three separate volumes of her collected newspaper columns were published in 1853 and 1854. She ceased newspaper writing when she signed a contract to write a novel in 1854. In nine months' time she produced *Ruth Hall*, the semi-autobiographical story of a young, ambitious, once-married woman who overcomes great hardship and defies societal restrictions hindering the freedom of enterprising women wishing to achieve wealth and independence.

Her novel *Ruth Hall*, her serialized novella "Fanny Ford," and her second novel, *Rose Clark*, all enjoyed popular success, though the critics wrote scathing reviews. She was criticized for her failure to draw female protagonists who epitomized the cultural mandate that women be submissive, pious, and seek the protection of men while remaining safely ensconced in the domestic world of "women's sphere."

Fern resumed her work for newspapers when she agreed to write regularly for the *New York Ledger* in 1855. She enjoyed the accolades from her readership much more than the scorn the literary critics lavished on her novels. When she began writing for the *Ledger* at $100 a column, she was earning more than any other newspaper writer at the time. Phenomenally popular, less than a year after Fern was hired to write for the *Ledger*, the paper's circulation gained more than 100,000 readers. In 1856, Fern created a sensation when she married the author and biographer James Parton, a man 11 years her junior.

In the pages of the *Ledger*, Fern came into her own as a columnist, concentrating on women's rights and other topics of concern to women, while also reflecting on pressing social issues that few writers—male or female—dared to address: the squalor of New York City's slums, the predicament of women forced into prostitution because of their inability to find jobs that paid a living wage, sexually transmitted diseases, prison reform, and the failure of social reform to effect change in society. Fern urged her middle-class female readers to grasp as much independence as they could achieve in their lives, to educate themselves and their daughters, and to read and write. She criticized and often lampooned the married male, exposing what she perceived as the most common male presumptions, pretensions, and thoughtlessness creating inequalities in the marital relationship.

Within the first few months of the Civil War, Fern embraced the patriotism sweeping the North. In June 1861, she chastised men who chose not to enlist, calling their masculinity into question.

> We have no words to express our disgust … of the spectacle of a young man thus yawning away existence… . His well knit limbs should be encased in a petticoat, and a subscription should be immediately raised to present him with a sewing-machine, unless, indeed the *steel* used in the machinery should be objectionable to his sensitive organization. (quoted in Warren 1992, 241)

When Northern men were drafted after passage of the Conscription Act of 1863, she had nothing but contempt for men who bought their way out of the Union army, paying either the $300 mandated or hiring a substitute. In a later column on the subject, she wished she'd been called upon to serve.

> "Don't you think it wrong for a *woman* to hold up her hands for war?" she imagined being asked. She answered frankly, "Bless you, not I; I enjoy the fight; I am only sorry that, being a woman, I am necessarily counted out. You wouldn't catch me hiring a `substitute': in fact, you couldn't get a substitute for *me*." (quoted in Sizer 2000, 134)

In 1863, Fern voiced her frustration that propriety prevented her, as a woman, from directly interviewing soldiers about their experiences. In 1864, however, came the opportunity she had been seeking. While visiting Union Major General Benjamin Butler at Fortress Monroe in Virginia, she toured the frontlines with Union Brigadier

General William Birney, spoke with the wounded in the army hospital, and talked with Union soldiers who had been prisoners of war. Her experiences reinforced her patriotic fervor and her sense that the war was worth fighting. In her column of September 17, 1864, she blasted Northern men who called for an end to the war for economic reasons, and who, by doing so, failed to appreciate all that the Union had sacrificed.

> I have little patience with your "men of today," who, with no thought or care for the future of their children or their country, seeing only the increased cost of living and increased taxation … clamor like grown-up babies for "peace" … as if a country that was worth living in was not worth fighting for; as if more than three years of battling, two hundred and fifty thousand lives, and four thousand million of dollars, were to have their finale in inglorious subjection to rebeldom. The men who hold these views, whether in Wall Street or behind drygoods-counters, in pulpits or in colleges, had better go home and tend the babies while the women finish the fighting. (quoted in Warren 1992, 253–254)

In numerous columns, Fern praised the bravery of women laboring on the home front. She revealed the problems of soldiers' wives who raised their children in poverty while trying to survive on the pittance the federal government paid their husbands. Fern also emphasized that the war created unprecedented opportunities for women to broaden their horizons beyond their domiciles. As many women stepped forth into public life, she argued, they were removing the major obstacle that men claimed should bar them from the ballot: "want of intelligence." The war and its impact on women's lives had made Fern confident about one fact: "… this war won't leave *women* where it found them, whatever may be said of *men*" (quoted in Warren 1992, 245).

As the battle raged, Fern concerned herself with social issues exacerbated by the war. After observing the desperate poverty in parts of New York City in June 1864, she wrote an article in which she made certain that her readers visualized and smelled the "slimy alleys" and the "slaughter-houses, with pools of blood in front." She posed questions that few middle-class Americans were considering in the midst of the war, even though the conflict spawned disastrous economic conditions that prohibited the urban working class from earning a subsistence wage. At the conclusion of the article, she castigated the business interests and the city of New York for squandering money that might otherwise be used to improve the slums.

> Alas! If some of the money spent on corporation-dinners, on Fourth of July fireworks, and on public balls, where rivers of champagne are worse than wasted, were laid aside for the cleanliness and purification of these terrible localities which slay more victims than the war is doing, and whom nobody thinks of numbering. (quoted in Warren 1992, 325–326)

After the war, and until her death from cancer in 1872, Fern continued to write her column for the *New York Ledger*, again focusing on women's rights and social issues. She particularly called attention to the economic and social problems of poor working women. During these years, three volumes of her collected articles were published. In 1868, she was one of the founders of Sorosis, an organization of women newspaper writers and the first women's club in the United States.

See also **Literary Women**

Selected Reading

Warren, Joyce W. *Fanny Fern: An Independent Women*. New Brunswick, NJ: Rutgers University Press. 1992.

Fort Sumter

[A]t half past four this morning, the heavy booming of cannons woke the city from its slumbers … not a sign of fear or anguish is seen. Every body seems relieved that what has been so long dreaded has come at last … Though every shot is distinctly heard & shakes our house, I feel calm and composed.

—Emma Holmes, Charleston, South Carolina, April 12, 1861 (Holmes 1979, 25)

From April 12 to April 14, 1861, the Confederate bombardment of Fort Sumter, located in Charleston Harbor, South Carolina, marked the first military action of the Civil War. Federal troops had occupied the fort since December 26, 1860, six days after South Carolina became the first state to secede from the Union. The occupation of Fort Sumter enraged the white men and women of South Carolina. Citizens and state leaders insisted the fort belonged to the Palmetto State, not the federal government. As news of the attack spread, men and women throughout the North and South recognized it as the watershed event that transformed what had been a sectional conflict into a civil war. The writings of Southern and Northern women reflect their sense that a momentous change was underway.

MARY BOYKIN CHESNUT, a native of South Carolina, witnessed the attack as did thousands in Charleston. In a fever of anticipation and anxiety, she was awake the entire evening and early morning of April 12 to April 13. Her husband, Colonel James Chesnut, a South Carolina politician and Confederate leader, was acting upon Confederate President Jefferson Davis's direct order when he (Chesnut) and Captain Stephen D. Lee rowed across Charleston Harbor to Fort Sumter. Early in the morning of April 13, they demanded that Union Major Robert Anderson and his 127 troops surrender the fort to the Confederacy.

Boykin Chesnut remained purposefully awake all that night, knowing that if Anderson did not agree to President Davis's terms, Fort Sumter would be attacked. Finally, at 4:30 on the morning of April 13, the "heavy booming of a cannon" jolted her out of bed and onto her knees, and she said she prayed as never before. As she listened to the entire household scamper to the housetop, she hurriedly dressed to join them. On the roof, with the harbor spread out before her, she looked on in horror as the bursting of shellfire lit up the night sky. "I knew my husband was rowing about in a boat somewhere in that dark bay. And that the shells were roofing it over—bursting toward the fort …. And who could tell what each volley accomplished of death and destruction" (Chesnut 1981, 46).

Once the firing on Fort Sumter began, young Emma Holmes of Charleston found it difficult to wait for daylight to visit her cousin Sallie's home, which had a "splendid" view of the harbor. When Holmes arrived, she and Sallie "could distinctly see the flames amidst the smoke. We could only tell when a gun was fired by the smoke or a white cloud as 'big as a man's hand' floating for a few moments along the blue sky marked where a shell had burst …" (Holmes 1979, 26). To Holmes, the dramatic attack was "intensely exciting."

In the North, news of the attack on Fort Sumter immediately ignited a firestorm of war preparations. Until newspapers printed Major Anderson's surrender, most Northern men and women had been hoping against hope that war could be averted by continued diplomacy. According to MARY ASHTON LIVERMORE, the firing on Fort Sumter transformed Bostonians' opinions. As she recalled, on Sunday, April 14, the pulpits throughout Boston "thundered with denunciations of the rebellion" as "ministers counselled war rather than longer submission to the imperious South. Better that the land should be drenched with fraternal blood than that any further concessions should be made to the slaveocracy" (Livermore 1995, 88–89).

After the surrender of Fort Sumter, many Northern and Southern women were convinced that divine intervention had played a crucial role in the outcome of the battle. This type of religious conviction was ever-present in most women's reflections about the battles and campaigns of the war, regardless of their national or religious affiliation. On April 15, 1861, Catherine Devereux Edmondston of North Carolina, an ardent secessionist, faithfully reported the details of the attack in her diary as she learned of them. To her mind, the most peculiar aspect of the entire affair was that despite the intense cannon fire, neither side sustained any casualties inflicted by the enemy, although one Federal soldier was killed and five wounded when one of their own cannons exploded. Of this death, Devereux Edmondston reflected,

> Does it not seem wonderful? Truly as tho' the hand of Providence had been inter-posed, as tho' God himelf had said "Ye shall not shed thy brother's blood." Thank God for it. The breach not being yet stained with blood we may separate in Peace. The Union is gone, but it may fall apart from its own want of cohesion & we be spared a protracted civil struggle. (Edmondston 1979, 49)

For the next few weeks, while some Northern and Southern women managed to cling to the belief that the conflict could be solved without all-out warfare, the Union and Confederate war machines quickly mobilized and men and women from every state made preparations to support their soldiers.

See also **Patriotism; Religion; Secession**

Selected Readings

Holmes, Emma. *The Diary of Miss Emma Holmes*. Edited by John F. Marszalek. Baton Rouge: Louisiana State University Press. 1979.
Jones, Katharine M. *Heroines of Dixie: Confederate Women Tell Their Story of the War*. Indianapolis: Bobbs-Merrill. 1955.

Forten, Charlotte (1837–1914)

Charlotte Forten was one of the first African-American teachers from the North to join the TEACHERS OF THE FREEDPEOPLE in the South. She was also the only black teacher on St. Helena Island in the South Carolina Sea Islands, part of the Port Royal Experiment. She was a member of one of the most prestigious abolition-ist families in Philadelphia. Raised in a protected upper-middle-class environment,

Forten grew up surrounded by strong female relatives who were antislavery activists and lifelong students of literature and the arts.

During her youth in the 1850s, Forten received her secondary schooling and teacher-training in Salem, Massachusetts. After graduating from the Salem Normal School in 1856, Forten became the first black teacher hired to teach in the public schools of Salem. Throughout the rest of the 1850s, she repeatedly tried to launch a career in education, but her attempts were interrupted by lengthy bouts of serious illness.

Although Forten regularly attended antislavery meetings, was an avid reader of William Lloyd Garrison's *The Liberator*, and expressed abolitionist sentiments in her journals, abolition was not the focus of her life as it was for many of her family members and friends. She was far more captivated by her scholarly projects, including her study of modern languages, the classics, and contemporary literature, and her own writing. Immersed as she was in the humanitarian reform culture of her family and friends, Forten's self-focused attention to the development of her intellect created considerable internal conflict as well as an overwhelming sense that she must make a contribution to society.

In 1861, she acted on the advice of her friend, the poet and abolitionist John Greenleaf Whittier, to take a post teaching the freedpeople in the South Carolina Sea Islands. Sponsored by the organization that would soon become the Pennsylvania Freedmen's Relief Association, she arrived in Port Royal, South Carolina, in October 1862. From her journal entries written in the weeks before her departure, it appears that Forten was motivated to brave the dangers of teaching in this embattled Union-occupied region by a conviction that she ought to be contributing more to the advancement of her race. As she expressed in her journal on August 17, 1862, she hoped that by going to the Sea Islands, she would find herself filled with purpose.

> The accomplishments, the society, the delights of travel which I have dreamed of and longed for all my life, I am now convinced can never be mine. If I can go to Port Royal, I will try to forget all these desires. I will pray that God in his goodness will make me noble enough to find my highest happiness in doing my duty. Since Mrs. J. has given me such sad accounts of the sufferings of the poor freed people my desire of helping them has increased. (Grimké 1988, 376)

Without the robust health and driving sense of mission that the freedmen's aid organizations demanded, Forten was poorly suited to face the rigors of such a difficult assignment. Yet, once settled into the routine of teaching, she rose to the challenge she set for herself.

Of all the diaries and journals written by female teachers in the Port Royal Experiment, Forten's is the most compelling in terms of the frank discussion of her emotions and perceptions of the island and its people. While other teachers' letters and diaries focus on describing the outer world they confronted, Forten's dialogue with her inner self—her fears, loneliness, and empathy for the freedpeople coupled with her emotional reactions to the strangeness of their culture—provides insight to what a sensitive, caring young woman experienced in educating the formerly enslaved.

In August 1864, Forten's severe headaches, exhaustion, and respiratory problems forced her to return to Boston and Philadelphia. She was also mourning the recent death of her father. In October 1865, while waiting for her health to improve, she became secretary of the Teachers Committee of the New England Freedmen's Union Commission. For $10 per week, she communicated with the teachers sponsored by this organization. During her six years with the commission, she never lost hope that one day she would be strong enough to return to teaching the freedpeople. In the early 1870s, she was well enough to teach in Charleston, South Carolina, and in Washington, DC, before accepting a position in the U.S. Treasury Department in 1873. After marrying the minister Francis J. Grimké in 1878, she no longer worked outside of their home as she turned her attention to writing and publishing her poetry and essays.

See also **Abolitionists; African-American Women; Contraband Women**

Selected Readings

Grimké, Charlotte Forten. *The Journals of Charlotte Forten Grimké*. Edited by Brenda Stevenson. New York: Oxford University Press. 1988.
McKay, Nellie Y. "Charlotte Forten Grimké." In *Notable Black American Women*. Volume 1. Detroit: Gale Research. 359–364.
Sterling, Dorothy. *We Are Your Sisters: Black Women in the Nineteenth Century*. New York: W.W. Norton. 1984.

Frémont, Jessie Benton (1824–1902)

The enemy have already occupied, & in force... . Mr. Frémont says send anything in the shape of arms—but arms we must have. Send money, & both arms & money by the most rapid conveyance. It is also my own to say that I don't like this neglect & I look to you & the President to see that it has not a fatal effect.

—Jessie Benton Frémont, letter from Jessie Benton Frémont to Montgomery Blair (Lincoln's postmaster general), July 28, 1861, St. Louis, Missouri (Frémont 1993, 256)

As the wife of "The Pathfinder" John Charles Frémont, Union major general and 1864 presidential candidate, Jessie Benton Frémont was politically active through much of the Civil War. From the early years of her marriage, Benton Frémont had advised and assisted her husband with most of his literary and political endeavors. During the Civil War, she continued to perform these roles, hoping to ensure his success on the battlefield and in national politics. Despite her intense involvement in her husband's affairs, almost all of her political work took place out of the public eye. In addition to her work behind closed doors, Benton Frémont also worked tirelessly on behalf of the Western Sanitary Commission and the UNITED STATES SANITARY COMMISSION in New York City.

As the daughter of the prestigious statesman Missouri Democratic Senator Thomas Hart Benton, Jessie Benton developed an enthusiastic interest in national politics as a young girl living in Virginia and St. Louis. As the result of her father's influence, she opposed the expansion of slavery into Missouri and the territories. Intellectually curious and articulate, she received a thorough education from the tutors her father handpicked for her. He took seriously his role in her education and enjoyed instructing her in history and politics.

When Benton was 17 years old, she defied her father and created a scandal when she secretly married John Frémont, a then undistinguished, underpaid explorer serving with the U.S. army's Topographical Corps. From the beginning of their marriage, they formed a working partnership. She assisted Frémont with the writing of government documents reporting on his expeditions to the West. The second of these reports, which she and Frémont wrote after his 1844 exploration of Oregon and California, was published for the U.S. Senate and the public, making Frémont a celebrity. The book captivated Americans and inspired dreams of westward migration.

Following Frémont's third expedition, he was court-martialed as a result of a controversial command conflict in California. In 1848, he and Jessie settled in California on a large estate that Frémont had purchased years earlier. In 1850, he was elected to the U.S. Senate and traveled with Jessie to Washington, DC.

In 1856, when John Frémont was chosen as the first presidential candidate of the Republican Party, Jessie Benton Frémont became deeply involved in his campaign. Running on a platform embodied in the slogan "Frémont, Free Speech, Free Soil, and Free Kansas," John Frémont had a strong base of support in the Northeast and the West, and had the strong backing of abolitionists. For the first time, a candidate's wife was a prominent part of national campaign advertising. The enormously popular "Frémont and Jessie" were featured on banners and campaign buttons.

Away from the spotlight, Benton Frémont played a much more integral role in the campaign than the public realized or would have accepted, had they any inkling. She was in charge of her husband's correspondence, supervised and helped prepare the writing of Frémont's biography, and devised strategies to minimize the fallout from rumors circulating about her husband's past (Herr 1987, 290).

In May 1861, President Abraham Lincoln commissioned Frémont a major general in the Union army. In July, Lincoln appointed him commander of the Western Department. Benton Frémont and their three children immediately joined Frémont at the Western Department's headquarters in St. Louis. From the time of her arrival, she assumed an active role at headquarters. Unlike MARY BOYKIN CHESNUT and VARINA HOWELL DAVIS who acted in a secretarial capacity for their husbands, Benton Frémont, with her husband's blessing, took charge.

In addition to bolstering her husband's embattled position with Washington and the president, Benton Frémont helped him improvise the means of securing the arms and funding he needed to oust invading Confederate forces that were determined to make pro-slavery Missouri a Confederate state. She wrote most of Frémont's letters and messages and censored communications that might wound or unduly discourage him. She received and addressed the needs of his visitors and played an active role in staff meetings. This intense involvement in her husband's military business did not pass unnoticed. Reports of her unorthodox role reached the press, and before long, she was dubbed "General Jessie."

The beginning of the end for Frémont and his political future occurred on August 30, 1861, when he issued what came to be known as the Frémont Emancipation Proclamation. By this declaration, Frémont instituted martial law in Missouri and freed all Confederate-owned slaves in the state. He took this step without notifying or discussing the matter with Lincoln, which was a bold and fatally impulsive move. At first, antislavery Northerners were thrilled with Frémont's proclamation. Abolitionists hailed him a hero for finally grasping the initiative they believed Lincoln was too weak to take—that is, to make the war a struggle to emancipate the slaves.

Lincoln, perhaps realizing his Northern support was weakening, asked Frémont to annul his proclamation. When he refused, Benton Frémont hurried to Washington to explain her husband's position to the president. Her emphatic manner of persuasion did not win Lincoln's support. According to Benton Frémont, he dismissed her out of hand, called her "quite a female politician," and refused to trust her with his reply to Frémont. Years later, she described Lincoln's refusal to accept her as an intermediary, saying that she "felt the sneering tone and saw there was a foregone decision against all listening" (Herr 1987, 338–339).

Although she believed Lincoln's treatment of her was largely a result of her gender, there was much more at stake for Lincoln than his displeasure at having to deal with a female emissary. John Frémont was undermining Lincoln's firm political position that the civil conflict was "a war for a great national object and the Negro has nothing to do with it" (quoted in Herr 1987, 339). Even more crucial for Lincoln was the fact that Frémont was looming as a formidable political challenger for the 1864 Republican Party nomination.

Upon Benton Frémont's return to Missouri, Frémont realized that he must take action to stabilize his shaky political position by securing several victories on the battlefield. While Frémont moved his army south to rout the Confederates out of Missouri, Benton Frémont remained in St. Louis to manage army headquarters. She gathered munitions and other supplies and made all the arrangements to transport them south. But Frémont's critics and enemies in Washington were working against him. Weeks later, Lincoln dismissed him from his command.

Exhausted and embittered by their defeat, the Frémonts settled in New York City. To clear her husband of charges of ineptitude and corruption, Benton Frémont immediately devoted herself to writing *The Story of the Guard: A Chronicle of the War*, a book about one unit of courageous soldiers of the Missouri campaign. It was published in the spring of 1863.

In the North, the pro-Frémont clamor had gained so much strength that in March 1862, Lincoln was forced to give in to public pressure and appoint Frémont commander of the Union army's Mountain Department based in western Virginia. Given Frémont's considerable defects as a military leader, his troops could not match those led by the brilliant Confederate Lieutenant General Thomas J. "Stonewall" Jackson. By late June, Frémont spared himself the embarrassment of another dismissal by resigning.

Once again, the Frémonts retreated to New York City where Benton Frémont threw herself into work for the local auxiliary of the United States Sanitary Commission (USSC). By the early months of 1864, she was fully occupied with plans for the Metropolitan Sanitary Commission Fair to be held in New York City on April 4, 1864, a gala event involving the labors of thousands of women. It raised over a million dollars for the USSC. Benton Frémont produced and directed a children's production of Cinderella that involved close to 200 young people. This one event yielded $2,500 for the commission.

In May 1864, John Frémont was chosen as the candidate of a third party, the Radical Democratic Party. Once again, Benton Frémont participated. Frémont's platform called for a constitutional amendment that would liberate all enslaved African Americans. He also proposed a policy of reconstruction that would redistribute Confederate-owned land while safeguarding the new civil and political rights of the freed slaves (Venet 1991, 137). Even though most Northern abolitionists agreed with his positions, his military blunders and the ensuing months of rumors and allegations had sown distrust. Aside from the rallying of a few strong supporters, including the abolitionists SUSAN B. ANTHONY, ELIZABETH CADY STANTON, and Wendell Phillips, there was little public enthusiasm for his campaign. In September, Frémont pulled out of the race to lend strength to Lincoln's candidacy.

After the war, Benton Frémont retired from the political scene to immerse herself in domestic concerns and in New York society. Despite her extensive experience encountering the prejudice against women who involve themselves in public life, she refused to become involved in the woman suffrage movement after the war. Following her husband's bankruptcy in 1873, Benton Frémont supported her family with the proceeds from her magazine travel writing and reminiscences of the West.

See also **Women and Politics**

Selected Readings

Frémont, Jessie Benton. *The Letters of Jessie Benton Frémont.* Edited by Pamela Herr and Mary Lee Spence. Urbana, IL: University of Illinois Press. 1993.
Herr, Pamela. *Jessie Benton Frémont.* New York: Franklin Watts. 1987.

G

General Order No. 28

I cannot express ... the indignation this thing awakened .... The cowardly wretches! to notice the insults of ladies! But the news will get abroad & then we shall be praised for our actions.

—Clara Solomon, New Orleans, May 17, 1862 (Solomon 1995, 369–370)

On April 25, 1862, U.S. Navy Captain David G. Farragut's West Gulf Blockading Squadron succeeded in capturing the city of New Orleans. Believing the city was well fortified, the nearly 170,000 inhabitants of the South's largest city were shocked by the suddenness of the fall of New Orleans.

Citizen resistance began immediately. The occupying forces of Union Major General Benjamin Franklin Butler faced hostile, unruly crowds. As military governor of Louisiana, Butler recognized that he must quell all civil unrest if he were to execute the tightly organized administration he had in mind. Butler ordered that rounds of artillery be used to repel mobs of men and women who refused to disband. He demanded that a man who destroyed a U.S. flag be hanged for treason. He also refused to tolerate other, more passive modes of resistance. Storeowners who refused to sell goods to Unionists had their shops impounded and their goods confiscated. Clergymen who were unwilling to lead prayers for President Abraham Lincoln were arrested and deported to the North (D. Faust 1997, 208–209).

Despite the resistance of a number of men in New Orleans, contemporary accounts emphasize the hostile reactions of the city's white women. Upper-class, middle-class, and working-class women publicly expressed disdain for the occupying Union troops. Surviving diaries and letters of elite women reveal the intensity of their rage about the Union invasion and occupation of their city. Following the surrender, they were horrified to discover that Confederate troops had left the city completely undefended. Women were further enraged when the Confederate government did not send reinforcements to oust the invaders or to provide protection. As the days of occupation wore on, women were forced to confront their own powerlessness as they realized that civilian men were helpless to strike back at Union forces. For many women in New Orleans, the realization did not paralyze them. Denied of the protection that Southern society insisted was their birthright as women, they found a way to fight back.

White women of New Orleans flaunted their patriotism and their disdain of their Union occupiers whenever confronted with their presence. Elite and middle-class ladies pinned or sewed small Confederate flags to their dresses or wore black arm-bands as they walked about town or attended church services. Teachers encouraged their students to sing "The Bonnie Blue Flag" and taught them other songs celebrating the Confederacy. Women of all classes walked in the middle of the street to avoid passing soldiers on the sidewalk. As Benjamin Butler later described one such encounter in his autobiography, a woman took "great pains to hold her skirts aside as if she feared they might be contaminated if they touched the soldier" (Butler 1892, 415). When officers and soldiers boarded the city's streetcars, women abandoned their seats and headed for the streets. They lifted their chins, "turned their noses up," and wore facial expressions of disgust and revulsion. A few hurled insults, and one woman dumped the contents of a chamber pot out into the street on top of Captain Farragut's head.

As benign as most of the women's behavior appeared to be, it was effective in disturbing Union officers and troops. Early in the war, throughout the Union-occupied regions of the Confederacy, Federal troops had been reluctant to retaliate against women's passive acts of resistance. Union forces in New Orleans managed to tolerate most abuses until a few women and girls spat at them. Upon hearing of the spitting incidents, Butler retaliated. On May 15, 1862, after some deliberation, he issued the infamous General Order No. 28, also known as the "Woman Order."

Although all women were included in the order, Butler especially targeted the upper-class ladies whose defiance riled him. To Butler's mind, these women not only took advantage of the immunity of their gender and class from censure and imprisonment, but also believed they were members of an aristocratic class superior to all Yankees, a pretension that Butler could not stomach. Through General Order No. 28, he believed he struck a crippling blow at their arrogance and forced them to bear responsibility for their public actions. His attack, then, was an assault on the women of New Orleans's notions of gender as well as a broadside against the entire Southern master class. By threatening to declass women by branding them prostitutes—a terrifying fate in caste-ridden New Orleans society—Butler was certain that he restored Yankee supremacy.

If women were angry before the issuance of General Order No. 28, afterward their blood boiled. Only a few women ignored the order while the rest fumed and stormed in private. When Southern newspapers caught up with the story, they blasted "The Beast" who dared to defile Southern womanhood. Even Northern newspapers expressed outrage on behalf of the women of New Orleans. Their reporting, however, frequently misconstrued Butler's order, interpreting it as giving free license to the Union military to ravish any disrespectful Confederate woman. This interpretation had no role in the intention or proposed execution of the order, and Butler made certain his troops knew it.

Clara Solomon, a young Jewish woman of New Orleans, had no sympathy for women who refused to abide by General Order No. 28. But in June 1862, when Butler issued General Order No. 76, her ire knew no bounds. The order required all citizens, men and women, to swear an oath of allegiance to the U.S. government. Thousands of residents packed up their belongings and fled the city rather than pledge their loyalty to the Union. The event spurred Solomon to wish that an epidemic of "Yellow Jack" (yellow fever) would descend upon Butler's troops. She also declared in her diary entry of June 22, 1862,

> Old Butler! If he could only have as many ropes around his neck as there are ladies in the city & each have a pull! Or if we could fry him! Or give him many salty things to eat, & have water in sight, & he unable to obtain it! (Solomon 1995, 419–420)

In December 1862, the people of New Orleans were jubilant to learn that General Nathaniel Banks would replace Butler as military governor. Also in December, President Davis vowed to have Butler executed, should he be captured. As the early months of 1863 passed, residents relaxed under Banks's more lenient rule. Before long, women resumed singing and playing Confederate songs and insulting Union troops.

See also **Battle of the Handkerchiefs; Invasion and Occupation**

Selected Readings

Faust, Drew Gilpin. *Mothers of Invention: Women of the Slaveholding South in the American Civil War.* New York: Vintage Books. 1997.

Rable, George. "'Missing in Action': Women of the Confederacy." *In Divided Houses: Gender and the Civil War.* Edited by Catherine Clinton and Nina Silber. New York: Oxford University Press. 1992. 134–146.

Ryan, Mary P. *Women in Public: Between Banners and Ballots, 1825–1880.* Baltimore: Johns Hopkins University Press. 1990.

Solomon, Clara. *The Civil War Diary of Clara Solomon: Growing Up in New Orleans, 1861–1862.* Edited, with an introduction, by Elliott Ashkenazi. Baton Rouge, LA: Louisiana State University Press. 1995.

Gettysburg, Battle of

The Battle of Gettysburg, waged from July 1 to July 3, 1863, in the southern Pennsylvania hamlet of Gettysburg, involved more than 165,000 Union and Confederate troops. By the time the three days of fighting were over, there were over 50,000 casualties, including at least 4,000 Union and 3,000 Confederate dead. This Union victory, coupled with the Union conquest of Vicksburg, Mississippi, on July 4, proved to be the turning point of the Civil War. At Gettysburg, Union Major General George Gordon Meade's Army of the Potomac repulsed Confederate General Robert E. Lee's Army of Northern Virginia's recent invasion of the North, placing the Confederate armies on the defensive for the remainder of the war. Historians differ as to the strength of the armies that fought at Gettysburg. The Army of the Potomac is believed to have consisted of 85,000 to 97,000 men; Lee's Army of Northern Virginia numbered from 70,000 to 75,000.

As was the case with other Civil War engagements, civilians living in the battle zone were swept up in the violence and chaos of the fighting. Even though Gettysburg residents—men, women, and children—were helpless to protect their property from destruction by artillery and cannon fire, they volunteered to assist wounded Union and Confederate soldiers.

Weeks after the stunning Confederate victory at the Battle of Chancellorsville (Virginia) in early May 1863, Lee persuaded President Jefferson Davis and other top leaders of the Confederate government and military that the Army of Northern Virginia should undertake an invasion of the North in June 1863. Despite its recent triumphs, the Confederate military was struggling with problems that were overwhelming its fighting force. A lack of supplies—particularly food, clothing, shoes, and horses—was draining the military's strength. Lee reasoned that a campaign into the fertile farmland of Pennsylvania would feed and strengthen his troops while providing them with desperately needed supplies. Lee also argued that battle victories in the North would convince Britain and France to recognize and assist the Confederacy. He also claimed that decisive Confederate victories in the North would enable the Northern peace movement to gain strength and would convince the Northern public that the war must come to an end.

Prior to the battle, Gettysburg's population stood at 2,400. As soon as it became clear that a major battle was to be fought in the Gettysburg vicinity, many male civilians abandoned the area to avoid confrontation with enemy troops, leaving their womenfolk to endure the battle alone. When the cannon fire commenced, women and children ran to their cellars for protection, where many remained until the hostilities were over. Not all women stayed hidden, however. Some emerged to share their food with hungry soldiers while others left their homes to care for the wounded.

Like a number of courageous Gettysburg women who baked to feed the famished soldiers, Mary Virginia "Jenny" Wade made biscuits in her sister's kitchen during the battle. She was kneading the dough for a batch of biscuits when a stray bullet pierced the door of her sister's house, killing her instantly. She was the only Gettysburg civilian to be killed during the battle.

Not long after the fighting began in earnest, Mary McAllister left her home in the town of Gettysburg to assist the Union and Confederate wounded who were filling the church near her home. Although the presence of Confederate "Greybacks" startled many a volunteer at first, most civilians gave whatever they had to their wounded invaders. Elizabeth Plank, who lived on a farm outside of town, was dismayed when she discovered that Confederate Major General John Bell Hood had commandeered her house for a hospital for his wounded troops. A total of 1,542 soldiers were treated there during and after the battle. Gettysburg residents Mary and Sally Witherow, possibly Southern sympathizers, helped to nurse them. Several pro-Confederate women from Baltimore also arrived to volunteer at the Plank home in the days after the battle (Conklin 1993, 15–16).

Union and Confederate women attached to the armies—nurses, laundresses, cooks, servants, and a few soldiers—worked feverishly during the engagement. ANNIE ETHERIDGE, a nurse for the 3rd Michigan Volunteer Infantry, and Marie Tepe, vivandière of the 114th Pennsylvania Volunteer Infantry, both of whom had recently received the Kearny Cross for valor on the battlefield, aided fallen soldiers during the battle. Laundress, cook, and nurse Rose Quinn Rooney, an Irish immigrant, dodged bullets and shellfire to assist her comrades in the 15th Louisiana Volunteer Infantry. Another Confederate woman served with the military at Gettysburg as a soldier. Although never identified, she was killed in the disastrous Confederate assault known as Pickett's Charge, when nearly 12,000 Confederate soldiers were mown down by Union firepower toward the conclusion of the three-day battle. A group burying the dead after the battle found her body (Conklin 1993, 97–98, 112, 134).

Following the battle, Lee's army retreated, leaving Gettysburg by the night of July 4. Relief workers, civilians, chaplains, reporters, soldiers, and officers—all remarked on the human devastation covering the battlefield in their letters, memoirs, diaries, and other writings. As UNITED STATES CHRISTIAN COMMISSION (USCC) volunteer Jane Boswell Moore testified, "No human pen can adequately depict the horrors of a battlefield" (quoted in Hoisington 2002, 113). Like Moore, most writers declared their incapacity to express what they had witnessed. Sophronia Bucklin, an army nurse in Dorothea Dix's corps, did not arrive in Gettysburg until July 18, two weeks after the battle ended. Even after this length of time, the battlefield continued to be littered with potent reminders of the suffering and death that had transformed the landscape. In her memoir, Bucklin described what she observed when she visited the battlefield.

> Earlier in life it would have been almost impossible for me to walk over such a field of horror, but I had grown familiar with death in every shape …. [A]t one place, so close that it touched me, hung a sleeve of faded army blue—a dead hand protruding from the worn and blackened cuff—I could not but feel a momentary shudder …. In fancy I saw the long procession of widows, and orphans, and kindred, who mourned for the slaughtered heroes. Every grave had its history. (quoted in Conklin 1993, 328)

For days following the battle, the sights and sounds that confronted Gettysburg civilians were difficult to tolerate. Most relief workers stated that they had to struggle to avoid being overcome by the masses of maimed and mutilated soldiers and the shrieks and screams of men undergoing amputations.

Shortly after the battle, on the morning of Sunday, July 5, congregants in Northern churches received a summons to travel to Gettysburg to attend to the thousands of survivors. Appeals were also made for women to quickly gather food, clothing, rags for bandages, and medicines to be shipped to Pennsylvania. Women from all over the North immediately responded.

While Gettysburg civilians waited for workers and supplies to arrive, they toiled day and night to save lives. The most severe problem facing them was the absence of supplies. The Army of the Potomac's supply train was 25 miles away. The UNITED STATES SANITARY COMMISSION (USSC) stores were also many miles distant, but like the army train, were encumbered by multiple obstacles en route. The USCC was trying to respond as well, but encountered similar hurdles. In time, however, both organizations contributed much to the care of the Union and Confederate wounded. In the meantime, residents of Gettysburg and surrounding villages carted their own supplies from home, exhausting their resources. Some subsisted on crackers and water so that the wounded could eat more nourishing food. Women were agonized when they reached the bottom of their flour barrels and there was no food left to fortify the soldiers.

Private homes, barns, churches, schools, and other buildings were hastily transformed into hospitals sheltering wounded Union and Confederate soldiers and officers. Those whose wounds were not life-threatening walked or were transported to trains to be treated in military hospitals some distance from the battle site. The most severely wounded remained in Gettysburg.

Some male and female relief workers from the North and a number from Maryland and northern Virginia poured into Gettysburg. A group of approximately 14 Sisters of Charity of Saint Vincent de Paul from Emmitsburg, Pennsylvania, also arrived to rescue as many lives as possible.

USSC volunteers Georgeanna Woolsey and her mother, Jane Eliza Newton Woolsey, both from New York City, operated a refreshment station and lodge for Union and Confederate soldiers who were soon to embark trains leaving Gettysburg. Twice daily the cars departed for Baltimore and Harrisburg, Pennsylvania, and as each group of soldiers endured the long wait for their departure, the Woolseys served soup and coffee as well as one hot meal to soldiers of both armies. The two women also supervised the work of the African-American men who actually cooked the soup and the meals. They also distributed clothing and bandages. Georgeanna's memoir *Three Weeks at Gettysburg* was published as a USSC pamphlet to encourage Northern women to continue contributing their donations for the front to the USSC. At this time, the USSC had cause to worry as its rival the USCC persuaded many Northern women that it was the more responsible, responsive organization.

Charlotte Johnson McKay, a volunteer from Massachusetts, worked in a field hospital for six weeks after the battle. A widow, she had lost her only child two months before the war began. From the time the first shots were fired and throughout nearly the entire war, she devoted herself to caring for soldiers. While at Gettysburg, she journeyed to town each day to acquire food and supplies from the USSC, the USCC, and any other source that would provide the raw materials she needed to feed the wounded in her care for that day.

> I would take butter, eggs, and crackers by the barrel, dried fish by the half kentle, and fresh meat in any quantity, and having seen them loaded on an army wagon, would return in my ambulance ... in time to give some attention to dinner. The remainder of the day would be devoted to the distribution of such stimulants as eggnog and milk punch ... or supplying them [the soldiers] with clothing, pocket-handkerchiefs, cologne, bay rum, anything that could be had to alleviate their sufferings. (quoted in Conklin 1993, 240)

Not all Gettysburg women contributed by nurturing the living. Elizabeth Masser Thorn, a German immigrant and mother of three, had assumed her husband's duties as caretaker of Gettysburg's Evergreen Cemetery when he enlisted in the Union army in 1862. Sometime after the battle, the president of the cemetery informed her that the dead were to be buried at Evergreen until further notice. Thorn, pregnant at the time, and her elderly father commenced digging and burying the rapidly decomposing bodies. Although a few friends arrived to assist them, these helpers became ill and soon departed, leaving Thorn and her father alone with their labor. Amidst the overpowering stench, the father and daughter team buried 105 soldiers before the Gettysburg National Cemetery was available for burials in late October 1863 (Conklin 1993, 172).

On November 19, 1863, the Gettysburg National Cemetery was officially dedicated in a lengthy ceremony that included a two-minute speech by President Abraham Lincoln, which only later came to be known as "The Gettysburg Address." The night before this event, Jane Boswell Moore reflected on the significance of the occasion for her and for others who had experienced what transpired at Gettysburg in the summer of 1863.

> I write these lines in the solitude of my chamber, on the eve of the National celebration at Gettysburg. Gettysburg! Can I ever hear that name without a thrill of indescribable emotion? … Good God, how many thousands of those to whom we once ministered during our month sojourn are now sleeping in bloody graves, whose eternal silence the archangels trumpet alone can break …. Truly this ground has already been consecrated by the very extremity of human suffering; the amputating tents are gone, pitched elsewhere, the woods once resounding with shrieks are silent now, but the agony once endured, the buried limbs and bodies call to heaven for judgment on the authors of this rebellion. (quoted in Hoisington 2002, 117–119)

Selected Readings

Conklin, Eileen. *Women at Gettysburg 1863*. Gettysburg, PA: Thomas Publications. 1993.

Hoisington, Daniel John. *Gettysburg and the Christian Commission*. Roseville, MN: Edinborough Press. 2002.

Gibbons, Abby Hopper (1801–1893)

At age 60, the Quaker Abby Hopper Gibbons had three decades of reform activism behind her when the Civil War began. With her husband, James Sloan Gibbons, she was a chief fund-raiser for the Manhattan Anti-Slavery Society during the 1840s and 1850s. When her father, Isaac Tatem Hopper, formed the Prison Association of New York, Hopper Gibbons directed the organization's Female Department. In 1846, she and other reformers founded the Isaac T. Hopper Home that provided housing for women released from prison.

At the outset of the Civil War, Hopper Gibbons and her daughters sewed "shirts, drawers, havelocks, and dear knows what all the summer and autumn" of 1861 (Gibbons 1897, 1: 292–293). By December, she decided to investigate the destination of the supplies they were sending to the troops. With her daughter Sarah Gibbons (Emerson), Hopper Gibbons toured the army hospitals in Washington and northern Virginia. For the next three years, she and Sarah nursed the sick and the wounded soldiers at hospitals in Virginia, Maryland, and New Jersey.

What distinguished Hopper Gibbons's work in the army hospitals was her intolerance of incompetence and corruption among the surgeons and the military bureaucracy. She was enraged by evidence of surgical blundering, particularly when she cared for soldiers whose amputations had been so crudely executed that the bones were left exposed, leaving the victims vulnerable to massive infections and "doomed to die" (Gibbons 1897, 1: 306). Following the fighting at Winchester, Virginia, in 1862, she wrote, "There are about 20 of the wounded ones who, I think, must die; and many of them, because of the unskilful [sic] and positively ignorant butchery of men calling themselves surgeons. Oh, it is too sad, to see fine men sacrificed, whose lives might have been saved (Gibbons 1897, 1: 324). Whenever possible, she demanded that military administrators address surgical incompetence.

Throughout the time that she was a nurse in the army hospitals, she devoted whatever time she could spare to visiting the contraband camps to bring aid and assistance to the freed African-American men, women, and children sheltered there. Within the army hospitals, she made it clear to all staff, army brass, and the wounded that racism in any and all forms would not be permitted as long as she was on the premises. While she was chief nurse at the army hospital at Point Lookout, Maryland, she protested vehemently when several African-American men were tied to a tree for stealing. She "upbraided the officer of the day himself," she explained, "and threatened to publish such an account of the affair, as would make all concerned regret it" (Gibbons 1896, 2: 24).

During her tenure at Point Lookout, Hopper Gibbons had conflicts with the military staff concerning the CATHOLIC NUNS who were nursing the wounded. Hopper Gibbons's major objection to the Catholic sisters was their "coldness"—specifically their refusal to talk with their soldier patients. With the support of DOROTHEA DIX, superintendent of Union army nurses, Hopper Gibbons maintained that "the presence of Protestant women, with ability to regard the need of the sick, and to sympathize with suffering humanity is a treasure beyond price." Catholic nurses, she pointed out, "are the machinery of an Institution and do not minister to the broken-down in spirit" (Gibbons 1897, 1: 347–348).

Following the war, Hopper Gibbons continued her humanitarian work until she was in her early nineties. In the immediate postwar years, she helped veterans and war widows find jobs. She also helped establish the New York Diet Kitchen Association, which provided food for the needy. She continued women's prison reform work and was a leader in the movement to eliminate prostitution in New York State.

See also **Abolitionists; Draft Riots; Nurses**

Selected Readings

Bacon, Margaret Hope. *Abby Hopper Gibbons: Prison Reformer and Social Activist.* Albany, NY: State University of New York Press. 2000.

Gibbons, Abby Hopper. *The Life of Abby Hopper Gibbons: Told Chiefly Through Her Correspondence.* 2 volumes. Edited by Sarah Hopper Emerson. New York: G.P. Putnams. 1897, 1896.

Girlhood and Adolescence

Regardless of race, social class, or ethnic identity, the lives of American girls of all ages were deeply affected by the Civil War. Southern girls and boys were more profoundly influenced by war than children living in relative security in the North. Southern children's experience of Union invasion, bombardment, and occupation, and their suffering as a result of wartime food shortages and widespread school closings deprived them of a normal childhood. Yet Northern children did not survive unscathed. Like Southern children, they grieved the losses of fathers, brothers, uncles, cousins, and neighbors who were killed in battle or perished from disease. Many girls and boys were forced by necessity to assume responsibilities at home that would have been unthinkable before the war. Based on the hundreds of diaries, memoirs, and other personal writings of women who were girls from 1861 to 1865, it is evident that the Civil War was the most significant, life-altering event of their youth.

Children and adolescents absorbed the volatile political climate of the immediate prewar and war years. As soon as the war began, Southern and Northern girls and boys attended parades and rallies to bolster the troops. Girls sewed flags to honor their local regiments. Encouraged by their teachers, schoolgirls and boys sang patriotic songs at the top of their lungs, and in the South, often in the presence of the enemy. Girls boasted of their fierce patriotism in their diaries and in their correspondence with friends and loved ones, voicing their passionate loyalty to their country. In her diary entry of December 31, 1861, Lucy Rebecca Buck of Grove Hill, Virginia, reflected on the tumultuous political events of the past year and, with anger and resentment, expressed her opinion of the national conflict, particularly her disdain for the federal government's tyranny over the Southern states, which forced them, against their will, to unite as a separate nation.

> I saw a great and glorious Government [the United States] … the pride and the boast of a free and happy people … become a by-word of hissing and reproach …. I saw it trample upon the laws, desecrate the symbols and outrage every principle upon which this government was founded. Then I saw the oppressed [the South] rise up and assert its rights …. I saw … efforts for compromise, but the strong would [have] none of it. *Might* was *right*, and the only compromise to be accepted was entire submission and resignation of self-respect by the weak (Buck 1997, 9).

During the final months of the war, when hope for the future of the Confederacy was nearly extinguished, 16-year-old EMMA LECONTE of Columbia, South Carolina, confided her thoughts to her diary. As Union Major General William Tecumseh Sherman vowed to invade and lay waste to her home state, LeConte held fast to her Confederate patriotism, even when all seemed lost.

> All that is between us and our miserable fate is a handful of raw militia assembled near Branchville [South Carolina]. And yet they may say there is a Providence who fights for those who are struggling for freedom—who are defending their homes, and all that is held dear! Yet these vandals—these fiends incarnate, are allowed to overrun our land! Oh my country! Will I live to see thee subjugated and enslaved by these Yankees—surely every man and woman will die first. (LeConte 1957, 4)

Northern and Southern girls longed to be part of the action as the nation prepared itself for war. A young girl from Yonkers, New York, could not bear to be left behind when her brother marched off to join a Zouave regiment. She managed to find "a soldier's cap, a drum, and canteen" and journeyed alone by ferry and train to New York City to convince her brother's colonel to accept her as a "daughter of the regiment." When he refused, she returned home, heartbroken, though her patriotic zeal was not quenched a bit (Marten 1998, 162). She was not alone in her ambition to join the army as hundreds of girls and young women donned men's clothing and became MILITARY WOMEN.

Most young people in the North never saw a Confederate soldier or heard the guns of battle. Yet they sympathized with the struggles of the Union soldier. Older girls followed the war news in adult newspapers and magazines. Younger children were avid readers of magazines published especially for them. These publications urged girls and boys to become involved in the war effort, particularly by taking part in fund-raising events in their communities. Girls worked with their mothers in SOLDIERS' AID SOCIETIES, scraping lint to be used for dressing bandages, knitting socks, making shirts, and sewing havelocks to shield soldiers' heads and necks from the sun. Northern girls and boys raised funds for the UNITED STATES SANITARY COMMISSION, which sent food, clothing, and medical supplies to the front. Girls and boys staged their own SANITARY FAIRS in their backyards, inviting their neighbors and friends to spend their money and enjoy concerts and other staged entertainments, games, baked goods, fruits, and candy. In Philadelphia, 72,000 schoolchildren participated in fund-raising for the Great Central Sanitary Fair in Philadelphia.

In both the North and South, the war changed children's lives by increasing their workload at home. With their fathers absent, their mothers struggled to manage the household, the family business, or the farm chores of both parents. Girls stepped in to relieve their mothers of some of these duties, including heavy farm labor that ordinarily would not have been allotted to them. In the South, as slaves fled from their slaveholders, white girls and boys kept busy doing the menial work household slaves had performed. After her mother gave birth in December 1864, ten-year-old Carrie

Berry of Atlanta, Georgia, was filled with pride when she managed all the cooking and cleaning. Carrie managed the entire household for several days until an adult was brought in to relieve her. When the slaves vanished from young Sally Hawthorne's home in Fayette, North Carolina, she had to learn to bathe and dress herself. Once she mastered these tasks, she pitched in to help with the domestic labor. Twelve-year-old Céline Frémaux's mother was overwhelmed by stress when the family became refugees in Louisiana. Céline found that she had to become an adult overnight when much of the care for her six siblings, including an infant, fell on her shoulders. Her only breaks from the never-ending childcare were her hours spent at school.

In the South, children were forced to cope with a multitude of privations. The Union blockade of Southern ports and the collapse of the Confederate rail transportation system caused serious food shortages. Poor crop yields diminished food supplies even further. By 1863, and more extensively by 1864, many girls and boys were suffering from hunger. By late 1864 and 1865, children in devastated regions of the Confederacy were starving. As schools were forced to close their doors due to a lack of teachers and buildings, and as communities became engrossed in struggling for their survival, girls and boys had little in their lives to relieve the grim day-to-day, hand-to-mouth existence. As the war drew to a close and Confederate defeat appeared imminent, children suffered from the knowledge that their country had no future and that the Confederacy's economic system was in a state of collapse. At a time in their lives when young people look with hope to the future, there was none to be found. Emma LeConte voiced the despair of a generation in this diary excerpt written in late January 1865.

> How dreadfully sick I am of this war. Truly we girls, whose lot it is to grow up in these times, are unfortunate! It commenced when I was thirteen, and I am now seventeen and no prospect yet of its ending. No pleasure, no enjoyment—nothing but rigid economy and hard work—nothing but the stern realities of life. … We have only the saddest anticipations and the dread of hardships and cares, when bright dreams of the future ought to shine on us. I have seen little of the light-heartedness and exuberant joy that people talk about as the natural heritage of youth …. I often wonder if I will ever have my share of fun and happiness. (LeConte 1957, 21–22)

The war made it impossible for many Southern girls to mingle and begin courting boys of their own age. Instead of enjoying parties and entertainments as they had before the war, elite and middle-class Southern girls found that they spent most of their evenings at home. Their most frequent social occasion was attending church services on Sunday. The death of hundreds of thousands of young men in the South meant that the postwar years did not promise a brighter future as far as social and marital opportunities were concerned.

For some children in the South, the worst the war had to offer was the weeks of bombardment prior to INVASION AND OCCUPATION by Union troops. The trauma of shells imploding day after day terrified, traumatized, and sometimes wounded children and adults. In her diary, young Carrie Berry recorded her experiences of living day after day with shells dropping all around their home in August 1864, during the siege of Atlanta.

> We had no shells this morning ... and thought that we would not have any to day (but, my, when will they stop) but soon after breakfast Zuie and I were standing on the platform between the house and the dining room. It made a very large hole in the garden and threw the dirt all over the yard. I never was so frightened in my life. Zuie was as pale as a corpse and I expect I was too. It did not take us long to fly to the cellar. (Berry 2000, 9)

For the most part, Northern girls did not suffer from invasion to the extent that girls like Carrie Berry did, but in July 1863, Confederate troops did come north to invade southern Pennsylvania prior to the BATTLE OF GETTYSBURG. Tillie Pierce was 15 years old when she witnessed the horrors of the Battle of Gettysburg that raged near her home. Her first glimpse of Confederate soldiers came as a shock.

> What a horrible sight! There they were, human beings! clad almost in rags, covered with dust, riding wildly, pell-mell down the hill toward our home! shouting, yelling most unearthly, cursing, brandishing their revolvers, and firing right and left.

Several days into the battle, as the scores of wounded mounted, farmhouses were called upon to act as surgeries and hospitals. Tillie Pierce had taken shelter at a neighbor's house in a supposedly safe part of town, a location that proved to be one of the most dangerous. She never forgot the sights and sounds that surrounded her there.

> I fairly shrank back aghast at the awful sight presented. The approaches were crowded with wounded, dying and dead. The air was filled with moanings, and groanings. As we passed on toward the house, we were compelled to pick our steps in order that we might not tread on the prostrate bodies.

Tillie Pierce joined the women and men of the household by assisting the surgeons in whatever ways they could. As she did so, she observed the amputating benches placed about the house.

> I must have become inured to seeing the terrors of battle, else I could hardly have gazed upon the scenes now presented. I was looking out one of the windows facing the front yard. Near the basement door, and directly underneath the window I was at, stood one of these benches. I saw them lifting the poor men upon it, then the surgeons sawing and cutting off arms and legs, then again probing and picking bullets from the flesh .... I saw the surgeons hastily put a cattle horn over the mouths of the wounded ones .... [I] soon learned that that was their mode of administering chloroform, in order to produce unconsciousness. But the effect in some instances was not produced; for I saw the wounded throwing themselves wildly about, and shrieking with pain while the operation was going on. (Alleman 1889)

Such experiences forever changed young people, and for many served as a traumatic demarcation between childhood and adulthood.

Children of all ages grieved deeply for family and friends killed in battle. After all the songs, parades, and patriotic hurrahs, children found it difficult to comprehend the grim realities of battle. The sudden loss of a father, brother, relative, or friend often came as a blow that shook young people to their roots. For 17-year-old Clara Solomon, a Jewish girl living in Union-occupied New Orleans, the death of an officer friend, one about whom she had romantic feelings, struck her hard and was perhaps her first confrontation with death.

> Oh! I fear our worst fears are confirmed! I do not think that there is a shadow of a hope remaining. I am miserable! My whole life seems to be departed. I have no energy, no spirit for anything! It is so painfully, acute a subject, that I refrain from mentioning it to you & prefer to think, think! Think .... Oh! God! How uncertain is life .... Died! Can I ever realize it! How distinctly do I remember every event of those happy days, which have been followed by such anguish .... Everything we love is doomed to destruction. (Solomon 1995, 433–434)

Of all children, slave children were the most vulnerable during the war. As food shortages became severe, the bodies of growing children suffered the most from hunger and starvation. Although children were spared the hazards of flight to Union encampments when they stayed with their families on the plantations, they were subject to the whims of the slaveholders who worked girls and boys hard to make up for the absence of slave men who had been impressed into the Confederate military. Of the slaves who decided to chance fleeing the plantations, children were safest if they traveled in large family groups to the relative security of a Union army camp. Older girls in the camps might obtain employment as a laundress, servant, or cook as 12-year-old SUSIE BAKER KING TAYLOR did. Behind Union lines, thousands of former slave girls and boys attended schools organized by Northern white and African-American missionaries who became TEACHERS OF THE FREEDPEOPLE. Union encampments were not always safe havens, however, as young female slaves were sometimes the victims of rape and abuse at the hands of white Union soldiers, just as they had been at the mercy of white male slaveholders and overseers on the plantations.

See also **Courtship and Marriage; Education; Family Life; Guerrilla War; Morgan, Sarah**

Selected Readings

King, Wilma. *Stolen Childhood: Slave Youth in Nineteenth-Century America.* Bloomington: Indiana University Press. 1995.

Marten, James. *The Children's Civil War.* Chapel Hill: University of North Carolina Press. 1998.

Werner, Emmy E. *Reluctant Witnesses: Children's Voices from the Civil War.* Boulder, CO: Westview Press. 1998.

Government Girls

When male government clerks in federal offices in Washington, DC, abandoned their posts to enlist in the Union army in 1861, many government offices suffered severe labor shortages. In 1862, Francis Elias Spinner, the United States Treasurer, solved the labor deficit in the Treasury Department by hiring young women to count treasury bills and to perform other duties. New wartime monetary policies made the shortage especially critical in the Treasury Department. According to Spinner, a woman could "use scissors better than a man" and, he added, she could be paid less than a man, thereby saving the government money at a time when the Union needed to conserve its financial resources (Baker 1977, 84). Moreover, Spinner declared, men "ought to be handling muskets instead of shears" (quoted in Deutrich 1971, 68).

Although Spinner is often credited as being the first government administrator to employ women (or "government girls" as they were commonly called) to work in federal offices, female clerks, including CLARA BARTON, held positions in the United States Patent Office prior to 1861. Although he was not the first, Spinner's support of the employment of women in government offices was instrumental to their assuming these jobs during the Civil War.

Spinner hired hundreds of women as "currency trimmers," who cut long sheets of currency into individual bills, at a salary of $600 per year. (Male clerks earned from $1,200 to $1,800 per year.) Government girls in the Treasury Department worked from 9 AM until 3 PM with a half-hour lunch break. During the five-and-a-half-hour interval, a single clerk likely handled up to 50,000 bills at a rate of 9,090 notes per hour (Baker 1977, 82).

Also in 1862, the War Department and the Quartermaster General's Office hired female clerks and copyists. 447 women worked in the Treasury Department during the war, 107 of them in Spinner's office. In 1862, 80 women were on the payroll in Secretary of the Treasury Salmon Chase's office. By 1863, 30 women were clerks in the Quartermaster General's Office and 13 in the United States Patent Office, where Clara Barton had worked in the mid-1850s as a copyist.

The propriety of women clerks working alongside men was an ever-present issue during the war, so much so that administrators felt compelled to establish separate rooms and work spaces for women workers. In 1864, charges of immorality within the Treasury Department shocked newspaper readers, but a Congressional investigation proved them false. Nevertheless, public anxiety concerning women office workers persisted. The quartermaster general was so concerned about the female clerks in his offices that he posted a guard at the door of their workroom.

In 1864, Congress passed a bill that established the employment of female clerks in federal offices "at an annual compensation not exceeding six hundred dollars per year." By the end of the war, this ceiling had been raised to $720.

Not until 1870 did Congress pass a law allowing female government clerks to be paid on an equal basis with men. In practice, however, men and women were not assigned to the same work. Male clerks were given positions that were higher paying while women were usually relegated to the most menial jobs. By 1880, more than a thousand women were employed in the Treasury Department while their numbers had also vastly increased in other federal offices.

See also **Treasury Girls**

Selected Readings

Baker, Ross K. "Entry of Women into Federal Job World—At a Price." *Smithsonian*. 8(4) (July 1977): 82–91.

Deutrich, Bernice M. "Propriety and Pay." *Prologue*. 3(2) (Fall 1971): 67–72.

Greenhow, Rose O'Neal (1817–1864)

Rose O'Neal Greenhow, Confederate patriot and spy, was a key member of an espionage ring targeted at the most prominent politicians in Washington, DC. Her tragic death, occurring at the height of the war, helped establish her as one of the most celebrated of all Confederate heroines. Born a Roman Catholic of Irish descent in Montgomery County, Maryland, Rose O'Neal nurtured a passion for politics early in life. From childhood on, she was a staunch advocate of states' rights.

While living in Washington, DC, in the 1840s with her husband Robert Greenhow, a diplomat in the State Department whom she had married in 1835, O'Neal Greenhow developed numerous friendships with leading politicians. Following the death of her husband in 1854, O'Neal Greenhow cultivated these relationships and emerged as one of the capital's most powerful society hostesses. Renowned for her intellect and self-assured beauty, politicians, diplomats, and judicial officials flocked to her salon. Influential men valued her insight, and a few confided their ambitions, ideas, and plans to her.

During the SECESSION crisis of 1860 to 1861, O'Neal Greenhow made no secret of her conviction that every state in the Union possesses the constitutional right to secede. Yet her favorite Northern congressmen and Union military leaders never suspected that her political beliefs would lead her to betray them. As early as the final months of 1860, months before the fall of Fort Sumter, she was relaying information about federal military and naval operations to Southern secessionist leaders. At some point during the first half of 1861, Confederate Lieutenant Colonel Thomas Jordan urged her to become an integral member of his espionage ring. Her mission was to continue information-gathering among her Washington contacts and to extend her circle of Northern informants. To assist her in her espionage work, Jordan instructed her in the use of a 26-symbol code.

Early in July 1861, O'Neal Greenhow discovered that Union Brigadier General Irvin McDowell was preparing to launch an assault on Confederate troops outside of Manassas, Virginia. She then lured a young, inexperienced military official into revealing the strength of McDowell's fighting force and its anticipated battle route. With no time to spare, O'Neal Greenhow enlisted Betty Duvall, a young female friend, to carry a message wrapped in her hair to Confederate Brigadier General Pierre Gustave Toutant (P. G. T.) Beauregard's encampment. Aided by the forewarning, Beauregard's forces, though vastly outnumbered, resoundingly defeated the Union army at the First Battle of Manassas (known to the Union army as the First Battle of Bull Run) on July 21, 1861.

Following the massive Union rout, rumors multiplied in Washington that O'Neal Greenhow was a Confederate spy. Despite the talk about her, she did not recognize the need to be more cautious or circumspect in her behavior, and she persisted in carrying on her espionage activities as normal. After weeks of surveillance, federal agent Allan Pinkerton arrested her on her doorstep and imprisoned her and her youngest daughter, Rose, in their home. Though surrounded by guards day and night, she managed to collect her most sensitive intelligence documents and stuff them into the stockings and boots of a close friend who smuggled them to Confederate leaders. For the next three months, O'Neal Greenhow claimed that she received and relayed dozens of coded messages past her frequently inebriated guards. To halt the flow of information, on January 18, 1862, federal officials sent her and her daughter to Old Capitol Prison in Washington where they were held for over five months.

In the early spring of 1862, after nearly two years' imprisonment, federal officials arranged to deport O'Neal Greenhow and her daughter. In early June, they first sent her to Baltimore, Maryland, and then to Richmond, Virginia, the Confederate capital. At the request of President Jefferson Davis, she traveled to England and France to raise political and financial support for the Confederacy. While abroad, she wrote a memoir, *My Imprisonment, and the First Year of Abolition Rule at Washington*. She returned home in September 1864, in a British blockade runner named *The Condor*, carrying vital diplomatic papers and gold valued at $2,000, worn in a large reticule around her neck. Off the coast of Wilmington, North Carolina, the vessel ran aground while fleeing from a Union gunboat. Desperate to avoid capture, she convinced several men to row her and two other Confederate agents to shore. When high seas capsized the boat, she alone drowned, perhaps weighed down by the gold sovereigns. News of her death provoked a deluge of grief throughout the South, and she was buried in Wilmington on October 1, 1864, with full military honors.

See also **Spies and Espionage**

Selected Readings

Leonard, Elizabeth D. *All the Daring of the Soldier: Women of the Civil War Armies*. New York: Penguin Books. 2001.

Guerrilla War

As I reached the corner below the post office, I noticed an unusual crowd …. I stopped and in a moment a ruffianly looking fellow came riding out … with a revolving pistol in his hand, and flourishing it round, ordered one man in sight to come out and fall into line …. I can't say I never was cooler in my life. I know I was never whiter or felt weaker, for it was the bushmen!

—Eliza C. Draper, letter from Eliza C. Draper to her sister, Clarksville, Missouri, November 1, 1864 (Draper 1993, 51–52)

As the Civil War progressed, and as the amount of Southern territory occupied by Union forces increased, groups of citizens in specific regions of the Confederacy turned to guerrilla warfare to resist and take revenge on their Union occupiers and pro-Union neighbors. In areas controlled by Confederate military forces, Unionist civilians likewise engaged in guerrilla violence against Confederate soldiers and their sympathizers. Missouri, East Tennessee, and western North Carolina were among the areas that experienced the harshest guerrilla violence.

Guerrilla warfare turned rural farm communities upside down and inside out. When a civilian population was divided in its political allegiances, neighbor became pitted against neighbor, and family against family. Union (or Confederate) military forces, in an attempt to restore order, frequently resorted to the same guerrilla tactics. As discord and violence escalated, more and more civilian men and women found themselves forced to take sides. As the number of combatants increased, it became increasingly difficult for any individual to distinguish their allies from their enemies. Both women and men living in guerrilla-ravaged communities, whether or not they or their families were guerrillas, found their lives consumed by years of uninterrupted trauma and violence.

When a gang of men on horseback charged up to the front door of a home in Missouri or western North Carolina, the occupants often had no idea whether the raiders were local guerrillas, Confederate troops, Union soldiers, or a band of outlaws or deserters. Similarly, when a gang of bushwhackers demanded that the woman of a house state her family's political loyalty (a common guerrilla strategy), she often had no clue which response would ensure the survival of her menfolk and the security of her family's farm. Sometimes a family's loyalty mattered not; Missouri guerrillas who were supposedly pro-Confederate were known to rob and terrorize Confederate sympathizers as well as Unionists. To complicate matters further, Missouri guerrillas sometimes disguised themselves as Union soldiers and Union soldiers dressed as guerrillas. Union soldiers, disguised as Missourians, conducted raids on Unionist and Confederate farmhouses, stealing horses and forcing civilians (many of them women) to give information, surrender their foodstuffs, and feed them.

Civilian men often reasoned that it was safer to join a guerrilla force and eliminate their enemies than to remain at home waiting for their murders. Women found themselves locked in a similar struggle. With guerrillaism engulfing their menfolk and their communities, women aided whomever shared their loyalties. In western Missouri, in the large town that would one day be called Kansas City, ten teenage girls and young women, all under age 20 and relatives of known guerrillas, were imprisoned by Union military officials for "giving information" to their menfolk. By federal order, women who aided their guerrilla family members in any way—by providing meals, clothing, or nursing care—were subject to execution (Harris 1995, 294). Although four girls and women of this group were killed when the prison building they were jailed in collapsed, no woman or girl is known to have been executed for aiding guerrillas.

In western North Carolina, Unionist women took huge risks when they assisted Union soldiers traveling to federally occupied areas of Tennessee and Kentucky. They gave the soldiers food and shelter, and, in some cases, acted as their mountain guides. The Hollinger sisters of Flat Rock, North Carolina, ranging in age from 16 to 24, were part of an underground railroad for prisoners escaping from a Confederate prison in South Carolina. The sisters took an enormous risk, considering that two of them were married to Confederate soldiers (Inscoe and McKinney 1998).

Female Unionists in western North Carolina participated in raids against their Confederate neighbors. Pro-Union women also risked their lives to protect their husbands, fathers, brothers, and sons from guerrilla gangs, and, when not successful, were witnesses to their brutal murders. When Unionist women tried to protect their families, guerrillas sometimes tortured them until they revealed the whereabouts of their menfolk. Guerrillas brutalized a group of Unionist women living in Madison County, North Carolina, when they refused to divulge their male relatives' hideout. They were whipped and beaten, and then hung or strung up until nearly dead. As a woman approached death, the men cut her down, tried to force her to talk, and if she did not speak, hung her up again (McKinney 1992, 44; Paludan 1981, 96). Confederate women suffered as well in this region, enduring the destruction and horror of Unionist attacks on their homes and farms.

In addition to the atrocities confronting women living in the midst of guerrilla war, they had the additional burden of wrestling with all the problems facing women living in other parts of the Confederacy. They had to take over their husbands' and fathers' farm labor and management and become the sole protectors of their children and elderly relatives, all while maintaining their regular domestic duties. Death by starvation was a constant threat in the guerrilla-ridden mountain villages of western North Carolina because food and crops were frequently destroyed, stolen, or consumed in raids. To feed their children and families, mountain farm women stole food and rioted as they did in a few other areas of the Confederacy. They wrote impassioned letters to North Carolina Governor Zebulon Vance. Women also banded together to write and sign petitions to demand aid from the state and Confederate government.

Some Missouri guerrillas prided themselves on the fact that they did not kill or physically or sexually attack white women. Yet, like Union and Confederate soldiers, they felt no compunctions about beating, raping, and killing African-American and Native American women.

There are surprisingly few accounts of the activities of women guerrillas even though it is widely accepted that women joined male bushwhackers in leading and participating in guerrilla raids. There is evidence that women, like MALINDA PRITCHARD BLALOCK of North Carolina, led their own guerrilla groups or acted violently on their own. Union soldiers in Kansas and Missouri recorded their fears of armed women in their journals and letters. Henry Dysart, a Union private from Iowa, noted that women were the leaders of a mixed band of outlaws who stole wounded soldiers' weapons, money, and clothing (Fellman 1989, 215–216). Despite the undeniable presence of women among guerrilla warriors, many of their individual stories have not been uncovered, nor have any personal writings emerged.

See also **Invasion and Occupation; Patriotism**

Selected Readings

Ash, Stephen V. *When the Yankees Came: Conflict and Chaos in the Occupied South, 1861–1865*. Chapel Hill: University of North Carolina Press. 1995.

Fellman, Michael. *Inside War: The Guerrilla Conflict in Missouri During the American Civil War*. New York: Oxford University Press. 1989.

Harris, Charles F. "Catalyst for Terror: The Collapse of the Women's Prison in Kansas City." *Missouri Historical Review*. 89 (3) (1995): 290–306.

McKinney, Gordon B. "Women's Role in Civil War Western North Carolina." *North Carolina Historical Review*. 69 (January 1992): 37–56.

Gunboat Societies

Following the historic naval battle between the two ironclad warships, the USS *Monitor* and the CSS *Virginia* (formerly the USS *Merrimack*) on March 9, 1862, the building of ironclad gunboats for Confederate civilian defense became a cause célèbre in Southern coastal cities. In fact, months before the battle, in December 1861, the women of New Orleans formed an association to raise money to construct ironclad warships (Coski 1996, 82).

All during the spring of 1862, white women in Norfolk and Richmond, Virginia; Savannah, Georgia; Mobile, Alabama; Charleston, South Carolina; and several ports along the Mississippi River formed gunboat societies to raise money to assist the Confederate Navy in building these technological marvels. Women capitalized on their traditional arsenal of money-raising projects—raffles, fairs, bazaars, elaborate entertainments—and also solicited contributions from prominent citizens to support the defense of their communities from Union naval attacks and invasion. As in the SOLDIERS' AID SOCIETIES, men assumed supportive roles in the gunboat societies. They assisted with fund-raising, financial management, and occasionally acted as intermediaries between Confederate naval officials and the societies' female leaders.

In the Confederate capital of Richmond, Virginia, located on the James River, a group of elite women established a gunboat society in April 1862. At a meeting with President Jefferson Davis and Secretary of the Navy Stephen Mallory, the society's president, Maria Gaitskell Clopton, wife of a distinguished judge, received official support for its gunboat project. At a meeting on April 24, 1862, the Ladies' Gunboat Association (also known as the Ladies' Defense Association and the Ladies' Aid and Defence Society) agreed to work toward "building a gunboat for the defence of the James River." They also asserted their political purpose for such an endeavor, resolving, "That we, as the weaker sex, being unable actively to join in the defence of our country, will encourage the hearts, and strengthen, the hands of our husbands, brothers, fathers and friends by all means within our power" (Ladies Gunboat Association Papers, Southern Women's History Collection, Museum of the Confederacy).

Despite their need to enlist the assistance of male supporters, the women agreed that they wanted the work and the contributions of their gunboat society to be "peculiarly ours as women." Toward this goal, they determined that they would "give such ornaments of gold, and articles of silver, as are our private personal property." Then they articulated the purpose of such sacrifice: to be able, as women, to pass on a patriotic legacy to their children by ensuring the safety and survival of historic Richmond.

> For should it be our sad fate to become slaves, ornaments would ill become our state of bondage; while if God in his infinite mercy shall crown our efforts with success, we will be content to wear the laurel leaves of victory, and point our children to our civil and religious liberty so gloriously achieved and say "These be thy jewels." (Southern Women's History Collection, Museum of the Confederacy)

The Richmond gunboat society was successful in achieving its goal. It is estimated that members raised $30,000 toward the construction of the CSS *Virginia II*, which was launched in Richmond on the James River in June 1863 (Coski 1996, 85). On April 3, 1865, the *Virginia II* was destroyed, along with other Confederate gunboats on the James River, during the Union invasion of Richmond.

Selected Readings

Coski, John M. *Capital Navy: The Men, Ships, and Operations of the James River Squadron*. Campbell, CA: Savas Publishing. 1996.

Faust, Drew Gilpin. *Mothers of Invention: Women of the Slaveholding South in the American Civil War*. New York: Vintage Books. 1997.

H

Hale, Sarah Josepha
(1788–1879)

From 1827 to 1877, Sarah Josepha Buell Hale influenced public opinion through the pages of the women's magazines she edited, the *Ladies' Magazine* and *Godey's Lady's Book*. As literary editor of *Godey's Lady's Book*, the leading women's magazine in the United States, she promoted numerous social and political causes, among them women's education, the advancement of women in the medical profession, women's property rights, unity between the North and South, and colonization for African Americans. In addition to her career as an editor, she wrote extensively, publishing novels, essays, poems, short stories, plays, anthologies, cookbooks, etiquette pamphlets, and a women's biographical dictionary. As the conflict over slavery increasingly divided the North and South during the 1850s, she promoted programs that would foster national unity, all through the pages of *Godey's Lady's Book*. She lent her editorial support to the project to rescue Mount Vernon, George Washington's home in Virginia in the mid-1850s. During the Civil War, her 17-year campaign to install a nationally celebrated Thanksgiving Day was realized when President Abraham Lincoln proclaimed the last Thursday in November 1863, as a day of National Thanksgiving.

A native of Newport, New Hampshire, Sarah Josepha Buell was the daughter of farmers. She was educated first by her mother, and then by her brother Horatio who tutored her during his vacations from Dartmouth College. In 1806, Buell established her own school and taught until she married attorney David Hale in 1813. Hale encouraged and assisted his wife as she continued her education at home in the evenings. When he died in 1822, Buell Hale was pregnant with their fifth child. With her young family to support, she engaged in a millinery business with her sister-in-law. She published her first book, a volume of poetry, in 1823. Soon literary journals were accepting her short stories and poetry. In 1827, her novel *Northwood: or, Life North and South; Showing the True Character of Both* was published to critical acclaim.

The success of *Northwood* brought Buell Hale to the attention of a Boston publisher planning the nation's first magazine for women. He hired her to edit the *Ladies' Magazine* in 1827. While editor, Buell Hale instituted a number of innovations unique to American periodical publishing of that era. She made it clear from the outset that the magazine would be a truly American publication and would not reprint articles from British magazines, a common practice at the time. She also accepted only original contributions for publication. The *Ladies' Magazine* was also unique in that it encouraged the work of women writers, publishing their fiction, essays, poetry, and scholarly articles.

In 1837, Buell Hale entered into a partnership with Louis Godey, publisher of the Philadelphia-based woman's magazine *Godey's Lady's Book*. When the *Ladies' Magazine* was absorbed into *Godey's Lady's Book*, she became the magazine's literary editor.

In 1852, in reaction to the publication of *Uncle Tom's Cabin* by HARRIET BEECHER STOWE, Buell Hale republished *Northwood* in a revised, expanded edition, hoping that it would counteract the divisiveness produced by the national furor over Beecher Stowe's book. The 1852 edition of *Northwood* included a discussion of one of Buell Hale's pet projects, her support of colonization as a solution to the problem of slavery. Buell Hale detested slavery, but unlike many Northern abolitionists, she did not believe that the slaves, once freed, could be assimilated into white society. In particular, she supported the plan to emancipate the slaves and send them to Liberia, the African colony founded by the American Colonization Society in West Africa. To this effect, in 1853, she published *Liberia; or Mr. Peyton's Experiment*, a fictional work that further delineated her views on colonization. Based on this story, it is clear that she believed that the slaves should be educated to prepare them for freedom and independent life in Liberia. In the pages of *Liberia*, she endorsed the concept that Southern slaveholders should be compensated for their financial loss after abolition. According to Buell Hale, the federal government should either reimburse slaveholders or the slaves should earn the money to buy their freedom. The colonization solution had many supporters in the South and a following among Northern conservatives. It appealed particularly to white Americans who believed as Buell Hale did that "two races who do not intermarry can never live together as equals" (Finley 1938, 176).

Although Buell Hale delved into political writing, such topics were taboo in *Godey's Lady's Book*. Louis Godey prohibited the inclusion of religious or political material in the magazine. In terms of the volatile 1850s, he wanted to make sure that no Southern subscriber was offended or inclined to cancel a subscription. In 1860, on the eve of the Civil War, *Godey's Lady's Book*'s circulation was 150,000, higher than any other woman's magazine, which ranked it among the top-circulating general-interest periodicals of the era. Shortly after the war began, its circulation dropped precipitously when mail delivery ceased between the North and South. Despite the lack of Southern readers, Godey still did not permit political opinion to seep into the pages of his magazine. Nevertheless, the war did creep into the fiction section. As literary editor, Buell Hale published numerous short stories on war-related themes.

Through the war years, she supported higher education for women. *Godey's Lady's Book* continued to publish its ever-popular song sheets, colored fashion plates, articles of interest to women, recipes, household hints, and pages devoted to children. In acknowledgment of the war raging in the South, one of Buell Hale's editorials explained,

> If the physical world were convulsed with storms, and all the elements of nature charged with destructive power, would it not be a blessed relief to find a "lodge in the wilderness"? An oasis in the desert? A quiet, cultured garden on which the burning lava had not even breathed? (quoted in Finley 1938, 193)

As much as she hoped that *Godey's Lady's Book* would be that "lodge," its circulation declined during the war as other publications embraced the national conflict and attracted Northern women's attention.

During the Civil War, Buell Hale's ambition to establish Thanksgiving as a national holiday was finally realized. Her early attempts to promote the holiday began in the late 1820s in the *Ladies' Magazine*. First formally endorsed by George Washington, the observance of a national Thanksgiving Day was met with apathy in many regions of the country. Through the late 1820s and 1830s, Buell Hale kept the celebration alive, first in the *Ladies' Magazine* and then in *Godey's Lady's Book*. In 1846, she initiated an active campaign for the nationalizing of the November holiday by publishing editorials and writing letters to state and territorial governors, several presidents, and other influential politicians throughout the nation. All through the 1850s, she advocated the holiday, in the hopes that the national celebration would unify the North and South. By the time of the Civil War, she had written thousands of letters in the hope that all states and territories would recognize Thanksgiving Day. In 1861, she implored her readers to observe a Thanksgiving Day of Peace, asking that "we lay aside our enmities and strifes on this one day" (Finley 1938, 197). In 1863, after having sent several letters to President Lincoln, she received a response from Secretary of State William H. Seward, indicating that he had forwarded her letters to the president. Weeks later, Lincoln proclaimed that the nation would observe a day of Thanksgiving on the last Thursday of November 1863. She then hoped that Congress would officially designate a national Thanksgiving Day, but this did not occur in her lifetime. Not until 1941, during Franklin Delano Roosevelt's administration, did Congress issue a joint resolution instituting Thanksgiving Day as the fourth Thursday in November.

All through the Civil War, Buell Hale publicized the building of Vassar Female College. From its inception, she published articles and editorials highlighting the details of the educational experiment as they unfolded. Although she had endorsed hundreds of schools for women in the past, she was particularly involved in the plans for Vassar because of its goal to offer young women a collegiate education equal to that offered by the best men's colleges. When college founder Matthew Vassar's plan to hire an all-women faculty met with opposition, she rallied to support his intention. Her editorials roused public support for the inclusion of women professors, and although women faculty were a minority at Vassar, they were not excluded as most of the college's administrators wished. She also pushed for the inclusion of domestic science in Vassar's curriculum. Though this proposal was ignored at Vassar, other colleges and universities adopted domestic science programs. As much as she approved of knowledge of the classics, higher mathematics, and the sciences for women, she insisted that women needed grounding in the domestic arts because the private realm of the household remained women's dominant sphere of influence. As she explained to her readers,

> The young lawyer or merchant who has had the good fortune to carry off to his new home a fair graduate of Vassar College will doubtless be not a little proud of the intellectual acquirements of his bride. But when he comes down with a limp collar to an ill-cooked breakfast, the idea will be likely to occur to him that it would be well if the idol of his heart ... had acquired something more of that practical training for her actual sphere. ... (Rogers 1985, 108)

After the war, Buell Hale continued as literary editor at *Godey's Lady's Book*, though more and more of her duties were delegated to other editors. She was, after all, in her late seventies. In 1870, at the age of 81, she published a volume of verse titled *Love: or, Woman's Destiny*. In the book's preface, she indicated that her purpose was to oppose the efforts of women who wished to engage in the professions—to do, as she put it, "the proper work of men." She opposed the suffrage for women, though she never turned her back on the necessity of expanding women's educational opportunities.

In December 1877, Buell Hale retired from her work at *Godey's Lady's Book*. She was 89. She died in Philadelphia in April 1879.

See also **Literary Women**

Selected Readings

Hoffman, Nicle Tonkovich. "Legacy Profile: Sarah Josepha Hale." *Legacy.* 7 (Fall 1990): 47–54.

Okker, Patricia. *Our Sister Editors: Sarah J. Hale and the Tradition of Nineteenth-Century American Women Editors*. Athens: University of Georgia Press. 1995.

Rogers, Sherbrooke. *Sarah Josepha Hale: A New England Pioneer 1788–1879*. Grantham, NH: Tompson & Rutter. 1985.

Hamilton, Gail (1833–1896)

Gail Hamilton, the pseudonym of the prominent mid- to late-nineteenth-century journalist Mary Abigail Dodge, wrote passionately about politics, religion, and the role of women in society. The author of more than 25 books, she was best known for her essays, which were published in several of the most widely circulated newspapers of the day. During the late 1850s, while residing in Washington, DC, she became acquainted with leading politicians and witnessed the political turmoil in Congress as the North and South collided toward war. During the Civil War, her political opinion pieces brought her to the center of a controversial debate about the proper role of women during wartime.

Mary Abigail Dodge was the daughter of well-to-do farmers in Hamilton, Massachusetts. An unusually intelligent child, she was encouraged by her parents to read, write, and develop her intellect. Her mother, a former teacher, guided her daughter's education. Mary loved book-learning and the outdoors but resisted all forms of domestic training. Throughout her life, she abhorred housework of any kind. Her parents appear to have accepted her inclinations and did not force her to become domestically competent as most adolescent girls of her era were expected to do. After attending the local public school, she went on to acquire an excellent education at Ipswich Female Seminary in Ipswich, Massachusetts. After graduation in 1850, she taught at the school for four years. She then acquired a job teaching for one year at the prestigious Hartford Female Seminary in Hartford, Connecticut, followed by several years of teaching at the public high school in Hartford.

While Dodge was in the classroom, she seriously contemplated a writing career and began writing and publishing essays in a few newspapers. The first noteworthy recognition of her skill as a writer came in 1856 when the editor of the antislavery newspaper the *National Era*, Gamaliel Bailey, agreed to publish her work. From that point on, writing became the focus of her professional life. Sandwiched in between long hours teaching and preparing lessons, Dodge wrote essays and poetry for the *National Era* and for the *Independent*, the most prominent literary Christian newspaper in the country.

By 1858, Dodge was weary of teaching and anxious to dedicate herself full time to her writing. She resigned from her position at Hartford High School and agreed to become governess to Gamaliel Bailey's children in Washington, DC. Her duties did not consume all of her waking hours, leaving ample time for writing and for observing the Washington political and social scene. By this time, in addition to her work for the *National Era* and the *Independent*, she was a contributor to the *Congregationalist*, another important national religious newspaper. Unusually protective of her private life, she assumed the pen name "Gail Hamilton" and fought to keep her identity a secret. As she watched the political drama in Washington unfold, she read avidly, conversed with prominent Republicans and Democrats, and wrote political essays for the *Congregationalist*, using a different pen name "Cunctare."

In 1860, Hamilton reluctantly returned to Massachusetts to help care for her ailing mother. Despite her mother's ill health, she managed to keep her editors satisfied. Her first book of collected essays, *Country Living and Country Thinking*, appeared in 1862. During the next six years, she published seven more volumes of her opinion pieces on women's rights, travel, and rural life. Unlike many LITERARY WOMEN concerned with their reputations, Hamilton gave herself permission to write as boldly and as forcefully as she dared, seemingly without the concern that she was "unsexing" herself, a freedom that may have stemmed from her use of pseudonyms. As she described it, "There is about my serious style a vigor of thought, a comprehensiveness of view, a closeness of logic, and a terseness of diction, commonly supposed to pertain only to the stronger sex" (quoted in Coultrap-McQuin 1990, 117). Yet, despite her fame and her confidence in her innate talent, she privately doubted her abilities. In 1864, she confided her misgivings in a letter to her friend, the author Henry James.

> I think I am better than any book I ever wrote, or, I fear, any that I ever shall write. Nothing satisfies me. I catch glimpses of the beautiful Truth. I know I hear her voice and feel her coming, but I only lay hold of the hem of her robe as she passes by. … The lovely form escapes me. … I write because I do write, because I must write, because I will write. Yet nothing I have ever written has seemed to me adequate when it was accomplished. My life gives me great joy, but also great unrest. (Hamilton 1901, 1: 408–409)

In March 1863, her best-known writing on the war appeared in the *Atlantic Monthly*. The publication of the political essay "A Call to My Country-Women" created an immediate sensation and prompted other women to step forward and publish their views of the appropriate mission for Northern women in the Civil War. "A Call to My Country-Women" was reissued as a pamphlet and was widely available throughout the North.

From the beginning of "A Call to My Country-Women," Hamilton makes clear that she is addressing the ordinary, middle-class white woman of the North, the women who were "at this moment darning stockings, tending babies, sweeping floors," rather than the famous few who were already crusading at the front. She commends all that Northern women have accomplished for the war effort through SOLDIERS' AID SOCIETIES, while pointing out that "stitching does not crush rebellion, does not annihilate treason, or hew traitors in pieces before the Lord." Noting that "[t]he war cannot be finished by sheets and pillow-cases," she argues that a crucial element—patriotic passion—is missing from women's war work. Without "this soul of fire ... burning white and strong and steady," she maintains, there can be no true victory (Hamilton 1863, 346).

If patriotic fervor was not evident in soldiers' aid societies, then how should it be manifested? According to Hamilton's vision, women's letters to husbands, sons, and lovers at the front should be the primary vehicle of women's love of country and hopes for peace. She urged women to fill their correspondence with optimism and strength rather than "tears and sighs" about their hardships on the home front. To avoid weakening their soldier-husbands by revealing their troubles at home, Hamilton offered the following advice:

> Fill your letters with kittens and Canaries, with baby's shoes, and Johnny's sled, and the old cloak which you have turned into a handsome gown. ... Show him that you clearly apprehend that all this warfare means peace. ... Help him to bear his burdens by showing him how elastic you are under yours. Hearten him, enliven him, tone him up to true hero-pitch. (Hamilton 1863, 347)

In "A Call to My Country-Women," Hamilton also waged war on what she termed "weak talk," the growing public debate on the merits of compromise with the South, a solution that she believed posed a grave danger to democracy and liberty. She appealed to women to stamp out talk of "buying peace," to rise up and demand that the North live up to its moral obligation.

> Will you fail the world in this fateful hour by your faint-heartedness? Will you fail yourself, and put the knife to your own throat? For the peace which you so dearly buy shall bring to you neither ease nor rest. You will but have spread a bed of thorns. Failure will write disgrace upon the brow of this generation, and shame will outlast the age. ... Let compromise, submission, and every form of dishonorable peace be not so much as named among us. ... Wherever the serpent's head is raised, strike it down. (Hamilton 1863, 349)

For some women, "A Call to My Country-Women" improperly demanded that women take political responsibility. Women belonged in the domestic world of "women's sphere," where they could exert a quiet influence on their loved ones and, at the most, nurture soldiers far from home with their good works. The suggestion that women shoulder a political mission was an anathema to many of the women who stepped forward to object to Hamilton's "Call."

Hamilton's essay embodied much of what she believed was the proper role of women in society. In her essays on women's rights throughout her career, she encouraged women to communicate their beliefs and convictions, political and otherwise, and to be independent and strong minded. She urged women to develop their characters and intellects, pointing out that self-improvement was a duty they owed to God. Hamilton also promoted the expansion of women's educational opportunities and equality for women in the workplace. In general, she believed that the concept of separate spheres for men and women diminished the lives of both genders. As for herself, she once commented, "I shall not confine myself to my sphere. I hate my sphere. I like everything that is outside of it,—or, better still, my sphere rounds out into undefined space. I was born into the whole world. I am monarch of all I survey" (quoted in Sizer 2000, 125).

After the war, Hamilton continued to promote women's rights though she never supported woman suffrage, believing that it would not change women's lives for the better. Beginning in 1871 and continuing through the mid-1890s, she spent the winter seasons living in Washington, DC, with her cousin Harriet Stanwood Blaine and her husband, the Republican Congressman and Speaker of the House James G. Blaine. Back amid the nation's political scene, she wrote political commentary for several newspapers, including the *New York Tribune*. She also authored three biographies, a novel, some poetry, and some stories for children. Following a massive stroke, she died in Hamilton, Massachusetts, in 1896.

Selected Readings

Coultrap-McQuin, Susan. "Legacy Profile: Gail Hamilton (1833–1896)." *Legacy.* 4(2) (Fall 1987): 53–58.

Sizer, Lyde Cullen. *The Political Work of Northern Women Writers and the Civil War, 1850–1872*. Chapel Hill: University of North Carolina Press. 2000.

Harper, Frances Watkins (1825–1911)

One of the most distinguished African-American poets and writers of the nineteenth century, Frances Watkins Harper began a prolific career in social reform as an abolitionist orator in 1854. As the national conflict over slavery heightened during the 1850s, she gained renown as an eloquent antislavery speaker. During the Civil War, despite desperate personal circumstances, she traveled from city to city hammering home to her audiences her political message that the mission of the war was not just to abolish slavery, but to make a place for the freedpeople in American society.

Born free in Baltimore, Maryland, Frances Ellen Watkins was raised and educated by her uncle, a clergyman. She became a teacher in Ohio in 1850. After relocating to Pennsylvania in 1853, she involved herself in the abolitionist movement, becoming an antislavery orator, poet, and writer in 1854.

In 1860, after more than six years on the lecture circuit, Watkins was exhausted from being on the road and was longing for a family life. In November of that year, she married Fenton Harper, a free black man and father of three children. She bought a small farm in Grove City, Ohio, for her new family, using money she had saved from her years of lecturing. The following year, she gave birth to a daughter, Mary. During the time of her brief marriage, Watkins Harper continued to write poetry and occasionally lectured, though for the most part she devoted herself to domestic concerns and to her small business making and selling butter.

Even while immersed in the care of her husband and their children, she kept a watchful eye on national political developments. She lectured in Columbus, Ohio, regarding President Abraham Lincoln's Emancipation Proclamation. A passage from a letter to her friend, the Underground Railroad leader William Still, portrays her poetic, emphatic style of expression.

> Well, thank God that the President did not fail us, that the fierce rumbling of democratic thunder did not shake from his hand the bolt he leveled against slavery. Oh, it would have been so sad if, after all the desolation and carnage that have dyed our plains with blood ... had the arm of Executive power failed us in the nation's fearful crisis! (quoted in Boyd 1994, 53)

When her husband died in May 1864, Watkins Harper was shocked to learn of his extensive debt. As soon as his estate was settled, creditors claimed the farm and all of their belongings. She was destitute, losing even the equipment she used to make butter. She immediately traveled east and resumed her lecturing career to support herself and her daughter.

As an orator, few women speakers either before or during the war were considered the equal of Watkins Harper. An excerpt from the *Portland Advertiser* (Maine) is typical of the accolades she received from abolitionist audiences.

> ... [T]he deep fervor of feeling and pathos that she manifests, together with the choice selection of language which she uses arm her elocution with almost superhuman force and power over her spellbound audience. (quoted in Boyd 1994, 43)

As in the late 1850s, many of her Civil War speeches were read by abolitionists all over the North and Midwest. *The Liberator*, the *National Anti-Slavery Standard*, the *Anti-Slavery Bugle* (Ohio), and the African-American newspapers the *Christian Recorder* and the *Anglo-African Magazine* regularly published her lectures.

After the war, Watkins Harper courageously embarked on a lecture tour of the South, an especially perilous time for African Americans as Southern whites struggled to reassert white supremacy. Although there is no record detailing her personal experiences as she traveled in the South during this time, it is known that she lectured African Americans on the challenges confronting them as a result of Reconstruction. She also advocated women's rights. During the late 1860s and for the rest of the century, she devoted herself to her writing, and to the causes of woman suffrage, African-American civil rights, and international peace. She helped form the National Association of Colored Women and served for a time as its vice president.

See also **Abolitionists; African-American Women; Literary Women**

Selected Readings

Bacon, Margaret H. "'One Great Bundle of Humanity': Frances Ellen Watkins Harper (1825–1911)." *Pennsylvania Magazine of History and Biography.* 113(17) (January 1989): 21–44.

Boyd, Melba Joyce. *Discarded Legacy: Politics and Poetics in the Life of Frances E. W. Harper, 1825– 1911.* Detroit: Wayne State University Press. 1994.

Hine, Darlene Clark. "Harper, Frances Ellen Watkins." In *Black Women in America: An Historical Encyclopedia.* Edited by Darlene Clark Hine, Elsa Barkley Brown, and Rosalyn Terborg-Penn. Brooklyn, NY: Carlson Publishing. 532–537.

Haviland, Laura Smith (1808–1898)

By the time of the Civil War, Laura Smith Haviland had already devoted many years to the abolitionist cause and to helping enslaved African Americans escape to freedom. In 1863, she continued her long record of humanitarian activism by becoming a leader of freedpeople's relief in the South and in Kansas. During the last years of the war, she braved the hazards of travel throughout the Southern states to help the African-American and white refugees, to inspect refugee camps and army hospitals, to assist Union prisoners, and to expose and eliminate corruption in federal and military institutions. Confident, audacious, and self-righteously religious, Haviland commanded respect wherever she went—a characteristic that ensured her success as an activist.

Laura Smith spent her youth in a Quaker agricultural community in western New York State. Four years after marrying fellow Quaker Charles Haviland, she moved to Raisin Township, Michigan Territory, to open that frontier to farming. She became involved in the abolitionist movement very early; in 1834, she and Elizabeth Chandler established the Logan Female Anti-Slavery Society. When the community's Quaker elders objected that the society's antislavery affairs were too political, the Havilands withdrew from the Society of Friends and joined the Wesleyan Methodist Church, a faith that encouraged abolitionist activity.

An 1845 erysipelas epidemic (a streptococcal disease of the skin that is also known as St. Anthony's Fire) caused the deaths of Smith Haviland's husband, daughter, parents, and sister. Following this tragedy, she immersed herself in assisting fugitive slaves via the Underground Railroad.

During the early years of the war, Smith Haviland continued directing Raisin Institute, the school she and her husband founded in 1837. Open to white and African-American male and female students, the secondary school prepared many of its graduates for careers in education. In 1863, following the departure of 17 male students to the Union army, she gathered 1,800 to 2,000 items of clothing to be distributed among the freedpeople, and collected medical and food supplies for the army hospitals. She traveled down the Ohio River, dispensed some of her aid at Cairo,

Illinois, and then steamed south on the Mississippi River to Tennessee. There she visited hospitals, distributed her stores, and offered assistance wherever possible. An important component of the help she offered was in the form of religious ministering and proselytizing. Whenever she tended wounded and ill soldiers, she read from her Bible and prayed by their bedsides. When offering food and clothing to the freedpeople, she quoted liberally from scripture and proffered advice on how they could live morally and devoutly as free Christians.

Like most Northern abolitionists of the East and West, Smith Haviland was convinced that the Civil War was God's way of assigning retribution to the South for its refusal to surrender the evils of slavery. In her mind, God was vengeful and the North's destruction of the South was his way of reinstituting justice.

In her autobiography, Smith Haviland reveals that she could summon no sympathy for the trials and privations of a former slaveholding woman she met on a Mississippi steamboat. Hoping for a sympathetic ear, the woman told her,

> "I tell you it is mighty hard, for my pa paid his own money for our niggers; and that's not all they've robbed us of. They [Union soldiers] have taken our horses and cattle and sheep *and every thing*." As I [Smith Haviland] had my little Bible in my hand, I turned to the predicted destruction of Babylon in Revelation, and read, "Fine flour, and wheat, and beasts, and sheep, and horses, and chariots, and slaves, and souls of men." "You see here," I said, "are the very articles you have named. And God is the same unchanging Lord to-day."

The ex-slaveholder repeated her refrain, certain that she had not made her point, "[B]ut I tell you, madam, its [sic] mighty, mighty hard" (Haviland 1881, 256).

Smith Haviland's bluntness and her ability to state her opinion forcefully and without mincing words set her apart from the majority of women Civil War activists. Many women believed that they made more headway in a man's world when they adhered to societal conventions for women's speech. Smith Haviland made no concessions to propriety, and given her success in effecting bureaucratic change, her bold, emphatic approach achieved her goals.

Once, when asked by a high-ranking military official to give her opinion of the army surgeon in charge of a Memphis hospital, she declared, "I think he is an unfeeling tyrant. The white of his eyes had the color of red flannel, and the unmistakable brandy breath made standing near him very unpleasant" (Haviland 1881, 261). Within weeks, the surgeon was dismissed.

In 1864, Smith Haviland returned to Michigan to raise funds and supplies. She helped organize the Freedmen's Relief Association in Detroit. In the early spring, she traveled south again, this time to Vicksburg and Natchez, Mississippi, followed by trips to Baton Rouge and New Orleans, Louisiana.

In New Orleans, she championed 3,000 Union prisoners incarcerated on Ship Island and Dry Tortugas, two Union prison encampments. When she toured Ship Island, she was outraged. She found the filth and overcrowded living conditions, the inadequate diet, and the untreated outbreak of scurvy intolerable. What infuriated her most was her discovery that almost all of the prisoners were serving long sentences for trivial offenses—mild verbal insubordination and petty theft among them. One prisoner had swapped his surplus rations with another soldier and for that offense had been charged with selling government property. As she pointed out in a letter to one government official, while the army was declaring itself desperate for enlistees, it was permitting thousands of able-bodied men to languish in the Gulf of Mexico. Smith Haviland persisted, going from one elected official to the next, until the prisoners were released and were returned to their regiments.

After another trip to gather supplies and funds in Michigan in mid-1864, she set out with the $4,000 in proceeds to dispense aid to freed African Americans and white Southern refugees in Kansas, most of whom were women and children. To her horror, she found white and black families dying from starvation. During late 1864 to 1865, tens of thousands of white and African-American refugees poured into Kansas from the South, many of them on a desperate search for food and shelter. She traveled throughout Kansas to provide whatever assistance she could.

Although she had nothing but praise for the freedpeople she helped, she scorned many of the Southern poor whites she met, especially those who refused to work when she demanded they do so in return for the aid they were given. She described this group as "the most ignorant, listless, and degraded of any people I had ever met." When a local official asked what she recommended be done for them, she recalls that she replied, "I would keep body and soul together till Spring opens ... and then load up your great army wagons, and take them out upon the rich prairies and dump them out, giving them the homely adage, 'Root, pig, or die.' " The Southern women's feelings for Haviland were mutual. Their comments, as recorded by the Michigan reformer, indicate that the manner in which she delivered her charity, as much as their lives depended on it, was insufferable. As Smith Haviland commented, "They swore they would not be tyrannized over by that Yankee woman any longer, and left, very much to my relief" (Haviland 1881, 371, 376).

Immediately after the war, Smith Haviland escorted more than 100 men, women, and children to Michigan to help them find jobs and to settle, perhaps in connection with SOJOURNER TRUTH's mission to place freed African Americans in Battle Creek, Michigan (Stanton and Anthony 1886, 3: 532).

See also **Abolitionists; Contraband Women; Teachers of the Freedpeople**

Selected Readings

Ambler, Effie K. "Haviland, Laura Smith." In *American National Biography, Vol. 10*. Edited by John A. Garraty and Mark C. Carnes. New York: Oxford University Press. 335–337.

Dillon, Merton L. "Haviland, Laura Smith." In *Notable American Women, 1607–1950*. Volume 2. Edited by Edward T. James et al. Cambridge, MA: Belknap Press of Harvard University Press. 1971. 159–160.

Hawks, Esther Hill (1833–1906)

Educator, physician, abolitionist, and women's rights activist, Esther Hill Hawks served the Northern cause in multiple capacities throughout the Civil War. A native of New Hampshire, Hill Hawks left teaching to pursue a career in medicine in the mid-1850s. One of six graduates of Boston's New England Female Medical College in 1857, she spent the years immediately prior to the war attempting to gain acceptance as a physician in southern New Hampshire. With her physician husband, John Milton Hawks, an active member of the American Anti-Slavery Society, she involved herself in the abolitionist movement. From the first days of the war in April 1861, Hill Hawks devoted hours of her time to the Women's Aid Society of Manchester, New Hampshire, organizing women from the region to sew the 2,000 shirts needed by New Hampshire soldiers.

The early years of the Civil War were filled with frustration for Hill Hawks who desperately sought to contribute her medical skills to the Union cause. During the summer of 1861, she traveled to Washington, DC, determined to serve as a doctor or, failing that, as a nurse. When she discovered that the federal government was refusing to hire female doctors, she applied for a nursing position. DOROTHEA DIX, superintendent of Union army nurses, rejected Hill Hawks's request, most likely because, at the age of 28, she fell two years short of the age required of women nurses. Refusing to be turned away, Hill Hawks stayed on in Washington working as a volunteer in the army hospitals. She discovered she had to settle for a job serving the soldiers tea, coffee, and snacks.

Hill Hawks returned to her fledgling medical practice in Manchester in late 1861 and continued to act as secretary of the Women's Aid Society. When her husband became superintendent of a U.S. government–controlled plantation on the South Carolina Sea Islands, she joined him there.

In January 1863, she was officially enlisted as a teacher attached to the 1st South Carolina Volunteer Infantry, one of the first all-black regiments. Her husband was the surgeon for the regiment. Over the next two years, she traveled with this unit, instructing African-American soldiers, workers, and children. During this period, she had numerous opportunities to employ her medical skills, though always on a temporary basis. When her husband accompanied the regiment on raids and missions, she was occasionally left in charge of medical care at the regimental hospital.

Hill Hawks reported in her diary that she derived enormous satisfaction from teaching the soldiers and the children of the freedpeople, though she continued to be troubled that her medical expertise, which was so sorely needed, was not being utilized. Following several experiences doctoring the wounded after battles that left soldiers "all mangled and ghastly," she doubted her will to pursue a medical career.

> I often wonder … if I am wasting time which should be devoted to my profession.
> Shall I ever resume its duties—sometimes I say *no* to the question, in my own mind.
> There is a feeling of *dread* connected with my experience, which I cannot shake off.
> I never wish to go through the same scenes. (Hawks 1984, 71)

During the final months of the war and the early years of Reconstruction, Hills Hawks was a school administrator and teacher working for the federally operated Freedmen's Bureau. Until 1870, she resided in Florida with her husband who was determined to open up Florida to business and settlement. In September of that year, Hill Hawks returned to New England to resume her medical career. She entered into practice with two other women doctors in Lynn, Massachusetts. In 1874, she established her own practice and assumed a role as a distinguished, active member of the Massachusetts medical community. Throughout the late nineteenth century, in addition to her professional work, she was deeply involved in social reform as an activist and philanthropist. Among the many causes she supported were public education, health care, and woman suffrage. In 1899, her medical service in the Civil War was acknowledged when she was elected an honorary member of the New Hampshire Association of Military Surgeons.

See also **Doctors; Teachers of the Freedpeople**

Selected Reading

Hawks, Esther Hill. *A Woman Doctor's Civil War: Esther Hill Hawks' Diary.* Edited by Gerald Schwartz. Columbia: University of South Carolina Press. 1984.

Hopkins, Juliet Opie (1818–1890)

As the superintendent of hospitals for Alabama soldiers and officers in Richmond, Virginia, during the first three years of the war, Juliet Opie Hopkins wielded more power in the realm of military hospital administration than most women working in Southern or Northern hospitals during the Civil War. Although other women directed Confederate military hospitals, most notable of whom was Captain SALLY TOMPKINS, they did not have the authority that Hopkins commanded. On the Union side, Northern women working in Union military hospitals did not fulfill comparable, leading positions of responsibility in hospital operations.

Juliet Ann Opie was born and raised at "Woodburn," her family's plantation in Jefferson County, Virginia. Her father was a wealthy slaveholder owning approximately 2,000 slaves, securing him a place in the most elite social circles. Although little information about her youth is available, it is known that she was tutored at home during her childhood. As a young adolescent, she attended Miss Ritchie's school in Richmond, Virginia. At the age of 16 when her mother died, Opie returned to Woodburn, reportedly to help superintend the plantation. It is more likely that she took charge of all domestic affairs on the estate, including managing the care of the slaves.

In 1837, when Juliet was 19 years old, she married Alexander George Gordon, a naval lieutenant. He left her a widow, though accounts differ widely as to the date of his death. She married again in 1854, this time to a prominent Alabama politician and former United States senator, Arthur Francis Hopkins, who served as chief justice of the

Alabama Supreme Court. The couple, residing in Mobile, Alabama, did not have children of their own, though they adopted a niece whom they considered their daughter.

Once the Civil War began in the spring of 1861, Opie Hopkins and her husband volunteered to help found hospitals for Alabama soldiers in Virginia, the seat of the early conflicts. With their own funds, and with money raised from members of their elite society and from the state of Alabama, they established three military hospitals in Richmond, known as the First, Second, and Third Alabama Hospitals. Because her husband was in his late sixties, Opie Hopkins, then in her early to mid-forties, performed the labor of administering the hospitals.

She was also called upon to establish hospitals in Warrenton, Culpepper Court House, Yorktown, Bristow Station, and Monterey, Virginia. On November 9, 1861, the vast numbers of soldiers crowding the Alabama hospitals spurred the Alabama state legislature to enact a law formalizing the institution of hospitals for wounded and sick soldiers of that state. The legislation also introduced the positions of hospital superintendent and hospital agent, appointments soon conferred on Opie Hopkins and her husband, respectively. In the role of superintendent, she was charged with the management of the existing Alabama military hospitals and all the new hospitals that she and her husband were to create. Once again, her husband's role was minimal while Opie Hopkins's duties were extensive. At the Third Alabama Hospital, she is known to have requisitioned all purchases of supplies. She scrutinized all incoming shipments that Alabama SOLDIERS' AID SOCIETIES and individual citizens sent to her. She inspected all the wards daily, ensuring that patients were receiving proper care and nourishment. She hired nurses; wrote letters for soldiers; handled their petitions for furloughs; collected and distributed newspapers, magazines, and books; recorded the names of the dead; and shipped their personal belongings home to their families. In a caring, personal gesture appreciated by the families of soldiers in this era, she carefully wrapped a lock of hair from each deceased soldier to be enclosed with his other possessions.

Fannie Beers, matron of the Third Alabama Hospital, reminisced in her memoir about Opie Hopkins. "I have never seen a woman better fitted for such work," Beers wrote. "Energetic, tireless, systematic, loving profoundly the cause and its defenders, she neglected no detail of business or other thing that should afford aid or comfort to the sick and wounded" (Beers 1889, 34). According to Beers, one morning, when she and Opie Hopkins arrived at the tobacco warehouse that was to be transformed into the Third Alabama Hospital, they discovered 50 soldiers lying in filth on the floor. The two women set to work immediately. By that night, Opie Hopkins had acquired a surgeon; hired nursing staff; obtained beds, clean bedding, and food; and had patients in their wards all fed and tucked in (Beers 1889, 43–45).

Although Opie Hopkins did not perform any nursing duties in the hospitals, she did care for soldiers on the battlefield during the Battle of Seven Pines near Fair Oaks, Virginia, on May 31 to June 1, 1862. As she was tending to fallen soldiers, she was wounded twice. Her injuries were serious enough to warrant surgery to extract bone fragments from her leg. She returned to her duties after healing from the operation, though she was encumbered with a limp from then on.

Late in 1863, the state of Alabama mandated the closing of its hospitals. As they were dissolved, the wounded and sick were transferred to the large Confederate military hospitals. After Opie Hopkins completed the transfers and finished her work, she returned to Alabama. A precise accounting of her activities after this time is not available. It is known that she managed a hospital at Camp Watts near Tuskegee, Alabama, at some point in 1864. In January 1865, she traveled to Montgomery, the state capital, to work in a hospital there until the final days of the Confederacy in April 1865. In the week after the Confederate defeat, as Union Brigadier General James H. Wilson's troops attacked the region, she and her husband became refugees, escaping to Newnan, Georgia.

When Opie Hopkins and her husband returned to their home in Mobile, they faced a dismal financial future. In addition to their property losses in Mobile, they each had given lavishly to the Alabama hospitals during the war. It is not clear how much they contributed, though some have conjectured that they donated hundred of thousands of dollars. Judge Hopkins died during the year after the war. A widow once again, Opie Hopkins moved to New York City where her husband had purchased property. Nothing definite is known of her years in the North, except that she often visited her adopted niece in Washington, DC. She died at the age of 71 in 1890, while visiting Washington. She was honored with a full military burial in Arlington National Cemetery where she was buried in the same gravesite as her niece's husband, Union General Romeyn Beck Ayers, who also served in the Civil War. Not until 1987 was a gravestone added to mark her burial site.

See also **Nurses**

Selected Readings

Griffith, Lucille. "Mrs. Juliet Opie Hopkins and Alabama Military Hospitals." *The Alabama Review*. 6(2) (April 1953): 99–120.

Schafer, Elizabeth D. "Hopkins, Juliet Ann Opie." In *American National Biography*. Volume 11. Edited by John A. Garraty and Mark C. Carnes. New York: Oxford University Press. 1999. 178–180.

Sterkx, H. E. "The Angel of the South." In *Some Notable Alabama Women During the Civil War*. University, AL: Alabama Civil War Centennial Commission. 1962. Online. Oakwood Military Cemetery. Richmond, Virginia. http://www.mindspring.com/~redeagle/Oakwood/Hopkins.htm

Hospital Ships

The hospital ships, or "floating hospitals" as they were often called, were critical to the survival of fallen Union soldiers in the aftermath of battles. These boats, most of them steamships, transported the wounded from the battlefields and rail depots to military hospitals further north or to Union-occupied cities of the South. The UNITED STATES SANITARY COMMISSION (USSC), through its Hospital Transport Service (HTS), and the Western Sanitary Commission (WSC) were the largest relief organizations maintaining hospital ships. The Union navy and army also operated hospital boats, including those on the rivers in the Trans-Mississippi Theater. AFRICAN-AMERICAN WOMEN (mostly CONTRABAND WOMEN), CATHOLIC NUNS, and white elite and middle-class women labored alongside the largely male medical and support staff on the hospital steamers, struggling to keep the wounded and ill soldiers alive until their transfer to Northern hospitals.

From the time of the Civil War's first battles in the summer of 1861, the Union army's Medical Bureau was overwhelmed by the medical needs of its troops. Especially during the first year of the war, it was common for the wounded and the sick to lie for days untended, without food or water, on or near the battlefields. Following the Battle at Fort Donelson in Tennessee in February 1862, the side-wheel steamer *City of Memphis* carried the wounded to hospitals in St. Louis.

The USS *Red Rover*, the U.S. Navy's first hospital ship, served the Mississippi Squadron from mid-1862 until the end of the war. According to one historian, African-American men and women most often formed the majority of the *Red Rover*'s crew, sometimes outnumbering white crew members by more than two to one (Roca 1998, 108). In addition to the many female contraband cooks and laundresses, white Catholic sister nurses and a select, specially trained group of female contraband nurses cared for the sick and wounded. The logs of the *Red Rover*'s commander indicate that the ship's medical officers (two of whom were Bostonians) provided nurses' training to the most competent of the contraband women—Sarah Bohannon, Ellen Campbell, Betsy Young, and Georgina Harris, among them (Roca 1998, 105–106). The Catholic sisters and the African-American women were the first women to have official status on board a U.S. naval vessel.

At the beginning of the Army of the Potomac's Peninsular Campaign (Virginia) in April 1862, USSC General Secretary Frederick Law Olmsted persuaded Secretary of War Edwin Stanton to permit the USSC to use government-owned steamships to provide emergency care to the wounded. This fleet of boats and ships came to be named the HTS.

As Union Major General George McClellan embarked on the Peninsular Campaign, the USSC improvised its vessels, floating them on the York and James Rivers in Virginia. Although very little is known about the experiences of the African-American women and men who served as cooks, servants, laundresses, and general custodians of all dirty work for the HTS, a number of the white elite and middle-class volunteer "matrons" wrote letters, journals, and memoirs detailing their experiences. Unlike the female army NURSES working in Union military hospitals, the HTS's matrons possessed considerable autonomy over their activities. The USSC male administrators acted as buffering agents between the women and the surgeons, allowing the white matrons to make their own decisions concerning the best means of providing care. For these women, the hospital ship successfully operated as an extension of the Victorian household, where women could expect to rule on domestic issues (Ross 1992, 101).

At the beginning of the Peninsular Campaign, the primary task of the white female matrons was to supervise the labor of the male and female contrabands and the convalescent soldiers who served as orderlies and servants. Matrons Katharine Prescott Wormeley and Harriet Whetten reassured their friends at home that they had nothing disagreeable to do. They could, in effect, maintain their dignity and class superiority as white ladies of position and stature.

> As far as I can judge, our duty is to be very much that of a housekeeper. We attend to the beds, the linen, the clothing of the patients; we have a pantry and storeroom, and are required to do all the cooking for the sick, and see that it is properly distributed according to the surgeon's orders; we are also to have a general superintendence over the condition of the wards and over the nurses, who are all men. ... There are eight medical students on board ("dressers," they are called), and perhaps twenty other young men, wardmasters and nurses—all volunteers. (quoted in Dannett 1959, 162)

Yet as soon as the wards and decks of the ships filled with wounded and sick soldiers, the USSC matrons' role broadened to include plenty of hands-on nursing. The influx of 245 soldiers stricken with typhoid fever was the matrons' first crisis. Immediately Wormeley and the other white female volunteers took on nursing duties as the male nurses on board were soon overwhelmed by the epidemic. Although HTS nurses dressed wounds, their first duty was to supply the sick and the wounded with stimulants and nourishment. As Wormeley explained, "Our work is not like regular hospital work. It is succoring men just off the battle-field, and making them easy, clean, and comfortable before we turn them over to other hands ... we can do little beyond the mere snatching from physical death" (Wormeley 1889, 115). Given that most of the soldiers had lain exposed on the beaches and marshes of the Peninsula for several days without food or water, the nurses played a critical role in the soldiers' survival.

> In my ward, as each man was laid in his berth, I gave him brandy and water, and after all were placed, tea and bread and butter, if they could take it, or more brandy or beef-tea if they were sinking. (Wormeley 1889, 20)

Hundreds of patients in various stages of deliria proved an enormous challenge to the entire medical staff, prompting Wormeley and her colleagues to admit that caring for hundreds of the wounded was far less taxing than caring for the very ill.

The most overwhelming emergency the HTS faced during the Peninsular Campaign followed the Battle of Seven Pines (Virginia) in early June 1862. During a period of approximately one week, the entire fleet of the HTS took on board approximately 5,000 wounded men. The entire staff worked day and night. Both Wormeley and Whetten refused to describe the horrors they experienced and the torment of the wounded. In a letter home, Wormeley explained, "To think or speak of the things we see would be fatal. No one must come here who cannot put away all feeling. Do all you can, and be a machine,—that's the way to act; the only way" (Wormeley 1889, 102).

The demands on the female contrabands in the HTS were just as intense, though most white women's accounts ignore their activities but for the rare occasions when they found their assistance deficient. The contrabands, male and female, while working for little or no pay, washed the decks and walls of the ships, washed the mountains of laundry, performed all the scut work in the kitchens and the wards, and frequently served as nurses.

When Wormeley was later transferred to the boat that transported the surgical cases, she was horrified to discover that there was no food or drink to sustain the soldiers, many of whom had been without food or water for at least 48 hours. Wormeley and her female crew improvised by concocting a drink of molasses, vinegar, water, and ice. They then struggled to locate food stores and served crackers and milk, or tea and bread, depending on the condition of the soldier. The barely averted disaster left Wormeley's confidence in the Union army and the government shaken, an experience that afflicted countless women who worked on or close to the battlefields all through war. She wrote, "We were … bitterly asking why a Government so lavish and perfect in its other arrangements should leave its wounded almost literally to take care of themselves" (Wormeley 1889, 104–105).

The organization of the army's first fully functioning ambulance service in the summer of 1862 signaled the end of the HTS, but not the end of the Union army's and navy's hospital ships. Wormeley, Whetten, and many of the white matrons went on to volunteer in the military hospitals in the North and in the Washington, DC, area.

Selected Readings

Roca, Steven Louis. "Presence and Precedents: The USS *Red Rover* During the American Civil War, 1861–1865." *Civil War History.* 44 (2) (1998): 91–110.

Ross, Kristie R. "Arranging a Doll's House: Refined Women as Union Nurses." In *Divided Houses: Gender and the Civil War.* Edited by Catherine Clinton and Nina Silber. New York: Oxford University Press. 1992.

Wormeley, Katharine Prescott. *The Other Side of War: With the Army of the Potomac.* Boston: Ticknor, 1889.

Howe, Julia Ward (1819–1910)

Mine eyes have seen the glory of the coming of the Lord:
He is trampling out the vintage where the grapes of wrath are stored;
He hath loosed the fateful lightning of His terrible swift sword:
His Truth is marching on.
Glory! Glory! Hallelujah!
Glory! Glory! Hallelujah!
Glory! Glory! Hallelujah!
His truth is marching on.

—Julia Ward Howe, excerpt from "The Battle Hymn of the Republic"

As author of the cherished Union anthem "The Battle Hymn of the Republic," Julia Ward Howe was one of the most celebrated women of the North during the Civil War and during the last half of the nineteenth century. Although she was a publicly prominent, active social reformer after 1868, during the 1850s and most of the 1860s, she was a poet, scholar, philosopher, and essayist. During these two decades of national turmoil, many of her fellow upper-middle-class Unitarian women of Boston became involved in benevolent activity or political and social reform work outside the home. Ward Howe's more restricted life was not of her choosing. Her husband, the prestigious reformer Samuel Gridley Howe, 18 years her senior, demanded that her activities remain confined to the home and to their social circle. Despite these constraints and considerable marital discord, she did manage to publish her poetry and essays throughout the 1850s and 1860s.

Though her husband was an ardent abolitionist, Ward Howe was not prominent in the movement nor did she harbor much in the way of antislavery sentiment until late in 1859. She believed that emancipation was necessary but rejected any suggestion that racial equality was a desirable or possible goal. John Brown's raid at Harpers Ferry, Virginia, in October 1859, galvanized her spiritually, though it did not transform her into an abolitionist. What astounded and moved her most about the event was Brown's apparent surrender to divine will and his unswerving commitment to follow the voice of God, as he heard it. As one of her biographers explains, Brown's mission became comprehensible to her because his actions translated the unfamiliar domain of politics into religion, a language and a world that she knew intimately (Grant 1994, 138).

From the first days of the war in April 1861, Ward Howe felt compelled to serve her country, a difficult task for a mother of six children. She and her two oldest daughters participated in soldiers' relief work, scraping lint to be used for the dressing of bandages. For a time, Ward Howe also worked within a Boston sewing circle to produce clothing for the troops. But domestic pursuits left her frustrated and dissatisfied. She admitted that she possessed neither the skills nor the aptitude for sewing or for the collecting and packaging of food and medical supplies for the New England Sanitary Commission. She yearned to make a more distinctive contribution, one that would tap her literary powers.

As Ward Howe recalled in her memoir *Reminiscences 1819–1899*, during the early months of the war, her youngest child was only two years old. "I could not leave my nursery to follow the march of our armies. ... Yet, because of my sincere desire, a word was given me to say, which did strengthen the hearts of those who fought in the field and of those who languished in the prison" (Howe 1969, 273–274).

This "word" was "The Battle Hymn of the Republic," a poem that came to her in a rush of inspiration one November morning before dawn in a Washington, DC, hotel. The day before, she had accompanied her husband and several other New England dignitaries on a grand tour of Union troops in northern Virginia. While they were visiting, Confederate soldiers attacked the encampment, forcing Ward Howe and her group to return to Washington. On the long road back, they sang army songs, including "John Brown's Body," a popular army tune that is believed to have originated among Massachusetts soldiers stationed at Fort Warren on Georges Island in Boston Harbor. James Freeman Clarke, abolitionist and Boston Unitarian minister, suggested to Ward Howe that she write new lyrics for the song.

Once "The Battle Hymn of the Republic" was committed to paper, Ward Howe was convinced that it had been divinely inspired. The poem had come to her so quickly and effortlessly that no other explanation seemed possible. Almost no editing was required; she made only 13 changes to the original. In December 1861, once she was home again in Boston, she sent it to the *Atlantic Monthly*, a previous publisher of her work. It appeared on page one of the February 1862 issue. She was paid only $5.

By the end of 1862, a few Union regiments were singing "The Battle Hymn of the Republic," but it never replaced the lighthearted, irreverent "John Brown's Body" as the favorite Union marching tune. "The Battle Hymn" was much more beloved by Northern civilians. Its popularity derived from its embodiment of widespread Northern sentiments and attitudes toward the war and the South. In particular, the song's image of a militant, angry, all-powerful God intervening in war and national affairs to institute justice and freedom was a powerful concept at the time.

Following this success, while enfolded in her new celebrity, Ward Howe became bolder in claiming her right to be a public person and to develop her strengths and talents as she felt moved to do. In the midst of her grief following the death of her youngest son, Sammy, to diphtheria in May 1863, she returned to her study of philosophy with renewed energy, reexamining the works of Spinoza, Swedenborg, Comte, Hegel, and Kant. In 1864, she delivered a series of six lectures on "Practical Ethics," her own blend of philosophy and ethics, at her home and in Washington, DC. Through this experience, she discovered her enthusiasm for oratory, which became her chosen vehicle for expressing her ideas and personal beliefs.

In November 1864, she undertook another highly successful venture, editing *The Boatswain's Whistle*, the daily newspaper for the National Sailors Fair in Boston, a 12-day event to raise funds for a home for handicapped and elderly seamen. The paper included essays, poetry, short stories, letters to the editor, as well as classified advertisements. Best of all from her point of view, she exercised complete control of the product. The accolades she received as editor were immensely satisfying, in large part because she had found a way to contribute her talents to the war effort while advancing her literary career.

In April 1865, when she announced her intention to speak to inmates at the Charlestown Prison, her husband forbade her to proceed. She submitted to his demand, though anguished that she was making the wrong choice (Williams 1999, 232). In her journal entry discussing her emotional reactions to this event, it becomes clear that all of her activities during the war years—a time when she reached beyond the confines of her home and her intimate circle of friends to express her deepest beliefs and personal vision—were transforming her. No longer would she allow her voice to be stifled or deny herself the chance to fulfill what she believed was her divinely directed mission.

In 1868, in addition to her literary endeavors, Ward Howe embarked on her career as a leader of the woman suffrage movement. At various times she served as president of the Massachusetts Woman Suffrage Association and the New England Woman Suffrage Association. Three years later, she launched the women's club movement when she became president of the New England Women's Club, a post she would hold, with few interruptions, from 1871 until her death in 1910.

See also **Literary Women**

Selected Readings

Clifford, Deborah Pickman. *Mine Eyes Have Seen the Glory: A Biography of Julia Ward Howe.* Boston: Little Brown. 1978.

Grant, Mary H. *Private Woman, Public Person: An Account of the Life of Julia Ward Howe from 1819 to 1868.* Brooklyn, NY: Carlson Publishing. 1994.

Williams, Gary. *Hungry Heart: The Literary Emergence of Julia Ward Howe.* Amherst, MA: University of Massachusetts Press. 1999.

I

Immigrant Women

Between 1840 and 1880, more than ten million people immigrated to the United States. Most were Europeans—predominantly from Ireland, the German-speaking countries and principalities of central and Eastern Europe, Scandinavia, and Great Britain. Although the chaos of the Civil War curbed the flood of immigration somewhat, hundreds of thousands continued to arrive. During the war years, the nation—especially the Union states and territories—was assimilating the 4.2 million immigrants who arrived between 1840 and 1860. Although the circumstances of life in their countries of origin differed, most immigrant women and men left their homelands because of inhospitable economic conditions and because the possibility of prosperity and advancement in their native lands was poor.

From the outbreak of hostilities, European immigrants were vital to the war effort. Large numbers of Irish, German, and Scandinavian immigrant men voluntarily enlisted or were drafted into both the Union and Confederate militaries. And in the North, especially, immigrant male and female workers kept agricultural and industrial production at peak levels.

Despite differences, all immigrant groups formed close-knit communities, whether in the cities or in rural areas. They established their own churches and preferred to form their own schools, primarily to pass on religious and cultural teachings. They worked hard to acquire capital, property, and, in many cases, land. Although men were the most involved in establishing civic, public, and religious organizations, the correspondence of female immigrants indicates that women of all ethnic groups formed close bonds with other immigrant women of their own nationalities. These cooperative female networks helped women to acculturate and to build new lives in the cities, rural villages, and in sparsely populated farming regions.

Irish immigrants composed the largest percentage of newcomers already living in the United States during the Civil War era. Nearly 40 percent of the 4.2 million who immigrated from 1840 to 1860 were from Ireland. Irish immigrants arriving during the Civil War were significantly fewer in number than those immigrating during the years of the Great Famine from 1848 to 1854. From 1861 to 1870, 435,778 million Irish entered the country, down from 914,119 during the years 1851 to 1860 (Daniels 1991, 127).

In 1860, Irish men and women formed the largest immigrant group living in many Northern cities, including Boston, New York, and Philadelphia. In the large mill cities of Massachusetts and Rhode Island, where large numbers of women were needed to operate the textile factories, Irish women predominated among all other immigrant groups of both genders. In general, Irish immigrants preferred to settle in cities where jobs were abundant.

The largest percentage of Irish immigrants during the Civil War years were older teens and young adults ages 15 to 24. Young women left Ireland because their futures in that country were bleak. Farmers and landholders passed their land on to only one son. Ordinarily, only one daughter received a dowry. The remaining daughters and sons had poor prospects if they remained in Ireland, their opportunities consisting of working as hired hands for siblings or neighbors, or as seasonal migrant workers in England.

Unlike German, Jewish, and Scandinavian immigrants who migrated in family groups, Irish women of the late 1850s, 1860s, and later tended to migrate in groups of female relatives. Aunts, sisters, and female cousins traveled together, settled in an American city, found jobs, and sent money home to Ireland, often to assist additional female kin to cross the ocean to join them.

Irish women worked as domestic servants, factory workers, sewers, laundresses, and keepers of boarding houses. Girls, single women of all ages, and widows predominated in the Irish female labor force. When compared with women of other immigrant groups, Irish women highly valued work outside the home and played a powerful economic role in their families. They worked at jobs that native-born and other immigrant women scorned, forming the highest percentage of domestic servants.

Irish immigrant women received the most support from family members, friends, and neighbors. Although Irish men were active in promoting civic and political life and formed all sorts of mutual aid and benevolent societies, these groups did not effectively meet the needs of women in the Irish community. Irish lay women did not form their own charitable organizations at mid-century, though they did strongly support the Catholic Church. Religious orders of CATHOLIC NUNS, most of them made up of Irish immigrant women, assisted women in the Irish community. They instituted schools for girls, and aided widows, the elderly, and the sick. In Boston, the Sisters of Notre Dame de Namur created an industrial school in 1858 to help working girls find jobs that paid more than a pittance. They provided relief to the impoverished, operated a home for working girls, and in 1868 established St. Elizabeth's Hospital, an institution that specialized in treating women's diseases (Diner 1983, 131).

During the early and mid-nineteenth century, German-speaking immigrants did not originate from a single country. Before 1871, there was no one German nation. So-called "German-born" speakers originated from twelve large states and numerous smaller principalities, which in 1871 would unite to form the German imperial nation. "German" immigrants also hailed from Switzerland, Austria, and other lands in central Europe.

German-speaking immigrants preferred settling in rural areas of the Midwest, particularly Missouri, Illinois, Wisconsin, and Iowa. In the 1850s, they rushed to establish farms in Kansas and Nebraska. They also favored settling in Pennsylvania, New York State, and New Jersey, and, although as a rule they did not prefer urban life, sizable numbers made their homes in eastern cities. When German immigrants settled in the cities, the stay for many families was temporary; they immediately found jobs, collectively shared their earnings with relatives and friends from their home communities in Europe, and eventually moved to farming regions to buy land. Those who bypassed city life altogether went immediately to the countryside and became farmhands and servants, again sharing resources so that they could purchase farmland.

German-born women who performed wage labor outside the home did so primarily to earn money so that they, their husbands, and their families could purchase farmland. Wieschen Swehn saved $200 after two and a half years laboring on farms in Iowa. Combined with her husband's earnings of $350, the couple was able to buy their own farm. Once a family owned their own land, German women worked alongside their menfolk to turn the land to arable acreage. German men, women, and children all worked long, grueling hours to build and sustain their farms. Once their farms were established, German women's roles were remarkably similar to those of native-born AGRICULTURAL WOMEN. German farm women planted and tended large vegetable gardens, shared the dairying with their menfolk, churned butter, supervised their own poultry operations, assisted men with the harvest and haying, preserved foods, and, during the butchering of livestock, took charge of making sausages and head cheese (Pickle 1996, 53, 57).

German immigrants pushed their children to work hard. Young boys and girls as young as eight years of age herded cows and cattle and tended younger children, often working and boarding with neighbors or relatives on nearby farms. Older girls were often hired out as domestic servants. Children's wages were then collected to enrich their family's farm. For girls, this labor had an additional benefit as they learned how to run a farming household, the only education that their community believed they needed. German immigrants did not spend time or resources educating girls beyond instructing them in basic reading, writing, and arithmetic, and the tenets of the German Lutheran religion.

German immigrants preferred living in farming communities with relatives and other German newcomers. Families who immigrated as a group often tried to stay together, first in the cities, then in the countryside. German women thrived on the interdependent relationships they maintained with other women of their own ethnic background. In Illinois in the early 1860s, Susanna Ruth Krehbiel and Barbara Lehmann, two Mennonite women, supported each other when their husbands contracted malaria and they had to assume their husbands' farm duties. At harvest time, they set aside some of their domestic tasks to work in the fields together. After the men used the reaper to cut the grain, the women were left to bind it and shock it into piles of sheaves. Susanna Krehbiel especially appreciated the companionship because her husband, a traveling minister, frequently left her in charge of the farm (Pickle 1996, 116–118).

Unlike Irish women, German women did not involve themselves in public life. As a general rule, they held fast to their domestic occupations. Although male religious leaders did not permit women to actively participate in religious affairs, they supported the religious life in their communities, joining forces with other women to keep churches clean, to cook for church-related events, and to raise funds for the maintenance of their congregations.

By 1860, approximately 150,000 European Jews had arrived in the United States. Although many Jewish immigrants of the early to mid-nineteenth century spoke German, and although immigration agents often classified them as part of the German migration, Jews immigrating between 1820 and 1880 hailed from regions throughout central and Eastern Europe. Jews from Germanic principalities did form a slight majority before 1860, although large numbers also immigrated from Poland, Bohemia, Moravia, Galicia, Lithuania, Slovakia, and Alsace. By the 1860s, the majority of Jews entering the United States were from these lands in Eastern Europe (Diner 1992, 49).

Despite their disparate geographic origins, immigrant Jews shared many commonalities—their motivations for leaving their homelands, their work in the United States, the types of communities they formed, and the role of women in the workplace, in the home, and in the neighborhood. Like all other groups immigrating to the United States during this period, almost all Jews left Europe for economic reasons. The poorer classes of Jews also left because legal codes in many regions prohibited those without means from marrying. Only men who could demonstrate they had the resources and the skills to earn a "good" livelihood were permitted to wed.

Young, single Jewish men typically immigrated first. Once well established in the United States, they returned to their towns and villages in Europe to find women to marry, or they arranged, through social networks at home, to have young women immigrate to become their wives. In another common immigration pattern, brothers and sisters traveled together, settled down, and then sent for additional family members to join them.

Most young Jewish men were peddlars once they arrived in the United States, though a minority became workers in the garment industry, glassworks, and cigar manufacturing. Once a peddlar or laborer accumulated enough capital, he commonly established a dry goods business or a general store. Immigrant Jewish women—wives, daughters, and sisters—worked in these family businesses, usually combining their labor with domestic chores and childrearing responsibilities. They also managed boarding houses and took in sewing. Jewish immigrants preferred to settle in Jewish neighborhoods in the largest cities, though they also established communities in towns large and small throughout the country, including in the South and Far West.

Despite their workload, immigrant Jewish women devoted time and energy to community building. In particular, they were active in their own female benevolent societies. With the dues collected from members and from fund-raisers, these organizations cared for the Jewish poor, subsidized "Sunday schools," supported synagogue building, and provided entertainment and socialization. During the Civil War, these associations were active as SOLDIERS' AID SOCIETIES.

Approximately 125,000 Scandinavians from Norway, Sweden, and Denmark immigrated to the United States by 1860. During the Civil War, most Scandinavian immigrants were Norwegian, and immigration from Norway exceeded those of the other two countries. (The flood of Swedish immigration did not begin until the late 1860s.) To an even greater extent than German immigrants, Scandinavian immigrants, traveling in family groups, settled in farming regions, particularly in northern sections of the Midwest and Great Plains.

Norwegian women labored alongside men to prepare the northern forested wilderness and the tough prairie grasslands for agriculture. Women helped to remove trees and brush from their homesteads. When it was time to plant the crops, Norwegian immigrant women participated, as they had in Norway. Young, single Norwegian women and teenaged girls worked for hire on neighboring farms. Whether they assisted their employers with domestic tasks, farm chores, or a combination of the two, young female Norwegians headed straight for the fields at harvest time when they could earn nearly as much money as men (Lagerquist 1991, 59, 73).

The Chinese tide of immigration to California and other regions of the Far West began during the Gold Rush era of the late 1840s and 1850s. During this early period, almost all Chinese immigrants were male, and they arrived to work in mining and railroad construction. The very few women who appeared in the United States at this time worked primarily as prostitutes and operated as independent, successful entrepreneurs. By 1854, prostitution in California came under the control of the male leaders of the tongs, secret organizations that vied for power and control of the Chinese business community. As the tongs took over management of prostitution, Chinese women lost control of their trade, income, and lives.

Most Chinese women immigrating during the 1850s and 1860s were from the poorest families of peasants in Kwangtung Province in southern China. The numbers of Chinese women immigrating remained small. By 1860, the total Chinese population in California stood at 34,933. Approximately 1,700 to 2,000 of this number were women (Hirata 1979, 227; Peffer 1999, 24). Enticed by promises of wealth, freedom, and a copious supply of good husbands, some women boarded ships sailing for the United States. Others were sold by their families, were kidnapped, or were otherwise coerced into making the journey. Although many women realized their powerless condition on board ship, others did not learn of their fate until several weeks after docking in the United States. Wong Ah So was one young Chinese woman who was kept ignorant of her future for weeks.

> I was nineteen when this man came to my mother and said that in America there was a great deal of gold. … He was very nice to me, and my mother liked him, so my mother was glad to have me go with him as his wife. I … was very grateful that he was taking me to such a grand, free country, where everyone was rich and happy.

Several weeks after settling in San Francisco, Wong Ah So discovered that not only would she never be the man's wife, but that to survive she must live as a prostitute (Ling 1998, 24).

Shortly after Chinese women arrived in the United States, male traders sold them to male brothel owners in San Francisco and in the mining camps and towns. Women were then forced to sign a work contract or a comparable "bill of sale" agreement. In general, they then were obligated to serve as prostitutes for a number of years, usually without pay (Tong 1994, 72–73).

Chinese prostitutes fared far worse than white prostitutes in California. Chinese women not only earned less (once they completed their years of wageless servitude), but their living conditions were worse and they were more vulnerable to violence and abuse, more apt to be arrested by police, and more likely to be treated harshly by the courts.

Not all Chinese women became prostitutes. Although approximately 85 percent of Chinese women in 1860 San Francisco were sex workers, women in the city and throughout California also labored as laundresses, miners, domestic servants, seamstresses, and laborers in other industries. By the 1870s and as the years passed, fewer and fewer Chinese women worked as prostitutes.

Although immigrant women of all nationalities rarely figure in most histories of the Civil War period, their labor was vital to industry, agriculture, and the businesses in their communities. Historians have only recently begun to uncover the experiences of mid-nineteenth-century immigrant women.

See also **Businesswomen; Industrial Women**

Selected Readings

Diner, Hasia R. *A Time for Gathering: The Second Migration 1820–1880.* Series: The Jewish People in America. Baltimore: The Johns Hopkins University Press. 1992.

Diner, Hasia R. *Erin's Daughters in America: Irish Immigrant Women in the Nineteenth Century.* Baltimore: Johns Hopkins University Press. 1983.

Lagerquist, L. DeAne. *In America the Men Milk the Cows: Factors of Gender, Ethnicity, and Religion in the Americanization of Norwegian-American Women.* Brooklyn, NY: Carlson Publishing. 1991.

Ling, Huping. *Surviving on the Gold Mountain: A History of Chinese American Women and Their Lives.* Albany: State University of New York Press. 1998.

Pickle, Linda Schelbitzki. *Contented Among Strangers: Rural German-Speaking Women and Their Families in the Nineteenth-Century Midwest.* Urbana: University of Illinois Press. 1996.

Industrial Women

As the Civil War created and expanded industries that required an increased labor force in the North and South, women in ever-increasing numbers became industrial workers. According to the 1860 U.S. census, 15 percent of all women were engaged in wage labor. Of these women workers, approximately 271,000 worked in manufacturing, including the poorest classes of white women, free African-American women, and slave women. Largely as the result of the Civil War's galvanizing effect on industry, the overall number of women wage earners increased during the 1860s, causing the number of women working in manufacturing to swell to 358,950 (Kessler-Harris 1982, 76; Foner 1979, 109). By 1870, women composed one-fourth of all wage laborers. (Of this group of wage earners, 70 percent were engaged in domestic service. Four-fifths of the remaining 30 percent were sewing women in textile manufacturing and one-fifth were teachers, shopclerks, or workers in non-sewing manufacturing occupations, such as cigar manufacturing, paper box making, and printing, to name a few [Turbin 1979, 204].)

The rapid industrialization of the war years created economic conditions and labor practices that decreased women's earning power. Despite the importance of women's wages to their families, women during the Civil War earned less than 50 percent of the wages men received for the same work (Foner 1979, 110). Falling wages and harsh practices pushed women to collaborate to demand higher wages and better working conditions. Through various types of labor organizations, including trade unions, women built stronger networks among themselves that would pave the way for stronger collective action in the late 1860s and 1870s.

In the 1860s, the predominant popular image of the woman worker was the young single woman who labored at some form of industrial work for several years until she married and exited the labor market. In reality, young single women represented only one group of female workers. Young girls, widows, single women with children, and married women also worked in industry.

Contrary to another popularly held view, the income of young single women— however temporary—was critical to their livelihoods and to the mainstay of their families. In 1872, a groundbreaking Massachusetts state government study revealed that the average male worker could not earn enough to keep his family out of debt without the income of other family members (Turbin 1979, 206). The wages of a family's daughters (and sons) were crucial to a working-class family's subsistence. Even though the report from this study was not published until seven years after the Civil War, it reveals the challenges of subsistence for working men and women throughout the 1850s and 1860s.

During the first half of the nineteenth century, women and girls were the principal laborers in textile manufacturing in New England and the Northeast. Vast changes in the textile industry during the Civil War diminished the earning power of its women workers. In one part of the industry, seamstresses' working conditions were so poor that they formed small labor organizations by the early 1850s. The increasingly hostile work environment during the Civil War pushed thousands more women to work collectively to improve their labor conditions and raise their wages through petitions, rallies, appeals to the public and the press, trade unions, and strikes.

On the eve of the Civil War, two events in Massachusetts altered the Northern public's view of the life circumstances of factory women, fostering public acceptance of female workers' need to organize and unionize.

Late one bitterly cold January afternoon, the Pemberton Mill in Lawrence, Massachusetts, collapsed. While rescue efforts were underway, a fire broke out. Many of the trapped and injured victims were burned, most of them young women and girls. A total of 88 people died and many of the mill's 600 employees were injured (Kessler-Harris 1982, 64). The tragedy made headlines in newspapers all over the country. All through the winter and spring of 1860, the press coverage continued, provoking public criticism of factory owners. Articles, editorials, and stories focused on the working and living conditions of women factory workers. Journalists related stories of young teenage girls supporting their mothers and siblings, of daughters as the chief bread-winners in male-dominated households, of single women struggling to care for their sick and elderly relatives, and of single women struggling to survive on their own.

The writer Elizabeth Stuart Phelps, at the time a young, impressionable, well-edu-cated girl of fifteen years, explained in her autobiography that the fall of the Pemberton Mill brought the problems of mill workers to the attention of her middle-class family and community. Before the mill collapse, she wrote, "We did not think about the mill-people; they seemed as far from us as the coal-miners of a vague West. ... One January evening we were forced to think about the mills with curdling horror, which no one living in that locality ... will forget." Phelps's brother, "being of the privileged sex," was permitted to witness the scene that night. Elizabeth, forced to remain at home, spent years re-creating the scene from the details she gathered from eyewitnesses and from factory documents. Following a thorough investigation, she wrote the short story "The Tenth of January," which was published in the *Atlantic Monthly* (Phelps 1896, 89, 91, 92).

Also, in the winter of 1860, in the seaside city of Lynn, Massachusetts, approximately 30 miles from the Pemberton Mill, young, single shoe factory women briefly organized under the leadership of 21-year-old Clara H. Brown. This coalition of female workers stated that their objective was to increase wages for all women shoe workers who labored in the factories and who did piecework in their homes. The wage increases were intended to compensate workers for their employers' new demand that employees buy their own thread and lining material for the shoes they manufactured (Blewett 1987, 43).

Not all women shoe workers joined the women's coalition. Most female home workers joined male shoemakers (many of whom were their husbands, fathers, and brothers) in promoting men's interests. This group protested wage increases for women, insisting that a strike's priority must be to increase male earnings. They argued that this was the best means to increase the family wage and to support the work of women in the home. When male leaders declared at a women's coalition rally that women's wages should be secondary to their husbands, a chorus of Clara Brown's followers shouted, "We have no husbands!" Brown then stood up and demanded,

> Girls of Lynn, do you hear that and will you stand it? Never Never, NEVER. Strike then—strike at once; DEMAND 8 1/2 cents for your work ... don't work your machines; let 'em lie still till we get all we ask, and then go at it. (Blewett 1991, 82)

On March 2, 1860, the pro-male wage earners took control of the women's strike meetings and advanced their own agenda, swaying many in the women's coalition to shift their allegiance. When a vote was taken, the women's alliance lost despite Brown's efforts (Blewett 1987, 43–45). Despite the young women's failure in Lynn, press cov-erage, especially by labor newspapers, broadcast the issues to workers nationwide.

The majority of male workers and trade unionists during the Civil War rejected supporting women workers, in the belief that the presence of women would undercut men's wages and oust male workers from their jobs. Yet other male labor leaders had the foresight to realize that if they did not encourage women's efforts to increase their earnings, men's wages would likely fall to match women's. For these men, pushing employers to increase women's wages was an important strategy to increase wages and improve working conditions for all.

Sewing Women

Of all women in industry, sewing women, or women in the needle trades, had the most difficulty avoiding penury and starvation. In 1863, a New York newspaper reported that the wages of sewing women had decreased 25 to 50 percent since 1860, while the cost of living in the city had risen more than 50 percent during the same time period (Massey 1994, 145). In 1864, New York City underwear sewers earned only $.17 per day, in a city where board could not be had for under $3 per week (Foner 1979, 113). Moreover, seamstresses had been barely subsisting before the war. In 1858, physician and health reformer William Sanger conducted a survey of 2,000 prostitutes incarcerated in New York City. Of this group of women, approximately 25 percent had been in the sewing and dressmaking trades. Over half of the 2,000 prostitutes had been earning only $1 a week before they turned to prostitution; another 336 women had earned no more than $2 a week (Wertheimer 1977, 101–102).

The emergence of subcontractors was the biggest problem for women sewing garments under government contracts during the war. These middlemen collected material from government arsenals and parceled it out to sewing women. Subcontractors paid workers less than what the average sewer had been earning. The subcontractors made enormous profits, while the sewing women drew wages that were on average less than 50 percent of what they had been earning. In addition to undercutting wages, the subcontractors were habitually late in doling out earnings. Some unscrupulous middlemen collected completed clothing and refused to pay seamstresses, charging that the work was defective. Others demanded that workers pay large fines for returning work late. When the cost of thread doubled, the middlemen forced women to purchase their own, diminishing their wages further.

Out of desperation, sewing women in large Northern cities did more than grumble. Many female sewers, close to starvation, organized to petition legislators and government officials to pressure employers to pay a fair wage. The Working Women's Relief Association of Philadelphia, a protective society made up of sewing women, factory women (including arms and munitions workers), and shopclerks, sent a petition to Secretary of War Edwin Stanton to request that women working on government contracts be paid a wage commensurate with the cost of living. They also asked that they be spared the intervention of subcontractors. As a result, a small percentage—1,000 to 2,000 women—received their work directly from the government and all workers on government projects obtained a 20 percent pay hike. In January 1865, female arsenal workers from the protective society met with President Lincoln to have him address their grievances. He interceded for them immediately (Foner 1979, 116).

Successful petitioning led women to organize with more fervor. In October 1863, umbrella sewers in New York City and Brooklyn established a trade union and went on strike demanding an additional $.02 for each completed umbrella cover. Although employers agreed to the demands some women workers made others refused (Foner 1979, 114).

In November 1863, women shirtmakers in New York City organized and went on strike, but failed to increase their wages. Later that month, with the assistance of several men's trade unions, the Working Women's Union of New York City was formed. Although the union was created to unite all working women of the city for the purpose of raising wages, it did not succeed in this goal, though the organization did manage to establish the Sewing Women's Protective and Benevolent Union, which worked to improve the living conditions of women workers (Foner 1979, 114).

Concerned middle- and upper-class women of New York City established the Working Women's Protective Union. More of a benevolent association than a trade union, the protective union gave working women legal assistance free of cost. With this help, the organization settled thousands of working women's grievances and collected wages owed to them (Wertheimer 1977, 155).

During the Civil War, working women's protective associations appeared in many other Northern cities, including Boston, Troy, Buffalo, Detroit, Chicago, and Worcester and Woburn, Massachusetts. Unlike New York City's Working Women's Protective Union, most were organized by working women or by male trade unionists. Although these societies did much to improve working women's lives, they were not trade unions and were not able to obtain higher wages or shorter working hours (Foner 1979, 120–121).

The Sewing Women's Protective Association of Detroit was a particularly powerful protective union that managed to make inroads when many women's trade unions and protective unions did not. With the advice and assistance of male trade unionists, in early 1865, the Detroit association posted a list of prices for garments and piecework, and demanded that all employers adhere to it. If employers neglected to follow the schedule, the men's trade unions were notified. Male union representatives then visited the offending employer to insist that he abide by the pay scale the association established. If the employer still refused to cooperate, the trade unions broadcast the name and business(es) of the employer and called for union members to boycott his goods and business(es) (Foner 1979, 117–118).

Another effective innovation of the Detroit association during the war was its effort to eliminate the subcontractors and other middlemen. The all-male Detroit Trades' Assembly purchased eight sewing machines for women workers. They also paid the rent for a hall where women worked. This cooperative workspace allowed some women to collect higher wages by bypassing the middlemen.

Black women suffered the most of all Northern industrial workers. White women excluded free African-American working women from trade and protective unions.

Black workers were not only paid the least, but they were also the first to be laid off or fired, and were generally the group most vulnerable to hostility and violence meted out by white co-workers (Foner 1979, 118).

As the South took its first tentative steps toward industrialization before the Civil War, slaveholders hired out slave women and men to white factory owners. By the eve of the Civil War, 5,000 slave women and girls worked in the South's textile mills. Slave women also labored in sugar refineries, rice mills, in hemp manufacturing, and in food and tobacco processing. They also performed hard physical labor at tasks ordinarily reserved for men in foundries and mines (Wertheimer 1977, 118). The living conditions of factory slaves were even more squalid than that of poor white Southern workers. Slaves worked 12- to 16-hour days and a minimum of a six-day week, sometimes laboring a seventh day. They were given a poor, restricted, and unvaried diet, which left them vulnerable to nutritional and infectious diseases. Factory owners, always mindful of keeping their costs low, preferred female slaves and their children as workers because they ate less and were less expensive to maintain. Slave women and men resisted the efforts of manufacturers to exploit their labor by resorting to work stoppages and slowdowns. They also sabotaged production by ruining tools and machinery.

Poor white women and girls also worked as factory operatives throughout the South. Confederate government contractors cut into Southern sewing women's wages, using the same strategies as Union manufacturing contractors. Southern women's wages on average were higher than Northern women's, but the exorbitant inflation of Confederate currency more than consumed whatever wage advantage Southern workers appear to have had. Southern women factory operatives experienced hazards that Northern women workers did not. Although Northern women were idled by a scarcity of textiles during the early months of the war, Southern women lost work due to the lack of raw materials and the work stoppages resulting from the Union blockade of Southern ports and INVASION AND OCCUPATION.

Some Southern women workers attempted to strike but most were unsuccessful. They lacked organization and formed no trade unions or protective associations as Northern women did. Southern women were much more apt to petition the Confederate and state governments to increase their wages. Also unlike Northern women workers, Southern industrial women did not have the support of male workers.

Ordnance Workers

As in the North, poor white women and girls worked in munitions factories. Higher wages were the rule in these workplaces due to the hazardous nature of the labor. In Richmond, Virginia, on Friday, March 13, 1863, an explosion rocked parts of the city, destroying portions of the Confederate State Laboratory. At least 45 workers, mostly young girls, were killed by the blast and fire. The laboratory manufactured ammunition—cartridges, fuses, percussion caps, fixed ammunition, signal rockets, grenades, and friction primers (the intensely explosive items that "ignited" the powder in large weaponry and cannons). Other ordnance works employing women and girls were located in Atlanta, Georgia, and Selma, Alabama (Coulter 1950, 208). According to eyewitnesses, Mary Ryan, an 18-year-old woman from Ireland precipitated the blast. While she worked on a friction primer, it stuck to the varnishing board. To remove it, she hit the board to free the primer. Another munitions explosion killed 35 men, women, and children in Jackson, Mississippi.

In December 1863, about nine months after the explosion, women workers at the Confederate States Laboratory went on strike to raise their wages from $2.40 to $3 a day, an extremely modest increase considering the rampant inflation of Confederate currency. These women were eventually successful in achieving their goal and their wage hikes. In 1864, however, because unmarried women earned $5 per day and married women $7, single women demanded that they be paid the same wage as married women. When all female workers decided to strike, the Confederate government fired all the women and hired 300 new workers to replace them (Coulter 1950, 237).

In the closing months of the war, the press and the public voiced their expectation that women prepare to leave their jobs in the factories to make way for returning veterans. The most prominent rationale for the exodus of women was that male workers contributed greater stability to the workforce than women who were often temporary workers.

Widows of veterans and single women protested. In January 1865, the *Boston Daily Evening Voice*, a labor newspaper that supported working women's issues, printed a letter written by a woman worker. "Many are shocked that we should insist on trying to keep our occupations, and charge us with masculinity," she wrote. "Perhaps it would be more feminine to fold our hands and starve in graceful indolence; or pass through life an object of charity" (Foner 1979, 122).

After the war, working women pursued more vigorously the formation of their own trade unions and enthusiastically responded to invitations to join a few previously all-male unions. In November 1865, working women took courage from the efforts of New York City ballet dancers to increase their wages from $5 to $9 per week. When the dancers' demands were not met, they called a strike and refused to work until their employers agreed to the increase.

Kate Mullaney, a young, single woman and sole supporter of her mother and two younger sisters, was a "collar laundress" in the collar manufacturing center of Troy, New York. Troy was the manufacturing capital for the detachable collar, invented by a minister's wife, Hannah Lord Montagu, in 1827. The work of laundering and starching the new collars required skill and was exhausting, difficult, and sometimes dangerous work. In February 1864, Mullaney organized the Troy Collar Laundry Union, in large part a response to plummeting wages caused by the development of commercial steam laundries prior to the Civil War (Turbin 1979, 208). With the support of male trade unionists in Troy, by the early months of 1866, Mullaney and her fellow laundresses raised their wages from $2 to $3 per week to $8 to $14 per week, reaching a pay scale that gave them equity with male workers.

Black laundresses in the South submitted a petition of demands for increased wages to the *Daily Clarion*, a newspaper in Jackson, Mississippi, in June 1866. As far as is known, this petition represents the first collective action of African-American female workers in the United States. Although the *Daily Clarion*'s editor printed a strong rebuttal, it did not snuff out black laundresses' labor protests as many more African-American women posted their demands throughout the country.

In the immediate postwar period, working-class women encountered trying economic times, tougher than those they faced during the war. The infiltration of men back into the labor force and the postwar decrease in production pushed many women out of the factories just as the numbers of women dependent on themselves to earn their living increased. War widows and other female family members of disabled veterans were forced to be breadwinners in a society that denied them work. Although these developments caused some women to organize and join labor unions, it would be decades before women demanded change through their activism in the trade union movement. For the time being, outspoken working-class women resorted to petitions, speeches, and other requests to pressure legislators and the public to act to increase wages and improve their working and living conditions.

Selected Readings

Foner, Philip S. *Women and the American Labor Movement: From Colonial Times to the Eve of World War I.* New York: Free Press. 1979.

Kessler-Harris, Alice. *Out to Work: A History of Wage-Earning Women in the United States.* New York: Oxford University Press. 1982.

Wertheimer, Barbara M. *We Were There: The Story of Working Women in America.* New York: Pantheon Books. 1977.

Invasion and Occupation

Now the soldiers, with hateful leers from their red eyes, would walk up to the steps ... and throwing down the hams and shoulders of our meat ... would cut them up with savage delight, in our very faces. ... Like statues mother and I ... saw them ... kill the milk cows and other stock ... [we] stood silent and sad as we saw the "potato hill" robbed, and knew that now our last hope for food was gone.

—Mrs. "L. F. J.," south of Macon, Georgia,
November 1864 (quoted in Jones 1964, 42)

Thousands of volumes have been written about men's experiences on the battlefields of the Civil War. Among these are the studies, published diaries, letters, and memoirs that focus on Union and Confederate soldiers' individual confrontations with combat. Very few books explore or mention the experiences of women and other civilians who encountered violent aggression during the invasion and occupation of enemy troops. Most Northern and Southern women who recorded the stories of their survival, declared that the weeks surrounding invasion and occupation were the most overwhelmingly difficult and unforgettable days of their lives.

More women than men experienced the trauma of invasion. In fact, Southern and Northern white and African-American women and children of all ages formed the vast majority of those who met the Union or Confederate invaders on their own doorsteps. From 1861 through the spring of 1865, Southern women bore the brunt of the onslaught of advancing Union armies. Although many Southern locales never glimpsed an invading Union regiment, parts of Virginia, South Carolina, North Carolina, Georgia, Louisiana, Mississippi, and Tennessee suffered greatly from Union invasion. Since nearly the entire war was fought on Southern territory, the Confederate army only rarely penetrated Northern lands. Confederate officers occasionally led raids into southern Pennsylvania, Kansas, and Unionist areas of Maryland and Kentucky. Confederates also raided the town of St. Albans, Vermont, from Canada.

Despite variations in women's personal stories of invasion, in general, most Southern women shared a similar set of experiences when their homes and properties were invaded by Union soldiers. In the days and weeks prior to their arrival, civilians were inundated by an avalanche of conflicting rumors. These stories, many exaggerated or erroneous, swore as to the numbers of approaching troops and the direction of their intended route. They also described in horrifying detail the army's destructive activities in nearby communities. This pre-invasion period and its concomitant burden of anticipation and terror were extremely wearing emotionally. Women frequently reported sleeplessness, exhaustion, severe anxiety, and an increased incidence of illness during this time.

The actual invasion of a community was the most harrowing time for its women residents, especially when Union soldiers advanced onto a family's property. They ripped apart farm fencing; burned, slashed, or harvested crops in the field; tore down or torched barns and outbuildings; and, on rarer occasions, cut well ropes or befouled wells. On campaigns in which a "scorched earth" policy was in effect, as in SHERMAN'S MARCH TO THE SEA and other Union military operations in 1864 and 1865, the destruction of property and land was the primary military objective.

The most terrifying part of any incursion on a woman's land was the moment when soldiers entered her household. Once inside a woman's home, soldiers often disregarded or reinterpreted their commanders' orders to suit their own whims and desires. Some soldiers waged a war of psychological terror on the women, children, and slaves they found within. These renegades threatened children with the deaths of their pets, their parents, or themselves. Others terrified women with threats of rape or with the promise to rape their daughters. Men often demanded that women cook a meal for them—at gunpoint, if necessary (Rable 1989, 160).

While soldiers consumed the household's alcohol supply, they frequently stole or destroyed furniture, family pictures and mementos, and jewelry. Once inside a woman's bedroom, they sometimes slashed her bedding or rifled through her clothing, destroying or stealing whatever they fancied, including her underwear. Some shouted every blasphemous and obscene curse in their vocabulary, while others took the opportunity to expose themselves before their traumatized female audience.

For the women who suffered these attacks, Union invasion was an intrusion that penetrated deep inside a woman's most personal and intimate space. Minerva Rowles McClatchey of Marietta, Georgia, stoically endured the massive destruction of her property and crops, but when soldiers "Took all the children's books—and valuable files of newspapers—pictures, slates, everything out of the office. … My feelings of loneliness, helplessness and dread cannot be described" (Bryan 1967, 203).

Women occasionally reacted aggressively, meeting their attackers at the door with weapons in hand. To do so, however, sometimes attracted more reprisals and violence. Elite women, especially early in the war, prided themselves on their attempts to shame soldiers for their ungentlemanly behavior. Regardless of a woman's response, one commonality that all women shared was their powerlessness to repel the invader.

When given the opportunity, Confederate soldiers could be just as brutal as Union troops. Confederate Lieutenant General Jubal A. Early's men destroyed much of Chambersburg, Pennsylvania, in July 1864. Although General Robert E. Lee had tightly restrained his army in 1863 when it occupied Chambersburg in the weeks prior to the Battle of GETTYSBURG, a year later Confederate officers lost control of their troops when drunken soldiers burned, robbed, and terrorized the entire town, rendering 3,000 women, children, and men homeless.

Although Confederate and Union troops did not kill white women (except in a few rare instances) and, for the most part, did not rape them, many modern historians agree that the rape of Southern white women by Union soldiers was undoubtedly more common than reported (Rable 1989, 161; Ash 1995, 201). Both free and enslaved African-American women, on the other hand, experienced rape and murder far more frequently during the Civil War years than white women, as slave women had all through the centuries of slavery in the United States.

Regardless of their race or class, Southern women feared rape and sexual assault more than any other terror a Yankee could inflict. In the mid-nineteenth century in both the South and the North, rape was considered to be an atrocity so horrendous that men and women rarely addressed it in specific terms. In a letter to her cousin Blanche, Roxa Cole of Mississippi described how Union soldiers broke into her house in the middle of the night, brandishing their pistols: "I should not have suffered so that night had I known that mere robbery was all I had to fear, but I had seen and heard so much of their lawless deeds and worse threats that we knew not what to fear" (quoted in Ash 1995, 198). Rape engendered tragic social consequences as well. Being a victim of rape degraded and declassed a woman, even when society agreed that she had been a powerless victim. Consequently, reporting a rape rarely held any advantages for a woman or her family. Union soldiers found guilty of rape were executed; in all, at least 18 men were put to death during the Civil War for this crime.

In the first days and weeks after invasion, women's letters, diaries, and memoirs reveal that as women struggled to care for their families and properties, nearly all were suffering at least somewhat from the aftereffects of the psychological trauma inflicted during the invasion. Judith Herman, a foremost authority on the effects of trauma on women, has stated that feelings of "intense fear, helplessness, loss of control, and threat of annihilation" are the emotions common to survivors of traumatic events—emotions that are ever-present in the personal papers of women who endured Union invasion (Herman 1992, 33).

Herman also stresses that not all of a trauma survivor's pain occurs at the time of the traumatic event. She explains that the aftereffects of trauma—the sometimes crippling reactions that occur in the weeks and months following a traumatic experience, "when action is of no avail. ... When neither resistance nor escape is possible"—are just as debilitating (Herman 1992, 33–34). During the weeks after an invasion, women frequently described their anxiety, physical and emotional exhaustion, sleep disturbances and nightmares, depression, apathy, and rage against their Yankee invaders as well as the emotional turmoil of their children and elderly relatives. Rachel Cormany, a resident of Confederate-invaded Chambersburg, Pennsylvania, was not one of the thousands burned out of their homes on July 30, 1864, but was deeply affected by it nevertheless. On August 6, 1864, a week after the siege, she wrote in her journal, "We live in constant dread. I never spent such days as these few last. ... I feel as if I could not stay in the country any longer. I feel quite sick of the dread and excitement" (Mohr 1982, 446).

Despite the tremendous strain that white and African-American women of all classes endured during and after invasion and occupation of Union forces, most were successful in keeping their children and elderly relatives safe and alive. Many families also managed to continue living on their land without being forced to become REFUGEES.

Women living in towns, cities, and in less isolated rural areas depended heavily on their female support networks. Women relatives, neighbors, friends, and, in some cases, female slaves cooperatively sustained one another physically, spiritually, and emotionally. In the weeks and months after Sherman's March to the Sea, Georgian women of all classes worked cooperatively to share the few food stuffs and resources that had not been destroyed.

Young women and girls appear to have been more likely than older women to channel their sense of violation and rage into the creation of revenge fantasies. Teen-aged Clara Solomon of New Orleans fervently hoped that an epidemic of yellow fever would decimate occupying Union troops. Confederate women enjoyed folk-lore of women sporting jewelry made from the bones of Union soldiers and visiting the battlefields and hospitals to celebrate among the mangled bodies of the Union dead. PHOEBE LEVY PEMBER noted in a letter to her sister EUGENIA LEVY PHILLIPS that a Christian friend received satisfaction from displaying the bones of a Union soldier in her yard (D. Faust 1997, 206).

A variant on the revenge tale was the well-circulated "power story" in which a woman successfully repelled Union aggression or harassment by outwitting, outclass-ing, or shaming her tormentors. In one such story, Evelyn Smith of North Carolina reported that when a Union officer taunted her, "Madam, do you know we sometimes divest Southern women of their clothes?," she retorted that he better not attempt it, or "he would never ride a horse again" (quoted in Rable 1989, 163).

For all the Union soldiers who behaved destructively and aggressively toward Southern women, many others treated them respectfully, even chivalrously. There were Yankees who risked their lives to help Southern civilians facing extreme dan-ger and officers who scrupulously enforced their orders and restrained their troops' treatment of civilians. And there were those who, no matter how much verbal abuse women heaped upon them, held their emotions in check and never resorted to vio-lence or psychological terror. Tales of the Yankee "Good Samaritan" are not uncom-mon in Southern memoirs and diaries. In general, however, especially in areas of the Confederacy that endured the most savage invasions, the presence of a kind, caring Union soldier is viewed only as a miraculous or aberrant event.

Occupation

Once the invasion phase of Union occupation was over, the most extreme threats to civilian survival came to an end. The civilian population then tried to adjust to the continual presence and power of federal authority. Although everyday life eventually settled into a routine, civilians were not living in the same community that existed prior to invasion. In some cities, women had to acquire a pass in order to leave their property and to return to it. They were not free to express their opinions or to talk defiantly to Union soldiers, and they were forbidden to sing Confederate songs. In many occupied cities and towns, the federals demanded that civilians swear to an oath of loyalty to the U.S. government. And there was an unwritten expectation that Southern women should respect and like Union officers, or at the very least, behave genially toward them. As Emma LeConte of Columbia, South Carolina, observed,

> These Yankee officers … take it rather hard that they are treated so coldly. … They invade our country, murder our people, desolate our homes, conquer us, subject us to every indignity and humiliation—and then we must offer our hands with pleasant smiles and invite them to our houses. … Are they crazy? (LeConte 1957, 108–109)

For many women, the worst aspect of occupation was that Union officers and soldiers could enter a civilian's home at any time of the day or night without warning. Usually they commandeered food and other supplies. Sometimes they stole furniture and items of value while cursing and threatening the female occupants should they try to resist. Occasionally a home was appropriated to provide housing for a Union officer and his family. Consequently, women's fear and anxiety did not diminish after an invasion. Instead they became hyper-vigilant—acutely sensitive to every sound and arrival. Some women slept fitfully and continued to sleep fully dressed, so that they could be ready at a moment's notice to protect their children and their belongings. And they continued to fear rape.

Yet in some parts of the Confederacy, particularly in the Unionist regions of Maryland, northern Virginia, and Tennessee, civilians greeted the arrival and occupation of Union forces with enthusiasm. In sections of East Tennessee, Unionist women developed cordial, trusting relationships with Union officers and troops. Young women responded favorably to offers of courtship. Civilians loyal to the Union were favored in other areas, too. In areas where women were initially wary and cool to the Yankees, over a period of months, and after examples of kind, humane treatment from individual officers or soldiers, women and other civilians eventually tolerated their presence.

See also **Battle of the Handkerchiefs; General Order No. 28; Guerrilla War; LeConte, Emma; Morgan, Sarah; Roswell Women; Vicksburg**

Selected Readings

Ash, Stephen V. *When the Yankees Came: Conflict and Chaos in the Occupied South, 1861–1865.* Chapel Hill: University of North Carolina Press. 1995.

Jones, Katharine M. *When Sherman Came: Southern Women and the "Great March."* Indianapolis: Bobbs-Merrill. 1964.

Rable, George C. *Civil Wars: Women and the Crisis of Southern Nationalism.* Urbana: University of Illinois Press. 1989.

J

Jacobs, Harriet (1813–1897)

During the Civil War and Reconstruction, Harriet Jacobs committed herself to assisting the African-American refugees in the overcrowded contraband camps outside of Washington, DC. As a former slave and as the author of the popular slave narrative and autobiography *Incidents in the Life of a Slave Girl: Written by Herself,* Jacobs was in a unique position to raise funds and gather support from Northern abolitionists for the fugitive slaves. Despite her years of leadership in freedpeople's relief, she is best known for her autobiography. Published in 1861, this volume earned a broad readership among abolitionist women and men, but it has never been more popular than it is today. Though neglected for much of the twentieth century, as a result of the erroneous assumption that the white abolitionist LYDIA MARIA CHILD was the author, the past 20 years has seen the book's reemergence. It is now considered a classic of antebellum American literature and has been acknowledged as "the most important slave narrative by an African-American woman" (Yellin 1993, 627).

Born a slave in North Carolina, Harriet Jacobs lived in bondage in the town of Edenton until 1835 when she escaped and went into hiding at her grandmother's home. The single mother of two spent the next two decades as a fugitive in both the South and North. In 1849, she became involved in antislavery activism in Rochester, New York, where her brother John Jacobs was an antislavery orator. She worked in the Anti-Slavery Office Reading Room, an establishment managed by her brother. Once the Fugitive Slave Act became law in 1850, she moved to New York City, where her former North Carolina owners once again attempted to capture her and her children and return them to slavery. Finally, in 1852, her former New York employer, Cornelia Grinnel Willis, purchased the Jacobs family's freedom.

For five years during the mid-1850s, while working full time as a domestic servant, Jacobs wrote her life story. She exposed topics that mid-nineteenth-century Americans rarely alluded to, let alone discussed. She revealed her experiences of her North Carolina owner's sexual domination of her and of her resistance to him, including her successful attempt to control her own sexuality and reproduction by having an intimate relationship with a white neighbor. Jacobs's close friend in Rochester, the white Quaker abolitionist Amy Kirby Post, encouraged Jacobs to write about her experiences as a slave.

In her preface to *Incidents*, Jacobs states her purpose in publishing an account of her life.

> I do earnestly desire to arouse the women of the North to a realizing sense of the condition of two millions of women at the South, still in bondage ... to convince the people of the Free States what Slavery really is. Only by experience can any one realize how deep, and dark, and foul is that pit of abominations. (Jacobs 1987, 1–2)

At first Jacobs encountered difficulty in finding a publisher for her book. After an unsuccessful trip to England, she received the assistance of Lydia Maria Child, who edited her manuscript.

Early in the Civil War, Jacobs was alarmed by news reports describing the living conditions of fugitive slaves in the contraband camps in and around Washington, DC. In 1862, she began raising money among her white and black abolitionist acquaintances. She traveled to Alexandria, Virginia, in 1863 to bring this aid to the freedpeople. She distributed food and clothing, dispensed medical care, and advocated on the freedpeople's behalf among Northern white abolitionists who exercised power in the freedmen's aid societies. To both Northern whites and freed African Americans, Jacobs strongly asserted the need for African Americans to self-determine their own institutions.

Toward this end, with financial backing from the New England Freedmen's Aid Society, she and her daughter Louisa Jacobs founded the Jacobs Free School. Unlike most schools for the freedpeople that were operated by middle-class whites who imposed Northern educational standards, the Jacobs Free School was directed by African Americans. In 1863, while still engaged in freedpeople's relief, Jacobs volunteered as a Union army recruiter of African-American men on an unofficial basis. Despite the long hours of backbreaking work, she found the time to pen letters to Northern newspapers, apprising the public of the extreme needs of the refugees and of the deplorable conditions of the contraband camps.

In 1864, she served on the membership committee of the WOMAN'S NATIONAL LOYAL LEAGUE (WNLL). Established by SUSAN B. ANTHONY and ELIZABETH CADY STANTON, the WNLL was the first national political organization established by women. Its goal was to collect a million signatures to convince Congress to pass the Thirteenth Amendment guaranteeing the freedom of African Americans.

From 1866 until 1868, Jacobs and her daughter continued their work among the freedpeople in Savannah, Georgia. In 1868, they traveled to England to raise money for two homes—one for African-American orphans and the other for the elderly in Savannah, a project that was never realized as a result of the chaos and hazards presented by racial tensions in the Reconstruction South.

See also **Abolitionists; African-American Women; Contraband Women; Teachers of the Freedpeople**

Selected Readings

Forbes, Ella. *African American Women During the Civil War.* New York: Garland. 1998.

Jacobs, Harriet A. *Incidents in the Life of a Slave Girl: Written by Herself.* Edited by Jean Fagan Yellin. Cambridge, MA: Harvard University Press. 1987.

Yellin, Jean Fagan. "Jacobs, Harriet Ann." In *Black Women in America: An Historical Encyclopedia.* Edited by Darlene Clark Hine, Elsa Barkley Brown, and Rosalyn Terborg-Penn. New York: Carlson Publishing. 1993.

K

Keckley, Elizabeth
(c. 1818/24–1907)

African-American author, dressmaker, and former slave Elizabeth Keckley is best known for her memoir, *Behind the Scenes, or, Thirty Years a Slave, and Four Years in the White House*, originally published in 1868. As the fashion designer, seamstress, and closest confidante of MARY TODD LINCOLN during the Civil War, Keckley resided in the White House and observed much of the Lincolns' private lives. Although she traces her own personal history in her book, she also focuses her gaze on her revelations about the Lincolns, especially Todd Lincoln. She also includes an exposé of Todd Lincoln's disastrously ill-conceived plan to sell her dresses and other finery in 1867.

Despite Keckley's mission to "place Mrs. Lincoln in a better light before the world," Keckley's narration of her life is fascinating in its own right, as it portrays the determination of an oppressed woman who achieved her most ambitious goal (Keckley 1988, xiv). Although her creation and leadership of the CONTRABAND RELIEF ASSOCIATION (later renamed the Ladies' Freedmen and Soldiers' Relief Association) rarely receives more than passing mention in most accounts of her life, her labors on behalf of the freed slaves add a vital dimension to the understanding of this extraordinary woman.

Born a slave in Dinwiddie Court House, Virginia, Elizabeth Hobbs was first owned by the Burwell family. While an adolescent, a white man, whom Keckley never names, repeatedly forced himself on her sexually over a period of four years. The unwanted liaison resulted in the birth of her only child, George.

She developed exceptional skill as a seamstress while owned by Anne Burwell Garland and her husband, whom Keckley claims that she supported for over two years with the proceeds from her dressmaking. Following several years of marriage to James Keckley, an alcoholic slave who had led her to believe that he was free and sober, she struck out on her own. In 1855, one of her devoted customers purchased her freedom for $1,200, a debt Keckley soon repaid.

In 1860, she established a dressmaking salon in Washington, DC. She then purposefully cultivated the wives of the most politically connected men of the capital, hoping eventually to sew for the occupants of the White House. Immediately prior to the war, she designed and made dresses for VARINA HOWELL DAVIS, wife of Senator Jefferson Davis, as well as Adele Cutts Douglas, wife of Senator Stephen Douglas, and Ellen Hutchison Stanton, wife of Secretary of War Edwin M. Stanton. She secured an interview with Todd Lincoln just two weeks after she moved into the White House and soon proved to the First Lady that she could not do without Keckley's exceptional designs.

Keckley had been sewing for Todd Lincoln for a brief time when she was also pressed into service as her personal maid and nurse. When Todd Lincoln professed that Keckley was her "very best friend," she never meant that she considered Keckley her equal. Although Todd Lincoln confided all her troubles to Keckley, Todd Lincoln remained the exacting, demanding employer while Keckley dovetailed as the dedicated employee who submerged her own needs in the fulfillment of Todd Lincoln's.

What is least known about Keckley's Civil War experiences is her organization of the Contraband Relief Association. As fugitive slaves escaped from bondage during the Civil War, they poured into the nation's capital. Frequently harbored in contraband camps, they subsisted in desperate want of nutritious food, clothing, bedding, and medical supplies. Upon witnessing their need, Keckley conceived of a relief society run by free African-American women volunteers, who would raise money and gather supplies for the contrabands. She also believed that free African Americans, by their own example and by their refusal to accept white society's limited conception of the former slaves' capabilities, would be the most effective group to guide the contrabands into their new lives as free people. With Todd Lincoln's support and encouragement behind her, Keckley developed an efficient, thriving society.

Writers and historians have long pondered Keckley's motivation in publishing *Behind the Scenes*. Her stories and anecdotes portray Todd Lincoln in an unflattering light and reveal many of her faults. Because of Keckley's decision to include many of Todd Lincoln's postwar letters, particularly those that emphasize her desperation and pathetic vulnerability, one cannot take too seriously Keckley's claim that she intended the book to "help" Todd Lincoln. Indeed, many writers and scholars have vastly overstated Keckley's claim that she wrote *Behind the Scenes* to improve Todd Lincoln's public image. In the book's preface, Keckley makes no pretense of having written the memoir solely to assist the former First Lady. Keckley repeatedly explains that her involvement in organizing the sale of Todd Lincoln's finery had harmed her own reputation as well as her employer's and as such, she shares the need to establish the truth behind their actions.

> My own character, as well as the character of Mrs. Lincoln, is at stake, since I have been intimately associated with that lady in the most eventful periods of her life. I have been her confidante, and if evil charges are laid at her door, they also must be laid at mine, since I have been a party to all her movements. To defend myself I must defend the lady that I have served. The world have judged Mrs. Lincoln … and through her have partially judged me, and the only way to convince them that wrong was not meditated is to explain the motives that actuated us. (Keckley 1988, xiv)

Keckley's dressmaking business never recovered from the firestorm of negative press over the dress-sale affair. As it continued to falter, she eventually closed it. She later taught domestic art at Wilberforce University. Back in Washington, DC, during her final years, she resided at a charity she helped establish, the Home for Destitute Women and Children.

Selected Readings

Garrett, Marie. "Elizabeth Keckley." In *Notable Black American Women*. Edited by Jessie Carney Smith. 616–621.

Keckley, Elizabeth. *Behind the Scenes, or, Thirty Years a Slave, and Four Years in the White House*. New York: Oxford University Press. 1988. Orig. Pub. New York: G. W. Carleton. 1868.

Quarles, Benjamin. "Keckley, Elizabeth." In *Notable American Women, 1607–1950: A Biographical Dictionary. Volume 2*. Edited by Edward T. James et al. Cambridge, MA: Belknap Press of Harvard University Press. 1971. 310–311.

Kemble, Fanny (1809–1893)

The state of the country is very sad, and I fear will long continue to grieve and mortify its well wishers; but of the ultimate success of the North, I have not a shadow of a doubt. I hope to God that neither England nor any other power from the other side of water will meddle in the matter—but, above all, not England …. With the clearing away of this storm, slavery will be swept from among the acknowledged institutions of America.

—Fanny Kemble, letter to Arthur Malkin, September 15, 1861 (Clinton 2000, 188)

Fanny Kemble, the renowned British-born actress and author, spent much of her adult life in the United States. An immensely popular stage celebrity during her lifetime, Kemble is more often remembered for her influential eyewitness account of the cruelty and brutality of slavery on her husband's Georgia plantations. *Journal of a Residence on a Georgian Plantation 1838–1839*, published in 1863, helped to persuade the British government and public from supporting the Confederacy.

Frances (Fanny) Ann Kemble was born in London, the daughter of Charles Kemble and Marie-Therese deCamp, both actors on the London stage. Charles also worked as a theatrical manager, though without much success. In 1829, after years of struggle, the family faced financial disaster. Marie-Therese determined that Fanny was the family's best chance for economic survival. Coaching her daughter in the art of the theater, she prepared Fanny for her first appearance as Juliet in *Romeo and Juliet* in 1829. Fanny instantly dazzled audiences and was an immediate sensation. Despite the fact that she packed the theater night after night, the family continued to teeter on the edge of bankruptcy. To stave off ruin, Charles decided that Fanny should tour the United States and Canada for two years. In 1832, she made her debut in American theaters and soon achieved stardom.

For Fanny, attaining financial security was a priority, which may have influenced her in 1834 to abandon her career to marry Pierce Butler, a member of a wealthy Philadelphia family. From the start, she was bewildered by all the changes that marriage obligated her to make. Her husband expected her to be obedient and subservient at all times. To her dismay, she lost control of her finances to him, a condition she held in common with all American married women at the time. Butler also refused to allow her to entertain her theatrical friends, on account of their lower social status. Even the welcome birth of a daughter, Sarah, in 1835 did not relieve her oppressive emptiness and loneliness.

In 1836, Butler inherited two rice and cotton plantations on the Sea Islands off the coast of Georgia, making him the second largest plantation owner in the state. Kemble, greatly influenced by abolitionist leaders in Philadelphia and New England, longed to visit the plantations so that she could inspect the institution of slavery firsthand. Butler finally consented to allow her, Sarah, and second daughter, Frances (Fan), born in 1838, to accompany him to the islands in December of that year. Before she departed, she decided to keep a journal of her experiences, which she planned to compile from letters written to her friend Elizabeth Sedgwick in Massachusetts. Kemble, already a well-known author, undoubtedly hoped that her observations of life on a Southern plantation might one day be published.

Although Kemble suspected that the living conditions of the slaves on her husband's plantations might not be as rosy as the Butler family and the plantations' reputation had led her to believe, she was not prepared for the desperate squalor and suffering she found when she inspected the slave quarters and the plantation hospital after her arrival. In particular, her first contact with the hospital shocked and overwhelmed her. In letters to Sedgwick, Kemble detailed the conditions she discovered there and recorded the emotional upheaval she experienced and the conflicts the situation created in her marriage.

In the slave hospital, Kemble found that,

> ... [T]he sick women ... were cowering, some on wooden settles, most of them on the ground, excluding those who were too ill to rise; and these last poor wretches lay prostrate on the floor, without bed, mattress, or pillow, buried in tattered and filthy blankets, which, huddled round them as they lay strewed about, left hardly space to move upon the floor .... Now pray take notice that this is the hospital of an estate where the owners are supposed to be humane, the overseer efficient and kind, and the Negroes remarkably well cared for and comfortable. (Kemble 2000, 104–105)

Kemble immediately resolved to do what she could to improve hygiene, and upon first inspection, ordered the slaves to clean the four large rooms while she directed and assisted. When she took the matter to her husband, she discovered for the first time that she was powerless to effect any substantive, lasting change in slave conditions. From this point forward, whenever she attempted to grapple with slave health and family issues, she raged with the realization of her "impotent indignation and unavailing pity" (Kemble 2000, 129).

Kemble soon realized that as long as the institution of slavery remained, pleading with her husband and the overseer to change the system was doomed to failure. As downcast and despairing as she was about this fact, she did not stop recording in intricate detail her observations and experiences of plantation life, nor did she flee or turn away from the slaves whose lives she attempted to make easier.

When a slave woman named Die came to Kemble asking for red flannel cloth and meat—two of the few things that as a plantation mistress she could offer the slaves—Kemble learned that the woman had given birth to 16 children, 14 of whom were dead. The woman also had endured four miscarriages, one caused by a fall sustained while carrying a heavy load on her head, the other "from having her arms strained up to be lashed." When Die, upon Kemble's prompting, explained what this punishment entailed, Kemble wrote, "And to all this I listen—I, an English woman, the wife of the man who owns these wretches, and I can not say 'That thing shall not be done again; that cruel shame villainy shall never be known here again'" (Kemble 2000, 157).

When the Butler family returned to their home in Philadelphia, Kemble, now an impassioned abolitionist, renewed her antislavery acquaintances and, over the next few years, read aloud from her journal of plantation life at abolitionist gatherings. While in England in 1840 or 1841, Kemble received a letter from LYDIA MARIA CHILD, then editor of the *National Anti-Slavery Standard*, asking her to submit portions of the journal for publication in the abolitionist newspaper. Kemble dearly wanted to publish but understood all that her husband and his family had to lose from the negative publicity her account would create. Following a long struggle with Butler over the matter, she did not publish the journal at this time, to her grave discontent.

Back in the United States in 1843 to 1844, Kemble discovered that Butler was and had been engaging in extramarital affairs. In 1845, she left him and her daughters to return to England. She returned to the stage in 1847 when the income Butler promised was not forthcoming. A year later, realizing that she did not have the stamina she once enjoyed, she retired from acting and began giving Shakespearean readings throughout England. In the summer of 1848, she returned to the United States when she learned that Butler was divorcing her and trying to obtain sole custody of their daughters. The divorce became final in 1849, giving Kemble custody of her daughters for only two months of the year. Throughout the 1850s, she lived in the United States, earning an admirable living conducting readings from city to city.

At the outset of the Civil War, like most abolitionists, Kemble believed that the conflict would ultimately eliminate slavery. As optimistic as she was at first about the North's chances of victory, her family was sharply divided between North and South. Her younger daughter, Fan Butler, supported the pro-Confederate views of her slaveholding father, who was imprisoned briefly for treason. Sarah Butler Wister, Kemble's older daughter, married to a Philadelphia doctor, backed the North.

From 1861, Kemble was concerned about the fate of the North should England decide to uphold the Confederacy. When she returned to England in 1862, her anxiety about the issue intensified as she observed the British public's hatred for the North and witnessed how susceptible her British acquaintances were to the arguments of Confederate advocates residing in England. Desperate to do what she could to prevent England from recognizing the Confederacy, she quickly edited her journal and submitted it for publication. As she explained in a letter to her lifelong friend Harriet St. Leger, it was her "imperative duty, knowing what I know, and having seen what I have seen, to do all that lies in my power to show the dangers and the evils of this frightful institution" (Clinton 2000, 8–9). Now that she was divorced, Butler had no power to stop her from sharing all she knew about slavery in the South. In May of 1863, *Journal of a Residence on a Georgian Plantation* was published in England.

Although the full impact of the *Journal*'s influence on the course of events is not known, it was widely acclaimed and received a broad readership. Portions of it were read during debates in the House of Commons. The Ladies' Emancipation Society of London included passages from the journal in its antislavery pamphlet "The Essence of Slavery," of which hundreds of thousands of copies were printed. (The British government ultimately chose not to back the Confederacy.) When the *Journal* was published in June of 1863 in the United States, the Northern press and public eagerly embraced it. With the success, however, came heartache. In a letter to Kemble, Fan declared that she would never forgive her mother for publishing a book that so harmed her father's reputation.

After the war, Kemble once more turned to delivering dramatic readings in England and the United States. In 1874, Harriet St. Leger returned over 40 years' worth of correspondence to Kemble. With this treasure trove in hand, Kemble resolved to write her memoirs, a venture that proved highly successful. *Records of a Girlhood* was published in 1878, *Records of Later Life* (her most widely read memoir) in 1882, and *Further Records* in 1891. In 1877, following her last visit to the United States, Kemble returned to England where she resided for the rest of her life until her death in 1893.

See also **Abolitionists**

Selected Readings

Blainey, Ann. *Fanny and Adelaide: The Lives of the Remarkable Kemble Sisters*. Chicago: Ivan R. Dee. 2001.

Clinton, Catherine. *Fanny Kemble's Civil Wars*. New York: Simon and Schuster. 2000.

Kemble, Fanny. *Fanny Kemble's Journals*. Edited by Catherine Clinton. Cambridge, MA: Harvard University Press. 2000.

Kemble, Frances Anne. *Journal of a Residence on a Georgian Plantation in 1838–1839*. Edited by John A. Scott. Athens: University of Georgia Press. 1984.

L

Larcom, Lucy (1824–1893)

It was the only time in my life that I ever thought I would rather be a man than a woman, that I might go and fight and perhaps die for my country and freedom. I had to content myself with knitting blue army socks and writing verses.

—Lucy Larcom (Marchalonis 1989, 136)

One of the nation's leading poets during the mid- to late nineteenth century, Lucy Larcom's renown faded during the twentieth century. Yet during the 1860s and 1870s, New England's most celebrated literary figures welcomed her into their midst. The poets John Greenleaf Whittier, Henry Wadsworth Longfellow, and Oliver Wendell Holmes lauded her writing, and novelist HARRIET BEECHER STOWE declared that Larcom was the American equivalent of Britain's Elizabeth Barrett Browning. The Civil War inspired Larcom to write numerous patriotic poems, though she is best known for her poetry focusing on nature and religious themes. As intent as she was on supporting the Union cause, the early war years found her enmeshed in a personal conflict—whether to remain in teaching or to devote herself full time to her writing.

Lucy Larcom was born in the coastal community of Beverly, Massachusetts. Following her father's death when she was seven years of age, her mother moved the family from Beverly to the nearby city of Lowell, Massachusetts, where she secured a position operating a boarding house for young female mill workers. A financially inept manager, she discovered that to make ends meet she would have to send yet another of her daughters to work in the mills. She selected Larcom who, though not yet an adolescent, was eager to leave school and start work as a "doffer." In this position, Larcom removed and replaced bobbins on the mill's spinning frames.

When Larcom returned to public school (state law mandated that child mill operatives attend school for three months each year), she progressed so swiftly that at the end of the three months, she was fully prepared for high school, a startling achievement. Though she longed to attend the high school in Lowell, one of the first in the nation, the family depended on her wages and she could not attend. Now 13 years of age, Larcom was promoted to the job of operating the spinning frames. In her leisure hours, she was a voracious reader and writer of poetry and essays for the *Lowell Offering*, a newspaper published by mill workers. She continued to work in the mills throughout the remainder of her adolescence.

As a young woman, Larcom traveled to the frontier of Illinois with an older sister and her husband. Although at the time Larcom had no formal education beyond grammar school, the studies she had pursued on her own more than qualified her to teach in an Illinois district school. She wrote verse in the time she could spare and continued to publish her poems in the *Lowell Offering* as well as in the *New England Offering* and several other newspapers.

In 1848, she submitted an antislavery poem to the *National Era*, an abolitionist newspaper in Washington, DC. Larcom had first come to the attention of the editor, the New England writer and poet John Greenleaf Whittier, back in her Lowell days. It was her first poem in a national newspaper. Its publication also initiated Whittier's mentorship of Larcom, a relationship that lasted for decades. During this period, Larcom became engaged to the brother of her sister's husband. The attachment endured for many years, but she never married, in part out of concern for her and her fiancé's divergent interests and her fears of the restrictions of marriage.

Larcom could not believe her good fortune when she enrolled in Monticello Seminary in Godfrey, Illinois, in 1849. At last she would obtain the higher education she'd been yearning for. At first she paid her way by performing domestic chores at the school. Not long afterward, she was appointed to teach in the seminary's preparatory department as a means of paying her tuition and board. Fatigued by life on the frontier, she returned to Massachusetts after graduation in 1852.

With Whittier's help and encouragement, a small volume of Larcom's essays or "prose poems" were published under the title *Similitudes, from the Ocean and Prairie* in 1853. She was writing and publishing her poetry regularly at this time but earning nothing for it. Like other female writers of the 1850s and 1860s, she only gradually came to realize that she would have to take the initiative in securing payment from publishers. Although she began requesting remuneration, she did not demand it, nor did she refuse to permit her work to be published if no money were forthcoming, a strategy some women writers of the time used successfully. Yet Larcom understood that, as an unmarried woman, she must have income if she were to maintain her independence. Her family urged her to marry, but Larcom resisted, choosing instead to assume a faculty position at Wheaton Seminary in Norton, Massachusetts, in 1854.

Following passage of the Kansas-Nebraska Act in 1854, antislavery activists from New England migrated to Kansas Territory to settle the region and to prevent it from becoming a slave state. In full sympathy with the emigrants, Larcom composed new lyrics to a familiar tune and submitted them to a song–writing competition intended to motivate abolitionist men and women to join the emigrants. Her "Call to Kansas," to be sung to the tune of "Nelly Bly," was chosen as the best song, earning her the $50 prize.

As the violent conflict between pro-slavery Missourians and antislavery Kansans intensified in 1856, Larcom became passionate about the political issues involved, so much so that she considered immigrating to Kansas herself. Like many abolitionist men and women in the North, she believed that the North would be justified in seceding from the Union so long as the South remained determined to maintain slavery, which she considered an intolerable evil. She endorsed the new Republican Party's candidate John C. Frémont for president in 1856, hoping that he would usher in an antislavery government in Washington, DC. It disturbed her that she could not become more actively involved in the struggle, and she believed her failure to do so was at least in part the result of her being a woman. As she explained in a letter to Whittier, "We are indeed living in a revolution. … It makes me ache to think that I am doing nothing for the right, holy cause. What can one do? It is not very agreeable to sit still and blush to be called an American woman" (quoted in Helmreich 1990, 111).

In the mid- to late 1850s, as the national crisis over slavery escalated, Larcom devoted herself to her teaching while also managing to create numerous poems. She was still publishing her verse in newspapers that paid very little or nothing at all while she sought better-paying markets for her work. In 1856 to 1857, she began writing for *The Congregationalist*, a religious newspaper that paid her $1 to $2 per poem. In 1857, a poem brought her instant celebrity. "Hannah Binding Shoes" was widely acclaimed and became popular with the public. As much as Larcom enjoyed receiving recognition, she was dismayed that a verse that she considered inferior to much of her other work should be heralded.

As her poetry received more attention, Larcom became increasingly frustrated with teaching, resenting its limitations on her time and energies, which she felt could be better spent dedicated to her writing. By the late 1850s, Larcom had the literary connections to support herself as a writer, but she chose not to do so. For almost all of her years at Wheaton (1854 to 1862), she agonized over her inclination to leave teaching to pursue her writing, yet she clung to the security of the teaching position, partly because she did not believe that she could succeed as an independent writer.

With the onset of the Civil War came a turning point in Larcom's career. Her poem "The Rose Enthroned" was published in the June 1861 issue of the *Atlantic Monthly*, ushering her into the center of New England's literary culture. During the war, she became a regular contributor to the *Atlantic Monthly* while also submitting poems, many of them on patriotic themes, to newspapers and other publications.

In April 1861, as the North began its mobilization for war, Larcom explained her changing attitude toward armed conflict to Whittier who, as a Quaker, could not, under any circumstances, accept warfare. Any reservations she had about the call to arms were swept away when she visited Boston during the first days after war was declared. In her journal entry for April 21, 1861, she wrote,

> The few days I have passed at Boston this week, were the only days in which I ever carried my heart into a crowd, or hung around companies of soldiers, with anything like pleasure. But I felt a soldier-spirit rising within me, when I saw the men of my native town armed and going to risk their lives for their country's sake; and the dear old flag of our Union is a thousand times more dear than ever before. (quoted in Helmreich 1990, 114)

On April 23, she tried to explain her new position toward war to Whittier. Larcom acknowledged her own revulsion at the prospect of war but asserted that, given the political situation, war was justified and worthy of her involvement.

> Yet, although I cannot bring myself to think of the waste of noble and precious lives which must result from this conflict ... although I cannot think of that without deepest sorrow, yet it seems as if my whole being had turned from peaceful to warlike. I wish I were a man, that I might offer my life for my country; I have urged my friends to go,—and I will work night and day, if it is needed, for the success of our cause,—for is it not freedom's and truth's and God's. ... If ever there was a cause for fighting, there is now. (quoted in Marchalonis 1989, 134–135)

As Larcom later noted, there was little she could do for the cause other than spend her time "knitting blue army socks and writing verses" (quoted in Marchalonis 1989, 136). She produced a number of patriotic poems throughout the war. Although present-day writers have criticized the sentimentality of her war poems, they were well received at the time and are representative of the patriotic prose and poetry filling Northern and Southern newspapers during the conflict's early months. Larcom's poem "The Nineteenth of April" commemorates the beginnings of two wars—the Revolutionary War and the Civil War. The poem praises the rallying of Northerners to the Union cause while mourning the fratricidal conflict dividing the nation. In the final stanzas of the following excerpt, the narrator laments the need to fight yet points out that the Union is battling for justice and freedom, a cause sanctioned by God.

Along the whole awakening North are those bright emblems spread;
A summer noon of patriotism is burning overhead.
No party badges flaunting now,—no word of clique or clan;
But "Up for God and Union!" is the shout of every man.

O, peace is dear to Northern hearts; our hard-earned homes more dear;
But Freedom is beyond the price of any earthly cheer;
And Freedom's flag is sacred;—he who would work it harm,
Let him, although a brother, beware our strong right arm!

A brother! ah, the sorrow, the anguish of that word!
The fratricidal strife begun, when will its end be heard?
Not this the boon that patriot hearts have prayed and waited for;—
We loved them, and we longed for peace: but they would have it war. ...

To war,—and with our brethren, then—if only this can be!
Life hangs as nothing in the scale against dear Liberty!
Though hearts be torn asunder, for Freedom we will fight:
Our blood may seal the victory, but God will shield the Right!

(Larcom 1869, 130–131)

In 1862, with literary success to bolster her decision, Larcom left Wheaton. She spent the war years living among various friends and relatives, immersed in her writing. She became a regular contributor to the *Atlantic Monthly* and continued to publish in newspapers. Her patriotic poems "Re-enlisted," "Waiting for News," "The Sinking of the Merrimack," and "The Flag," to name a few, are not considered her finest work, yet they convey the emotion and strength of purpose and righteousness that Northerners presented in their patriotic writings. She applied several times for a position teaching the freedpeople in the South, but each application she made was rejected, perhaps because of her history of ill health. During the 1850s and early 1860s, Larcom suffered from scrofula, a tuberculosis of the lymph nodes. Groups sending teachers to the South admitted only the healthiest candidates.

After the war, Larcom's literary career burgeoned. In addition to writing poetry, she was an editor of Our Young Folks, a literary magazine for children. She assembled several poetry anthologies, wrote An Idyl of Work (a novel in blank verse), and published a number of volumes of her collected poems. Her most widely known work, A New England Girlhood, published in 1889, is a memoir of her youth. In her final years, she published three books communicating her religious belief that God resides in nature. She died in Boston in 1893.

See also **Literary Women; Patriotism**

Selected Readings

Helmreich, Paul C. "Lucy Larcom at Wheaton." *New England Quarterly.* 63 (1) (1990): 109–120.

Marchalonis, Shirley. *The Worlds of Lucy Larcom 1824–1893*. Athens: The University of Georgia Press. 1989.

LeConte, Emma (1847–1932)

We give up to the Yankees! How *can* it be? … Why does not the President call out the women if there are [not] enough men? We would go and fight, too. … I never loved my country as I do now. I feel I could sacrifice everything to it.

—Emma LeConte, Columbia, South Carolina,
April 16, 1865 (LeConte 1957, 90–91)

Emma LeConte wrote the first entry of her Civil War diary on December 31, 1864, when she was 17 years old, a month before Union Major General William Tecumseh Sherman's troops invaded South Carolina. Her diary concludes in August 1865, as she and her family confront the grim burden of resuming their lives in a society destroyed by war, under federal occupation during Reconstruction. Her colorfully vibrant descriptions of war-ravaged Columbia, her ease of language, and her outspoken candor distinguish her diary as a major work of Civil War literature. It is also one of the clearest articulations of the patriotic ideals and emotions of Southern white girls and women who clung to their faith in the future of the Confederacy.

LeConte's diary also provides one of the most vivid portraits of the burning of Columbia, South Carolina, in February 1865. When Union Major General Oliver O. Howard, acting on Sherman's orders, directed the bombardment of the city on February 16, Columbia quickly surrendered. As Union troops marched into the city the next day, retreating Confederate forces ignited bales of cotton in city warehouses. The weather turned blustery as the day progressed, spreading the fire from building to building and house to house throughout the entire central part of the city.

> Imagine night turned into noonday, only with a blazing, scorching glare that was horrible—a copper-colored sky across which swept columns of black, rolling smoke glittering with sparks and flying embers, while all around us were falling thickly showers of burning flakes. (LeConte 1957, 45)

On the night of February 17, the inner city of Columbia burned to the ground as thousands of drunken Union soldiers caroused in the streets. According to LeConte, surviving the fire was traumatic enough without having to witness the glee of Union soldiers as women and children were burned out of their homes. Although no one has ever determined all the parties responsible for the blaze, LeConte and the residents of Columbia were convinced that the Yankees burned the city.

It was not until after the surrender to the Union in April 1865 that the grief-stricken LeConte gradually let go of her romantic dream of a victorious Confederacy. A month later, during which time she recorded nothing in her diary, LeConte was still overwhelmed by the defeat. On May 17, 1865, she wrote that she could not describe the intensity of this loss and that "perhaps it is best not to put all I felt and suffered on paper." She then silences herself on the subject, adding, "And so I had better not write about it all—only of personal and family matters, if I can keep back the expression of what fills my heart and thoughts" (LeConte 1957, 98).

After the war, LeConte's father moved his family to Georgia. Though the rest of LeConte's family emigrated west in 1869, LeConte remained and married Farish Carter Furman, a Confederate veteran and plantation owner who became a lawyer, judge, and agricultural scientist in Scottsboro near Milledgeville, Georgia. When he died in 1883, LeConte Furman was left alone to raise their two daughters and to run their 1,000-acre plantation on her own, an operation she managed successfully.

See also **Diaries; Girlhood and Adolescence; Invasion and Occupation; Patriotism; Sherman's March to the Sea**

Selected Readings

Faust, Drew Gilpin. *Mothers of Invention: Women of the Slaveholding South in the American Civil War.* New York: Vintage Books. 1997.

LeConte, Emma. *The Diary of Emma LeConte.* Edited by Earl Schenck Miers. New York: Oxford University Press. 1957.

Lewis, Edmonia
(c. 1840–after 1909)

Edmonia Lewis was the first African-American sculptor, male or female, to achieve success on an international scale. During the Civil War, when she was launching her career, white women sculptors in the United States were just beginning to overcome the prejudices that prevented women from prospering as professional artists. For an African-American female sculptor to attain celebrity was an extraordinary accomplishment in an era when most black artists were male and were struggling to earn a living. Lewis's early work honored prominent male abolitionists. After settling in Rome, her sculptures celebrated the emancipation of African Americans and portrayed figures from ancient history, the Bible, mythology, and Native American culture.

Edmonia Lewis was born in Greenbush, near Albany, New York. Her father was a free African-American servant and her mother, of mixed African-American and Chippewa (Native American) ancestry, originated from an area that is now the site of the city of Mississauga, Ontario, Canada. Very little of Lewis's childhood has been authenticated. It is known that her mother and father died when she was a young child. According to Lewis, she grew up among the Chippewas, "fishing, swimming, and making moccasins," although most historians doubt the veracity of her stories of her Native American upbringing (quoted in Bearden and Henderson 1993, 55). Her stepbrother, at least eight years her senior, went west as an adolescent and thrived as a gold prospector in California. He paid for her to be educated at the preparatory school of New York Central College at McGrawville, New York. In 1859, her stepbrother again paid the tuition when Lewis enrolled in the Ladies' Preparatory Department at Oberlin College in Ohio, the first college to admit African Americans.

Although Oberlin had 31 other African-American students in 1859, she was the only black student among the 13 girls boarding at the home of a respected abolitionist minister. From all accounts, Lewis was well liked, was a diligent student, and enjoyed an active social life. In late January 1862, she became embroiled in a scandal that inflamed the college community, the town of Oberlin, and the neighboring region. One evening she offered a hot wine beverage to two white girls who were about to embark on a sleigh ride with two young men. During the outing, both girls were seized by severe abdominal pains. Both doctors called in to examine the girls concurred that a well-known aphrodisiac—cantharides or Spanish fly—had made them ill. The girls immediately accused Lewis of poisoning them.

Although the incident was not reported in the local newspapers for three weeks, rumors spread throughout Oberlin overnight, stirring racial animosity among whites. Lewis was not apprehended by police, nor was any action taken against her in the early days after the incident, though friends of the ill girls demanded that Lewis be brought to justice. Days later, as Lewis left her boarding house one night, white vigilantes abducted her. They forced her to accompany them to a neighboring field where they brutally beat her, leaving her battered body exposed to the bitter February cold. Hours later, when she was discovered missing, a search party located her and carried her to safety.

It took weeks for Lewis to recover from her injuries. While she was recuperating, a preliminary date was set for a hearing on the charges brought against her. John Langston, a well-known African-American attorney and Oberlin graduate, offered to take on her legal defense. At the two-day hearing preliminary to her trial, the case was dismissed due to the absence of evidence.

A year later, in the late winter of 1863, Lewis left Oberlin without completing the final term of her college education. She had been twice accused of theft, causing the head of the Oberlin Ladies' Department to reject her enrollment for the spring term of 1863. Although both claims were unproven and lacking in evidence, Lewis nevertheless was prevented from graduating.

Lewis departed for Boston where she met the white abolitionist leader William Lloyd Garrison. When he learned of her artistic talents and aspirations, he made it possible for her to be introduced to Edward A. Brackett, a noted Boston sculptor. Lewis studied under Brackett, gradually learning how to model in clay. In a matter of months, she was making plaster medallions of the martyred white militant abolitionist John Brown, which she sold at abolitionist gatherings.

In May 1863, Lewis joined crowds lining the streets of Boston to watch the 54th Massachusetts Colored Regiment, the first all-black regiment to be raised in the North, march out of the city. Leading them was the white officer Union Colonel Robert Gould Shaw, the son of prominent Boston abolitionists. Twenty-one of the soldiers in the regiment were men who had attended Oberlin College. Less than two months later, in the Union attack on Battery Wagner on Morris Island, South Carolina, Shaw and many soldiers of the 54th were killed. In memoriam, Lewis sculpted a highly acclaimed bust of Shaw, capturing the attention of other well-known sculptors, including Harriet Hosmer and Anne Whitney. Lewis then created 100 plaster copies of the bust to be sold at the Soldiers' Relief Fund Fair, an event intended to raise money to boost the wages of black soldiers. (Black Union soldiers were paid less than their white counterparts.)

Like most successful sculptors of the mid-nineteenth century, Lewis was eager to study in Italy. By the summer of 1865, she had raised enough money to finance the journey. After spending a year in Florence, she settled in Rome, becoming the compatriot of Harriet Hosmer, Emma Stebbins, and other white American female sculptors in the city. In this environment, Lewis fully immersed herself in neoclassicism, the style of art commemorating the classical sculpture of ancient Greece, which predominated in the mid-nineteenth century. In 1867 to 1868, Lewis created the two-figure sculpture titled *Forever Free*, which memorialized the Emancipation Proclamation of 1863, one of the first steps leading to the liberation of all enslaved African Americans. During this period, she also honored her Native American ancestry by carving a number of sculptures inspired by Henry Wadsworth Longfellow's narrative poem *Hiawatha*.

In 1876, Lewis shocked the American public with her sculpture the *Death of Cleopatra*, an acutely realistic portrayal of death. Although many American sculptors left Italy in the mid- to late 1870s, Lewis remained, her work still in demand. She is known to have been a close friend of SARAH PARKER REMOND and her sisters. Aside from Frederick Douglass's discussion of his meeting with Lewis in 1887, almost nothing is known of her later years. A faithful Roman Catholic, she is mentioned in a Catholic periodical in 1909, yet information about her death has not been located.

See also **Artists**

Selected Readings

Bearden, Romare and Harry Henderson. "Edmonia Lewis." In *A History of African-American Artists from 1792 to the Present*. New York: Pantheon. 1993.

Richardson, Marilyn. "Lewis, Edmonia." In *American National Biography*. Volume 13. Edited by John A. Garraty and Mark C. Carnes. New York: Oxford University Press. 1999.

Rubinstein, Charlotte Streifer. "Pioneering Sculptors." In *American Women Sculptors: A History of Women Working in Three Dimensions*. Boston: G.K. Hall. 1990.

Lincoln, Mary Todd (1818–1882)

Of all prominent public women during the Civil War, none suffered more from a hostile press than Mary Todd Lincoln. More than a century after her death, she is still remembered, not for her accomplishments or contributions, but for what many historians and biographers have chosen to emphasize—her emotional instability, her "difficult" personality, her compulsive shopping, and her "meddlesome" involvement in her husband's political activities. According to biographer Jean Baker, however, Todd Lincoln was a politically ambitious woman, determined to do whatever necessary to advance her husband's career, in an era when society strictly relegated women to the domestic world of "women's sphere" and chastised those who dared to encroach on the all-male territory of politics and public life.

Born into a distinguished, slaveholding family in Lexington, Kentucky, in 1818, Mary Todd grew up living a privileged, upper-class existence. Her father, Robert Smith Todd, provided the best education that could be obtained for all his children, including his daughters. By the time Mary left school at 17, she had completed an extraordinary 12 years of formal schooling, unusual for a young woman of her era in the South or North.

Mary Todd's precocious interest in politics distinguished her from the girls of Lexington. From the time she was a young girl, she followed Whig party politics closely, as did her father. He encouraged her political interest and knowledge, a passion that led her as a young adult to become interested in the Illinois lawyer and politician Abraham Lincoln. Following their marriage in 1842, and during their nearly 20 years living in Springfield, Illinois, Todd Lincoln immersed herself in her domestic duties. Although she had been raised to expect that slaves would spare her the drudgery of almost all domestic tasks, Todd Lincoln cooked, cleaned, sewed, and did most of the onerous household chores of the mid-nineteenth-century household with a minimum of hired help.

What was most unusual about Todd Lincoln, however, was her political partnership with her husband. From the early days of his political career in Springfield, she cultivated his most important political relationships. She entertained lavishly on a limited budget, wrote thousands of letters, helped him to garner influence and to strategize his campaigns, and encouraged him when he faltered after his defeats and setbacks.

By the time Lincoln was elected president in 1860, Todd Lincoln had a long history of assisting her husband with his political duties. But unlike Springfield, where her ambition was grudgingly tolerated, Washington society was shocked when they encountered her immersion in her husband's career. Political wives in the nation's capital traditionally shied away from the limelight. They retired to their boudoirs and emerged only for social engagements. Todd Lincoln was harshly criticized in the press for her interference in her husband's affairs and her "unseemly" deviance from her proper feminine role. She was acutely sensitive to the criticism, in part because she was already dealing with the Washington establishment's prejudice against her and her husband's "uncivilized" western ways.

As would any savvy politician, she attempted to placate her critics by vehemently denying that she had abandoned her traditional role. "My character is wholly domestic," she protested (quoted in Baker 1987, 181). As she told James Gordon Bennett, publisher of the *New York Herald*, "I have a great terror of *strong* minded Ladies" (quoted in Turner and Turner 1972, 138).

In her own way, Todd Lincoln attempted to master both the domestic and public spheres while in the White House. Her domestic mission to rejuvenate and redecorate the White House stimulated enormous controversy. She was the first wife of a president to direct and manage a redecoration project. She quickly overspent the four-year $20,000 allowance granted by Congress. In addition to disproving the notion of her uncouth westernness, she had a grand design in mind in making the White House the showplace of Washington. She reasoned that since the Civil War threatened to tear the Union apart, it was imperative that the White House be a symbol of federal strength and majesty. Her political critics and the press lambasted her for her extravagance at a time when the nation needed to conserve its resources to fight a war.

Her wish to bolster Lincoln's and her own popularity and her concern for the Union also drove her to maintain an exhausting schedule of White House receptions during all of 1861. Whether she was ill or fatigued, she refused to miss a single occasion. Always attired elegantly, she extended a warm, gracious welcome to the thousands of citizens and foreigners who wished to meet the president.

Eventually her most vocal male critics accused her of being a Confederate sympathizer and spy. Although three of her half-brothers fought and died for the Confederacy and several of her other siblings supported it, she was always devoted to the Union cause. She was tormented by the calumny, yet the attacks did not sway her from her course. She campaigned just as vigorously for Lincoln's reelection in 1864. As ELIZABETH KECKLEY, her African-American dressmaker and closest confidante, claimed Todd Lincoln did not see herself as having a choice; she had to ensure Lincoln's reelection so that she could continue to hide the debts from her spending sprees.

Todd Lincoln's devotion to public service has been frequently overlooked. Few biographers have emphasized the time or the money she spent aiding the army hospitals in Washington. Although she never nursed the wounded, she visited the hospitals frequently, providing support and encouragement to the wounded and ill, reading to them, writing their letters, serving meals, and organizing special holiday dinners (Baker 1987, 186). Unlike most Washington political wives, the sight of amputated limbs and smell of putrefying flesh did not abbreviate or deter her from her visits. And, unlike her peers, she looked forward to reviewing the troops on the frontlines with her husband.

Elizabeth Keckley persuaded the First Lady to help her organize relief for the thousands of African-American contrabands in Washington. Though the daughter of a slaveowner, Todd Lincoln had become decidedly antislavery in her views through her contacts with Northern abolitionist politicians. She was dismayed when she found it difficult to raise funds in Washington for Keckley's CONTRABAND RELIEF ASSOCIATION. She also helped a number of former slaves to acquire government jobs as clerks, nightwatchmen, and lamplighters (Turner and Turner 1972, 145).

In a letter to the editor of the *Chicago Tribune*, written five days after Todd Lincoln's death in 1882, the abolitionist journalist JANE GREY SWISSHELM asserted that the First Lady had been "more radically opposed to slavery" than Lincoln. Swisshelm also claimed that Todd Lincoln pushed her husband toward enacting emancipation before he had fully committed himself to the slaves' freedom (Turner and Turner 1972, 145).

As far as Todd Lincoln's mental health is concerned, there is no question that she was emotionally unstable during the Civil War. The death of her young son Willie Lincoln, the Lincolns' second child lost to illness, incapacitated her for many months. Her suffering seems to have been compounded by a battery of unrelieved stressors that dominated her four years as the president's wife: repeated assassination threats on her husband's life, the recurring prospect of Confederate invasion, the presence of armed military troops within the White House walls, and, of course, the ceaseless barrage of negative press. Todd Lincoln is reported to have said, "Ah, no one knows what it is to live in constant dread of some fearful tragedy" (Keckley 1988, 178). She also sabotaged her attempts to bolster her public image. She was carelessly indiscreet, trusting servants and acquaintances with her personal feelings and opinions about high-ranking politicians and officials.

After Lincoln's assassination, Todd Lincoln's political life was over. Grief and anxiety further undermined her emotional health. The last 16 years of her life were spent moving from one set of rented hotel rooms to others, fighting for her independence and integrity. Her attempt to raise money selling her dresses, Elizabeth Keckley's tell-all memoir, the newspapers' endless fascination with her wartime extravagances, her son Robert's mission to commit her to an asylum, and her insanity trial, all contributed to her decision to travel and live abroad for long periods.

Selected Readings

Baker, Jean H. "Mary Todd Lincoln (1818–1882)." In *Portraits of American Women: From Settlement to the Present.* Edited by G. J. Barker-Benfield and Catherine Clinton. New York: St. Martin's Press. 1991. 241–257.

Baker, Jean H. *Mary Todd Lincoln: A Biography.* New York: Norton. 1987.

Turner, Justin G. and Linda Levitt Turner. *Mary Todd Lincoln: Her Life and Letters.* New York: Knopf. 1972.

Literary Women

A dozen [stories] a month were easily turned off, and well paid for, especially while a certain editor labored under the delusion that the writer was a man. The moment the truth was known the price was lowered; but the girl had learned the worth of her wares, and would not write for less, so continued to earn her fair wages in spite of sex.

—Louisa May Alcott, commenting on her early years as a writer for the magazine *The Critic*, March 17, 1888 (quoted in Stern 1998, 58).

By the advent of the Civil War, women writers were an established, influential force in the nation's literary marketplace. They supplied a print-hungry populace with novels, short stories, poems, essays, articles, and nonfiction narratives. During the war, women's writing increasingly dominated magazines and newspapers, especially in the North, where no significant disruption in press circulation occurred. Through their writings, women of the North and South expressed their political beliefs and helped to shape the way their respective nation viewed its mission. A crucial part of their political agenda was to highlight all the ways in which women were contributing to the war effort.

As educational opportunities for women expanded and as women's literacy rates soared in the early to mid-nineteenth century, women became important literary consumers. An array of women's magazines appeared and prospered. *Godey's Lady's Book*, edited by the author SARAH JOSEPHA HALE, was the most popular women's magazine for several decades before the war. It achieved a circulation of 150,000 by 1860, rivaling that of the most widely sold general-interest periodicals (Fahs 2001, 42). Although men controlled the manufacture and business of mainstream publishing, book publishers had recognized the economic power of women readers and were increasingly catering to their tastes by the 1850s. By this time, women purchased the majority of the novels published. Many of these popular works were written by women for women. By the time of the Civil War, women made up nearly half of all writers of popular literature in the country (Petrino 1998, 23).

Despite the successes of professional women writers, they faced prejudices and obstacles that male writers did not have to endure. Although women published nearly as much printed material as male writers, women writers did not enjoy the status or prestige of their male colleagues, largely because male publishers and critics did not regard women's literary products to be as significant or as worthy as men's. Moreover, male commentators criticized successful women writers for their supposed deficiencies as women—for having strong opinions, for being scholarly, and for delving into topics that ranged beyond the narrow domestic arena of "women's sphere." Women writers were stereotyped as being brainy, selfish, unladylike, and unattractive (Coultrap-McQuin 1990, 16).

At the time of the Civil War, as in previous decades, the nation's literary women were almost exclusively white and middle class. Most were Protestant and were residents of the North, especially the Northeast. In the South, white elite and middle-class women contributed fiction and essays to women's magazines and general-interest periodicals, although in far fewer numbers than Northern women. At mid-century and during the Civil War, African-American women were being published, though rarely in the mainstream press. Their poems, speeches, essays, songs, and letters to the editor were primarily published in white abolitionist newspapers and in the African-American press. It was not until the twentieth century that black women's work appeared with any regularity in periodicals and newspapers not owned and operated by African Americans.

At mid-century, only a small percentage of women who contributed their poetry, fiction, and essays to the press and publishing houses made their living by their pens. Most professional women writers in the North—women who supported either themselves or their families—did not begin their careers as writers. Well-known poets, essayists, and authors were once teachers, domestic servants, or seamstresses who discovered that they could not adequately provide for their families on the paltry wages from the few occupations open to women. HARRIET BEECHER STOWE was a teacher in her youth, as was LOUISA MAY ALCOTT, Sarah Josepha Hale, novelist E.D.E.N. Southworth, poet LUCY LARCOM, and essayist GAIL HAMILTON (Mary Abigail Dodge). Off and on throughout the 1850s and early 1860s, Alcott found it necessary to work as a servant or governess to provide for her family. All of these women were aspiring writers who longed to make a living by their writing, though they spent their early careers laboring in other capacities.

Successful literary women of the mid-nineteenth century shared a powerful sense of vocation. They typically launched their careers by submitting their work, again and again, to many newspaper and magazine editors. When a fledgling writer's first work was published, it was invariably without payment. Writers in the apprenticeship phase of their careers needed to publish many times over, building up solid relationships with a variety of editors, before they could demand payment. Most writers found that they had to develop an impressive following or a popular demand for their literary product before they could negotiate with editors and publishers. Some talented women found that they lacked the confidence in their abilities that enabled other, more successful writers to assert themselves with editors. It took years before Lucy Larcom felt empowered to negotiate. Fellow poet EMILY DICKINSON, for unknown reasons, never reached this level of professionalism and chose not to pursue publication.

Literary women of the nineteenth century found that they suffered from a lack of firsthand knowledge of business practices. Most encountered obstacles in their business dealings with their editors and publishers at some point in their careers. Beecher Stowe learned about the importance of establishing international copyright only after selling a million-and-a-half copies of *Uncle Tom's Cabin* in Britain. She earned no royalties for the copies sold abroad. When her second and third novels were published, she traveled to Britain on each occasion to obtain copyright. Women writers often learned of the advantages of negotiating written contracts only after years of accepting the verbal terms and low payments publishers offered. Even so, many women experienced occasions when they believed they were cheated of the money rightfully due them. Essayist Gail Hamilton was stunned when she discovered that her publisher, a man of excellent reputation, had been underpaying her royalties for years. When months of acrimonious relations did not resolve the matter, independent arbiters settled the affair to Hamilton's satisfaction. She then engaged two other firms to publish her subsequent books. When a writer settled into a relationship with an honest and square-dealing publisher, she was likely to accept an offer to publish her works exclusively with that firm. Editorialist FANNY FERN and novelist E.D.E.N. Southworth entered into exclusive contracts with Robert Bonner, publisher of the *New York Ledger*, because he paid them highly and treated them respectfully.

Successful women writers learned early in their careers that they must conform to the expectations of the market. Yet it was the male publisher who sometimes interpreted consumers' expectations, rather than the writer herself. If a novelist wanted to keep her royalties flowing, she soon learned to accede to the publisher's demands about what she wrote. During the Civil War, Alcott noted in her journal that the editor of the *Atlantic Monthly* wanted war stories. She vowed to write " `great guns' Hail Columbia & Concord fight" if only he would publish her work, because, as she put it, "money is the staff of life" (quoted in Moyle 1985, 220).

There is no doubt that the business of publishing controlled the lives of professional writers. The editors and publishers of Beecher Stowe, Fanny Fern, Alcott, Southworth, and other leading authors and essayists pressured them to keep producing without respite. Most professional women writers who supported themselves or their families worked furiously, and often to the breaking point. Many, including Alcott, Beecher Stowe, and Southworth, found that they had to write through illness and disability to maintain their publisher's expectations, occasionally working themselves into a state of collapse.

Much of the popular literature women created at mid-century has since been labeled domestic fiction. These popular novels and short stories written by women for women focused on themes of direct interest to women's live, especially the private, domestic world of women's sphere. Although many romance novels and moralistic potboilers of the period were firmly entrenched in the conventional lives of mid-nineteenth-century women, some literary women were producing best-selling novels that deviated from these norms. Beecher Stowe's *Uncle Tom's Cabin*, though embracing family-oriented themes, was a political indictment against slavery. Unlike most domestic fiction, it was acclaimed by both men and women. Rebecca Harding Davis's and Alcott's war stories for the *Atlantic Monthly*, portraying the impact of the war on race relations, grappled with national issues of importance to both sexes. Moreover, many of the so-called "sentimental novels," though labeled domestic fiction, actually embodied strong political statements about the roles and status of women in society. These novels portray the experiences of girls and young women who must find a means to survive on their own, after family, friends, and all other supports have failed them. At the conclusion of these novels, the central characters discover that they have become strong, independent women who depend on themselves to thrive in a hostile world (Coultrap-McQuin 1990, 19–20).

From the beginning of the Civil War, women writers in the North and South communicated their convictions about the war in periodicals, newspapers, and books. The war emboldened many women to expand on their customary domestic themes to tackle political subjects and engage in debate about the war and the proper role of men and women within it. Early in the war, women writers focused on patriotic subjects, writing poetry, stories, and essays that encouraged men to enlist. They urged women to support the decision of their menfolk to fight and to goad reluctant men to sign up. "The Laggard Recruit," by Kate Sutherland, published in *Arthur's Home Magazine* in January 1862, was typical of stories published early in the war that modeled the ideal patriotic woman's behavior. In this tale, two young women use shame to push a beau into enlisting. "If we ladies cannot fight for our country, we can at least organize ourselves into a band of recruiting sergeants, and bring in the lukewarm and the laggards. ... Men who stay at home, court our smiles in vain" (quoted in Fahs 2001, 127–128). Although fiction by women was filled with patriotic women supporting a nation at war, women, for the most part, were not portrayed as active participants during the first two years of the conflict.

By the middle of the war, from 1863 on, the way women were presented in both fiction and nonfiction radically changed. Women writers began producing realistic and sensational fiction that cast women in active roles on the home front and on or near the battlefields. They created female characters who worked hard for the war effort—becoming nurses, vivandières (women attached to regiments), spies, and soldiers. Published in 1864, the immensely popular book *Unsexed; or the Female Soldier* (renamed *Nurse and Spy in the Union Army* in 1865) by SARAH EMMA EDMONDS, described her real-life adventures when she disguised herself as a soldier and male nurse for the Union army. *Hospital Sketches*, by Louisa May Alcott, was a fictional account, based on her experiences as an army nurse in Washington, DC. Women on the home front are portrayed as struggling bravely in their menfolks' absence to carry on despite great hardships. In the South, novelist AUGUSTA JANE EVANS reconfigures what might otherwise have been construed as a passive role for her female protagonist in her pro-Confederate novel *Macaria*. As Evans's heroine Irene watches and waits by her dead father's side, she reveals that she has absorbed the suffering of the war wounds that have killed him. Irene's "face was chill and colorless as death, the eyes were closed, and a slender stream of blood oozed slowly over the lips, and dripped upon the linen shroudings of the table" (quoted in Fahs 2001, 136). Irene could not go to battle for the Confederacy, but she could endure the agony of fallen soldiers as if she had.

In both fiction and nonfiction, women writers advanced their conviction that women's contributions to the war effort were as important as men's. With the exception of Evans and a few others, the war prevented Southern women writers from publishing books during the war. Margaret Junkin Preston managed to publish her volume of verse *Beechenbrook: A Rhyme of the War* in the early spring of 1865. Within weeks, all but 450 copies of the first printing were burned in fires that raged through Richmond in the final days of the war in April 1865. In 1866, the book was reprinted, selling so well that it was reissued seven more times. Like most women's war literature, *Beechenbrook* espoused a political message. The heroine, despite all the adversity that she and her husband have endured, never turns her back on the Confederacy, believing to the end that the "South MUST BE FREE!" (quoted in Fahs 2001, 145–146).

A number of Northern women writers addressed social issues in their fiction during the final years of the war. Harding Davis was the forerunner of this realistic fiction, publishing stories and novels that exposed the miserable living conditions of the working poor in 1861 to 1862. From 1863 to 1865, more writers attended to this theme. Fanny Fern protested the plight of working women in several of her editorial essays in the *New York Ledger*. Virginia Townsend's serialized novel *The Story of Janet Strong*, published in 1863, relates the story of an orphaned domestic servant who suffers from class prejudice, poverty, and cruelty in the middle-class home where she labors. As Townsend became more knowledgeable about the living conditions of working women, she went on to publish an essay promoting fair wages for working women (Sizer 2000, 135–136).

The conclusion of the war did not signal the end of the public's appetite for fiction and nonfiction about the Civil War. In the years and decades after the Confederacy's surrender at Appomattox, women (as well as men) in the North and South published their memoirs, journals, and diaries detailing their wartime experiences. Histories and fictionalized adventure tales also flooded the market.

See also **Businesswomen; Child, Lydia Maria; Harper, Frances Watkins; Jacobs, Harriet; Kemble, Fanny**

Selected Readings

Coultrap-McQuin, Susan. *Doing Literary Business: American Women Writers in the Nineteenth Century*. Chapel Hill: University of North Carolina Press. 1990.

Fahs, Alice. *The Imagined Civil War: Popular Literature of the North and South, 1861–1865*. Chapel Hill: University of North Carolina Press. 2001.

Sizer, Lyde Cullen. *The Political Work of Northern Women Writers and the Civil War, 1850–1872*. Chapel Hill: University of North Carolina Press. 2000.

Livermore, Mary Ashton Rice (1820–1905)

Mary Ashton Rice Livermore, one of the most publicly prominent women of the Civil War era, was a powerful force driving the work of the UNITED STATES SANITARY COMMISSION (USSC) in the northern Midwest. A resident of Chicago during the late 1850s and 1860s, Rice Livermore's creative ideas, initiative, hard work, and zest for fund-raising powerfully influenced USSC work throughout the North. During a career that spanned more than half a century, she worked as a committed humanitarian reformer, temperance activist, suffragist, journalist, celebrated lecturer, and author.

Born in Boston, Massachusetts, of modest middle-class origins, Mary Ashton Rice completed her education at a female seminary in neighboring Charlestown in 1836. In 1839, over the protests of her father, she accepted a position as a tutor to the children of a plantation owner in southern Virginia. Her observations of slavery and plantation life swayed her to abhor slavery. Although she had a lively interest in the antislavery movement, she was never fully involved in abolitionism.

Not long after returning to Massachusetts, she met Daniel Parker Livermore, a Universalist minister. Rice was transformed by Daniel's Universalist beliefs, and the two eventually married in 1845. During her early years as a minister's wife and while raising her two daughters, writing became an integral part of her life. She wrote stories and poems for religious publications, and after she and Daniel settled in Chicago, she helped him edit and write the *New Covenant*, a Universalist monthly. In May 1860, she had the distinction of being the only woman journalist at the Republican Party's convention in Chicago.

From the moment the war began, Rice Livermore was infused with a patriotic fervor that demanded immediate involvement. As a volunteer to the newly formed Chicago Sanitary Commission (CNC) in the spring of 1861, she gathered supplies and packed boxes to be sent to Union regiments further south. Rice Livermore's involvement deepened when, shortly after the Battle of Fort Donelson in February 1862, she and colleague Jane Hoge, a fellow Chicago social reformer and sanitary worker, toured the military medical wards in St. Louis, Missouri, for the CNC. While gathering information intended to help sanitary workers meet the medical and supply needs of Union troops in the West, Rice Livermore battled nausea and fainting spells when confronted with the suffering of the wounded for the first time. She overcame her revulsion with what she later described as an "iron control," forcing herself to "become habituated to the manifold shocking sights that are the outcome of the wicked business men call war" (Livermore 1995, 188).

By the end of 1862, Rice Livermore and Hoge had emerged as the managers of the CNC. In November, the two women met with other regional leaders of the USSC in Washington, DC. Although the CNC had been supporting the Western Sanitary Commission based in St. Louis, Rice Livermore and Hoge agreed to loosen those ties and permit the CNC to become a full-fledged auxiliary of the USSC, bearing the new name, the Northwestern Sanitary Commission (NSC). Included in the NSC's region were local SOLDIERS' AID SOCIETIES in Illinois, Indiana, Michigan, Wisconsin, Minnesota, and parts of Iowa.

With political astuteness, Rice Livermore and Hoge negotiated the merger with the USSC. They managed to hammer out a relationship with the USSC that allowed them to balance their need for autonomy with their desire to unite with other sanitary workers in a powerful, centralized organization that would benefit masses of Union soldiers, not only those in their own region. Rice Livermore and Hoge convinced male USSC leaders that the NSC must retain its prerogative to make its own decisions on issues and policies that affected the Northwest region.

According to Rice Livermore, the "[g]rand passion" of the Union army in the West was to control the entire length of the Mississippi River. As Grant's army moved southward toward Vicksburg, Mississippi, the ranks were devastated by "swamp fever" (malaria), scurvy, and measles. In March 1863, Rice Livermore and Hoge traveled by boat—"a little, rickety, wheezy, crowded, unsafe craft"—down the Mississippi River to bring food and supplies to Grant's troops (Livermore 1995, 285). They also planned to inspect and lend assistance in the military hospitals from Cairo, Illinois, to Young's Point, Louisiana, the Union stronghold on the opposite side of the Mississippi River from Vicksburg, Mississippi. Along the way, they distributed 3,500 packages.

In the course of her sanitary inspections, only rarely did Rice Livermore assume the duties of a nurse, unlike many sanitary commission hospital visitors. She did not perceive hands-on nursing to be part of her role, though she strongly identified herself as an alleviator of suffering. A tireless, meticulous administrator, she did not allow wretched hospital conditions to sidetrack her from her goals on these tours, which were to assess hospitals and their staff, deliver supplies, seek solutions to problems in the delivery of care and food, and offer words of comfort and encouragement to soldiers in her spare moments. In her memoir *My Story of the War*, she describes a Wisconsin regimental hospital in Milliken's Bend, Louisiana, as "a sadder sight I never witnessed during the war." There she discovered,

[T]wo hundred men, all of them very sick, all lying … on the bare floor, with their knapsacks for pillows, with no food but army rations, no nurses but convalescent soldiers, themselves too sick to move except on compulsion, the sick men covered with vermin … and their surgeon dead-drunk in bed. (Livermore 1995, 302)

Confronted with this disaster, Rice Livermore first offered comfort—she made tea and dispensed it with crackers, speaking words of sympathy to each soldier. Then she dashed off to medical headquarters where she informed the military brass about the conditions of the hospital and its surgeon. Shortly thereafter, the Wisconsin sick and wounded were boarding a hospital boat bound for Nashville, Tennessee.

To Rice Livermore, the poverty of soldiers' families was an important concern of the NSC, though it was definitely not a part of the USSC's official mission. Female auxiliary leaders in New York, Philadelphia, Boston, and Chicago were determined to make it their business, however. In 1863, Rice Livermore was shocked to discover the desperate squalor of immigrant and African-American soldiers' wives, widows, and mothers in Chicago. A black Union private's pay, insufficient to support a family, was commonly months late in arriving. Poor women, left to fend for themselves, barely subsisted on the money they earned from jobs as laundresses and domestic servants. Some had no choice but to leave their children alone in box-like tenement rooms while they worked. By allocating NSC funds to provide them with food, coal, and other necessities, Rice Livermore and Hoge broadened the scope of USSC work, just as Louisa Schuyler of the WOMAN'S CENTRAL ASSOCIATION OF

RELIEF, Abby May of the New England Woman's Auxiliary Association, and other women were to do in their communities. For Rice Livermore, benevolent work for poor women went beyond the scope of her involvement in the NSC. During the war years, she also helped to establish the Home for Aged Women (1861) and the Chicago Hospital for Women and Children (1865).

Historians agree that Rice Livermore's crowning achievement was her role in the creation and organization of the Chicago Sanitary Fair held in the fall of 1863. This extravaganza became the prototype and inspiration for SANITARY FAIRS in dozens of Northern cities, which contributed millions of dollars to USSC coffers. When Rice Livermore and Hoge broached the idea of the fair to the leading men in the NSC, they "laughed incredulously at our [Rice Livermore's and Hoge's] proposition to raise twenty-five thousand dollars" for the commission's work. Thus rebuffed, the two women called on female leaders of every society affiliated with the NSC and got their enthusiastic support. As soon as thousands of dollars of saleable goods and pledges flowed in to the warehouses Rice Livermore rented, men from all walks of life became involved in the massive project. In all, this fair collected over $86,000 for the USSC (Schnell 1975, 42).

Toward the end of the war, Rice Livermore and Hoge collaborated on establishing a soldiers' home. After the war, Rice Livermore became deeply involved in the woman suffrage movement. She later explained that her involvement in the Civil War had made her realize that without political power, women could do little to improve social conditions or their own lives. In 1868, she served as the first president of the Illinois Woman Suffrage Association. In 1869, she became editor of her own women's rights newspaper *The Agitator*, which she later merged with Lucy Stone's and Henry Browne Blackwell's *The Woman's Journal* in Boston. In 1870, she helped found the Massachusetts Woman Suffrage Association and from 1875 to 1878, served as president of the American Woman Suffrage Association. She remained an active lyceum lecturer until she was in her mid-seventies.

See also **Patriotism**

Selected Readings

Attie, Jeanie. *Patriotic Toil: Northern Women and the American Civil War*. Ithaca, NY: Cornell University Press. 1998.

Giesberg, Judith Ann. *Civil War Sisterhood: The United States Sanitary Commission and Women's Politics in Transition*. Boston: Northeastern University Press. 2000.

Livermore, Mary A. *My Story of the War: A Woman's Narrative*. Hartford, CT: A.D. Worthington. 1887. Reprint, New York: Da Capo Press. 1995.

Venet, Wendy Hamand. "The Emergence of a Suffragist: Mary Livermore, Civil War Activism, and the Moral Power of Women." *Civil War History*. 48 (2) (June 2002): 143–163.

M

McCord, Louisa Cheves
(1810–1879)

During the volatile decade preceding the Civil War, Louisa Cheves McCord was fully engaged as a political and social essayist, respected scholar and intellectual, poet and dramatist, plantation mistress, slaveholder, and mother of three. By the time the first shot was fired on Fort Sumter in April 1861, she had abandoned her intellectual life to dedicate herself to supporting the Confederacy.

Born to wealth and privilege in Charleston, South Carolina, Louisa Susanna Cheves was the daughter of a plantation owner and politician who served as a president of the Bank of the United States from 1819 to 1829. Her father recognized her quicksilver intellect at a young age and permitted her to receive instruction in mathematics and the classical languages in addition to the standard "female curriculum."

In 1840, she married David James McCord, a former state legislator, attorney, and president of the Bank of the State of South Carolina.

Cheves McCord was an anomaly among Southern women. Although she staunchly defended her society's most cherished notions of Southern womenhood, she was anything but the typical Southern lady. In Southern antebellum society, politics was a realm reserved strictly for men, and the ideal woman was expected to remain removed from it. Despite the cultural stereotype, Southern women of the upper classes were interested and involved in political issues, particularly as the sectional conflict intensified during the mid- to late 1850s. Women discussed politics with their family and neighbors, expressed their political views in their personal correspondence and diaries, and by the late 1850s and early 1860s, were seeing their letters to the editor published in a number of leading Southern newspapers. Yet no Southern woman entered the political sphere as Cheves McCord did, publishing essays that significantly influenced Southern political leaders, political thought, and intellectual tradition.

During the 1850s, Cheves McCord's essays on political economy and on women's proper social roles were published in the most distinguished of Southern journals. Her articles reveal her facile grasp of the key issues of her day as well as the depth of her legal, political, and classical knowledge. Conforming to society's expectations of her, she did not assert her authorship. She used only her initials to sign her works or contributed them anonymously.

As far as her own political activity was concerned, Cheves McCord, the self-proclaimed guardian of Southern notions of womanhood, declared that a woman may think, learn, talk, write, and even publish her thoughts about politics without reaching beyond her proper sphere; but she added, "She does not rule, she cannot rule, by stump-speech, convention, or ballot-box" (McCord 1995, 152). She dismissed Northern women's rights "convention women," proclaiming that a "Woman's task is, to make herself the perfected woman, not the counterfeit man" (quoted in Fox-Genovese 1988, 283).

Northern attacks on the institution of slavery and the Southern way of life awakened her ire and her eloquence as she set out in her essays to persuade Northerners, especially abolitionists, to the errors in their political and economic attacks on slavery. In discourse after discourse, Cheves McCord defended slavery, arguing that "the negro" desperately needed the support and protection of his white superiors. The institution of slavery, she insisted, was a divinely ordained and expeditious solution to the problems of both blacks and whites. In her essay "Diversity of the Races," Cheves McCord states,

> The dark [race] ... needs, and in slavery obtains, the governing mind and protection of the white. ... The white, in and near the tropics, cannot live and progress without the labour and bodily endurance of the dark race. Thus ... through the beneficent institution of slavery a hitherto unknown phenomenon in history occurs:

a barbarous people lives peaceably, happily, and improvingly, in connection with a superior one. (McCord 1995, 183)

She was obsessed with counterpunching what she believed were the vicious attacks of abolitionists. Although her readers were primarily Southerners, Northern antislavery advocates were her intended audience. She wanted to make Northerners understand "the truth" about slavery, to correct the fables and answer the "foul load of slander and villainous aspersion so often hurled against us." HARRIET BEECHER STOWE's *Uncle Tom's Cabin* was a particularly heinous assault, to her mind, and one that she discredited for its ignorance of the South, its culture, dialect, geography, and people (McCord 1995, 245).

Even before the war interrupted daily life on her plantation, Cheves McCord was spending less time on her literary activities, particularly after the death of her husband, David James McCord, in 1855 and her father's illness and death in 1857. Her failing eyesight also made it difficult to read and write. As Confederate leaders urged all plantation owners, she ceased planting cotton and cultivated food crops instead, a sacrifice most planters were unwilling to make. She served as president of the Soldiers' Relief Association in Columbia, South Carolina, and as president of the Soldiers' Clothing Association. From this position, she directed the outfitting of the soldiers in the regiment her son was commanding.

She did not remain a leader of soldiers' relief for long. By late 1861, she was devoting all of her time to nursing at the army hospital established at South Carolina College in Columbia, where she eventually assumed control of much of the hospital's management. In addition to nursing, she wrote letters for soldiers, read to them, soothed the mortally wounded, and sometimes helped to bury them. Following her son's death from a head wound in 1863, she invested herself more deeply in hospital work.

In July 1863, Cheves McCord's brother and two nephews were killed—successive tragedies that threatened to overwhelm her. Her daughter Louisa McCord Smythe recalled in her memoir the intensity of her mother's hospital work at this time: "I have known her to drive all over the town to find a minister of some particular denomination for some poor dying creature who could not be quite comforted by the chaplain." Her daughter also noted that her mother knit three pairs of soldiers' socks a day throughout the war. "My mother knit day and night, walking, driving, under all circumstances. ... I used to wake at night and listen to the click, click of her needles, and shudder at the groans and sobs that accompanied them when she supposed no one heard her" (McCord 1996, 371–372).

In February 1865, as Union Major General William Tecumseh Sherman's troops roared into South Carolina, Cheves McCord discovered that Columbia was one of their destinations. Instead of fleeing with her neighbors, she decided to endure the invasion with her daughters. Though her neighbors laughed at her, she devised what proved to be a foolproof method of hiding food supplies and heirlooms from Union marauders. She made the back section of her house into a sealed-off warehouse by having all access to a second-floor piazza removed. Her home was one of the few in her neighborhood that did not burn when Union troops invaded Columbia, in large part because Union Major General Oliver Otis Howard made it his headquarters. Even so, the house narrowly escaped being engulfed by fire several times.

After the war, Cheves McCord was physically, emotionally, and spiritually exhausted. Her home in Columbia, though still standing, was ruined inside. Her plantation manor, too, had been stripped of its interior, its lands devastated. She divested herself of ownership of her properties and lived with her daughter and son-in-law. She did not resume her prewar political writing, nor did she engage in any other activity outside the home. As her daughter explained, her mother never recovered from the loss of her son and the "failure of the cause she loved so well. After that, she only waited patiently for the welcome release" (McCord 1996, 464–465).

See also **Women and Politics**

Selected Readings

Fox-Genovese, Elizabeth. *Within the Plantation Household: Black and White Women of the Old South*. Chapel Hill: University of North Carolina Press. 1988.

McCord, Louisa. *Louisa S. McCord: Poems, Drama, Biography, Letters*. Edited by Richard C. Lounsbury. Publications of the Southern Texts Society. Charlottesville: University Press of Virginia. 1996.

McCord, Louisa. *Louisa S. McCord: Political and Social Essays*. Edited by Richard C. Lounsbury. Publications of the Southern Texts Society. Charlottesville: University Press of Virginia. 1995.

Mexican-American Women

Native Americans were not the only established population living in the West when white American gold seekers and settlers arrived in California and in the rest of the U.S. Southwest in the 1850s. Mexicans inhabited parts of the region, particularly southern California, New Mexico Territory, and Texas. Prior to 1848, the year that the United States defeated Mexico in the Mexican-American War, much of the land that would become the U.S. Southwest belonged to Mexico. When the United States defeated Mexico in 1848, both countries accepted the terms of the Treaty of Guadalupe Hidalgo. According to the treaty, Mexico sold its lands in northern Mexico (California and New Mexico) to the United States for $15 million. (At this time, New Mexico included lands that in the future would encompass the U.S. states of New Mexico, Arizona, Nevada, and Utah.)

The Spanish-speaking Mexican inhabitants of the new U.S. Southwest were primarily the mixed-race descendants of Spanish colonists and Native Americans. A small percentage, mostly among the Mexican elite, claimed that they were purely of Spanish descent. Following the Mexican-American War, Mexicans suddenly found themselves living in the United States and subject to its laws and customs. They clashed repeatedly with Euro-American (white American) settlers who originated from the northern, southern, and midwestern United States.

During the Civil War, 9,900 Mexican-American men enlisted in the U.S. military, serving primarily in the Southwest. Overall, the Civil War era was a tumultuous period for Mexican-American men and women as they struggled to maintain their culture in the midst of pressure from Euro-American newcomers to accommodate themselves (Mexican Americans) to Euro-American society, institutions, and way of life.

The Civil War was also a time of major transition for Mexican-American women of the Southwest. When U.S. laws and its legal system became established in the West in the 1850s, Mexican-American women lost some of the legal rights they had exercised under Mexican law. Mexican-American women's family roles were transformed when they and their families suffered huge losses of farm and grazing land to Euro-Americans. Despite the upheaval that these land losses cost their families, and the vast changes that they created in the lives of all Mexican Americans, caring for family members remained the central focus of women's lives. In spite of the forces working to annihilate their Hispanic culture, Mexican-American women held fast to Mexican traditions and to the Catholic religion, inspiring their children to remain true to their traditional way of life.

Before the Mexican-American War, women living under the laws of Mexico had the right to own their own property separate from their husbands, a privilege denied to American women in the early to mid-nineteenth century. Mexican women also had the right to be heard in a court of law and the right to sue and be sued. They also could be executors of estates and were permitted to superintend the inheritances of their children (Gonzalez 1999, 6, 93–94). Following the Mexican-American War, according to the laws established by Euro-Americans in each state and territory in the Southwest, women lost many of these rights. They did retain one property right that they used to their families' advantage, the right to make a will and to leave their land and property to their children. Wealthy, middle-class, and poorer women all made wills. The will of Barbara Baca of Santa Fe, New Mexico Territory, is representative of a woman's will at mid-century. Besides her house and land, Baca left her son "two cows, a mule, four burros, ten bottles, six jars, six bowls, two forks, five mattresses, five sheets, ten coverlets … two storage boxes, three chairs, one bedstead, nine saints … two cast-iron skillets, two spoons, two cooking pans … and a tablecloth" (Gonzalez 1999, 96). Through will-making, Mexican-American women helped their children retain family wealth at a time when Euro-Americans were utilizing every resource and institution to claim it.

The loss of Mexican Americans' farming and ranching lands was the most overwhelming long-term consequence of the Mexican defeat in the Mexican-American War. The Treaty of Guadalupe Hidalgo clearly stated that the United States would uphold all Mexican land titles and claims. Despite this provision, former Mexican citizens soon discovered all the ways that the new ruling class of Euro-Americans could claim Mexican lands. A major stumbling block for some Mexican-American farmers and ranchers was that they could not produce evidence that they held title to their lands. Without this proof, their land fell into the hands of Euro-Americans. Other Mexican Americans lost their land when they could not pay the high, ever-increasing Euro-American taxes, or the unusually high interest rates on loans. To make matters worse, Spanish-speaking Mexicans were at a disadvantage in U.S. courts of law because of the language barrier and because they lacked an understanding of the U.S. justice system.

Mexican Americans in southern California experienced a tremendous amount of land loss during the Civil War years. Cattle prices dropped in the 1850s and stayed low, causing Mexican-American cattle ranchers to lose capital. Then, a severe flood followed by years of drought (1862 to 1865) resulted in huge losses of livestock and successive crop failures, forcing ranchers and farmers to mortgage their lands so that they could pay for supplies and high taxes and other legal fees instituted by Euro-Americans. When Mexican Americans could no longer keep up with their mortgage payments, millions of acres of Mexican-American lands were sold at public auction to the only group with the necessary funds, Euro-Americans.

Without land, many Mexican Americans were forced into lives of poverty. Mexican-American men became itinerant farmworkers on Euro-American ranches and farms. Other men flocked to the mining camps or migrated to the growing cities to look for work. Mexican-American women, in ever-increasing numbers, entered the labor force. Although most married women continued to stay at home close to their families, widows, single women with children, and a small percentage of single women without children worked outside the home as laundresses, cooks, and domestic servants. A small number of married women took laundry and sewing into their homes. All of this wage labor did not remove these women or their families from poverty, at least partly because Mexican-American women received much less remuneration for their work than Euro-American women. (Although wage figures for the 1860s are not available, in 1880, Mexican-American women in Santa Fe earned less than half of the wages of Euro-American women.) In the years before 1870, less than 1 percent of Mexican-American women in Santa Fe, New Mexico Territory, possessed net worths over $100. The census found that most Mexican-American women had net worths of less than $50. The women of Santa Fe and elsewhere in the Southwest cultivated chickens, laying hens, and sheep to earn extra cash, yet this enterprise did not lift them above a bare subsistence (Gonzalez 1999, 86–87).

Just as the loss of land and the strengthening Euro-American society impacted Mexican-American women's work lives, these two factors also had a profound effect on the traditional structure of the Mexican-American family. Before the Mexican-American War, the father or male head of household was the absolute source of power in the family. Children, including adult children in large, extended families, obeyed the father or patriarch without question. Women were expected to be subservient to their husbands and the patriarch. Despite the hierarchy of male power in the family, all family members understood that women ruled in the domestic arena. They cared for children and the elderly, and directed all domestic arrangements.

After the Mexican-American War and the huge losses of land, the father remained the most powerful figure in the family, yet the need for income often compelled Mexican-American men to leave their families to find work, often at a great distance from their homes. During their absences, women frequently assumed the role of temporary heads of household, thus giving them more authority than they had before. When their menfolk returned home, however, women returned to their subservient role.

In spite of all the changes occurring in women's work and home lives, Mexican-American women's domestic duties remained the same throughout the Civil War years. Mexican-American women cooked, manufactured the family's clothing, did all the laundry, and supplied food and board to travelers. Women also whitewashed their adobe homes, carried wood and water (sometimes over a great distance), ground corn and wheat by hand on millstones known as *metates*, and collected herbs for medicinal use and plants for dyes. On farms and ranches, women and children often assisted with the planting and harvesting of crops and the herding of sheep and other livestock (Miller 1997, 154–155).

Because Mexican Americans tended to live with their extended families, women had the opportunity to form close-knit bonds with their female relatives. Mexican-American women also reduced their isolation through their friendships with female neighbors and through their special relationships with their children's godparents, particularly their godmothers or *comadres*. Visiting comadres, friends, and relatives was the most important social activity of women. In times of hardship, childbirth, illness, and disaster, women stepped in to help one another.

Both Mexican-American men and women had to contend with the pervasive prejudice and racism of Euro-Americans. In 1859, the San Francisco *Herald* declared that "the Californios [Mexican Americans of California] are a degraded race; a part of them are so black that one needs much work to distinguish them from Indians; there is little difference between them and the Negro race" (Pitt 1966, 204). Euro-Americans also passed laws and resorted to violence to "control" Mexican Americans just as they used these two methods to dominate Native Americans and African Americans throughout the United States. In California, an antivagrancy law hampered Mexican Americans' freedom of mobility, so necessary to their ability to earn a livelihood after being dispossessed of their lands. Another California law was aimed at eliminating an important aspect of Mexican-American culture. The "Sunday Law" prohibited traditional Mexican-American Sunday festivities, such as "the operation of any bull, bear, cock or prize fights, horse race, circus, theatre, bowling alley, gambling house, room, or saloon, or any place of barbarous or noisy amusements" (Pitt 1966, 197). Euro-Americans also disparaged Mexican-American women for their supposed licentiousness or lack of sexual restraint, concerns based largely on the low-cut blouses that Mexican-American women wore, their dancing in public, and their gambling. Euro-American women and men also scorned poor Mexican-American women living with men out of wedlock, a situation that was common because the poor could not afford the costs of church marriage ceremonies.

In some areas of the Southwest, Mexican-American men and women lived more harmoniously with Euro-Americans. In the 1850s and 1860s, in Lincoln County, New Mexico Territory, Mexican-American men and women assisted Euro-Americans with the construction of adobe homes and with farming and irrigation methods in the extremely arid climate. Mexican-American women taught Euro-American newcomer Barbara Jones how to cook chili peppers and how to grind corn using a *metate*. When Mexican-American women instructed Jones on the healing power of local herbs, Jones offered to share her medicines with them. Jones also served as midwife to her Mexican-American neighbors (Miller 1997, 153).

After the Civil War, Euro-Americans continued to gain in economic and political power in California, Texas, and New Mexico, crowding Mexican

Americans into the margins of society. Increasingly, Mexican Americans suffered from poor working conditions, low wages, poverty, segregation, and negligible educational opportunities. As Mexican Americans became sequestered in their own neighborhoods and locales, and experienced more prejudice and discrimination from Euro-Americans, the family home became more of a refuge. Women, in their domestic lives, made the cultivation of Mexican culture and the Catholic religion their priorities, ensuring that future generations would not lose their proud, rich heritage.

See also **Native American Women; Western Women**

Selected Readings

Gonzalez, Deena J. *Refusing the Favor: The Spanish-Mexican Women of Santa Fe, 1820–1880*. New York: Oxford University Press. 1999.

Griswold del Castillo, Richard. *North to Aztlán: A History of Mexican Americans in the United States*. New York: Twayne Publishers. 1996.

Griswold del Castillo, Richard. *La Familia: Chicano Families in the Urban Southwest, 1848–Present*. Notre Dame, IN: Notre Dame Press. 1984.

Jiménez, Alfredo, ed. *Handbook of Hispanic Cultures in the United States: History*. Houston, TX: Arte Publico Press. 1994.

Military Women

I am convinced that a larger number of women disguised themselves and enlisted in the service … than was dreamed of. Some startling histories of these military women were current in the gossip of army life; and extravagant and as unreal as were many of the narrations, one always felt that they had a foundation in fact.

—Mary Ashton Rice Livermore, from her memoir,
My Story of the War: A Woman's Narrative (Livermore 1995, 120)

In nearly every state in both the South and North, young women disguised themselves as men to enlist in the military during the Civil War. Although their exact numbers are not known, researchers specializing in the history of women soldiers during the Civil War estimate that hundreds of women were involved. DeAnne Blanton and Lauren M. Cook have been intensively researching this subject since the early 1990s. They have data confirming the presence of approximately 250 enlisted women in the Union and Confederate armies (Blanton and Cook 2002, 6). Blanton and Cook acknowledge that it is probable that many more women served than those that they have identified.

Of the women soldiers Blanton, Cook, and other scholars have documented thus far, most were young women from farming communities or impoverished urban areas. Many were from poor or modest middle-class families, had limited educations, and were accustomed to hard, physical labor, whether from farm or factory work. A number of women soldiers had prior experience with guns, and were accustomed to hunting, camping, and horseback riding. Although the mid-nineteenth-century ideal of domestic femininity did not sanction heavy agricultural labor, the work of unmarried teenaged girls and young AGRICULTURAL WOMEN was critical to the survival of small family farms in both the North and South, unless the farms were unusually prosperous or had a surplus of slave or male labor available.

As Blanton and Cook point out, the piecemeal education and arduous nature of agricultural women's and girls' lives did not provide them with the skills or the leisure for letter-writing and literary self-expression. The researchers suggest that these factors may help explain why historians have failed to uncover much in the way of personal documents of female soldiers. In addition to the collection of letters written by SARAH ROSETTA WAKEMAN (alias Union Private Lyons Wakeman), the correspondence of only two other women soldiers has been located. No diaries have been found and only two military women—SARAH EMMA EDMONDS and LORETA JANETA VELAZQUEZ—published memoirs of their experiences in uniform (Blanton and Cook 2002, 2).

Although insufficient evidence exists to determine the precise reasons why women were motivated to leave their homes for the battlefields, it is known that a large number of women soldiers enlisted with their menfolk—their husbands, lovers, and male relatives—which suggests that women did not want to be separated from their loved ones and wished to share the military experience with them. The data available also indicates that patriotism inspired many women to join up. Other women were enticed by soldiers' wages and the promise of escape from the monotony of their home lives.

How did so many women soldiers manage to conceal that they were female, especially during the process of enlistment? Neither the Confederate nor the Union armies required proof of identity, nor did most of the physical examinations demand that recruits remove their clothing. As long as prospective soldiers' hearing, eyesight, and teeth were functioning, and their hands, arms, and legs were operational, recruits were considered fit for duty. In donning disguises, women bound their breasts if they needed to and attached extra material to their undergarments to increase their girth and the size of their waists. Loreta Velazquez invested time and money to ensure that her uniform would not betray her. To add heft to her shoulders, she placed "six wire net shields" under her jacket, secured with straps crossing her chest and shoulders (Blanton and Cook 2002, 48).

Women soldiers' lack of facial hair and broad shoulders did not make them as conspicuous as one might expect. In addition to the boys younger than 18 years of age in the ranks, there were men 18 years and slightly older from the slums and poor rural areas who were undersized and who were likely experiencing delays in physical maturation as a result of chronic malnutrition. Women soldiers' efforts to conceal their gender also benefited from the fact that soldiers usually did not remove their uniforms or their underclothing for days and, quite often, weeks at a time.

More women attempted to enlist than those who actually succeeded. Whether due to feminine characteristics that could not be disguised or a lack of skill in deception, many would-be women soldiers had difficulty concealing their gender for very long. One woman gave herself away by the way she pulled on her stockings. Some failed by neglecting to maintain a low profile or by overly fraternizing with male recruits. Of the women who evaded detection for months or longer, their sex was sometimes discovered when they fell ill or were wounded on the battlefield. As soon as military authorities learned of a woman soldier's gender, she was removed from service regardless of her military record. Not to be deterred, a number of discharged women marched off to reenlist as soon as they recovered from illness or healed from their wounds. Although Loreta Velazquez was wounded three times, no surgeon learned of her sex, largely because the location of her injuries did not necessitate the removal of much of her clothing (Blanton and Cook 2002, 97). Edmonds so feared detection that she refused treatment for her war injuries. When she became extremely ill from malaria, she abandoned the military hospital where she was being treated and deserted the army lest her female identity be uncovered.

Newspaper accounts of women soldiers fighting and living side by side with men fascinated and shocked the public during the Civil War. Women who dressed in men's clothing, for whatever reason, were considered aberrant, unsexed, and morally deficient. Their motives were presumed to be impure rather than patriotic. MARY ASHTON RICE LIVERMORE met a number of women soldiers during her tenure as a UNITED STATES SANITARY COMMISSION leader. Her attitude, expressed more than 20 years later, was more forgiving but made clear that women soldiers upset the natural balance when they chose to join men in the destructive business of war. "Such service was not the noblest that women rendered the country," she wrote, ". . . and no one can regret that these soldier women were exceptional and rare. It is better to heal a wound than to make one" (Livermore 1995, 120). Yet despite the prevalence of these views, the Northern press often applauded the heroism of women soldiers. The male comrades of women soldiers, if they became aware of their gender, commended their service and their bravery. There is ample evidence that male soldiers were aware that women were serving with them, accepted their contributions, and chose not to reveal their secrets.

There is scanty evidence that African-American women served in the military. Maria Lewis of Virginia was a respected soldier in the 8th New York Cavalry where she served for 18 months. An unknown black woman, a member of the 29th Connecticut Colored Infantry, endured the siege of Petersburg, Virginia, at the end of the war. In late February 1865, an unidentified black woman in the same regiment gave birth. (It is not known if this was the same or two different women.) The gender of African-American soldier Lizzie Hoffman from Alexandria, Virginia, was discovered when she and the rest of the 45th U.S. Colored Infantry embarked on a steamboat (Blanton and Cook 2002, 23, 105, 123). Another African-American woman, Mary Dyson of Philadelphia, has also been assumed to have fought in uniform in a number of battles (Forbes 1998, 41). It is likely that there were other black women soldiers, but there is no doubt that thousands of African-American women were an essential part of military CAMP LIFE, serving as cooks, nurses, and laundresses. In the Union military, most of these women were fugitive or CONTRABAND WOMEN, traveling in family groups, who attached themselves to the Union army camps for protection. In the Confederate army, black women were predominantly enslaved.

See also **Cashier, Albert D. J.; Mountain Charley; Turchin, Nadine Lvova**

Selected Readings

Blanton, DeAnne and Lauren M. Cook. *They Fought Like Demons: Women Soldiers in the American Civil War.* Baton Rouge: Louisiana State University Press. 2002.

Leonard, Elizabeth D. *All the Daring of the Soldier: Women of the Civil War Armies.* New York: Penguin Books. 2001.

Mitchell, Maria (1818–1889)

The Civil War era proved to be a decisive turning point in astronomer Maria Mitchell's career. As the first American woman to be elected to the American Academy of Arts and Sciences in 1848 and the first woman to become a member of the American Association for the Advancement of Science in 1850, Mitchell's future as a scientist of international repute appeared bright at the beginning of the Civil War. In 1862, an unexpected overture from a trustee of the soon-to-be-built Vassar Female College transformed her life. Appointed professor of astronomy at Vassar shortly before its doors opened in 1865, Mitchell became an impassioned educator and a leader in the movement advocating higher education for women.

Born on the island of Nantucket in Massachusetts, Maria Mitchell was the daughter of devout Quakers. Her father, employed first as a teacher and then as a banker, was a well-known amateur astronomer throughout his life. Her mother was a well-educated woman who had worked for a time as a librarian. Mitchell attended her father's school as a young child and was cultivated to be a close observer of the natural world. Though she would attend another school before completing her formal education, her training at her father's side continued. As a girl, she spent the evenings assisting him as he made astronomical calculations. He supplied Nantucket whalers with the data that helped them to correct their chronometers, the exceptionally accurate timepieces then in use.

In 1835, at the age of 17, Mitchell taught at her own school for a year. A year later, she left teaching to work as a librarian at Nantucket's new library, the Atheneum, where she found the time to further her studies in mathematics, navigation, French, German, and Latin. She assisted her father by night, studying the positions of the stars and the moon to determine time, latitude, and longitude for the U.S. Coast Survey. Together she and her father also surveyed the Nantucket coast so that more accurate maps could be produced.

On October 1, 1847, while studying the night sky by telescope, Mitchell discovered a comet. Although others also recorded their sightings of it, Mitchell's was determined to be the first observation and she was credited with its discovery. The king of Denmark awarded her a gold medal, and she received acknowledgment from the scientific community. As a result of the recognition, she became acquainted with other scientists, and was soon appointed to the American Academy of Arts and Sciences and to membership in the American Association for the Advancement of Science. Now less isolated, she began traveling to meetings and met other scientists, although the all-male memberships kept her on the boundaries of their organizations.

In 1849, Mitchell obtained a job as a computer—performing astronomical calculations each night—for the *American Ephemeris and Nautical Almanac*, a position that enabled her to be self-supporting. She finally had the opportunity to satisfy her craving for extensive travel when she became chaperone to a wealthy banker's daughter. With this young girl by her side, she traveled throughout much of the South in 1857, and months later, in Europe. In her journal, Mitchell noted her observations of slaves and slaveholders. The elite white men and women she encountered eagerly shared their rationale for the institution of slavery, informing her that giving freedom to the slaves would be cruel. Evidently Mitchell declined to engage in debate on the subject with those she met, choosing instead to record her thoughts in her journal.

> One argument which three persons have bro't up to me, is the superior condition of the blacks now to what it would have been had their parents remained in Africa and they been children of the soil. I make no answer to this, for if that is an argument, it would be our duty now, to enslave the heathen, instead of attempting to enlighten them. (quoted in Albers 2001, 81)

From her limited exposure to slavery, Mitchell concluded—however erroneously—that slaves were content with their lot. "It does not follow because the slaves are sleek and fat and really happy—for happy I believe they are—that slavery is not an evil," she wrote, "and the great evil is, as I always supposed, in the effect upon the whites" (quoted in Kendall 1896, 76). Like many Northerners with antislavery convictions, Mitchell believed that slavery had a corrupting influence on whites. In particular, she believed that the childishness and fussiness that she observed among elite Southern men was a result of their having been pampered by slaves for all of their lives.

Not long after Mitchell arrived in Europe, the banker's daughter was called back to the United States as a result of the financial panic of 1857. Mitchell took immediate advantage of her newfound freedom and hastened to meet a number of prominent astronomers and scientists, which included an inspiring visit with the British astronomer and physicist Mary Somerville.

After returning from Europe, Mitchell returned to Nantucket to continue her observations and work for the *American Ephemeris and Nautical Almanac*. She soon received the gift of approximately $3,000 for the purchase of an equatorial telescope, the funds raised by educator ELIZABETH PALMER PEABODY among her women friends and acquaintances in Boston. With her new telescope, Mitchell wrote articles in 1860 for the *American Journal of Science and Arts* and other publications regarding her investigations of double stars, sunspots, and globular comets. In 1861, following the death of her mother, she and her father moved to Lynn, Massachusetts. Mitchell and her father immediately installed an observatory at the rear of their house where they settled back into their habit of watching the heavens and making calculations.

In 1862, Rufus Babcock, a trustee of Vassar Female College, approached Mitchell to determine if she would be an asset to Vassar's faculty. Mitchell assumed he visited her to consult her about the future of women's education at Vassar. Three months later, he wrote her that he was certain she was suited to serve as professor of astronomy at the college when it opened. Although privately she hesitated, primarily because she doubted her ability to teach due to her lack of higher education, she wrote Babcock that she would be honored to accept the position should one be offered.

The Civil War protracted the building of Vassar, and during the months of waiting, the trustees argued about the advisability of appointing women professors and instructors. Philanthropist Matthew Vassar lobbied hard for women teachers, insisting that he wanted the college to be an institution of higher learning for women taught by the best female minds the country had to offer. By 1864, still no decision had been made in Mitchell's case, yet she was hopeful, given the college's acquisition of a remarkable 12-inch telescope. In 1865, Mitchell endured a discouraging visit from Vassar President John Howard Raymond in Lynn. She detected that he was not enthusiastic about the prospect of women teaching at the college. Moreover, he informed her that he was not certain that her appointment was critical to the college's overall mission. Yet despite the resistance of the president and some of the trustees, the college ultimately invited her to teach. They offered her the position of professor of astronomy and superintendent of the astronomical observatory. In addition to her salary, they promised to provide board for both her and her father.

Despite her fears about her capabilities as a teacher, Mitchell devoted herself to introducing her students to the demands of astronomy. She insisted that her students acquire a thorough background in mathematics, declaring that astronomy without mathematics was mere stargazing, a pseudoscience that she dubbed "Geography of the Heavens." As she explained in 1866, "The laws which govern the motions of the sun, the earth, planets, and other bodies in the universe, cannot be understood and demonstrated without a solid basis of mathematical learning" (quoted in Kendall 1896, 177, 185). She was a firm believer in small-group instruction rather than formal lectures. In a letter to Caroline H. Dall, a fellow proponent of education for women, she described her instruction in the early months of the college.

> I have a class of pupils, seventeen in number, the youngest 16 the eldest 22. They come to me for 50 m. every day. I am no teacher, but I give them a lesson to learn and the next day the recitation is half a conversational lecture and half questions and answers. I allow them great freedom of questions and they puzzle me daily. They show more mathematical ability than I had expected and more originality of thought. I doubt if young men of that age would take as much interest in science. Are there 17 students in Harvard College who take Mathematical Astronomy do you think? (quoted in Albers 2001, 160–161)

Mitchell also made regular observation of the night sky mandatory for all students. She ignored the college rulebook that stated that students must remain in their rooms after 10 pm, encouraging them to spend the nighttime hours making observations. When unexpected astronomical events took place, she was also known to awaken students in the middle of the night.

Mary W. Whitney, one of Mitchell's students who eventually replaced her at Vassar, explained,

> Miss Mitchell's gift was that of stimulus, not that of drill. She could not drill; she would not drive. But no honest student could escape the pressure of her strong will and earnest intent. The marking system she held in contempt, and wished to have nothing to do with it. "You cannot mark a human mind," she said, "because there is no intellectual unit;" and upon taking up her duties as professor she stipulated that she should not be held responsible for a strict application of the system. (Kendall 1896, 179–180)

In addition to her debates with the administration concerning the grading system, Mitchell preferred to rule her own department and remain as remote as possible from President Raymond's strict rule over every aspect of the faculty's and the students' lives. She was impatient with his cautious, stand-back-and-wait approach to every problem. "We wait and ask for precedent," she once complained. "If the earth had waited for a precedent, it never would have turned on its axis!" (quoted in Kendall 1896, 174). She chafed over the requirement that she be present at the daily chapel service. On one occasion in January 1866, she wished to observe the moon pass over the star Aldebaran rather than sit through one of Raymond's lengthy sermons. "Can't you let me do both?" she wrote in a note to Raymond. "*Will* you stop at eleventhly or twelfthly? Oh why need you show us all sides of the subject?" (quoted in Vassar College 1961, 11–12).

By the 1870s, Mitchell was thoroughly immersed in the education of her students, sacrificing her own astronomical research. Her chief concern had become the advancement of higher education for women. Mitchell was also an advocate of the women's rights and woman suffrage movement. She invited women's rights activists JULIA WARD HOWE, Lucy Stone, and others to Vassar to speak to students. In 1875, she helped establish the Association for the Advancement of Women. In that year and in 1876, she served as president of the organization. Throughout her years at Vassar, she urged the scientific community to accept women scientists. In 1888, after 23 years of educating women at Vassar, she retired, returning to her home in Lynn where she died the following year.

See also **Education**

Selected Reading

Albers, Henry, ed. *Maria Mitchell: A Life in Journal and Letters*. Clinton Corners, NY: College Avenue Press. 2001.

Morgan, Sarah (1842–1909)

[O]ur troops have resolved to burn the town down, since they cannot hold it under
the fire of the gunboats. … Think of wandering around houseless and homeless,
with not even the chance of making one for myself, for nothing is to be done! Beg-
gared! How shall I endure it? … O my home! Shall I never see you again?

—Sarah Morgan, June 3, 1862, Baton Rouge, Louisiana (Dawson 1991, 199–200)

The diary of Sarah Morgan, first published posthumously as *A Confederate Girl's
Diary* in 1913, is among the most articulate, insightful nineteenth-century literary
portrayals of a young woman on the threshold of adulthood. As a work of Civil War
literature, it has been acclaimed as one of the most important diaries of the period.
Charles East, editor of the most recent and most complete edition of the diary, asserts
that its power resides in the "character and force" of Morgan's personality (Dawson
1991, xxii). In 1862, as Morgan begins her diary, she is 19 years old. By the time the
diary concludes in June 1865, she is a grown woman of 23 and has endured the worst
war has to offer—the invasion and occupation of Union troops, the loss of her cherished childhood home, the harried existence of a refugee, and, in the final weeks of
the war, the deaths of two brothers, Gibbes and George Morgan.

Sarah Ida Fowler Morgan was born in New Orleans, Louisiana, the daughter
of the city's customs collector. In 1850, when Morgan was eight years old, her family moved to the state capital at Baton Rouge where her father served as judge in the
District Court. As a child and adolescent, she was extremely close to her father. After
enduring the anguish caused by his death in 1861, Morgan, her mother, and several
sisters fled Baton Rouge in 1862 following Union occupation of the city. For the next
several years, and especially after the destruction of their home in August 1862, they
were forced to become refugees.

Morgan's diary is distinctive because, unlike other male and female war diarists, she does not merely report military and political news, family doings, local
events, or rail against the Yankees. She elaborates on the war's impact on her family,
her community, and, most of all, on herself. A month after the Union invasion of
Baton Rouge, Morgan encounters one of the first of many unlivable dwellings she,
her mother, and her sisters must reside in. Without her slaves or a mother capable of

helping her, she tackles the job at hand and realizes that the war is transforming her and the world of privilege she once knew.

> What a day I have had! Here mother and I are alone, not a servant on the lot. ... The dirt and confusion was extraordinary in the house. I could not stand it, so I applied myself to making it better. I actually swept two whole rooms! ... I discovered I could empty a dirty hearth, dust, move heavy weights, make myself generally useful and dirty, and all this is thanks to the Yankees! (Dawson 1991, 103)

Morgan dwells on her internal emotional life and is far more introspective than most mid-nineteenth-century women diarists. In an entry dated August 18, 1862, she recalls her reaction to the death of Hal, the most beloved of all her brothers, who was killed in a duel just before the war. As she describes her wish to follow him into the grave, she then addresses the torturous dilemma of a Southern girl who believes she cannot mold her strong, intellectual, opinionated self into the conventional role of Southern lady. She believes the teachings of her culture—that she is selfish because she wishes to be independent and shape her own identity.

> Spared, but for what? Is my life to be spent in selfishly sacrificing the comfort of others, to my own? [am] I only to seek my own comfort, and follow my own selfish impulses? ... What labor is it I am to turn to? What am I fit for? What can I do?

Although she has not an answer to any of these questions, one thought dominates all others. When Morgan responds, she does so with a spirit and strength that pulses throughout the entire diary.

> There is but one question ... which is plain before me. That question is Shall I be dependent? and the answer comes with an energy that makes my head throb, Never! take drudgery, take teaching which you abhor ... take hard crusts and bitter words; take poverty, and hardships; take all that God sends, cheerfully, bear all patiently; but dependence, Never! Death first! (Dawson 1991, 217)

At the same time as she reaches toward a vision of independence, Morgan fully accepts her role as a member of the white elite. She disdains the "rabble"—lower-class white women, Yankees of all classes, and free and enslaved African Americans. She accepts without question the privileges and authority of her class. Even though she knows she has no choice but to become a lady, she envisions a future in which she will carve out her own interpretation of that role. She will be an unreproachable lady while also continuing to develop her intellect and her reputation as a fiercely independent thinker.

Whatever her future or her circumstances, Morgan knows she cannot wear the cloak of her mother's ladyhood. She rejects her mother's dependencies, her emotional volatility, and her inability to cope and rise above adversity. As she struggles to define her future role, she is determined to incorporate her father's virtues, especially his calm, thoughtful, and well-balanced approach to problems. When she injures her lower spine in a carriage accident, she refuses to play the role of a helpless victim even when she is one. Unable to rise or walk, she sits up at the roadside, and though dazed by the intense pain, is determined to maintain a dignified calm while waiting for assistance. She cannot reveal the location of the injury in the presence of men, and, to reassure them, attempts to carry on their lighthearted banter. Having won her battle to be her own woman, she later notes with pride that she won their admiration. As one young soldier remarked, "I am afraid the young lady is seriously injured, only she won't acknowledge it. … She is the coolest, most dignified girl you ever saw" (Dawson 1991, 336).

Toward the end of the war and for a time afterward, Morgan lived in Union-occupied New Orleans with her Unionist half-brother Judge Philip Hicky Morgan. As the years passed, the restricted roles of women in Southern society continued to concern her. In 1872, after a move to South Carolina, she met the British-born Francis Warrington Dawson, who had immigrated to the South early in the war to fight for the Confederacy. As editor of the Charleston *News* (in 1873, the Charleston *News and Courier*), Dawson encouraged Morgan to write editorials for his paper. For six months in 1873, using the pseudonym "Mr. Fowler," Morgan raised men's and women's consciousnesses about the unnecessarily rigid gender roles for women and men in Southern society. In such essays as "Old Maids," "The Use and Abuse of Widows," "The Property of Married Women," and "Work for Women," Morgan emphasized how narrow, limited concepts of women's roles prevented women from developing their individual identities and achieving equality with men. From the time she married Dawson in January 1874, she focused on her roles as wife and mother. The couple had three children, one of whom died in infancy.

Following Morgan Dawson's death in 1909 in Paris, her son, Francis Warrington Dawson, published his edited version of his mother's war diary, *A Confederate Girl's Diary*.

See also **Diaries; Girlhood and Adolescence; Invasion and Occupation; Refugees**

Selected Readings

Clark, E. Culpepper. "Sarah Morgan and Francis Dawson: Raising the Woman Question in Reconstruction South Carolina." *South Carolina Historical Magazine.* 1 (81) (1980): 8–23.

Dawson, Sarah Morgan. *The Civil War Diary of Sarah Morgan.* Edited by Charles East. Athens: University of Georgia Press. 1991.

Juncker, Clara. "Behind Confederate Lines: Sarah Morgan Dawson." *Southern Quarterly.* 30 (1) (Fall 1991): 7–18.

Mormon Women

In 1847, Mormon Church leader Brigham Young led his followers westward to settle in the region known as the Great Basin, west of the Rocky Mountains, in the valley of the Great Salt Lake in present-day Utah. Persecuted and driven from settlements in the Midwest, the Church of Jesus Christ of Latter-day Saints sought to reestablish its center in the new settlement to be named Salt Lake City. There, and in the surrounding territory, Mormon men and women created farming communities in their new "Zion."

Isolated from the critical eyes of the rest of nineteenth-century America, Mormons founded their own spiritually based communities free from persecution and governmental interference. By 1857, 40,000 Mormon pioneers had migrated to the Great Salt Lake region.

Mormon women were directly involved in the settlement process. To survive in the harsh, arid environment, Mormon men and women had little time to dwell on their religious concerns in the late 1840s and early 1850s. Women and men toiled together, constructing homes of sun-dried adobe, digging irrigation ditches and canals, and planting and harvesting crops.

As soon as the initial colony was established in Salt Lake City and in the neighboring farming communities, church authorities urged all able-bodied adult men to leave their wives and families to create new Mormon settlements in outlying areas of the Great Basin, in parts of present-day southern Utah, Nevada, Idaho, and western Wyoming. Some Mormon men spent anywhere from two to six years on these missions. Eventually, individual families were encouraged to colonize these new communities. The Mormon Church also directed men to participate in public works projects clearing the land, erecting public buildings, and digging networks of irrigation ditches.

The journals and letters of Mormon women of the 1850s and 1860s attest to the fact that their menfolk were frequently absent from their homes. Consequently, Mormon women managed their homesteads on their own, combining domestic duties with agricultural and livestock production. Because men were not able to provide for their families while working on missions for the church and community, Mormon women were sometimes obligated to earn enough money for themselves and their children to live on, to supplement whatever subsistence their farms provided. To a large extent, women engaged in home-based industries, earning cash by weaving cloth, making candles, cooking and baking, sewing, quilting, and producing and selling agricultural products, including butter, eggs, and cheese. Other women marketed a particular skill, such as midwifery or teaching.

Although Mormon women found it necessary to farm and manage small businesses for long periods of time independently of their husbands, all Mormons of the mid-nineteenth century believed that a woman's most important roles were as mother and wife. Women were highly praised for their nurturing and domestic abilities as well as for their obedience to their husbands. Brigham Young and other church leaders stressed the subservient position of women in Mormon society. In 1862, Young declared, "Let our wives be the weaker vessels, and the men be men, and show the women by their superior ability that God gives husbands wisdom and ability to lead their wives into his presence" (quoted in Arrington 1992, 225). Despite Mormon men's involvement in church activities far from home, their religion decreed that they share the emotional, moral, and spiritual upbringing of their children with their wives. Mormons also placed a high spiritual value on the marital relationship. Men, in particular, were responsible for maintaining a close marital bond and were expected to "court" their wives throughout their marriages.

From the early days of Mormonism, Mormon women visited the sick, aided the impoverished, and comforted the recently bereaved, tasks that women often shared by working in groups. Even during the busiest days of settlement in the 1850s, men and women spared the time to help the needy in their communities. Lucy Meserve Smith described how her village gathered together to assist newly arrived settlers who had nearly expired from exposure to cold on the last leg of their journey west.

> We did all we could, with the aid of the good brethren and sisters, to comfort the needy as they came in with Hand-carts late in the Fall. They got their hands and feet badly frosted. Br. [Brother] Stephen Nixon and wife nursed and took care of them til they were better ... the four Bishops could hardly carry the bedding and other clothing we [women's relief society] got together the first time we met. We did not cease our exersions til all were made comfortable. ... The sisters stripped off their Peticoats stockings and every thing they could spare, right there in the Tabernacle [house of worship] and piled into the wagons to send to the saints [Mormons] in the mountains. (quoted in Godfrey 1982, 268–269)

Church leaders first openly encouraged Mormon men to engage in polygamy—the marrying of multiple wives—beginning in 1852, though the practice was common among church leaders long before that date. Once formally established, polygamy was the church-honored ideal of marriage until 1890. Although polygamous marriages were essential for any man wishing to assume greater authority in the Mormon Church, no more than 15 to 20 percent of Mormon men and women in the 1850s and 1860s entered into plural unions (Goodson 1976, 109).

In most cases, Mormon men did not make the decision themselves to marry an additional wife or wives. Church leaders encouraged particularly devout, prosperous men who could afford the economic burden of additional wives and children to choose polygamy. Usually, a man's first wife had to agree to the plan before a plural union could take place. At the wedding ceremony, the first wife customarily stood between her husband and the new bride. The first wife was also responsible for taking the new wife's right hand and placing it into her husband's (Goodson 1976, 99).

The advantages of polygamous marriage were many, especially for women. With their husbands far from home, a man's wives could share the often burdensome workload of domestic chores, childcare, farm duties, and wage labor. Martha Cragun Cox became the third wife of Isaiah Cox sometime in the late 1860s. From her point of view, the division of labor among wives was one of the sterling features of her marital situation. She explained these benefits in a testimonial she wrote for her children and grandchildren.

> We had our work so systematized and so well ordered that we could with ease do a great deal. One [wife] would for a period superintend the cooking and kitchen work with the help of the girls. Another make beds and sweep, another comb and wash all the children. At 7:30 all would be ready to sit down to breakfast. Lizzie was the dressmaker for the house. ... She was also the best sales woman of the house. She generally did most of the buying, especially the shoes. She was a good judge of leather. Auntie did darning and repairing. ... When wash day came all hands were employed except the cook ... we had in our home an almost perfect United Order. ... We enjoyed many privileges that single wifery never knew. (quoted in Godfrey 1982, 285–286)

Polygamous wives enjoyed the companionship and the close bonds they formed with each other, which they considered a blessing on the isolated frontier. Martha Cragun chose to marry Isaiah Cox, not because she was in love with him, but because she "loved his wives and the spirit of their home" (quoted in Godfrey 1982, 278). Even if a man's wives did not share the same household, each woman could be assured that her children would be cared for in the event of her death or severe illness.

From the Mormon Church leadership's perspective, polygamy provided homes for older, unmarried women who could not find husbands. In the 1850s and 1860s, many immigrant women had converted to Mormonism and migrated to the Salt Lake City area. Plural marriage extended the economic and spiritual advantages of the wedded state to more women while increasing the strength of the Mormon Church through the births of more children.

Non-Mormons throughout the United States were scandalized when they learned of the Mormon predilection for polygamy. Legislators, government officials, newspaper reporters, and the general public denounced Mormonism as a practice that they considered to be as corrupt, evil, and morally contemptible as prostitution. Brigham Young's pronouncements about polygamy and Mormon power also frightened and repulsed most Americans, stirring them to form strong negative opinions. Typical of

Young's rhetoric was his 1856 declaration, "The sound of polygamy is a terror to the pretended republican government. Why? Because this work is destined to revolutionize the world and bring all under subjection" (quoted in Sheldon 1976, 115).

Non-Mormons were also concerned that polygamy oppressed and degraded women, turning them into powerless, sexual slaves. In 1861, a Dr. Samuel S. Cartwright made an assertion that would become a common non-Mormon belief about polygamy, stating that it caused women to be "incapable of breeding any other than abortive specimens of humanity" (quoted in Sheldon 1976, 123).

Beginning in the 1860s and continuing for more than 25 years, the anti-polygamy forces in Congress and the nation debated how the government should handle the "Mormon problem." Mormon women were among the first women in the United States to gain the right to vote when Utah gave women the suffrage in 1870. In the 1870s and 1880s, Mormon women were instrumental in defending polygamy through petitions and vehement speeches at their "indignation meetings" or rallies. Yet Mormon women's efforts did not deter Congress from passing legislation prohibiting polygamy in 1882 and 1887. In 1890, due to unceasing government pressure and a firm consensus among Mormon men and women, Mormon Church leaders abolished polygamy.

Selected Readings

Arrington, Leonard J. and Davis Bitton. *The Mormon Experience: A History of the Latter-Day Saints*. Urbana: University of Illinois Press. 1992.

Bushman, Claudia, ed. *Mormon Sisters: Women in Early Utah*. Cambridge, MA: Emmeline Press Limited. 1976.

Godfrey, Kenneth W., Audrey M. Godfrey, and Jill Mulvay Derr. *Women's Voices: An Untold History of the Latter-Day Saints*. Salt Lake City, UT: Deseret Book Co. 1982.

Mountain Charley

In the years immediately preceding and during the Civil War, stories of an adventurous young woman named Mountain Charley circulated throughout the West. Historians agree that it is likely that the actions of more than one woman have been ascribed to the legendary Mountain Charley. In 1861, Elsa Jane Guerin published her autobiographical work, *Mountain Charley or the Adventures of Mrs. E.J. Guerin, Who Was Thirteen Years in Male Attire*, revealing her experiences in the 1850s as a wagon-train emigrant to California and as a Denver saloon owner during the Colorado Gold Rush. In 1885, George West, publisher of the *Colorado Transcript* in Golden, Colorado, immortalized a Mountain Charley of his acquaintance when he published the account of another young woman's experiences as a "girl-mountaineer" and as a Union soldier in the Iowa Cavalry from 1859 to 1864. It is this latter woman's experiences that are the subject of this entry.

Although it is impossible to authenticate the narrative West presents, it is evident from newspaper accounts and stories of the Colorado Gold Rush era that a number of armed women in male attire, traveling alone, roamed the West. According to West's narrative, Charlotte, or "Charley" (West never reveals her surname ostensibly at her request), left her hometown in Iowa in 1859 when she was 22 years old. In 1859, her husband abandoned her following the death of their first child and departed for the West with another woman. Charley vowed to seek revenge on them both and headed first to St. Joseph, Missouri, a popular jumping-off site for emigrants traveling to Colorado and California. After earning $600 there, she began to wear men's clothing, bought a mule, and traveled to Pikes Peak. She wandered the mountains from Colorado to New Mexico and back, doing some prospecting along the way. After meeting Charley in Colorado in 1859, West was surprised to meet her again in Denver, this time dressed as a woman, dealing cards in a Denver saloon to earn money so that she could return to Iowa.

In 1862, Charley once again disguised herself as a man and was hired as a "mule-whacker" on a government wagon train heading east from Colorado to Leavenworth, Kansas. When the assistant wagon-master proved unfit due to drunkenness, she was promoted to take his place. Although offered the position of wagon-master at the end of this tour, she returned to Iowa where she resisted the impulse to resume her female identity.

In September 1862, West claims that Charley enlisted in a regiment of the Iowa Cavalry as Charles Hatfield. Her legible handwriting prompted her commanding officers to make her a clerk, though she also acted as a spy on nearby Confederate regiments. In the Battle of Westport, Missouri, in October 1864, she transported messages to the frontlines and back, and was commended for her courage in the line of fire. Following the battle, Confederate soldiers found her lying wounded and carried her in for medical treatment. The Confederate doctor who treated the wound in her leg and the saber slash in her shoulder never reported his discovery of her sexual identity.

When Charley was returned to her regiment following a prisoner exchange, Union Major General Samuel R. Curtis arranged to have her awarded the rank of first lieutenant and made her aide-de-camp to his adjutant-general. After the war, she returned to Des Moines, Iowa, with her regiment and resumed civilian life as a woman.

Although the veracity of this particular account is in question, the proliferation of legends and stories told about Mountain Charley and women like her suggest that some western women were having similar experiences and that the public had a fascination for information about their unconventional activities.

See also **Military Women; Western Women**

Selected Readings

Guerin, E. J. *Mountain Charley or the Adventures of Mrs. E.J. Guerin, Who Was Thirteen Years in Male Attire.* Norman: University of Oklahoma Press. 1968.

Hall, Richard. *Patriots in Disguise: Women Warriors of the Civil War.* New York: Paragon House. 1993.

N

Native American Women

For many mid-nineteenth-century Native American women living in the United States, the Civil War was an extremely difficult, turbulent period. Although each Native American tribe's relationships with white Americans and the federal government differed, many tribes experienced one or more of the following during the war years: the trauma of broken treaties and devastating losses of land, forced marches to new homelands, unfulfilled promises of government-subsidized food, hostile attacks by vigilante bands of white settlers, massacres perpetrated by the U.S. army, starvation, and disease. For women, these disasters and dislocations made their daily lives a never-ending struggle to survive. Although women's roles varied according to each tribe, all Native American women were concerned with food gathering and food production, the building and maintenance of shelters, childcare, and clothing manufacture. War, forced marches, and moves to new lands made these responsibilities much more arduous, and sometimes impossible to perform adequately.

Of the many myths nineteenth-century white Americans harbored about Native American women, one major assumption permeated all of white society. As one historian has portrayed the white viewpoint, "The Anglo-American image of the ignoble squaw was of a squat, haggard, ugly, papoose-lugging drudge who toiled endlessly while her husband sported in the hunting fields or lolled about the lodge" (Smith, 1987, 65). White Americans also were convinced that Native American women were powerless slaves. In reality, as hard as all Native American women worked, most male and female Native Americans perceived women to be vital members of their communities. Although the men, as the tribes' hunters and warriors, had the strongest voices politically, women participated in tribal affairs and were accustomed to having men listen to their opinions.

In a number of tribes, women traditionally took part in the all-important activity of warfare, though this participation had decreased by the mid- to late nineteenth century. In general, it was more common for Native American women to support military affairs by participating in ceremonies and special dances honoring male warriors than to engage in warfare themselves.

Women gained status in some tribes through their membership in female and male sodalities. Typically each sodality or group focused on a particular interest. Some female sodalities were craft related, encouraging women to become expert in quillwork, painting, or basketry. By perfecting a particular skill through their associations with other sodality members, Native American women could gain considerable wealth, status, and power in their communities. Other sodalities, including those belonging to men, focused on the performance of celebratory rituals related to warfare, hunting, and religion. Men invited women to join some of their sodalities, in which women played ritualistic roles in ceremonies before and after hunting trips and battles.

Women of the Blackfoot Tribe of the northern Plains were recognized for their integral role in many of the tribe's most important activities. In addition to their food-related tasks, childcare, and other domestic duties, Blackfoot women sometimes hunted alongside their menfolk, accompanied war parties on horseback, and participated in combat. The Blackfoot also had special ceremonies to venerate women who were exceptionally skilled and independent (Kehoe 1983, 69).

Despite Native American women's varied activities, their principal roles revolved around domestic concerns. As the battles with white Americans over land intensified, and as warfare, disorder, and hunger dominated their lives, Native American women found that they had to devote almost all of their time and energy to gathering food.

California's Indian Wars

In California, the problems of Native Americans intensified beginning in 1849 when white American gold seekers rushed into the region. As more and more white settlers arrived from the East and Midwest during the 1850s, they pushed many of California's Native American tribes from their fertile lands into the mountains, the deserts, and the nearly impenetrable forests where game, fish, and other traditional food sources were scarce or nonexistent. As starvation and disease became a new way of life for these Native Americans, northern California tribes, such as the Hoopas, the Shastas, the Yukis, the Wiyots, and others, were driven by their desperate circumstances to invade the fertile valleys to rob livestock and sometimes attack and kill white settlers.

The violence so outraged white settlers that they immediately fought back, murdering and scalping every Native American they could hunt down. White vigilantes captured Native American women and children, often raping the women or forcing them into concubinage. The children, if they survived, were usually sold as slaves. This brutality on both sides—each white reprisal instigating further Native American attacks—intensified into an all-out war in the late 1850s which continued throughout the entire Civil War. The northern California region was not peaceful until after June 1865 (Josephy 1991, 241–243).

Native American Refugees

The Five Civilized Tribes—the Cherokees, Creeks, Chickasaws, Choctaws, and Seminoles—originally resided in the southeastern United States. In the 1830s, the federal government forced them to relocate hundreds of miles to the west on lands that the government set aside for them in Indian Territory (site of the present-day state of Oklahoma). In 1861, the Civil War brought disorder to these tribes once again as each tribe split into pro-Union and pro-Confederate factions and as the men became soldiers for either the Union or the Confederate army. From 1861 to 1863, pro-Union and pro-Confederate women, children, and elderly men were forced to flee and become refugees when troops of the opposing army entered their communities. While they were refugees living in camps far from their homes, many died from starvation, cold, and disease. Both the Confederate and Union armies neglected to provide adequately for their own refugees.

Sioux Uprising of 1862

The Sioux Uprising of 1862 had a devastating impact on all the Native American tribes of Minnesota. In late summer, warriors of the Dakota tribes (part of the Sioux nation), massacred hundreds of white settlers in the southern part of the state. The Dakota tribes were desperate; having suffered huge losses of land, crop failures from the previous growing season, and months of starvation, they were enraged by the federal government's failure to pay the annuities it owed them. To add to the crisis, white traders refused to sell food to the Dakota tribes on credit, enraging them further.

U.S. army troops retaliated, crushing the Dakotas after several bloody battles. Following the hostilities, the federal government dissolved all its treaties and obligations to the Dakota tribes. In November 1862, Dakota women, children, and elderly men who had not participated in the massacre or battles were herded to Fort Snelling near St. Paul. During the winter of 1862 to 1863, many of the captives, already weak and ill from starvation, died from disease. The rest of the Dakota and several other Minnesota tribes, including the hundreds of warriors who were not executed, were forced into Dakota Territory.

Bear River Massacre

In the fertile valleys surrounding Salt Lake City, Utah Territory, the Mormons made settlements throughout the 1850s, forcing Native Americans out of their lands into the deserts and mountains where food was difficult to obtain. As hunger and starvation spread among them, Native Americans raided Mormon farms, stole livestock, and killed settlers. When the Civil War began, this violence increased as a consequence of the region's U.S. army troops' departure for eastern battlefields.

The Shoshoni, living north of Salt Lake City, was one of several tribes menacing Mormon settlements. On January 22, 1863, Union Brigadier General Patrick Edward Connor became so frustrated by the task of policing the region that he led a massacre on the Shoshoni Tribe at Bear River in Idaho Territory, just north of the Utah Territory border. With 70 soldiers in his command, Connor and his troops surprised the Shoshoni encampment, quickly slaughtering 250 men, women, and children. As the soldiers hacked and bayoneted the bodies, they also raped the women, some of whom lay dying. The soldiers also led away 160 women prisoners, separating them from their families.

The "Long Walk"

Increasingly during the 1850s, Navajo warriors attacked white ranchers and farmers in the Rio Grande River valley in northern New Mexico Territory where whites had been seizing the Navajos' best grazing and farming land. By the late 1850s and early 1860s, the violence intensified into war, causing Union Brigadier General James H. Carleton to take action against the Navajo Tribe in 1862. When Colonel Christopher

"Kit" Carson's effort to capture or kill Navajo warriors proved unsuccessful, Carleton ordered Carson to sweep through Navajo territory in 1863. According to Carleton's orders, Carson employed a "scorched earth policy" in which his troops burned and destroyed all Navajo villages, crops, livestock, and other possessions. As Carson carried out this winter campaign, Navajo men, women, and children suffered from starvation and the bitter cold. Without shelter, food, or blankets, they soon succumbed to disease. Carleton then ordered Carson to round up all surviving Navajos and march them to Fort Sumner and Bosque Redondo in eastern New Mexico Territory. Known to the Navajos as the "Long Walk," during the winter months of 1864, more than 8,000 Navajo women, men, and children—nearly three-fourths of the entire tribe— trekked the 400 miles to Bosque Redondo. Along the way, hundreds died of starvation, disease, and exposure to the cold.

Once the Navajos arrived at their destination, there was not enough food to nourish the entire population. Although the federal government had planned that the Navajos would farm the reservation lands of Bosque Redondo, the land proved unsuitable and the climate too arid for intensive agriculture. In June 1868, after years of privation, the U.S. government permitted the Navajos to return to their ancestral lands where the government set aside a reservation for them (Josephy 1991, 284–287; Sparks 1995, 135–149).

The Sand Creek Massacre

In Colorado Territory, white settlers panicked when warriors from a number of Native American tribes attacked white homesteads and stole livestock and horses. News of the 1862 Sioux uprising in Minnesota, in which hundreds of white farmers and their families were massacred, increased white Colorado residents' fears that a war with Native Americans was inevitable in their region. Colorado Governor John Evans traveled to Washington to plead for extra troops to protect the territory, but was refused due to the Union army's urgent need of soldiers in 1863 to 1864. When Evans returned to Colorado, he and Union Colonel John M. Chivington decided to provoke hostilities with the Cheyennes, in the hopes that increased violence would lead Washington to send troops. When Chivington's troops killed Cheyenne men, women, and children in their villages in retaliation for Cheyenne attacks on whites, other tribes joined the Cheyenne and raided white ranches and farms and attacked emigrants traveling on the Santa Fe Trail. To Evans's and Chivington's frustration, Washington still did not send reinforcements.

In the fall of 1864, Black Kettle, leader of the Southern Cheyennes, accepted Evans's offer of protection to Native American tribes willing to lay down their arms. Acting according to the military's order, 500 of Black Kettle's people and 50 members of the Arapaho tribe established an encampment on Sand Creek in eastern Colorado.

Without any Native American provocation, on November 29, 1864, Chivington and his troops launched a surprise attack on the Southern Cheyennes and the Arapaho at Sand Creek. Prior to the assault, many of Chivington's officers objected to attacking a peaceful, cooperative group of Native Americans who had been promised protection.

Despite the dissent, Chivington's troops stormed the Cheyenne encampment, massacring all those who did not manage to escape. In all, more than 150 Cheyenne and Arapaho were slaughtered, two-thirds of whom were women and children. The soldiers were not content to leave the dead and dying, remaining instead to rape the women, and mutilate and scalp the bodies of the dead. Taking no prisoners, they left only after burning the entire village.

Unlike the massacre at Bear River, Idaho Territory, the Sand Creek Massacre made headlines across the nation, resulting in a tremendous public outcry and demands that the federal government respond. The U.S. Congress undertook two investigations while the Union army led one as well. The news of the massacre also spread like wildfire among Native American tribes of the West, triggering more tribes to engage in warfare with whites.

Despite the intense violence of the Native American wars of the Civil War era, not all tribes experienced war, starvation, and suffering at this time. Some tribes coexisted peacefully, living alongside white Americans. These tribes survived by adapting to the changes white Americans created in the environment. These adaptations did not come without an enormous cost, however. Most Native Americans found it nearly impossible to keep their culture intact when confronted by white Americans' insistence that they abandon their way of life and become "civilized" members of white society. Even so, the women and men of the many tribes faced with this situation managed to keep alive their religious beliefs and cultivate their traditional art forms, sometimes by doing so in secret.

The Northern Paiutes of Nevada Territory experienced upheaval in their tribal society when white American miners flooded the state in the 1850s. The digging of mines and the building of mining camps and boomtowns stripped trees from the hills while farmers and ranchers claimed the valleys for agriculture and herding livestock. Without the traditional Northern Paiute food sources—pine nuts from the region's pinyon trees and native plants growing in the valleys—the tribe faced acute food shortages.

Although some Northern Paiutes attacked white farms and ranches in the early 1860s, the violence did not intensify or continue as occurred elsewhere in the West. Instead, many members of the tribe ceased fighting and constructed new villages on the outskirts of the mining towns. In Virginia City, Nevada Territory, Northern Paiute women adapted to this new environment by becoming wage earners—working for whites as laundresses, domestic servants, and seamstresses—while their menfolk worked as lumberjacks. Women continued to gather food, though not in the same way as they had in the past. They now collected day-old, and discarded vegetables from the town's vendors. By living in their own settlements just outside of town, the Northern Paiutes were able to uphold much of their own culture (Hattori 1998, 230–234).

After the Civil War, the federal government, through open warfare and military force, continued its mission to compel most Native Americans to live on reservations and to assimilate into white society. Despite the government's demands, Native American women and men from many tribes reluctantly assumed aspects of white American culture while struggling to preserve features of their own tribal religion, mythology, crafts, and overall civilization.

See also **Western Women**

Selected Readings

Albers, Patricia and Beatrice Medicine, eds. *The Hidden Half: Studies of Plains Indian Women*. Washington, DC: University Press of America. 1983.
Josephy, Alvin M. *The Civil War in the American West*. New York: Knopf. 1991.

Nurses

Our women appear to have become almost wild on the subject of hospital nursing …. Women, in our humble opinion, are utterly and decidedly unfit for such service. They can be used …as the regular administrators of prescribed medicines, and in delicate, soothing attentions which are always so grateful to the sick …. But as hospital nurses for wounded men, they are by nature, education, and strength totally unfitted when we consider *all the duties* surgical nurses are called upon to perform.

—Letter to the editor of the *American Medical Times*, July 18, 1861 (quoted in Baxandall and Gordon 1995, 76–77)

White and African-American women of all ages, social classes, ethnic groups, and religions nursed Union and Confederate soldiers and sailors during the Civil War.

Although historians' estimates of the numbers of female nurses vary, it is likely that at least 20,000 women of the North, South, and West served in the military hospitals, field hospitals, military camps, and on the battlefields (Leonard 1994, xix). The actual total is undoubtedly far greater. What has not been calculated is the number of women who cared for the sick and wounded in an unofficial capacity. Southern women (and Northern women after the Battle of GETTYSBURG) nursed soldiers in their homes, churches, local schools, and on the battlefields adjoining their communities. Northern and Southern women visiting their husbands and menfolk in camp also attended the sick and wounded. White and black Northern women attached to the military camps—cooks, laundresses, servants, prostitutes, and wives of soldiers and officers—cared for the ill and injured whenever the need arose. Because records of African-American nurses—free black women, CONTRABAND WOMEN, and slave women—were only sporadically maintained, their numbers will never be known. Yet from the letters, journals, and memoirs of white nurses and soldiers, it appears that the number of African-American hospital staff—both male and female—was extensive. They formed the backbone of hospital staffs, performing the most physically demanding, distasteful labor that white medical personnel did not want to do. In some hospitals, African-American women composed half of the nursing staff (McPherson 1982, 267).

In April 1861, at the outset of the war, the U.S. (Union) army scarcely had a medical department. There were no general military hospitals other than one 40-bed hospital in Leavenworth, Kansas, and there were less than 100 surgeons (Brown 1998, 287). The Union army's medical bureau had no professional nurses and no established means of distributing food, medicines, and other supplies. Many of the army's surgeons had received a substandard medical education and little or no professional training. Although a Confederate medical service was nonexistent when its army was organized, the Confederate government foresaw the need for a highly organized medical department and established one within the first year of the war.

DOROTHEA DIX, Superintendent of Female Nurses for the Union army, appointed a minimum of 3,200 white nurses to serve in the military hospitals (Leonard 1994, xix). Hundreds of white women who volunteered to serve as hospital relief workers under the auspices of the UNITED STATES SANITARY COMMISSION (USSC) and the Western Sanitary Commission frequently performed nursing duties in addition to their official tasks. USSC matrons also nursed soldiers on the Hospital Transport Service's HOSPITAL SHIPS. The UNITED STATES CHRISTIAN COMMISSION (USCC) supplied female volunteer nurses and approximately 600 CATHOLIC NUNS, representing 12 religious orders, nursed for the Union and the Confederacy.

Based on pension records in the National Archives, it has been determined that at least 4,500 black and white women served as nurses in the field and in the hospitals without the sanction of Dix, the USSC, the WSC, or the USCC. Some of these women enlisted in regiments in their own communities and states. Yet personal narratives and other primary source documents reveal that many additional female nurses in the North and South and hospital workers never claimed a pension. No official records document their service and their numbers will never be known.

Determining the number of white and black nurses in the South will never be possible, in part because the Confederate Surgeon General's records were burned during the fall of Richmond in April 1865. In the South, slave women nursed and worked in the hospitals. Their white owners either donated their services or hired them out, the government paying the slaveholder all wages due.

The vast majority of female nurses in the North and South had no prior professional training or hospital experience. The notable exceptions were the Catholic sisters and the nurses trained by Doctors Elizabeth and Emily Blackwell at Bellevue Hospital in New York City under the auspices of the WOMAN'S CENTRAL ASSOCIATION OF RELIEF (WCAR) and by Dr. MARIE ZAKRZEWSKA at the New England Hospital for Women and Children in Boston. Despite the lack of medical training, many women volunteered, believing that their experiences caring for their families at home qualified them for military nursing. Although they may have overestimated their abilities, they had more experience caring for the sick than most male nurses, who formed approximately 75 percent of the Union and Confederate hospital ranks. Male nurses were usually convalescent soldiers with no aptitude or medical credentials. They were ordered to serve as nurses because of their physical inability to return to their regiments.

Despite the Blackwells' insistence that nurses need training to be effective, Dorothea Dix, USSC male leaders, and the Union military thought otherwise. Dix had no experience nursing, but believed, based on her knowledge of hospitals and Florence Nightingale's directives, that she could select the best women to take on the challenge.

Based on Nightingale's theories and observations, Dix determined the qualities essential to military nurses. "No young ladies should be sent at all," she wrote to Louisa Schuyler of the WCAR in New York City. Dix made it clear that only "those who are sober, earnest, self-sacrificing, and self-sustained; who can bear the presence of suffering and exercise entire self control, of speech and manner," would be considered (Leonard 1994, 16). By 1862, she ordained that she would only select plain-looking, mature women over the age of 30, with preference given to those between the ages of 35 and 50. She also mandated that her nurses wear simple black or brown-colored clothing. Hoopskirts, the height of women's fashion in the Civil War era, were forbidden.

What motivated women to leave home for an uncertain future at the front or in the military hospital? Many middle-class women ventured forth from a sense of patriotic duty and love of country, declaring that since they were not permitted to fight in uniform, they would assist those who could. The popularity of British nurse Florence Nightingale's books detailing her experiences nursing in the Crimean War (1853 to 1856) influenced American women who wished to save the lives of their brothers in arms. Women who volunteered their services to the regiments enlisting their husbands, lovers, and brothers often stated that they went to war to look after their menfolk. White working-class women and free black women nursed because they needed the income to survive, while slaves labored in the hospitals because they were forced to do so. A conviction that nursing was doing God's work inspired religious middle-class women to volunteer. A desire for adventure sometimes prompted young women to sign up, although it was rarely acknowledged as being a primary motivator.

DIARIES are the best source of information about the experiences and emotions of Civil War nurses. Women tended to mask their feelings when writing home to families and friends, but were more apt to reveal the truth to their journals. Like other nurses, 23-year-old Cornelia Hancock's letters to her worried family in Pennsylvania avoided all unpleasantness. A woman did not have to concern herself with others' reactions when confiding to her diary. Ada Bacot, a young widow from South Carolina, candidly summed up her reaction to her first day as a nurse at Monticello Hospital in Charlottesville, Virginia.

> I have been all day runing up & down stairs, attending to poltices, giving medicine & answering questions .... I am thourely sick of the sight of men, & would gladly get away for a time to rest, but I know these are not the right feelings and will suppress them. (Bacot 1994, 76)

A critical period in every nurse's experience was her first confrontation with the grisly realities of wounds and disease. Those who kept diaries, those who wrote memoirs, and many who wrote letters described the sometimes overwhelming challenge of coming face to face with bone-shattered limbs, pus-filled and gangrenous wounds, epidemic disease, and squalid hospital conditions. Elvira Powers was overpowered by her first day confronting the horrifying specter of nursing in a hospital filled with 800 smallpox patients. "The unsightly, swollen faces, blotched with eruption, or presenting an entire scab, and the offensive odor," she wrote, "require some strength of nerve in those who minister to their necessities" (quoted in Ross 1993, 195–196).

As nursing historian Kristie Ross points out, women coped with the initiation process by various means. Some called on their reservoir of religious faith, asking God for the strength and the will to continue. Others relied on their sense of duty and patriotism and their awareness that the soldiers desperately needed their help, and some leaned on their female colleagues' support to pull them through (Ross 1993, 193–197). Other women could not withstand the suffering before them. Cornelia Peake McDonald of Winchester, Virginia, explained that as much as she wished to nurse the wounded, she could not. When a surgeon instructed her to wash a bullet-shattered face, "I thought I should faint," she wrote in her diary. "I could only stagger towards the door. As I passed, my dress brushed against a pile of amputated limbs heaped up near the door" (McDonald 1992, 38).

While some women never returned to the hospitals after their first encounter with severed limbs and blood-strewn linens, others, though shaky and uncertain, forced themselves to face the wounded day after day until they became inured. MARY ASHTON RICE LIVERMORE's first nursing experience made it necessary for her to be escorted from the wards three times in a single day.

Nurses' duties varied widely, depending on the medical setting they worked in, their proximity in time and place to battles and the battlefields, and the individual initiative of the nurses themselves. Most female nurses of the North were responsible for maintaining the soldiers' cleanliness. Care for the soldiers' nutritional needs became the special province of women nurses and sanitary agents. In both the South and North, female nursing staffs cooked and dispensed food and medicine as the surgeons directed. They spent hours of their day comforting their patients: talking with them, supplying them with reading and writing material, and writing letters for them. Those closest to the scenes of battle distributed water, stimulants, and food to revive the weak and wounded. They often dressed wounds and assisted surgeons in operations and amputations. In many hospitals, middle-class white matrons and nurses were also in charge of supervising the work of male and female African-American staff—nurses, laundresses, cooks, and those who performed all the heavy physical labor of keeping a hospital clean. In the absence of black workers, lower-class white women performed these tasks. Middle-class white women engaged in these chores only when there was no other hospital staff available.

At her first hospital, Union army nurse Sophronia Bucklin's duties

…were to distribute food to the patients …wash the faces and hands and comb the heads of the wounded; see that their bedding and clothing was kept clean and whole, bring pocket handkerchiefs, prepare and give various drinks and stimulants …

By contrast, Bucklin explains how her tasks changed when 1,100 wounded soldiers were brought in for treatment.

Beds were to be made, hands and faces stripped of the hideous mask of blood and grime, matted hair to be combed out over the bronzed brows, and gaping wounds to be sponged with soft water, till cleansed of the gore and filth preparatory to the dressing …. Then with all my resolution I nerved myself to the task and bound up the aching limbs. (quoted in Leonard 1994, 19)

Dorothea Dix's nurses earned $.40 per day or approximately $12 per month. Many white, middle-class Northern nurses worked as volunteers, never receiving payment for their services. In the Confederacy, nurses' wages were much higher, but so were the inflation-driven prices of food, clothing, and other necessities. The Confederacy also instituted a pay scale for nurses before the Federal government.

Because the war was fought primarily in the Confederacy, Southern women had a greater opportunity to nurse soldiers in their homes and in their own communities. Especially during 1861 and 1862, a number of Southern women established hospitals in private homes. Caroline Mayo operated the Good Samaritan Hospital in her Richmond, Virginia, home. Maria Foster Clopton created a hospital in the residence of her daughter and son-in-law. Throughout the war, SALLY TOMPKINS superintended a first-rate hospital in the home of a Richmond judge (Barber 1997, 84). The soldier-patients who recuperated in these small hospitals fared far better than their counterparts in the large military hospitals. At the sprawling Chimborazo Hospital in Richmond, 41.2 percent of the 17,000 soldiers treated there died. In contrast, Maria Clopton's hospital experienced only 11 deaths among the 565 soldiers sheltered there (Barber 1997, 91).

In September 1862, the Confederate Congress passed the Hospital Act, which officially established the roles and hierarchy of women within its military hospitals, a development that the federal government never took. On account of the well-publicized successes of the small, private, women-led hospitals, the Confederate government supported and encouraged the work of women within its military hospitals.

In the South, white elite and middle-class matrons superintended all of the military hospital's domestic details as they did in the North. Southern matrons supervised the preparation of the patients' diets and the work of all other domestic and female nursing staff, earning $40 per month. Assistant matrons, for $35 per month, were in charge of all clothing, bedding, and laundry for the wards. Ward matrons were paid $30 per month to make beds and care for the sheets and other bedding, give medications, and oversee the work of the more lowly nurses. For $25 per month, the female nurses were assigned the most menial and disagreeable tasks (Barber 1997, 103–104; D. Faust 1997, 97). In the South, only middle- and upper-class women were matrons and only working-class women, free black women, and slaves were nurses.

Civil War nursing was an extremely hazardous occupation. Disease was ever-present. Like the military camps, the military hospitals were filled with soldiers suffering from typhoid fever, dysentery, cholera, erysipelas (a streptococcal infection of the skin), smallpox, scarlet fever, and venereal diseases. In fact, two out of three soldiers and officers who did not survive died from disease rather than wounds (Adams 1952, 194). Although statistics concerning the health of female nurses are not available, women who kept personal records reported episodes of severe illness in themselves and in their fellow nurses. Some returned home, never to recover. Others died. LOUISA MAY ALCOTT contracted what was believed to be typhoid pneumonia and nearly died. Hannah Ropes, head matron at Union Hotel Hospital in Washington, DC, died of the disease during Alcott's illness. Soldiers' infected wounds also put nurses at risk. Elida Rumsey Fowle of Massachusetts developed a septic carbuncle (a severe, localized infection of the skin) on her face, a result of cleansing wounds on the battlefield. She was permanently disfigured. A number of nurses reported serious skin infections erupting as a result of blood and pus splashing on them (Holland 1897, 75).

Nurses' diaries reveal that they worked excruciatingly long hours, often laboring all day and into the night on a regular basis. After battles, field nurses frequently reported that they worked without cease, stopping only to sleep a few hours when they dropped from exhaustion. Not infrequently, the grueling schedules resulted in physical collapse, illness, and disability, forcing a nurse to be sent home, never to return. Battlefield nurses were also threatened by their proximity to weaponry. Nurses were wounded and sometimes killed during engagements as they tended to soldiers' wounds.

The relationships and conflicts between male medical officers and staff and female nurses was a frequent topic of discussion in nurses' writings. From the very beginning of the war, women encountered stiff resistance from army medical staff. The Union army Medical Department did not want women nurses. Surgeons and military officials preferred to rely on convalescent soldiers to distribute food and medicine. They were also concerned about civilians interfering in military matters. When it was determined that women nurses would be assigned to Union military hospitals, surgeons resented their presence in what had been a strictly male domain.

Complicating the surgeons' unwillingness was the behavior of female nurses. Unaccustomed to following military protocol and obeying military authority, some women disregarded surgeons' orders when they believed those prescriptions were harming patients or hindering their recoveries. Georgeanna Woolsey of New York City, one of the nurses trained under the auspices of the Woman's Central Association of Relief at Bellevue Hospital in New York, traveled to Washington, DC, in 1861. From there, she and her sister Eliza Woolsey Howland followed the army to Alexandria, Virginia, where they found a military camp sheltering a number of sick soldiers. Believing they had found a site that needed their skills, the two sisters set up a makeshift hospital in a shanty.

> We asked no one's permission, but went to work; had the house cleaned from top to bottom, shelves put up and sacks filled with straw; then we prescribed the diet and fed them just as we pleased. All this was a shocking breach of propriety, and I have no doubt the surgeon of the regiment was somewhere behind a fence, white with rage. (Bacon 1899, 120)

Patients' diets were a frequent source of conflict. Surgeons and nurses had opposing agendas when it came to nutrition for the sick and wounded. Female nurses and male and female sanitary agents insisted that diet was a critical, primary element in patient care. Surgeons disagreed as to the importance of diet and the type of foods and beverages that should be served. In addition to dietary concerns, female nurses placed a high priority on making soldiers comfortable by keeping them clean and providing them with warm clothing, concerns that the surgeons dismissed as trivial.

Some nurses scorned surgeons for resorting so frequently to amputation. The women who expressed this frustration in their diaries and memoirs often complained that surgeons did not try to see if they could save a limb, but amputated without considering other possibilities. Abby Woolsey, another of Georgeanna Woolsey's sisters, sums up the opinion of many women who worked in the hospitals.

It grieves me ...to think of how many men are ruined for life by surgeons who with savage glee hurry to chop off arms and legs *ad libitum,* who might by a slower and more skillful process have been saved such humiliation. (Bacon 1899, 173–174)

Nurses and surgeons sometimes differed as to the treatment of dying soldiers. After battles, with hundreds of the wounded needing attention, surgeons were apt to devote their time to soldiers who had the best chances for survival, to the endless frustration of the nurses. Soldiers with devastating wounds were often left to die unattended. When women nurses witnessed what they perceived as the surgeons' callous abandonment of the sickest and most severely wounded patients, they frequently became enraged and insisted on nursing the dying. Ruth Helena Sinnotte, "nurse at large" on the hospital steamship *Imperial,* did not leave the side of a dying young man the surgeon had declared was hopeless. Later, when the soldier was out of danger, the doctor approached her, asking, "Why, ain't he dead yet?" When the surgeon inquired how she had helped her patient, she said, "I attended to him as though he were my own, and in our own home" (quoted in Holland 1897, 130).

After the war, most nurses returned home to resume the domestic lives they had left behind. A small percentage, however, continued to be active in the public sphere: teaching, attending medical school, running businesses, or pursuing volunteer work to assist destitute families, war orphans, and the freedpeople. Several Civil War nurses, Georgeanna Woolsey among them, worked to professionalize nursing by establishing nurses' training schools. In 1873, nursing schools were founded at Bellevue Hospital in New York City, Massachusetts General Hospital in Boston, and Connecticut Hospital in New Haven, Connecticut. Also in 1873, Linda Richards became the first person to be granted a nursing degree, from the first nursing school in the United States, the New England Hospital for Women and Children in Boston. The first African-American nurse to be so honored was Mary Eliza Mahoney in 1879, also at New England Hospital (Schneider and Schneider 1993, 191, 309).

See also **Antietam (Sharpsburg), Battle of; Barton, Clara; Bickerdyke, Mary; Cumming, Kate; Doctors; Hawks, Esther Hill; Pember, Phoebe Levy; Taylor, Susie Baker King; Tubman, Harriet; Walker, Mary Edwards**

Selected Readings

Faust, Drew Gilpin. *Mothers of Invention: Women of the Slaveholding South in the American Civil War.* New York: Vintage Books. 1997.

Leonard, Elizabeth D. *Yankee Women: Gender Battles in the Civil War.* New York: Norton. 1994.

Schultz, Jane E. "'Are We Not All Soldiers?' Northern Women in the Civil War Hospital Service." *Prospects.* 20 (1995): 39–56.

P

Patriotism

I devote all my red, white, and blue silk to the manufacture of Confederate flags. As soon as one is confiscated, I make another, until my ribbon is exhausted .... Henceforth, I wear one [a miniature flag] pinned to my bosom ... the man who says take it off will have to pull it off for himself; the man who dare attempt it—well! a pistol in my pocket fills up the gap. I am capable, too.

—Sarah Morgan, Baton Rouge, Louisiana, May 9, 1862 (Dawson 1991, 64–65)

During the weeks and months following the firing on FORT SUMTER in April 1861, white men and women of the North and South reveled in effusive public displays of patriotism. As men of military age rushed to form regiments, women and men organized parades, flag presentations, dances, and parties to support and fortify the troops. Women composed patriotic songs, prose, and poetry, which newspapers and magazines eagerly published. In SOLDIERS' AID SOCIETIES and local sewing circles, Northern and Southern women manufactured clothing for their respective militaries. As time passed, many women found that the hardships created by war forced them to redefine their patriotic obligations. For most women, fulfilling the needs of their families superseded their duty to their government. In the North, many women found that they had to reduce or eliminate the hours and resources spent on soldiers' aid so that they could give their all to their children, their farms, and their livelihoods. Women faced a greater challenge in the Confederacy as they waged a grim daily battle to feed their families. Many Southern women found that the struggle to keep their children alive demanded that they openly protest the Confederate government's expectations of them.

In the first flush of war, in the spring and summer of 1861, men and women of the North and South staged lavish ceremonies to celebrate the departure of soldiers from their communities. At these events, women presented the battle flags and regimental banners that they had designed and sewed themselves. They also delivered elaborate presentation speeches. Even in towns and villages that had never experienced the novelty of a woman speaking in public, no voice dared to question its propriety in the impassioned patriotic climate. The press supported women's involvement and their speechmaking, a departure from the past. Hassie Anderson's speech, given to the soldiers of Pike County, Alabama, typifies the romantic, patriotic language of the time: "Arise, grasp your sword and wield your steel, and drive your enemies from the field. Onward, onward, you gallant band, save us! Save our cherished land. Gird on your armor, lift your hearts, and God will shield you from the darts" (quoted in Dinkin 1995, 54).

MARY ASHTON RICE LIVERMORE, who was to become a dynamic leader within the UNITED STATES SANITARY COMMISSION, was visiting her native city of Boston in April 1861 when President Abraham Lincoln called for 75,000 volunteers to enlist for three months' military service. In her memoir of the war, Rice Livermore recorded her impressions of the day she and her elderly father stood at Faneuil Hall to observe the city overtaken by a storm of patriotism.

> As they [the recruits] marched from the railroad stations, they were escorted by crowds cheering vociferously. Merchants and clerks rushed out from stores ... saluting them as they passed. Windows were flung up; and women leaned out into the rain, waving flags and handkerchiefs. Horse-cars and omnibuses halted for the passage of the soldiers, and cheer upon cheer leaped forth from the thronged doors and windows.

As Rice Livermore recalled being swept up in the passion of the crowd, the rising of the Stars and Stripes provided the catalyst that sparked her own patriotic feelings, leaving her to reflect anew on the republic, the government, and the nation.

> I saw the dear banner of my country, rising higher and higher to the top of the flag-staff ... Oh, the roar that rang out from ten thousand throats! ... I had never seen anything like this before. ... Never before had the national flag signified anything to

me. But as I saw it now, kissing the skies, all that it symbolized as representative of government and emblematic of national majesty became clear to my mental vision. (Livermore 1995, 90–92)

For the Union and the Confederacy, the national flag was the all-important rallying symbol during the first months of the war. In the North, women adorned their houses with the Stars and Stripes, hanging flags from all the windows. Men and women attached miniature flags to their clothing and wore Union badges. Women sewed flags onto their bonnets, and some made "Union bonnets," designed in red, white, and blue. New York City girls decorated their stationery paper and envelopes with red-, white-, and blue-striped borders. They also sported flag pins and wove ribbons of red, white, and blue through their hair (Attie 1998, 26–27).

For Sallie Brock, an arch-secessionist, the appearance of the Confederacy's new flag transformed the city of Richmond, Virginia.

> Suddenly—almost as if by magic—the new Confederate flag was hoisted on the Capitol, and from every hill-top, and from nearly every house-top in the city, it was soon waving. The excitement was beyond description; the satisfaction unparalleled … At last Virginia was free from the obligation that bound her to a Union which had become hateful. Cannons were fired, bells rang, shouts rent the air, the inhabitants rushed to and fro to discuss the joyful event. (Putnam 1996, 20)

In the fall of 1861, Confederate Brigadier General Pierre Gustave Toutant (P.G.T.) Beauregard asked three young women to create a new battle flag for the Confederate Army of the Potomac (later renamed Army of Northern Virginia). Two sisters, Hetty and Jennie Cary, and their cousin Constance Cary each constructed a flag from the design Beauregard presented to them. In her memoir decades later, Constance described the flag as "jaunty squares of scarlet crossed with dark blue, the cross bearing stars to indicate the number of the seceding states" (Harrison 1885, 609). Hetty presented the flag she made to Brigadier General Joseph E. Johnston, Constance gave hers to Major General Earl Van Dorn, and Jennie offered hers to General Beauregard. Women in sewing circles throughout Richmond, Virginia, were then enlisted to sew battle flags for the army.

When the spring and summer of 1861 were over, the staggering number of casualties from the first battles dampened the euphoria in the South and North. Women, urged on by the press and their governments, continued to contribute their time and resources to their local soldiers' aid societies. The federal and Confederate governments encouraged women's participation and directed the national appeals for goods squarely at women's patriotic loyalties. Throughout the war, both governments made it clear that it was women's duty to volunteer to produce and collect food, clothing, and other home-manufactured items needed by the troops. In the early months of the war, women in the North and South responded overwhelmingly. By 1863, however, the numbers of women participating dwindled as many women needed to devote all their waking hours to the care of their families, their farms, and their family businesses while their male relatives served in the military.

As the battles waged and the death toll mounted, the press exhorted women to take special care with their letters to their loved ones in the military. In the North and South, women were instructed to demonstrate their loyalty by writing heartening letters to their husbands and sweethearts. As an Alabama newspaper writer instructed his female readers, "When you write to soldiers, speak words of encouragement; cheer their hearts, fire their souls, and arouse their patriotism. Say nothing that will embitter their thoughts or swerve them from the path of patriotic duty" (quoted in Clinton 1995, 59). According to the federal and Confederate governments, a woman could best show her patriotism by silently shouldering her cares and burdens at home on her own. Although some women may have taken these directives to heart, surviving letters of military wives indicate that many women did not want their communications with their loved ones to be the vehicle of their patriotism. Women on both sides of the conflict used letters to openly communicate their struggles with their husbands and male family members and asked for guidance and support.

By 1863, and increasingly as the war wore on, women protested the absence of their menfolk. Especially in the Confederacy, where women watched helplessly as their children became weak and malnourished from the lack of food, women petitioned their state governors, President Jefferson Davis, and Confederate government officials for assistance. When help did not arrive, when the government neglected to take the steps to alleviate women's distress, or when the measures taken were insufficient to meet their needs, some women implored their soldier-husbands to leave their posts and come home. In late 1864, two-thirds of Confederate soldiers from North Carolina were listed as being absent without leave (Bynum 1992, 130). As desertion depleted the Confederate army, Confederate officials demanded that women remember their patriotic duty to the Confederacy, reminding them that the survival of the Confederacy was in their hands. Yet, by this time, women were not listening to a government that had failed to help them meet their most basic needs. In her letter to North Carolina Governor Zebulon Vance, Nancy Mangum explained that runaway inflation was putting food out of her family's reach. She demanded that prices be lowered or "we wimen will write for our husbands to come …home and help us we cant stand it" (D. Faust 1992 [Altars], 194–195).

As desperate women urged their husbands to return home, the Confederate press and the government charged that women were staging the ruin of the Confederacy. One man from North Carolina declared, "Desertion takes place because desertion is encouraged …And though the ladies may not be willing to concede the fact, they are nevertheless responsible …for the desertion in the army and the dissipation in the country" (D. Faust 1992 [Altars], 195). Yet women, when faced with the potential loss of their families and farms, chose to put their family's interests first. And they were not alone. Their husbands agreed that the survival of their families must come first.

Not all Confederate women felt forced by circumstances to abandon their patriotism. Many remained as steadfast in their support of the government when the last shots were fired as they had been on the first. In the final weeks of the war, when two Union soldiers entered South Carolina refugee Emma Holmes's domicile, she "fired volley after volley of rebel shot at them," taunting them for their "warring on women & children." "In fact," she added, "I hurled so many keen sarcasms, such home thrusts, that the Pennsylvanian said 'I was the best rebel he had met, and that it was such women as I who kept up this war by urging on our brothers and friends.' I told him I considered it a high compliment, that I was delighted to find I was able to do so much for my country" (Holmes 1979, 402). Two months after the defeat of the Confederacy, Sarah Morgan wrote, "Our Confederacy has gone with a crash .... What tears we have shed over it, it is not necessary to mention. I only pray never to be otherwise than what I am at this instant—a Rebel in heart and soul" (Dawson 1991, 611).

Devastated by the collapse of the Confederacy, young EMMA LECONTE found it unthinkable to surrender her patriotism. On April 16, 1865, she wrote, "Let us suffer still more, give up yet more—anything, anything that will help the cause, anything that will give us freedom .... I never loved my country as I do now. I feel I could sacrifice *everything* to it, and when I think of the future, oh God! It is too horrible" (LeConte 1957, 91).

In the months and years following the Confederate defeat, Southern women channeled their grief and sense of devastating loss into monument dedications, memorial exercises, and other celebrations that venerated the war dead. Although the North honored its fallen soldiers as well, Southern women in particular took an active role in encouraging postwar Southern society to revere the lost glory of the Old South and the Confederacy.

See also **Secession**

Selected Readings

Faust, Drew Gilpin. "Altars of Sacrifice." In *Divided Houses: Gender and the Civil War*. Edited by Catherine Clinton and Nina Silber. New York: Oxford University Press. 1992.

Faust, Drew Gilpin. *Mothers of Invention: Women of the Slaveholding South in the American Civil War*. New York: Vintage Books. 1997.

Paludan, Phillip Shaw. *"A People's Contest": The Union and Civil War 1861–1865*. New York: Harper and Row. 1988.

Peabody, Elizabeth Palmer (1804–1894)

In 1860, on the eve of the Civil War, pioneer of early childhood education Elizabeth Palmer Peabody established in Boston the first English-speaking kindergarten in the United States. Throughout the 1860s and 1870s, Peabody strove to perfect kindergarten education and the training of early childhood teachers, a mission that had her traveling throughout much of Europe and the U.S. Peabody is not only remembered for her kindergarten crusade as she was also a significant contributor to transcendentalism, a liberal philosophical, spiritual, and literary movement in Boston during the 1840s.

Possessed of a rare intellect, Peabody was the daughter of two highly learned scholars. Born and brought up in Massachusetts, she became a teacher in her mother's school at age 15. Thoroughly educated by her parents in religion, philosophy, history, literature, and Latin, she continued to educate herself throughout her life, ultimately learning to read and write in ten languages.

During her young adulthood, she was a governess and teacher, and established two schools of her own. She was a friend of the philosopher and writer Ralph Waldo Emerson, and was a colleague of Emerson's friend Bronson Alcott (philosopher, educational reformer, and father of LOUISA MAY ALCOTT), becoming an assistant teacher in his experimental school. Peabody also was an intellectual compatriot of the leader of American Unitarianism William Ellery Channing, educational reformer Horace Mann, and noted author and thinker Margaret Fuller. As a close associate of this group, she became deeply involved in the transcendentalist movement of the 1840s. During this time, she established and operated a bookstore and lending library in Boston that became a primary gathering place of the transcendentalists.

Peabody may have been the first female publisher in the United States. As such, she is credited with having published her brother-in-law Nathaniel Hawthorne's early writings. Also in the 1840s, she was a frequent contributor to the *Dial*, the chief magazine of the transcendentalists. In 1849, she launched her own journal *Aesthetic Papers*, which primarily published essays on educational reform. In this magazine, she published fellow transcendentalist Henry David Thoreau's essay "Civil Disobedience."

After the flurry of her activities of the 1840s, Peabody involved herself in various radical political and social causes during the 1850s. By the late 1850s, she was an ardent antislavery advocate, though she was never an active member of any abolitionist organization. In October 1859, she carefully followed the events surrounding the abolitionist John Brown's raid on the federal arsenal in Harpers Ferry, Virginia. With the financial support of numerous African-American and white abolitionists in the North, Brown intended to ignite a slave insurrection in the South. In early March of 1860, Aaron Stevens, who had struggled to maintain Kansas as a free state in the mid-1850s, was one of only two direct participants who had not been killed in the raid or executed afterward. In early March, Peabody traveled to Richmond, Virginia, to persuade Virginia Governor John Letcher to spare Stevens's life. She was unsuccessful and on March 16, Stevens was hanged.

In the midst of all the national turmoil in 1859, Peabody met Margarethe Schurz, who introduced her to the work of the German educational reformer Friedrich Froebel, who specialized in teaching very young children. Although Froebel had died in 1852, his followers in Europe and the United States continued to practice his philosophy of early childhood education. Margarethe Schurz, as one such devotee, had opened a German-speaking kindergarten in Watertown, Wisconsin, in 1856.

After meeting Schurz, Peabody studied Froebel's writings and the next year, in 1860, opened a Froebel-inspired kindergarten in Boston. With 30 youngsters in her schoolroom, Peabody, her two assistant teachers, a French instructor, and a gymnastics teacher began the experiment. In a report that Peabody issued concerning her kindergarten venture, she described her implementation of Froebel's educational philosophy. "The idea of Kindergarten is organized play," she explained. Peabody defined the kindergarten as "children in society,—a commonwealth or republic of children,—whose laws are all part and parcel of the Higher Law alone. It may be contrasted, in every particular, with the old-fashioned school, which is an absolute monarchy." To Peabody's mind, the teacher was a critical element of Froebel's educational plan. She believed that the model kindergarten instructor was a mature woman who could nurture all aspects of a child's development—physical, mental, and moral (Ronda 1999, 274).

In 1863, Peabody and her sister Mary Peabody Mann (widow of Horace Mann) wrote and published their *Moral Culture of Infancy and Kindergarten Guide*, a volume intended to instruct and inspire women throughout the country to organize kindergartens.

Although Peabody spent the war years immersed in her work developing kindergarten programs and training teachers, she contributed to the war effort and kept abreast of all the war news. Like many Northern abolitionists, she was convinced that the war was ordained by God and was being fought principally to free the slaves. She assisted in the raising of funds to tend to the sick and wounded Union soldiers by assisting in auctions of memorabilia (Ronda 1999, 271).

In January 1865, Peabody was thrilled to be present when the U.S. House of Representatives held its debates on the Thirteenth Amendment, which was to guarantee the freedom of African Americans. She was also on hand when the House finally passed the amendment. In a letter to her nephew Horace Mann, Jr., she described the jubilation of everyone present.

> But it was something to see the Amendment pass the House which I did! ...When the vote was declared it was found to be 7 above the majority of 2/3rds and then such a shout—while the floor on the right side of the house seemed to *blaze* with excitement—& the galleries wholly sympathized—On the *opposition* side the members threw themselves back and bore as quietly as they could .... But the eyes on the right side somehow showed out like stars—Some embraced—most shook hands—So we did in the gallery—Tears & smiles contended for mastery. (Quoted in Ronda 1999, 278)

After the war, Peabody, still engrossed in her educational mission, perceived that she had not fully attained Froebel's ideal for the kindergarten, a realization that came to haunt her. "Seven years of experience with my so-called kindergarten," she wrote, "though it had a pecuniary success and a very considerable popularity ...convinced me that we were not practicing Froebel's Fine Art" (Peabody 1984, 311). Peabody believed that the only way that she could remedy the defects was to travel to Europe to meet Froebel's disciples and to see their kindergartens in practice. In June 1867, she embarked on her European trip, traveling to Switzerland, Germany, France, Italy, and England.

Following an exhausting journey, Peabody returned to the United States in the fall of 1868, dedicated to pursuing what had been revealed to her as the true ideals of Froebel's theories of early childhood education. She now realized that structured, supervised play was necessary for learning to take place because only through organized play could children learn about their bodies and their creative selves (Ronda 1999, 301). Peabody also more fully recognized that the strictest attention must be paid to the training of kindergarten teachers. Toward these ends, she revised the book *Moral Culture of Infancy and Kindergarten Guide*, deleting entirely the section on the teaching of reading. She now believed that teaching children to read was not an appropriate function of the kindergarten.

In 1870, at the age of 66, Peabody traveled throughout the North and Midwest to disseminate her kindergarten vision. By this time, she was at the center of the Froebellian movement in the United States. During the early 1870s, she contributed to and edited the periodical *Kindergarten Messenger*. In 1877, she served as president of the American Froebel Union. Despite her advanced years, in the 1880s, she continued to read and study as she always had and still had the strength to lecture on transcendentalism. She remained devoted to a host of liberal causes, perhaps most notable among them her advocacy of education for Native Americans. Intellectually vital at 84 years of age, in 1888, she published her *Lectures in Training Schools for Kindergartners*.

Selected Reading

Ronda, Bruce A. *Elizabeth Palmer Peabody: A Reformer on Her Own Terms*. Cambridge, MA: Harvard University Press. 1999.

Pember, Phoebe Levy (1823–1913)

As chief matron at Hospital Number Two at Chimborazo Hospital in Richmond, Virginia, from 1862 to 1865, Phoebe Levy Pember was among the most prominent of Confederate Civil War NURSES. As a woman of elite social stature, she daily challenged traditional Southern society that regarded with distaste and suspicion any "lady" who lowered herself to engage in the "coarse" and "dirty" work within military hospitals.

Phoebe Yates Levy was born in Charleston, South Carolina, to Jacob Clavius Levy, a prosperous Jewish merchant, and to Fanny Yates Levy, a well-known actress. The Levys were well accepted among the elite in Charleston and appear not to have experienced significant prejudice or discrimination on account of their religious background. All that is known of Levy's childhood is that she was well educated. The younger sister of fiery Southern rights' advocate EUGENIA LEVY PHILLIPS, Phoebe moved with her family to Savannah, Georgia, in the late 1840s. In 1856, she married Thomas Pember of Boston. When Pember fell ill with tuberculosis, the couple settled in South Carolina where it was hoped the warmer weather would improve his health. Following Pember's death in 1861, Levy Pember rejoined her father and other family in Marietta, Georgia. This living arrangement did not agree with Levy Pember who encountered friction and hostility among her relatives from the moment she arrived.

In November 1862, Levy Pember received a letter from a woman of her acquaintance, Mrs. George W. Randolph, wife of the Confederate Secretary of War, urging her to accept the post of matron at one of the large Confederate military hospitals.

Not hesitating long, Levy Pember agreed to assume a post at Chimborazo Hospital in Richmond. In her memoir, *A Southern Woman's Story*, she fully acknowledged that the untenable circumstances of her home life motivated her to accept the position: "I look forward with pleasure to any life that will exempt me from daily jealousies and rudenesses" (Pember 1959, 150). As a chief matron, she would draw a salary and be able to live independently of her family. With some trepidation, though not at all lacking in courage, she journeyed to Richmond.

The Chimborazo Hospital, where Levy Pember was the first matron to report for duty in December 1862, was an enormous institution that had been treating soldiers since the early months of that year. During the Civil War, Chimborazo was the largest military hospital in the world, treating 76,000 patients from 1862 to 1865. As the war progressed, Chimborazo continued to grow and eventually included 150 wards, each able to hold 40 to 60 patients. Each ward had its own one-story building. Of the hospital's five divisions, Levy Pember was chief matron for Hospital Number Two, which treated up to 600 sick and wounded soldiers at any given time. Chimborazo's size made it vulnerable to a host of administrative snarls that reduced efficiency and compromised the treatment of soldiers. Incompetent administrators, petty rivalries, and infighting also hampered the hospital's effectiveness.

As chief matron, Levy Pember supervised the cooking and feeding of 600 patients. She superintended all housekeeping details, making sure that the hospital orderlies and other staff swept the wards on a daily basis, washed the bed linens and changed the beds, and dispensed medicines. In her memoir, Levy Pember rarely mentions the staff that worked under her direction, and when she does, she neglects to identify their race or class. She does discuss, however, the unsatisfactory habits of three white working-class women whom she hired and trained to be nurses and whom she hoped would take direction well. Although the hospital's cooks, laundresses, and orderlies were almost entirely African American, she omits them from her memoir.

When the hospital was flooded with new arrivals of wounded soldiers, Levy Pember washed and bandaged wounds and occasionally attended surgeons during amputations, although these duties were by no means her regular tasks. Male nurses, most of them convalescent soldiers, usually performed these chores. Levy Pember, like most female Civil War nurses of the North and South, traveled from ward to ward offering words of comfort and solace to soldiers. Although not specifically part of her job description, she viewed the constant surveillance of patients to be one of the most important aspects of her role. When stopping to chat at a soldier's bedside, she could "remedy any apparent evils overlooked by the surgeons" and inquire about each patient's nutrition (Pember 1959, 35). She despaired that a large majority of soldiers did not eat the food provided. Always battling the limited variety of foods available, she tried novel recipes and menus to make food palatable and to provide soldiers of varying backgrounds with the comfort foods they craved.

Being constantly confronted with dying men and their endless suffering was extremely difficult, Levy Pember admitted, despite her seemingly endless reserve of self-discipline. Yet as other Civil War nurses learned, "There was too much work to be done, too much active exertion required, to allow the mental or physical powers to succumb …. There was, indeed, but little leisure to sentimentalize, the necessity for action being ever present" (Pember 1959, 45).

Although Levy Pember was no different from other female war nurses who believed at times that the surgeons were not providing the proper medical treatment, she declared that "no temptation could induce me to interfere in any way with medical treatment, not even to offering the slightest alleviation to suffering men" (Pember 1959, 80). One harsh reprimand from a surgeon after she altered a patient's treatment ensured that she would not stray from the surgeons' orders again. Perhaps because the surgeons knew that they could trust her to follow their treatment protocols, she enjoyed good working alliances with a number of them who permitted her to work "hand in hand" with them (Pember 1959, 81). Not all of her relationships with male surgeons and administrators were genial. As the first matron to be appointed at Chimborazo Hospital, her entrance was greeted with resentment and dismay by a number of men.

Levy Pember's most troublesome conflict with male medical staff arose over her control of the hospital's whisky supply. According to Confederate law, matrons were to control medicinal spirits. Not long after she arrived at Chimborazo, she submitted a requisition for the one-month supply of whiskey to which Hospital Number Two was entitled. Only when she insisted on her legal right to have it did the surgeon-in-charge release it. When she finally received the barrel, her problems with surgeons and male administrators began. In this battle of wills, Levy Pember discovered that even with a lock and key, she could not control the supply as surgeons and other staff used every ruse possible to siphon off whiskey for their own personal use. After one particularly grueling conflict, she wrote, "I recompensed myself from that time till the end of my sojourn by acting exactly as I thought right, braving the consequences, and preferring to being attacked to attacking" (Pember 1959, 73).

The evils of alcohol were evident enough. While inebriated, one surgeon operated on a patient with a broken leg by setting the wrong limb. The soldier did not survive. Throughout the entire length of her service, she never gave up trying to protect the patient's liquor supply or to ensure that patients who truly needed it received it. At the end of the war, after the Union invasion and destruction of Richmond, Levy Pember struggled to maintain her control of the liquor cabinet. When a group of "hospital rats," devious malingerers she had endured all through the war, tried to wrest the whiskey from her possession, she flashed the pistol Confederate officers had given her to protect herself from Union troops and secured the supply.

Unlike Union nurses, Levy Pember and all Confederate medical personnel struggled with increasing scarcities as the war progressed—privations that compromised the survival rates of the wounded and sick. When Union forces cut Confederate rail lines, food from the countryside spoiled on the tracks and never reached the hospitals. Then Levy Pember found that trying to make a nourishing, strengthening meal from herb tea, arrowroot (a tasteless starch), and rancid bacon was a challenge. As she described it, one of her most painful frustrations was learning "to count the number of mouths to be fed daily, and then contemplating the food, calculate not how much but how little each man could be satisfied with" (Pember 1959, 84). Rats were a persistent plague, diminishing meager food supplies even further. They also gobbled the poultices and absorbent, bran-stuffed bandaging right off the patients' bodies.

After the retreat of Confederate forces and the invasion of Union troops, Levy Pember was alone in her decision to remain at Chimborazo with those wounded and ill soldiers who could not be moved. She continued to nurse them, remaining by their side even when Union soldiers moved them to another hospital. Once the last of her patients departed, Levy Pember reported that she was left "houseless, homeless, and moneyless" in Richmond.

Her destitute postwar condition does not appear to have lasted long. Although little is known of her later activities, it is evident that following the war, and for the rest of her life, Levy Pember traveled widely throughout Europe and the United States. She died at the age of 89 in 1913.

See also **Nurses**

Selected Reading

Pember, Phoebe Yates. *A Southern Women's Story: Life in Confederate Richmond.* Jackson, TN: McCowat-Mercer Press. 1959.
Original text is also available online at http://www.jewish-history.com/Pember/

Phillips, Eugenia Levy (1820–1902)

I listened in respectful attention to my banishment to Ship Island, to be fed on soldiers' rations, to be denied communication with everyone, to be allowed one servant to cook my rations …. I replied by asking if Gen. Butler had finished with me …. I was commanded to follow some individual, who locked me up … while Mr. Phillips found his way home to a heartbroken family.

—Eugenia Levy Phillips, from *The Journal of Mrs. Eugenia Phillips* (Marcus 1955, 163)

An arch-secessionist and defiantly outspoken proponent of Southern rights, the Jewish-American Eugenia Levy Phillips is best known for her refusal to kowtow to Union might and power. As the wife of Philip Phillips (1807–1884), a former Alabama congressman and prominent attorney in Washington, DC, Levy Phillips was well known in the nation's capital as a society hostess and as a bitterly outspoken opponent of Northern politicians and federal authority. The mother of nine children, she was twice imprisoned during the early months of the Civil War, paying a heavy price for her political allegiances and her refusal to remain quiet about them. Her journal written in 1861 to 1862 and her memoir written after the war provide not only a record of her experiences but a fascinating glimpse of New Orleans under the administration of Union Brigadier General Benjamin F. "The Beast" Butler.

Eugenia Levy was born in Charleston, South Carolina, the daughter of Jacob Levy, a prosperous businessman and railroad developer who made his fortune selling insurance. As a girl and young teenager, Eugenia received an outstanding education. She began her adult life early by marrying Philip Phillips when she was 16 years old. With her husband a leading figure in Alabama state politics from the 1830s through the early 1850s, Levy Phillips molded herself into a political wife as a young woman. Phillips was elected to Congress in 1852, but after one term in the House of Representatives, returned to the practice of law, in Washington, DC.

Once the Civil War began, Levy Phillips's fiery antagonism toward the North and her closeness to Southerners suspected of espionage made her the subject of surveillance by the federal government. In late August 1861, she was informed that she and her family were under arrest. Though kept in the dark about the nature of her purported crimes, she was imprisoned in her own home. Shortly thereafter, Levy Phillips, two of her daughters, and her sister Lina were moved to Fort Greenhow in Washington, the federal prison and home of the Confederate spy ROSE O'NEAL GREENHOW.

Banished to the South, Levy Phillips and her family settled in New Orleans where her husband hoped to reestablish his law practice. According to several sources, her resentment of her incarceration inspired her to engage for the first time in the crime of which she had been accused—espionage. On her way to New Orleans, she carried Confederate documents to Richmond.

Life in the Deep South, though satisfactory at first, did not remain calm as the Phillipses had hoped. Following three days of chaos and mob rule after New Orleans surrendered to the Union on April 29, 1862, General Butler's iron-fisted grip on the city's population kept Levy Phillips and her family at home day and night. Though she remained strictly within the confines of her own household, she was arrested once again and made to appear before Butler because laughter had been heard coming from her home as a Union funeral procession passed her house. Although most accounts maintain that she claimed her laughter sprung from her gaiety during a children's party, she states in her memoir that she told Butler, "I was in good spirits the day of the funeral," a response that intensified his rage (Marcus 1955, 187).

Butler, already fed up with the rebellious female population of New Orleans, ordered Levy Phillips to be incarcerated on Ship Island, situated off the Mississippi coast. Her prison (as she described it, a "box, or small room, fixed upright on a hill of sand") on this mosquito-infested, hot, and treeless sandbar of an island was so intolerable as to be life-threatening (Marcus 1955, 190). Deprived of water and edible food on many occasions, Levy Phillips and her Irish servant woman Phoebe (who suffered all of her employer's privations) focused all their energies on survival. After three months, with Levy Phillips's health nearly destroyed, she and Phoebe were released and they returned to her family. Soon afterward, when Levy Phillips and her husband refused to sign an oath of allegiance to the federal government, they were forced to become refugees, eventually settling in La Grange, Georgia. For the remainder of the war, Levy Phillips and her daughters were soldiers' aid volunteers and nurses to the Confederate sick and wounded. In their elder years, the Phillipses made their home in Washington, DC.

See also **General Order No. 28**

Selected Readings

Marcus, Jacob Rader, ed. "Eugenia Levy Phillips." In *Memoirs of American Jews, 1775–1865.* Volume 3. Philadelphia: The Jewish Publication Society of America. 1955. 161–196.

Rable, George. "'Missing in Action': Women of the Confederacy." In *Divided Houses: Gender and the Civil War.* Edited by Catherine Clinton and Nina Silber. New York: Oxford University Press. 1992. 134–146.

Pleasant, Mary Ellen (1814–1904)

African-American abolitionist, civil rights activist, and millionaire entrepreneur Mary Ellen Pleasant lived most of her adult life in San Francisco, California. From the Gold Rush of the early 1850s until the 1890s, Pleasant amassed a fortune by operating her businesses and investing in real estate and mineral mines. Her life story has been the subject of numerous myths and legends, so much so that her biographers have not been able to confirm many of the details of her life and work, especially those involving her birth and her life before she migrated to California.

In a brief autobiography, Pleasant stated that she was born in 1814 in Philadelphia, though this fact cannot be authenticated. According to Pleasant, her father, Louis Alexander Williams, was a native Kanakan (Hawaiian) and her mother was a free African American from Louisiana. At the end of her life, Pleasant insisted she had never been a slave, though rumors to the contrary persisted throughout her lifetime and after her death. She spent her girlhood separated from her family, working for a Quaker family on Nantucket, an island off the coast of Massachusetts. She labored as a clerk in the Hussey family's "huckster shop," a small general store. Although she learned basic reading, writing, and arithmetic while she lived with them, she never attended school.

As a young woman, Pleasant is believed to have worked for a tailor in Boston. At some point in the late 1830s or early 1840s, she married the African-American abolitionist, carpenter, and businessman James Smith. After his death, Pleasant was a wealthy woman. She married again in 1847, wedding another African-American abolitionist John James Pleasants (the "s" was later removed). Although the details of the Pleasants' marriage are not known, it seems that they shared a commitment to abolitionism and a passion for securing civil rights for African Americans. Despite their mutual interests, it appears that they lived together only sporadically.

Once Pleasant arrived in San Francisco in the early 1850s, she immediately opened several businesses, operating a number of commercial laundries while working as a housekeeper, and later, as a cook. By the late 1850s, the Pleasants were leaders in San Francisco's African-American community. Well known for her philanthropy, Pleasant donated funds to help create the 800-volume library at the San Francisco Athenaeum Institute, a club for African-American men.

California's version of the Fugitive Slave Act was passed in 1852. For the next three years until the law expired in 1855, the Pleasants and their fellow black abolitionists sheltered fugitive slaves and assisted them on their way to safe settlement. The black community also raised money to defend African Americans who had been captured and enslaved according to the provisions of this law.

Fed up with the mounting racism in California, the Pleasants left the state in 1858 to become part of an active black community in Canada West, located in what is present-day western Ontario, Canada. As members of the Chatham Vigilance Committee, they joined African-American leaders Martin Delany and MARY ANN SHADD CARY, helping fugitive slaves who had successfully completed their journey north on the Underground Railroad. While living in Canada West, the Pleasants met the white American abolitionist John Brown, who was organizing a mission intended to instigate a massive slave uprising in Virginia. Throughout her life, Pleasant maintained that she provided financial assistance to Brown for this plan, which culminated in Brown's 1859 raid on the federal arsenal at Harpers Ferry, Virginia. Although two of Brown's children concurred that a black woman gave their father a large sum of money prior to the raid, it cannot be confirmed that Pleasant was the donor. According to blacks who were living in San Francisco in the late 1850s, the money Pleasant donated to Brown had been raised among members of the African-American community in that city. Pleasant also asserted that she rode on horseback along the Roanoke River in Virginia in advance of the raid, alerting slaves that an insurrection was imminent. This claim, too, has not been substantiated (Hudson 1996, 62).

By the time the Civil War began, Pleasant had returned to San Francisco. During the war years, she worked as a domestic servant for a prominent family. The extent of her wealth at this time is not clear—did she still possess the capital she acquired in the 1850s or had she donated all her funds to John Brown when she was in Canada? In any event, the Civil War years was not an active period for her as an entrepreneur or as an investor as she appears to have focused her energies on giving assistance to escaped slaves and participating in civil rights activism. In California, African Americans were prohibited from testifying in the courts. Pleasant continued the struggle she had begun in the 1850s to repeal this law, at this time leading the initiative. In 1863, she and her abolitionist colleagues' work came to fruition when state legislators passed the Testimony Bill of 1863, which permitted blacks to testify in both civil and criminal trials.

Like HARRIET TUBMAN and SOJOURNER TRUTH, Pleasant protested discrimination and segregation on public transportation. Although a judge outlawed segregation on San Francisco's streetcars in 1864, the ruling was not enforced. Streetcar drivers still refused to stop for African Americans who wanted to board. In 1866, Pleasant sued two transit companies, one for ejecting her from a streetcar and the other for a driver's refusal to accept her as a passenger. She dropped her charges against the first company when its managers vowed to permit African Americans to ride in the future. Her suit against the latter company, the North Beach and Mission Railroad Company, dragged on for two years. In 1867, a jury awarded her $500 in punitive damages as compensation for the company's refusal to allow her to ride. By January 1868, however, the California Supreme Court ruled that the damages in the 1867 case were excessive since there was no proof of injury or other special damage (Hudson 1996, 92). Although Pleasant lost what the district court had awarded her, the case set an important precedent, confirming that African Americans had the right to equal access to public transportation.

In 1867, Pleasant became a boarding house operator in San Francisco and soon resumed her career as a real estate investor. It is also likely that she invested heavily in gold and silver mines. During this time, rumors multiplied that she operated as a madam, procuring prostitutes for her boarding house customers, an accusation that has never been proven.

In the 1870s, Pleasant reached the pinnacle of her success as an entrepreneur, with holdings amounting to at least $1 million and probably exceeding that amount many times over. It is impossible to gauge the extent of her fortune because she co-owned so much of her property and mining stock with other investors. Lengthy court battles in the 1890s against the family of her deceased white business partner Thomas Bell marked a decade in which Pleasant lost most of her capital and her property. By the turn of the century, her fortune was vastly reduced. At the time of her death in 1904, her estate was valued at approximately $10,000, a fraction of its original value.

See also **African-American Women; Businesswomen**

Selected Reading

Hudson, Lynn M. "When 'Mammy' Becomes a Millionaire: Mary Ellen Pleasant, An African-American Entrepreneur." Ph.D. dissertation. Indiana University. 1996.

Prostitutes

Prostitution flourished during the Civil War. At no other time in the nineteenth century did it increase as much or as rapidly. The rallying of large armies and the establishment of vast military camps spawned a vital sex trade, especially in the camps located near cities and large towns. Most of the women and adolescent girls who catered to soldiers were from the South, largely because most Union army encampments occupied Southern soil. Northern prostitutes traveled to the South to be near the Union army, but they were a minority. The Civil War also marked the first time that prostitution was legalized in the United States, in the cities of Nashville and Memphis, Tennessee.

Most of the women sex workers of the Civil War era were poor, white, and young, although women and girls from all races, cultures, and ages engaged in the sex trade. Little is known of the experiences of prostitutes because very few left any personal documents. What has been learned about their lives has been gleaned from court and police records, newspapers, military documents, census returns, and cemetery lists. These sources indicate that prostitutes of the North, South, and West struggled with poverty much of the time. Whether they plied their trade in brothels or wandered the streets, they were vulnerable to criminals, the violence of drunken men, the caprices of brothel madams and male owners, and the whims of police, judicial, and military authorities.

The landmark study of New York City's prostitutes, conducted in 1858 by Dr. William Sanger of the Venereal Disease Hospital on Blackwell's Island, New York, reveals that even before the war prostitution was rampant in the nation's largest city. His investigation discovered that most women were sex workers because they were poverty-stricken and needed income. Half of those he interviewed were mothers who needed to feed and clothe their children. Many were widows or women whose husbands had deserted them. Sixty-two percent were immigrants, most without skills. The average income of a New York prostitute was $10 per week, almost five times the wages of domestic servants (Clinton 1999, 12; Lowry 1994, 61). New York City's sex trade expanded during the Civil War; in the 1860s, there were almost 600 brothels (Clinton 1999, 14). City authorities did not overlook the proliferation of the illegal trade. In 1866, the police conducted 6,000 arrests related to prostitution.

Washington, DC, was a bustling center of prostitution during the war, due to the proximity of numerous Union encampments. In 1862, city records indicate that there were 450 registered brothels. A Washington newspaper claimed that there were at least 5,000 prostitutes in the city, with 2,500 more residing in neighboring George-town and Alexandria, Virginia. Richmond, Virginia, the capital of the Confederacy, experienced a similarly thriving sex trade.

According to one young man working in City Point, Virginia, for the UNITED STATES SANITARY COMMISSION toward the end of 1864, this port on the James River was the site of Union General Ulysses S. Grant's headquarters, seven military hospitals, and an enormous Union army supply depot as well as being home to "a whole city of whores." In one section of the huge military reservation, prostitutes inhabited "three parallel streets" filled with block after block of one-story wooden brothels, "all built with Army supplies." As he described it, "At pay time, the lines before these houses are appalling and men often fight each other for a place. The average charge is three dollars and on paydays some [prostitutes] make as much as $250 to $300" (quoted in Lowry 1994, 29). What this observer failed to note is that most women earned much less. Moreover, in between the soldiers' meager monthly paychecks, prostitutes had to live on much less, waiting another month until the next payday.

While officers as well as soldiers frequented prostitutes, some officers became alarmed at the toll venereal diseases were taking on their troops. Although venereal disease did not incapacitate soldiers to the extent that dysentery, typhoid, and other epidemic diseases did, syphilis and gonorrhea did disable soldiers to a significant extent. During the Civil War, Union army surgeons recorded 73,382 cases of syphilis and 109,397 cases of gonorrhea (James Jones 1985, 270). All in all, one in eleven Union soldiers was infected with a venereal disease during the war (Clinton 1999, 22). African-American troops contracted syphilis and gonorrhea less frequently than white soldiers.

Venereal disease was a particular worry of Union officers in Nashville, Tennes-see. Beginning in mid-1863, they attempted to eject prostitutes from the city. In early July 1863, the army forced Nashville's prostitutes to board the steamship *Idahoe* to be shipped North. The *Idahoe* tried to unload its passengers in Louisville, Kentucky; Cincinnati, Ohio; and in two other Kentucky riverport towns. At each stop, city offi-cials rejected the ship's female cargo. Finally, after its one-month journey, the *Idahoe* steamed its way back to Nashville where the angry, disgruntled women disembarked. At no time did the army take responsibility for the feeding or the health of its pas-sengers, leaving the captain of the ship to provide all meals and medical care.

After the *Idahoe*'s failed mission, Union Provost Marshal Lieutenant Colonel George Spalding devised another plan to ease the venereal disease problem in Nash-ville. Prostitutes were ordered to receive medical examinations and be licensed before plying their trade. According to this system of legalized prostitution, the first ever in the United States, all Nashville prostitutes were given licenses. They were obligated to appear before a surgeon once a week for medical inspection. If a woman was clear of venereal disease, she obtained a health certificate. If she was infected, she was obligated to go to a hospital. If a prostitute did not comply with these regulations, she was sent to the workhouse for 30 days. Once this program was instituted, a hospital for women with venereal diseases was organized (James Jones 1985, 273).

Nashville's system of legalized prostitution was successful, according to army officials. An unexpected consequence of the licensing program was an increase in the number of prostitutes in the city. Women welcomed the opportunity to receive medical treatment for venereal diseases. Although the system did not eliminate venereal disease, it did control it (James Jones 1985, 275). Army officers in Memphis, Tennessee, implemented a similar legalized prostitution plan in late September 1864. Unlike Nashville, Memphis prostitutes were restricted to working in brothels.

After the armies disbanded in 1865, it is not known what became of the thousands of prostitutes who catered to soldiers. Some women undoubtedly flocked to the cities where prostitution burgeoned throughout the late nineteenth century. Others likely emigrated to the West to become sex workers in the booming frontier towns. Some wartime prostitutes may have married, turned to factory work, or resorted to employment in domestic service.

See also **Immigrant Women**

Selected Readings

Clinton, Catherine. *Public Women of the Confederacy*. Milwaukee, WI: Marquette University Press. 1999.

Jones, James Boyd, Jr. "A Tale of Two Cities: The Hidden Battle Against Venereal Disease in Civil War Nashville and Memphis." *Civil War History*. 31 (3) (September 1985): 270–276.

Lowry, Thomas P. *The Story the Soldiers Wouldn't Tell: Sex in the Civil War*. Mechanicsburg, PA: Stackpole Books. 1994.

R

Ream, Vinnie (1847–1914)

Vinnie Ream achieved celebrity in 1866 as the first woman artist to be awarded a Congressional commission. Her full-length sculpture of Abraham Lincoln, creating enormous controversy in the post–Civil War era, is still on display in the U.S. Capitol Rotunda. Ever since Ream was awarded the commission, critics, scholars, and historians have debated how a young novice sculptor with no formal education in the art was chosen over a field of established, predominantly male professional sculptors. When she received the commission, Ream was a month shy of her nineteenth birthday and had only been sculpting for approximately two years.

Ream was born in Madison, Wisconsin, the daughter of a government surveyor. As a child, she lived with her family on the frontier in Missouri, Iowa, and Kansas, moving from place to place as her father's occupation required. As a young adolescent, she briefly attended Christian College in Columbia, Missouri, where she enjoyed courses in music, poetry, and painting. In 1861, due to the poor health of Ream's father, the family settled in Washington, DC, where her parents found it difficult to stay out of poverty. The following year, Ream was hired to work in the Dead Letter Office of the Post Office Department. To land the clerkship, she claimed she was older than 16, though in reality she was only 14 years of age. Earning $500 a year, her income helped improve her family's financial situation.

In 1863, Ream met Clark Mills, the acclaimed Washington sculptor, when she toured his studio in the basement of the Capitol. In her memoir, Ream asserted that on this visit, she made a clay medallion of an Indian chief's head in a period of several hours, which so stunned Mills that he agreed to take her on as a student and apprentice. During the next year, she produced busts of a number of Washington politicians who frequented Mills's studio, including one of Pennsylvania Representative Thaddeus Stevens and one of Oregon Senator James Nesmith. While working and studying in Mills's studio, Ream was befriended by scores of senators and congressmen.

Ream yearned to sculpt a bust of President Abraham Lincoln. In 1864, two congressmen approached Lincoln on her behalf but the president rejected the idea. According to Ream, when Lincoln discovered that she was a poor girl trying to support her family, he agreed to sit for her. During the last five months of Lincoln's life, Ream states that she sat with the president daily for 30 minutes while shaping a clay model bust. Although most writers accept the veracity of Ream's story, several historians have questioned it, pointing out that MARY TODD LINCOLN claimed that the young sculptor could not have met with the president as she claimed. Todd Lincoln asserted that she knew the names of all her husband's friends and regular visitors, and Ream's name was not among them. According to Todd Lincoln,

> With his life of toil, he had no opportunities and far less inclination, to cultivate the acquaintance of any save those who were compelled to be with him daily in saving our great nation from the hands of its enemies. (quoted in Prioli 1989, 4)

One historian suggests that Ream's bust of Lincoln may have been sculpted from her study of Clark Mills's life mask of the president, which he crafted in February 1865. The truth may never be known. In any case, Ream's bust of Lincoln was well received and looked upon with favor by many in Washington.

In the early months of 1866, the U.S. Congress established a $10,000 commission to be paid to the chosen sculptor of a full-length statue of Lincoln. Nineteen sculptors applied for the job, including Clark Mills and the highly acclaimed woman sculptor Harriet Hosmer. Ream submitted her bust of Lincoln to the competition. The nation's politicians stood firmly behind the selection of Ream and voiced their support in a petition presented to Congress. Among the names signing the petition were President Andrew Johnson, the members of his Cabinet, 31 senators, 110 representatives, and 31 other well-known national personalities (Jacob 2000, 108).

Representative Thaddeus Stevens proposed a resolution in the House to offer the commission to Ream, which passed with ease. Although many in the Senate could not be persuaded to endorse her, the measure was accepted and Ream became the recipient of the commission.

As soon as the news became public, the press made Ream a national celebrity. Newspaper reports delighted in emphasizing Ream's modest upbringing in the West, comparing it to Lincoln's humble frontier background. Not all journalists were captivated by Ream. Women's rights advocates questioned her selection, noting that the professionally trained, internationally heralded Harriet Hosmer was passed over. Some women journalists suggested that Ream was chosen not so much for her skill as her youth, beauty, and charm. In a press commentary, journalist JANE GREY SWISSHELM observed that Ream

> is a young girl of about twenty who has been studying her art for a few months, never made a statue, has some plaster busts on exhibition … has a pretty face, long dark curls and plenty of them …. [She] sees members [of Congress] at their lodgings or in the reception room at the Capitol, urges her claims fluently and confidently, sits in the galleries in a conspicuous position and in her most bewitching dress. (quoted in Stathis and Roderick 1976, 47)

Despite the deluge of criticism, Ream set to work in the studio that had been Clark Mills's workplace in the Capitol. When the Lincoln statue was completed in plaster, Ream sent it in 1869 to Rome where she sculpted it in white Carrara marble.

In late 1870, Ream returned with the finished sculpture to Washington. The press was wildly enthusiastic about the statue at its presentation in the Capitol Rotunda in January 1871. Once again, a number of male and female journalists and art critics panned it. Hiram Powers, perhaps the most noteworthy of U.S. sculptors, declared that Ream possessed "no more talent for art than the carver of weeping willows on a tombstone" (quoted in Jacob 2000, 110).

Ream used all of her political influence to land another federal commission in 1875, when she was selected from a large group of artists to sculpt a statue of Admiral David G. Farragut, the brilliant naval commander of the Civil War. While working on this monumental bronze statue, she married Lieutenant Richard Hoxie in 1878. Following the unveiling of the Farragut statue, she did not work again as a sculptor until 1906, when at the age of 59, she accepted a commission to sculpt a statue of Iowa Governor Samuel Kirkwood. She suffered from kidney disease late in life and died in 1914 in Washington, DC, after completing a plaster model of her final work, a statue of the Cherokee leader Sequoyah.

See also **Artists**

Selected Readings

Jacob, Kathryn Allamong. "Vinnie Ream." *Smithsonian*. 31 (5) (August 2000): 104–115.

Prioli, Carmine A. " 'Wonder Girl from the West': Vinnie Ream and the Congressional Statue of Abraham Lincoln." *Journal of American Culture*. 12 (Winter 1989): 1–20.

Refugees

It had been decided that we must go if the army retreated, and so I sadly went about preparing to take my flight …. I got a chest packed with the house linen and winter clothes and the silver, rolled up a few carpets and waited …. And thus I left my pleasant home, to see it never again. Heavy-hearted I was, for I knew nothing of what was before me, and I felt that I had let go the only hold I had on anything.

—Cornelia Peake McDonald, Winchester, Virginia,
July 1863 (McDonald 1992, 163,165)

Throughout the Civil War, Southern men, women, and children of all classes abandoned their homes to avoid facing the INVASION AND OCCUPATION of Northern armies. Wealthy slaveholders fled their plantations with their slaves, hoping to protect their labor force from seizure by Union soldiers. Many refugees departed quickly and took few possessions, convinced that they were leaving for only a brief time. Others had the time to carefully prepare their departures. Depending on the transportation that could be arranged, those about to flee packed as much as they could carry, including kitchenware, bedding, clothing, furniture, and treasured mementos. In the majority of cases, once refugees left their properties, they did not return for months or years, and often never occupied their homes again.

Not all Southerners became refugees. Many women determinedly remained at home unless they were forcibly removed by Union troops. Yeoman farm wives were among those who were reluctant to leave their properties, primarily because they had no money or resources other than what was invested in their land, crops, and livestock. Landless poor whites and African Americans were transient throughout the war, particularly from 1864 on. Often forced to leave their home communities by the lack of food, they took to the road in search of work, charitable aid, and sustenance.

As the war progressed, fewer and fewer men were available to accompany women when they fled their homes. The absence of men compounded the difficulties of middle- and upper-class women refugees. Prior to the war, propriety dictated that "respectable" Southern women be accompanied by a male relative or protector whenever venturing outside of the confines of their property. Many middle- and most upper-class women had never traveled on their own before the war, not even to church or to a social function within their own neighborhoods. (Poor white women, urban working women, and free African-American women in the South suffered no such restrictions.)

By 1862 and 1863, more middle- and upper-class women were forced to overcome this handicap. For the first time, they made their own travel arrangements and fled alone or with their children, female relatives, and one or more trusted slaves to head for safety at the home of a relative or to a large city or town (Cashin 1996, 32–33).

Safety in the Confederacy proved to be elusive for many refugees. Travel was difficult and dangerous. Train derailments were commonplace and the overcrowded trains were unreliable to an extreme. On the road, groups of Confederate or Union soldiers as well as bands of guerrillas were apt to impress from refugees food, horses, wagons, carts, and household goods.

Once safely delivered in a town or city, refugees without relatives to shelter them never knew how they would be received. Early in the war, many Southerners resented refugees, especially those of the slaveholding aristocracy, believing that the upper classes were foolish to leave their homes and wrong to foist themselves on the charity of others. Although some communities were generous to all newcomers, others regarded them suspiciously, and made it difficult for them to integrate successfully.

Women who escaped to the largest cities found that the surge in refugee populations made habitable, vermin-free rooms and dwellings nearly impossible to find. The inflation of Confederate currency quickly drained refugees' financial resources, reducing many to poverty. Women, whatever their social class, sought work as teachers, government workers, seamstresses, ordnance workers, and domestics.

Once a refuge was found, it was rarely permanent. SARAH MORGAN faced the necessity of yet another move in late March 1865, when food became so scarce in Clinton, Louisiana, that her mother's health was threatened. The only dwelling available was her Unionist half-brother's home in Union-occupied New Orleans, a prospect the pro-Confederate Morgan would not have considered had she any alternative. As was true for Morgan, ensuring the immediate survival of family members dominated refugee women's decision-making. In her diary, Morgan reflected,

"To be or not to be; that is the question," Whether 'tis nobler in the Confederacy to suffer the pangs of unappeasable hunger and never ending trouble, or to take passage to a Yankee port, and there remaining, end them .... But to go to New Orleans; to live surrounded by Yankees; to cease singing Dixie; to be obliged to keep your sentiments to yourself .... Even if I did not go crazy, I would grow so restless, homesick and miserable, that I would pray for even Clinton again. (Dawson 1991, 449–450)

The Confederate government did little to assist refugee families despite the impassioned letters that women wrote to officials. Although Confederate President Jefferson Davis was made aware of the refugee crisis at various points throughout the war, he did not consider it a problem serious enough to warrant the attention of the already-overwhelmed national government. Several state governments made attempts to address the needs of refugees, but the agencies they established and the measures passed by the state legislatures often came too late and were too limited in scope to adequately relieve the suffering. Most of the aid that benefited refugees originated from private sources, but as generous as some communities, churches, and individuals were, the amount of private charity was inadequate to meet the enormity of the need.

Beginning in late 1864, the entire South was in motion. Thousands more displaced women, their children, and elderly relatives took to the road seeking food, safety, and shelter. Starving poor white and African-American women and children as well as destitute yeoman farm families wandered from town to town, gathering scattered corn kernels and greens from the fields. When no food could be found, they resorted to begging and stealing. Not all refugees survived. Many perished from starvation and disease in the final months of the war and the remainder of 1865.

Once the war was over, those refugees who were physically able and who possessed the means struggled to return to their home communities. Many found their former homes uninhabitable and faced finding temporary shelter once more.

Selected Readings

Cashin, Joan E. "Into the Trackless Wilderness: The Refugee Experience in the Civil War." In *A Woman's War: Southern Women, Civil War, and the Confederate Legacy.* Edited by Edward D. C. Campbell, Jr., and Kym S. Rice. Richmond and Charlottesville: The Museum of the Confederacy and the University Press of Virginia. 1996.

Massey, Mary Elizabeth. *Refugee Life in the Confederacy.* Baton Rouge: Louisiana State University Press. 1964.

Rable, George C. *Civil Wars: Women and the Crisis of Southern Nationalism.* Urbana: University of Illinois Press. 1989.

Religion

In both the North and South, religion was a predominant focus of men's and women's lives during the Civil War. Even before the heightened religious fervor of the war years, religious participation had been on the increase in the United States. From 1800 to 1850, the numbers of church members increased from one in fifteen Americans to one in seven (Paludan 1988, 339). The sectional conflict of the mid- to late 1850s and the hostilities of the war inspired many more women and men to actively practice religion. At this time, the overwhelming majority of Americans considered themselves Protestant. Of the many Protestant denominations active in the United States at this time, the Methodists had the largest membership, counting nearly 1.5 million congregants in the North alone. In urban areas, Roman Catholicism was widely practiced as the numbers of European immigrants increased. Immigration also boosted the membership of Jewish synagogues.

The war brought enormous change to the religious practices of African Americans in the South. With emancipation, the freedmen and women flocked to form their own Protestant churches, where they worshiped freely and openly, in contrast to the past when, as slaves, their only options were to attend white churches or to hold clandestine religious meetings in the slave quarters.

Throughout the nineteenth century, the American public perceived women to be innately more religious than men. Being pious and being an active church member was viewed as being an important part of a woman's natural role. Women attended church and became church members in greater numbers than men and were also the more active church fund-raisers. Although involvement in female church charity organizations brought women out of their homes, the practice was widely accepted as a part of women's domestic sphere. Despite women's numbers and their contributions to religious life in the United States, they possessed little decision-making power in their congregations as men formed the clergy and controlled the lay leadership.

Although it would be many decades before women entered the ministry in sizable numbers, two women were ordained in the mid-nineteenth century. Antoinette Brown Blackwell, an Oberlin College graduate, is often credited as the first woman minister in the United States. She was ordained as the minister of a Congregational church in Wayne County, New York, in 1853. In 1863, Olympia Brown of Michigan became the first woman to be ordained by the leadership of a recognized denomination—in this case, Universalism. She served her first parish ministry in Weymouth, Massachusetts. Both women were women's rights activists.

Beginning in the Civil War era, women for the first time served as independent foreign missionaries. In the early to mid-nineteenth century, the wives of male missionaries accompanied and helped their husbands in the foreign missions, frequently working with native women and children. In 1861, the Woman's Union Missionary Society of America for Heathen Lands was established, sending the first unmarried women missionaries abroad.

Women's diaries and letters are a testament to the depth of their religious faith, the role religion played in their lives during wartime, and the intensity of their personal relationships with their God. Most of the surviving women's Civil War diaries contain the voices of white Protestant elite and middle-class women. Few personal documents delineate how the war affected non-Protestant women's religious experiences.

From the outset of the war, ministers of both the North and South reassured their congregations that God fully supported their nation's cause and bestowed His blessings on their respective militaries. Northern and Southern ministers' sermons consistently blended religion and politics, which encouraged many women to become more politically aware. In desperate times, as in the South during the INVASION AND OCCUPATION of Union troops, ministers dispensed hope and comfort to exhausted, war-weary women and men, proclaiming that God favored the Confederacy and would not abandon them. In her diary, Lucy Rebecca Buck of northern Virginia, living in the midst of Union occupation in the spring of 1862, revealed several occasions when her minister's sermons gave her hope.

> Mr. Berry's sermon was such a good one—the subject, the contest between David [the Confederacy] and Goliath [the Union], in which he so plainly proved the superiority of the physically weak, who rely upon a Higher power, to the might of the strong, who confide entirely in their own strength. It was so comforting. (Buck 1997, 39)

As the war wore on in the South, many churches stopped holding services as clergymen enlisted or served as chaplains in the military. The Confederate impressment and the Union seizure of Southern horses and carriages kept many churchgoers at home on Sundays. In response, women sometimes organized their own prayer services in their homes. They also relied increasingly on their Bibles for religious inspiration and their diaries for communications with God.

Northern women did not suffer the interruptions in organized religious services as Southern women did. The hardships of war inspired many Northern women to become members of their churches. In her diary, Margaret Vedder Holdredge of Berlin, Wisconsin, repeatedly wrote of her loneliness during her husband's absence. On July 1, 1865, she committed herself to her religious faith by becoming a member of the Presbyterian Church, an action that she suspects her husband would not endorse.

This has been a very pleasant day and doubly so to me for I feel I have done right in confessing Christ. Oh I should be so happy if Eliza and Mary had joined with me and my dear husband, if he was only a Christian …. I hope and pray I shall never forget my duty before God. (quoted in Bunkers 2001, 170)

During the war years, Ann Lewis Hardeman of Mississippi, like many Northern and Southern women, used her diary to record her special prayers to God. In May 1861, she prays for two of her nephews who have enlisted in the Confederate military.

Our cause is a just & Holy one—& God will protect the right—O that they [her nephews] may ever be the objects of *His Peculiar care*—& while our aching hearts are sending up prayers for them … may they be sustained by that grace which will enable them to be true to themselves …. God help me for Christs sake. (O'Brien 1993, 332)

In times of trial and desperation, women's faith in God helped them to endure overwhelming hardships and grief. Lucy Breckinridge of Grove Hill, Virginia, was devastated to learn that a beau had been wounded and was not expected to live.

… I won't tell of those hours of wicked despair! I will tell how when I opened my Bible that night, my eyes rested on the scene of Christ's agony in Gethsemane, when he prayed, saying, … "not my will but Thine be done". Then how a feeling of hope and comfort came over me, and I used that same prayer, and God in His infinite mercy heard me. (Breckinridge 1979, 24)

Cornelia Peake McDonald of northern Virginia found that her journal tracked her descent into despair and her struggle to regain hope. By 1865, she was worn out from her three-year battle to scrounge food to keep her seven children from starvation. "I felt so weak and helpless and every thing seemed so dark," she wrote, "that for a time …I felt that God had forsaken us, and I wished, oh! I wished that He would at one blow sweep me and mine from the earth." After hours of lying prostrate, unable to move, she noted that "the remembrance of the goodness my God had shown me in the former dark hours I had passed through" imbued her with the resolve to continue (McDonald 1992, 242).

When Harriet Person Perry of east Texas lost her beloved husband in the Red River Campaign in 1864, she wrote a eulogy for him in which she asserted her conviction that the afterlife offered a joyous compensation for the agonies of war.

… it is a consolation to them [her husband's family and friends] which they would not barter for all the fading horrors of the world, to know that he died a christian, that the toil, the privations and hardships of a soldier's life are now exchanged for the splendors and glories of a brighter world—the roar of cannon and clash of arms for the songs and shouts of the New Jerusalem. (Perry 2000, 244)

Emilie Riley McKinney of Mississippi clung to her faith in God during the Union's siege on Vicksburg, Mississippi. "Oh! may we have strength and purpose to outlive these times," she wrote in May 1863. "If Vicksburg stands we can and will endure anything. But I know God will not desert us. He will not deliver us over into the hands of our enemies" (McKinley 2001, 13–14). Yet Vicksburg did not stand. By July 1863, Union soldiers occupied the region. In times of devastating defeat, when women put all their trust in God to protect them and were not protected, they had to struggle to hold on to their faith. Two months after the defeat of the Confederacy in June 1865, the once devout Grace Elmore of Columbia, South Carolina, described how she was tempted to turn away from God.

> Our lot darkens every day .... Sometimes I feel so wicked, so rebellious against God, so doubtful of his mercy .... But as day by day only increases our care, as under the rule of our *conquerors* evil after evil unfolds itself ... the mind will rise and question ... the goodness, the mercy of it's [sic] maker. (Elmore 1997, 123)

Like most Southern women, despite defeat, the death of loved ones, the loss of property, the depredations of the Union army, and the loss of a way of life, Catherine Devereux Edmondston's faith in God was unshaken. The wife of a plantation owner in North Carolina, she thanked God for the few blessings remaining. Faith in God helped women to face the harsh realities of the postwar Reconstruction era in the South.

> So ends this terrible year of 1865! ... It has brought us untold misery, unhappiness, care, & anxiety, but God has mercifully preserved us ... & spared us much .... Praised be His name for the blessing He has left us & may we be enabled to see His hand in all His future dealings with us! (Edmondston 1979, 725)

See also **Diaries**

Selected Readings

Faust, Drew Gilpin. *Mothers of Invention: Women of the Slaveholding South in the American Civil War.* New York: Vintage Books. 1997.
Miller, Randall M., Harry S. Stout, and Charles Reagan Wilson, eds. *Religion and the American Civil War.* New York: Oxford University Press. 1998.

Remond, Sarah Parker (1826–1894)

Let no diplomacy of statesmen, no intimidation of slaveholders, no scarcity of cotton, no fear of slave insurrections, prevent the people of Great Britain from maintaining their position as the friend of the oppressed negro, which they deservedly occupied previous to the disastrous civil war.

—Sarah Parker Remond, lecture delivered in London, England, 1862 (Remond 1942, 218)

Thousands of miles from the United States, the African-American abolitionist Sarah Parker Remond spent the Civil War years working to eradicate slavery and to ensure the defeat of the Confederacy. Her abolitionist speeches, delivered throughout England, Scotland, and Ireland, helped to awaken the British public to the evils of slavery in the United States. As Confederate agents and British pro-Confederate sympathizers struggled to influence the British government to recognize the Confederacy as an independent government, Remond and other Northern abolitionists just as urgently tried to persuade middle- and working-class British men and women to support the Union and to oppose slavery in the United States. Her oratory, and that of her fellow abolitionists—both American and British—helped to sway public opinion to support the Union.

Born in Massachusetts, Sarah Parker Remond was a member of a distinguished, well-to-do, free African-American family that was active in the abolitionist movement. The Remond home was an important gathering place for black and white abolitionist leaders. At a young age, Sarah joined the Remond women in becoming a member of the Salem Female Anti-Slavery Society. She later joined both the Essex County Anti-Slavery Society and the Massachusetts Anti-Slavery Society. Her older brother Charles Lenox Remond, a celebrated abolitionist orator, was an important mentor for her as she grew to maturity and aspired to her own career in the movement.

Even though Massachusetts was one of the least restrictive states as far as racially discriminatory practices and policies were concerned, African Americans still experienced limitations of their freedoms. Remond protested racial discrimination and segregation in Massachusetts, and in 1853, sued the managers of the Howard Athenaeum in Boston for the injury she received when she was removed from the whites-only seating section at an operatic performance she was attending.

In 1856, she officially launched her career as an abolitionist orator when she toured New York State with her brother Charles and a troupe of American Anti-Slavery Society (AASS) abolitionists led by SUSAN B. ANTHONY, the organization's general agent for the state of New York. Although the experience caused Remond to gain in strength and poise as a speaker, she found that she did not grow accustomed to the racial prejudice and discrimination she encountered wherever they traveled. Following Charles's successful lecture tour of England in the late 1850s, Sarah decided to brave European audiences herself, but as eager as she was to try life abroad, she feared the reception she would receive as a black woman who dared to raise her voice in public.

Early in January 1859, Remond arrived in Liverpool, England, and immediately began educating the British people about slavery in the United States. From her first public appearance, audiences thronged to hear her, partly out of curiosity to see an African-American woman lecture. In her speeches, Remond concentrated on making the institution of slavery a living reality for her listeners who understood slavery only in the abstract. When speaking to gatherings of women, Remond described the sufferings of female slaves. She especially emphasized the ways in which slaveholders destroyed families and ruptured the bonds between mothers and their children. In addition, she boldly exposed a fact of enslaved women's lives that she knew would be of keen interest to women—the widespread sexual exploitation of female slaves by white men, a subject Remond turned to again and again to rouse women to violent opposition against slavery.

> If English women and English wives knew the unspeakable horrors to which their sex were exposed on southern plantations, they would freight every westward gale with the voice of their moral indignation, and demand for the black woman the protection and rights enjoyed by the white. (Quoted in Bogin 1974, 139)

After more than a year on the lecture circuit, Remond studied at the Bedford College for Ladies in London. In addition to lecturing, she was a member of the Executive Committee of the Ladies London Emancipation Society, which supported the newly freed slaves in the United States. She also wrote the pamphlet *The Negroes and Anglo-Africans as Freedmen and Soldiers*.

Life abroad so appealed to Remond that she did not return to the United States until after the Civil War, and then she remained only briefly. During this time, she cooperated with other abolitionists to secure equal rights for African Americans. By 1867, Remond had returned to England, primarily because she found relief from the racial hatred that so disturbed her in the United States She ultimately settled in

Florence, Italy, where she married and studied and practiced medicine. She remained abroad for the rest of her life.

See also **Abolitionists; African-American Women**

Selected Readings

Bogin, Ruth. "Sarah Parker Remond: Black Abolitionist from Salem." *Essex Institute Historical Collections.* 110 (2) (April 1974): 120–150.

Humez, Jean McMahon. "Sarah P. Remond." In *Notable Black American Women.* Edited by Jessie Carney Smith. Detroit: Grale Research. 1992. 929–931.

Porter, Dorothy B. "Remond, Sarah Parker." In *Dictionary of American Negro Biography.* Edited by Rayford W. Logan and Michael R. Winston. New York: Norton. 1982.

Roswell Women

Until July 1864, Roswell, Georgia, was a thriving textile manufacturing town on the Chattahoochee River, 18 miles north of Atlanta. More than a thousand textile workers were employed in Roswell's factories, most of them white, native-born Southern women and girls who needed the work because the male breadwinners in their households were enlisted in the Confederate military. Although Roswell factory owners were reaping huge profits through military contracts with the Confederacy, millworkers' pay was abysmally low. Earning just $1.50 a week, the women were scarcely subsisting, considering severely inflated Confederate prices (D. Evans 1987, 38).

As Union Brigadier General William Tecumseh Sherman's forces advanced through Northern Georgia toward Atlanta, his troops invaded Roswell and burned every factory on July 6, 1864. Sherman then issued several orders that marked a radical departure from the Union military's standard treatment of Southern civilians.

I repeat my orders that you arrest [for treason] all people, male and female, connected with those factories, no matter what the clamor and let them foot it, under guard, to Marietta, whence I will send them by cars [trains] to the North .... The poor women will make a howl. Let them take their children and clothing .... We will retain them until they can reach a country where they can live in peace and security. (quoted in H. Bynum 1970, 170)

The "poor women" not only had their factory-owned homes burned to the ground and their livelihoods eliminated, but they were now forced into exile. On July 10, they traveled to Marietta, Georgia, a distance of approximately thirteen miles. Some soldiers' accounts disclose that the deportees were taken by Union soldiers on horseback while other reports state that they were transported in large wagons. In the meantime, Sherman was frustrated by subordinates who questioned his Roswell orders or asked him to clarify them. When the Virginia-born Union Brigadier General George H. Thomas told Sherman that it seemed "hard" to turn the Roswell women and children out to shift for themselves in Nashville, Tennessee (the intended rail destination), Sherman retorted, "I have ordered General Webster at Nashville to dispose of them. They will be sent to Indiana" (H. Bynum 1970, 174).

From the time that this order was entered into military documents, official records concerning the deportation of the Roswell workers cease. Yet, just as military records became silent, newspapers in Nashville; Louisville, Kentucky; and Indiana began reporting the unwelcome arrival of hundreds of Confederate refugees. While church groups and other humanitarian societies reported their trials to find the resources to feed and house the Georgia millworkers, newspaper editorials exposed the injustice of the Union military's and the federal government's decision to unload hundreds of starving rebels on their war-impoverished communities.

The historians and investigators who have attempted to track down the fate of the hundreds of women, girls, and men of Roswell have unearthed very little. More than a decade after the Union invasion of Roswell, scattered, unsubstantiated newspaper articles appeared that hinted at the destinies of a handful of Roswell women. For the most part, however, family stories, theories, and guesswork have had to substitute for historical fact. Late nineteenth- and twentieth-century writers have suggested that the Roswell women were probably too poor to travel to the South after the war and may have remained in the North, in Indiana and Ohio. Others are convinced that most Roswell survivors eventually returned to the South. As more and more historians turn their attention toward investigating the history of the civilians of the Civil War, particularly the lives of poor white Southern women and men, it is probable that more of the stories of the Roswell women and their families will be uncovered.

See also **Industrial Women; Invasion and Occupation; Sherman's March to the Sea**

Selected Readings

Bynum, Hartwell T. "Sherman's Expulsion of the Roswell Women in 1864." *Georgia Historical Quarterly.* 54 (2) (1970): 169–182.

Evans, David. "Wool, Women, and War." *Civil War Times Illustrated.* 26 (5) (1987): 38–42.

Hitt, Michael D. *Charged with Treason.* Monroe, NY: Library Research Associates. 1992.

S

Sanitary Fairs

From the fall of 1863 through 1865, the North was host to a profusion of fund-raising fairs designed to fill the coffers of the UNITED STATES SANITARY COMMISSION (USSC) and its many local branches. Although women were the principal movers and shakers of these multi-day and often multi-week events, men eagerly participated, and in many cities and towns they shared the burden of executing the events with women. These "sanitary fairs," as they were known, sold donated items of every description, provided entertainments, and operated restaurants to feed the legions of fair visitors. The sanitary fairs appeared at a time when the North was beginning to rejoice over a number of the Union army's decisive victories. By projecting a mood of hopeful celebration, the fairs motivated citizens throughout the North to contribute to the effort to achieve a final victory. The fairs were also important because they enabled Northern women to express their patriotism in the public sphere rather than the domestic arena, as had typified much of their previous war work.

For decades before the Civil War, fund-raising fairs and bazaars had been one of the most common ways for women in church benevolent and social reform organizations to raise money for charitable or for social and political causes. Female members of the antislavery societies kept their organizations solvent and their male lecturers in the field by offering annual bazaars. Hosting fairs was a socially accepted means for women to act in the public sphere. Based on this prewar precedent, during the early months of the Civil War, women naturally turned to the staging of festivals, fairs, concerts, and parties to raise money to provide goods for departing soldiers.

By the summer of 1863, the Northwestern Sanitary Commission (NSC), the Chicago-based branch of the USSC, had nearly depleted its funds by fulfilling the needs of Union soldiers at a crucial time in the war. Having already exploited nearly every traditional means of raising money, MARY ASHTON RICE LIVERMORE and Jane C. Hoge, leaders of the NSC, initiated their plans for "a grand fair, in which the whole Northwest would unite" (Livermore 1995, 410). Rice Livermore and Hoge had watched the children of Chicago enjoy treating their friends and neighbors to fairs on the grounds of their homes. Over the course of the summer, the children had raised $300 for the soldiers.

In planning a fair to be held in Chicago, Rice Livermore and Hoge set their fund-raising goal at $25,000, which would be contributed to the NSC and the USSC's central treasury. Although Chicago's city leaders and USSC male officials scoffed that the figure was unattainable, the two women went to work. Writing thousands of letters, they enlisted the assistance of the region's women, politicians, clergy, military officers, businessmen and -women, and teachers (Attie 1998, 200). Rice Livermore and Hoge then commandeered the building of huge structures to display exhibits and booths containing donated items to be sold.

On the day the fair opened, Chicago schools, city offices, courtrooms, and businesses were closed. Men, women, and children lined the city streets to observe the three-mile-long parade opening the celebrations. Regiments of marching soldiers were followed by a procession of farmers carrying cartloads of agricultural products. Other conveyances held children singing "John Brown's Body," one of the most popular Union marching tunes of the Civil War. Once participants arrived at the fair buildings, tickets to the fair sold for $.75, a price that also bought a full-course meal in the fair's restaurant.

In gathering donations for the Northwestern Fair, Livermore and Hoge did not turn down any contributor's offer of goods. Manufacturers, business owners, farmers, and city dwellers donated,

> ploughs, stoves, furnaces, millstones, nails by the hundred kegs. Wagons and carriage-springs, plate glass, and huge plates of wrought iron ... block tin, enamelled leather, hides, boxes of stationery, cases of boots, cologne by the barrel, native wine in casks, refined coal oil by the thousand gallons, a mounted howitzer, a steel

> breech-loading cannon, a steam-engine w. boiler, boatloads of rubble-stone, loads
> of hay and grain and vegetables, horse, colts, oxen. (Livermore 1995, 416)

President Abraham Lincoln contributed the original draft of his Emancipation Proclamation, which sold for $3,000.

At the end of the fair, Rice Livermore and Hoge were satisfied with the result:
they had raised nearly eighty $80,000 in net profits over the course of nearly two
weeks, more than three times their original goal (Thompson 1958, 52–53). A portion of the funds was set aside to establish the Chicago Soldiers' Home while the rest
replenished the NSC and USSC treasuries.

The success of the Chicago fair was heralded throughout the Northern press.
Soon women in other cities were planning their own versions of Chicago's extravaganza. In Cincinnati, not long after the Chicago fair, the Western Sanitary Fair raised
nearly three times the amount its predecessor had gathered. From Maine to the Midwest to California, women and men staged sanitary fairs in large and small cities, and
in towns and villages.

Despite the vast sums that sanitary fairs raised, USSC leaders were not enthusiastic about the fair mania. Louisa Schuyler of the WOMAN'S CENTRAL ASSO-
CIATION OF RELIEF in New York City, Abby May of the New England Woman's
Auxiliary Association, and other female USSC branch leaders lamented the way in
which the sanitary fair craze adversely affected women's home production for the
war effort. Women who had dutifully sewn shirts, knitted socks, and donated their
homemade jams and jellies were now devoting all their spare time to the planning
and execution of sanitary fairs. USSC male leaders watched nervously as goods in the
central supply depots disappeared and were not replaced. As a result, the USSC found
that it had to spend the dollars that the sanitary fairs raised to buy clothing and supplies for the troops. Had it not been for the spiraling inflation sweeping the North,
this would not have been as overwhelming a difficulty. Just as the USSC leaders
feared, money raised in December 1863 could not buy nearly as much by the middle
of 1864 (Thompson 1958, 65).

The sanitary fairs created other problems for the USSC. The women branch
leaders noticed that following a sanitary fair, women did not return to home production. With the newspapers full of stories of the millions raised by the fairs, women
reasoned that there was no need for them to return to their homebased work for the
troops. The public assumed that the USSC had more money than it could ever use.
In reality, much of the money raised never reached the USSC central bureau because
it was utilized by the local auxiliaries instead. These groups bought supplies for the
soldiers and sent them to the USSC for distribution. The USSC central treasury, however, was so depleted that leaders had difficulty summoning the resources they needed
to distribute the goods to the frontlines.

The commissioners of the USSC knew they were powerless to halt the sanitary fair phenomenon. In an attempt to exert some measure of control, they backed a fair that proved to be the most prosperous of all—the Metropolitan Fair held in New York City in April 1864. Unlike other sanitary fairs, this event was largely controlled by men. Women, many the wives or kin of USSC leaders, led the women's committees while prominent upper-middle-class men were selected to supervise the business aspects of the fair. From the start, the women and the men clashed, the men protesting many of the decisions made by women in their committees. Their differences persisted throughout the planning phase and into the time of the proceedings. At the opening celebration, the men refused to allow women to share the platform with them, much to the women's distress. As disgruntled as the women were, they had no redress (Attie 1998, 205).

The Metropolitan Fair's entrance fees were so expensive that only the well-off could afford to attend. The fair raised nearly $1.2 million. Philadelphia's fair, held shortly after the Metropolitan Fair, raised over a million dollars. In total, sanitary fairs throughout the North collected nearly $4.4 million (Thompson 1958, 64).

Despite the USSC's misgivings about the sanitary fairs, they were an enormous boon to Northern women. By creating and hosting fairs on their own, women, rather than men, made the decisions about the type of charity they would contribute to the war effort. Unlike their previous work for the USSC through their local SOLDIERS' AID SOCIETIES, women responded to their own directives and sponsored events that knitted their local communities together in a groundswell of patriotic goodwill.

Selected Readings

Attie, Jeanie. *Patriotic Toil: Northern Women and the American Civil War*. Ithaca, NY: Cornell University Press. 1998.

Thompson, William Y. "Sanitary Fairs of the Civil War." *Civil War History*. 4 (1) (March 1958): 51–57.

Secession

Day after tomorrow the vote of Virginia on secession will be taken, and I who so dearly loved this Union, who from my cradle was taught to revere it, now most earnestly hope that the voice of Virginia may give no uncertain sound; that she may leave it with a shout.

—Judith White McGuire, Alexandria, Virginia (McGuire 1889, 16–17)

Of all the events that galvanized elite white Southern women during the Civil War era, none so thoroughly engaged their hearts and intellects as the secession crisis of 1860 to 1861. Yet the popular image of the fervently patriotic Confederate lady who supported and nurtured the birth of the Confederacy and its armies—an ideal immortalized by secessionists and the Southern press as "Confederate Womanhood"—reflected only a portion of Southern women's responses to the crisis. Although there is ample evidence to prove that elite women fulfilled this role at various times during the secession crisis and the Civil War, most Southern women of every social class were much more ambivalent about disunion, the future of the Confederacy, and the prospect of a war fought on Southern soil than the popular ideal suggested. Even women who were strongly pro-secessionist in public trembled in private, voicing their doubts and fears to their DIARIES and in their letters to family and friends.

On December 20, 1860, South Carolina officially seceded from the Union. Once one state severed its ties to the federal government, six other states in the Deep South followed suit by the end of February 1861: Mississippi, Florida, Alabama, Georgia, Louisiana, and Texas. In the weeks following the firing on FORT SUMTER in April 1861, Virginia, Arkansas, North Carolina, and Tennessee seceded and joined the Confederate States of America. In most states, public and private debate had raged for months prior to any official action. As in South Carolina, male and female secessionists agitated the issue everywhere—in private homes, in the marketplace, at political rallies and social events, in the press, and in the state legislatures. And throughout most of the South, women were active participants in the political debate.

Although disunionists were a minority in most Southern states in the months preceding December 1860, they were extremely vocal, politically well connected, and successful in utilizing the press and in generating masses of pro-secessionist literature.

But despite the secessionists' high visibility, Southern men and women were by no means of one mind on the issue in 1859 to 1860. Many Southerners were pro-Unionist, refusing to consider disunion as a viable solution. Moderate men and women hoped that diplomacy and compromise with the federal government would settle sectional differences and quiet secessionist demands. While slaveholders generally tended to be more pro-secessionist than non-slaveholders, both groups were by no means unified in their views. An individual's stance on secession depended on a multitude of complex factors, among them, social class, extent of slaveholding and land ownership, state of residence, region and locality, and family political affiliations.

What were Southern women's responses to the secession crisis? Among women of the slaveholding planter elite, the issue came to dominate their daily lives, particularly after the raid on the federal arsenal at Harpers Ferry, Virginia, in October 1859. The militant Northern abolitionist John Brown's attack was a catalytic event that sent shockwaves throughout the South. The horrifying specter of slave insurrection (always a fear simmering below the surface of Southern society) suddenly gripped slaveowners as a terrifying reality. The raid jolted moderate men and women into considering secession as a solution to the conflicts between the North and South. Constance Cary (Harrison), at the time an impressionable girl, years later recalled the all-pervasive fear—the "dark, boding, oppressive, and altogether hateful" terror of slave revolt that transformed her once tranquil world.

> I can remember taking it to bed with me at night ... The notes of whip-poor-wills in the sweet-gum swamp near the stable, the mutterings of a distant thunder-storm, even the rustle of the night wind in the oaks that shaded my window, filled me with nameless dread. In the day-time it seemed impossible to associate suspicion with those familiar tawny or sable faces that surrounded us ... they were so guileless, so patient, so satisfied. What subtle influence was at work that should transform them into tigers thirsting for our blood? The idea was preposterous. But when evening came again ... the ghost that refused to be laid was again at one's elbow. Rusty bolts were drawn and rusty fire-arms loaded .... Peace, in short, had flown from the borders of Virginia. (Harrison 1885, 606)

Following the raid, in the fall of 1859, elite women throughout Virginia sponsored a boycott of all Northern products. In the cities and larger towns, upper- and middle-class women formed "Homespun Clubs" that encouraged women to shun Northern-made textiles in favor of spinning and weaving their own cloth at home. As men rushed to organize volunteer militias in response to the prospect of Northern aggression, women formed SOLDIERS' AID SOCIETIES to sew uniforms, shirts, and tents. They also designed and created colorful banners and flags for their local military companies to rally around.

The election of Abraham Lincoln in November 1860, and, to a greater extent, his inaugural speech on March 4, 1861, intensified secessionist sentiment. Finally, the crisis at Fort Sumter, South Carolina, on April 12 to April 14, 1861, swayed many former Unionist, moderates, and undecided men and women to view secession as an inevitability. Elite women reported that they spent hours scouring newspapers for information; engaged in heated discussions with family, neighbors, and friends; recorded their opinions in their diaries; and spent long, anxious hours waiting for the next piece of news.

Of the women diarists who articulated their reasons for favoring secession, most voiced their longing for freedom from the federal government's tyranny, coercion, and condemnation of the Southern way of life, particularly concerning slaveholding. The North, by refusing to recognize secession, rejected the freedom and sovereignty of its citizens to conduct their business affairs as they saw fit and as they had for decades. The celebrated author AUGUSTA JANE EVANS expressed a typical secessionist viewpoint in her reply to fellow author L. Virginia French of Tennessee who had requested Evans's assistance in funding a memorial dedicated to preserving the Union.

> The South asks but her *sacred constitutional rights*: these, have been grossly and persistently violated … the law of *self-preservation* is imperative; and as the thirteen States cut the chains of Great Britain to regain their birth-right—*Freedom*; so we of the South sever the galling links that bind us to a people who guided by the Demon of Fanaticism have insanely destroyed the noblest government which the accumulated wisdom of centuries has ever erected. (Evans 1941, 65)

Catherine Devereux Edmondston of North Carolina spent countless hours detailing the political developments of 1860 and 1861 in her diary. Like her South Carolina–born husband, she was an ardent secessionist, a devotion that cost her the peace she had once known in her relationships with her Unionist parents and her sister Frances. When Frances declared, "This glorious Union, broken up for the sake of a few negroes! Rather let them go than destroy the Union," Edmondston had fits. "This is to me treason against Liberty," she wrote in February 1861. "In the first place, it is not a `few negroes.' It is the country, for I should like to know who could live here were they freed?—& then the principle involved! I yeild [sic] nothing—no compromise—where my liberty, my honour, dearer than life is concerned! (Edmondston 1979, 36–37). As a planter's wife, well versed in the plantation's operation, Edmondston knew only too well that everything her husband and she owned—in fact, their entire world—would collapse without the labor of their slaves. So, too, Susan Bradford, a 14-year-old diarist in northern Florida, faithfully recorded the conflicting opinions about secession among her family members, but she emphasized that "all agree on one point, if the negroes are freed our lands will be worthless" (quoted in K. Jones 1955, 5).

A trio of women from Broward's Neck, Florida, braved the societal taboo against women involving themselves in the political sphere when they publicly endorsed secession as a means of avoiding the social consequences of abolition. In their letter of protest to the *Jacksonville Standard*, they blasted the "submissive policy" of Southern politicians in Congress that left the South and its institutions—namely slavery—at the mercy of the North: "Will the South submit to the degradation of negroes [being] afforded a place on the same footing with the former owners, to be made legislators, to sit as Judges" (quoted in Proctor 1957, 269).

Regardless of elite women's reasons for advocating secession, they flocked to witness the secession conventions throughout most of the Southern state capitals. In Tallahassee, Florida, when Susan Bradford's father told her that she would accompany him to the state convention, she was so excited that she could barely hold her pencil steady to note the event in her diary. Her father did not think her attendance improper for a young girl, declaring, "This is history in the making, she will learn more than she can get out of books, and what she hears ... she will never forget." Not only did she not forget, each day when she returned home, she recorded every detail of what transpired. Even though much of what she learned was new and confusing, she clearly articulated what all secessionists believed—that "every state had the right to withdraw from the Union, if her rights and liberty were threatened" (quoted in K. Jones 1955, 6, 8).

In Richmond, Virginia, upper-class women joined men in crowding the galleries of the state's secession convention from February through April 1861. The Virginia secessionists were particularly absorbed in the task of enlisting women supporters. In the gallery specifically set aside for "ladies," women arrived so early in the morning that the seats were all taken by 8 AM, even though the proceedings did not begin until 10:30 (Varon 1998, 155, 159). In the early weeks of the convention, women were primarily observers and private recorders of the events. By the second month, they were actively promoting their political views in both the domestic and the public spheres. They attended political meetings and rallies and studied the debates in the newspapers. The Virginia press frequently published letters and appeals contributed by pro-secessionist women.

On the day following the Virginia convention's vote for secession, Richmond broke loose. As die-hard secessionist Sallie Brock (Putnam) recalled the event, the entire city was convulsed by a jubilant excitement.

> Suddenly—almost as if by magic—the new Confederate flag was hoisted on the Capitol, and from every hill-top, and from nearly every house-top in the city, it was soon waving .... Cannons were fired, bells rang, shouts rent the air, the inhabitants rushed to and fro to discuss the joyful event. (Putnam 1996, 19–20)

ELIZABETH VAN LEW, a Richmond Unionist and abolitionist, who would soon become the Union's most accomplished woman spy, could not comprehend why so many women leapt blindly on the secession bandwagon, nor could she fathom a "community rushing gladly, unrestrainedly, eagerly, into a bloody civil war!" She wrote, "The women became its [secession's] strongest advocates, unknowing and unreflecting. 'Ah, ladies, when you see your husbands, brothers, and fathers brought home dead, you'll think of this,' was said to them on every opportunity by a loyal statesman only to fall as idle words on deaf ears" (Van Lew 1996, 29, 33).

Despite Van Lew's worst fears about the South's female population, some women noted the occasion of their state's secession with a grim recognition of the sacrifices that war and the building of a new nation would exact. When Sarah Rousseau Espey, of Cherokee County, Alabama, heard the news that a local volunteer company had left for Mobile to confront 12 Union "war-vessels," she wrote, "I feel badly, for when the war commences when is it to end and what dire consequences will not fall on us! I fear our happy days are all gone" (quoted in Rice and Campbell 1996, 74).

VARINA HOWELL DAVIS, wife of the Confederate President Jefferson Davis, shared that dread. She knew, perhaps better than any other Southern woman, the nearly impossible task that lay before Confederate leaders. In February 1861, weighed down by a sense of gathering doom, Howell Davis traveled with her children to meet Davis in Montgomery, Alabama, where he had been recently sworn in as president. She recalled in her memoir that not even a serenade performed by a Captain Dreux and his battalion could lift her spirits. "I could not command my voice to speak to him when he came on the balcony; his cheery words and the enthusiasm of his men depressed me dreadfully," she wrote. "My journey up the Alabama River to join Mr. Davis in Montgomery was a very sad one, sharing his apprehensions, and knowing our [the Confederacy's] needs to be so many, with so little hope of supplying them" (quoted in K. Jones 1955, 15).

Judith McGuire poured out her worst fears in the days following Virginia's secession: "Can it be that our country is to be carried on and on to the horrors of civil war? I pray, oh how fervently do I pray, that our heavenly Father may yet avert it. I shut my eyes and hold my breath when the thought of what may come upon us obtrudes itself" (McGuire 1889, 9).

In the ensuing weeks, months, and years, Confederate women's secessionist passions would be sorely tested by the new nation's stumblings and a war waged on their doorsteps. Yet, during the first few months of the Confederacy, a solid belief in the rightness and justice of their cause pushed them forward. As Kate Stone of Virginia explained, "We should make a stand for our rights—and a nation fighting for its own homes and liberty cannot be overwhelmed. Our Cause is just and must prevail" (Stone 1955, 18).

See **Patriotism; Women and Politics**

Selected Readings

Rable, George C. *Civil Wars: Women and the Crisis of Southern Nationalism.* Urbana: University of Illinois Press. 1989.

Varon, Elizabeth R. *We Mean to Be Counted: White Women and Politics in Antebellum Virginia.* Chapel Hill: University of North Carolina Press. 1998.

Sherman's March to the Sea

Then we learned the truth, the fearful truth! We were not threatened with a mere raiding party, it was Sherman ... and we lay in the course of his march. We were indeed paralyzed .... Like a huge octopus, he stretched out his long arms and gathered everything in, leaving only ruin and desolation behind him.

—Miss A. C. Cooper, a refugee from Atlanta living in Milledgeville, Georgia
(quoted in K. Jones 1964, 26)

"I can make this march, and make Georgia howl!" So Union Major General William Tecumseh Sherman expressed his overriding goal for the March to the Sea in November and December 1864 (quoted in Rable 1989, 172). Commanding 62,000 hardened Union troops on a path 200 miles long and 50 to 60 miles wide from Atlanta to Savannah, Georgia, Sherman was convinced that the march would sever supply lines sustaining Confederate military forces, dissect and paralyze the Deep South, and annihilate civilian strength and resistance.

Who was this "Georgia" that Sherman vowed to set a-wailing? With white Georgian men and teenage boys enlisted in the Confederate military elsewhere in the South, the overwhelming majority of the region's civilians were women, male slaves, and children. Sherman was well aware of the gender, race, and class of those who lay in his path. But as he explained his purpose in military records, "We are not only fighting hostile armies, but a hostile people, and must make old and young, rich and poor, feel the hard hand of war." Although he did not include the word "women" among the groups that must be made to experience the brunt of war, the U.S. Congress, the federal government, and Union military leaders agreed that the civilian rebellion must be crushed (Ash 1995, 51–52).

By the end of 1864, the rank and file of Union soldiers expressed a common theme in their letters home—a peculiar yet persistent conviction that white "rebel" women initiated the Civil War, goaded their menfolk to continue it, and refused to permit them to surrender. According to this theory, white Southern women of the upper classes were viewed, not as the powerless, apolitical creatures of home and hearth that Southern society portrayed them to be, but as an omnipotent power directing the course of the Confederate government and military. For the seasoned

Union soldiers who were battle-scarred, angry, and fed up with a war that seemed endless, myths about Southern women provided a perfect outlet for their frustrations (Silber 1997, 123).

Some Union marauders, believing the popular propaganda that white elite women were the instigators of this war, tried to goad women into defending the Confederate cause. Most women reported that they struggled to resist these temptations to engage with a power which could only destroy them. Others were so overcome by the Yankees' wanton cruelty that they dealt their abusers a tongue-lashing. A Miss Maxwell in Dorchester, Georgia, could stand no more when a soldier who invaded her home hollered at her, "D—n you, I don' care, if you all starve" and pushed her out the door. She is reported to have shouted back, "[I]f I was a man I'd blow out every particle of your brains; if I had a pistol I'd do it anyhow, woman as I am" (quoted in K. Jones 1964, 73).

Of course, Sherman did not specifically order his troops to traumatize Georgia's women and children, destroy their homes, or run off with every scrap of food. In fact, he was so single-mindedly focused on his military objectives, that all civilians—white and African American—were insignificant obstacles to be brushed aside in pursuit of his overall mission. Yet the wording of his orders betrays what appears to be at best a well-deliberated strategy of callous disregard for civilians, and at worst, a master plan to pulverize a region, a culture, and a people that had thus far not suffered the brutality of war.

"The army will forage liberally on the country during the march," one of Sherman's orders stated (quoted in Kennett 1995, 265). In practice, this policy dictated that Union supply wagons would not accompany Union troops as they advanced so that they could "live off the land," a military euphemism that led to the destruction of farms, livestock, smokehouses, barns, corn cribs, wells, and household pantries and larders.

Sherman's orders concerning civilians were so unspecific that most troops either liberally interpreted them or, in some areas of the march, ignored them altogether. Although he ordered foraging troops to "endeavor to leave with each family a reasonable portion for their maintenance," the task of determining a "reasonable" amount was rarely made a part of any raid (quoted in Kennett 1995, 266). As marauders or "bummers" swooped down on farms at lightning speed, each group of soldiers interpreted the definition of "reasonable portion" for themselves. In the last result, only rarely did they leave any food for civilians.

As the sole protectors of their homes and farms, white and African-American women witnessed the burning and ruin of their buildings, land, and crops; the slaughter of their family pets and livestock; and the robbery and destruction of all their food, family heirlooms, pictures, and mementos. Women's and girls' eyewitness accounts of Sherman's March starkly portray the blitzkrieg tactics of Sherman's troops as well as their own individual experiences with the enemy and the trauma of invasion. Not all Union soldiers and officers were portrayed as monsters. Although the occasional kind and respectful "gentleman" bears passing mention in some memoirs, women focused their writings on tales of brutal and scurrilous Yankees.

On November 19, 1864, Dolly Lunt Burge, a widow and wealthy slaveholder living in Covington, Georgia, related her experience of a raid on her plantation hours after it happened. On that day, she had rushed home from town before Union soldiers arrived. After giving instructions to the slaves to hide, she hurried to the gate to protect her home and her land from Union soldiers.

> But like Demons they rush in. My yards are full. To my smoke house, my Dairy, Pantry, kitchen & cellar like famished wolves they come, breaking locks & whatever is in their way. The thousand pounds of meat in my smoke house is gone in a twinkling my flour my meal, my lard, butter, eggs, pickles of various kinds .... My eighteen fat turkeys, my hens, chickens & fowls. My young pigs are shot down in my yard, & hunted as if they were the rebels themselves. (Burge 1997, 159–160)

Union troops did not only prey upon the rich. Yeoman farm women, poor white women, and free and slave African-American women lost everything, too.

For the slave men and women who formed 44 percent of Georgia's population in 1860, news of Sherman's advance brought cries of jubilation. But in his wake, the reality of their encounter often proved devastating. Their shacks and gardens were torn apart, leaving many slaves with only the clothing they wore on their backs. As one African-American woman described it, "Dey've took ebry thing I had ... . Ebry body say de Yankees goin' to free us. Like a fool I belieb 'em an' now dis what dey do. I might a-knowed it. what kin you spec fum a hog but a grunt" (quoted in Drago 1973, 371). Thousands of slaves—men, women, and children—fled the plantations to join Sherman's troops as fugitive slaves had done elsewhere in the South since the early days of the war. Though Sherman refused to enlist male slaves in his army, he used them to help destroy railroads and as builders, scouts, servants, and cooks. As long as both male and female slaves were useful and did not hamper the advance of the army, they were tolerated. As soon as they became an encumbrance, they were abandoned, sometimes tragically.

In one particularly harrowing incident, Union Brigadier General Jefferson Columbus Davis was desperate to rid his troops of slaves who were impeding his troops' escape from Confederate cavalry. As soon as his men were safely across the Ogechee and Ebenezer Creek, Davis gave the order to raise the pontoon bridges to prevent slave families from following. As they were left to the mercy of the advancing Confederate cavalry at the creek's edge, a Northern journalist reported what he witnessed: "[Confederate Major General] Wheeler's cavalry charged on them, driving them, pellmell, into the waters, and mothers and children, old and young, perished alike!" (as quoted in Drago 1973, 369–370). Of the approximately 25,000 African Americans who followed Sherman's troops—most of them women and children—fewer than 7,000 completed the journey to the sea.

How did white Georgian women react to the trauma that Sherman's March inflicted? Based on surviving eyewitness documents from both sides, most historians agree that the majority avoided personal confrontation with Union troops. One historian asserts that by the time of Sherman's March, "the spirit of most female Rebels had been broken" (Rable 1989, 175). Yet this explanation of the absence of women's resistance does not shed light on the actual experiences of women who endured the invasion. Women's diaries, letters, and memoirs reveal that besides being too terrorized, traumatized, exhausted, and malnourished to resist, they were focusing all their energies on grappling with the bare facts threatening their immediate survival. With all their food gone, what would their families eat over the coming winter? Where would they find shelter? If forced to become refugees, how would they travel and find lodging, food, and fuel? And, just as important, how would their husbands, fathers, and sons ever find them again? The spirits of Georgian women were not broken but wholly redirected toward their immediate survival. And, although their numbers were very few, some women did fight back. The following Union soldier's description of a "Secesh woman" in battle, despite its exaggeration and mythic proportions, provides evidence that not all women failed to resist.

> Another She-Devil shot her way to our breastworks with two large revolvers dealing death to all in her path. She was shot several times with no apparent effect .... When the Corporal tried to shoot her she kicked him in the face smashing it quite severely. Then she stabbed three boys and was about to decapitate a fourth when the Lieutenant killed her. (Quoted in Campbell 1996, 93)

By the end of December, Sherman's troops reached the sea and Savannah, Georgia. From there, they immediately moved north through the heartland of South Carolina to the state capital at Columbia. Lest Georgian women think that they alone had endured overwhelming hardship, one Union officer told Nora M. Canning of Louisville, Georgia, before his unit shoved off, "God pity the people of South Carolina when this army gets there, for we have orders to lay everything in ashes—not to leave a green thing in the State for man nor beast" (K. Jones 1964, 57).

See also **Diaries; Invasion and Occupation; LeConte, Emma**

Selected Readings

Jones, Katharine M. *When Sherman Came: Southern Women and the Great March*. Indianapolis: Bobbs-Merrill. 1964.

Kennett, Lee. *Marching Through Georgia: The Story of Soldiers and Civilians During Sherman's Campaign*. New York: HarperCollins. 1995.

Silber, Nina. "The Northern Myth of the Rebel Girl." In *Women of the American South: A Multicultural Reader*. Edited by Christie Anne Farnham. New York: New York University Press. 1997.

Slater, Sarah Gilbert (1843– ?)

Of all female spies of the Civil War, perhaps the one most enshrouded in mystery is Sarah Gilbert Slater. Although she did not serve as a Confederate spy and courier for more than a few months, her missions to Canada, her shadowy connection to John Wilkes Booth and other conspirators in the plot to kill President Abraham Lincoln, and her abrupt disappearance have ensured that she will remain prominent in discussions of women Civil War spies.

Sarah Antoinette Gilbert was born in Middletown, Connecticut. As the daughter of a French woman and an American father who claimed French ancestry and was a teacher of the French language, Gilbert grew up speaking French fluently. In 1858 or 1859, she moved with her father and several brothers to North Carolina. Several years later, on June 12, 1861, she married Rowan Slater, a music and dance instructor. The young couple resided together in several North Carolina towns until Rowan enlisted in the 20th North Carolina Infantry in July 1864. According to all reports, once he marched off with his regiment, he never saw his wife again.

In January 1865, Gilbert Slater arrived in Richmond, Virginia, to obtain a pass to New York City where her mother was living. Whether she encountered difficulty or somehow aroused the attention of top Confederate officials is not clear, but she eventually was permitted to make her request to Confederate Secretary of War James A. Seddon. Although it is not known for sure what caused him to employ her as a courier and spy between Richmond and Confederate officials in Canada, her command of the French language was probably a decisive factor.

Her first mission was to carry money and documents to Confederate agents in Montreal. Canadian officials were detaining some of the Confederates who had invaded St. Albans, Vermont, in October 1864. Confederate authorities hoped that the money and official records proving that the men had been executing a military operation would influence the Canadians not to turn them over to the federal government. Gilbert Slater successfully transferred the package and the Canadians did not extradite those involved in the raid on St. Albans.

Gilbert Slater was then commissioned to carry papers to Richmond in mid-February 1865. Part of her mission involved meeting the Confederate agent John Harrison Surratt in New York. He was to assist her as she passed through the lines in southern Maryland back to the Confederacy. On April 1, 1865, the day before Richmond fell to Union troops, she traveled for the last time to Canada on behalf of the Confederate government. Her mission is believed to have involved the transfer of Confederate gold from Canada to Europe.

Gilbert Slater's activities on her trip north have been in dispute ever since. A number of sources claim that she spent several nights at MARY SURRATT's (the mother of John H. Surratt) boarding house in Washington, DC. While there, she may have spoken with John Wilkes Booth, just two weeks prior to his assassination of Lincoln on April 14, 1865. During the trials of those implicated in the conspiracy to kill Lincoln, several of the accused reported Gilbert Slater's presence at Surratt's boarding house early in April 1865. Although federal authorities pursued her for several years, she was never found. No trace of her or the Confederate gold has ever come to light.

See also **Spies and Espionage**

Selected Readings

Hall, James O. "The Lady in the Veil." *The Maryland Independent*. June 25, 1975.

Markle, Donald E. *Spies and Spymasters of the Civil War*. New York: Hippocrene Books. 1994.

Varon, Elizabeth. "Slater, Sarah." In *Encyclopedia of the Confederacy*. Volume 4. Edited by Richard N. Current. New York: Simon & Schuster. 1993. 1432.

Slavery and Emancipation

Albert … says he found quite a spirit of insubordination among the negroes who supposed they were free, but they are gradually discovering a Yankee army passing through the country and telling them they are free is not sufficient to make it a fact.

—Grace Brown Elmore, Columbia, South Carolina,
March 4, 1865 (Elmore 1997, 106–107).

But the light has come the Rebles is put down and Slavry is dead God Bless the union Forever more.

—Charlotte Ann Jackson, former slave (quoted in Starobin 1994, 144)

If the Civil War altered the lives of white Southern women, it profoundly transformed the world of enslaved women. No other event had more impact on AFRICAN-AMERICAN WOMEN and men than their emancipation. Although slave women have historically been viewed as passive observers and non-participants in the struggle for freedom, recent histories have documented their active involvement in achieving their emancipation. On the plantations and in the cities and towns, enslaved women rigorously attempted to ensure the welfare of their families while exploiting opportunities to resist, undermine, and thwart slaveholders' and the Confederacy's increased exploitation of them. By the tens of thousands, CONTRABAND WOMEN refused to wait for a formal decree of emancipation or the war's end to free them, thereby creating the pressure cooker that forced the reluctant federal government to confront the issues of slavery and emancipation.

From the beginning of the war in April 1861 until its conclusion in April 1865, the institution of slavery received successive blows that weakened it and eventually caused its collapse. The Confederacy's food crisis was one of the first of these emergencies. The Northern blockade of Southern ports and severe inflation made plantation maintenance prohibitively expensive for planters causing them to reduce slave rations. As a result, enslaved men, women, and children were the first to suffer from hunger. Enslaved African Americans faced malnutrition and an increased incidence of infectious diseases as their regular diet, already deficient in nutrients, became increasingly restricted.

When the costs of corn, bacon, and molasses tripled, resulting in prices that soared to nearly ten times their 1860 costs, several rice plantation owners in South Carolina decided to limit their slaves' diets to rice alone. Although an extreme case, many slaves died, their bellies and bodies swollen with fluid, as they fell victim to the severe protein deficiency now identified as kwashiorkor. Before the war, slave men and women had caught fish, cultivated small gardens, and hunted rodents and small mammals to add protein and other nutrients to their meager diets, but wartime shortages of fishhooks, netting material, shot, and gunpowder prevented them from obtaining these food sources (Schwalm 1997, 79–80).

As enslaved men were impressed into the Confederate military (and by 1862 into the Union military) to work in hospitals and army camps, and to build fortifications and roads, slave women were forced to assume a greater share of men's labor. Although slave women had always done "men's work" on the cotton, rice, tobacco, and sugarcane plantations, they were compelled to take on an ever-increasing burden of the heavy manual labor that male slaves no longer performed.

Throughout the war, slave women and men escaped from bondage. In the first few months of the conflict, and continuing throughout the war, fugitives from coastal rice plantations in South Carolina and Georgia fled to the Sea Islands off the coast of South Carolina, which came under federal occupation late in 1861. Tens of thousands of these African-American refugees, or "contrabands" as they were known, also settled in special encampments in and around Washington, DC, and in Union-occupied territory. As Union troops occupied more and more Southern territory, thousands of slaves, especially contraband women and their families, struggled to travel to Union-occupied territory to gain Union protection.

Despite the many tens of thousands who managed to flee from their owners during the war, the majority of enslaved women and men remained on the plantations and farms. Women often opted to keep their families safe by staying put rather than risk the dangers imposed by flight through Confederate territory. In remote rural areas, slave men and women were sometimes unaware of the forces driving toward their emancipation. In more populated regions, African-American communication networks operating from plantation to plantation, or the slave "grapevine," kept slaves informed about Union troop advances, slave escapes, and means of slave resistance. In this way, African Americans were alerted to the possibilities of ensuring their own emancipation.

The Civil War also metamorphosed the labor of plantation mistresses and slaveholding yeoman farm women. As white male planters and overseers enlisted in the Confederate military, plantation mistresses and farm women were left alone to manage crops, livestock, and slave production, roles that overwhelmed many white women who had these responsibilities added on to their extensive farm duties and domestic chores. Moreover, without the physical, coercive power that white men could bring to bear, planter women were frequently unable to assert the authority necessary to force slaves to work as they had before the war. As a result, planter women were often powerless to prevent slave women and children from escaping in ever-increasing numbers.

Even when enslaved African-American women decided that it was in their best interest to stay on the plantations rather than risk escape, planter women became incensed when their servants increased their resistance to their enslavement by producing less and working less diligently at tasks both in the fields and in the planter household. As a result, farms and plantations that were already depleted of male labor experienced diminished crop yields and crop failures, all of which seriously undermined the Confederacy's ability to sustain itself.

The DIARIES and letters of female slaveholders reveal their frustration in dealing with slave women's (and slave men's) resistance. Their journal entries portray their rage at the Confederate government which refused to acknowledge their need for assistance, at their enlisted husbands and other male relatives for abandoning them, and at their slaves for refusing to save them from financial ruin. In their writings, female slaveholders discuss their fears of the future, especially their growing realization that the war was destroying their investments in their plantations and farms and threatening their way of life.

Female slaveholders responded to the crisis of the slaves' resistance in a number of ways. For some white women, the realization of their powerlessness and their inability to succeed as farm managers led them to abuse their slaves more than in the past. Planter women increasingly relied on whippings, beatings, and other violent acts in an attempt to secure cooperation and obedience. As the enslaved Martha Glover of Mexico, Missouri, attested in a letter to her soldier-husband in December 1863, "I have had nothing but trouble since you left … . They [slaveholders] abuse me because you went & say they will not care of our children & do nothing but quarrel with me all the time and beat me scandalously the day before yesterday … they do worse than they ever did & I do not know what will become of me & my poor children (quoted in Forbes 1998, 176–177).

Emily Lyles Harris, the wife of a prosperous South Carolina yeoman farmer, was successful in maintaining the farm during her husband's absence, yet she continually fought to keep the slaves on task in the fields. In her journal, she noted the changes overtaking her labor force. "[N]egroes doing nothing but eating, making fires and wearing out clothes," she wrote in a journal entry from 1863. Later that year, she made a similar complaint, writing, "I am busy cutting our winter clothing, everything is behind time and I'm tired to death with urging children and negroes to work." By 1864 and 1865, Harris explained that she decided to use violence to keep the slaves in line, a decision that underscored her loss of influence over the women and men who worked for her. As she described it, the decision was "a painful necessity that I am reduced to the use of a stick but the negroes are becoming so impudent and disrespectful that I cannot bear it" (quoted in Racine 1980, 390, 394).

Other planters' wives coped by searching for a white man—any white man—to extract labor from their slaves. In Texas, Lizzie Neblett, wife of an aspiring yeoman farmer and mother of five children, worried when her farm's cotton production was down by nearly one-half after her first season managing the crop. According to her, the decline in crop yield was the result of a summer season in which the slaves had done nothing. The following season she hired a white male neighbor to drive her slaves, a decision that backfired when the man administered a near-fatal lashing of a male field hand, in violation of her order that no cruelty other than "a whipping or two" be employed. Rather than increasing crop production, the event made her slave management more unruly and chaotic. Her efforts to operate the farm on her own only served to reinforce her belief that "trying to do a man's business" was something at which she, as a woman, could not succeed (D. Faust 1992b, 201–205).

Many white planter women coaxed and cajoled their slaves as much as they could, though they were finally forced to devote their days and sometimes their nights to laboring in the fields alongside whatever workforce they could muster. Some white women's recognition of their loss of power caused them to relinquish all hope of controlling their slaves. These women grudgingly accepted whatever assistance their servants decided they were willing to give. The white women came to realize, however ruefully, that their husbands would not return to the world they had left in their wives' safekeeping. Mary Jones, a plantation mistress in South Carolina, commented, "Their [the slaves'] condition is one of perfect anarchy and rebellion. They have placed themselves in perfect antagonism to their owners and to all government and control. We dare not predict the end of all this, if the Lord in mercy does not restrain the hearts and wills of this deluded people … . What we are to do becomes daily more and more perplexing" (quoted in Weiner 1998, 175).

As slave resistance became more and more established as an accepted way of life in many regions of the South, enslaved women found additional ways to fight back and to capitalize on the world changing around them. They harbored and fed fugitive slaves traveling to freedom. They complained more, ducked tasks or refused to complete them, talked back and swore at their female owners, and made it nearly impossible for white women to extract the labor they had previously taken for granted. In North Carolina, Mary Bell's satisfaction and pride in finally becoming a slaveholder after years of hiring slaves was diminished when she discovered that the slave she bought to ease her household burdens "was so hateful." In a letter to her husband, Bell added that the woman "had made her braggs that if we kept her a hundred years she would never do us any good and she was making her words true" (Inscoe 1992, 401).

Female slaves also joined enslaved men in plotting revenge on their owners. Although slave violence directed against slaveholders was nothing new, it had never been common, nor did it become commonplace during the war. Even so, reports of scattered incidents of murder, poisonings, assault, and other destruction directed against slaveholding men and women spread like wildfire throughout the Civil War South, heightening slaveholders' anxieties that the South would be consumed by a massive slave insurrection.

Although slave women have traditionally been viewed as non-participants in violent conspiracies against slaveholders, recent histories have provided evidence that they sometimes either participated or were responsible for leading this type of resistance. In addition to slave women's involvement in several cases of murder, a number of enslaved women also appear to have been engaged in the preparation for a slave revolt. In September 1861, in Second Creek, Adams County, Mississippi, a group of male African-American carriage drivers were found to be planning a slave uprising. During the legal proceedings following the discovery, a number of the male conspirators named eight slave women who were fully cognizant of their plans. Although the few surviving documents do not reveal the roles these women may have played, it is likely that the identified enslaved women of Second Creek were directly involved—if not in the execution of the plot, then in its planning or in their intention to provide assistance to the leading conspirators (Jordan 1993, 172, 176, 177).

In the war's final months, as Union troops swept across large regions of the South, destruction and chaos completely altered the landscape. Although the Union army freed all African Americans in their wake, the formerly enslaved women and their children suffered the same attacks on their households, food, and property as did white women of all classes. Retreating Confederate troops, bands of Confederate deserters, Union troops, and guerrillas confiscated and destroyed property indiscriminately. In the midst of this chaos, as plantations in some areas of the Confederacy burned to ruins, the recently freed women and the few remaining freed men raided their former owners' plantation households, buildings, and lands. In coastal regions of South Carolina and Georgia, once the Union troops moved on, women and men stole furniture and rugs, and tore apart fences, barns, and the interiors of planter homes. Slave women ripped apart the wood-crafted interiors of the mansions they had once labored in. Banisters, ornately carved woodwork, doors, and door frames were carted off (Schwalm 1997, 127–128). In some cases, whether in fear of their lives or from the destructiveness of the raids, white families were driven off their own land.

These sieges were interrupted when former slaveholders, Confederate soldiers, deserters, overseers, and other white men banded together to reestablish white authority over blacks. These vigilantes, or "scouts" as they were often called, retaliated by exterminating entire families of freed African Americans. Rampages of murder, rape, and mass terror were the instruments they used to reinstitute white supremacy. Former slave Susan Merritt recalled, "Lots of Negroes was killed after freedom .... Their owners had them 'bushwhacked,' shot down while they was trying to get away. You could see lots of Negroes hanging to trees ... right after freedom" (quoted in Berlin et al. 1998, 270).

Emancipation

Despite the efforts of President Abraham Lincoln and Congress to free the slaves in various regions of the nation during the war, the majority of African Americans were not free until after the war was officially over. For others, freedom came later still as plantation owners in rural western regions managed to keep their slaves ignorant of their freedom until either the U.S. army or the Freedmen's Bureau arrived to enforce the law.

Despite the dangers imposed by their new status, African-American women and men were jubilant when they first realized they were free. A former slave in Mississippi described the moment in an interview many decades later: "After de war dere was a lot of excitement .... Dey [the freedpeople] was rejoicin' and singin'. Some of 'em lookd puzzled, sorter skeered like. But dey danced and had a big jamboree." Mary Anderson, who was freed by Union soldiers in North Carolina, had a similar recollection of unbridled joy: "They [the soldiers] called the slaves, saying, 'You are free.' Slaves were whooping and laughing and acting like they were crazy. Yankee soldiers were shaking hands with the Negroes and .... They [the soldiers] busted the door to the smoke house and got all the hams. The Negroes and Yankees were cooking and eating together …. The slaves were awfully excited" (quoted in Berlin et al. 1998, 214, 234).

The freedmen and women in some cities and towns staged "jubilees." In Charleston, South Carolina, on March 29, 1865, the U.S. 21st Colored Troops (3rd South Carolina Volunteers) supported local African-American men and women in presenting a jubilee parade. Thirteen African-American girls, one representing each of the 13 original American colonies, paraded on the "Liberty Float." Black schoolchildren, artisans, soldiers, and sailors all marched together (Kennedy 1995, 26). When black Charlestonians attempted to celebrate by holding another parade on Independence Day, white lawmakers enforced a law forbidding large gatherings of African Americans on national holidays.

As the weeks and months passed, freedwomen and men discovered that their daily lives after slavery closely resembled their days while enslaved. As Southern whites struggled to regain control of the African Americans in their districts during the final weeks of the war and immediately after, they reinstituted the Black Codes, laws that had restricted the activities of African Americans before emancipation. In some places, Southern legislators did little more than make minor changes in the old body of laws known as the slave codes, simply replacing the word "slave" with "freedmen" in many of the old laws on the books.

Although there were differences in these restrictive laws from one state to the next, they shared common features. Many laws prohibited African Americans from engaging in any but the most menial occupations, forbade them to bear arms, and forced them to abide by curfews and to obtain passes to travel a distance away from their workplaces. The enforcement of arbitrary vagrancy laws harassed African Americans of all ages and hampered their ability to move freely and to work at more than one job. If they wanted to work on a plantation, they often were forced to sign contracts that required them to live in plantation owners' housing on the plantation.

Even more crushing to the freedpeople's dreams of independence and their desire to own their own farms was the refusal of white landowners to sell them property. White property owners also pressured one another to deny African Americans' requests for loans. As a result, whites ensured that the freedpeople were economically dependent on them and were forced to work for them. When white planters, who had virtually no cash flow in the first few years after the war, neglected to pay the wages they promised their black employees, these workers complained to the federal government, particularly the Freedmen's Bureau. In most cases, however, the bureau would not and often could not redress their grievances. Without recourse through the courts or through the federal government administering Reconstruction, the only option open to African Americans was to move on and find work elsewhere.

Although freedwomen would have been hard-pressed to prove quantitatively that their lives after freedom were an improvement over their lives while enslaved, they capitalized on all the new freedoms they gained. As soon as they were free, African-American women and men rushed to make their marriages legal. If not bound by a labor contract, freedwomen traveled from state to state to locate their kinfolk. African-American women were largely responsible for uniting their immediate and extended families, which resulted in a resurgence of powerful black communities. With their menfolk, they established schools without any public funding and made literacy an attainable goal for children and adults. They were no longer forced to work for an employer who broke a contract, refused the wages promised, or who abused, brutalized, or sexually exploited them.

See also **African-American Women; Agricultural Women**

Selected Readings

Berlin, Ira, Barbara J. Fields, Steven F. Miller, Joseph P. Reidy, and Leslie S. Row-
land, eds. *Free at Last: A Documentary History of Slavery, Freedom, and the
Civil War.* New York: The New Press. 1992.
Jones, Jacqueline. *Labor of Love, Labor of Sorrow: Black Women, Work, and the
Family from Slavery to the Present.* New York: Basic Books. 1985.
Rable, George C. *Civil Wars: Women and the Crisis of Southern Nationalism.*
Urbana: University of Illinois Press. 1989.

Soldiers' Aid Societies

[T]he Ladies all through the country have been heart & soul in the cause. Never was there such universal enthusiasm ... which does not evaporate in words but shows itself in *work*, real hard work, steady and constant.

—Catherine Devereux Edmondston, North Carolina,
July 8, 1861 (Edmondston 1979, 88)

Notes accompanying supply packages sent to Union soldiers: My Dear Fellow,—
Just take your ease in this dressing gown. Don't mope and have the blues, if you
are sick. Moping never cured anybody yet … . I wish I could do more for you, and
if I were a man I would come and fight with you. Woman though I am, I'd like to
help hang Jeff Davis higher than Haman …. These cookies are expressly for the sick
soldiers, and if anybody else eats them, *I hope they will choke him!*

—(Livermore 1995, 138–139)

North and South, in every state and in nearly every territory, women swept aside their
household obligations to produce uniforms, tents, food, and other necessities for the
military. Before war was even declared, women and girls from Maine to Mississippi,
and from Florida to Iowa, quickly organized themselves into soldiers' aid societies.
More women of the North and South volunteered their time and labor in these societies than in any other type of war work. In the early months of the war, and throughout 1861, white middle-class women in the North as well as elite and middle-class
women of the South moved sewing machines to churches, schools, public buildings,
and private homes to collectively produce clothing for their respective militaries. As
soon as African-American regiments were formed in late 1862 to 1863, AFRICAN-
AMERICAN WOMEN rallied to organize their own soldiers' aid societies in the
North, the West, and in Union-occupied areas of the South.

Women formed the leadership in most soldiers' aid societies, regardless of region.
They wrote their own constitutions and elected women officers who delivered patriotic inaugural speeches. These associations operated at peak efficiency early in the
war, some members working all day at least five days a week. The intensity of the labor
in Concord, Massachusetts, caused LOUISA MAY ALCOTT to remark that she had
been spending her days "sewing violently on patriotic blue shirts" (Alcott 1987, 94).
When DOROTHEA DIX, superintendent of nurses for the Union army, urgently
needed 500 bedshirts for the sick and wounded, she contacted a Boston sewing circle.
By the end of the following day, the shirts were sewn and ready to be shipped (Young
1959, 69). Such responsiveness typified the work of the societies in 1861 when patriotic zeal was at its zenith and women were motivated to do their all.

Men and boys also performed important roles in the soldiers' aid societies. Since
no sewing hands could be spared, women enlisted men to assist with other duties.
Northern men helped with the packing and shipping of supplies, machine repair, and
fund-raising. In Alabama, the larger associations formed male auxiliaries to deal with
their finances and fund-raising. Yet neither Southern nor Northern women spared
themselves the onerous task of raising money. When women could no longer supply their own materials, they went door to door or stood on street corners to request
donations from businessmen and prominent citizens. And when private funds ran out,
they petitioned their governors, mayors, city council members, church leaders, and
legislators to provide materials. All over the South and North, soldiers' aid societies
also raised money for materials and supplies by producing large-scale entertainments,

SANITARY FAIRS, and bazaars within their communities. Girls and boys between the ages of nine and sixteen also added to the societies' coffers, organizing their own children's fairs and entertainments.

Of all women's war-related labor, work in the soldiers' aid societies did not conflict with popular convictions about women's roles and the domestic confines of "women's sphere." The sewing, knitting, fund-raising, and gathering of food and medical supplies all dovetailed harmoniously with what society expected of women. Yet marching off each morning to sew all day in a public hall in the company of dozens of other women *did* signal a radical departure in the lives of many women, even those who had a history of involvement in benevolent organizations. Home work—a woman's labor for her immediate family circle—had to assume back-burner status. When suppers were late and by necessity haphazardly prepared and when clothing in need of ironing and mending piled up, husbands, children, and aging parents were forced to recognize, however ruefully, that women's labor had a political value, aside from the family.

Moreover, unlike women's antebellum charity work, their labor within the soldiers' aid societies contributed to a political mission. Within this framework, women were unquestionably inside the body politic, a position they had rarely occupied. And, for the first time, charitable labor had extensive public support. During the early months of the war, when the need for soldiers' clothing was most extreme, the press in the North and South hammered home the message that women's work in the soldiers' aid societies was invaluable to the nation and government.

Yet, as SUSAN B. ANTHONY observed with annoyance, women all too often failed to perceive the political value of their labor. She longed for women to think "not only in terms of socks, shirts, and food for soldiers or of bandages and nursing, but in terms of the traditions of freedom upon which the republic was founded" (quoted in Lutz 1959, 100). Many women, according to their letters and diaries, were more often motivated by a profound sense of connection or kinship with the soldiers who received their supplies. As Catherine Edmondston observed from her vantage point in North Carolina, "one thing struck me throughout the whole progress of the summer [1861]; the universality & eagerness with which the women entered into the struggle! They worked as many of them had never worked before … . `The Soldiers' excited an enthusiasm in the bosoms of all! Every thing must be given to them, every thing done for them" (Edmondston 1979, 87).

Contrary to what many historians have stated, the Civil War did not introduce elite Southern women or free African-American women of the South to public charitable activity. Since the early nineteenth century, elite and middle-class white women and free African-American women in the cities and large, established towns of the South had been involved in women's benevolent organizations (Varon 1998, 10, 11, 16). In Alabama, thousands of women sewed and knitted for the troops in every county of the state. By the end of 1861, 91 societies were reported to be active by the Alabama governor's office (D. Faust 1997, 24). South Carolina also had nearly a hundred associations. And in the factory city of Augusta, Georgia, 225 elite women created the Ladies' Volunteer Association. In the summer of 1861, this society completed 4,185 items of clothing for the military (Whites 1995, 56).

Despite the Northern societies' greater numbers and superior organization, they were notorious for their misperceptions of what soldiers in the field needed. Early in the war, women shipped frosted cakes, soups, roasted chickens, and fresh fruit with predictably disastrous (and leaky) results. In 1861, when the havelock craze swept across the North, many societies produced them by the boxload. Named for General Havelock, this headgear was originally used by British soldiers in India. The material attached to the rear of the cap protected the back of the neck from the scorching sun. As enthusiastic as some Northern women were for the havelock, Union soldiers did not share their excitement. Soldiers showed an uncanny ingenuity in finding imaginative, often humorous uses for the havelock, converting them into turbans, sunbonnets, nightcaps, pouches, and cleaning rags (Young 1959, 113).

By the summer of 1861, Northern industry was quickly shifting its manufacturing toward production for the war effort. Unlike the North, the Confederacy was dependent on the volunteer work of women to outfit the Confederate army. Although this need was especially acute in the early months of the war, Southern textile production never came close to adequately providing for the needs of the Confederate military or the home front. In this crisis, poor urban women played a critical role in outfitting the military. The factories of the Confederate Clothing Bureau in major Southern cities produced and cut cloth for uniforms, then distributed the piecework for working-class women to sew in their homes. Two thousand wage-earning women were thus employed in Richmond in 1862; 3,000 in Atlanta, Georgia, in 1863; and many thousands more in the various branch factories in other parts of the South (Coulter 1950, 210). As the Union blockade of Southern ports continued, preventing the importation of cloth, Southern women had to add the time-consuming chore of spinning and weaving their own homespun cotton cloth to their sewing duties.

Toward the end of 1861, soldiers' aid societies in the North and South refocused their efforts on providing supplies for the army hospitals. These groups sewed bed linens, produced lint, made bandages, and collected food and medical supplies for hospitals. Scraping lint or "Lint Picks" were a major preoccupation in many societies. Women rubbed sharp knives or pieces of glass across cotton or wool materials to produce piles of lint. Early in the war, lint was believed essential to the sanitary packing of wounds, though in reality, the use of lint introduced infection to a wound rather than preventing it (Young 1959, 69). Some societies also dedicated resources to supplying food to troops traveling through their communities by rail or on foot.

In the South, women could not possibly keep up with the military's demand for supplies. Even though some soldiers' aid societies struggled to stay afloat, many groups disbanded by the end of 1862. A larger percentage of Southern women than

Northern women had to manage their own households, plantations, and farms without any male assistance during the war. Because of the Union blockade of Southern ports and the widespread disruption in food distribution, many Southern women had to spend their waking hours scrambling to find food for their families. As the war continued, still others had to cope with the chaos caused by invasions of Union troops. All disrupted the work of Southern societies.

In the North, most soldiers' aid societies did not sustain the level of production they experienced early in the war. Although a number of powerful city organizations maintained their strength and contributions, just as many others suffered from dwindling ranks that caused them to disband. Northern societies often chose to become auxiliaries of the UNITED STATES SANITARY COMMISSION (USSC), and, to a lesser extent, the UNITED STATES CHRISTIAN COMMISSION. By becoming part of a huge bureaucratic unit, local aid societies ensured that soldiers were supplied with the items they most needed. The Confederacy never organized to this level.

The defection of Northern women from the societies may have resulted from the realization that the federal government was adequately supplying the troops without their effort. Yet some groups, like the New England Women's Auxiliary Association, part of the USSC, succeeded in keeping their 1,050 auxiliaries in Maine, New Hampshire, Vermont, and Massachusetts active, raising nearly $315,000 and $1.2 million in supplies during the war (Brockett 1867, 553).

From 1863 to 1865, as some Northern white women turned away from war work, African-American women were eagerly joining societies to meet the needs of the 186,000 soldiers in the recently mustered all-black Union regiments. Although the activities of the African-American soldiers' aid organizations were very similar to those of the white societies, African-American volunteers had a different purpose. Their sense of duty and mission arose from their conviction that their contributions would help African-American men to elevate their race through their successful war service. As Louisa Jacobs, an African-American relief organizer in Washington, DC, explained, "Their cause is our cause. By their suffering and death our recognition as a people widens" (quoted in Forbes 1998, 95).

By 1864, Southern women of all classes were struggling, and often failing, to clothe their own families, a grim contrast to the war's early weeks when materials and energies had been plentiful. In the final months of the war, Confederate soldiers were desperate for every material need. If their own womenfolk could not supply them, they went without. In February 1865, an ailing, exhausted farm woman in Edgefield, South Carolina, had to disappoint her soldier husband's request. She answered him,

> [Y]ou rote to me for close but they is no chance for me to make them the children is all naked and me not able to work and if I was able I cant get a bit of woll and thays notelling when I will be able to work again. (Soldiers' Letters Collection, South Carolina Folder, Museum of the Confederacy)

Selected Readings

Faust, Drew Gilpin. *Mothers of Invention: Women of the Slaveholding South in the American Civil War.* New York: Vintage Books. 1997.

Massey, Mary Elizabeth. *Women in the Civil War.* Lincoln: University of Nebraska Press. 1966, 1994 reprint.

Spies and Espionage

White and African-American women as well as men performed critical roles in Civil War espionage that influenced the course of military campaigns. Although the stories of a few female spy legends are well known, thousands of other Northern and Southern women are believed to have acted as spies, informants, couriers, saboteurs, and smugglers throughout the war.

In recent decades, few professionally trained historians have dedicated research attention toward investigating or authenticating tales of female Civil War spies. In large part, this area has been neglected because official and personal documents that might have substantiated the activities of agents were destroyed at the end of the war. This was particularly true in the case of Confederate spies, who feared that the federal government might prosecute them. In many cases, it is difficult or impossible to determine which facts of a spy's written account are genuine and which are false, exaggerated, or fabricated. Even when scholars have conducted extensive research, they sometimes can verify only the major events of a spy's career, not the details that she used to create a marketable memoir for publication. When Confederate spies BELLE BOYD and ROSE O'NEAL GREENHOW and Union spies PAULINE CUSHMAN and SARAH EMMA EDMONDS embellished the facts of their histories, they were conforming to the demands of a mid-nineteenth-century audience that insisted on sensationalized, exotic adventures. Although spy memoirs may present an accurate overview of an agent's activities, they cannot be relied upon to consistently represent historical fact.

During the Civil War and for decades afterward, a popular stereotype of a woman spy consisted of a young, patriotic, fair-skinned beauty racing on horseback to deliver a crucial message to a general poised to send his troops into battle. Although Boyd and several other women claimed such a history, most female spies—elderly women, girls, and middle-aged women, as well as young women—never abandoned their traditional gender roles in the course of their work, managing to intermingle their spy activities with their domestic duties. A number of unmarried women—from the white Unionist ELIZABETH VAN LEW of Richmond, Virginia, to the African-American Union scout HARRIET TUBMAN—possessed the freedom to cast aside what society expected of them to try on non-traditional behaviors (and disguises) so that they could devote themselves fully to their undercover activities.

Early in the war, women spies had a distinct advantage over their male counterparts. Union and Confederate soldiers did not expect women to participate in the dangerous, male-oriented world of espionage. Women concealed information within their petticoats and blouses or rolled it up in their hair. They smuggled goods by attaching them to their hoopskirt frames or hid them in baskets or parcels. This period of relative ease for female spies and smugglers was short-lived, however. As soon as soldiers caught on, Northern and Southern women were frequently apprehended and searched as they crossed the lines dividing Union from Confederate territory. Although male spies were often executed after being captured, women escaped this fate—at worst suffering only imprisonment or deportation to the Deep South.

Most women spies, informants, and couriers who helped supply the Confederacy's or the Union's need for information did so for a limited time. They performed their missions well and were never identified. A few spies, like Belle Boyd and Pauline Cushman, became popular celebrities once their deeds became public, usually after they were detected or released from prison. Other famous female spies became well known after the press publicized their contributions.

Female smugglers, couriers, and those suspected of espionage were imprisoned for widely varying lengths of time, whether their guilt was established or not. Others were detained on the mere suspicion that they had been informants or smugglers, or because officials presumed they would soon resume covert behaviors. Mary M. Stockton Terry of Lynchburg, Virginia, was arrested and tried before a Union military commission when she tried to return home after settling her recently deceased husband's business affairs in New York City. Charged with the crimes of blockade running (smuggling) and spying (as one official told her, she was carrying "too many goods" to be considered anything but a blockade runner), she was imprisoned in Salem and in Fitchburg, Massachusetts, for 14 months (Mary M. Stockton Terry Diary, Virginia Historical Society).

Very little is known of the experiences of African-American female spies, primarily because so few documents have been found that confirm their activities. Yet free and enslaved African-American women, posing as slaves and freed servants, respectively, risked their lives for the Union and for the future of the freedom of their people. Because thousands of fugitive slaves were traveling to safety behind Union lines or to the North, African-American agents sometimes found it easier than their white counterparts to move about undetected. Harriet Tubman's disguise as an enfeebled, old slave woman and her unflinching daring enabled her to ferret out the intelligence that led to the Union army's raids on a number of Confederate ammunition warehouse sites. MARY ELIZABETH BOWSER relayed top-secret information from the White House of the Confederacy to Union spies stationed in Richmond. Mary Louveste, a Virginia slave woman owned by a Confederate naval engineer in Norfolk, Virginia, carried information to Gideon Welles, Secretary of the Union Navy, concerning the Confederacy's rebuilding of the USS *Merrimac* into the iron-clad vessel the CSS *Virginia* (Forbes 1998, 41).

See also **Edmondson, Belle; Phillips, Eugenia Levy; Slater, Sarah Gilbert; Velazquez, Loreta Janeta**

Selected Readings

Forbes, Ella. *African American Women During the Civil War.* New York: Garland. 1998.
Leonard, Elizabeth D. *All the Daring of the Soldier: Women of the Civil War Armies.* New York: Penguin. 2001.

Stanton, Elizabeth Cady (1815–1902)

Throughout the late 1840s and 1850s, Elizabeth Cady Stanton concentrated on advancing the status of women in society. As one of the most influential leaders of the antebellum WOMEN'S RIGHTS MOVEMENT, she spearheaded the first women's rights convention at Seneca Falls, New York, in 1848, and was instrumental in achieving passage of New York's Married Women's Property Law of 1860. During the Civil War, in close partnership with the abolitionist and women's rights leader SUSAN B. ANTHONY, she helped create an organization that would draw thousands of women into the center of the nation's hottest political issue—the effort to institute a constitutional amendment that would guarantee the freedom of enslaved African Americans.

During the antebellum era, Cady Stanton emerged as a key leader of the women's rights movement, despite the fact that she seldom was able to attend women's rights conventions or meetings. Between 1842 and 1859, she gave birth to seven children. Her domestic and child-rearing responsibilities, made all the more burdensome because of her husband's constant travel, necessitated that she remain close to home. Despite this obstacle, her writings and copious correspondence with women's rights activists established her as the philosopher and visionary of the women's rights movement.

During the Civil War, Cady Stanton became more involved in the struggle to emancipate the slaves. Like a number of leading women's rights leaders, she never viewed women's struggle for equality and civil rights as being separate from that of the slaves'. All of her abolitionist activity, including her leadership of the most politically significant Northern women's organization of the war—the WOMAN'S NATIONAL LOYAL LEAGUE (WNLL)—she linked to the cause of uplifting women in society.

Elizabeth Cady was born into a wealthy, socially prominent family in Johnstown, New York. In 1833, she graduated from Emma Willard's Troy Female Seminary in Troy, New York, where she received the most comprehensive education offered to women of that era. During her young adulthood, she spent a great deal of time at the home of her mother's cousin Gerrit Smith, a well-known abolitionist and social reformer. Through her cousin, she was introduced to the abolitionist movement. Smith was an adherent of the political abolitionist James Birney, leader of the Liberty Party. Political abolitionists were committed to finding political and constitutional solutions to the problems of slavery, whereas the followers of William Lloyd Garrison (Garrisonian abolitionists) believed that "moral suasion" was the one true means of securing emancipation.

At the Smith home, Cady met and fell in love with the abolitionist orator Henry Brewster Stanton whom she married in 1840. Because political abolitionists discouraged the involvement of women in the movement, Cady Stanton did not become actively involved as Anthony and many other female Garrisonians did. Instead she turned her activism toward relieving the oppression of women in society.

In October 1859, as the nation was torn apart over John Brown's raid at Harpers Ferry, Virginia, Cady Stanton was recovering from the difficult birth of her last child. She was weak with exhaustion, depressed, and grieving the death of her father. All through the 1850s, she had looked forward to the time when her childbearing days would be over and she would be able to turn more of her attention toward her writing and her women's rights activism. With Susan B. Anthony's encouragement, Cady Stanton was on her feet by 1860 and was agitating once more for women's rights on the issues of marriage and divorce reform and women's property rights. Anthony, an American Anti-Slavery Society (AASS) leader in New York State, convinced Cady Stanton to join her troupe of abolitionist orators as they toured New York during the winter of 1861, a time that Anthony would one day refer to as "the winter of mobs."

This abolitionist tour was Cady Stanton's first, although she was by no means an inexperienced speaker. She had delivered eloquent orations before both houses of the New York State legislature, and before women's rights and antislavery conventions when free from her domestic duties. She was an accomplished, natural orator who captivated audiences—qualities that Anthony knew she needed on this tour. The AASS intended the lectures to keep the issue of immediate emancipation before the public by agitating the issue in public meetings and rallies. AASS abolitionists hoped to stir up antislavery sentiment among the public and thereby compel Lincoln to take decisive action against slavery. And rouse the public they did, creating a furor wherever they spoke.

Cady Stanton delivered speeches in Buffalo and Rochester, the first two cities on the tour. In both cities, the group encountered hostile, violent mobs. After her experience in Rochester, her husband insisted that she return home for her own safety. When the tour reached its last stop in Albany, she rejoined her colleagues and spoke there.

In August 1861, Henry Stanton was appointed deputy collector of the Customs House in New York City. Cady Stanton was thrilled with the prospect of moving to the city. She had always hated the intellectual isolation of Seneca Falls. She settled their household in Brooklyn in the spring of 1862. As far as her women's rights work was concerned, she was at loose ends. Except for Anthony, all women's rights leaders agreed that the war emergency required a cessation of women's rights agitation. Cady Stanton busied herself with typical soldiers' relief work but longed to be embroiled in national political issues.

Out of this vacuum of unaccustomed inactivity, she and Anthony conceived of a revolutionary new role for women in the Civil War—participation in the first national women's political organization. It was a goal of both Cady Stanton's and Anthony's to involve women more directly in the political affairs of the nation. The new organization—which was later named the Woman's National Loyal League (WNLL)—would work toward the abolitionist movement's most cherished goal of emancipation while simultaneously advancing women's place in the public sphere. From March 1863 until late in 1864, the WNLL fully occupied Cady Stanton as she fulfilled her roles as the "philosopher and orator as well as its president" (quoted in Hamand 1989, 45).

Cady Stanton also yearned to involve women in electoral politics. Since at least September 1862, she had believed that Lincoln and his administration's blundering proved that they were incapable of leading the nation to victory. "It needs great faith to be calm now in this sea of trouble ...," she wrote her cousin Elizabeth Smith Miller. "Out of this struggle we must come with higher ideas of liberty, the masses quickened with thought, and a rotten aristocracy [the South] crushed forever. I have no misgivings as to the result. But I do hope the rebels will sack Washington, take Lincoln, Seward, and McClellan and keep them safe in some Southern fort until we man the ship of state with those who know whither they are steering and for what purpose" (Stanton and Blatch 1922, 2: 90–91).

In the spring of 1864, Cady Stanton and Anthony decided to support the presidential campaign of John C. Frémont, the celebrated explorer of the Far West and former Union army general who emancipated the slaves in Missouri in 1861. The Stantons had always been Frémont supporters and had backed his unsuccessful Republican bid for the presidency in 1856. Cady Stanton and Anthony wanted to encourage more women to become involved in political campaigns. Cady Stanton believed that if women made a significant political contribution during the war, they would be all the more likely to gain the franchise after the war. She and Anthony wanted the WNLL to endorse Frémont, a course that other abolitionists—male and female—urged them not to do. Although they followed their friends' advice, they opted to advocate his candidacy on their own. Both women helped institute the first chapter of the Freedom and Frémont Club. Cady Stanton distributed leaflets for Frémont in her New York neighborhood but soon discovered that she could persuade few women to endorse her candidate. She and Anthony had no luck converting their fellow women reformers, most of whom were gravitating toward supporting Lincoln's reelection (Venet 1991, 131–134, 138).

Following the success of the WNLL and Congress's approval of the Thirteenth Amendment guaranteeing the freedom of all African Americans in January 1865, Cady Stanton anxiously awaited the moment when male and female abolitionists would rally together to work toward achieving the suffrage for African-American men and all women. From the beginning of the war, Cady Stanton had felt assured of this postwar eventuality. Nothing had transpired during the war to alter her conviction that woman suffrage would be enacted after the war. Women from all walks of life had volunteered their time and energies to the war effort in a multitude of areas; they had been critical to the war effort and their contributions had been recognized and lauded in every leading newspaper. Wendell Phillips mounted the podium at the first anniversary of the WNLL in May 1864 and championed woman suffrage and had spoken of the necessity of women's moral judgment in politics (Venet 1991, 135).

In the immediate postwar era, however, the tide changed quickly. By August 11, 1865, Cady Stanton was urging Anthony to leave her freedpeople's relief work in Kansas. "I have argued constantly with Phillips and the whole fraternity," Cady Stanton wrote, "but I fear one and all will favor enfranchising the negro without us. Woman's cause is in deep water ... . Come back and help. I seem to stand alone" (Stanton and Blatch 1922, 2: 105).

In the rush to deliver civil and political rights to African-American men, Wendell Phillips and the majority of Cady Stanton's and Anthony's male and female abolitionist colleagues agreed that it was best to postpone the enfranchisement of women. From Cady Stanton's and Anthony's point of view, the fight was on to salvage some vestige of the promise to enfranchise women. As Cady Stanton explained to fellow activist Martha Coffin Wright,

> We have fairly boosted the negro over our own heads, and now we had better begin to remember that self-preservation is the first law of nature. Some say, "Be still, wait, this is the negro's hour." But I believe this is the hour for everybody to do the best thing for reconstruction. A vote based on intelligence and education for black and white, man and woman—that is what we need. Martha, keep your lamp trimmed and burning, and press in through that constitutional door the moment it is opened for the admission of Sambo. (Stanton and Blatch 1922, 2: 108–109)

Historians do not agree whether Cady Stanton's reference to African-American men as "Sambo" was more an indication of her racism or an indicator of the depth of her fury at her fellow abolitionists who were willing to sweep aside the political rights of all women the moment it became politically inconvenient. From 1865 to 1869, with Anthony's close collaboration, Cady Stanton marshaled all her forces toward making woman suffrage a part of the Fourteenth and then the Fifteenth Amendments. When these tactics failed, she and Anthony formed the National Woman Suffrage Association in 1869.

See also **Abolitionists; Frémont, Jessie Benton**

Selected Readings

Griffith, Elisabeth. *In Her Own Right: The Life of Elizabeth Cady Stanton.* New York: Oxford University Press. 1984.

Venet, Wendy Hamand. *Neither Ballots Nor Bullets: Women Abolitionists and the Civil War.* Charlottesville: University Press of Virginia. 1991.

Stowe, Harriet Beecher (1811–1896)

From the early 1850s until the Emancipation Proclamation of January 1863, most of Harriet Beecher Stowe's creative energies were directed toward the abolition of slavery. As a novelist, columnist, and essayist, she strove to alert the nation to the evils of the South's "peculiar institution." Of all her writings, her novel *Uncle Tom's Cabin*, published in 1852, had the greatest and most enduring influence on the hearts and minds of the reading public. A best-seller of immense proportions, *Uncle Tom's Cabin* helped solidify Northerners' antipathy toward slavery by portraying the ways in which slaveholders robbed their slaves of their humanity. As a political writer of newspaper columns and essays, Stowe was outspoken, and often self-righteously so, without a care for the consequences. In the 1850s, she made certain that her readers understood that slavery was the all-important issue for the nation to address. A profoundly religious woman, she hammered home her conviction that the war was nothing other than a holy war to emancipate the slaves.

The seventh of nine children born to the eminent evangelical minister Lyman Beecher and his first wife, Roxana Foote, Harriet Beecher spent her youth in Litchfield, Connecticut. Her mother died when she was five years old. From that time on, her sister Catharine, 11 years her senior, acted as her most important maternal figure. Harriet started attending Litchfield Female Academy when she was eight, and soon developed a love of composition and writing. In 1824, she enrolled in her sister Catharine's school, Hartford Female Seminary, and later served as a teacher there from 1829 to 1832.

When her father accepted the presidency of Lane Theological Seminary in 1832, the Beecher family moved to Cincinnati, Ohio. Harriet became a teacher in Catharine's new school, the Western Female Academy. She also devoted herself to writing essays and stories, which were published in the *Western Monthly Magazine*. In January 1836, she married Calvin Ellis Stowe, also a New Englander, who was a professor of biblical studies at Lane. From 1836 to 1850, Beecher Stowe gave birth to seven children. Although fully occupied by her domestic duties, she persevered at her writing, and in 1843, *The Mayflower*, a collection of her stories, was published. During the remainder of the 1840s, however, motherhood and illness prevented her from making the commitment to writing that she longed for.

In 1849, Beecher Stowe's youngest child at the time, Samuel Charles, died of cholera. It was this experience that led her, a white woman, to identify with a common tragedy that slaveholders forced upon slave families—the loss of family members when they were sold. "It was at *his* dying bed, and at *his* grave ... that I learnt what a poor slave mother may feel when her child is torn away from her" (quoted in Hedrick 1994, 193).

In 1850, the Stowe family moved to Brunswick, Maine, where Calvin Stowe joined the faculty of Bowdoin College. In her new home, Beecher Stowe found that with some domestic help she could dedicate brief periods to writing. Passage of the Fugitive Slave Act in 1850 outraged antislavery Northerners as the law required the capture and return of escaped slaves. Beecher Stowe was so angered by the new law that she believed she must strike out against its injustice, but realized that as a mother with a new baby to consume her hours, her options were limited (her youngest child was born in 1850). As the months passed, and as she pored over newspaper accounts of fugitive slaves, her determination to act mounted. In a letter to her husband in December 1850, Beecher Stowe vowed that she would write something on the slaves' behalf that would make an indelible impact on the American public: "[A]s long as the baby sleeps with me nights I can't do much at any thing—but I shall *do it at last*. I shall write that thing if I live" (quoted in Hedrick 1994, 207).

With the support of her husband and her extended family, Beecher Stowe began writing *Uncle Tom's Cabin* in 1851. The novel was serialized in the antislavery newspaper the *National Era* from June 5, 1851 to April 1, 1852, and was published as a book in March 1852, at about the time the Stowes moved to Andover, Massachusetts. The story riveted the nation–North and South. Beecher Stowe's biographer attributes the power of *Uncle Tom's Cabin* to its combination of "freedom narrative" and "bondage narrative" (Hedrick 1994, 212). Beecher Stowe's slave characters Eliza and George Harris successfully escape North to Canada while the enslaved Tom is sold from a kind family to a cruel plantation owner who brutally beats and kills him.

Beecher Stowe knew nothing of slavery firsthand. Her sources were mainstream and abolitionist newspapers, published slave narratives, and the accounts of her African-American domestic servants, several of whom had direct knowledge of slavery. The novel sold 10,000 copies during its first week, and within a year's time, sold 300,000. Three months after *Uncle Tom's Cabin* was available in bookshops, Beecher Stowe had earned $10,000. No author before *Uncle Tom's Cabin* had profited as much from the publication of a single work as Beecher Stowe (Hedrick 1994, 223). In Great Britain, the novel was even more of a success, selling one-million-and-a-half copies the first year, though she did not earn any royalties from the international sales of this book.

Greatly admired in the North, Beecher Stowe was despised in the South as Southern critics condemned the book for its purportedly inaccurate presentation of slavery. The outcry was so vociferous that Beecher Stowe felt she must respond. With help from her brothers, she compiled *A Key to Uncle Tom's Cabin* (1853). This work contained a host of documents, most originating from slaveholders, that supported her presentation of slavery in the novel.

In 1853, Beecher Stowe voyaged to England to engage in what proved to be a triumphant celebrity tour. The highlight of her journey was the moment when she was presented with a petition signed by 562,448 British women from every social class. This letter, "An Affectionate and Christian Address of Many Thousands of Women of Great Britain and Ireland to Their Sisters the Women of the United States of America," urged American women to publicly denounce slavery.

Not long after Beecher Stowe returned to the United States, the nation was once again mired in political controversy. When the congressional debate concerning the pending Kansas-Nebraska Act of 1854 ensued, Beecher Stowe was horrified that the proposed law would cause slavery to proliferate throughout the territories of the United States. She immediately wrote "An Appeal to the Women of the Free States of America, On the Present Crisis in Our Country," published in the *Independent*, a leading religious newspaper of the mid-nineteenth century. In her address, she incited women to protest using the few political means available to them. She called on women to circulate petitions and arrange political lectures to educate the public. She also exhorted women to gather and pray that slavery spread no further.

Throughout the 1850s, the *Independent* published Beecher Stowe's political essays. In 1856, at the peak of the violence in Kansas, as free-state settlers battled pro-slavery forces, she wrote her second abolitionist novel in an impassioned three months. *Dred: A Tale of the Great Dismal Swamp*, the story of an attempted slave insurrection, did not resonate with the Northern public as *Uncle Tom's Cabin* did, and it did not prove to be as politically influential as she had hoped.

Following the death of her 19-year-old son Henry in 1857, Beecher Stowe's fiction veered away from antislavery subjects. Her novel *The Minister's Wooing*, published in 1859, was set in New England and reflected her religious interests. The novel was serialized in the *Atlantic Monthly* prior to publication as a book.

The Civil War broke out during a time when Beecher Stowe was in the midst of one of the most prolific periods of her career. In addition to her fiction, she continued to contribute front-page columns of political opinion to the *Independent*. Shortly after war was declared, on April 25, 1861, her essay "Getting Ready for a Gale" made it clear that despite President Lincoln's assertion that the war was being fought to preserve the Union, the war must be waged to eliminate slavery.

> We are married to this cause; we have taken it for better or worse, for richer or poorer, til death do us part. It is one part of the last struggle for liberty—the American share of the great overturning which shall precede the coming of Him whose

right it is—who shall save the poor and needy, and precious shall their blood be in his sight. (quoted in Gossett 1985, 312)

In June 1861, when most abolitionists agreed to cease their activism in the belief that antislavery agitation would divide rather than unite the North, Beecher Stowe refused to quiet her pen.

[W]e of the free states of the North will fight this battle through to the end. While there is a brick in our chimneys, a tile on our roofs, a drop of blood in our hearts, every man, woman and child of us are of one mind to give it all to this cause—for it is the cause of God and liberty—the cause of human rights and human equality. (quoted in Gossett 1985, 314)

Beecher Stowe also declared that "this is a cause to die for—and, thanks to God our young men embrace it as a bride, and are ready to die" (quoted in Gossett 1985, 312). On a personal level, however, she found the crusade's human cost dreadful to contemplate, especially when it involved the enlistment of her son Frederick.

From the beginning of the war, Beecher Stowe was bewildered by Britain's neutrality. She was even more flummoxed to learn that some British politicians wanted their government to recognize the Confederacy. This was all the more difficult for her to comprehend because Britain had a history of being more antislavery than the United States. Fearful lest Britain officially recognize the South, she reprimanded the British nation in a letter to Lord Shaftesbury in July 1861, which was published in many newspapers in England and the United States. She was condemned for the letter on both sides of the Atlantic. Her Northern abolitionist colleagues claimed that her action would only breed dissension in the North and harm the Union's mobilization for war. Beecher Stowe did not allow the criticism to steer her away from her mission. She continued to press for abolition and immediate emancipation.

In November 1862, still concerned about Britain's refusal to support the North, she began writing a reply to the "Affectionate and Christian Address" that British women promoted in 1853. Before she completed it, she traveled to Washington, DC, to visit the president, to make certain that he planned to follow through on his prior announcement that he would issue the Emancipation Proclamation on January 1, 1863. Her meeting with him assured her that she should complete her "Reply." Published in the *Atlantic Monthly* and reprinted in many British newspapers in January 1863, the fourteen-page letter reprimanded Britain for its lack of commitment to the abolition of slavery in the United States and implored British women to support the Union. In her "Reply," Beecher Stowe leaves no doubt as to why the North is sending a generation of young men into battle: "Why does not the North let the South go?" Beecher Stowe asks.

What! give up the point of emancipation for these four million slaves? Turn our backs on them, and leave them to their fate? What! leave our white brothers to run a career of oppression and robbery, that, as sure as there is a God that ruleth in the armies of heaven, will bring down a day of wrath and doom? . . .

Who among you would wish your sons to become slave-planters, slave-merchants, slave-dealers? And shall we leave our brethren to this fate? Better a generation should die on the battle-field, that their children may grow up in liberty and justice. Yes, our sons must die, their sons must die. We give ours freely; they die to redeem the very brothers that slay them; they give their blood in expiation of this great sin, begun by you in England, perpetuated by us in America, and for which God in this great day of judgment is making inquisition in blood. (Stowe 1863, 132–133)

Although the majority of British newspapers criticized her "Reply," a number validated her positions. It is not known to what extent her views influenced British public opinion, yet it is clear that following publication of her "Reply" and other writings disseminated by American men and women, the British viewpoint began to shift. Later in 1863, after lengthy debates in Parliament, the British government finally gave its official backing to the North.

While immersed in news of the war and her political writing, Beecher Stowe was busy, nearly franticly so, writing several works of fiction during the early war years. In 1861 and 1862, she was in the midst of two serialized novels—*Agnes of Sorrento*, which she began during a trip to Italy in 1860, and *The Pearl of Orr's Island*, set in Maine. *The Pearl of Orr's Island*, based in part on themes relating to Beecher Stowe's adolescence, is the story of a young girl who, as she matures, comes to realize the ways in which society restricts women's opportunities (Hedrick 1994, 297). Both novels were published in book form in 1862.

In July of 1863, Beecher Stowe's son Frederick was wounded during the Battle of GETTYSBURG when a piece of shell entered his ear. Concern about him dominated her life for many months afterward and made writing difficult. Beecher Stowe was also engrossed in the details of building a mansion in Hartford, Connecticut. By 1864, she discovered that she desperately needed a change. To prevent herself from obsessing about the horrors of war, she felt pulled toward writing comforting articles about home life. In a letter to the editor of the *Atlantic Monthly*, she explained, "It is not wise that all our literature should run in a rut cut thro our hearts & red with our blood—I feel the need of a little gentle household merriment & talk of common things ..." (quoted in Hedrick 1994, 312). The editor agreed and so began her monthly column "House and Home Papers," including articles on entertaining, household economics, servant management, cooking, the care of houseplants, the importance of modern plumbing, and other home-related subjects. In 1865, she continued writing about domestic topics in her new "Chimney Corner" series, also published in the *Atlantic Monthly*.

After the assassination of President Lincoln and the war's conclusion in April 1865, she briefly turned to politics once again, writing a long essay, "The Noble Army of Martyrs." She vented her fury over the assassination and the inhumane conditions that Union soldiers were forced to endure in Confederate prisons. She denounced Northerners who suggested that Confederate General Robert E. Lee and former Confederate President Jefferson Davis should be treated leniently when the victims of the war were either dead or suffering. Like many abolitionists, she advocated that the federal government severely punish former Confederates (Hill 1992, 270).

> There has been, on both sides of the water, much weak, ill-advised talk of mercy and magnanimity to be extended to these men, whose crimes have produced a misery so vast and incalculable …. It is no feeling of personal vengeance, but a sense of the eternal fitness of things, that makes us rejoice, when criminals, who have so outraged every sentiment of humanity, are arrested and arraigned and awarded due retribution at the bar of their country's justice. There are crimes against God and human nature which it is treason alike to God and man not to punish …. If there be those whose hearts lean to pity … [l]et them think of the thousands of fathers, mothers, wives, sisters, whose lives will be forever haunted with memories of the slow tortures in which their best and bravest were done to death. (Stowe 1865, 236)

Beecher Stowe, however, did not champion civil rights for the freedpeople as many former antislavery activists did. Once the Emancipation Proclamation of 1863 was declared, her activism on behalf of African Americans ended.

In her mid-fifties at war's end, Beecher Stowe continued to be prolific. As the lone breadwinner of her large family, she needed to keep writing. She continued writing on domestic topics, authored stories for children, published a volume of religious poetry, wrote a compilation of biographies of well-known men, and, in 1869, published a novel *Oldtown Folks*. In the 1870s, the last decade that she was fully productive, she wrote three novels set in New York—*Pink and White Tyranny*, *My Wife and I*, and *We and Our Neighbors*—and one—*Poganuc People*—based on her memories of her youth in Litchfield, Connecticut. She died in 1896 at the age of 85 in Hartford.

See also **Abolitionists; Literary Women**

Selected Readings

Hedrick, Joan D. *Harriet Beecher Stowe: A Life.* New York: Oxford University Press. 1994.

Venet, Wendy Hamand. *Neither Ballots Nor Bullets: Women Abolitionists and the Civil War.* Charlottesville: University Press of Virginia. 1991.

Surratt, Mary (c. 1823–1865)

On July 7, 1865, when Mary Surratt was hanged for her involvement in the conspiracy to assassinate President Abraham Lincoln, she became the first woman executed by the federal government. She was one of eight convicted in the conspiracy and the only woman; three men were also executed. From the time of her 1865 trial until the present day, historians have debated the circumstances of Surratt's case and the extent of her knowledge and participation in the plot to assassinate Lincoln. Her trial also revived public debate about the execution of women, a controversy that continued to erupt in the years after her death.

Mary Jenkins was born and lived almost all of her life in southern Maryland. In the 1830s, she briefly attended a Catholic girls' academy run by the Sisters of Charity in Alexandria, Virginia. At some point during her early teenage years, she converted to Catholicism. In 1840, at age 17, she married John Surratt, the owner of a grist mill, with whom she had three children. Her religious faith, though not shared by her husband, was the focus of her life. In the late 1840s, she devoted many hours to the raising of funds for the building of a Catholic church in her community.

As the Surratts grew more prosperous, John Surratt purchased farmland, several slaves, and a tavern. When hostilities erupted between the North and South during the 1850s, the Surratts were strong advocates of the Southern cause, as were most of their neighbors in southern Maryland. Prior to the war and in the first few years of the conflict, the Surratts' tavern served as a waystation for Confederate couriers traveling back and forth from Richmond, Virginia, to Northern cities and to Canada. Beginning in 1861, the Surratts' oldest son John, Jr., was a Confederate blockade runner. After her husband's death in 1862, Mary Surratt struggled with the debts he left her. At least in part because of her reduced financial circumstances, she moved to Washington, DC, in November 1864. She operated her own boarding house in the city, which soon became a meeting place for John Wilkes Booth, her son John, and others involved in a plot to abduct President Lincoln.

On April 17, three days after President Lincoln was assassinated at Ford's Theater, Mary Surratt, her daughter Anna, and two other women living in the Surratt boarding house were arrested and sent to Old Capitol Prison. John Surratt, Jr., who had traveled to Canada in March, remained there throughout his mother's trial. On

April 30, Mary was transferred to Old Arsenal Penitentiary, the site of the conspiracy trial. In all of the interrogations of Mary Surratt, she maintained her innocence and is said to have consistently, coolly, and calmly told the same story—that she knew nothing about the assassination.

It was not until the first day of the trial, May 9, 1865, that Surratt and the others learned of the charges against them. Surratt's charge stated that she did "receive, entertain, harbor, and conceal, aid and assist" John Wilkes Booth and the alleged co-conspirators "with intent to aid, abet, and assist them in the execution" of the assassination plot and in their attempts to conceal it (quoted in Trindal 1996, 146).

The testimonies of two men—Surratt's boarder Louis Weichmann and the manager of her Surrattsville tavern John Lloyd—strongly implicated her. One historian notes that the most damaging evidence against her was the testimonies of several witnesses, avowing that she had spoken privately with Booth on several occasions, including a conversation on the day of the assassination (Chamlee 1990, 439; Turner 1991, 155).

As to the legitimacy of Weichmann's and Lloyd's testimonies, both men feared being implicated in the conspiracy and were threatened during their pre-trial interrogations. According to journalist David Rankin Barbee, who dedicated decades to researching the Lincoln assassination, John Lloyd was strung up by his thumbs when he declined to incriminate Surratt. Only when he could tolerate the pain no longer did he offer damaging testimony against her (Trindal 1996, 133).

Surratt and the other seven co-defendants did not receive the benefits of a trial in the civil courts and were deprived of their civil rights during the proceedings. With President Andrew Johnson's approval, the government ordered that a military tribunal try the accused. Of the nine male military judges who tried the alleged conspirators, six were brigadier generals and three had served in the Union army. According to Judge John Bingham, the rationale for a military trial rather than a civil trial was based on the premise that the accused were enemies of the Union army and that they had committed their crimes while martial law was still in effect. Bingham declared that the war was not officially over on April 14, even though the Confederacy had formally surrendered on April 12 (Schuetz 1994, 48).

During the trial, Surratt sat next to the seven male co-defendants. She was heavily veiled and dressed entirely in black each day, despite the oppressive summer-like heat. Eyewitnesses report that she appeared calm and in control, except for the very end of the trial when she was ill and in extreme pain. Unlike the men, she was neither handcuffed nor were her ankles chained (Chamlee 1990, 215, 219).

The trial attracted a large audience, many of them women. Several newspaper journalists reported that the women in attendance subjected Surratt to a constant barrage of negative commentary. Journalist JANE GREY SWISSHELM, special correspondent to the *Pittsburgh Daily Commercial*, reported that hundreds of persons made "the most insulting remarks in her hearing" (Trindal 1996, 169). As the trial proceeded, and as the evidence increasingly appeared to incriminate her, Surratt's initially positive press coverage turned against her. The *New York Times* referred to her as the "female fiend incarnate" (Chamlee 1990, 237). Although the Northern public demanded that the accused be severely punished, this opinion did not extend to a widespread conclusion that Surratt should be executed.

Surratt's defense team focused on character and gender issues, emphasizing that she embodied the nineteenth-century cultural ideal of "True Womanhood." Defense witnesses revealed her devotion to God; her Christian, moral nature; her neighborliness; and the fact that she had offered food to Union soldiers. They argued that justice in her case ought to be based on a respect for the ideals of motherhood and womanhood in American society and thus ought to protect "the privacy of home life" from the defilation of "arrest and incarceration" (Schuetz 1994, 59).

It was expected that Surratt would be sentenced to life imprisonment. When her attorneys learned that she was to be hanged, they were stunned. They immediately applied for a writ of habeas corpus. When the court granted the writ, President Johnson suspended it, reversing the court's decision. As Johnson explained to Reverend George Butler after Surratt's execution, he pressed for her death because she "maintained the nest that hatched the egg" (Turner 1991, 175). Regarding the morality of executing women, he said that people should learn that "if women committed crimes they would be punished." If Surratt were spared, Johnson explained, "conspirators and assassins would use women as their instruments. It would be a mercy to womankind to let Mrs. Surratt suffer the penalty of her crime" (Chamlee 1990, 444).

When the evidence against Surratt is compared with the evidence condemning the three men who were executed with her, Surratt's deeds pale in comparison. All of the three men sentenced to die actively participated in the assassination conspiracy: Surratt did not. (Historians believe that it is possible that she may have played a minor role in the original abduction conspiracy.) Lewis Payne severely wounded Secretary of State William H. Seward in an attempt to assassinate him. George Atzerodt planned to kill Vice President Johnson, but failed due to drunkenness. And David Herold acted as Payne's guide on the night of the assassination, helping him to flee into southern Maryland. Herold then caught up with Booth and fled with him. So why was Surratt executed?

A number of historians believe that Surratt suffered the penalty intended for her son John Surratt, Jr., hiding in Canada. Several scholars have emphasized the role that the "excited and violent nature of the times" played in the decision to execute Surratt (Turner 1990, 181). Surratt's execution occurred at a time of an extraordinary national crisis and at the end of a brutal war, when sectional hatred—North and South—was at a fever pitch.

In 1867, during the trial of John Surratt, Jr., the public learned that of the nine military judges who sentenced Surratt to death, five had added a plea for clemency. President Johnson always insisted that he had never seen their plea. Several members of his Cabinet, however, left records indicating otherwise. The revelation of Johnson's decision to execute Surratt damaged his reputation and increased the public sentiment against the use of capital punishment for women.

Selected Readings

Chamlee, Roy Z., Jr. *Lincoln's Assassins: A Complete Account of Their Capture, Trial, and Punishment*. Jefferson, NC: McFarland. 1990.

Trindal, Elizabeth S. *Mary Surratt: An American Tragedy*. Gretna, LA: Pelican Publishing. 1996.

Turner, Thomas Reed. *Beware the People Weeping: Public Opinion and the Assassination of Abraham Lincoln*. Baton Rouge: Louisiana State University Press. 1991. Orig. Pub. 1982.

Swisshelm, Jane Grey (1815–1884)

From the 1840s through 1866, Jane Grey Swisshelm achieved celebrity as a writer and journalist. In the late 1830s, her exposure to the brutality and cruelty of slavery in Louisville, Kentucky—"that dark, bloody ground"—converted her to the cause of abolitionism, which became the most frequent subject of her essays, editorials, and speeches. She was also an outspoken women's rights advocate. Her writings revealing Pennsylvania women's powerlessness regarding their own property helped influence the state's legislators to pass a women's property rights bill in 1848. During her career, she was the editor and publisher of three newspapers. Her first, the Pittsburgh *Saturday Visiter* (1848–1857) claimed 6,000 subscribers at its peak, a circulation that rivaled those of the most highly respected abolitionist newspapers.

In 1857, Swisshelm left her husband and her troubled marriage to move to the frontier town of St. Cloud, Minnesota, where her sister was living. She immediately published the *St. Cloud Visiter* (1857–1858), followed by the *St. Cloud Democrat* (1858–1863). Through her lively, humorous, often caustic rhetoric, she made enemies and gained vigorous supporters while acquiring a reputation for stimulating debate on national political issues in a frontier region far removed from Washington, DC.

Beginning in 1858, Swisshelm discovered she had the aptitude and the appetite for lecturing. Most often speaking on political subjects, particularly abolition and women's rights, she crisscrossed Minnesota. She was a political abolitionist who rejected the disunionism of the Garrisonians and other eastern abolitionists. She believed that the Constitution was intrinsically an antislavery document and tried to convince her audiences that the best way to eradicate slavery was "by and through it" (Swisshelm 1880, 200). For these unorthodox views, she was declared "the mother of the Republican party" and was burned in effigy.

Settlers of the Minnesota wilderness experienced a devastating Sioux massacre during the summer of 1862. Soldiers garrisoned in the federal forts of the region departed for the Civil War battlefields, leaving pioneer farmers vulnerable. Although the precise number of settlers killed is not known, historians believe that at least 450 and perhaps as many as 750 were murdered in this attack. The massacre was experienced as a calamity of enormous proportions in this thinly populated area. Swisshelm, whose adopted hometown of St. Cloud was nearby some scenes of the destruction, blamed the federal government for its lackadaisical handling of the "Indian problem" and its lack of responsiveness to mass murder and what she viewed as white genocide.

Swisshelm rushed to the lecture circuit to publicize her and other Minnesotans' opinions and experiences of the crisis. In January 1863, she departed on the tour, speaking in Chicago, Philadelphia, Brooklyn, and Washington, DC. Through her oratory, she portrayed the realities and perils of frontier life to easterners and urbanites, in the hope that they would help pressure the federal government to take a harsher, more punitive stance in all dealings with Native Americans. Swisshelm had not always been so anti–Native American. Prior to her life in Minnesota, she had idealized them, wholeheartedly embracing, as she described it, James Fenimore Cooper's "idea of the dignity and glory of the noble red man of the forest" (Swisshelm 1880, 223). Life in Minnesota so dashed these romantic images that she swung from lofty admiration to scorn and bitter hatred.

While in Washington, DC, Swisshelm encountered Secretary of War Edwin M. Stanton, who had long admired her for her women's rights essays and editorials in Pennsylvania. He offered her a position as a clerk in the War Department, which she accepted. Prior to her clerkship, she devoted herself to nursing soldiers. She attempted to get a nursing opportunity through Dorothea Dix, superintendent of nurses for the Union army. When this move failed, she walked into Campbell Hospital, one of the larger army hospitals in Washington. Noticing the absence of female nurses, she set to work immediately, comforting the dying and assisting the sick and wounded men. As she explained in a letter to the *St. Cloud Democrat* back home,

> I have been here in the hospital ten days, dressing wounds, wetting wounds, giving drinks and stimulants, comforting the dying, trying to save the living …. The doctors have committed to my special care wounded feet and ankles, and I kneel reverently by the mangled limbs of these heroes, and thank God and man for the privilege of washing them. I want whiskey—barrels of whiskey—to wash feet, and thus keep up circulation in wounded knees, legs, thighs, hips. I want a lot of pickles, pickles, pickles, lemons, lemons, lemons, oranges. No well man or woman has a right to a glass of lemonade. We want it all in the hospitals to prevent gangrene. (Swisshelm 1976, 233)

After the war, in December 1865, Swisshelm began publication of the *Reconstructionist* in Washington, DC, a newspaper espousing the views of the Radical Republicans in Congress. So vituperative were her attacks on President Andrew Johnson that she was fired from her job in the War Department. Without the income from her federal employment, she could not keep the *Reconstuctionist* afloat, and in March 1866, she had to terminate publication. At this point, she had no means to support herself and was on the verge of becoming completely destitute. She then learned that she had a legitimate claim to her husband's family's estate near Pittsburgh. She succeeded in gaining control of the Swisshelm property, and was thus guaranteed a home and a modest income to sustain her for the rest of her life. In 1880, she published her memoir, *Half a Century*.

See also **Abolitionists; Literary Women; Surratt, Mary**

Selected Readings

Swisshelm, Jane Grey. *Crusader and Feminist: Letters of Jane Grey Swisshelm 1858–1865*. Saint Paul: The Minnesota Historical Society. 1934. Reprint: Westport, CT: Hyperion Press. 1976.

Tyler, Alice Felt. "Swisshelm, Jane Grey Cannon." In *Notable American Women, 1607–1950: A Biographical Dictionary*. Volume 3. Edited by Edward T. James et al. Cambridge, MA: Belknap Press of Harvard University Press. 1971. 415–417.

T

Taylor, Susie Baker King (1848–1912)

It seems strange how our aversion to seeing suffering is overcome in war,—how we are able to see the most sickening sights, such as men with their limbs blown off and mangled by the deadly shells, without a shudder; and instead of turning away, how we hurry to assist in alleviating their pain, bind up their wounds, and press the cool water to their parched lips, with feelings only of sympathy and pity.

—Susie Baker King Taylor, excerpt from A Black Woman's Civil War Memoirs, originally published as Reminiscences of My Life in Camp: With the 33rd United States Colored Troops, late 1st S.C. Volunteers (Taylor 1988, 87–88)

Susie Baker King Taylor's 1902 memoir is the only account of an African-American girl's life on the frontlines during the Civil War. It relates her experiences while attached to the 1st South Carolina Volunteers, one of the first black regiments. Although Susie took on the challenging roles of a grown woman all through the war—she was teacher, nurse, laundress, and soldier's wife—she was only 12 years of age when the first shot was fired on FORT SUMTER and 16 years when the surrender was signed at Appomattox.

Though born a slave on August 6, 1848, Susie Baker spent much of her childhood living with her grandmother, who, though enslaved herself, was living much like a free woman, in Savannah, Georgia. Although education for African Americans was prohibited by law, Baker received lessons from Mrs. Woodhouse, a free black woman who operated a secret school near her grandmother's home. Baker also managed to sneak instruction from another African-American woman, a white girl, and her grandmother's landlord's son, a high-school student.

In April 1862, Baker followed her uncle and his family to the Georgia Sea Islands, which came under Union occupation on April 12, 1862. Baker was there only a few days when officers of the naval command learned of her literacy and asked her to establish a small school. According to her memoir, she instructed approximately 40 children during the day and taught adults how to read in the evenings.

At the age of 14, in October 1862, Baker became officially attached to the military when she was enlisted as a laundress for soldiers of the 1st South Carolina Volunteers at Camp Saxton in Beaufort, South Carolina. At some point during this year, she married fellow Georgian Edward King, a sergeant in the regiment. Because they were both literate, their skills were in great demand by the dozens of black soldiers who were desperate to learn to read. The young couple spent most of their evenings teaching.

Although Baker King was never trained as a nurse, she used what basic knowledge she possessed as well as her common sense and ingenuity when pressed into service as a nurse. She also participated in other chores of the regiment, and especially enjoyed cleaning and reloading the soldiers' weapons.

> I learned to handle a musket very well while in the regiment, and could shoot straight and often hit the target. I assisted in cleaning the guns and used to fire them off, to see if the cartridges were dry.... I thought this great fun. (Taylor 1988, 61)

Baker King remained working alongside her regiment at least through its participation in the capture of Charleston, South Carolina, in February 1865. After the war, she lived with her husband in Savannah until his death in 1866, at a time when she was pregnant with their first child. After their son was born, Baker King taught for a time in rural Georgia. She later moved back to Savannah where she instructed the freedpeople in the evenings. To make ends meet, she entered domestic service as a laundress and cook.

In the 1880s, after relocating to Boston and after marrying Russell Taylor, she became a leader in the Woman's Relief Corps, an auxiliary of the Grand Army of the

Republic, a patriotic organization dedicated to honoring war veterans, the national government, and the American flag.

See also **African-American Women; Military Women**

Selected Readings

Baum, Rosalie Murphy. "Taylor, Susie." In *African-American Women: A Biographical Dictionary.* Edited by Dorothy C. Salem. New York: Garland. 1993. 491–493.

Taylor, Susie King. *A Black Woman's Civil War Memoirs.* Reprint. Edited by Patricia W. Romero. New York: Markus Wiener Publishing. 1988. Original Edition. *Reminiscences of My Life in Camp: With the 33rd United States Colored Troops, late 1st S.C. Volunteers.* 1902.

Teachers of the Freedpeople

It seems to me that God has committed to us, the missionary teachers, the future of these people, the destiny of immortal souls is in our hands, plastic minds are to be molded by our hands, for good or evil, in beauty or deformity.... Oh! "who is sufficient for these things?"

—Excerpt from a letter written by Sara G. Stanley, African-American teacher to the freedpeople, 1864 (quoted in DeBoer 1995, 24)

As Northerners became aware of the desperate needs of the African-American refugees living in the contraband camps in 1861 and 1862, they sent them food, clothing, medicine, and other supplies while also planning for their future as a free people in a postwar society. White and free African-American abolitionists formed the vanguard of Northerners who sought to prepare the freedpeople for their new lives. They believed that education was the crucial component of the program to transform the freedpeople from slaves to independent, self-sufficient members of society.

As historian Ronald Butchart has pointed out, the recently freed African Americans "needed land, protection, and a stake in society." In most cases, they were given none of these things. What they received instead were schoolhouses and teachers to instruct them (Butchart 1980, 9). Northerners who promoted freedpeople's education were determined to prove to a prejudiced North that African Americans were not intellectually deficient. With education, these reformers argued, the freedpeople would prove themselves capable of managing productive lives.

Northern women—white and black—formed more than two-thirds of the teaching force that instructed the freedpeople during the Civil War and Reconstruction (Morris 1981, 58). Most were single middle-class women, white and Protestant, from New England and the Midwest. For the most part, freedmen's aid societies, affiliated with both nonsectarian organizations and the Protestant denominations, sponsored the teachers during the Civil War. They were almost all experienced educators, and many had received higher education in the colleges or in the state normal schools. By December 1865, the freedmen's aid associations (and after February 1865, the federal Freedmen's Bureau) had placed teachers and established schools in every Southern state as well as in Maryland, Washington, DC, Kentucky, Kansas, and Missouri. At the time of the surrender of the Confederacy in April 1865, there were more than 900 Northern women and men instructing the freedpeople. After the Civil War, the mission to educate the formerly enslaved expanded further and became an important part of Reconstruction in the South.

Not all of the educators were Northerners. A number of literate former slaves—both women and men—conducted their own classes. As soon as the brightest scholars in the freedpeople's schools gained a minimal competency, they, too, stepped forward to fill teaching posts. After the war, educated white Southern women, under strict Northern supervision, also instructed the formerly enslaved.

The American Missionary Association (AMA) sponsored the greatest number of teachers sent to the South and border states—approximately 5,000 women and men from 1861 through 1876. The AMA's male administrators selected women who possessed "a true missionary spirit." Only those who were strong enough in mind, body, and spirit "to do hard work, go to hard places, and submit if need be, to hard fare" were chosen (quoted in DeBoer 1995, 10). Most female teachers left positions in the North that paid higher wages and most embarked fully aware of the discomforts and dangers they would endure by settling in battle-ravaged areas. Although many female teachers were either abolitionists or were women inspired by strong antislavery convictions, others were motivated by a profound sense of religious mission and social duty—to aid the suffering and to bring the word of God to the "heathen."

The first contingent of Northern teachers traveled to the South Carolina Sea Islands as part of the "Port Royal Experiment" in early 1862, a New England–based program designed to prove that the freedpeople, as free laborers, could produce more cotton on government-managed and Northern-owned plantations than they had as slaves (Morris 1981, 6). Although the male-dominated agricultural aspects of the experiment took precedence, by the end of 1862, 1,727 African-American children were attending school on the three largest islands and hundreds of adults were learning to read in the evenings.

The Port Royal teachers' educational program, like all freedpeople's instruction to follow, tried to instill "Northern" values as it provided instruction in the 3Rs. The necessity of working for a wage, the value of hard work, and the qualities of industriousness, self-sufficiency, and cleanliness were integral to the overall educational plan.

The challenges that faced the Port Royal teachers upon their arrival to the islands resembled those that would soon face all teachers of the freedpeople during the Civil War. Although the Port Royal teachers' accommodations in the abandoned plantation manors appeared more luxurious than the spartan, bare-bones quarters most teachers were allotted on the mainland, the island houses had been stripped of furniture, carpeting, and nearly every other household amenity. They were also infested with fleas, rats, and other vermin. Food for the teachers was almost always in insufficient supply. Meat, eggs, and milk were rarely available, and a general scarcity of all other foodstuffs made hunger a constant problem.

Few teachers who decided to remain on the islands complained of the discomforts once they became aware of the squalid living conditions of the freedpeople. The 10,000 former slaves were severely malnourished, diseased, and in desperate need of food, housing, and medical care. For the first six months, the Northern women were not able to teach. They spent their days and evenings distributing food, clothing, and other supplies sent from freedmen's aid societies in the North, providing medical care, coping with a smallpox epidemic, and helping the freedpeople to find ways to provide for their basic needs in an environment devoid of resources.

Despite the freedpeople's misery, they flocked to the classrooms the teachers established in the fall of 1862. Children attended classes whenever they were free from their daily labor on the Northern-run cotton fields and were joined in their lessons by a few adult women nursing babies and toddlers. Most adults wanting reading instruction gathered in the evenings or were instructed in their shanties by teachers who visited them.

The teaching conditions were daunting at first for most of the teachers who were accustomed to the discipline and order of Northern schools. Laura Towne, an energetic Unitarian abolitionist from Philadelphia, described the challenge that faced her when she first confronted her young pupils, crammed into the small church that was to serve as their school for over two years.

> They had no idea of sitting still, of giving attention, of ceasing to talk aloud. They lay down and went to sleep, they scuffled and struck each other. They got up by the dozen, made their curtsies, and walked off to the neighboring field for blackberries,

coming back to their seats with a curtsy when they were ready. They evidently did not understand me, and I could not understand them, and after two hours and a half of effort I was thoroughly exhausted. (Towne 1969, xiv–xv)

The teachers worked grueling hours. Most taught hundreds of pupils for five to six hours during the day. The late afternoons they devoted to instruction in sewing and other domestic skills. The evenings were reserved for teaching adults to read. Sunday Sabbath schools introduced the islanders to the Bible and religious instruction.

Though deprived of adequate space, books, and supplies, and despite being overtaxed by the long hours of teaching and assisting the freedpeople, women educators emphasized their job satisfaction. Most of the Port Royal teachers were inspired by the freedpeople's eagerness for education, and echoed in their letters and diaries an observation CHARLOTTE FORTEN made in her journal. "I never before saw children so eager to learn, although I had had several years' experience in New-England schools," she wrote. "Coming to school is a constant delight and recreation to them" (Grimké 1988, 71).

Outside of the classroom, however, the teachers' lives were fraught with obstacles. Male and female missionaries—white and black—suffered the harassment of Union soldiers stationed on the islands, many of whom were anti-abolitionists who rejected the mission to educate the freedpeople. The never-ending threat of Confederate attack rattled nerves, especially when several of the surrounding islands experienced rebel invasions. Charlotte Forten coped by keeping a revolver at her bedside. Elsewhere in the Union-occupied South, teachers endured the bullying and hatred of Southerners who pushed and jostled them in the streets, spat at them, and refused to rent them housing or serve them in stores.

Mosquito-borne diseases, scurvy and malnutrition, and overwork all took their toll on the teaching force. Even the most dedicated teachers sometimes found that their failing health compelled them to return North. In 1865, Mary Ames, a teacher in Charleston, South Carolina, confided to her diary that she felt weak after three weeks subsisting on nothing but crackers and tea. No matter how rewarding the teachers found the work, those with frail constitutions did not last long.

Despite the autonomy that the Port Royal women teachers had in their own classrooms, men were the unquestionable leaders of the experiment just as male administrators governed the freedmen's aid societies and the Freedmen's Bureau during the war and Reconstruction. Women teachers were also paid less than male teachers doing the same work, a fact of life in Northern schools as well. At Port Royal and on the other South Carolina Sea Islands, men were the superintendents and the military leaders who made all the decisions and who determined the futures of the freedpeople.

As Laura Towne's diary and letters attest, she frequently disagreed with the men's supervision of the experiment. She objected to the methods male cotton agents, plantation supervisors, and the military used to coerce the freedpeople into going along with Northerners' money-making schemes, particularly when these plans were counter to the freedpeople's interests. Towne boldly expressed her objections on several occasions, but the most she could do was to plant a seed of doubt in an administrator's or an army officer's ear. Worst of all from her point of view was her obligation to go among the freedpeople to convince them to accept a superintendent's edict when she believed it was morally wrong.

In her opinion, Northern leaders of the experiment were permitting unscrupulous agents to replace the slaveholders' tyranny with other equally oppressive edicts. The agents threatened to withhold the freedpeople's government rations, to reclaim land that had been given to them, and to reenslave them. According to Towne,

> The mischief has been that ... the gentlemen have been determined to make the negroes show what they can do in the way of cotton, unwhipped. But they have only changed the mode of compulsion. They *force* men to prove they are fit to be free men by holding a tyrant's power over them. (Towne 1969, 55)

Going South to teach was not the only way that Northern black and white women contributed to the effort to educate the freedpeople. Female members of the freedmen's aid societies, female antislavery societies, and other secular and religious benevolent organizations—women who never left their communities—raised the funds that made the educational programs possible. The money they collected paid teachers' salaries; purchased books, Bibles, and other educational supplies; built schoolhouses; and even provided the schoolbell that brought both young and old to class on time. These organizations raised over one million dollars from the time of the Port Royal Experiment until the end of the war (Butchart 1980, 9).

See also **Abolitionists; African-American Women; Contraband Women; Hawks, Esther Hill**

Selected Readings

Forbes, Ella. *African American Women During the Civil War*. New York: Garland. 1998.

Morris, Robert C. Reading, *'Riting, and Reconstruction: The Education of Freedmen in the South, 1861–1870*. Chicago: University of Chicago Press. 1981.

Towne, Laura M. *Letters and Diary of Laura M. Towne*. Edited by Rupert Sargent Holland. 1912. Reprint: New York: Negro Universities Press. 1969.

Tompkins, Sally (1833–1916)

A native of Virginia, Sally Tompkins was the only woman in the North or South to receive a commission as a military officer during the Civil War. Her commission as a captain in the Confederate cavalry enabled her to continue to direct the private military hospital she established during the summer of 1861. Tompkins was a member of the plantation elite who was successful in enlisting the aid of other elite white women in Richmond, Virginia, to assist her in operating the hospital and supplying it with food and other necessities when Confederate hospital supplies were low or nonexistent. Although she has been recognized as the most well-known Confederate nurse, few details of her life and work have been published.

Sally Louisa Tompkins was born in Poplar Grove in Mathews County, Virginia. Very little is known of her childhood and upbringing, although it is clear that as a child and young adult she lived with her parents on their Virginia plantation. When her father died, she and her mother and sister relocated to Richmond.

After the First Battle of Manassas (known in the North as the First Battle of Bull Run) on July 21, 1861, the Confederate military was overcome by the enormous number of wounded requiring medical attention. As they arrived in Richmond, there were not enough hospitals to accept them. The Confederate government urged the city's civilians to take the wounded into their homes and to open their churches and commercial buildings. Tompkins was only one of the many Richmond women and men to step to the forefront of this mission. Judge John Robertson suggested that she take over his town house and transform it into an army hospital. On August 1, 1861, Tompkins opened the Robertson Hospital with space available for 25 patients. As the hospital's administrator, she placed a stringent emphasis on cleanliness. Within weeks, Robertson Hospital had achieved a reputation for being extraordinarily successful in healing soldiers and preventing death.

In early September 1861, Tompkins was distressed when she learned that the Confederate government had ordered that all military medical departments and hospitals be centralized. As a result, the small private hospitals were to be dissolved and replaced by much larger institutions. With the help of Judge William W. Crump, assistant secretary of the Confederate Treasury, Tompkins managed to meet with President Jefferson Davis. As she made her appeal to keep Robertson Hospital's doors open, she displayed hospital records that proved that Robertson sent more soldiers back to the ranks than any other hospital in Richmond. Davis did not dare thwart the will of the Confederate Congress, but decided to establish Robertson Hospital as a military institution. To achieve this designation and to ensure that she remain the hospital's director, he ordered that she become a commissioned officer in the Confederate army. On September 9, 1861, Tompkins received her commission as captain.

Robertson Hospital operated throughout the war, closing its doors two months after the defeat of the Confederacy on June 13, 1865. Of the 1,333 patients treated at Robertson, there were only 73 deaths, an astonishingly low percentage of 5.5 percent when compared with the number of fatalities at other Confederate military hospitals. Of the 17,000 soldiers treated at Chimborazo, one of the largest military hospitals in Richmond, 41.2 percent did not survive (Holzman 1959, 130; Barber 1997, 91).

Patients at Robertson Hospital were fortunate because it was the beneficiary of the largesse of Richmond's elite. When Confederate food and medical supplies were inadequate, Tompkins purchased them with her own funds and asked for help from the elite community in Richmond. Tompkins employed both free African-American women, slave women, and white women as nurses. She also had the support of the upper-class volunteer nurses known as the "Ladies of Robertson Hospital."

In addition to cleanliness, Tompkins stressed the importance of spirituality to promote health in her patients. She ministered to soldiers, guiding them in prayer whenever possible. Judge Crump reported that she "ruled her hospital with a stick in one [hand] and a Bible in the other" (quoted in Coleman 1956, 40).

After Robertson Hospital closed in 1865, Tompkins continued to make her home in Richmond. She devoted her time and finances to a number of charitable causes. She was active in her local Episcopal church and contributed to the Association for the Preservation of Virginia Antiquities. She was honored with membership in the United Confederate Veterans organization and occasionally hosted reunions for veterans.

In 1905, Tompkins took up residence at the Home for Confederate Widows. Housing was made available for her because her finances were depleted and her health was poor. When she died in 1916 at the age of 83, she was given full military honors at her burial.

See also **Nurses**

Selected Readings

Coleman, Elizabeth Dabney. "The Captain Was a Lady." *Virginia Cavalcade.* (Summer 1956): 35–41.

Cook, Cita. "Tompkins, Sally Louisa." In *American National Biography.* Volume 21. Edited by John A. Garraty and Mark C. Carnes. New York: Oxford University Press. 1999. 740–741.

Treasury Girls

The Confederacy's "Treasury Girls" were the first Southern women to find work as government clerks in the South. From mid-1862 until April 2, 1865, several hundred middle- and upper-class women and teenage girls found much-needed employment signing notes in the Treasury Department of the Confederacy in Richmond, Virginia, and in Columbia, South Carolina. After the first Conscription Act became law in April 1862, the supply of male treasury clerks diminished, leading Confederate Secretary of the Treasury Christopher Memminger to pursue the hiring of women. Once the Treasury Department had accepted female clerks, the Post Office, Commissary General, Quartermaster, and War Departments followed suit.

Treasury Girls were the envy of women seeking remunerative labor during the Civil War. Although not paid as highly as women ordnance workers or male clerks, female government workers' salaries, at $65 per month, exceeded that of most soldiers in the military. Even so, their wages never kept pace with the runaway inflation of Confederate currency. The clerkships were in extraordinarily high demand, particularly among impoverished upper-class refugees from outlying areas who flooded into the Confederate capital. Secretary Memminger reported that for every position there were a hundred applicants.

Jobs for women in the Treasury Department were intended only for those who were the sole support of their families or themselves, including soldiers' wives, war widows, teenage girls, and refugees. A demonstration of need was usually not enough to gain a woman employment, however. Besides the prerequisites of intelligence, education, and perfect handwriting, an applicant needed to present testimonials of her moral character, usually from a member of the clergy or a prominent public official. In fact, competition for the clerkships was so intense that women often had to garner support from every distinguished man that they could find, including members of the Confederate Congress, high-ranking government and military officials, and President Jefferson Davis. All too often, women with the loftiest political and social connections won out over other equally qualified candidates who were in greater need.

Malvina Black Gist, the young war widow of the son of the South Carolina governor, was delighted to find work in the Treasury Note Department in Columbia.

An entry from her diary reveals that she was by no means dependent on the job for her survival.

> Took my vocal lesson and paid Signor Torriani for my last quarter.... I also sent check to the milliner for the $200 due on my new bonnet, and paid $80 for the old lilac barege bought from Mary L———. Miss P——— does not yet agree to let me have the congress gaiters for $75.... 'Tis a pretty come to pass when $75 of confederate currency is not the equivalent of an ordinary pair of Massachusetts made shoes. (Quoted in K. Jones 1955, 357)

Although upper-class ladies were employed as treasury clerks, there was a stigma attached to a member of the elite working in such a menial, middle-class position. On May 24, 1862, Mary Boykin Chesnut vehemently protested the prospect of work in a "department."

> Mrs. Preston and I have determined ... we will not go into one of the departments. We will not stand up all day at a table and cut notes apart, ordered round by a department clerk. We will live at home with our families and starve in a body. Any homework we will do. Any menial service—under the shadow of our own rooftree. Department—never! (Chesnut 1981, 350)

To be subordinate to her husband and other elite men was one thing, but to be subordinate to a male of a lower class was intolerable.

Work in the Treasury Department was not overly taxing. A female treasury clerk's workday began at 9 AM and concluded at 3 PM, five days a week, and she either signed notes or clipped them. Note signers were required to number or write their signature on 3,200 bills a day. Should ink smudge, blot, or otherwise spoil a note, the government deducted $.10 from a woman's wages. The women's shorter workday was used as the justification for paying them half of a male clerk's salary. By late 1864, however, women treasury workers were given pay increases that made their wages the equal of men's.

Once the war was over, Southern women left their government positions as male clerks once more filled these positions. Although Northern "GOVERNMENT GIRLS" continued to work in government offices after the Civil War, Southern women would not do so for several more decades.

Selected Readings

Kaufman, Janet E. "Treasury Girls." *Civil War Times Illustrated*. 25 (May 1986): 32–38.

Rable, George C. *Civil Wars: Women and the Crisis of Southern Nationalism*. Urbana: University of Illinois Press. 1989.

Truth, Sojourner (c. 1797–1883)

Look there above the center, where the flag is waving bright;
We are going out of slavery, we are bound for freedom's light;
We mean to show Jeff Davis how the Africans can fight,
 As we go marching on.
Chorus.—
Glory, glory, hallelujah! Glory, glory, hallelujah!
We hear the proclamation, massa, hush it as you will;
The birds will sing it to us, hopping on the cotton hill;
The possum up the gum tree couldn't keep it still,
As he went climbing on.

> —Excerpt from the song lyrics composed by Sojourner Truth for the
> 1st Michigan Colored Regiment, February 1864, to be sung to the
> tune of "John Brown's Body" (quoted in Painter 1996, 183)

Former slave, preacher, abolitionist, and women's rights advocate, Sojourner Truth spent the 1850s captivating Northern social reformers with her homespun, yet profound rhetoric. Like the majority of black and white female abolitionists during the Civil War, Truth's activism shifted from a focus on antislavery activism toward work to aid the freedpeople and African-American soldiers.

At the beginning of the war, Truth continued her lectures on abolition that had brought her fame during the 1850s. Truth was adamant about supporting the Union cause from the beginning of the conflict. In April 1861, she ventured from her home in Battle Creek, Michigan, with her white abolitionist friend Josephine Griffing and a host of supporters to lecture in Indiana, a hotbed of pro-Confederate sentiment. Truth, dressed in a red, white, and blue shawl, sash, and apron, mounted the platform and began expounding on her antislavery and pro-Union rhetoric. The crowd mobbed her and threatened to attack her and her advocates. She was then arrested and charged with violating an Indiana state law that barred those of African descent from entering the state. After being detained on and off for ten days, she was allowed to return home (Painter 1996, 179–180).

By the latter half of 1863, Truth was devoting much of her time to soldiers' aid for the all-black 1st Michigan Regiment. In the spring of 1864, she traveled to Washington, DC, to assist the freedpeople as hundreds of other Northern abolitionists were already doing. Not long after arriving in Washington, Truth prevailed upon her friends to help her set up a meeting with President Abraham Lincoln. A devout Lincoln supporter, Truth emerged from her visit glowing with admiration for the president. For years afterward, she told and retold the events that transpired during that encounter.

According to Truth, Lincoln was warm and responsive to her, and he was humble when she acknowledged him as the emancipator of African Americans. Lucy Colman, Truth's white abolitionist friend who accompanied her when she visited Lincoln, reported in her 1892 memoir that the meeting was not all that Truth claimed. Colman revealed that the president had been civil but had responded in a condescending and dismissive manner toward Truth, addressing her as " 'Aunty' …as he would his washerwoman" (quoted in Painter 1996, 207).

From Truth's point of view, the actual demeanor of the president and the content of their conversation may have been the least important aspects of their meeting. What was more significant was that she succeeded in gaining an audience with Lincoln, a connection that she could use to publicize her presence in Washington and to promote her current cause—aid for the freedpeople.

Truth devoted herself to assisting the freedpeople from November 1864 through most of 1868. Soon after arriving in Washington, she visited the camp established for fugitive slaves at Mason's Island. Her first official refugee work was at Freedmen's Village, a camp established by the National Freedmen's Relief Association, at Arlington Heights, Virginia. Later, in 1865, she worked at the Freedmen's Hospital in Washington.

At the Freedmen's Village, Truth mingled with the former slaves, visiting and talking with them. She taught the women how to sew, knit, and cook. She also preached to them, imparted moral instruction, and demanded that they be more self-reliant. Her message was not always well received. According to Truth, when she "told them to get off the government and take care of themselves" and "they were in disgrace living in the poor house off the government," they forced her out of the church where she was speaking (quoted in Mabee 1990, 7).

Although African Americans were permitted to ride the streetcars of Washington, DC, for the first time in March 1865, many conductors refused to obey the new law and would not allow African Americans to board. Truth was determined to take advantage of her right to use public transportation, despite the dangers. On one occasion, when she was traveling with Griffing, the conductor allowed Griffing to climb aboard safely but tried to prevent Truth from doing so. She was dragged a few yards as the vehicle picked up speed. According to Truth, Griffing complained to the president of the streetcar company, and he fired the conductor. Shortly thereafter, Truth ran into difficulty again when she stepped onto another streetcar: "As I assended [sic] the platform of the car, the conductor pushed me, saying 'go back—get off here.' I told him I was not going off, then 'I'll put you off' said he furiously, clenching my right arm with both hands, using such violence that he seemed about to succeed" (quoted in Sterling 1984, 254). Truth's right arm was injured in the process. This time Truth not only had the man fired, but she also filed criminal charges and had the man arrested. He was ultimately convicted of assault and battery (Painter 1996, 210–211).

Immediately after the war, Truth struggled to find jobs for the freedpeople in Rochester, New York, and in Battle Creek. Of all her efforts during the Civil War era, this mission proved the least successful. Potential employers were interested primarily in young, single male and female workers, and were reluctant to hire freed African Americans, most of whom were living in family groups. Truth and her co-workers also had difficulty persuading many African Americans to relocate to cities so far North. Even so, she reported that she was able to place at least 100 men and women in these two cities.

See also **African-American Women; Contraband Women**

Selected Readings

Mabee, Carleton. "Sojourner Truth and President Lincoln." *New England Quarterly.* 61 (4) (1988): 519–529.

Painter, Nell Irvin. *Sojourner Truth: A Life, a Symbol.* New York: Norton. 1996.

Tubman, Harriet (1821–1913)

You have without doubt seen a full account of the Combahee expedition. We weakened the rebels by bringing away seven hundred fifty-six heads of their most valuable livestock. Of these seven hundred and fifty-six contrabands, nearly or quite all the able-bodied men have joined the colored regiments here.

—Harriet Tubman, June 30, 1863, Beaufort, South
Carolina (quoted in Sterling 1984, 260)

By the time of the Civil War, Harriet Tubman was a venerated figure among Northern black and white abolitionists and free and enslaved African Americans. Her success as a slave rescuer had been well publicized in the antislavery press. From 1849 on, she undertook at least 15 expeditions to the South and border states, escorting over 200 slaves to freedom in the Northern United States and Canada.

By the late 1850s, Tubman's rising influence as an abolitionist orator elevated her to near-celebrity status in New York and Boston. During the Civil War, she shifted her activism to assume new roles in her work to support and uplift the newly freed slaves and as a nurse, scout, and spy for the Union army. Despite the stock of oft-told stories and legends about Tubman, many of the facts of her life remain in the shadows. No definitive, modern biography exists as of this writing, and no thorough attempt has yet been made to sort out the verifiable details of her life from the folklore that has inevitably seeped into accounts of her heroism.

In 1858 and 1859, Tubman helped the militant abolitionist John Brown to obtain financial support and recruits for his planned assault on the federal arsenal at Harpers Ferry, Virginia. Historians past and present do not agree about Tubman's role in the raid. All acknowledge Brown's outspoken admiration of Tubman and the fact that they met several times during the 18 months prior to the attack in October 1859. Yet stories circulated among New England abolitionists that Tubman was intending to participate in the raid (and ultimately did not due to illness) have not been substantiated by modern scholars of the Brown conspiracy.

What remains clear, however, is that Tubman's role in the conspiracy was vital. Even recent investigators who have downplayed her impact have upheld the importance of her role in raising support for Brown among Afro-Canadians and abolitionists in New England. One conspiracy scholar has documented her pivotal role in boosting the flagging support of four of Brown's major financial supporters and co-conspirators—Samuel Gridley Howe, Thomas Wentworth Higginson, Frank Sanborn, and George Stearns (Rossbach 1982, 205).

From the outset of the national conflict, Tubman regarded the Civil War as the final culmination of African Americans' centuries-long quest for freedom. And, like a number of black and white abolitionists, she distrusted President Abraham Lincoln and scorned his policies, particularly his lack of resolve concerning the future of the slaves and his reluctance to allow African Americans to enlist in the Union military. In January 1862, Massachusetts abolitionist LYDIA MARIA CHILD recorded a conversation she had with Tubman concerning these issues. According to Child, Tubman stated that Lincoln should apply the old saying, "Never wound a snake but kill it," to his policies concerning the institution of slavery. She believed that the most expedient means of winning the war was for Lincoln to set the slaves free immediately.

In March 1862, Tubman traveled to Beaufort, South Carolina, to assist the recently freed slaves in the Union-occupied South Carolina Sea Islands, where she made her home for the next three years. Immediately after her arrival, she nursed the ill and severely malnourished contraband men, women, and children. She also helped the CONTRABAND WOMEN to adapt to their new lives as self-sufficient providers and caretakers of their families. She helped them find ways to eke out a living in the severely overcrowded conditions of the camps by teaching them how to make a living as laundresses and how to make and sell items that the soldiers wanted to purchase. Tubman was a teacher who instructed by her own example; during the evenings she earned the money for her own subsistence by baking pies and brewing root beer to sell to Union troops (Conrad 1943, 161, 163).

At some time during 1862 or early in 1863, Tubman began operating as an intelligence agent for the Union army. Under the direction of Union Major General David Hunter and Brigadier General Rufus Saxton, she executed numerous intelligence-gathering expeditions, working both as a scout and spy. She eventually became the leader of a group of freedmen who were intimately familiar with the rivers penetrating the inland coastal region. At a height of just five feet, Tubman's unprepossessing appearance (most contemporary descriptions emphasize her "ordinariness") combined with her art of subterfuge acquired from her years on the Underground Railroad enabled her to gather the information the army needed to launch successful attacks on Confederate outposts and ammunition sites.

On June 2, 1863, Tubman embarked on her most challenging and successful mission. With Colonel James Montgomery and the African-American soldiers of the 2nd South Carolina Volunteers, she guided Union gunboats up the Combahee River in South Carolina. During this mission, Tubman was instrumental in encouraging hundreds of enslaved men and women to abandon the inland plantations to flee to the Union-occupied coast. In all, 756 African-American men and women were liberated via this mission. Of this group, Tubman estimated that approximately 400 men enlisted in the U.S. Colored Troops.

On July 18, 1863, Colonel Robert Gould Shaw, white Union commander of the 54th Massachusetts, the first black regiment mustered in a Northern state, agreed to have his regiment lead the Union assault on Fort Wagner, one of the Confederate batteries protecting Charleston, South Carolina. Tubman is believed to have been nearby during the scene of carnage that decimated Union troops in that battle. She is known to have nursed the wounded and tended the dying following the battle.

Tubman continued military nursing until July 1865. During her journey home to Auburn, New York, she carried a pass that entitled her, as a nurse of the Union army, to travel at half fare by rail. As she made her way North, she encountered racism among the railway personnel, who chose to ignore her credentials. Although most sources agree that her arm was permanently injured when a rail worker ejected her from a train, a speech given by FRANCES ELLEN WATKINS HARPER in 1866 states otherwise.

The last time I saw that woman [Tubman], her hands were swollen. That woman who had led one of Montgomery's most successful expeditions, who was brave enough and secretive enough to act as a scout for the American army, had her hands all swollen from a conflict with a brutal conductor. (Quoted in Boyd 1994, 85)

After the war, Tubman dedicated herself and all her financial resources to improving the lives of those who had once suffered enslavement. At her home in Auburn, she established a home for elderly former slaves who could no longer earn a living. She also raised money for schools for the freedpeople and became involved in a number of social reforms, including the woman suffrage movement. Always a stirring orator, Tubman spoke often at suffrage conventions. In 1896, at the age of 75, she was the oldest delegate attending the National Federation of Afro-American Women in Washington, DC, the first national organization of African-American women's clubs in the United States.

Although Tubman served the U.S. army throughout most of the Civil War, she never succeeded in obtaining a pension to compensate her for her service, despite the efforts of many prominent men and women who intervened for her. In 1890, after decades of effort, several women's organizations finally managed to secure her a federal pension as the widow of the Civil War veteran Nelson Davis, her second husband who died in 1888.

See also **African-American Women; Military Women; Spies and Espionage**

Selected Readings

Bradford, Sarah. *Harriet Tubman: The Moses of Her People*. 1886. Reprint: Gloucester, MA: Corinth Books. 1981.

Conrad, Earl. *Harriet Tubman*. New York: Paul S. Eriksson. 1943.

Hine, Darlene Clark. "Tubman, Harriet Ross." In *Black Women in America: An
Historical Encyclopedia*. Edited by Darlene Clark Hine, Elsa Barkley Brown,
and Rosalyn Terborg-Penn. Brooklyn, NY: Carlson Publishing. 1993.
1176–1180.

Turchin, Nadine Lvova (1826–1904)

Nadine Lvova Turchin, a Russian immigrant of noble birth, was celebrated for her heroism in leading the 19th Illinois Infantry into battle, nursing the regiment's soldiers, and devoting herself to her husband's health and military career. As she accompanied him and his regiment from 1861 until his retirement from active service in 1864, she kept a diary, written in French, of which only one volume survives. A well-educated, widely read intellectual, her writings reveal the experiences of an officer's wife living close to the frontlines. Her diary is especially significant because it provides a fresh, incisive, and often acerbic outsider's analysis of American society at mid-century.

Born Nedezhda Lvova, "Madame" Turchin (as she was most commonly known) grew up the daughter of a colonel in the czar's army. She and her husband, Ivan Vasilivetch Turcheninov (later changed to John Basil Turchin), an accomplished military officer and member of the Imperial Guard, are believed to have been inspired by their democratic ideals to immigrate to the United States in 1856. They settled in Illinois.

When the Civil War began, John Turchin immediately sought an army commission and became colonel and commanding officer of the 19th Illinois Infantry in 1861. His regiment saw action early in the war, in Missouri, Kentucky, Tennessee, and Alabama. From the beginning of the war, Lvova Turchin traveled with her husband. According to reports and stories circulating during the war and after, when Union Colonel Turchin fell ill in the spring of 1862, she briefly assumed command of his regiment at a critical point during an assault on Confederate forces in Tennessee. The 19th Illinois Infantry's officers and enlisted men supposedly acquiesced to her leadership while she led them into some of the fiercest fighting of the campaign. When her husband recovered, he resumed his leadership while she returned to her volunteer duties nursing the wounded. Although the veracity of these accounts has not been substantiated, it is likely that Lvova Turchin engaged in battle at some point during the early part of the war.

One fact supports the legends of Lvova Turchin's military involvement. In July 1862, Union Brigadier General Don Carlos Buell court-martialed John Turchin on three counts. Turchin pled guilty to only one specification of the third charge, which cited his failure to obey the army regulation forbidding women (his wife) from the battlefield. The other two counts involved his failure to control his troops during the destruction and pillage of the town and lands of Athens, Alabama.

Postwar published accounts of women's contributions to the war effort agree that Lvova Turchin defended her husband's commitment to the necessity of waging total war by traveling to Washington, DC, to meet with President Abraham Lincoln. Though other forces were at work on her husband's behalf, these nineteenth-century sources credit her with securing a pardon for him and with bringing him the news of his promotion to brigadier general.

From 1863 until the autumn of 1864 (when John Turchin retired from military service), Lvova Turchin no longer participated in military action, though she moved with the Union troops her husband was leading. Within the pages of the surviving volume of her 1863 to 1864 diary, she bemoans the tedium of her life as an officer's wife. As grateful as she was to be close enough to her husband to care for him, she chafed at being denied the opportunity to fill her days with more productive activity (Leonard 2001, 137). In this environment, her diary proved to be an outlet for her frustrations as well as a vehicle through which she could express her views on life in the United States. In these pages, she championed the poor, the illiterate, the worker, and the enlisted man. As she explains in one entry, she used the journal as a means of privately venting her disillusionment with the American political system, and the nation's leaders and generals who, in her opinion, corrupted the democratic principles on which the nation was founded.

The details of the Turchins' postwar experiences have not been uncovered. It is known that they were impoverished toward the end of their lives. John Turchin died in 1901 and Lvova Turchin in 1904. They had been living in Radom, Illinois.

See also **Camp Life**

Selected Readings

Leonard, Elizabeth D. All the Daring of the Soldier: Women of the Civil War Armies. New York: Penguin Books. 2001.

Livermore, Mary A. My Story of the War: A Woman's Narrative. Hartford, CT: A.D. Worthington. 1887. Reprint: New York: Da Capo Press. 1995.

McElligott, Mary Ellen, ed. " 'A Monotony Full of Sadness': The Diary of Nadine Turchin, May 1863–April 1864." Journal of the Illinois State Historical Society. 70 (February 1977): 27– 89.

U

United States Christian Commission

The Young Men's Christian Association (YMCA), founded in 1851, established the United States Christian Commission (USCC) on November 16, 1861, seven months after the Civil War began. The original mission of the USCC was to attend to the moral and religious needs of Union soldiers. After its first year, the USCC expanded its role by providing for the physical well-being of soldiers in the military camps, in the hospitals, and at the front, thus rivaling the work of the UNITED STATES SANITARY COMMISSION (USSC).

The USCC primarily relied on clergymen volunteers to serve as its delegates, although scores of laymen also served. By the end of 1863, 12 women had been selected to act as USCC delegates. They were a distinct minority as most women who worked as volunteers for the organization did so without any official status. The

USCC leadership was composed entirely of men. By the conclusion of the war, the organization stated that a total of 5,000 clergymen had served under its auspices. The number of women volunteers, though considerable, is not known.

During the Civil War, USCC delegates distributed millions of religious publications directly to the soldiers, including religious newspapers, magazines, tracts, Bibles, New Testaments, and hymnbooks as well as secular books and periodicals (Paludan 1988, 353). The USCC established reading rooms and libraries for the soldiers and encouraged them to write home by providing stationery and stamps. Delegates set up coffee wagons and refreshment stations in an effort to steer soldiers away from peddlars of whiskey and other spirits. When a regiment marched out of camp, male delegates accompanied the troops, ministering to their spiritual and physical needs. After battles, USCC volunteers greeted returning soldiers with food and refreshing beverages. The emphasis on direct, one-on-one contact with individual soldiers distinguished the USCC from the USSC. It is this characteristic, emphasized in USCC promotional literature, that was instrumental in winning the support of men and women on the Northern home front.

Women volunteers for the USCC were most likely to be found working in the military hospitals. These white, middle-class women prepared food and drink for the wounded and sick, bandaged wounds, offered comfort, wrote letters for soldiers, distributed religious literature, sang hymns, and prayed with the dying. After the Battle of GETTYSBURG in July 1863, USCC female volunteers rushed to the battle-scarred Pennsylvania town to nurse the wounded. Emily Bliss Souder and Clarissa Fellows Jones of Pennsylvania, Isabella Fogg of Maine, Charlotte McKay of Massachusetts, and Jane C. Moore and her daughter Jane Boswell Moore of Maryland offered drinks and nourishment to the wounded lying within the houses and tents serving as makeshift field hospitals. They remained on duty in the hospitals for weeks afterward. Jane Boswell Moore's article about her experiences at Gettysburg, published in the *Second Annual Report of the Maryland Committee of the Christian Commission*, portrays the distinctly spiritual nature of the USCC nurse's contact with soldiers. Moore, writing within months after the battle, recorded her conversation with a dying 17-year-old soldier. The dialogue indicates that Moore ministered to the boy, consoling him, questioning him gently about his religious faith, and assisting him to have "faith in the power of the Lord Jesus to save you" (quoted in Hoisington 2002, 108).

The spiritual component of USCC volunteerism was central to all its activities. As its leadership declared, the organization believed its mission was to "persuade [the soldiers] to become reconciled to God through the blood of His Son, if they have not already done so, and if they have, then to be strong in the Lord, resolute for duty, earnest and constant in prayer, and fervent in spirit, serving the Lord" (quoted in Woodworth 2001, 168). For every female volunteer working directly with soldiers, there were thousands more women on the home front contributing food, clothing, and money to the USCC. In many Northern states, the USCC competed with the

USSC for women's attention and resources. Competition between the two organizations was fierce at times, and in rural and other religiously conservative regions, the USCC's devout, evangelical religiosity won out.

When Annie Turner Wittenmyer, leader of the Keokuk (Iowa) Ladies' Soldiers' Aid Society, visited her brother in a Missouri military hospital in 1862, she was appalled to see the breakfast he was served: "On a dingy-looking wooden tray was a tin cup full of black, strong coffee; beside it was a leaden-looking tin platter, on which was a piece of fried fat bacon, swimming in its own grease, and a slice of bread" (quoted in Leonard 1994, 88). Wittenmyer's subsequent work in the military hospitals convinced her that the food the army served was not only unhealthy but was also so unappetizing that the sick and wounded often refused to eat. In 1864, after leaving her position as Iowa State Sanitary Agent, she convinced USCC leaders to fund a new project she proposed, which she called "special diet kitchens." In these kitchens, Turner Wittenmyer explained, nourishing, health-promoting food would be prepared in a manner that would mimic as closely as possible meals prepared at home. According to her reasoning, meals similar to those prepared by mothers and wives would tempt the soldier-patients to eat, thus hastening their recoveries.

The USCC male leadership endorsed the plan and agreed that Turner Wittenmyer should be the diet kitchens' Supervisory Agent. As such, she superintended the creation of over a hundred special diet kitchens in Union military hospitals. She hired approximately 200 mature, capable, Protestant white women to manage the kitchens and their all-male, largely African-American cooking staffs at a salary of $20 per month. Turner Wittenmyer scrutinized her prospective managers cautiously. An applicant had to demonstrate that she was a pious Christian and was prepared to sacrifice herself for the good of the soldiers. The diet kitchens, though short-lived, were a resounding success. By the end of the war, they had served over two million rations (Leonard 1994, 89–93).

Over the course of the war, the USCC collected and disbursed $6 million toward the spiritual and physical care of Union soldiers, a mere 40 percent of the $15 million the USSC estimated it raised. The USCC concluded its operations during 1865, and held its last meeting in February 1866.

See also **Gettysburg, Battle of**

Selected Readings

Hoisington, Daniel John. *Gettysburg and the Christian Commission.* Roseville, MN: Edinborough Press. 2002.

Leonard, Elizabeth D. *Yankee Women: Gender Battles in the Civil War.* New York: Norton. 1994.

United States Sanitary Commission

The United States Sanitary Commission (USSC) was a civilian-run national government relief organization that provided food, clothing, medical supplies, white female nurses, and other assistance to the Medical Department of the Union army. During the Civil War, more women volunteered their labor under the auspices of this organization than any other. Thousands of Northern white women worked in local SOLDIERS' AID SOCIETIES that were affiliated with the USSC. They gathered and manufactured supplies, raised funds, and provided support to enlisted soldiers, veterans, and their families. Approximately 3,200 Northern women—most of them white, Protestant, and middle class—served as USSC nurses in the army's Union military hospitals and HOSPITAL SHIPS. The Western Sanitary Commission (WSC) and a number of independent soldiers' aid societies also sent female nurses to the military hospitals and to the "floating hospitals." At the end of the war, Alfred Janson Bloor, Corresponding Secretary of the USSC, estimated that $15 million dollars' worth of goods were "collected, assorted, despatched, and re-collected, reassorted, and re-despatched by women, representing with great impartiality, every grade of society in the Republic" (Attie 1998, 262).

According to various USSC reports, the commission included thousands of soldiers' aid societies, a large percentage of them in the Northeast. Estimates vary widely as to the total number of USSC-affiliated soldiers' aid societies. In its official history, the USSC reported that approximately 7,000 societies had been auxiliaries (Attie 1998, 3). At the conclusion of the war, the USSC estimated 32,000 societies (Giesberg 2000, 4). At one point, the USSC stated that it included 10,000 to 12,000 relief organizations. The number of soldiers' aid societies that never served under the umbrella of an official organization is not known.

Chicago was the hub of the Northwestern Sanitary Commission (NSC), an auxiliary of the USSC, which provided links to societies in much of the northern Midwest, including Ohio, Illinois, Wisconsin, Iowa, Michigan, Indiana, and Minnesota. The Western Sanitary Commission (WSC) was completely independent of the USSC. It coordinated the efforts of pro-Union women and men in Missouri, in much of the Mississippi River Valley and in parts of the West. The WSC performed many of the same functions as the USSC, but it also focused on feeding, clothing, and sheltering the tens of thousands of white and black civilian REFUGEES who wandered the trans-Mississippi region.

Even while responding to the directives of the USSC, local soldiers' aid societies managed to maintain some autonomy, to the disapproval of Washington bureaucrats. Like the WSC, many women in the small soldiers' relief societies valued controlling their labor and production so that they could address the needs of soldiers and their families from their own hometowns and states.

In April 1861, a week after the outbreak of the war and two months prior to the USSC's formation, physicians Elizabeth and Emily Blackwell of New York City established the WOMAN'S CENTRAL ASSOCIATION OF RELIEF (WCAR). Through this organization, they originated the concept of a centralized agency to dispense women's home front productions and to train nurses for the military hospitals.

When the USSC was formally established in June 1861, its male leadership expected that the organization's primary functions would be to assist the federal government and the U.S. army in the establishment and management of military hospitals and in the promotion of up-to-date medical and sanitary practices. There was no question in the minds of the elite, urban male directors that such help was essential. When sanitary leaders Reverend Henry Whitney Bellows, Frederick Law Olmsted, and George Templeton Strong toured the military camps and hospitals in the first weeks of the war, they learned of the military's desperate need of medical assistance.

After the Union defeat at the First Battle of Bull Run (First Manassas), Olmsted, the general secretary of the USSC, inspected the condition of Union troops. In his "Report on the Demoralization of the Volunteers," a paper that helped USSC leaders to focus the organization's priorities, he observed,

> Our army, previous to and at the time of the engagement [Bull Run], was suffering from want of sufficient, regularly-provided, and suitable food, from thirst, from want .... of refreshing sleep, and from the exhausting effects of a long, hot, and rapid march, the more exhausting because of the diminution of vital force of the troops due to the causes above enumerated (quoted in Rybczynski 2000, 201).

Despite the pressing need and prospect of imminent disaster, Union military leaders and federal officials resisted the prospect of a civilian organization interfering in the military hospitals. President Abraham Lincoln, though persuaded to approve the formation of the USSC, insisted that there was no need of such intervention. The USSC, he said, would be a "fifth wheel to the coach" (quoted in Rybczynski 2000, 204).

It became clear to USSC leaders in 1861 and 1862 that a major challenge involved the encouragement and management of women's volunteer production and the collection of clothing, bedding, food, medicines, and other supplies for Union soldiers—a massive effort that assumed center stage in the eyes of the Northern public. Regardless of the importance of the USSC's other functions, by war's end the public was convinced that the USSC's primary role had been the gathering and distribution of these goods (Attie 1998, 88).

While Northern white upper-middle-class men superintended the USSC bureaucracy in Washington, DC, white upper-middle-class women directed its largest branch organizations in the North's urban centers. These women had the most direct influence over the production of the largely female soldiers' aid societies. Women branch leaders Louisa Lee Schuyler of the WCAR in New York, Abigail (Abby) Williams May of the New England Woman's Auxiliary Association (NEWAA) in Boston, and MARY ASHTON RICE LIVERMORE and Jane Hoge of the NSC in Chicago were among the highest-ranking USSC female leaders who orchestrated the network of production and delivery that enabled clothing, bedding, and food produced by Northern women to reach the central distribution centers in and around Washington, DC. From these centers, USSC agents, most of them male, dispensed the supplies to the soldiers in the military camps and hospitals.

Shortly after the USSC was in operation, during the summer of 1861, its male leaders issued a directive to women throughout the North, urging them to form USSC-sponsored soldiers' aid societies in every village and town. The USSC's call to Northern women emphasized the nation's urgent need of their voluntary labor and their duty to supply it.

By the time the USSC distributed this call, women in thousands of soldiers' aid societies were already producing supplies to soldiers on the frontlines, sending them directly to local regiments or to state relief agencies. Although pleas from the USSC to coalesce under its auspices met with cooperation in many regions, there was a lack of compliance in others. A number of women's groups preferred to maintain control over their own operations and insisted on giving to community and state agencies.

Women in Keokuk, Iowa, developed their own centralized network of soldiers' aid societies in the first few weeks of the war, before the USSC was fully operative. By the time USSC leaders in Washington contacted them, the Iowa women were leagues ahead of the USSC in production and efficiency. In addition to supplying military camps and hospitals, they had placed nurses in the regimental and general hospitals further South.

USSC leaders pressured the governor of Iowa to corral the state's civilian relief for the USSC, but the women of Keokuk fought to retain their independence. Led by Annie Turner Wittenmyer, a woman with a long history of involvement in benevolent reform, the Keokuk Ladies' Soldiers' Aid Society continued to operate as a self-sufficient network until late in 1863 when they succumbed to pressure to merge with the USSC (Leonard 1994, 60–80). Not long afterward, Wittenmyer defected to the USSC's arch rival, the UNITED STATES CHRISTIAN COMMISSION, where she once again had the freedom to determine what soldiers from her region needed most, leading her to establish special diet kitchens in western hospitals.

Convincing women to give to a national organization rather than to a state or local agency was only one of the challenges the USSC faced in its work with women on the home front. By 1863, with the cloudburst of production in 1861 and the flurry of activity in the fall of 1862 long past, many soldiers' aid societies ceased to operate. USSC branch directors Louisa Schuyler and Abby May were determined to convince Northern women of the importance of contributing to the USSC. Both women spent countless hours, writing letters long into the nights, to encourage local society leaders to stay productive.

Schuyler, May, and other women leaders of the largest auxiliary societies devised their own strategies that they knew would operate most fruitfully in their regions. Unlike the male leaders' USSC circulars that chided women because they were not producing enough to fulfill their patriotic duty, Schuyler and May listened to women's problems, respected their decisions, and strategized new methods of securing supplies from women. Instead of following the USSC directive that the societies' limited funds should purchase soldiers' clothing from manufacturers, May decided that the money the women raised would stretch farther if she were to purchase the material wholesale and send it directly to them to be made into clothing (Giesberg 2000, 77–78). By so doing, May respected New England women's demand that the USSC be frugal with their hard-earned funds. In Boston, Helen Gilson used USSC money to hire needy working-class and immigrant women, many of them soldiers' wives, to manufacture soldiers' clothing, thereby satisfying the desires of middle- and upper-class women in her community to help poor women on the home front.

Most women in the Northeast who responded to Schuyler's and May's appeals asserted that the pressing nature of their home responsibilities—care of children, the sick, and the elderly—prevented them from contributing. As the war wore on, increasing numbers of middle-class women were juggling their household and family duties while maintaining family farms and businesses in their husbands' absence. A woman from New Hartford, New York, wrote, "it seems to me if I had not a family of 5 small children and health very poor, that I would spend my whole time for a few weeks at least, in trying to mitigate such suffering [on the battlefields and in the military hospitals]" (quoted in Giesberg 2000, 70). Single women were equally stressed. An unmarried woman explained her situation to Schuyler.

> I am shut in school from 8 1/2 untill 4 p.m. every day. I have all my own housekeeping to do and we have no baker here …. I have an acre and three quarters of land to take care of out of school and in winter all my wood to saw and split at least I had to do it until a week since I found it was injuring my health … you must see I have not much leisure. (quoted in Attie 1998, 103–104)

The lack of financial resources to buy cloth and supplies plagued women's societies as hard economic times made fund-raising difficult. Rampant inflation and tax increases in the North from 1863 on pushed many families into poverty and made conservation of resources a priority for the middle class. In difficult economic times, some women reported that they had to channel the little charity they could spare toward the impoverished in their own communities.

Besides the economic concerns, by 1863, Northern women had also become concerned about the possibility of fraud and corruption within the USSC in Washington. Rumors and newspaper reports circulated stories of supplies being sold to soldiers instead of donated, of surgeons and military officers hoarding homemade goodies and spirits intended for the sick, and of USSC agents siphoning off goods for their own profit. Despite several public relations initiatives, female branch leaders were never able to shake off these charges. Their inability to do so led many women's societies to either halt operations or transfer their allegiance to the United States Christian Commission.

Schuyler was convinced that a broad-scale public relations campaign would persuade women that the USSC was a vital organization and that women's contributions were essential to the Union war effort. She and May sent male lecture agents into the field to inform the Northern public about the urgency of the USSC mission. Schuyler also persuaded Washington leaders to publish a newspaper to encourage women on the home front. The male writers and editors of the *USSC Bulletin* did not follow her recommendations. The publication's articles did little to validate Northern women's needs and problems and did not sufficiently acknowledge their criticisms or their contributions (Attie 1998, 187).

In Chicago in the fall of 1863, Mary Ashton Rice Livermore and Jane Hoge staged the first of the SANITARY FAIRS, the gala fund-raising events that were enormous moneymakers for the USSC. Although the male leaders in Washington issued stern recommendations that the regional branches and local societies not squander their energies and resources in what they believed were frivolous, madcap affairs, female leaders and their male cohorts in many cities and towns paid the advisory no heed and organized the fairs anyway, confident that they could raise huge sums. In all, sanitary fairs raised more than $4 million.

At the end of the war, the male USSC directors in Washington disbanded the organization and moved on to other work. Yet the women branch leaders and many women in the soldiers' aid societies continued to relieve the war-related suffering in their communities. For some Northern women, the wartime habit of collective work and organization with other women, once begun, was nearly impossible to relinquish. And for women who had never been involved in antebellum reform movements or benevolent work, the experience of soldiers' aid made them acutely aware of the needs of war veterans, the poor, the infirm, and the elderly in their own communities. This awareness, coupled with a raised political consciousness about their power as women working together for common goals, galvanized women who had wielded the most power in the USSC, and paved the way for postwar women's reform efforts.

See also **Hospital Ships; Nurses**

Selected Readings

Attie, Jeanie. *Patriotic Toil: Northern Women and the American Civil War*. Ithaca, NY: Cornell University Press. 1998.

Giesberg, Judith Ann. *Civil War Sisterhood: The United States Sanitary Commission and Women's Politics in Transition*. Boston: Northeastern University Press. 2000.

Ginzberg, Lori D. *Women and the Work of Benevolence: Morality, Politics, and Class in the Nineteeth-Century United States*. New Haven, CT: Yale University Press. 1990.

V

Van Lew, Elizabeth
(1818–1900)

You asked me my opinion of the cause of this war … He [a fellow spy] has endeavored to convince me that Democracy was the whole and sole cause, but I always told him I thought it was slavery …. Slave power is arrogant—is jealous and intrusive—is cruel—is despotic—not only over the slave, but over the community, the State.

—Elizabeth Van Lew, c. late February 1864, Richmond, Virginia (Van Lew 1996, 63)

Of all spies, male and female of the North and South, Elizabeth Van Lew is considered to have been among the most skilled, innovative, and successful. Operating from her mansion in the Confederate capital of Richmond, Virginia, Van Lew supplied essential information to Union Generals Ulysses S. Grant, George H. Sharpe, George G. Meade, and Benjamin F. Butler. She directed an espionage ring of approximately a dozen white and African-American women and men operating in and around Richmond. Van Lew was a fervid abolitionist dating from her school days in Philadelphia. When war was declared in 1861, she was determined to do everything in her power to help the Union cause. Since many pages are missing from Van Lew's 1861 diary entries, the motivation for her decision to become a Union spy cannot be precisely determined. Those pages that have survived emphasize her intense loyalty to the U.S. government and her passion for freedom for African Americans.

A member of the Richmond elite, Van Lew was raised as a Virginia aristocrat, even though her parents were both born in the North. Her mother and her father, both well-educated intellectuals, cultivated a love of learning in their daughter. They also sent her to be educated in Philadelphia. After her father died, Van Lew persuaded her mother to free their nine slaves. She also used a portion of her inheritance to purchase and then liberate a number of their servants' family members. By the 1850s, it was no secret in Richmond that Van Lew was an antislavery advocate. Her outspokenness about her abolitionism disturbed members of the elite and caused them to shun her, "as if I were plague-stricken," she once wrote (Van Lew 1996, 20).

Van Lew was particularly adept at devising and adapting espionage methods and strategies to meet the challenge of constantly changing situations. To secure the routing of messages, she instituted five relay sites between her home and the destination of most of her messages, south of Richmond. The first site was her family's small farm outside of the city. The four others were the homes of Unionist friends who were assisted by servants of her household or by other Unionist friends from Richmond. Her system was so successful and her spies so well trained and skilled that none were ever seized by the Confederates.

Van Lew also devised her own cipher system or code. She used a colorless liquid concoction to pen her messages, writing between the lines of ordinary correspondence. When the recipient added milk to a page, the invisible writing appeared. Van Lew was careful to tear messages into several parts before relaying them, sending each piece via a different courier. Her female spies also carried baskets of eggs in which one hollow egg carried a message (Markle 1994, 182).

From the early months of the war, Van Lew habitually visited Union soldiers and officers in the Confederate prisons in Richmond. This devotion to the enemy raised eyebrows and aroused suspicion in Richmond. Yet most of her neighbors appear to have concluded that her behavior merely betrayed a mental imbalance. Van Lew capitalized on their assumption to draw attention away from her activities. By muttering to herself as she walked to the prison, and by dressing untidily and far beneath her station, she earned the nickname "Crazy Bet" and lost her neighbors' notice.

In 1862, Van Lew directed her volunteer efforts and much of her information-gathering to the new prison for Union officers, Libby Prison, not far from her home. As many as 50,000 officers were incarcerated there at some point during the war. Van Lew, her elderly mother, and their African-American servants brought food to the starving soldiers, helped bandage the wounded, and read to the prisoners. Inside the spines of books she lent to officers, she inserted and received coded messages. Using this ruse, she sent and gathered information from recently captured Union officers and relayed the data to the appropriate military command. In 1864, with help from fellow spies Abby Green and Lucy Rice, she assisted 109 prisoners to escape from Libby by providing them with safe routes and locations of shelters (Barber 1997, 243–244).

When Union troops invaded Richmond on April 2, 1865, Grant made sure that a Union guard protected Van Lew's home. When he became president in 1869, he appointed her postmistress of Richmond, a position that she held until the end of his administration in early 1877. Soon after Rutherford B. Hayes became president, she was demoted to the position of a clerk. She then moved to Washington, DC to assume a postal clerkship. She eventually returned to Richmond, though she had little money to keep her going. She had spent her inheritance years before by assisting her former slaves and by funding her espionage activities during the war. Although several generals tried to obtain a $15,000 payment for her from the federal government as a tribute to her extensive war service, their efforts were unsuccessful. Van Lew did receive some money from the well-known Boston family of Paul Joseph Revere, a soldier she assisted at Libby Prison in 1862, as well as from other prominent citizens of Massachusetts (Van Lew 1996, 21).

See also **Patriotism; Secession; Spies and Espionage**

Selected Readings

Leonard, Elizabeth D. *All the Daring of the Soldier: Women of the Civil War Armies.* New York: Penguin Books. 2001.

Van Lew, Elizabeth. *A Yankee Spy in Richmond: The Civil War Diary of "Crazy Bet" Van Lew.* Edited by David D. Ryan. Mechanicsburg, PA: Stackpole Books. 1996.

Velazquez, Loreta Janeta (1842–?)

Since the 1876 publication of Loreta Janeta Velazquez's Civil War memoir, controversy, skepticism, and debate have dominated discussions of her experiences as a Confederate soldier and spy. Her sensationalized portrayal of her adventures, related in her best-seller *The Woman in Battle: A Narrative of the Exploits, Adventures, and Travels of Madame Loreta Janeta Velazquez, Otherwise Known as Lieutenant Harry Buford, Confederate States of America* has led many historians to conclude that much of her account is fabricated. In-depth research of Civil War era sources, however, reveals that many of the basic facts of her life in uniform are supported by press accounts, government records, and the memories of the Confederate soldiers who served with her. Nevertheless, as was common among adventure memoirs of the era, Velazquez undoubtedly embellished and exaggerated her history (Blanton and Cook 2002, 2, 178).

According to Velazquez, she was born into a family residing in Havana, Cuba. She states that she immigrated to the United States in 1849 to live with an aunt and to receive her education in New Orleans, Louisiana. Velazquez (her birth name) married an officer in the U.S. army in 1856 when she was 14 years old. Not long after her husband enlisted in the Confederate military in 1861, Velazquez, guided by her pro-Confederate passions and inspired by her childhood and adolescent desire to be a second Joan of Arc, claims that she perfected her ability to spit and swagger, disguised herself as a Harry T. Buford, and pronounced herself a lieutenant in the Confederate army. In Arkansas in the early weeks of the war, she managed to recruit enough men to form a company. Following this effort, she traveled on her own to Virginia. After the battle at Blackburn's Ford (Virginia) on July 18, 1861, Lieutenant Buford assumed the command of a company that had lost its officers. She was present at the First Battle of Manassas (known in the North as the First Battle of Bull Run) and again led a company of soldiers at the Battle of Balls Bluff in northern Virginia in October 1861.

After rejecting a job as a recruiting officer, Velazquez longed for greater adventure. She headed west where she joined Confederate combatants fighting near Woodsonville, Kentucky, in December 1861. During the wintry weeks prior to her participation in the Battle of Fort Donelson in western Tennessee in February 1862, she boasted that she wooed a number of young ladies. In early April 1862, toward the conclusion of the Battle of Shiloh in Pittsburg Landing, Tennessee, Velazquez was burying the dead when she was struck by shrapnel in the arm and shoulder. Following this crushing Confederate defeat, her final battle, Velazquez reports that she was overwhelmed by exhaustion, depression, and a revulsion against armed combat. After spending some weeks recuperating, she struggled to obtain a position as a spy. In 1862, she passed several weeks operating as a military passport agent and conductor on Confederate railways.

When Velazquez decided her career as a soldier had come to an end, she worked as a spy for the Confederate Secret Service. Her first assignments brought her to New Orleans and Havana. Twice captured and incarcerated, Union authorities in New Orleans deported her. She resumed her espionage activities in Richmond, Virginia, and, when suspected of being a Union spy, was imprisoned in Castle Thunder Prison in June 1863. Confederate officials soon remedied the error and, following a brief stint working in Atlanta, Georgia, she served as a double agent in Washington, DC. After six months on this detail, she claims in her memoir that she traded counterfeit federal stocks and bonds in Canada and Britain to obtain monies to bolster the Confederate government's treasury funds. There is evidence that she also was a collaborator in the conspiracy to assassinate President Abraham Lincoln (Blanton and Cook 2002, 119).

After the war, Velazquez traveled in Europe and throughout the South. She married for the third time to a former Confederate officer. (She supposedly wed her second husband during the war after her first husband was killed in an accident.) In 1867, she settled in New Orleans to assist in efforts to establish a community of Confederate exiles in Venezuela. When her third husband died, she eventually returned to the United States. After an unsuccessful career mining in the West, she and her son from her fourth marriage relocated to Rio de Janeiro, Brazil, with the proceeds from her 1876 memoir. There she found work as a journalist. Nothing is known of her later life and death.

See also **Military Women; Spies and Espionage**

Selected Readings

Blanton, DeAnne and Lauren M. Cook. *They Fought Like Demons: Women Soldiers in the American Civil War.* Baton Rouge: Louisiana State University Press. 2002.

Leonard, Elizabeth D. *All the Daring of the Soldier: Women of the Civil War Armies.* New York: Penguin Books. 2001.

Vicksburg

The screams of the women of Vicksburg were the saddest I have ever heard. The wailings over the dead seemed full of a heartsick agony. I cannot attempt to describe the thrill of pity, mingled with fear, that pierced my soul, as suddenly vibrating through the air would come these sorrowful shrieks!—these pitiful moans!—sometimes almost simultaneously with the explosion of a shell.

—Mary Ann Loughborough, Vicksburg, Mississippi (Loughborough 1864, 131–132)

For six weeks from May 22 until July 4, 1863, Union troops and artillery besieged the city of Vicksburg, Mississippi. Situated high on steep-banked bluffs on the east side of the Mississippi River, Vicksburg was a leading commercial port. As Union forces struggled to gain and retain control of the entire river from Illinois to the Gulf of Mexico, the capture of Vicksburg emerged as a key strategic goal that had eluded Union efforts for more than a year. When Confederate Brigadier General John Pemberton's troops refused to give up the city during the spring of 1863, Union Brigadier General Ulysses S. Grant's forces began attacking the Confederate entrenchment with artillery day and night.

Although Pemberton repeatedly demanded that Vicksburg citizens flee the city for their safety, not everyone heeded the warning. Many white women insisted that there was no need to leave. From their point of view, the war had been fought all around them since the early months of the war and Vicksburg had remained virtually untouched. The outskirts of the city and surrounding areas had been shelled, but because the residential area of the city was still intact, many women assumed that the hills provided protection from bombardment. In their diaries and memoirs of the siege, a number of women explained that abandoning the city for an uncertain future as a refugee was just as hazardous as remaining. If they had to suffer the cruelties of war, they reasoned, at least in Vicksburg they would be among friends and familiar surroundings.

The white women and men of means who chose to stay arranged for caves to be dug into the hillsides for their families and slaves to retreat to during bombardments. Male slaves did most of the digging. As Lida Lord Reed explains, "Now, the caves of Vicksburg were not, as many suppose, natural caverns, but hastily dug passages, like the burrows of rabbits, running straight into the hillsides, and many of them in the heart of the city (Reed 1908, 923). Loughborough described her cave as "an excavation in the earth the size of a large room, high enough for the tallest person to stand perfectly erect, provided with comfortable seats, and altogether quite a large and habitable abode ... were it not for the dampness and the constant contact with the soft earthy walls" (Loughborough 1864, 17). Besides the dampness, women reported that they minded the claustrophobic atmosphere of cave life: "When we went in this evening and sat down, the earthy, suffocating feeling, as of a living tomb, was dreadful to me" (Cable 1885, 767).

Of all women's portrayals of the siege, Loughborough best captures the fear and terror of a lengthy bombardment—especially the horrific assault on the mind and senses.

> As it [the shell] neared, the noise became more deafening; the air was full of the rushing sound; pains darted through my temples; my ears were full of the confusing noise; and, as it exploded, the report flashed through my head like an electric shock, leaving me in a quiet state of terror the most painful that I can imagine—cowering in a corner, holding my child to my heart—the only feeling of my life being the choking throbs of my heart, that rendered me almost breathless .... Again and again the terrible fright came over us in that night. (Loughborough 1864, 56–57)

Enduring one barrage after another left many women prostrate with exhaustion in the days following a lengthy attack. Women writers recorded the aftereffects of severe trauma and stress that they and their friends experienced. As Loughborough observed, "Many women were utterly sick through constant fear and apprehension" (Loughborough 1864, 131–132). Other diarists and memoirists noted that the extreme lethargy and apathy was accompanied by an increase in the incidence of disease. As women struggled to survive the worst crisis they had ever encountered, their increasingly deficient diet compromised their resiliency. Because the city was completely cut off, food quickly disappeared. Women and their families subsisted on rice or cornmeal, supplemented occasionally by milk and a bit of bacon, mule meat, or, by the end of the siege, rat meat.

However meager civilians' rations or miserable their existence, Vicksburg women were painfully aware that the Confederate soldiers entrenched nearby were experiencing far worse conditions, including death from starvation. One diarist recalled the words of a Confederate soldier after the surrender of Vicksburg.

> The men [Confederate soldiers] in Vicksburg will never forget Pemberton! ... A child would have known better than to shut men up in this cursed trap to starve to death like Useless vermin .... Starved to death because we had a fool for a general. (Cable 1885, 774)

On July 4, 1863, when Pemberton formally surrendered Vicksburg to Grant, the city became another Union-occupied city on the Mississippi. White women and their families returned to their battle-scarred homes. As food became more available, everyday life appeared to normalize, though the world of white prewar Vicksburg was shattered. For the African-American men and women who were now free, those who did not gain employment or enlistment in Union regiments, entered the federal contraband camps, received aid from freedmen's relief societies, or labored on plantations confiscated by the federal government.

See also **Contraband Women; Invasion and Occupation**

Selected Readings

Cable, George Washington, ed. "A Woman's Diary of the Siege of Vicksburg." *Century Magazine*. 30 (September 1885): 767–775.

Loughborough, Mary Ann. *My Cave Life in Vicksburg*. New York: D. Appleton and Co. 1864.

Reed, Lida L. "A Woman's Experience During the Siege of Vicksburg." *Harper's Monthly Magazine*. 118 (December 1908): 45–53.

Walker, Peter F. *Vicksburg: A People at War, 1860–1865*. Chapel Hill: University of North Carolina Press. 1960.

W

Wakeman, Sarah Rosetta (1843–1864)

I don't know how long before i shall have to go into the field of battle. For my part i don't Care. I don't feel afraid to go. I don't believe there are any Rebel's bullet made for me yet. Nor i don't Care if there is. I am as independent as a hog on the ice. If it is God will for me to fall in the field of battle, it is my will to go and never return home.

—Sarah Rosetta Wakeman (Pvt. Lyons Wakeman),
August 5, 1863, Washington, DC (quoted in Burgess 1994, 42)

In 1991, Lauren M. Cook (formerly Burgess), a leading authority on women soldiers during the Civil War, gained access to the letters that Sarah Rosetta Wakeman (alias Union Private Lyons Wakeman) wrote home during her two years in the Union army.

These documents are among the few known surviving personal papers of a woman soldier who fought during the Civil War. As Cook points out in her introduction to her edited volume of Wakeman's letters, *An Uncommon Soldier*, these documents "represent the most complete, contemporary account of a woman's experiences as a Civil War soldier that has been discovered thus far." (Burgess 1994, 7).

Sarah Rosetta Wakeman was born in Afton, a farming hamlet in south central New York State, in 1843, the daughter of farmers. As the oldest of nine children, only two of whom were boys, Wakeman's labor was undoubtedly critical to the survival of her family's farm. Census records reveal that she attended school, but, as was common for children in rural farm communities in the 1840s and 1850s, she probably attended school sporadically, perhaps only during the winter months.

When Wakeman was 19 years old, she left home, striking out on her own dressed in men's clothing. From her subsequent letters to her family, it appears that she may have left home and her employment as a domestic servant to find a means to help her father repay his debts. She found a job on a coal barge navigating the Chenango Canal, a waterway that provided passage from Binghamton to Utica, New York. Working as a man, Wakeman was able to earn much more than she could have as a domestic or from any of the few other occupations open to her as a woman.

In late August 1862, not long after she started work on the canal, she enlisted in the 153rd Regiment, New York State Volunteers in Canajoharie, New York, receiving a bounty of $152. The 153rd was first posted to the Washington, DC, area and remained there until February 1864, to help bolster Union forces defending the nation's capital from Confederate attack.

From the letters Wakeman wrote home, army life appears to have agreed with her. Her self-confidence soared as she proved herself more than equal to the demands of a soldier's existence. She fulfilled her duties competently, enjoyed military drills, remained healthy, and managed to gain weight on camp food. She also was able to return in kind what pugnacious fellow soldiers dealt her. Despite the satisfactions of camp life, Wakeman found herself waiting and hoping for the day her regiment would engage in battle. As she and her fellow soldiers languished from boredom, she envisioned the day when the war would be over and she would be on her own once again. Though she could not imagine returning to live with her family, she dreamed of owning her own farm in Wisconsin.

In February 1864, her regiment joined forces with the troops of Union Brigadier General Nathaniel Banks as they prepared to embark on the Red River Campaign in Louisiana. From early March on, her regiment was on the move, marching hundreds of miles in less than two months. The campaign was fraught with hardships and disasters, the worst of which were the physical conditions the soldiers had to endure. Prolonged, often forced marches in the sun and the sweltering, high humidity of Louisiana were oppressively difficult, but it was the ingestion of the murky, infested waters of the region that proved disastrous for thousands of soldiers.

On April 9, 1864, Wakeman participated in the Battle of Pleasant Hill and in the Battle of Monett's Ferry on April 23 in central Louisiana. In her last letter home dated April 14, 1864, Wakeman reported the facts of the battle but did not reveal her personal reactions or emotional responses to the combat.

> Our army made an advance up the river to pleasant hill about 40 miles …. The first day of the fight our army got whip[ped] and we had to retreat back about ten miles. The next day … There was a heavy Cannonading all day and a Sharp firing of infantry …. I was under fire about four hours and laid on the field of battle all night. (Quoted in Burgess 1994, 71)

Wakeman did not write home again. At some point during the next few weeks, she contracted dysentery, the most common and most deadly disease afflicting soldiers during the Civil War. On May 3, she entered the regimental hospital and on May 7 was transferred to a military hospital in New Orleans. The trip, probably traversing an arduous overland route, took over two weeks. She entered the hospital May 22 and died a month later on June 19, 1864.

See also **Military Women**

Selected Readings

Blanton, DeAnne and Lauren M. Cook. *They Fought Like Demons: Women Soldiers in the American Civil War.* Baton Rouge: Louisiana State University Press. 2002.

Burgess, Lauren Cook, ed. *An Uncommon Soldier: The Civil War Letters of Sarah Rosetta Wakeman, Alias Pvt. Lyons Wakeman, 153rd* Regiment, New York State Volunteers, 1862–1864. Pasadena, MD: The Minerva Center. 1994.

Walker, Mary Edwards (1832–1919)

[Mary Edwards Walker] … faithfully served as contract surgeon in the service of the United States, and has devoted herself with much patriotic zeal to the sick and wounded soldiers, both in the field and hospitals, to the detriment of her own health, and has endured hardships as a prisoner of war for four months in a southern prison while acting as a contract surgeon.

—President Andrew Johnson, November 11, 1865, upon signing the bill to present Mary Edwards Walker with the Congressional Medal of Honor for Meritorious Service (quoted in Leonard 1994, 155)

Throughout the Civil War, physician Mary Edwards Walker pursued a commission as a surgeon in the Union army. This ambition spurred her to contribute her medical expertise in field and general military hospitals in Washington, DC, Virginia, Tennessee, and Ohio. Though she never stopped trying to achieve her goal, and though the military willingly accepted her medical services, the army never recognized her with the commission she craved. Her battle to win acceptance as a full-fledged army surgeon was not a complete failure, however. In November 1865, President Andrew Johnson awarded her the Congressional Medal of Honor. She was the first woman to be so recognized.

Mary Edwards Walker was born and raised on a farm in Oswego, New York. As a young woman, she vowed to become a doctor and at age 22, she graduated from the Syracuse Medical College in 1855. One of her professors later acknowledged that she was a "faithful and diligent student" who had made "rapid and meritorious progress," graduating "with honor" (quoted in Leonard 1994, 251).

From her graduation until the Civil War, Walker practiced medicine in New York State. She married, but separated from her husband after a short time. During the 1850s, she was an ardent advocate of dress reform, although her parents had championed the health benefits of nonrestrictive attire for women long before this time. Walker's costume varied over her lifetime, but in the 1850s and 1860s, she often wore a modified version of the bloomer costume (named for temperance and women's rights activist Amelia Bloomer), which included a full knee-length skirt worn over trousers.

As soon as the war began in 1861, Walker traveled to Washington, DC. Like physician ESTHER HILL HAWKS and other female DOCTORS, she failed to convince military officials to permit her to serve as an army surgeon. Undeterred, she volunteered her services at the Indiana Hospital in Washington where she assisted the head surgeon. The Quaker nurse ABBY HOPPER GIBBONS encountered Walker at this time. She commented, not unkindly, that Walker was "a character." Gibbons added, "She has a keen eye, a cheerful manner, and the patients believe in her" (Gibbons 1897, 1: 299).

In the fall of 1862, as fierce battles raged around the nation's capital, Walker expected that the army's medical crisis would supersede its concerns about her gender and its automatic assumptions about her lack of competence. Upon arriving in the midst of a typhoid epidemic among the ranks in Warrenton, Virginia, she immediately set to work to save as many lives as she could. From there, she rushed to tend to the amputees and severely wounded following the Battle of Fredericksburg, in Virginia, again as a volunteer. Though her surgeon superiors and co-workers attempted from time to time to acquire a commission for her or, at the least, some remuneration, their requests were always denied.

Walker had strong opinions about the efficacy of amputations, the treatment of choice for severe arm and leg wounds. Like many female nurses and doctors in the field hospitals, she believed that some soldiers were unnecessarily maimed for life or killed by the inevitable post-operative infections. She shared these views with her fellow surgeons and counseled soldiers whose wounds she believed did not require amputation to refuse the operation. She urged these men to threaten any surgeon who refused to heed their wishes. If need be, she told them, threaten non-compliant surgeons with murder after the war is over (Leonard 1994, 124).

In 1863, Walker offered her time to an organization that assisted Northern women who came to the capital to care for their soldier relatives in the military hospitals. In late 1863, she journeyed to Chattanooga, Tennessee, to tend to fallen soldiers at the Battle of Chickamauga. Though the head surgeon allowed her to perform only as a nurse, she did what she could to relieve the suffering of the wounded. Her hard work impressed Brigadier General George H. Thomas, commander of the Army of the Cumberland. In January 1864 he pushed through her first official appointment. In February, she became a civilian contract surgeon for the 52nd Ohio Volunteers stationed in Tennessee. This post was not the commission she longed for, but it was official recognition of her status as a doctor.

Two months later, in April 1864, Confederate soldiers captured her while she was en route to doctor civilians in the area. She spent the next five months in Castle Thunder Prison in Richmond, Virginia. Although she had always been physically strong and healthy, inadequate food and squalid prison conditions spawned health problems that plagued her for the rest of her life. In August, she was released as a result of a prisoner exchange.

Despite her weakness from her ordeal, in September, Walker managed to convince Major General William Tecumseh Sherman to give her a post at Louisville Female Military Prison, where Confederate female spies and insurgents were incarcerated. She bore the title "Surgeon in Charge," yet remained a civilian contract surgeon. After years of earning nothing for her war efforts, she now earned a salary of approximately $100 per month. Walker and the military officers at the prison clashed repeatedly, leaving Walker in a difficult, isolated position that subverted her authority. During the final weeks of the war, she accepted a transfer to become a director of a home for orphans and refugees in Clarksville, Tennessee.

Lee's surrender at Appomattox did not end Walker's quest for a commission as a military surgeon. She and her advocates petitioned President Andrew Johnson after the war, to no avail. On November 11, 1865, Johnson presented Walker with the Congressional Medal of Honor.

Immediately after the war, Walker immersed herself in the causes of dress reform and woman suffrage. She also lectured for a brief time on her Civil War experiences. In her later years, her determination to wear trousers and other vestiges of male attire caused most women and men to dismiss her as an eccentric. She did not pursue the practice of medicine to any great extent after the war.

In 1918, at age 86, the U.S. government withdrew the Congressional Medal of Honor from 910 individuals, including Walker, when it decided to issue the medal only for heroic acts "involving actual conflict with the enemy." In 1977, President Jimmy Carter reissued the medal to Walker posthumously.

See also **Nurses**

Selected Readings

Filler, Louis. "Walker, Mary Edwards." In *Notable American Women, 1607–1950: A Biographical Dictionary.* Volume 3. Edited by Edward T. James et al. Cambridge, MA: Belknap Press of Harvard University Press. 1971. 532–533.

Leonard, Elizabeth D. *Yankee Women: Gender Battles in the Civil War.* New York: Norton. 1994.

Western Women

Six thousand white and African-American men, women, and children emigrated west during the Civil War, far fewer than during any other four-year period in the 1840s and 1850s. From 1841 to 1867, 350,000 people made the trek west on the overland trails, becoming newcomers in lands already inhabited by Native Americans, Mexicans, and Mexican Americans.

Western women and men rarely figure in histories of the Civil War, adding to the popular misconception that Americans living west of the Mississippi River were completely isolated from the war, cared little about it, and lived peaceful lives during the war years. Although hundreds and sometimes thousands of miles away from the major battlefields, large sections of the West were in turmoil during the war. A number of Native American tribes revolted to protest the loss of their lands, the decimation of buffalo herds, and their resulting starvation. On the Rio Grande River, Mexican-American volunteer soldiers assisted the Union army in ousting the Confederate army from New Mexico Territory. In Minnesota, several tribes of Sioux Indians attacked and killed hundreds of white settlers in 1862. In Colorado and Idaho Territories in 1864, the Union army massacred Indian men, women, and children, which motivated many more tribes throughout the West to retaliate against white settlers. In the midst of all this upheaval, western women of all races, ethnic groups, and social classes struggled—as nineteenth-century American women did throughout the nation—to maintain stable, comfortable homes and care for their families, to sustain their family farms and businesses, to uphold and build strong communities, and, when possible, to aid the war effort.

For all the hazards and trials of the journey west on the overland trails, from 1861 to 1865, the trip was less taxing and difficult for most emigrants than it was for earlier migrants. By this time, general stores and trading sites were well established, providing opportunities to replenish supplies and trade livestock. Trail improvements shortened the travel by nearly a month. Telegraph communication allowed travelers to send and receive messages. And Salt Lake City in Utah Territory, by this time a thriving community, made it possible for emigrants to make repairs, rest, and relax in comfortable surroundings.

Confrontation with hostile Native Americans was the threat the overlanders feared most during the Civil War. Despite Indian attacks on small, isolated groups of emigrants, the vast majority of travelers never experienced any serious problems with the Indian tribes they encountered. White marauders, however, presented a constant danger. These thieves and outlaws, occasionally disguised as Indians, attacked wagon trains and small groups of migrants throughout the West.

For other travelers, the war itself disrupted the journey. In 1863, the white GUERRILLA WAR between pro-Confederate Missouri Bushwackers and pro-Union Kansas Jayhawkers disrupted the overland journey in Kansas. Mary Barnard Aguirre, a young white woman, was traveling with her Hispanic husband and newborn on a mule-drawn wagon train. She commented on the fears she experienced as her family passed through hostile territory.

> Our road lay thro' Kansas which was then in a fearful state of exasperation against the Bushwackers on account of Quantril [Confederate Colonel William C. Quantrill] having just burnt Lawrence & murdered a great many people in revenge for something the Jayhawkers had done to his people. So we could literally feel the *blood* in the air & were thrown into a terrible state …. (quoted in Moynihan 1998, 246)

In the midst of their anxieties on the trail, women kindled new friendships with other women traveling with them on the overland journey. For most women, separation from their family members, the homes, and their female support networks they left behind was the greatest trial they faced on the road west. When frontier women reached their final destinations in the West and began the work of settlement, they were often isolated from other adult women for the first time in their lives. The first months and years of settlement were emotionally the most difficult and was the hardship they lamented most in their diaries and letters. In 1866 in Colorado Territory, Amelia Buss poured out her distress to her diary.

> George went to the mountains yesterday morning to be gon all week … after he had gon gave vent to my feelings in a flood of tears. It may seem foolish to those that have neighbors and friends around them. I get a long very well through the day but the long evening and nights are horrible. (Quoted in Armitage 1987, 12)

Louise A. K. Clappe described the shock of frontier life in early California for female newcomers in her "Dame Shirley" letters, which she published for those back East. According to Clappe, life in the West could be defined by its deficiencies, which included,

> no newspapers, no churches, lectures, concerts, or theaters; no fresh books; no shopping, calling nor gossiping little tea-drinkings; no parties, no balls, no picnics, no tableaus, no charades, no latest fashions, no daily mail … no promenades, no rides or drives; no vegetables but potatoes and onions, no milk, no eggs, no *nothing*. (Quoted in Armitage 1987, 182)

The first essential chore of settlement for women and men was the clearing of land and the planting of food crops, if the land was arable. At first, families lived in tents or in the wagons they had traveled in. Once a food supply was assured, a family's main concern turned toward the building of a dwelling that would enable them to survive the winter. On the prairie and the plains, the first home was usually a simple earthen dugout to be followed years later by a more permanent sod house or "soddy." In forested regions, men, women, and children all pitched in to construct a log cabin, often containing no windows.

Whether clearing land, felling trees, or planting and plowing crops, women always had a regular assortment of never-ending domestic duties to attend to. Cooking meals was a daily challenge on the frontier. Without the cookstoves that had been too heavy to haul west, women had to master the time-consuming art of cooking over an open fire. Baking in a Dutch oven, substituting baking soda biscuits for yeast breads, and baking cakes without butter or eggs were all skills a frontier woman needed to add to her culinary repertoire. The most difficult domestic chore—the laundry—was made more arduous by the necessity of carrying water, often over a great distance. If no store or source of supply was at hand, women had to manufacture their own lye soap from a concoction of water, lime, and ashes. This product, combined with kitchen grease, was boiled over the open fire until the soap was made (Myres 1982, 146–148, 152).

Even when a family became firmly established with a permanent winter-secure home, women continued to juggle the same domestic tasks that had challenged them when they were living back East or in the Midwest. Rachel Haskel lived with her family in the established mining town of Aurora, Nevada. On March 21, 1867, she recorded the details of a hard day's work in her diary, but also took the time to note that she had seized some literary leisure.

> Swept and dusted house prior to beginning the great domestic dread of the household; washing. Made bread and washed, back ached thought I should not attempt to do this another week but suppose when the day comes shall do so rather than send clothes up town … Had beans cooking all day. Made rolls to eat hot with them. Bread rather a failure, would not rise well. Scrubbed kitchen nicely and read Harper by stove while waiting Mr. H's return to supper …. Children playing their author game …. I read "Laura's lovers" and finished "Brace of boys" in Harper. (Quoted in Fischer 1977, 65)

As was the case for Rachel Haskel, not all pioneers venturing west became farmers. Some women followed their husbands or journeyed alone to the mining camps and boomtowns in the Pacific Northwest and Nevada, or to mines in the Rocky Mountains, where gold rushes were ongoing during the Civil War. Women composed no more than 20 percent of adults in the West's mining camps (and often far fewer), and their domestic services were always in high demand. Single and married women earned wages either at home or in the community at large. Even though census takers recorded that 90 percent of all women in the mining towns "kept house," a non-wage-earning occupation, many middle-class and lower-income women did work for wages at home, baking bread and pies for miners, taking in boarders, doing laundry, or sewing. The 10 percent of women who were independent wage earners were primarily single white women who worked as teachers, restaurant owners, cooks, hotelkeepers, domestic servants, and laundresses (West 1987, 181). NATIVE AMERICAN WOMEN and married AFRICAN-AMERICAN WOMEN also worked for wages as poorly paid domestic servants and laundresses.

Mining camps and towns varied widely. The newest camps, created hastily as soon as gold or silver was discovered, were rough-hewn, often filthy settlements. As the population grew with the arrival of more prospectors, service providers—storekeepers, saloon owners, bankers, and other professionals—arrived with their families, eventually making a more orderly community. Thirteen-year-old Harriet Hitchcock traveled with her family to the Colorado Rockies during the Colorado Gold Rush of the early 1860s. In her diary, she describes the primitive nature of a brand new mining "city."

> Rode to Cache Creek on my pony .... This is a city composed of ten or twelve log cabins. It is the largest city on the western side of the snowy range. Population this summer one hundred ... Mining is the principle occupation of the inhabitants .... On the principle street (which by the way is the only one) there are two hotels and one store containing a few yards of calico plenty of flour and whiskey. Bread is considered the staff of life. Whiskey the life itself. (Quoted in Holmes 1999, 252)

By the 1860s, women new to the frontier were usually not isolated for long. Neighbors arrived, and though farms may have been distant from each other, opportunities to socialize with other women soon materialized. Women traveled to visit with each other, to help with childbirth or illness, or to cooperate on a major sewing or cooking project. Frontier families socialized at barn raisings, quilting bees, church services, potluck gatherings, and dances. As a settlement became larger and more organized, annual Fourth of July celebrations, speeches, debating clubs, and theatrical groups brought neighbors together (Haarsager 1997, 45).

Finding a way to worship with others was a craving that most isolated frontier women yearned to satisfy. Before a fledgling community had the means to erect a church building and pay for a minister, men, women, and children gathered on Sundays at each other's homes to engage in prayer and to sing hymns. Women were often the planners and leaders of these religious meetings. They often kept their leadership roles until a formal church was established. Women read sermons and led congregations in prayer and singing. Women also directed and carried out church fund-raising as well (Jeffrey 1979, 96–97).

Once a formal church was organized and leadership was turned over to a minister, men then assumed control of the church organization and were pivotal to its politics while women, through their church benevolent societies, continued to raise funds, operate Sunday schools, and care for the poor, the elderly, and the sick. In the mining town of Idaho City, Idaho Territory, female church members formed the

Ladies' Mite Association in 1864, primarily to raise money to repay the $3,000 debt of their First Baptist Church congregation. The association organized concerts and tableaux, held food and bake sales, operated an express service for city residents, published a newspaper, and solicited new members for the church. The women managed to raise $1,080, while simultaneously providing their members, the congregation, and the entire community with good fellowship, entertainments, and evidence of the community's growing strength (Haarsager 1997, 56).

Although news of Civil War developments was often slow in coming to some western locations, western women were well aware of the needs of soldiers and of the work of the UNITED STATES SANITARY COMMISSION (USSC). SOLDIERS' AID SOCIETIES, though not as ubiquitous as in the Northeast and Midwest, were present in many towns and cities of the West. Women residing in the small hamlet of McMinnville, Oregon, established their Ladies' Sanitary Aid Society in 1863. To raise money to send to the USSC, they met regularly to knit socks, produce quilt tops, and organize special dinners and entertainments. Despite the minuscule population of McMinnville, the society's members managed to raise hundreds of dollars (Haarsager 1997, 54).

Women were also the driving force propelling the founding of schools in the West. At first, women organized lessons at home, for their own and their neighbors' children, the better educated among them serving as the teachers. Women then joined forces to raise the funds needed to erect school buildings and to pay teacher salaries. On occasion, women assisted in the actual building of schoolhouses (Myres 1982, 184). Despite their being the instigators of all community building, women stepped into the background when the time came for formal school boards to be established. In any case, women maintained their active interest in the education of their children and continued as a powerful fund-raising force in local education projects.

By the time of the Civil War era, few African Americans had emigrated west. Barred from joining most wagon train companies, those who struggled to make the journey found it extremely difficult and dangerous. Most African-American men and women, however, did not possess the funds necessary to launch themselves on the overland trail.

Of the African Americans who successfully settled in the West during the Civil War, very few were women. The population of black men exceeded that of black women by ratios of two or more to one. Of the black women who did emigrate, 40 to 50 percent were wage earners outside the home as compared to 12 to 25 percent of white women. Most black women worked in very low-paying domestic capacities as maidservants, cooks, nursemaids, and laundresses (Riley 1994, 160, 169). In the towns and cities of the West, African-American women gathered together to support their schools, churches, and the poor, and to build their communities, just as they did in all other parts of the country. Wherever they settled, African-American men and women confronted white and Hispanic westerners' racial prejudice and discrimination, which relegated them to the most menial jobs.

African Americans were not the only group that encountered prejudice in the West. Mexican Americans, Chinese Americans, and the Mormons of Utah and Idaho Territories suffered as well. Although some white newcomers to the West were favorably impressed by the MEXICAN-AMERICAN WOMEN and men they met, many others were convinced that Mexican Americans were ignorant, unintelligent, lazy, and dishonest. This prejudice encouraged whites or "Anglos" to take over Mexican lands and communities and made it easier for whites to justify pushing Mexican Americans from power. The "California for Americans" obsession caused white westerners to discriminate against immigrant Chinese men and women as well.

Although the Mormons were white and Protestant, non-Mormon white westerners reviled them. Non-Mormons considered the followers of Mormon leader Brigham Young to be dangerously immoral, depraved, and crude, primarily because of their practice of polygamy. Non-Mormon white women were particularly harsh in their attitudes toward Mormon men and women and often wrote in their diaries and letters that they could not fathom how MORMON WOMEN could approve of and participate in polygamous relationships. To accept such an evil arrangement, non-Mormon women argued, a woman must be a slave, a prostitute, or mentally deficient.

Of all groups that white westerners encountered during the Civil War, Native Americans proved to be the group that stimulated the strongest fears and emotions. Nineteenth-century white Americans' appetite for literature and press accounts about Native Americans was insatiable. Published alongside a modicum of accurate information were reams of fabricated stories, myths, legends, and news reports having little basis in reality. They misinformed the public about Native Americans' physical appearance, character, morality, and intelligence (Myres 1982, 49). As a result, emigrants traveling west carried a sizable baggage of negative attitudes and prejudice, all of which influenced their first encounters with Native Americans. Whites often described Indians as cruel, sneaky, troublesome, hostile "savages," even when most of the Native Americans they encountered were peaceable and only wanted food, medicine, or the opportunity to trade. Thirteen-year-old Harriet Hitchcock wrote in her diary, "We have seen quite a number of Indians today they appeared friendly but they are an ignorant miserable race of beings" (quoted in Holmes 1999, 239).

Rumors of Native American hostility were rampant on the overland trails, especially during the Civil War when Native American attacks on white settlers increased in frequency. Although only a small percentage of whites were harmed, travelers feared for their lives throughout the entire journey and during settlement. When Jane Holbrook Gould and her emigrant party discovered a deserted wagon and three dead men, she and her group immediately concluded that they had been killed by Native Americans, even though white marauders attacked emigrants as well. "Oh! it is a horrid thing," she wrote. "I wish all of the Indians in Christendom were exterminated ...

. It is not an enviable situation to be placed in, not to know at night when you go to bed, whether you will all be alive in the morning or not" (quoted in Schlissel 1982, 225–226). Harriet Hitchcock, writing in 1864, commented, "Reports say that the Indians are murdering the whites on the plains at a rapid rate. It is sad news but we hope they [the Indians] will soon be drawn to the Pacific coast and then pushed in" (quoted in Holmes 1999, 255).

Despite the salutary dealings that the majority of white Americans enjoyed with Native Americans, the four years of the Civil War was an intensely turbulent period in the history of white westerners' relationships with Native Americans. From 1861 to 1865, whites decimated more Native American tribes and grabbed more of their land than during any other four-year period in U.S. history (Josephy 1991, xiii). White men, women, and children also experienced a greater number of Native American attacks and massacres and were captured more frequently than at any other time during the nineteenth century. Yet most whites during the Civil War never encountered any hostile Native Americans.

Centuries of white Americans' poor treatment of Native Americans fueled the tribes' desperate actions. In the mid-nineteenth century, white men slaughtered huge herds of buffalo to force Native American tribes to become dependent on whites. Some white men and women cheated Indians in their trading relationships. And white men abused and raped Native American women throughout the West (Riley 1984, 107–108). The federal government and the U.S. military repeatedly broke treaty agreements, forced tribes to move farther and farther west, and reneged on promises of food deliveries, thereby triggering mass starvation.

At the beginning of the war, when U.S. army regiments abandoned many of the forts and garrisons located on the western outposts in order to head east for the Civil War battlefields, a number of Native American tribes took advantage of the troops' absence to strike back and reclaim their lands. This was certainly the case in Minnesota in 1862 when, following years of living peacefully with white settlers, several of the Sioux tribes—known to themselves as Dakotas—perpetrated the largest Native American massacre of whites in U.S. history (Josephy 1991, 98). On August 18 of that year, Dakota warriors unleashed a rampage of murder and mayhem, burning homes and carrying off livestock and other goods. Hundreds of white men, women, and children (including infants) were killed or taken into captivity. Guri Olsdatter Endreson, a Norwegian immigrant, wrote her family in Norway about her ordeal.

> Guri and Britha [Endreson's daughters] were carried off by the wild Indians ... when the savages gave them permission to get some food, these young girls made use of the opportunity to flee and thus they got away alive, and on the third day after they had been taken, some Americans came along who found them on a large plain or prairie .... I myself wandered aimlessly around on my land with my youngest daughter and I had to look on while they shot my precious husband dead, and in my sight my dear son Ole was shot through the shoulder .... We

also found my oldest son Endre shot dead, but I did not see the firing of this death shot .... To be an eyewitness to these things and to see many others wounded and killed was almost too much for a poor woman; but, God be thanked, I kept my life and my sanity, though all my movable property was torn away and stolen. (Quoted in Seller 1981, 60–61)

The terror soon spread to eastern Dakota Territory where the U.S. army finally engaged the Dakotas in fierce fighting and put an end to the attacks. In 1863, the U.S. Congress retaliated by canceling all treaties with the Dakotas and ordering their removal from Minnesota. This uprising, combined with bitter attacks on white settlers in Texas, Kansas, Colorado, California, Nevada, and Utah and Idaho Territories created mass panic and near hysteria throughout the West. The press exaggerated and embellished all accounts of Native American hostilities, stimulating the public to demand that the U.S. army put an end to the "Indian problem" once and for all.

Minnesota journalist JANE GREY SWISSHELM was outraged that the federal government failed to send the U.S. army to deal with the Dakotas after the massacre. On January 8, 1863, she embarked on a lecture tour, traveling to Chicago, Philadelphia, Brooklyn, New York, and Washington, DC, to inform the eastern public about the savagery of the massacre and to convince them that the Dakotas must be removed from Minnesota and subdued so that they could no longer revolt (Swisshelm 1976, 26–27).

Despite the violence and temper of the times, in other regions of the West, white men and women continued to coexist peacefully with Native Americans as they had since the opening of the overland trails in the 1840s. As in earlier years, Native Americans acted as guides, and assisted emigrants in the fording of streams and rivers. White women developed warm relationships with Native American women in many regions, sharing information, food, herbs, medicines, and recipes. Christina Phillips Campbell, the only white woman in Salina, Kansas, during the early years of the war, maintained that if she had not had the friendship of neighboring "squaws," she did not see how she would have survived the intense loneliness of her first months in Kansas (Stratton 1981, 116).

After the Civil War, and throughout the 1870s and 1880s, white Americans poured into the West. They continued to transform it, building communities and governments that resembled those they had left behind in the East, the South, and the Midwest. They fought and won the last of the Indian wars and pushed nearly all Native Americans onto reservations while relegating Mexican Americans, African Americans, and Asian Americans to the margins of white society.

See also **Brown, Clara; Mountain Charley; Pleasant, Mary Ellen**

Selected Readings

Billington, Monroe Lee and Roger D. Hardaway, eds. *African Americans on the Western Frontier.* Niwot: University Press of Colorado. 1998.

Josephy, Alvin M. *The Civil War in the American West.* New York: Knopf. 1991

Moynihan, Ruth B., Susan Armitage, and Christiane Fischer Dichamp, eds. *So Much to Be Done: Women Settlers on the Mining and Ranching Frontier.* Lincoln: University of Nebraska Press. 1998.

Myres, Sandra L. *Westering Women and the Frontier Experience 1800–1915.* Albuquerque: University of New Mexico Press. 1982.

Riley, Glenda. *Women and Indians on the Frontier 1825–1915.* Albuquerque: University of New Mexico Press. 1984.

Woman's Central Association of Relief

On April 25, 1861, a week after President Abraham Lincoln called for the mustering of 75,000 volunteer troops for the Union, pioneering physicians Elizabeth and Emily Blackwell called a meeting of New York City women to discuss plans for an organization that would stimulate and coordinate the production of SOLDIERS' AID SOCIETIES and that would supply the Union army with professionally trained NURSES. On April 29, between 2,000 and 3,000 New York women responded to the Blackwells' call to action and convened to organize women's war work.

The Woman's Central Association of Relief (WCAR), as Elizabeth and Emily Blackwell originally envisioned it, was to be an organization in which women and men would work together to make critically important civilian contributions to the Union war effort. Elizabeth intended that the WCAR would 1) train professional female nurses for the military hospitals and 2) coordinate and administrate the work of the hundreds of soldiers' aid societies that had sprouted in the New York region in the days since war was declared. According to the Blackwells' plan, prominent, politically well-connected male leaders of the WCAR would open and maintain channels of communication between the women of the WCAR and military and government officials. It was Elizabeth's hope that the male WCAR leaders would lobby the government so that all obstacles to the acceptance of professional female nurses would be overcome.

At the April 29 meeting of the WCAR, the well-known Unitarian minister Henry Whitney Bellows was elected president. Twelve women and twelve men were also selected to form the committee that would operate the WCAR. Bellows and three other male leaders—all physicians—traveled to Washington, DC, to meet with federal officials. While in the nation's capital, they inspected the poorly nourished recruits, the squalid, overcrowded military camps, and the hastily prepared, dank rooms that served as the first Union military hospitals. Bellows's exposure to the early days of the nation's mobilization convinced him that the Blackwells' conception of the WCAR would not adequately address the most pressing medical and sanitary needs of the Union army. His discussions with DOROTHEA DIX, (appointed by Secretary of War Simon Cameron to supervise nurses for military hospitals), and his confrontation with Cameron's resistance to female nurses persuaded him that a large, national, civilian-run organization located in Washington, DC, was essential to meet the enormity of the Union army's medical and supply crisis.

When the Blackwells learned of Bellows's decision to push aside the WCAR's agenda, they tolerated the upset in plans and continued in their own way to carry out the work of the WCAR as they intended. The nurses' training program continued as planned. With some reservations, Elizabeth agreed to select nurses according to Dix's specification, although she was disturbed that Dix, a health reformer rather than a medical professional, did not see the need for a professionally trained nursing corps.

Georgeanna Woolsey, a single, elite young woman from New York City, was one of the nurses the WCAR selected in May of 1861. She described the training she was about to receive in a letter to her sister Eliza Woolsey Howland: "We are to learn how to make beds for the wounded, cook food properly for the sick, wash and dress wounds, and other things as they come along in the proper care of the wards—fresh air, etc." (Bacon 1899, 1:85). When Woolsey first arrived, she was assigned an entire ward of patients before receiving a single instruction: "I shall never forget the hopeless state of my mind at this exact point. To be left standing in the middle of a long ward, full of beds, full of sick men—it was appalling! ... Such a month we had of it, walking round from room to room, learning what we could" (Bacon 1899, 1:81). Woolsey, who went on to have a distinguished nursing career all through the war and after, was only one of the approximately 100 women the WCAR was responsible for training.

As one of the country's leading public health experts, Elizabeth Blackwell fully expected that when the new national sanitary commission was finally formed, she, at the least, would be asked to serve on the advisory board. As spring became the summer of 1861, no such plan materialized. Dorothea Dix was officially commissioned Superintendent of Female Nurses on June 10, 1861, the day after the UNITED

STATES SANITARY COMMISSION (USSC) was formally established. The medical department of the the Union army and the Secretary of War had made their choice. Although all parties were well aware of the superior medical backgrounds of the Blackwells and their offer to train nurses to work in the military hospitals, officials chose Dix, a woman with no professional training in medicine or science.

The all-male medical establishment was not ready to accept women doctors as government or military advisors, though they did accede to Dix whose career in prison reform had made her well versed in public health administration. The male doctors on the USSC advisory board refused to allow the Blackwells to sit on any committee and would not consider Elizabeth's ideas about training professional nurses. As Blackwell explained in a letter to a friend in England,

> ... we soon found that jealousies were too intense for us to assume our true place. We would have accepted a place on the health commission which our association is endeavoring to establish in Washington, & which the government will probably appoint—but the Doctors would not permit us to come forward ... & they refused to have anything to do with the nurse education plan if the Miss Blackwells were going to engineer the matter. (quoted in Attie 1998, 84–85)

In September 1861, the WCAR ceased to be an independent organization when it became an auxiliary of the USSC. As Dix took over the job of selecting nurses, Elizabeth's role in the WCAR gradually receded as she redirected her energies toward her work at the New York Infirmary for Women and Children.

Louisa Lee Schuyler, the 24-year-old daughter of wealthy New York humanitarian reformers, assumed command of the WCAR. It was the largest and, politically speaking, the most significant branch of the USSC. It administered the work of soldiers' aid societies in New York, Connecticut, and parts of New Jersey and Massachusetts. By the fall of 1861, the WCAR received from hundreds of soldiers' aid societies a total of 30,000 items of hospital patient clothing, 15,147 bedding items, 6,112 havelocks, and more than 2,000 packages of jellies and preserves (Attie 1998, 83). During the war years, Schuyler kept up a voluminous correspondence with female leaders of the 1,400 WCAR's soldiers' aid societies. In the final year of the war, the WCAR's efforts shifted toward assisting veterans and their families find food, fuel, shelter, and obtain employment.

See also **Doctors; United States Sanitary Commission**

Selected Readings

Attie, Jeanie. *Patriotic Toil: Northern Women and the American Civil War.* Ithaca, NY: Cornell University Press. 1998.

Giesberg, Judith Ann. *Civil War Sisterhood: The United States Sanitary Commission and Women's Politics in Transition.* Boston: Northeastern University Press. 2000.

Woman's National Loyal League

> While the mass of women never philosophize on the principles that underlie national existence, there were those in our late war who understood the political significance of the struggle: the "irrepressible conflict" between freedom and slavery; between national and State rights …. Accustomed as most women had been to works of charity, to the relief of outward suffering, it was difficult to rouse their enthusiasm for an idea, to persuade them to labor for a principle …. This Woman's Loyal League voiced the solemn lessons of the war: liberty to all; national protection for every citizen under our flag; universal suffrage, and universal amnesty.
>
> —Elizabeth Cady Stanton and Susan B. Anthony, *History of Woman Suffrage*, 1881 (Stanton et al. 2: 2–3)

Early in 1863, two New York abolitionists and women's rights activists, SUSAN B. ANTHONY and ELIZABETH CADY STANTON, initiated plans for a new political organization, to be composed entirely of women, and that would execute the most extensive petition campaign ever attempted in the hope of persuading Congress to approve a Thirteenth Amendment guaranteeing the freedom of African Americans. During 1863 and 1864, the Woman's National Loyal League (WNLL) introduced thousands of women to political activism while making a critical contribution to the abolitionist movement's quest for the "immediate emancipation" of the slaves.

Since petitioning the government was the only political means open to mid-nineteenth-century women, Anthony and Cady Stanton vowed that the WNLL would exploit it to the fullest. Anthony's petition drive to expand the Married Women's Property Law in New York State in the mid- to late 1850s was so successful that she and Cady Stanton felt confident in setting the WNLL's goal at a million signatures. Throughout every Northern state, from Maine to California, women distributed petitions in their communities. They sent the signatures of men and women on reams of parchment to the WNLL's office in New York City. Anthony and Cady Stanton then delivered the petitions to Massachusetts Republican Senator Charles Sumner, the congressional leader of the drive for the Thirteenth Amendment, who then exhibited them before both houses of Congress.

In April 1864, in response to the 250,000 signatures on WNLL petitions and a groundswell of popular support, the Senate passed the Thirteenth Amendment. Because the House of Representatives delayed its action, Anthony kept the pressure on WNLL members to circulate petitions all through the summer of 1864. By August, with 400,000 signatures collected, Sumner informed Anthony that since full congressional approval seemed imminent, the WNLL's primary mission had succeeded.

But what of Anthony's and Cady Stanton's other objective—their goal to involve the nation's women in a great political agenda that would continue after the war had ceased? Senator Sumner, though thankful for the WNLL's help in pushing through the Thirteenth Amendment, was alarmed by the prospect of thousands of women rolling up their sleeves and getting into the thick of political affairs. When he spoke to WNLL members in the autumn of 1864, he advised women to steer clear of the "strife of politics." As he informed them, it was acceptable that they work to "crush out the wicked rebellion," but that was as far as their efforts should extend (quoted in Massey 1994, 166).

Sumner's words did not dampen Anthony's or Cady Stanton's exhilaration over the success of the WNLL nor did it deter them from contemplating their postwar political plans. They closed the WNLL's New York office in the fall of 1864 while members continued their activism by encouraging their state legislators to ratify the amendment. In January 1865, the house voted in favor of the amendment, and in December 1865, following ratification of three-quarters of the states, the Thirteenth Amendment became law.

Besides having been a potent force in the enactment of the Thirteenth Amendment, and despite a mere sprinkling of male naysayers, the WNLL had made it more socially acceptable for women to engage in political work in the public sphere. Although the two feminists could not have foreseen it, the WNLL proved to be a vital link to a postwar era marked by women's increased political activity.

See also **Abolitionists**

Selected Readings

Hamand, Wendy F. "The Woman's National Loyal League: Feminist Abolitionists and the Civil War." *Civil War History.* 35 (1) (1989): 39–58.

Venet, Wendy Hamand. *Neither Ballots Nor Bullets: Women Abolitionists and the Civil War.* Charlottesville: University Press of Virginia. 1991.

Women and Politics

Although mid-nineteenth-century women could not vote and were expected to confine themselves to their domestic sphere, they engaged in party politics and sought to influence their local, state, and national governments. Only gradually did women penetrate the male sanctum of party politics. They supported their favorite candidates, formed all-women societies to promote political agendas, and participated in political campaigns. By the time of the Civil War, men and women in the North were becoming more accepting of public roles for women in the political process.

In the 1820s and 1830s, a national two-party system became organized, creating powerful party loyalties among male voters. During the 1830s and 1840s, the Whig Party (formerly the National Republican Party) and the Democratic Party encouraged men to bond around common political and economic issues in their communities. Men participated in campaign rallies honoring their party's candidates, read party newspapers, gambled on the outcome of elections, and donned campaign clothing, hats, and other gear proclaiming their party affiliation (Baker 1984, 628).

Although most political party activity was male oriented, men gradually sought out women's participation. In the early years of the two-party system, women encouraged men to become involved in the party of their choice. Women prepared food for party picnics and celebrations and occasionally marched alongside men in campaign parades. In the presidential campaign of 1840, male members of the Whig Party welcomed women to campaign meetings and asked them to urge their menfolk to vote for Whig candidates. In 1844, the Whig Party instituted all-women presidential campaign clubs to support the candidacy of Henry Clay. In a few cases, pro-Whig women gave campaign speeches honoring Clay. The Democratic Party, not to be outdone, also urged women to become involved in the 1844 election, though to a lesser degree than the Whigs.

For a time in the 1850s, a public debate raged over the propriety of women's involvement in political campaigns. Although strong feeling against women taking prominent public roles persisted, women again became politically active in the 1856 presidential campaign, particularly within the Republican Party. Newly established in 1854, the Republican Party courted women in 1856 to endorse the candidacy of its presidential candidate, John C. Frémont. Frémont and his wife JESSIE BENTON

FRÉMONT, both popular abolitionists, were the favorites of antislavery men and women in the North. The couple's female supporters sported badges and ribbons and carried campaign banners proclaiming their endorsement of "Frémont and Our Jessie" and "Jessie for the White House." For her part, Benton Frémont was deeply involved in the decision-making for her husband's campaign.

Also in 1856, the Republican Party employed Clarina Howard Nichols, an abolitionist and Kansas emigrant noted for her determination to make Kansas Territory a free state, to speak publicly on behalf of Frémont. Her efforts may have been the first occasion that a U.S. political party hired a woman to venture forth as a stump-speaker (Edwards 1997, 29).

ELIZABETH CADY STANTON and SUSAN B. ANTHONY attended Republican meetings and rallies in the 1850s. The journalist JANE GREY SWISSHELM, longtime champion of the political process, attended the first national convention of the Republican Party in 1856 in Philadelphia. As a woman, she found that she could exert the most influence on the political process by writing editorials and articles.

The fierce intensity of the presidential race of 1860 motivated the Republican Party to appeal to women to drum up support for its candidates. Girls and women endorsing the Republican candidate Abraham Lincoln marched in parades, gave speeches, organized barbecues, and formed all-women Republican clubs. In Kalamazoo, Michigan, approximately 50 pro-Lincoln young women proclaimed support for their candidate while parading on horseback wearing "Wide-Awake" uniforms. (The "Wide-Awakes" were a primarily male antislavery marching organization.) In Martinsville, Virginia, Republican women offered a flag to the men's Lincoln Club. During the flag presentation, 16 women clothed themselves in white and 16 in black to represent a nation split over the issue of slavery. An additional woman cloaked herself in red to symbolize "Bleeding Kansas," the state that went to war in its quest to become a free state (Gustafson 2001, 8). The Democratic Party had its share of female supporters as well. Women hosted picnics and participated in parades to honor the 1860 Democratic candidate, Stephen Douglas.

In 1864, Cady Stanton and Anthony strongly endorsed the candidacy of John C. Frémont, the choice of the new Radical Democratic Party. Through the WOMAN'S NATIONAL LOYAL LEAGUE (WNLL), the political organization that both women created, they longed to encourage thousands of other women to do likewise. To their mind, Frémont was the logical choice for WNLL members who were dedicated to securing a constitutional amendment guaranteeing the freedom of all African Americans. Frémont, unlike Lincoln, was unwavering in his demands for immediate emancipation. He also promoted a reconstruction program that promised to guard the rights of African Americans after the war. Yet, Frémont's platform proved too radical for most antislavery women's tastes. Most supported Lincoln. As a result, Cady Stanton and Anthony allowed their friends to persuade them to work for Frémont on their own, without involving the WNLL.

Women increasingly became campaign speakers during the Civil War years. The Republican ANNA DICKINSON was the most popular of all women who took to the stump in this period. Countering her views was the pro-slavery, anti-war Copperhead Democrat orator Emma Webb, a New York actress who attempted, but failed, to overshadow Dickinson in the 1864 presidential campaign. Two other Northern women who drew large audiences with their campaign rhetoric were the Democrat Teresa Esmonde and the Republican Cordelia Phillips.

Catherine "Kate" Chase Sprague, the daughter of the Republican Salmon P. Chase, assisted her father in his race for the presidency in 1860, 1864, and 1868. In 1868, she was the first woman to be directly involved in a political party's nominating convention. While behind the scenes at this convention, she attended private caucuses and lobbied delegates to urge them to support her father's candidacy (Dinkin 1995, 64). MARY TODD LINCOLN, renowned for her involvement in her husband's political career, advised her husband and met with his supporters behind closed doors during the 1860 election.

The vast majority of Southern women did not participate in party politics. Yet as the SECESSION crisis grew in severity in 1860 to 1861, they became deeply politicized. Southern women attended state secession conventions, expressed their political views on the crisis in letters to newspapers, and attempted to persuade their friends and neighbors to adopt their point of view.

After the Civil War, the fledgling woman suffrage movement vowed to add women to the electorate. Although only four states allowed women to vote in national elections by the end of the nineteenth century, women were increasingly visible in party politics. Women authored party pamphlets and disseminated them in their communities. They also traveled door to door to encourage men to vote for their party's candidates. Women gave campaign speeches, established party clubs for women, and, by the end of the century, in a few rare instances, served as delegates to state conventions (Freeman 2000, 21).

In 1866, Cady Stanton, always a devotee of partisan politics, wished to prove that she had the legal right to run a campaign for public office. She chose to launch her candidacy for Congress in the Eighth Congressional District of New York. She declared that she was running on a platform of "*free speech, free press, free men* and *free trade*—the cardinal points of democracy" (quoted in Gustafson 2001, 36). Cady Stanton vowed to secure universal suffrage—the vote for African-American men and all women—if elected. When the election results were in, she had obtained 24 votes.

In the late 1860s, when African-American men achieved the right to vote, African-American women became involved in the Republican Party in the South. They attended rallies, marched with men in party parades, and occasionally gave speeches. In some local Republican conventions and rallies, black women were sometimes permitted to cast votes for their chosen candidates. In South Carolina, where white supremacist groups used violence to prevent African Americans from participating in Republican politics, African-American women stood guard over Republican men's muskets while they attended party meetings (Edwards 1997, 35–36).

Even though women were engaging in party politics throughout the nineteenth century, they wielded no real power as men created all the strategies, executed all the decisions, and served as the only candidates. Not until later in the twentieth century, years after the 1920 ratification of the Nineteenth Amendment—the woman suffrage amendment—would women truly begin to venture into the heart of party politics.

Selected Readings

Dinkin, Robert J. Before Equal Suffrage: Women in Partisan Politics from Colonial Times to 1920. Westport, CT: Greenwood Press. 1995.

Freeman, Jo. A Room at a Time: How Women Entered Party Politics. Lanham, MO: Rowman & Littlefield. 2000.

Women's Rights Movement

The women's rights movement embraced all women's rights activity from the time of the first women's rights convention—the Seneca Falls Convention of 1848—to the establishment of the national woman suffrage associations in 1869. The movement was composed primarily of white middle-class Northern women although a minority of free African-American women participated. In 1861, all women's rights agitation came to an abrupt halt with the onset of the Civil War. With the exception of the WOMAN'S NATIONAL LOYAL LEAGUE, organized in 1863, there was no organized, formal activism for women's rights during the war years. By and large, women's rights supporters involved themselves wholeheartedly in the war effort. They believed that by vigorously engaging in activities to assist the soldiers and the Union cause, they could best demonstrate women's ability to share economic and political equality with men.

Although women had been trying to obtain their civil, political, and legal rights before 1848, the Seneca Falls Convention, held in Seneca Falls, New York, in July 1848, is generally recognized as the formal beginning of the women's rights movement and the woman suffrage movement. At this gathering, the convention's Declaration of Rights and Sentiments and its Resolutions encompassed women's demands for equality in the home, the workplace, education, religion, and public and political life (DuBois 1978, 23). Women's claim to the right to vote was the most radical demand made at the convention and was the one resolution nearly not accepted at the convention.

The antislavery movement was an important origin of the women's rights movement as female ABOLITIONISTS provided much of the women's rights leadership. To reach their goals, women's rights advocates employed the methods and strategies of the abolitionist movement. They organized conventions; wrote, published, and distributed informational pamphlets and other literature; established women's rights newspapers; and sent speakers forth on the lecture circuit to educate the public. Women's rights activists also utilized petition campaigns and lobbied legislators to pass new state property rights laws that would permit women to own property separate from their husbands. The presence of men was especially critical to the success of the movement in the early years. Men added credibility and legitimacy to the movement. Prominent male reformers also attracted attention to the cause of women's rights and boosted attendance at conventions.

ELIZABETH CADY STANTON and SUSAN B. ANTHONY, two key leaders of the women's rights movement, believed that educating the public was all-important to the progress of women in society. Women's rights conventions were one means of educating the public. At these local, state, and national meetings organized throughout the Northeast and the Midwest during the 1850s, the public was invited to meet with women's rights leaders to learn about the issues and to engage in discussion and debate. Among the subjects hotly contested at conventions were women's demands for civil and legal rights (especially property rights), women's right to vote, women's right to divorce, women's intellectual equality with men, the need for increased educational opportunities for women, and the right of women to enter the workplace and the professions.

Susan B. Anthony served as the organizer of the annual national women's rights conventions beginning in 1856. With the exception of 1857, she prepared and directed a national gathering each year through 1860. At the Tenth National Woman's Rights Convention in 1860, two major male women's rights leaders, William Lloyd Garrison and Wendell Phillips, opposed Cady Stanton's resolution proclaiming the right of women to divorce. The issue was intensely divisive and caused ill feeling to develop among the participants, a dissension that would not dissipate with time and that would ultimately contribute to the split in the women's rights movement in 1869.

The most significant legal victory of the pre–Civil War women's rights movement occurred in 1860 when the New York Married Women's Property Law was enacted. The law expanded the property rights of women as specified in New York's

Married Women's Property Law of 1848. The six-year campaign, waged principally by Anthony from 1854 to 1860, (with assistance from Cady Stanton and other women's rights activists) ensured that women could own property separately from their husbands, execute business transactions, control their own wages and other income, sue and be sued, and be joint guardian of their children with their husbands. The passage of the 1860 law also set an important precedent, that women as citizens were entitled to legal equality with men. In addition, the enactment of this law also stimulated other, similar property rights campaigns in other states.

In the spring of 1861, as Anthony was finalizing plans for the upcoming Eleventh National Woman's Rights Convention, the Civil War ensued. Although Anthony fully expected to pursue the event regardless, many of her male and female colleagues urged her to cancel it, against all her instincts. She predicted (with accuracy) that canceling the convention and postponing women's rights work would cause the male political establishment to chisel away at the hard-fought gains that women's rights activists had made all through the 1850s. As she explained in a letter to a close friend, "I am sick at heart, but I can not carry the world against the wish and the will of our best friends" (Stanton et al., 1881 1: 749).

Anthony and Cady Stanton were not idle long. Early in 1863, they organized the Woman's National Loyal League (WNLL), the first national women's political organization through which women petitioned Congress to pass a constitutional amendment guaranteeing the freedom of African Americans. Anthony and Cady Stanton enlisted the support of their women's rights colleagues. Lucretia Coffin Mott, Angelina Grimké Weld, Lucy Stone, Ernestine Potowski Rose, and Antoinette Brown Blackwell were among the women's rights leaders who enthusiastically participated.

At the founding meeting of the WNLL, Anthony and Cady Stanton attempted to interweave women's rights issues into the proceedings, an effort that caused controversy. Many women protested the resolution that stated, "There never can be a true peace in this Republic until the civil and political rights of all citizens of African descent and all women are practically established." Mrs. E. O. Sampson Hoyt from Wisconsin spoke for the dissenters.

> We all know that Woman's Rights as an *ism* has not been received with entire favor by the women of the country, and I know that there are thousands of earnest, loyal, and able women who will not go into any movement of this kind, if this idea is made prominent (Stanton et al., 1886 2: 59–60)

At that point, Potowski Rose, Stone, and other women's rights leaders resoundingly approved of the inclusion of women's rights in the WNLL's organizing resolutions, and the majority voted to carry the resolution. Although the decision did limit the number of women willing to be members of the WNLL, the leaders realized that the struggle for women's rights was crucially important to the entire WNLL mission and could not be omitted.

In May 1866, more than a year after the conclusion of the Civil War, Anthony and Cady Stanton organized the Eleventh National Woman's Rights Convention in New York City. Unlike all previous national meetings, this gathering focused on one issue: the drive to obtain universal suffrage—the vote for African-American men and all women. To that end, organizers and male and female women's rights activists established the American Equal Rights Association (AERA). The AERA aspired to alter state constitutions to eliminate race and gender restrictions on suffrage. By 1868, the organization had come under the control of male and female members who insisted that securing the ballot for African-American males must take priority over woman suffrage. They argued that African Americans in the South urgently needed the ballot to protect their civil and legal rights in the newly reconstructed, war-ravaged South and that women would have to wait. This faction of members made it impossible for Anthony, Cady Stanton, and other women's rights promoters to work for woman suffrage within the AERA. Anthony and Cady Stanton and their supporters did not deny that African Americans needed the ballot, but they did protest that this campaign be waged to the exclusion of securing the same right for women. Women, too, had desperate need of the ballot to remedy their crippling economic and social problems.

In 1869, the campaign for the Fifteenth Amendment, which promised to ensure the suffrage for African-American males only, was the issue that ultimately split the women's rights movement into two separate factions. Anthony and Cady Stanton, distressed by the AERA membership's refusal to support woman suffrage as part of the Fifteenth Amendment, left the AERA to establish the National Woman Suffrage Association. The activists who endorsed the Fifteenth Amendment, led by Lucy Stone and her husband, Henry Browne Blackwell, formed the American Woman Suffrage Association. These two organizations separately struggled to achieve national woman suffrage until they merged in 1890 to form the National American Woman Suffrage Association. As one dynamic organization, and in concert with the National Woman's Party and hundreds of other national, state, and local suffrage organizations, the woman suffrage movement achieved its final victory—the vote for American women—with the ratification of the Nineteenth Amendment on August 26, 1920.

Selected Readings

DuBois, Ellen Carol. *Feminism and Suffrage: The Emergence of an Independent Women's Movement in America 1848–1869*. Ithaca, NY: Cornell University Press. 1978.

Flexner, Eleanor and Ellen Fitzpatrick. *Century of Struggle: The Woman's Rights Movement in the United States*. Cambridge, MA: The Belknap Press of Harvard University Press. Enlarged Edition. 1996.

Z

Zakrzewska, Marie
(1829–1902)

Marie Zakrzewska is widely acknowledged as one of the most influential nineteenth-century women physicians in the United States. Throughout most of her nearly 50-year medical career, she provided young women DOCTORS with rigorous clinical training that was equal, if not superior, to the medical education offered to male doctors. A member of the pioneering generation of American women physicians, Zakrzewska spent the Civil War years establishing and keeping afloat a hospital expressly for poor, working-class Boston women—an enterprise that offered an excellent training ground for female medical school graduates. Zakrzewska is all too infrequently remembered for her advocacy of numerous mid-nineteenth-century reform movements, the most important and pivotal of which was her involvement in the radical political activism of a small community of intellectual German immigrants.

Marie Zakrzewska was born in Berlin, Germany, the daughter of Polish émigrés. Her grandmother was a veterinary surgeon and her mother worked as a midwife, largely because her father's salary as a civil servant was insufficient to support the family. From the age of 14, Zakrzewska accompanied her mother on her rounds and helped her deliver babies. When she was 18, she was determined to study midwifery and at age 20 attended the School for Midwives in Berlin. She decided to immigrate to the United States in the belief that American women had greater opportunities in medicine.

When she settled in New York City in 1853, she soon learned that openings for women in medicine were nearly nonexistent. When she found it impossible to make a living as a midwife, she formed a knitting business with her sister. She attempted to make connections with male physicians who might advise her on becoming a physician, but these contacts either discouraged or rebuffed her.

In 1854, Zakrzewska finally met the mentor she needed. Dr. Elizabeth Blackwell befriended Zakrzewska and helped her to apply to the medical school at Western Reserve College in Cleveland, Ohio. Blackwell and her women friends in Cleveland, most of them women's rights activists, provided Zakrzewska with books, meals, and lodging while she attended medical school. After graduating in 1856, she returned to New York City, operated a small private practice in the back parlor at the Blackwells', and collaborated with them to raise funds for a new hospital. In 1857, they opened the New York Infirmary for Women and Children.

Zakrzewska was resident physician at the New York Infirmary until 1859 when she agreed to become professor of obstetrics at the New England Female Medical College in Boston. By opening up a new obstetrical department at the school, she expected to employ the most up-to-date scientific methods to teach the next generation of women doctors. Samuel Gregory, the school's founder, did not share her vision and obstructed her efforts to broaden instruction beyond the traditional midwifery curriculum. When she asked for a microscope to assist her in the classroom, the request was rejected. A leader of the college and cohort of Gregory's dismissed her interest in microscopy, saying, "That is another one of those new-fangled European notions which she tries to introduce" (quoted in Vietor 1972, 251).

Fed up with Gregory's intransigence, Zakrzewska left the New England Female Medical College in the summer of 1862 to open the New England Hospital for Women and Children in Boston. She said of the decision to leave,

> not one of my expectations for a thorough medical education for women had been realized. … If it were the intention of the trustees to supply the country with under-bred, ill-educated women under the name of physicians … I think the New England Female Medical College is on the right track. (Quoted in Walsh 1977, 65)

As the founder and leading force behind the fledgling New England Hospital, an institution that would focus on the treatment of poor working-class women, Zakrzewska succeeded in implementing professional clinical training, based on the most up-to-date medical science, a goal that she acknowledged would not have been possible without support from prominent Boston reformers and a number of respected male physicians.

A close-knit network of female and male women's rights activists supported the New England Hospital for Women and Children from its earliest days. Boston reformers Abigail (Abby) Williams May of the UNITED STATES SANITARY COMMISSION, Caroline Severance, Ednah Dow Cheney, Henry Browne Blackwell (brother to Elizabeth and Emily) and his wife, the pioneering women's rights activist Lucy Stone, and Samuel Edmond Sewall gave freely of their money and time, and launched zealous fund-raising campaigns among reform-minded Bostonians, no easy feat given the effects of the Civil War economy on the home front.

Though the New England Hospital formed the central focus of Zakrzewska's medical career, she also maintained a private practice. Besides providing her with income, she was convinced that her vigorous handling of her own practice would demonstrate to male physicians who doubted whether women had the physical stamina to be in medicine that "a woman has not only the same (if not more) physical endurance as a man" (quoted in Drachman 1984, 39).

During the early 1860s, she called on her patients from one end of Boston to the other on foot, day and night, without regard for the weather. She insisted on making housecalls in the wee hours to disprove the prevalent notion that the female constitution was not hardy enough to handle nighttime work. For safety reasons, she did not walk alone at night. If the messenger who called on her could not escort her, she "walked with the policeman, and waited at the end of the different beats for the next one to take me to his limits. I was well known among them . . ." (quoted in Vietor 1972, 329). In 1865, as soon as she had the means, she purchased a horse and carriage, thereby taking on the trappings of male physicians. In this way, she deliberately tried to blend in with the male medical culture of the city.

Zakrzewska was unusual among mid-nineteenth-century women physicians in several respects. She did not agree with most of her colleagues that women possessed unique qualities that made them better doctors or natural healers. Sympathy and compassion were not qualities exclusive to women, she argued. She also challenged the widely held conviction that these "feminine" qualities, including a woman's "maternal instinct," made women morally superior to men (Tuchman 1999, 122–123).

In her later years, Zakrzewska questioned the overriding emphasis placed on bacteriology in medicine. Her view did not indicate a skepticism about the importance of pathogens in the cause of disease, but demonstrates her career-long conviction that preventive medicine and the support of patients' personal hygiene were the most critical aspects of health care (Tuchman 1999, 122–123).

Zakrzewska's involvement in the radical democracy of her circle of German political activists was a lifelong source of her intellectual interest. She was a member of the executive council of the Society for the Dissemination of Radical Principles.

With other German immigrants in this organization, she supported constitutional rights for all citizens, regardless of sex, race, or religion (Tuchman 1999, 129). She was also an ardent abolitionist and suffragist.

Zakrzewska remained an attending physician at the New England Hospital until 1887. From that date until 1899, she served there as an advisory physician, retiring at the age of 70.

Selected Readings

Drachman, Virginia G. *Hospital with a Heart: Women Doctors and the Paradox of Separatism at the New England Hospital, 1862–1969.* Ithaca, NY: Cornell University Press. 1984.

Tuchman, Arleen Marcia. "'Only in a Republic Can It Be Proved That Science Has No Sex': Marie Elizabeth Zakrzewska (1829–1902) and the Multiple Meanings of Science in the Nineteenth-Century United States." *Journal of Women's History.* 11 (1) (Spring 1999): 121–142.

Walsh, Mary Roth. *"Doctors Wanted: No Women Need Apply": Sexual Barriers in the Medical Profession, 1835–1970.* New Haven, CT: Yale University Press. 1977.

Glossary

The following is a list of terms that will be helpful to readers unfamiliar with the Civil War era.

Abolitionism: A political and social reform movement dedicated to the eradication of slavery.

American Anti-Slavery Society: One of the primary national abolitionist organizations in the United States, founded in 1833 by William Lloyd Garrison and Arthur and Lewis Tappan. Its members believed that if informed about the evils of slavery, northern citizens would demand that the government abolish it.

Antebellum: Pertaining to the period before the Civil War—for example, antebellum politics.

Black Codes: Laws enacted in the South following the Civil War that restricted the freedoms of African Americans. Among the Black Codes were state and local laws and policies that prohibited African Americans from voting, serving as jurors, giving testimony against whites, purchasing or selling property, and exercising their right to refuse to sign year-long labor contracts.

Blockade runner: A confederate military or commercial vessel that evaded the Union blockade of Southern ports.

Border states: States located on or near the boundary line that separated free and slave states including Delaware, Maryland, Kentucky, Missouri, and West Virginia (after it joined the Union in 1863). Border state residents were divided in their loyalties to the Union and the Confederacy.

Conscription Acts: Draft laws of the federal and Confederate governments that enforced the enlistment of men of military age.

Contraband: A term used during the Civil War to refer to fugitive slaves who escaped to Union-occupied areas. Most lived in or near Union military encampments.

Daughter of the Regiment: An honorary regimental position bestowed on a woman who usually marched and drilled with the enlisted men, encouraged them to fight in battle, and nursed them in camp and on the battlefield, carried the regimental flag.

Disunionist: One who believed that the Union must be dissolved. Most disunionists were Confederates, although a radical faction of abolitionists also believed that the Union should not remain intact if the federal government continued to uphold slavery.

Emancipation Proclamation: President Abraham Lincoln's decree of January 1, 1863, which declared freedom for all slaves living in states or regions under the control of the Confederacy.

Freedman's Bureau: A federal agency established in March 1865 that was designed to assist the newly freed slaves and protect their rights as citizens of the United States.

Freedpeople: Former slaves, including contraband women and men.

Fugitive Slave Act of 1850: A federal law which ordered that all escaped slaves be returned to their owners, thus prohibiting Northerners from harboring fugitive slaves.

Garrisonian abolitionists: Radical abolitionists who, like their leader William Lloyd Garrison, were committed to the immediate emancipation of all slaves. They rejected the possibility of political compromise as a solution to the issue of slavery.

Kansas-Nebraska Act: An act passed by Congress in May 1854 that overturned a mandate of the Missouri Compromise (1820) prohibiting slavery in the U.S. territories north of 36°/30⊠ latitude. The act paved the way for the establishment of two new territories—Kansas and Nebraska—and provided that the voters of a territory decide whether it be a free or a slaveholding territory.

Know-Nothing Party: A nativist, anti-Catholic party formed in the 1840s from a merger of the Union Whig Party faction and the anti-Catholic, anti-foreign American Party. In the early 1850s, the party's heyday, the Know-Nothings declared their intention to preserve the Union. In 1856, the party split into Northern and Southern splinter groups over the issue of slavery in the territories, leading to the party's dissolution.

Liberty Party: A political party formed in 1839 that sought to promote and elect antislavery presidential candidates as the best means of achieving emancipation. This third party had a small following in the North, but was never able to challenge the stronger Democratic and Whig Parties.

Planter; planter woman: A member of the elite plantation-owning, slaveholding class in the South.

Radical Republicans: A group of Northern Republican politicians who demanded that the federal government deal severely with the former Confederates. When the Radical Republicans gained control of Congress in 1866, they passed laws as well as the Fourteenth and Fifteenth Amendments to ensure the civil rights of African Americans.

Reconstruction: The post–Civil War period (1865 to 1877) when the federal government controlled the former states of the Confederacy prior to their being readmitted into the Union.

Secession: The formal withdrawal of a state from the Union. In 1860 and 1861, 11 Southern states withdrew, or seceded, from the United States and formed the Confederate States of America.

Suffragist: An individual who supported and promoted a woman's right to vote.

Thirteenth Amendment: An amendment to the Constitution that outlawed slavery and involuntary servitude. Ratified by the states in December 1865, it guaranteed the freedom of African Americans.

Transcendentalism: A philosophical and literary movement of liberal intellectuals in New England from the 1830s through the Civil War. Among the key leaders of the movement were Ralph Waldo Emerson, Bronson Alcott (father of LOUISA MAY ALCOTT), and Henry David Thoreau.

Unionist: An individual who supported the Union cause and who believed that the Union must not be divided.

Whig Party: The national political party formed after the reelection of Democratic President Andrew Jackson in 1832. The Whigs opposed Jackson and the Democratic Party and supported economic policies that were favorable to business, including high protective tariffs and a national bank. Presidents William Henry Harrison (elected in 1840) and Zachary Taylor (elected in 1848) were Whigs.

Writ of habeas corpus: A court order that directs officers of the law to show just cause for a prisoner's incarceration. Its purpose is to prevent citizens from being imprisoned unlawfully. According to the Constitution, during times of war or rebellion, government leaders may suspend prisoners' right to file a petition for a writ of habeas corpus as President Abraham Lincoln did during the Civil War. President Andrew Johnson suspended the writ of MARY SURRATT, who was convicted of conspiracy in the assassination of Lincoln.

Yeoman; yeoman farmer: Middle-income farmers of the South who grew crops and raised livestock principally for their own subsistence. Yeoman farmers were landowners, though most owned few or no slaves.

Bibliography

Abram, Ruth J., ed. *"Send Us a Lady Physician": Women Doctors in America, 1835–1920*. New York: Norton. 1985.

Adams, George Worthington. *Doctors in Blue: The Medical History of the Union Army in the Civil War*. Baton Rouge: Louisiana State University Press. 1952, 1996.

Albers, Henry, ed. *Maria Mitchell: A Life in Journals and Letters*. Clinton Corners, NY: College Avenue Press. 2001.

Albers, Patricia and Beatrice Medicine, eds. *The Hidden Half: Studies of Plains Indian Women*. Washington, DC: University Press of America. 1983.

Alcott, Louisa May. *Louisa May Alcott on Race, Sex, and Slavery*. Edited by Sarah Elbert. Boston: Northeastern University Press. 1997.

Alcott, Louisa May. *The Journals of Louisa May Alcott*. Edited by Joel Myerson and Daniel Sheahy. Boston: Little, Brown. 1989.

Alcott, Louisa May. *Selected Letters of Louisa May Alcott*. Edited by Joel Myerson and Daniel Sheahy. Introduction by Madeleine Stern. Boston: Little Brown. 1987.

Alcott, Louisa May. *Hospital Sketches*. Edited by Bessie Z. Jones. Cambridge, MA: Harvard University Press. 1960.

Alleman, Tillie Pierce. *At Gettysburg or What a Girl Saw and Heard of the Battle: A True Narrative*. New York: W. Lake Borland. 1889. http://cee.indiana. edu/gopher/Turner_Adventure_Learning/Gettysburg_Archive/Primary_ Resources/At_Getty sburg.txt

Armitage, Susan and Elizabeth Jameson, eds. *The Women's West*. Norman: University of Oklahoma Press. 1987.

Arrington, Leonard J. and Davis Bitton. *The Mormon Experience: A History of the Latter-Day Saints*. Urbana: University of Illinois Press. 1992.

Ash, Stephen V. *When the Yankees Came: Conflict and Chaos in the Occupied South, 1861–1865*. Chapel Hill: University of North Carolina Press. 1995.

Ash, Stephen V. "Poor Whites in the Occupied South, 1861–1865." *Journal of Southern History*. 57 (1) (1991): 39–62.

Attie, Jeanie. *Patriotic Toil: Northern Women and the American Civil War*. Ithaca, NY: Cornell University Press. 1998.

Attie, Jeanie. "Warwork and the Crisis of Domesticity in the North." In *Divided Houses: Gender and the Civil War*. Edited by Catherine Clinton and Nina Silber. New York: Oxford University Press. 1992. 247–259.

Austin, Anne L. *The Woolsey Sisters of New York 1860–1900: A Family's Involvement in the Civil War and a New Profession*. Philadelphia: American Philosophical Society. 1971.

Bacon, Georgeanna Woolsey and Eliza Woolsey Howland. *Letters of a Family During the War for the Union 1861–1865*. 2 volumes. Privately printed. 1899.

Bacon, Margaret Hope. *Abby Hopper Gibbons: Prison Reformer and Social Activist*. Albany: State University of New York Press. 2000.

Bacon, Margaret Hope. " `One Great Bundle of Humanity': Frances Ellen Watkins Harper (1825–1911)." *The Pennsylvania Magazine of History & Biography*. 113 (1) (January 1989): 21–44.

Bacot, Ada W. *A Confederate Nurse: The Diary of Ada W. Bacot, 1860–1863*. Edited by Jean V. Berlin. Columbia: University of South Carolina Press. 1994.

Baker, Jean H. "Mary Todd Lincoln (1818–1882)." In *Portraits of American Women: From Settlement to the Present*. Edited by G. J. Barker-Benfield and Catherine Clinton. New York: St. Martin's Press. 1991. 241–257.

Baker, Jean H. *Mary Todd Lincoln: A Biography*. New York: Norton. 1987.

Baker, Nina Brown. *Cyclone in Calico: The Story of Mary Ann Bickerdyke*. Boston: Little, Brown. 1952.

Baker, Paula. "The Domestication of Politics: Women and American Political Society, 1780–1920." *American Historical Review*. 89 (June 1984): 620–647.

Baker, Ross K. "Entry of Women into the Federal Job World—At a Price." *Smithsonian*. 8 (4) (July 1977): 82–91.

Baker, Tracey. "Nineteenth-Century Minnesota Women Photographers." *Journal of the West*. 28 (1) (January 1989): 15–23.

Barber, Edna Susan. " `Sisters of the Capital': White Women in Richmond, Virginia, 1860–1880." Ph.D. dissertation. University of Maryland at College Park. 1997.

Bardaglio, Peter. "The Children of Jubilee: African-American Childhood in Wartime." In *Divided Houses: Gender and the Civil War*. Edited by Catherine Clinton and Nina Silber. New York: Oxford University Press. 1992: 213–229.

Barry, Kathleen. *Susan B. Anthony: Biography of a Singular Feminist*. New York: New York University Press. 1988.

Barton, H. Arnold. *A Folk Divided: Homeland Swedes and Swedish Americans, 1840–1940*. Carbondale: Southern Illinois University Press. 1994.

Baxandall, Rosalyn and Linda Gordon, eds. *America's Working Women: A Documentary History 1600 to the Present*. Revised Edition. New York: Norton. 1995.

Baxandall, Rosalyn, Linda Gordon, and Susan Reverby. "Boston Working Women Protest, 1869." *Signs* 1 (3) (Spring 1976): 803–808.

Bearden, Romare and Harry Henderson. "Edmonia Lewis." In *A History of African-American Artists from 1792 to the Present*. New York: Pantheon. 1993. 54–77.

Beers, Fannie A. *Memories: A Record of Personal Experiences and Adventure During Four Years of War*. Philadelphia: J. P. Lippincott. 1889.

Benton, Josiah H., Jr. "What Women Did for the War, and What the War Did for Women: A Memorial Day Address, Delivered Before the Soldier's Club at Wellesley, Massachusetts." Pamphlet. Boston: [no publisher]. 1894.

Berkin, Carol Ruth and Mary Beth Norton, eds. *Women of America: A History*. Boston: Houghton Mifflin. 1979.

Berlin, Ira, Barbara J. Fields, Steven F. Miller, Joseph P. Reidy, and Leslie S. Rowland, eds. *Free at Last: A Documentary History of Slavery, Freedom, and the Civil War*. New York: The New Press. 1992.

Berlin, Ira and Leslie S. Rowland, eds. *Families & Freedom: A Documentary History of African-American Kinship in the Civil War Era*. New York: The New Press. 1997.

Berlin, Ira, Marc Favreau, and Steven F. Miller, eds. *Remembering Slavery: African Americans Talk About Their Personal Experiences of Slavery*. New York: The New Press. 1998.

Berlin, Ira. *Slaves Without Masters: The Free Negro in the Antebellum South*. New York: Pantheon. 1974.

Bernstein, Iver. *The New York City Draft Riots: Their Significance for American Society and Politics in the Age of the Civil War*. New York: Oxford University Press. 1990.

Berry, Carrie. *A Confederate Girl: The Diary of Carrie Berry 1864*. Mankato, MN: Blue Earth Books. 2000.

Billington, Monroe Lee and Roger D. Hardaway, eds. *African Americans on the Western Frontier*. Niwot: University Press of Colorado. 1998.

Bird, Caroline. *Enterprising Women*. New York: Norton. 1976.

Blackwell, Elizabeth. *Pioneer Work for Women*. New York: E.P. Dutton. 1914.

Blanton, DeAnne. "Women Soldiers of the Civil War." *Prologue*. 25 (Spring 1993): 27–33.

Blanton, DeAnne and Lauren M. Cook. *They Fought Like Demons: Women Soldiers in the American Civil War*. Baton Rouge: Louisiana State University Press. 2002.

Bleser, Carol, ed. *In Joy and in Sorrow: Women, Family, and Marriage in the Victorian South, 1830–1900*. New York: Oxford University Press. 1991.

Bleser, Carol and Frederick Heath. "The Clays of Alabama: The Impact of the Civil War on a Southern Marriage." In *In Joy and in Sorrow: Women, Family, and Marriage in the Victorian South, 1830–1900*. Edited by Carol Bleser. New York: Oxford University Press. 1991. 302–324.

Bleser, Carol K. and Lesley J. Gordon, eds. *Intimate Strategies of the Civil War: Military Commanders and Their Wives*. New York: Oxford University Press. 2001.

Blewett, Mary H. *We Will Rise in Our Might: Workingwomen's Voices from Nineteenth-Century New England*. Ithaca, NY: Cornell University Press. 1991.

Blewett, Mary H. "The Sexual Division of Labor and the Artisan Tradition in Early Industrial Capitalism: The Case of New England Shoemaking, 1780–1860." In *"To Toil the Livelong Day": America's Women at Work, 1780–1980*. Edited by Carol Groneman and Mary Beth Norton. Ithaca, NY: Cornell University Press. 1987. 35–46.

Blodgett, Geoffrey. "John Mercer Langston and the Case of Edmonia Lewis: Oberlin, 1862." *Journal of Negro History*. 52 (3) (July 1968): 201–218.

Bogin, Ruth. "Sarah Parker Remond: Black Abolitionist from Salem." *Essex Institute Historical Collections*. 110 (2) (April 1974): 120–150.

Boyd, Belle. *Belle Boyd in Camp and Prison*. Edited, with an introduction, by Curtis Carroll Davis. Cranbury, NJ: Thomas Yoseloff. 1968.

Boyd, Melba Joyce. *Discarded Legacy: Politics and Poetics in the Life of Frances E. W. Harper, 1825–1911*. Detroit: Wayne State University Press. 1994.

Bradford, Sarah. *Harriet Tubman: The Moses of Her People*. 1886. Reprint. Gloucester, MA: Corinth Books. 1981.

Breckinridge, Lucy. *Lucy Breckinridge of Grove Hill: The Journal of a Virginia Girl, 1862–1864*. Edited by Mary D. Robertson. Kent, OH: Kent State University Press. 1979.

Brewer, Eileen Mary. *Nuns and the Education of American Catholic Women, 1860–1920*. Chicago: Loyola University Press. 1987.

Brockett, Linus P. and Mary C. Vaughan. *Woman's Work in the Civil War: A Record of Heroism, Patriotism and Patience*. Philadelphia: Zeigler, McCurdy & Co. 1867.

Brown, Thomas J. *Dorothea Dix: New England Reformer*. Cambridge, MA: Harvard University Press. 1998.

Bruyn, Kathleen. *"Aunt" Clara Brown: Story of a Black Pioneer*. Boulder, CO: Pruett Publishing. 1970.

Bryan, T. Conn, ed. "A Georgia Woman's Civil War Diary: The Journal of Minerva Leah Rowles McClatchey, 1864–1865." *Georgia Historical Quarterly*. 51 (June 1967): 197–216.

Buck, Lucy Rebecca. *Shadows on My Heart: The Civil War Diary of Lucy Rebecca Buck of Virginia*. Edited by Elizabeth R. Baer. Southern Voices from the Past. Athens: University of Georgia Press. 1997.

Bunkers, Suzanne L. *Diaries of Girls and Women: A Midwestern American Sampler*. Madison: University of Wisconsin Press. 2001.

Burge, Dolly Lunt. *The Diary of Dolly Lunt Burge, 1848–1879*. Edited by Christine Jacobson Carter. Athens: University of Georgia Press. 1997.

Burgess, Lauren Cook, ed. *An Uncommon Soldier: The Civil War Letters of Sarah Rosetta Wakeman, Alias Pvt. Lyons Wakeman, 153rd* Regiment, New York State Volunteers, 1862–1864. Pasadena, MD: The Minerva Center. 1994.

Burton, David. "Friday the 13th: Richmond's Great Homefront Disaster." *Civil War Times Illustrated*. 21 (6) (October 1982): 36–41.

Bushman, Claudia, ed. *Mormon Sisters: Women in Early Utah*. Cambridge, MA: Emmeline Press Limited. 1976.

Butchart, Ronald E. *Northern Schools, Southern Blacks, and Reconstruction: Freedmen's Education 1862–1875*. Westport, CT: Greenwood Press. 1980.

Butler, Benjamin F. *Autobiography and Personal Reminiscences of Major-General Benjamin F. Butler: Butler's Book*. Boston: Thayer. 1892.

Bynum, Hartwell T. "Sherman's Expulsion of the Roswell Women in 1864." *Georgia Historical Quarterly*. 54 (2) (1970): 169–182.

Bynum, Victoria E. *Unruly Women: The Politics of Social and Sexual Control in the Old South*. Chapel Hill: University of North Carolina Press. 1992.

Cable, George Washington, ed. "A Woman's Diary of the Siege of Vicksburg." *Century Magazine*. 30 (September 1885): 767–775.

Camarillo, Albert. *Chicanos in a Changing Society*. Cambridge, MA: Harvard University Press. 1979.

Cameron, Ardis. *Radicals of the Worst Sort: Laboring Women in Lawrence, Massachusetts, 1860–1912*. Urbana: University of Illinois Press. 1993.

Campbell, Edward D. C., Jr., and Kym S. Rice, eds. *A Woman's War: Southern Women, Civil War, and the Confederate Legacy.* Richmond and Charlottesville: The Museum of the Confederacy and the University Press of Virginia. 1996.

Cashin, Joan E. "Into the Trackless Wilderness: The Refugee Experience in the Civil War." In *A Woman's War: Southern Women, Civil War, and the Confederate Legacy.* Edited by Edward D. C. Campbell, Jr., and Kym S. Rice. Richmond and Charlottesville: The Museum of the Confederacy and the University Press of Virginia. 1996. 29–53.

Cashin, Joan. " 'Since the War Broke Out': The Marriage of Kate and William McLure." In *Divided Houses: Gender and the Civil War.* Edited by Catherine Clinton and Nina Silber. New York: Oxford University Press. 1992. 200–212.

Cashin, Joan. "Varina Howell Davis (1826–1906)." In *Portraits of American Women: From Settlement to the Present.* Edited by G. J. Barker-Benfield and Catherine Clinton. New York: St. Martin's Press. 1991. 259–277.

Catton, Bruce. *The American Heritage New History of the Civil War.* Edited by James M. McPherson. New York: Viking. 1996.

Chamlee, Roy Z., Jr. *Lincoln's Assassins: A Complete Account of Their Capture, Trial, and Punishment.* Jefferson, NC: McFarland. 1990.

Chesnut, Mary Boykin Miller. *The Private Mary Chesnut: The Unpublished Civil War Diaries.* Edited by C. Vann Woodward and Elisabeth Muhlenfeld. New York: Oxford University Press. 1984.

Chesnut, Mary Boykin Miller. *Mary Chesnut's Civil War.* Edited by C. Vann Woodward. New Haven, CT: Yale University Press. 1981.

Chesson, Michael. "Harlots or Heroines? A New Look at the Richmond Bread Riot." *The Virginia Magazine of History and Biography.* 92 (April 1984): 131–175.

Chester, Giraud. *Embattled Maiden: The Life of Anna Dickinson.* New York: Putnam. 1951.

Child, Lydia Maria. *Lydia Maria Child, Selected Letters, 1817–1880.* Edited by Milton Meltzer and Patricia G. Holland. Amherst: University of Massachusetts Press. 1982.

Child, Lydia Maria. *Correspondence Between Lydia Maria Child and Gov. Wise and Mrs. Mason, of Virginia.* Boston: American Anti-Slavery Society. 1860.

Child, Lydia Maria. *The Duty of Disobedience to the Fugitive Slave Act: An Appeal to the Legislators of Massachusetts.* Boston: American Anti-Slavery Society. 1860.

Child, Lydia Maria. *The Right Way the Safe Way, Proved by Emancipation in the British West Indies, and Elsewhere.* New York: American Anti-Slavery Society. 1860.

Clark, E. Culpepper. "Sarah Morgan and Francis Dawson: Raising the Woman Question in Reconstruction South Carolina." *South Carolina Historical Magazine.* 81 (1) (1980): 8–23.

Clausius, Gerhard P. "The Little Soldier of the 95th: Albert D.J. Cashier." *Journal of the Illinois State Historical Society.* 51 (Winter 1958): 380–387.

Clifford, Deborah Pickman. *Crusader for Freedom: A Life of Lydia Maria Child.* Boston: Beacon Press. 1992.

Clifford, Deborah Pickman. *Mine Eyes Have Seen the Glory: A Biography of Julia Ward Howe.* Boston: Little, Brown. 1978.

Clinton, Catherine. *Fanny Kemble's Civil Wars*. New York: Simon & Schuster. 2000.

Clinton, Catherine. *Tara Revisited: Women, War, and the Plantation Legend*. New York: Abbeville Press. 1995.

Clinton, Catherine. "Maria Weston Chapman (1806–1885)." In *Portraits of American Women: From Settlement to the Present*. Edited by G. J. Barker-Benfield and Catherine Clinton. New York: St. Martin's Press. 1991. 147–167.

Clinton, Catherine and Nina Silber, eds. *Divided Houses: Gender and the Civil War*. New York: Oxford University Press. 1992.

Cohn, Jan. "The Civil War in Magazine Fiction of the 1860s." *Journal of Popular Culture*. 4 (2) (1970): 355–382.

Coleman, Elizabeth Dabney. "The Captain Was a Lady." *Virginia Cavalcade*. (Summer 1956): 35–41.

Conklin, Eileen F. *Women at Gettysburg 1863*. Gettysburg, PA: Thomas Publications. 1993.

Conrad, Earl. *Harriet Tubman*. New York: Paul S. Eriksson. 1943.

Cook, Adrian. *The Armies of the Streets: The New York City Draft Riots of 1863*. Lexington: University of Kentucky Press. 1974.

Coppin, Fanny Jackson. *Reminiscences of School Life, and Hints on Teaching*. New York: G.K. Hall. 1995.

Coski, John M. *Capital Navy: The Men, Ships, and Operations of the James River Squadron*. Campbell, CA: Savas Publishing. 1996.

Cott, Nancy F., ed. *No Small Courage: A History of Women in the United States*. New York: Oxford University Press. 2000.

Coulter, E. Merton. *The Confederate States of America, 1861–1865*. Baton Rouge: Louisiana State University Press. 1950.

Coultrap-McQuin, Susan. *Doing Literary Business: American Women Writers in the Nineteenth Century*. Chapel Hill: University of North Carolina Press. 1990.

Coultrap-McQuin, Susan. "Legacy Profile: Gail Hamilton (1833–1896)." *Legacy*. 4 (2) (Fall 1987): 53–58.

Culley, Margo, ed. *A Day at a Time: The Diary Literature of American Women from 1764 to the Present*. New York: The Feminist Press. 1985.

Cumming, Kate. *The Journal of a Confederate Nurse*. Edited by Richard Barksdale Harwell. Baton Rouge: Louisiana State University Press. 1998.

Current, Richard N., ed. *Encyclopedia of the Confederacy*. 4 volumes. New York: Simon & Schuster. 1993.

Daly, Maria Lydig. *Diary of a Union Lady, 1861–1865*. Edited by Harold Earl Hammond. Lincoln: University of Nebraska Press. 2000.

Dandurand, Karen. "New Dickinson Civil War Publications." *American Literature*. 56 (1) (March 1984): 17–27.

Daniels, Roger. *Coming to America: A History of Immigration and Ethnicity in American Life*. New York: Harper Perennial. 1991.

Dannett, Sylvia. *She Rode with the Generals*. New York: Thomas Nelson. 1960.

Dannett, Sylvia. *Noble Women of the North*. New York: T. Yoseloff. 1959.

Davis, Curtis Carroll. " 'The Pet of the Confederacy' Still? Fresh Findings About Belle Boyd." *Maryland Historical Magazine*. 78 (Spring 1983): 35–53.

Davis, Rebecca Harding. *A Rebecca Harding Davis Reader*. Edited, with an introduction, by Jean Pfaelzer. Pittsburgh: University of Pittsburgh Press. 1995.

Davis, Rebecca Harding. *Bits of Gossip*. Boston: Houghton Mifflin. 1904.

Dawson, Sarah Morgan. *The Civil War Diary of Sarah Morgan*. Edited by Charles East. Athens: University of Georgia Press. 1991.

Dean, Eric T., Jr. *Shook Over Hell: Post-Traumatic Stress, Vietnam, and the Civil War*. Cambridge, MA: Harvard University Press. 1997.

DeBoer, Clara Merritt. *His Truth Is Marching On: African Americans Who Taught the Freedmen for the American Missionary Association 1861–1877*. New York: Garland. 1995.

Deck, Alice A. "Whose Book Is This?: Authorial Versus Editorial Control of Harriet Brent Jacobs' Incidents in the Life of a Slave Girl: Written by Herself." *Women's Studies International Forum*. 10 (1) (1987): 33–40.

DeCredico, Mary A. *Mary Boykin Chesnut: A Confederate Woman's Life*. Madison, WI: Madison House. 1996.

De Pauw, Linda Grant. *Battle Cries and Lullabies: Women in War from Prehistory to the Present*. Norman: University of Oklahoma Press. 1998.

Deutrich, Bernice M. "Propriety and Pay." *Prologue*. 3 (2) (Fall 1971): 67–72.

Dickinson, Emily. *The Poems of Emily Dickinson*. Edited by Martha Dickinson Bianchi and Alfred Leete Hampson. Boston: Little, Brown. 1931.

Diner, Hasia R. *A Time for Gathering: The Second Migration 1820–1880*. Series: The Jewish People in America. Baltimore: The Johns Hopkins University Press. 1992.

Diner, Hasia R. *Erin's Daughters in America: Irish Immigrant Women in the Nineteenth Century*. Baltimore: Johns Hopkins University Press. 1983.

Dinkin, Robert J. *Before Equal Suffrage: Women in Partisan Politics from Colonial Times to 1920*. Westport, CT: Greenwood Press. 1995.

Dolensky, Suzanne T. "Varina Howell Davis, 1889 to 1906: The Years Alone." *Journal of Mississippi History*. 47 (2) (May 1985): 90–109.

Doyle, Elisabeth Johan. "Nurseries of Treason: Schools in Occupied New Orleans." *Journal of Southern History*. 26 (2) (May 1960): 161–179.

Drachman, Virginia G. *Hospital with a Heart: Women Doctors and the Paradox of Separatism at the New England Hospital, 1862–1969*. Ithaca, NY: Cornell University Press. 1984.

Drago, Edmund L. "How Sherman's March Through Georgia Affected the Slaves." *Georgia Historical Quarterly*. 57 (3) (1973): 361–375.

Draper, Arthur G., ed. " `Dear Sister:' Letters from War-Torn Missouri, 1864." *Gateway Heritage*. 13 (Spring 1993): 48–57.

DuBois, Ellen Carol. *Feminism and Suffrage: The Emergence of an Independent Women's Movement in America 1848–1869*. Ithaca, NY: Cornell University Press. 1978.

Edmondson, Belle. *A Lost Heroine of the Confederacy: The Diaries and Letters of Belle Edmondson*. Edited by Loretta and William Galbraith. Jackson: University Press of Mississippi. 1990.

Edmondston, Catherine Ann Devereux. *"Journal of a Secesh Lady": The Diary of Catherine Ann Devereux Edmondston*. Edited by Beth G. Crabtree and James W. Patton. Raleigh: North Carolina Division of Archives and History. 1979.

Edwards, Rebecca. *Angels in the Machinery: Gender in American Party Politics from the Civil War to the Progressive Era*. New York: Oxford University Press. 1997.

Eisenmann, Linda. *Historical Dictionary of Women's Education in the United States*. Westport, CT: Greenwood Press. 1998.

Elbert, Sarah. *A Hunger for Home: Louisa May Alcott and* Little Women. Philadelphia: Temple University Press. 1984.

Elmore, Grace Brown. *A Heritage of Woe: The Civil War Diary of Grace Brown Elmore, 1861–1868*. Edited by Marli F. Weiner. Athens: University of Georgia Press. 1997.

Ernst, Kathleen A. *Too Afraid to Cry: Maryland Civilians in the Antietam Campaign*. Mechanicsburg, PA: Stackpole Books. 1999.

Escott, Paul D. *Many Excellent People: Power and Privilege in North Carolina, 1850–1900*. Chapel Hill: University of North Carolina Press. 1985.

Escott, Paul D. "The Cry of the Sufferers: The Problem of Welfare in the Confederacy." *Civil War History*. 23 (September 1977): 228–240.

Evans, Augusta J. *Macaria; or, Altars of Sacrifice*. Edited by Drew Gilpin Faust. Baton Rouge: Louisiana State University Press. 1992.

Evans, Augusta J. "Augusta J. Evans on Secession." *Alabama Historical Quarterly*. 3 (Spring 1941): 65–67.

Evans, David. "Wool, Women, and War." *Civil War Times Illustrated*. 26 (5) (1987): 38–42.

Fahs, Alice. *The Imagined Civil War: Popular Literature of the North and South, 1861–1865*. Chapel Hill: University of North Carolina Press. 2001.

Fairbanks, Carol, ed. *Writings of Farm Women 1840–1940: An Anthology*. New York: Garland. 1990.

Farnham, Christie Anne. *The Education of the Southern Belle: Higher Education and Student Socialization in the Antebellum South*. New York: New York University Press. 1994.

Faust, Drew Gilpin. *Mothers of Invention: Women of the Slaveholding South in the American Civil War*. New York: Vintage Books. 1997.

Faust, Drew Gilpin. "Altars of Sacrifice." In *Divided Houses: Gender and the Civil War*. Edited by Catherine Clinton and Nina Silber. New York: Oxford University Press. 1992.

Faust, Drew Gilpin. " 'Trying to Do a Man's Business': Slavery, Violence and Gender in the American Civil War." *Gender & History*. 4 (Summer 1992): 197–214.

Faust, Patricia L., ed. *Historical Times Illustrated Encyclopedia of the Civil War*. New York: Harper Perennial. 1991.

Fellman, Michael. *Inside War: The Guerrilla Conflict in Missouri During the American Civil War*. New York: Oxford University Press. 1989.

Finley, Ruth E. *The Lady of Godey's: Sarah Josepha Hale*. Philadelphia: J.B. Lippincott. 1938.

Fischer, Christiane, ed. *Let Them Speak for Themselves: Women in the American West 1849–1900*. Hamden, CT: Archon Books. 1977.

Fladeland, Betty. "New Light on Sarah Emma Edmonds Alias Franklin Thompson." *Michigan History*. 47 (4) (1963): 357–362.

Flexner, Eleanor and Ellen Fitzpatrick. *Century of Struggle: The Woman's Rights Movement in the United States.* Cambridge, MA: The Belknap Press of Harvard University Press. Enlarged Edition. 1996.

Foner, Philip S. *Women and the American Labor Movement: From Colonial Times to the Eve of World War I.* New York: Free Press. 1979.

Forbes, Ella. *African American Women During the Civil War.* New York: Garland. 1998.

Fox-Genovese, Elizabeth. *Within the Plantation Household: Black and White Women of the Old South.* Chapel Hill: University of North Carolina Press. 1988.

Frémont, Jessie Benton. *The Letters of Jessie Benton Frémont.* Edited by Pamela Herr and Mary Lee Spence. Urbana: University of Illinois Press. 1993.

Furgurson, Ernest B. *Ashes of Glory: Richmond at War.* New York: Knopf. 1996.

Gallman, J. Matthew. "Anna Dickinson: Abolitionist Orator." In *The Human Tradition in the Civil War and Reconstruction.* Edited by Steven E. Woodworth. Wilmington, DE: Scholarly Resources. 2000. 93–110.

Gamber, Wendy. *The Female Economy: The Millinery and Dressmaking Trades, 1860–1930.* Urbana: University of Illinois Press. 1997.

Garcia, Céline Frémaux. *Céline: Remembering Louisiana, 1850–1871.* Edited by Patrick J. Geary. Athens: University of Georgia Press. 1987.

Garraty, John A. and Mark C. Carnes. *American National Biography.* New York: Oxford University Press. 1999.

Gates, Paul W. *Agriculture and the Civil War.* New York: Knopf. 1965.

George, Joseph, Jr. "Nature's First Law: Louis J. Weichmann and Mrs. Surratt." *Civil War History.* 28 (2) (June 1982): 101–127.

Gibbons, Abby Hopper. *Life of Abby Hopper Gibbons: Told Chiefly Through Her Correspondence.* 2 volumes. Edited by Sarah Hopper Emerson. New York: G.P. Putnam's. 1897, 1896.

Giesberg, Judith Ann. *Civil War Sisterhood: The United States Sanitary Commission and Women's Politics in Transition.* Boston: Northeastern University Press. 2000.

Gilmore, Donald. "Revenge in Kansas, 1863." *History Today.* 43 (Mar 1993): 47–53.

Ginzberg, Lori D. *Women and the Work of Benevolence: Morality, Politics, and Class in the Nineteeth-Century United States.* New Haven, CT: Yale University Press. 1990.

Glymph, Thavolia. " 'This Species of Property': Female Slave Contrabands in the Civil War." In *A Woman's War: Southern Women, Civil War, and the Confederate Legacy.* Edited by Edward D. C. Campbell, Jr., and Kym S. Rice. Richmond and Charlottesville: The Museum of the Confederacy and the University Press of Virginia. 1996. 55–71.

Godfrey, Kenneth W., Audrey M. Godfrey, and Jill Mulvay Derr. *Women's Voices: An Untold History of the Latter-Day Saints.* Salt Lake City, UT: Deseret Book Co. 1982.

Gollaher, David. *Voice for the Mad: The Life of Dorothea Dix.* New York: Free Press. 1995.

Gonzalez, Deena J. *Refusing the Favor: The Spanish-Mexican Women of Santa Fe, 1820–1880.* New York: Oxford University Press. 1999.

Goodson, Stephanie Smith. "Plural Wives." In *Mormon Sisters: Women in Early Utah*. Edited by Claudia Bushman. Cambridge, MA: Emmeline Press Limited. 1976. 89–111.

Gossett, Thomas F. *Uncle Tom's Cabin and American Culture*. Dallas, TX: Southern Methodist University Press. 1985.

Gould, Virginia Meacham, ed. *Chained to the Rock of Adversity: To Be Free, Black and Female in the Old South*. Athens: University of Georgia Press. 1998.

Grant, Mary H. *Private Woman, Public Person: An Account of the Life of Julia Ward Howe from 1819 to 1868*. Brooklyn, NY: Carlson Publishing. 1994.

Griffith, Helen. *Dauntless in Mississippi: The Life of Sarah A. Dickey 1838–1904*. South Hadley, MA: Dinosaur Press. 1965.

Griffith, Lucille. "Mrs. Juliet Opie Hopkins and Alabama Military Hospitals." *The Alabama Review*. 6 (2) (April 1953): 99–120.

Grimké, Charlotte Forten. *The Journals of Charlotte Forten Grimké*. Edited by Brenda Stevenson. New York: Oxford University Press. 1988.

Griswold del Castillo, Richard. *North to Aztlán: A History of Mexican Americans in the United States*. New York: Twayne Publishers. 1996.

Griswold del Castillo, Richard. *La Familia: Chicano Families in the Urban Southwest, 1848–Present*. Notre Dame, IN: Notre Dame Press. 1984.

Guerin, E. J. *Mountain Charley or the Adventures of Mrs. E.J. Guerin, Who Was Thirteen Years in Male Attire*. Norman: University of Oklahoma Press. 1968.

Gustafson, Melanie Susan. *Women and the Republican Party, 1854–1924*. Urbana: University of Illinois Press. 2001.

Haarsager, Sandra. *Organized Womanhood: Cultural Politics in the Pacific Northwest, 1840–1920*. Norman: University of Oklahoma Press. 1997.

Habegger, Alfred. *My Wars Are Laid Away in Books: The Life of Emily Dickinson*. New York: Random House. 2001.

Hagler, D. Harland. "The Ideal Woman in the Antebellum South: Lady or Farmwife?" *Journal of Southern History*. 46 (August 1980): 405–418.

Hall, James O. "The Lady in the Veil." *The Maryland Independent*. June 25, 1975.

Hall, Richard. *Patriots in Disguise: Women Warriors of the Civil War*. New York: Paragon House. 1993.

Hamand, Wendy F. "The Woman's National Loyal League: Feminist Abolitionists and the Civil War." *Civil War History*. 35 (1) (1989): 39–58.

Hamilton, Gail. *Gail Hamilton's Life in Letters*. 2 volumes. Edited by H. Augusta Dodge. Boston: Lee and Shepard. 1901.

Hamilton, Gail. "A Call to My Country-Women." *Atlantic Monthly*. 11 (March 1863): 345–349.

Hanchett, William. *The Lincoln Murder Conspiracies*. Urbana: University of Illinois Press. 1986. Orig. Pub. 1983.

Harper, Ida Husted. *The Life and Work of Susan B. Anthony*. 3 volumes. Indianapolis: Bowen-Merrill (volumes 1 & 2) and Hollenbeck Press (volume 3). 1899, 1908.

Harper, Judith E. *Susan B. Anthony: A Biographical Companion*. Santa Barbara, CA: ABC-CLIO. 1998.

Harris, Charles F. "Catalyst for Terror: The Collapse of the Women's Prison in Kansas City." *Missouri Historical Review*. 89 (3) (1995): 290–306.

Harris, Sharon M. *Rebecca Harding Davis and American Realism*. Philadelphia: University of Pennsylvania Press. 1991.

Harrison, Constance Cary. "A Virginia Girl in the First Year of the War." *Century*. 30 (August 1885): 606–614.

Harrison, Constance Cary (Mrs. Burton Harrison). *Recollections, Grave and Gay*. New York: Scribner. 1911.

Harzig, Christiane. *Peasant Maids, City Women: From the European Countryside to Urban America*. Ithaca, NY: Cornell University Press. 1997.

Hattori, Eugene. " 'And Some of Them Swear Like Pirates': Acculturation of American Indian Women in Nineteenth-Century Virginia City." In *Comstock Women: Making of a Mining Community*. Edited by Ronald M. James and C. Elizabeth Raymond. Reno: University of Nevada Press. 1998: 229–245.

Haviland, Laura. *A Woman's Life-Work: Labors and Experiences of Laura S. Haviland*. Cincinnati, OH: Walden & Stowe. 1881.

Hawks, Esther Hill. *A Woman Doctor's Civil War: Esther Hill Hawks' Diary*. Edited by Gerald Schwartz. Columbia: University of South Carolina Press. 1984.

Hays, Elinor Rice. *Those Extraordinary Blackwells: The Story of a Journey to a Better World*. New York: Harcourt. 1967.

Helmreich, Paul C. "Lucy Larcom at Wheaton." *New England Quarterly*. 63 (1) (1990): 109–120.

Herman, Debra. *College and After: The Vassar Experiment in Women's Education, 1861–1924*. Ph.D. dissertation. Ann Arbor, MI: University Microfilms International. 1982.

Herman, Judith Lewis, M.D. *Trauma and Recovery*. New York: Basic Books. 1992.

Herr, Pamela. *Jessie Benton Frémont*. New York: Franklin Watts. 1987.

Hill, Patricia R. "Writing Out the War: Harriet Beecher Stowe's Averted Gaze." In *Divided Houses: Gender and the Civil War*. Edited by Catherine Clinton and Nina Silber. New York: Oxford University Press. 1992. 260–278.

Hine, Darlene Clark. " 'Co-Laborers in the Work of the Lord': Nineteenth-Century Black Women Physicians." In *Send Us a Lady Physician: Women Doctors in America, 1835–1920*. Edited by Ruth J. Abram. New York Norton. 1985.

Hine, Darlene Clark and Kathleen Thompson. *A Shining Thread of Hope: The History of Black Women in America*. New York: Broadway Books. 1998.

Hine, Darlene Clark, Elsa Barkley Brown, and Rosalyn Terborg-Penn., eds. *Black Women in America: An Historical Encyclopedia*. New York: Carlson Publishing. 1993.

Hirata, Lucie Cheng. "Chinese Immigrant Women in Nineteenth-Century California." In *Women of America: A History*. Edited by Carol Ruth Berkin and Mary Beth Norton. Boston: Houghton Mifflin. 1979. 223–244.

Hitt, Michael D. *Charged with Treason*. Monroe, NY: Library Research Associates. 1992.

Hobbs, Catherine, ed. *Nineteenth-Century Women Learn to Write*. Charlottesville: University Press of Virginia. 1995.

Hoffman, Nicole Tonkovich. "Legacy Profile: Sarah Josepha Hale." *Legacy*. 7 (2) (Fall 1990): 47–54.

Hoisington, Daniel John. *Gettysburg and the Christian Commission*. Roseville, MN: Edinborough Press. 2002.

Holland, Mary A. Gardner. *Our Army Nurses*. Boston: Lounsbery, Nichols, & Worth. 1897.

Holland, Patricia G. "Legacy Profile: Lydia Maria Child." *Legacy*. 5 (Fall 1988): 45–52.

Holland, Patricia G. and Ann D. Gordon, eds. *The Papers of Elizabeth Cady Stanton and Susan B. Anthony*. Wilmington, DE: Scholarly Resources. 1991.

Holmes, Emma. *The Diary of Miss Emma Holmes*. Edited by John F. Marszalek. Baton Rouge: Louisiana State University Press. 1979.

Holmes, Kenneth L., ed. *Covered Wagon Women: Diaries and Letters from the Western Trails 1862–1865*. Volume 8. Lincoln: University of Nebraska Press. 1999.

Horton, James Oliver. *Free People of Color: Inside the African-American Community*. Washington, DC: Smithsonian Institution Press. 1993.

Howe, Julia Ward. *Reminiscences 1819–1899*. Orig. Pub. 1899. Reprint. New York: Negro Universities Press. 1969.

Huber, Leonard V. "The Battle of the Handkerchiefs." *Civil War History*. 8 (1) (1962): 48–53.

Hudson, Lynn M. "When 'Mammy' Becomes a Millionaire: Mary Ellen Pleasant, An African-American Entrepreneur." Ph.D. dissertation. Indiana University. 1996.

Inscoe, John C. "Coping in Confederate Appalachia: Portrait of a Mountain Woman and Her Community at War." *North Carolina Historical Review*. 69 (October 1992): 388–413.

Inscoe, John C. and Gordon B. McKinney. "Highland Households Divided: Familial Tensions in Southern Appalachia's Inner Civil War." Paper presented at the Families at War: Loyalty and Conflict in the Civil War South Symposium. April 1998.

Jacob, Kathryn Allamong. "Vinnie Ream." *Smithsonian*. 31 (5) (August 2000): 104–115.

Jacobs, Harriet A. *Incidents in the Life of a Slave Girl: Written by Herself*. Edited by Jean Fagan Yellin. Cambridge, MA: Harvard University Press. 1987.

James, Edward T. et al. *Notable American Women, 1607–1950: A Biographical Dictionary*. 3 volumes. Cambridge, MA: Belknap Press of Harvard University Press. 1971.

James, Janet Wilson, ed. *Women in American Religion*. Philadelphia: University of Pennsylvania Press. 1980.

Jameson, Elizabeth and Susan Armitage, eds. *Writing the Range: Race, Class, and Culture in the American West*. Norman: University of Oklahoma Press. 1997.

Jeffrey, Julie Roy. *The Great Silent Army of Abolitionism: Ordinary Women in the Antislavery Movement*. Chapel Hill: University of North Carolina Press. 1998.

Jeffrey, Julie Roy. *Frontier Women: The Trans-Mississippi West 1840–1880*. New York: Hill and Wang. 1979.

Jensen, Joan M. *With These Hands: Women Working on the Land*. Old Westbury, NY: Feminist Press. 1981.

Jentz, John B. and Richard Schneirov. "Chicago's Fenian Fair of 1864: A Window into the Civil War as a Popular Political Awakening." *Labor's Heritage*. 6 (3) (Winter 1995): 4–19.

Jiménez, Alfredo, ed. *Handbook of Hispanic Cultures in the United States.* Houston, TX: Arte Publico Press. 1994.

Jones, Jacqueline. *American Work: Four Centuries of Black and White Labor.* New York: Norton. 1998.

Jones, Jacqueline. *Labor of Love, Labor of Sorrow: Black Women, Work, and the Family from Slavery to the Present.* New York: Basic Books. 1985.

Jones, Jacqueline. "Women Who Were More Than Men: Sex and Status in Freedmen's Teaching." *History of Education Quarterly.* 19 (1) (Spring 1979): 47–60.

Jones, Katharine M. *When Sherman Came: Southern Women and the "Great March."* Indianapolis: Bobbs-Merrill. 1964.

Jones, Katharine M. *Heroines of Dixie: Confederate Women Tell Their Story of the War.* Indianapolis: Bobbs-Merrill. 1955.

Jordan, Winthrop D. *Tumult and Silence at Second Creek: An Inquiry into a Civil War Slave Conspiracy.* Baton Rouge: Louisiana State University Press. 1993.

Josephy, Alvin M. *The Civil War in the American West.* New York: Knopf. 1991

Juncker, Clara. "Behind Confederate Lines: Sarah Morgan Dawson." *Southern Quarterly.* 30 (Fall 1991): 7–18.

Karcher, Carolyn. *The First Woman in the Republic: A Cultural Biography of Lydia Maria Child.* Durham, NC: Duke University Press. 1994.

Katz, William Loren. *The Black West.* Seattle, WA: Open Hand Publishing. 1987

Kaufman, Janet E. "Treasury Girls." *Civil War Times Illustrated.* 25 (May 1986): 32–38.

Kaufman, Polly Welts. *Women Teachers on the Frontier.* New Haven, CT: Yale University Press. 1984.

Keckley, Elizabeth. *Behind the Scenes, or, Thirty Years a Slave, and Four Years in the White House.* New York: G.W. Carleton. 1868. Reprinted. New York: Oxford University Press. 1988.

Kehoe, Alice. "The Shackles of Tradition." In *The Hidden Half: Studies of Plains Indian Women.* Edited by Patricia Albers and Beatrice Medicine. Washington, DC: University Press of America. 1983: 53–76.

Kemble, Fanny. *Fanny Kemble's Journals.* Edited By Catherine Clinton. Cambridge, MA: Harvard University Press, 2000.

Kendall, Phebe Mitchell, ed. *Maria Mitchell: Life, Letters, and Journals.* Boston: Lee and Shepard. 1896.

Kennedy, Stetson. *After Appomatox.* Gainesville: University Press of Florida. 1995.

Kennedy, Susan Estabrook. *If All We Did Was to Weep at Home: A History of White Working-Class Women in America.* Bloomington: Indiana University Press. 1979.

Kennett, Lee. *Marching Through Georgia: The Story of Soldiers and Civilians During Sherman's Campaign.* New York: HarperCollins. 1995.

Kessler-Harris, Alice. *Out to Work: A History of Wage-Earning Women in the United States.* New York: Oxford University Press. 1982.

King, Wilma. *Stolen Childhood: Slave Youth in Nineteenth-Century America.* Bloomington: Indiana University Press. 1995.

King, Wilma. " `Suffer with Them Till Death': Slave Women and Their Children in Nineteenth-Century America." In *More Than Chattel: Black Women and Slavery in the Americas*. Edited by David Barry Gaspar and Darlene Clark Hine. Bloomington: Indiana University Press. 1996. 147–168.

Knight, Denise D., ed. *Nineteenth-Century American Women Writers: A Bio-Bibliographical Sourcebook*. Westport, CT: Greenwood Press. 1997.

Krowl, Michelle A. "For Better or For Worse: Black Families and the `State' in Civil War Virginia." In *Southern Families at War: Loyalty and Conflict in the Civil War South*. Edited by Catherine Clinton. New York: Oxford University Press. 2000: 35–57.

Kwolek-Folland, Angel. *Incorporating Women: A History of Women and Business in the United States*. New York: Twayne Publishers. 1998.

Lagerquist, L. DeAne. *In America the Men Milk the Cows: Factors of Gender, Ethnicity, and Religion in the Americanization of Norwegian-American Women*. Brooklyn, NY: Carlson Publishing. 1991.

Lammers, Pat and Amy Boyce. "Alias Franklin Thompson: A Female in the Ranks." *Civil War Times Illustrated*. 22 (9) (1984): 24–31.

Larcom, Lucy. *Poems*. Boston: Fields, Osgood. 1869.

Larson, C. Kay. "Bonny Yank and Ginny Reb." *Minerva: Quarterly Report on Women and the Military*. 8 (Spring 1990): 33–48.

LeConte, Emma. *The Diary of Emma LeConte*. Edited by Earl Schenck Miers. New York: Oxford University Press. 1957.

Le Grand, Julia. *The Journal of Julia Le Grand*. Edited by Kate Mason Rowland and Mrs. Morris L. Croxall. Richmond, VA: Everett Waddey. 1911.

Lensink, Judy Nolte, Christine M. Kirkham, and Karen Pauba Witzke, eds. " `My Only Confidante'—The Life and Diary of Emily Hawley Gillespie." *Annals of Iowa*. 45 (4) (Spring 1980): 288–307.

Leonard, Elizabeth D. *All the Daring of the Soldier: Women of the Civil War Armies*. New York: Penguin. 2001.

Leonard, Elizabeth D. *Yankee Women: Gender Battles in the Civil War*. New York: Norton. 1994.

Levine, Bruce et al. *Who Built America? Working People and the Nation's Economy, Politics, Culture, and Society. Vol 1. From Conquest and Colonization Through Reconstruction and the Great Uprising of 1877*. New York: Pantheon. 1989.

Lewis, Susan Ingalls. "Beyond Horatio Alger: Breaking Through Gendered Assumptions About Business `Success' in Mid-Nineteenth Century America." *Business and Economic History*. 24 (1) (Fall 1995): 97–105.

Lewis, Susan Ingalls. "Female Entrepreneurs in Albany 1840–1885." *Business and Economic History*. 21 (1992): 65–73.

Lindley, Susan Hill. *"You Have Stept Out of Your Place": A History of Women and Religion in America*. Louisville, KY: Westminster John Knox Press. 1996.

Ling, Huping. *Surviving on the Gold Mountain: A History of Chinese American Women and Their Lives*. Albany: State University of New York Press. 1998.

Livermore, Mary A. *My Story of the War: A Woman's Narrative*. Hartford, CT: A.D. Worthington. 1887. Reprint. New York: Da Capo Press. 1995.

Logan, Rayford W. and Michael R. Winston. *Dictionary of American Negro Biography*. New York: Norton. 1982.

Loughborough, Mary Ann. *My Cave Life in Vicksburg.* New York: D. Appleton and Co. 1864.

Love, Richard H. *Cassatt: The Independent.* Chicago: Milton H. Krienes. 1980.

Luft, Eric "Mid-Nineteenth Century Attitudes Toward Women Physicians: Reflections on Elizabeth Blackwell and the 150th Anniversary of Women in Medicine." Paper presented at the College of Physicians at Philadelphia as a Seminar of the Francis C. Wood Institute for the History of Medicine. March 23, 1999. http://www.hscsyr.edu/library/history/cppblackwell.html

Lutz, Alma. *Susan B. Anthony: Rebel, Crusader, Humanitarian.* Boston: Beacon Press. 1959.

Mabee, Carleton. "Sojourner Truth Fights Dependence on Government: Moves Freed Slaves off Welfare in Washington to Jobs in Upstate New York." *Afro-Americans in New York Life and History.* 14 (1) (January 1990): 7–26.

Mabee, Carleton. "Sojourner Truth and President Lincoln." *New England Quarterly.* 61 (4) (1988): 519–529.

Maher, Sister Mary Denis. *To Bind Up the Wounds: Catholic Sister Nurses in the U.S. Civil War.* New York: Greenwood Press. 1989.

Marchalonis, Shirley. *The Worlds of Lucy Larcom 1824–1893.* Athens: The University of Georgia Press. 1989.

Marcus, Jacob R. *The American Jewish Woman, 1654–1980.* New York: KTAV Publishing House. 1981.

Marcus, Jacob R. *The American Jewish Woman: A Documentary History.* New York: KTAV Publishing House. 1981.

Marcus, Jacob Rader, ed. "Eugenia Levy Phillips." In *Memoirs of American Jews, 1775–1865.* Volume 3. Philadelphia: The Jewish Publication Society of America. 1955. 161–196.

Markle, Donald E. *Spies and Spymasters of the Civil War.* New York: Hippocrene Books. 1994.

Marshall, Jeffrey D., ed. *A War of the People: Vermont Civil War Letters.* Hanover, NH: University Press of New England. 1999.

Marten, James. *The Children's Civil War.* Chapel Hill: University of North Carolina Press. 1998.

Massey, Mary Elizabeth. *Women in the Civil War.* 1966. Reprint. Lincoln: University of Nebraska Press. 1994.

Massey, Mary Elizabeth. *Refugee Life in the Confederacy.* Baton Rouge: Louisana State University Press. 1964.

Massey, Mary Elizabeth. *Ersatz in the Confederacy.* Columbia: University of South Carolina Press. 1952.

McCord, Louisa. *Louisa S. McCord: Poems, Drama, Biography, Letters.* Edited by Richard C. Lounsbury. Charlottesville: University Press of Virginia. 1996.

McCord, Louisa. *Louisa S. McCord: Political and Social Essays.* Edited by Richard C. Lounsbury. Charlottesville: University Press of Virginia. 1995.

McCurry, Stephanie. *Masters of Small Worlds: Yeoman Households, Gender Relations, and the Political Culture of the Antebellum South Carolina Low Country.* New York: Oxford University Press. 1995.

McDonald, Cornelia Peake. *A Woman's Civil War: A Diary, with Reminiscences of the War, from March 1862*. Edited by Minrose C. Gwin. Madison: University of Wisconsin Press. 1992.

McElligott, Mary Ellen, ed. " 'A Monotony Full of Sadness': The Diary of Nadine Turchin, May 1863–April 1864." *Journal of the Illinois State Historical Society*. 70 (February 1977): 27–89.

McGuire, Judith W. *Diary of a Southern Refugee, During the War, by a Lady of Virginia*. Richmond, VA: J.W. Randolph & English. 1889.

McKinley, Emilie Riley. *From the Pen of a She-Rebel: The Civil War Diary of Emilie Riley McKinley*. Edited by Gordon A. Cotton. Columbia: University of South Carolina Press. 2001.

McKinney, Gordon B. "Women's Role in Civil War Western North Carolina." *North Carolina Historical Review*. 69 (January 1992): 37–56.

McPherson, James M. *Ordeal by Fire: The Civil War and Reconstruction*. New York: Knopf. 1982.

Meltzer, Milton. *Tongue of Flame: The Life of Lydia Maria Child*. New York: Thomas Y. Crowell. 1965.

Meyer, Eugene L. "The Soldier Left a Portrait and Her Eyewitness Account." *Smithsonian*. 122 (January 1994): 96–104.

Miller, Darlis A. "The Women of Lincoln County, 1860–1900." In *Writing the Range: Race, Class, and Culture in the Women's West*. Edited by Elizabeth Jameson and Susan Armitage. Norman: University of Oklahoma Press. 1997. 147–171.

Miller, Kerby A. et al. " 'For Love and Liberty': Irish Women, Migration and Domesticity in Ireland and America, 1815–1920." In *Irish Women and Irish Migration*. Edited by Patrick O'Sullivan. New York: Leicester University Press. 1995. 41–65.

Miller, Randall M., Harry S. Stout, and Charles Reagan Wilson, eds. *Religion and the American Civil War*. New York: Oxford University Press. 1998.

Mohr, James C., ed. *The Cormany Diaries: A Northern Family in the Civil War*. Pittsburgh: University of Pittsburgh Press. 1982.

Moore, Frank. *Women of the War: Their Heroism and Self-Sacrifice*. Hartford, CT: S.S. Scranton. 1866.

Moorhead, James H. *American Apocalypse: Yankee Protestants and the Civil War 1860–1869*. New Haven, CT: Yale University Press. 1978.

More, Ellen S. *Restoring the Balance: Women Physicians and the Profession of Medicine, 1850–1995*. Cambridge, MA: Harvard University Press. 1999.

Morris, Robert C. *Reading, 'Riting, and Reconstruction: The Education of Freedmen in the South, 1861–1870*. Chicago: University of Chicago Press. 1981.

Mottus, Jane E. *New York Nightingales: The Emergence of the Nursing Profession at Bellevue and New York Hospital 1850–1920*. Ann Arbor, MI: UMI Research Press. 1981.

Moyle, Geraldine. "The Tenth Muse Lately Sprung Up in the Marketplace: Women and Professional Authorship in Nineteenth-Century America." Ph.D. dissertation. Ann Arbor, MI: University Microfilms International. 1985.

Moynihan, Ruth B., Susan Armitage, and Christiane Fischer Dichamp, eds. *So Much to Be Done: Women Settlers on the Mining and Ranching Frontier*. Lincoln: University of Nebraska Press. 1998.

Muhlenfeld, Elisabeth. *Mary Boykin Chesnut: A Biography*. Baton Rouge: Louisiana State University Press. 1981.

Muhn, James. "Women and the Homestead Act: Land Department Administration of a Legal Imbroglio, 1863–1934." *Western Legal History*. 7 (2) (Summer 1994): 282–305.

Murphy, Lucy Eldersveld. "Journeywoman Milliner: Emily Austin, Migration, and Women's Work in the Nineteenth-Century Midwest." In *Midwestern Women: Work, Community, and Leadership at the Crossroads*. Edited by Lucy Eldersveld Murphy and Wendy Hamand Venet. Bloomington: Indiana University Press. 1997. 38–59.

Murphy, Lucy Eldersveld. "Business Ladies: Midwestern Women and Enterprise, 1850–1880." *Journal of Women's History*. 3 (1) (Spring 1991): 65–89.

Murphy, Lucy Eldersveld. "Her Own Boss: Businesswomen and Separate Spheres in the Midwest, 1850–1880." *Illinois Historical Journal*. 80 (3) (Autumn 1987): 155–176.

Myres, Sandra L. *Westering Women and the Frontier Experience 1800–1915*. Albuquerque: University of New Mexico Press. 1982.

Oates, Stephen B. *A Woman of Valor: Clara Barton and the Civil War*. New York: The Free Press. 1994.

O'Brien, Michael, ed. *An Evening when Alone: Four Journals of Single Women in the South, 1827–1867*. Charlottesville: University Press of Virginia. 1993.

Ogilvie, Marilyn and Joy Harvey, eds. *The Biographical Dictionary of Women in Science: Pioneering Lives from Ancient Times to the Mid-Twentieth Century*. New York: Routledge. 2000.

Okker, Patricia. *Our Sister Editors: Sarah J. Hale and the Tradition of Nineteenth-Century American Women Editors*. Athens: University of Georgia Press. 1995.

Olin, Helen R. *The Women of a State University: An Illustration of the Working of Coeducation in the Middle West*. New York: G.P. Putnam's Sons. 1909.

Orpen, Adele. "Her Father's Right-Hand Man." In *Writings of Farm Women 1840–1940, An Anthology*. Edited by Carol Fairbanks. New York: Garland. 1990. 79–93.

Osterud, Nancy Grey. *Bonds of Community: The Lives of Farm Women in Nineteenth-Century New York*. Ithaca, NY: Cornell University Press. 1991.

Osterud, Nancy Grey. "Rural Women During the Civil War: New York's Nanticoke Valley, 1861–1865." *New York History*. 62 (4) (October 1990): 356–385.

Painter, Nell Irvin. *Sojourner Truth: A Life, a Symbol*. New York: Norton. 1996.

Palmquist, Peter E. "Pioneer Women Photographers in Nineteenth-Century California." *California History*. 71 (1) (Spring 1992): 110–127.

Paludan, Phillip S. *"A People's Contest": The Union and Civil War 1861–1865*. New York: Harper and Row. 1988.

Paludan, Phillip S. *Victims: A True Story of the Civil War*. Knoxville: University of Tennessee Press. 1981.

Parrish, William E. "The Western Sanitary Commission." *Civil War History*. 36 (1) 1990: 17–35.

Peabody, Elizabeth Palmer. *Letters of Elizabeth Palmer Peabody: American Renaissance Woman.* Edited by Bruce A. Ronda. Middletown, CT: Wesleyan University Press. 1984.

Peffer, George Anthony. *If They Don't Bring Their Women Here: Chinese Female Immigration Before Exclusion.* Urbana: University of Illinois Press. 1999.

Perkins, Linda M. *Fanny Jackson Coppin and the Institute for Colored Youth, 1865–1902.* New York: Garland. 1987.

Perry, Theophilus. *Widows by the Thousand: The Civil War Correspondence of Theophilus and Harriet Perry, 1862–1864.* Edited by M. Jane Johansson. Fayetteville: University of Arkansas Press. 2000.

Peterson, Carla L. *Doers of the Word: African-American Women Speakers and Writers in the North (1830–1880).* New York: Oxford University Press. 1995.

Petrino, Elizabeth A. *Emily Dickinson and Her Contemporaries: Women's Verse in America, 1820–1885.* Hanover, NH: University Press of New England. 1998.

Phelps, Elizabeth Stuart. *Chapters from a Life.* Boston: Houghton Mifflin. 1896.

Phifer, Louisa Jane. "Letters from an Illinois Farm 1864–1865." *Illinois State Historical Society Journal.* 66 (4) (Winter 1973): 387–403.

Pickle, Linda Schelbitzki. *Contented Among Strangers: Rural German-Speaking Women and Their Families in the Nineteenth-Century Midwest.* Urbana: University of Illinois Press. 1996

Pitt, Leonard. *The Decline of the Californios: A Social History of the Spanish-Speaking Californians, 1846–1890.* Berkeley: University of California Press. 1970.

Prieto, Laura. *At Home in the Studio: The Professionalization of Women Artists in America.* Cambridge, MA: Harvard University Press. 2001.

Prioli, Carmine A. " 'Wonder Girl from the West': Vinnie Ream and the Congressional Statue of Abraham Lincoln." *Journal of American Culture.* 12 (Winter 1989): 1–20.

Proctor, Samuel, ed. "The Call to Arms: Secession from a Feminine Point of View," *Florida Historical Quarterly,* 35 (January 1957), 266–270.

Putnam, Sallie Brock. *Richmond During the War: Four Years of Personal Observation.* Reprint. Lincoln: University of Nebraska Press. 1996.

Quattlebaum, Isabel. "Twelve Women in the First Days of the Confederacy." *Civil War History.* 7 (4): 370–385. 1961.

Rable, George. " 'Missing in Action': Women of the Confederacy." In *Divided Houses: Gender and the Civil War.* Edited by Catherine Clinton and Nina Silber. New York: Oxford University Press. 1992. 134–146.

Rable, George C. *Civil Wars: Women and the Crisis of Southern Nationalism.* Urbana: University of Illinois Press. 1989.

Rachal, John R. "Gideonites and Freedmen: Adult Literacy Education at Port Royal, 1862–1865." *Journal of Negro Education.* 55 (4) (1986): 453–469.

Racine, Philip N. "Emily Lyles Harris: A Piedmont Farmer During the Civil War." *South Atlantic Quarterly.* 79 (4) (1980): 386–397.

Ravage, John W. *Black Pioneers: Images of the Black Experience on the North American Frontier.* Salt Lake City: University of Utah Press. 1997.

Reed, Lida L. "A Woman's Experience During the Siege of Vicksburg." *Harper's Monthly Magazine.* 118 (December 1908): 45–53.

Remond, Sarah P. "The Negroes in the United States of America." *The Journal of Negro History.* 27 (April 1942): 216–218.

Renehan, Edward J., Jr. *The Secret Six: The True Tale of the Men Who Conspired with John Brown.* New York: Crown Publishers. 1995.

Rhodes, Jane. *Mary Ann Shadd Cary: The Black Press and Protest in the Nineteenth Century.* Bloomington: Indiana University Press. 1998.

Rice, Kym S. and Edward D. C. Campbell, Jr. "Voices from the Tempest: Southern Women's Wartime Experiences." In *A Women's War: Southern Women, Civil War, and the Confederate Legacy.* Edited by Edward D. C. Campbell, Jr., and Kym S. Rice. Richmond, VA: The Museum of the Confederacy and The University Press of Virginia. 1996. 73–111.

Richardson, Marilyn. "Lewis, Edmonia." In *American National Biography.* Volume 13. Edited by John A. Garraty and Mark C. Carnes. New York: Oxford University Press. 1999.

Richman, Irwin. "Pauline Cushman." *Civil War Times Illustrated.* 7 (February 1969): 39–44.

Riley, Glenda. *Frontierswomen: The Iowa Experience.* Ames: Iowa State University Press. 1981.

Roca, Steven Louis. "Presence and Precedents: The USS *Red Rover* During the American Civil War, 1861–1865." *Civil War History.* 44 (2) 1998: 91–110.

Rogers, Sherbrooke. *Sarah Josepha Hale: A New England Pioneer 1788–1879.* Grantham, NH: Tompson & Rutter. 1985.

Ronda, Bruce A. *Elizabeth Palmer Peabody: A Reformer on Her Own Terms.* Cambridge, MA: Harvard University Press. 1999.

Ropes, Hannah Anderson. *Civil War Nurse: The Diary and Letters of Hannah Ropes.* Knoxville: University of Tennessee Press. 1980.

Rose, Anne C. *Victorian America and the Civil War.* New York: Cambridge University Press. 1992.

Ross, Ishbel. *First Lady of the South: The Life of Mrs. Jefferson Davis.* New York: Harper and Bros. 1958.

Ross, Ishbel. *Rebel Rose: Life of Rose O'Neal Greenhow, Confederate Spy.* New York: Harper & Bros. 1954.

Ross, Kristie R. " 'Women Are Needed Here': Northern Protestant Women as Nurses During the Civil War, 1861–1865." Ph.D. dissertation. Columbia University. UMI Dissertation Services. 1993.

Ross, Kristie R. "Arranging a Doll's House: Refined Women as Union Nurses." In *Divided Houses: Gender and the Civil War.* Edited by Catherine Clinton and Nina Silber. New York: Oxford University Press. 1992. 97–113.

Rossbach, Jeffrey. *Ambivalent Conspirators: John Brown, the Secret Six, and a Theory of Slave Violence.* Philadelphia: University of Pennsylvania Press. 1982.

Rubinstein, Charlotte Streifer. *American Women Sculptors: A History of Women Working in Three Dimensions.* Boston: G.K. Hall. 1990.

Rubinstein, Charlotte Streifer. *American Women Artists from Early Indian Times to the Present.* New York: Avon Books. 1982.

Russell, Francis. "Butler the Beast?" *American Heritage Illustrated.* 19 (3) (April 1968): 48–53, 75–88.

Ryan, Mary P. *Women in Public: Between Banners and Ballots, 1825–1880*. Baltimore: Johns Hopkins University Press. 1990.

Rybczynski, Witold. *A Clearing in the Distance: Frederick Law Olmsted and America in the Nineteenth Century*. New York: Scribner. 1999.

Sacks, Benjamin. "Varina Howell Davis: A Wife's Vigil." *Journal of Mississippi History*. 56 (2) (May 1994): 107–127.

Sahli, Nancy Ann. *Elizabeth Blackwell, M.D. (1821–1910): A Biography*. New York: Arno Press. 1982.

Saxton, Martha. *Louisa May: A Modern Biography of Louisa May Alcott*. Boston: Houghton Mifflin. 1977.

Schafer, Elizabeth D. "Hopkins, Juliet Ann Opie." In *American National Biography*. Volume 11. Edited by John A. Garraty and Mark C. Carnes. New York: Oxford University Press. 1999. 178–180.

Schlissel, Lillian. *Women's Diaries of the Westward Journey*. New York: Schocken Books. 1982.

Schlissel, Lillian, Vicki L. Ruiz, and Janice Monk, eds. *Western Women: Their Land, Their Lives*. Albuquerque: University of New Mexico Press. 1988.

Schneider, Dorothy and Carl J. Schneider. *The ABC-CLIO Companion to Women in the Workplace*. Santa Barbara, CA: ABC-CLIO. 1993.

Schnell, J. Christopher. "Mary Livermore and the Great Northwestern Fair." *Chicago History*. 4 (1) (1975): 34–43.

Schuetz, Janice E. "Mary Surratt: The Logic of Conflicting Values." In *The Logic of Women on Trial: Case Studies of Popular American Trials*. Carbondale: Southern Illinois University Press. 1994.

Schultz, Jane E. " 'Are We Not All Soldiers?' Northern Women in the Civil War Hospital Service." *Prospects*. 20 (1995): 39–56.

Schultz, Jane E. "The Inhospitable Hospital: Gender and Professionalism in Civil War Medicine." *Signs*. 17 (2) (Winter 1992): 363–392.

Schultz, Jane. E. "Mute Fury: Southern Women's Diaries of Sherman's March to the Sea, 1864–1865." In *Arms and the Woman: War, Gender and Literary Representation*. Edited by Helen M. Cooper, Adrienne Auslander Munich, and Susan Merrill Squier. Chapel Hill: University of North Carolina Press. 1989. 59–79.

Schultz, Jane E. "Women at the Front: Gender and Genre in the Literature of the American Civil War." Ph.D. dissertation. University of Michigan. UMI Dissertation Services. 1988.

Schwalm, Leslie A. *A Hard Fight for We: Women's Transition from Slavery to Freedom in South Carolina*. Urbana: University of Illinois Press. 1997.

Schweninger, Loren. "Property Owning Free African-American Women in the South, 1800–1870." *Journal of Women's History*. 1 (Winter 1990): 13–44.

Scott, Anne Firor. *The Southern Lady: From Pedestal to Politics, 1830–1930*. Chicago: University of Chicago Press. 1970.

Seller, Maxine Schwartz, ed. *Women Educators in the United States 1820–1993: A Bio-Bibliographical Sourcebook*. Westport, CT: Greenwood Press. 1994.

Seller, Maxine Schwartz, ed. *Immigrant Women*. Philadelphia: Temple University Press. 1981.

Sewall, Richard B. *The Life of Emily Dickinson*. 2 volumes. New York: Farrar, Straus and Giroux. 1974.

Shaffer, Donald K. "In the Shadow of the Old Constitution: Black Civil War Veterans and the Persistence of Slave Marriage Customs." In *Southern Families at War: Loyalty and Conflict in the Civil War South*. Edited by Catherine Clinton. New York: Oxford University Press. 2000. 59–75.

Sheldon, Carrel Hilton. "Mormon Haters." In *Mormon Sisters: Women in Early Utah*. Edited by Claudia Bushman. Cambridge, MA: Emmeline Press Limited. 1976. 113–131.

Sherman, Joan R., ed. *African-American Poetry of the 19th Century: An Anthology*. Urbana: University of Illinois Press. 1992.

Shoemaker, Nancy, ed. *Negotiators of Change: Historical Perspectives on Native American Women*. New York: Routledge. 1995.

Silber, Nina. "The Northern Myth of the Rebel Girl." In *Women of the American South: A Multicultural Reader*. Edited by Christie Anne Farnham. New York: New York University Press. 1997. 120–132.

Silverman, Jason H. "Mary Ann Shadd and the Search for Equality." In *Black Leaders of the Nineteenth Century*. Edited by Leon Litwack and August Meier. Urbana: University of Illinois Press. 1988. 87–100.

Simkins, Francis Butler and James Welch Patton. *The Women of the Confederacy*. Richmond, VA: Garrett and Massie. 1936.

Sizer, Lyde Cullen. *The Political Work of Northern Women Writers and the Civil War, 1850–1872*. Chapel Hill: University of North Carolina Press. 2000.

Smith, Everard H. "Chambersburg: Anatomy of a Confederate Reprisal." *American Historical Review*. 96 (April 1991): 432–455.

Smith, Jessie Carney, ed. *Notable Black American Women*. Detroit: Gale Research. 1992.

Smith, Sherry L. "Beyond Princess and Squaw: Army Officers' Perceptions of Indian Women." In *Negotiators of Change: Historical Perspectives on Native American Women*. Edited by Nancy Shoemaker. New York: Routledge. 1995. 63–76.

Solomon, Barbara Miller. *In the Company of Educated Women: A History of Women and Higher Education in America*. New Haven, CT: Yale University Press. 1985.

Solomon, Clara. *The Civil War Diary of Clara Solomon: Growing Up in New Orleans, 1861–1862*. Edited, with an introduction, by Elliott Ashkenazi. Baton Rouge: Louisiana State University Press. 1995.

Sparks, Carol Douglas. "The Land Incarnate: Navajo Women and the Dialogue of Colonialism, 1821–1870." In *Negotiators of Change: Historical Perspectives on Native American Women*. Edited by Nancy Shoemaker. New York: Routledge. 1995. 135–156.

Stanton, Elizabeth Cady, Susan B. Anthony, and Matilda Joslyn Gage, eds. *History of Woman Suffrage, Vol. 2*. Rochester, NY: Susan B. Anthony. 1882. Reprint New York: Arno Press. 1969.

Stanton, Elizabeth, Susan B. Anthony, and Matilda Joslyn Gage, eds. *History of Woman Suffrage*. Volume 1 1881. Volume 2 1882. Reprint. New York: Arno Press. 1969.

Stanton, Theodore and Harriot Stanton Blatch, eds. *Elizabeth Cady Stanton as Revealed in Her Letters, Diary and Reminiscences.* Volume 2. New York: Harper and Bros. 1922.

Starobin, Robert S., ed. *Blacks in Bondage: Letters of American Slaves.* Princeton, NJ: Markus Wiener Publishers. 1994.

Stathis, Stephen W. and Lee Roderick. "Mallet, Chisel, and Curls." *American Heritage.* 27 (2) (February 1976): 45–47, 94–96.

Stephens, Lester D., ed. "A Righteous Aim: Emma LeConte Furman's 1918 Diary." *Georgia Historical Quarterly.* 62 (July 1978): 213–224.

Sterkx, H. E. *Partners in Rebellion: Alabama Women in the Civil War.* Rutherford, NJ: Fairleigh Dickinson University Press. 1970.

Sterkx, H. E. "The Angel of the South." In *Some Notable Alabama Women During the Civil War.* University, AL: Alabama Civil War Centennial Commission. 1962. Online. Oakwood Military Cemetery. Richmond, Virginia. http://www.mindspring.com/⊠redeagle/Oakwood/Hopkins.htm

Sterling, Dorothy. *We Are Your Sisters: Black Women in the Nineteenth Century.* New York: Norton. 1984.

Stern, Madeleine B. *Louisa May Alcott: From Blood & Thunder to Hearth & Home.* Boston: Northeastern University Press. 1998.

Stern, Madeleine B. *Louisa May Alcott.* Norman: University of Oklahoma Press. 1950.

Stevens, Peter F. *Rebels in Blue: The Story of Keith and Malinda Blalock.* Dallas, TX: Taylor Publishing Co. 2000.

Stevenson, Brenda. "Charlotte Forten (1837–1914)." In *Portraits of American Women: From Settlement to the Present.* Edited by G. J. Barker-Benfield and Catherine Clinton. New York: St. Martin's Press. 1991. 279–297.

Stillman, Rachel Bryan. *Education in the Confederate States of America, 1861–1865.* Ph.D. dissertation. University of Illinois at Urbana-Champaign. 1972.

Stone, Kate. *Brokenburn: The Journal of Kate Stone, 1861–1868.* Edited by John Q. Anderson. Baton Rouge: Louisana State University Press. 1955.

Stowe, Harriet Beecher. "The Chimney-Corner." *Atlantic Monthly.* 16 (August 1865): 232–237.

Stowe, Harriet Beecher. "A Reply to the Address by the Women of England." *Atlantic Monthly.* 11 (January 1863): 120–134.

Stowell, Daniel W. " 'A Family of Women and Children': The Fains of East Tennessee during Wartime." In *Southern Families at War: Loyalty and Conflict in the Civil War South.* Edited by Catherine Clinton. New York: Oxford Univ. Press. 2000. 175–191.

Stratton, Joanna L. *Pioneer Women: Voices from the Kansas Frontier.* New York: Simon and Schuster. 1981.

Stutler, Boyd B. *Glory, Glory Hallelujah! The Story of "John Brown's Body."* Harpers Ferry, WV: Eighth Day Press. 1960.

Sullivan, Walter, ed. *The War the Women Lived: Female Voices from the Confederate South.* Nashville, TN: J.S. Sanders. 1995.

Swint, Henry L., ed. *Dear Ones at Home: Letters from Contraband Camps.* Nashville, TN: Vanderbilt University Press. 1966.

Swinth, Kirsten. *Painting Professionals: Women Artists and the Development of Modern American Art, 1870–1930*. Chapel Hill: University of North Carolina Press. 2001.

Swisshelm, Jane Grey. *Crusader and Feminist: Letters of Jane Grey Swisshelm 1858–1865*. Saint Paul: The Minnesota Historical Society. 1934. Reprint. Westport, CT: Hyperion Press. 1976.

Swisshelm, Jane Grey. *Half a Century*. Chicago: Jansen, McClurg & Co. 1880.

Tager, Jack. *Boston Riots: Three Centuries of Social Violence*. Boston: Northeastern University Press. 2001.

Taylor, Susie King. *A Black Woman's Civil War Memoirs*. Edited by Patricia W. Romero. Reprint. New York: Markus Wiener Publishing. 1988. Orig. Ed. *Reminiscences of My Life in Camp: With the 33rd* United States Colored Troops, Late 1st S.C. Volunteers. 1902.

Thompson, William Y. "Sanitary Fairs of the Civil War." *Civil War History*. 4 (1) (March 1958): 51–67.

Thorp, Margaret Farrand. *Female Persuasion: Six Strong-Minded Women*. New Haven, CT: Yale University Press. 1949.

Tice, Douglas O. " 'Bread or Blood!' The Richmond Bread Riot." *Civil War Times Illustrated*. 12 (10) (1974): 12–19.

Tong, Benson. *Unsubmissive Women: Chinese Prostitutes in Nineteenth-Century San Francisco*. Norman: University of Oklahoma Press. 1994.

Toplin, Robert Brent, ed. *Ken Burns's the Civil War: Historians Respond*. New York: Oxford University Press. 1996.

Towne, Laura M. *Letters and Diary of Laura M. Towne*. Edited by Rupert Sargent Holland. 1912. Reprint. New York: Negro Universities Press. 1969.

Trefousse, Hans L. *Ben Butler: The South Called Him Beast!* New York: Twayne. 1957.

Trindal, Elizabeth S. *Mary Surratt: An American Tragedy*. Gretna, LA: Pelican Publishing. 1996.

Trotter, William R. *Bushwhackers! The Civil War in North Carolina*. Winston-Salem, NC: John F. Blair. 1988.

Tuchman, Arleen Marcia. " 'Only in a Republic Can It Be Proved That Science Has No Sex': Marie Elizabeth Zakrzewska (1829–1902) and the Multiple Meanings of Science in the Nineteenth-Century United States." *Journal of Women's History*. 11 (1) (Spring 1999): 121–142.

Turbin, Carole. "Beyond Conventional Wisdom: Women's Wage Work, Household Economic Contribution, and Labor Activism in a Mid-Nineteenth-Century Working-Class Community." In *"To Toil the Livelong Day": America's Women at Work, 1780–1980*. Edited by Carol Groneman and Mary Beth Norton. Ithaca, NY: Cornell University Press. 1987. 47–57.

Turbin, Carole. " 'And We Are Nothing But Women': Irish Working Women in Troy." In *Women of America: A History*. Edited by Carol Ruth Berkin and Mary Beth Norton. Boston: Houghton Mifflin. 1979. 202–222.

Turner, Justin G. and Linda Levitt Turner. *Mary Todd Lincoln: Her Life and Letters*. New York: Knopf. 1972.

Turner, Thomas Reed. *Beware the People Weeping: Public Opinion and the Assassination of Abraham Lincoln*. Baton Rouge: Louisiana State University Press. 1991. Orig. Pub. 1982.

Van Der Heuvel, Gerry. *Crowns of Thorns and Glory: Mary Todd Lincoln and Varina Howell Davis: The Two First Ladies of the Civil War*. New York: Dutton. 1988.

Van Lew, Elizabeth. *A Yankee Spy in Richmond: The Civil War Diary of "Crazy Bet" Van Lew*. Edited by David D. Ryan. Mechanicsburg, PA: Stackpole Books. 1996.

Varon, Elizabeth R. *We Mean to Be Counted: White Women and Politics in Antebellum Virginia*. Chapel Hill: University of North Carolina Press. 1998.

Vassar College. *The Magnificent Enterprise: A Chronicle of Vassar College*. Poughkeepsie, NY: Vassar College. 1961.

Venet, Wendy Hamand. "The Emergence of a Suffragist: Mary Livermore, Civil War Activism, and the Moral Power of Women." *Civil War History*. 48 (2) (June 2002): 143–163.

Venet, Wendy Hamand. *Neither Ballots Nor Bullets: Women Abolitionists and the Civil War*. Charlottesville: University Press of Virginia. 1991.

Venet, Wendy Hamand. " 'Cry Aloud and Spare Not': Northern Antislavery Women and John Brown's Raid." In *His Soul Goes Marching On: Responses to John Brown and the Harpers Ferry Raid*. Edited by Paul Finkelman. Charlottesville: University Press of Virginia. 1995. 98–115.

Vietor, Agnes C., ed. *A Woman's Quest: The Life of Marie E. Zakrzewska, M.D.* New York: Arno Press. 1972.

Walker, Henry. "Power, Sex, and Gender Roles: The Transformation of an Alabama Planter Family During the Civil War." In *Southern Families at War: Loyalty and Conflict in the Civil War South*. Edited by Catherine Clinton. New York: Oxford University Press. 2000. 175–191.

Walker, Peter F. *Vicksburg: A People at War, 1860–1865*. Chapel Hill: University of North Carolina Press. 1960.

Walsh, Mary Roth. *"Doctors Wanted: No Women Need Apply": Sexual Barriers in the Medical Profession, 1835–1970*. New Haven, CT: Yale University Press. 1977.

Warren, Joyce W. *Fanny Fern: An Independent Woman*. New Brunswick, NJ: Rutgers University Press. 1992.

Weiner, Marli F. *Mistresses and Slaves: Plantation Women in South Carolina, 1830–1880*. Urbana: University of Illinois Press. 1998.

Werner, Emmy E. *Reluctant Witnesses: Children's Voices from the Civil War*. Boulder, CO: Westview Press. 1998.

Wertheimer, Barbara M. *We Were There: The Story of Working Women in America*. New York: Pantheon Books. 1977.

West, Elliott. "Beyond Baby Doe: Child Rearing on the Mining Frontier." In *The Women's West*. Edited by Susan Armitage and Elizabeth Jameson. Norman: University of Oklahoma Press. 1987. 179–192.

Whetten, Harriet Douglas. "A Volunteer Nurse in the Civil War: The Letters of Harriet Douglas Whetten." *Wisconsin Magazine of History*. 48 (2) (1964): 131–151 and 48 (3) (1965): 205–221.

White, Deborah Gray. *Ar'n't I a Woman? Female Slaves in the Plantation South*. New York: Norton. 1985.

Whites, LeeAnn. *The Civil War as a Crisis in Gender*. Athens: University of Georgia Press. 1995.

Wiley, Bell Irvin. *Confederate Women*. Contributions in American History, no. 38. Westport, CT: Greenwood Press. 1975.

Williams, Gary. *Hungry Heart: The Literary Emergence of Julia Ward Howe*. Amherst: University of Massachusetts Press. 1999.

Wilson, Edmund. *Patriotic Gore: Studies in the Literature of the American Civil War*. New York: Oxford University Press. 1962.

Wolfe, Margaret Ripley. *Daughters of Canaan: A Saga of Southern Women*. Lexington: University Press of Kentucky. 1995.

Wolff, Cynthia Griffin. *Emily Dickinson*. New York: Knopf. 1986.

Wood, Ann Douglas. "The War Within a War: Women Nurses in the Union Army." *Civil War History*. 18 (2) (June 1972): 197–212.

Woodworth, Steven E. *While God Is Marching On: The Religious World of Civil War Soldiers*. Lawrence: University Press of Kansas. 2001.

Woody, Thomas. *A History of Women's Education in the United States*. Volume 1. New York: The Science Press. 1929.

Wormeley, Katharine Prescott. *The Other Side of War: With the Army of the Potomac*. Boston: Ticknor. 1889.

Wormeley, Katharine Prescott. *The United States Sanitary Commission: A Sketch of Its Purposes and Its Work*. Boston: Little, Brown. 1863.

Yellin, Jean Fagan. "Legacy Profile: Harriet Ann Jacobs." *Legacy*. 5 (Fall 1988): 55–60.

Young, Agatha. *The Women and the Crisis: Women of the North in the Civil War*. New York: McDowell, Obolensky. 1959.

Index

1st Michigan Cavalry, 62
1st Michigan Colored Regiment, 417
1st Rhode Island Volunteer Infantry, 54–55
1st South Carolina Volunteer Infantry, 63,
        405–6
2nd Michigan Infantry, 140, 151
2nd South Carolina Volunteers, 420
2nd Vermont Infantry, 96
3rd Michigan Infantry, 152
5th Michigan Infantry, 153
5th Rhode Island Infantry, 55
8th New York Cavalry, 294
10th Michigan Cavalry, 42
13th Virginia Infantry, 62
17th Illinois Infantry, 62
19th Illinois Infantry, 422
20th North Carolina Infantry, 372
21st Colored Troops (3rd South Carolina
        Volunteers), 379
26th North Carolina Infantry, 42
26th United States Colored Cavalry, 8
27th Pennsylvania Infantry, 63
29th Connecticut Colored Infantry, 294
29th Connecticut Volunteer Infantry, 70
45th U.S. Colored Infantry, 294
52nd Ohio Volunteers, 447
54th Massachusetts Infantry, 63, 269, 420
95th Illinois Infantry, 71, 73
114th Pennsylvania Infantry, 63
153rd Regiment, New York State Volunteers,
        444

A

AASS, *See* American Anti-Slavery Society
abolitionists, 2–4

Alcott, Louisa May, 17–21
Anne Whitney's sculpture, *Africa,* 30
Anthony, Susan B., 21–24
Cary, Mary Ann Shadd, 69–71
Child, Lydia Maria, 81–84
and Contraband Relief Association, 86
Davis, Rebecca Harding, 107–10
Dickinson, Anna, 121–24
draft riots and attacks on, 136
Forten, Charlotte, 171–73
freedpeople prepared for citizenship by, 408
and Frémont, John Charles, 175
Harper, Frances Watkins, 211–12
Haviland, Laura Smith, 213–16
Hawks, Esther Hill, 216–18
Kemble, Fanny, 256–59
Larcom, Lucy, 261–66
and Lewis, Edmonia, 268–70
McCord, Louisa Cheves, versus, 284–85
Pleasant, Mary Ellen, 337–39
political versus Garrisonian, 388, 402
Remond, Sarah Parker, 353–55
Stanton, Elizabeth Cady, 387–89
Stowe, Harriet Beecher, 392–97
Swisshelm, Jane Grey, 401–3
Truth, Sojourner, 417
Tubman, Harriet, 419
Van Lew, Elizabeth, 435–37
and Woman's National Loyal League,
        460–61
and women's rights, 466
abortion, 161
activists
        Anthony, Susan B., 21–24
        Cary, Mary Ann Shadd, 69–71
        Child, Lydia Maria, 81–84
        Gibbons, Abby Hopper, 187–88
        Haviland, Laura Smith, 213–16

Hawks, Esther Hill, 216–18
    Pleasant, Mary Ellen, 337–39
adultery, 97–98
Aesthetic Papers (journal), 328
Africa, 204
African Americans
    census figures for, 5
    courtship and marriage among, 99
    draft riots and attacks on, 136
    education of, 7, 8, 145, 192, 250, 408–11
    family life among, 164
    and higher education, 92–95, 120
    on hospital ships, 221–22
    literacy among, 145, 380
    opinions about, 3, 79–80, 90, 284–85, 296
    relief societies composed of, 85–86
    and religion, 349
    soldiers, 5, 63, 88, 123, 163–64, 269
    suffrage and, 390
    as teachers, 92–95, 171–73
    See also all-black regiments; contraband
        women; freedpeople; slaves
African-American women, 4–8
    Brown, Clara, 51–53
    as camp women, 63, 294
    Cary, Mary Ann Shadd, 69–71
    charitable activity of, 382
    collective action by, 241
    and Contraband Relief Association, 254
    Coppin, Fanny Jackson, 92–95
    Forten, Charlotte, 171–73
    free, 6–8
    Harper, Frances Watkins, 211–12
    on hospital ships, 221–22
    in industry, 239
    Jacobs, Harriet, 249–51
    John Brown supported by, 2
    Keckley, Elizabeth, 253–55
    Lee, Rebecca, 133
    Lewis, Edmonia, 268–70
    and medicine, 133
    in military, 294
    as nurses, 315–16, 322
    Pleasant, Mary Ellen, 337–39
    Remond, Sarah Parker, 353–55
    and Republican Party, 464
    slavery and, 373–80
    and soldiers' aid societies, 381, 383
    as spies, 386–87
    Taylor, Susie Baker King, 405–7

    as western emigrants, 453–54
    as writers, 275
    See also contraband women; freedpeople;
        slaves
African-American women's clubs, 421
African Methodist Episcopal Church, 94
Africa (Whitney), 30
Afro-Canadians, 69–70
Agitator, The (newspaper), 282
Agnes of Sorrento (Stowe), 396
agricultural women, 12–16, 56
    and gender roles, 12–13, 99
    German-speaking immigrants, 231
    as military women, 292
    Scandinavian immigrants, 233
    slave control by, 375
    slaves, 9
    and wage disputes, 90
Aguirre, Mary Barnard, 450
Alabama, 363, 381
Alabama Hospitals, Richmond, Virginia,
        218–19
alcohol, 333
Alcott, Bronson, 328
Alcott, Louisa May, 3, 17–21, 117, 274–78, 320,
        381
all-black regiments, 63, 86, 88, 217, 269, 381,
        383, 405–7, 417, 420
alternative medicine, 133
"Amazon of Secessia," *See* Boyd, Belle
ambulance service, 223
American Academy of Arts and Sciences, 295,
        296
American and Foreign Anti-Slavery Society, 2
American Anti-Slavery Society (AASS), 2, 18,
        22, 82–84, 215, 354, 389
American Association for the Advancement of
        Science, 295, 296
American Colonization Society, 204
American Ephemeris and Nautical Almanac, 296
American Equal Rights Association (AERA),
        468
American Froebel Union, 329
American Girl, An (A. Dickinson), 124
American Journal of Science and Arts, 296
American Medical Times, 315
American Missionary Association, 70, 120, 408
American Party, 66
American Red Cross, 33, 36
American Revolutionary War, 61–62, 74, 264

American Woman Suffrage Association, 282, 468

Ames, Mary, 410

Amherst Academy, Massachusetts, 125

amputations, 184, 186, 192, 321, 447

Anderson, Ellen, 8

Anderson, Hassie, 324

Anderson, Mary, 378

Anderson, Osborne Perry, 70

Anderson, Robert, 170

Andersonville, Georgia, prison for Union soldiers at, 35–36, 40

Andrew, Eliza Frances, 116

Angel of the Waters or Bethesda Fountain (Stebbins), 30

Anglo-African Magazine, 212

Anthony, Daniel Reed, 23

Anthony, Susan B., 2, 21–24, 146, 176, 354, 381, 388

Antietam (Sharpsburg), Battle of (1862), 25–28, 34, 141, 152

Antioch College, Ohio, 148

Anti-Slavery Bugle (newspaper), 212

Anti-Slavery Office Reading Room, Rochester, New York, 249

antislavery societies, 2, 86, 360, 411

See also specific societies

Appeal in Favor of That Class of Americans Called Africans, An (Child), 82

Arapaho tribe, 313

Arkansas, 363

Arlington National Cemetery, 153, 220

Army Medical Bureau, 129–30, 221, 316

Army of Northern Virginia (Confederate Army of the Potomac), 182, 325

Army of the James, 35

Army of the Potomac, 63, 140, 182, 221

Army of the Tennessee, 72

art clubs, 31

Arthur's Home Magazine, 277

artists, 28–31

    Cassatt, Mary, 29

    Hosmer, Harriet, 28

    Lewis, Edmonia, 268–70

    Martin Spencer, Lilly, 30–31

    Palmer, Fanny (Frances Flora Bond), 31

    Peale, Sarah Miriam, 30

    Ream, Vinnie, 343–46

    Stebbins, Emma, 29–30

    Whitney, Anne, 30

assimilation, Native American, 314–15

Association for the Advancement of Women, 298

Association for the Preservation of Virginia Antiquities, 413

astronomy, 295–97

Atlantic Monthly (magazine), 18, 107, 108–9, 126, 209, 226, 237, 264, 276–77, 395, 396

Atzerodt, George, 400

Augusta, Georgia, 383

Aurelian (A. Dickinson), 124

Ayers, Romeyn Beck, 220

B

Babcock, Rufus, 297

Baca, Barbara, 288

Bacot, Ada, 117, 318

Bailey, Gamaliel, 208

Baker, Jean, 271

Baker King, Susie Taylor, *See* Taylor, Susie Baker King

Ball's Bluff, Battle of (1861), 122, 438

Banks, Nathaniel, 37, 181, 444

Barbee, David Rankin, 399

Barton, Clara, 26–27, 33–36, 194

Bates, Edward, 67

Bates College, Maine, 148

Battery Wagner, Morris Island, South Carolina, 269

Battle Creek, Michigan, 418

"Battle Hymn of the Republic, The" (Howe), 224–25

Battle of the Handkerchiefs, 36–37

battles and campaigns

    Antietam (1862), 25–28, 34, 141, 152

    Ball's Bluff (1861), 122, 438

    Bull Run, First (1861), 54, 140, 152, 155, 196, 412, 429, 438

    Bull Run, Second (1862), 26, 34, 152

    Cedar Mountain (1862), 26

    Chancellorsville (1863), 152, 183

    Chantilly (1862), 152

    Chickamauga (1863), 447

    Cold Harbor (1864), 153

    Culpepper (1862), 34

    Fort Donelson (1862), 39, 68, 221, 280, 439

Fort Henry (1862), 68
Fredericksburg (1862), 34, 141, 152, 447
Gettysburg (1863), 152–53, 182–86, 192, 426
Lookout Mountain (1863), 40
Missionary Ridge (1863), 40
Mobile, Alabama (1865), 72
Monnett's Ferry (1864), 445
Peninsula (1862), 140, 222–23
Pleasant Hall (1864), 445
Red River (1864), 72
Seven Days' (1862), 140
Seven Pines (1862), 140, 219, 223
Shiloh (1862), 39, 103, 439
Spotsylvania Court House (1864), 35, 153
Vicksburg (1863), 40, 64, 72, 120, 182, 351, 440–42
Westport (1864), 306
Wilderness (1864), 153
Williamsburg (1862), 140, 152
bazaars, 360
Bear River Massacre, 312
Beauregard, P. G. T., 46, 155, 196, 325
Bedford College for Ladies, London, England, 354
Beechenbrook: A Rhyme of the War (Preston), 278
Beecher, Catherine, 146, 166
Beecher, Lyman, 392
Beecher Stowe, Harriet, *See* Stowe, Harriet Beecher
Beers, Fannie, 219
Behind the Scenes, or, Thirty Years a Slave, and Four Years in the White House (Keckley), 253–55
Bell, James, 99
Bell, Mary, 377
Bell, Thomas, 339
Belle Boyd in Camp and Prison (Boyd), 45, 46
Bellevue Hospital, New York, New York, 321
Bellows, Henry Whitney, 429, 458
benevolent associations
    African-American women and, 5, 8, 382
    and freedpeople, 411
    fund-raising for, 359–60
    Jewish women and, 233
    and trade unions, 239
    on western frontier, 452
Bennett, James Gordon, 272
Benton, Rosella, 15
Benton, Thomas Hart, 30, 174

Benton Frémont, Jessie, *See* Frémont, Jessie Benton
Berry, Carrie, 190–91, 192
Beulah (Evans), 154
Bible, 158, 162, 350, 413
Bickerdyke, Mary Ann, 38–40
Bingham, George Caleb, 30
Bingham, John, 399
Birney, David B., 152
Birney, James, 388
Birney, William, 167–68
birth control, *See* reproduction and birth control
Bits of Gossip (R. Davis), 109
Blackburn's Ford, skirmish at (1861), 152
Black Codes, 11, 379
Blackfoot Tribe, 310
Black Kettle, 313
black regiments, *See* all-black regiments
Blackwell, Antoinette Brown, 349, 467
Blackwell, Elizabeth, 130, 131, 133, 317, 429, 457–58, 470
Blackwell, Emily, 130, 131, 133, 317, 429, 457–58
Blackwell, Henry Browne, 133, 282, 468, 471
Blaine, Harriet Stanwood, 210
Blaine, James G., 210
Blair Etheridge, Annie, *See* Etheridge, Annie
Blalock, Malinda Pritchard, 41–43, 200
Blalock, William McKesson "Keith," 41–43
Blanton, DeAnne, 292
Bloomer, Amelia, 447
bloomer costume, 447
Bloor, Alfred Janson, 428
boarding houses, 6, 56
Boatswain's Whistle, The (newspaper), 226
Bohannon, Sarah, 221
Bonner, Robert, 276
Booth, John Wilkes, 372, 373, 399, 400
Bosque Redondo, New Mexico Territory, 313
Boston, Massachusetts
    draft riots in, 137
    patriotism in, 324
    reaction to Fort Sumter in, 170
Boston Daily Evening Voice (newspaper), 241
Boston Sanitary Fair, 19
Bowdoin College, Maine, 393
Bowen, James, 37–38
Bowles, Samuel, 125
Bowser, Mary Elizabeth, 44, 387
boycotts, of businesses, 239, 364

Boyd, Belle, 45–47, 385

Boykin Chesnut, Mary, *See* Chesnut, Mary Boykin

Brackett, Edward A., 269

Bradford, Susan, 365–66

bread rebellions, 47–50

Breckinridge, John C., 66, 67

Breckinridge, Lucy, 114, 351

Brewer, Eliza Jane, 51, 52, 53

British Honduras, 67

Brock (Putnam), Sallie, 49, 325, 366

Brooklyn and Long Island Sanitary Fair (New York), 127

Broward's Neck, Florida, 365

Brown, Charlotte, 8

Brown, Clara, 51–53, 237

Brown, George, 51–52

Brown, John, 2–3, 18, 70, 82, 100, 225, 269, 329, 338, 364, 388

Brown, Olympia, 349

Brownell, Kady Southwell, 54–55, 62

Brownell, Robert, 54

Browning, Elizabeth Barrett, 261

Brunner, Jacob, 52

Buck, Lucy Rebecca, 189, 350

Bucklin, Sophronia, 184, 319

Buell, Don Carlos, 422

Buell Hale, Sarah Josepha, *See* Hale, Sarah Josepha

Bull Run, First Battle of (1861), 54, 140, 152, 155, 196, 412, 429, 438

Bull Run, Second Battle of (1862), 26, 34, 152

bummers, 369

Burge, Dolly Lunt, 370

Burials

at Gettysburg, 186

of Juliet Opie Hopkins, 220

of Rose O'Neal Greenhow, 197

of Sally Tompkins, 413

See also Arlington National Cemetery

Burnside, Ambrose, 54

Burr, Aaron Columbus, 67

bushwhackers, *See* guerrilla war

businesswomen, 56–59

African-American women as, 7, 52

Brown, Clara, 52–53

and business characteristics, 57

Chesnut, Mary Boykin, 80

and gender roles, 99

Keckley, Elizabeth, 253–55

new opportunities for, 56–58

Pleasant, Mary Ellen, 337–39

successful, 58–59

underreporting of, 57

Buss, Amelia, 450

Butchart, Ronald, 408

Butler, Benjamin "Beast," 37, 87, 167, 179–80, 335, 435

Butler, Fran, 258

Butler, George, 400

Butler, Pierce, 257–58

C

Cady Stanton, Elizabeth, *See* Stanton, Elizabeth Cady

California

Chinese immigrants in, 233–34

Indians wars in, 311

Mexican Americans in, 288–90

California Supreme Court, 338

"Call to Kansas" (Larcom), 263

"Call to My Country-Women, A" (Hamilton), 209

Cameron, Simon, 129–30, 458

campaigns, *See* battles and campaigns

Campbell, Christina Phillips, 456

Campbell, Ellen, 221

Campbell Hospital, Washington, D.C., 402

camp life, 61–65

African-American women in, 294

attitudes toward camp women, 64, 88–89

contraband women and, 63, 88–89

effect on relationships of, 97–98

Kady Southwell Brownell and, 54

prostitutes and, 61, 88, 340

social class and, 64

women's duties in, 61–62

See also daughters of the regiment

Camp Nelson, Kentucky, 89

Canada, 69–71, 338, 372–73

Canning, Nora M., 371

capital punishment, 398–401

Carleton, James H., 312–13

Carroll, Anna Ella, 66–68

Carroll, Mary T., 57

Carroll, Thomas King, 66

Carson, Christopher "Kit," 312–13

Cartwright, Samuel S., 305

Cary, Hetty, 325

Cary, Jennie, 325

Cary, Mary Ann Shadd, 69–71, 338

Cary (Harrison), Constance, 325, 364

Case, Adelaide, 96

Cashier, Albert D. J. (Jennie Hodgers), 72–73

Castle Thunder Prison, Richmond, Virginia,
        439, 447

Catholicism

    and anti-Catholicism, 66, 75

    Irish immigrants and, 230

    Lewis, Edmonia, 270

    Mary Surratt and, 398

    Mexican Americans and, 287

    in urban areas, 349

    See also nuns, Catholic

caves, for Vicksburg siege, 440–41

Cedar Mountain, Battle of (1862), 26

celebrations, memorial, 327

celibacy, 99

cemeteries, *See* Arlington National Cemetery;
        Gettysburg National Cemetery

Central City, Colorado, 52

ceremonies, departure, 323–24

Chace, Elizabeth Buffum, 3

Chambersburg, Pennsylvania, 244, 245–46

Chancellorsville, Battle of (1863), 152, 183

Chandler, Elizabeth, 213

Channing, William Ellery, 82, 328

Chantilly, Battle of (1862), 152

chaperonage, 98

Chapman, Maria Weston, 2

charities, 349

    African-American, 5, 85–86

    food distribution by, 49

    Margaret Haughery and, 59

    See also benevolent associations; soldiers' aid
        societies

Charleston, South Carolina, 379

Charleston News (newspaper), 301

Charlestown Prison, 226

Chase, Lucy, 90

Chase, Salmon, 194, 464

Chatham Vigilance Committee, 338

Cheney, Ednah Dow, 133, 471

Cherry Creek, Colorado, 52

Chesnut, James, Jr., 78–79, 170

Chesnut, Mary Boykin, 77–81, 113, 116, 170,
        415

Chesson, Michael, 48

Cheves McCord, Louisa, *See* McCord, Louisa
        Cheves

Cheyenne, 313–14

Chicago Hospital for Women and Children,
        133, 282

Chicago Sanitary Commission (CNC), 39, 280

Chicago Sanitary Fair (1863), 282, 361

Chicago Soldiers' Home, 361

Chicago Tribune (newspaper), 273

Chickamauga, Battle of (1863), 447

Child, David Lee, 82

Child, Lydia Maria, 2, 81–84, 249, 250, 258,
        419

childbirth, 160–61

children

    and agriculture, 13

    diseases of, 65

    as focus of family life, 158

    of German-speaking immigrants, 232

    magazine for, 166

    in middle class families, 157–58

    raising, 161–65

    slave, 193

    See also girlhood and adolescence

Chimborazo Hospital, Richmond, Va., 332–33,
        413

"Chimney Corner" (Stowe), 396

Chinese Americans, 454

Chinese immigrants, 233–34

Chivington, John M., 313–14

cholera epidemics, 74

Christian College, Missouri, 343

Christian Recorder (newspaper), 212

churches, *See* religion

Church of Jesus Christ of Latter-day Saints, *See*
        Mormon women

Church of the United Brethren in Christ, 119

Cincinnati, Ohio, 361

City of Memphis (ship), 39, 221

City Point, Virginia, 341

"Civil Disobedience" (Thoreau), 328

civilian experience

    at Antietam, 25–28

    at Gettysburg, 182–86

    of girls, 192

    Sherman's March to the Sea, 368–71

    Siege of Vicksburg, 440–42

    See also girlhood and adolescence; invasion
        and occupation

civil rights
  African-American, versus woman suffrage, 390
  African American women and, 8
  Frances Watkins Harper and, 212
  of freedpeople, 23, 176
  John Charles Fremont and, 176
  of Lincoln assassination co-defendants, 399
  Mary Ann Shadd Cary and, 71
  Sarah Parker Remond and, 354
  Susan B. Anthony and, 23
civil service, *See* government girls
Clappe, Louise A. K., 450
Clarke, James Freeman, 225
Clay, Clement, 100
Clay, Henry, 462
Clay, Virgina Tunstall, 80, 100
Clayton, Henry, 100
Clayton, Virginia, 100
Cleveland Medical College, 133
Clopton, Maria Foster, 320
Clopton, Maria Gaitskell, 201
clothing, *See* dress
coeducation, 148
Cold Harbor, Battle of (1864), 153
Cole, Roxa, 245
colleges, *See* higher education
colonization, by freedpeople, 67, 204
Colorado Territory, 313–14
Colorado Transcript (newspaper), 306
color bearers, 54–55
Colored Ladies Freedmen's Aid Society of Chicago, 71
Colored Ladies' Relief Association, 86
Colored Orphan Infant Asylum, New York, New York, 135
Columbia, South Carolina, 266–67, 285–86
common schools, 145, 149, 170
communication, slave grapevine as, 375
communities
  African-American, 7
  female slave, 8–9
  immigrant, 230
  Jewish, 233
Comte, Auguste, 225
Condor, The (ship), 197
Confederate Army of the Potomac, *See* Army of Northern Virginia
Confederate Clothing Bureau, 383
Confederate Girl's Diary, A (Morgan), 299, 301

Confederate government, 78, 103, 240, 319–20, 322, 325, 347, 363
  See also treasury girls
Confederate States Laboratory, 241
Confederate States of America, formation of, 363
Confederate Womanhood, ideal of, 363
Confiscation Acts, 67
Congregational church, 349
Congregationalist (newspaper), 208, 263
Congress, and commission for Lincoln statue, 343
Congressional Medal of Honor, 446, 448
Connecticut Hospital, New Haven, 322
Connecticut (ship), 46
Connor, Patrick Edward, 312
Conscription Act (1863), 134–35, 167
Constitution of the United States, 67
Contraband Relief Association (CRA), 85–86, 254, 273
contraband women, 3, 87–91, 375
  Abby Hopper Gibbons and, 187–88
  and camp life, 63, 88–89, 294
  economic discrimination against, 90
  education of, 90
  Harriet Tubman and, 420
  on hospital ships, 221–23
  lives of, 10–11, 88, 164
  and pressure on federal government, 374
  provisions for, 408
  writings by, 8
contraceptives, *See* reproduction and birth control
Cook, Lauren M., 292, 443
cooks, African-American women as, 5, 6, 51
Cooper, James Fenimore, 402
Cooper, Mrs. A. C., 368
Cooper Union, New York, New York, 123
Copperhead Democrats, 464
Coppin, Fanny Jackson, 92–95
Coppin, Levi J., 94
copyright, 276
Cormany, Rachel, 117, 245–46
correspondence
  love letters, 96–98
  patriotism in, 209, 326
  Varina Howell Davis and Confederate government, 112
Country Living and Country Thinking (Hamilton), 208

courtship and marriage, 95–101
    among African Americans, 99, 100
    age of marriage, 159
    correspondence between lovers, 96–98
    courtship rituals, 98
    Fanny Fern on, 165
    freedpeople and legalization of marriage, 101,
        164–65, 380
    gender roles in, 95–96, 99–100
    Mexican Americans and, 290
    in Mormon church, 304, 454
    in stories of Rebecca Harding Davis, 110
    war interruption of, 191
    between whites and blacks, 204
    See also family life
Cox, Lucy Ann, 62
Cox, Martha Cragun, 304
CRA, *See* Contraband Relief Association
Crimea, 102–3, 130
Crown of Thorns, A (A. Dickinson), 124
Crump, William W., 412
Culpepper, Battle of (1862), 34
Cumming, Kate, 102–5
Cunctare (pseudonym of Mary Abigail Dodge),
    See Hamilton, Gail
Currier and Ives, 31
Curtis, Mattie, 91
Curtis, Samuel R., 307
Cushman, Charlotte, 29
Cushman, Pauline, 105–6, 385, 386
Customs House, New York, New York, 389

D

daguerrotypy, 58
Daily Clarion (newspaper), 242
Dakota tribes, 311–12, 455–56
Dall, Caroline H., 297
Daly, Maria Lydig, 115, 134
"Dame Shirley" letters (Clappe), 450
dancers, ballet, 241
Daniel Webster (ship), 152
daughters of the regiment, 63, 190
    Brownell, Kady Southwell, 54–55, 62
    Cox, Lucy Ann, 62
    Divers, Bridget, 62
    Etheridge, Annie, 62, 151, 153
    Reynolds, Arabella "Belle" Macomber, 62

"David Gaunt" (R. Davis), 109
Davis, Curtis Carroll, 47
Davis, Jefferson, 44, 46, 78, 106, 111, 170, 181,
        183, 197, 201, 254, 326, 348, 367,
        397, 412
Davis, Jefferson Columbus, 370
Davis, Lemuel Clark, 109
Davis, Nelson, 421
Davis, Rebecca Harding, 107–10, 277, 278
Davis, Varina Howell, 78, 111–14, 254, 367
Dawson, Francis Warrington, 301
Dead Letter Office of the Post Office
        Department, 344
death
    from childbirth, 160
    childhood experiences of, 193
    from disease, 5, 35–36, 320
    in military versus private hospitals, 320
    of refugees, 348
Death of Cleopatra (Lewis), 270
Deaver, Bridget, *See* Divers, Bridget
Delany, Martin, 70, 338
Democratic Party, 123, 136, 462–63
demonstrations, public, *See* Battle of the
        Handkerchiefs; bread rebellions; draft
        riots
Demorest, Ellen Curtis, 58
Denmark, king of, 295
Denver, *See* Cherry Creek, Colorado
depression, 124
desertion, soldiers', 326
Detroit Review of Medicine and Pharmacy, 161
Detroit Trades' Assembly, 239
Devens, Bridget, *See* Divers, Bridget
Dial (magazine), 328
diaries, 114–18
    Chesnut, Mary Boykin, 77–81
    Cumming, Kate, 102–5
    of farm women, 15
    of female slaveholders, 375
    Forten, Charlotte, 172
    LeConte, Emma, 266
    Morgan, Sarah, 299–301
    of nurses, 318
    religion in, 350
    Turchin, Nadine Lvova, 423
Diary from Dixie, A (Chesnut), 81, 117
Dickey, Sarah, 119–20
Dickinson, Anna, 121–24, 464
Dickinson, Emily, 125–28, 276

Dickinson, Lavinia, 125, 128
discrimination
    anti-Irish, 75
    economic, against contraband women, 90
    Susan B. Anthony on northern, 23
    against women artists, 30
    against women doctors, 459, 471
    See also racial discrimination
diseases
    casualties from, 5, 35–36, 320, 348
    children's common, 65
    in contraband camps, 85
    diet and, 374
    Louisa May Alcott and, 19
    Native Americans and, 311, 312, 313
    nurses' exposure to, 320
    on Sea Islands, 409, 410
    women's, 230
    See also specific diseases
Divers, Bridget, 62
divorce, 467
Dix, Dorothea, 75, 129–30, 188, 216, 316–17,
    381, 402, 458
doctors, women, 56, 131–34, 204
    Blackwell, Elizabeth, 457–58
    Blackwell, Emily, 457–58
    Hawks, Esther Hill, 216–18
    Walker, Mary Edwards, 446–48
    Zakrzewska, Marie, 469–72
    See also surgery and surgeons *for male doctors*
Dodge, Mary Abigail, *See* Hamilton, Gail
domestic art/science, in college curriculum, 206,
    254
domestic fiction, 277
domestic servants, 5, 6, 56, 230, 234
domestic slave economy, 10
Douglas, Adele Cutts, 254
Douglas, Stephen, 254, 464
Douglass, Frederick, 3, 86, 270
draft law, 123
draft riots, 134–37, 152–53
Draper, Eliza C., 198
Dred: A Tale of the Great Dismal Swamp (Stowe),
    394
dress
    of daughters of the regiment, 54, 62
    gender roles and, 72–73
    and guerrilla disguises, 198
    havelocks, 383
    industrial production for soldiers', 383

of nurses, 317
    reform of female, 446, 448
    women in men's, 42–43, 72–73, 106, 140,
        190, 291–94, 306–7, 438, 444
dressmaking, 56, 58–59, 85, 253–55
Dreux (Confederate captain), 367
Drum Beat (newspaper), 127
Dry Tortugas, 214
Duty of Disobedience to the Fugitive Slave Act, The
    (Child), 83
Duvall, Betty, 196
Dysart, Henry, 200
dysentery, 65, 445
Dyson, Mary, 294

E

Early, Jubal A., 244
East, Charles, 299
economy, 134, 167
    See also inflation
Edmonds, Sarah Emma (alias Frank Thompson),
    139–42, 278, 292, 385
Edmondson, Belle, 142–44
Edmondston, Catherine Devereux, 115, 170–71,
    352, 365, 380, 382
education, 144–50
    African-American, 8, 145, 193, 250, 408–11
    African-American women in, 94, 172
    art, 29, 30
    Catholic nuns and, 74, 231
    Clara Barton and, 34
    coeducation, 148
    curriculum, 147, 206, 283
    Dorothea Dix and, 129
    early childhood, 329
    Elizabeth Palmer Peabody and, 328–31
    Fanny Jackson Coppin and, 92–95
    father's role in, 161
    of females, 144–50, 204
    for freedpeople, 409
    higher, *See* higher education
    industrial and vocational, 94
    Maria Mitchell and, 295–98
    Mary Ann Shadd Cary and, 69–71
    Native Americans and, 330
    in Northern values, 91, 409
    nursing schools, 322

secondary, 146
in South versus North, 144
of teachers, 146, 148, 213, 329
on western frontier, 452
women teachers, 145–46, 205, 297
See also common schools; private schools;
    teachers of the freedpeople
Eldredge, Charles H., 166
Elmore, Grace, 352, 373
Emancipation Proclamation, 211, 270, 361, 395
Emerson, Ralph Waldo, 328
Emerson, Sarah Gibbons, *See* Gibbons, Sarah
emigration
by African Americans to Canada, 69–70
westward, 449–57
See also colonization, by freedpeople; refugees
employment
of Chinese immigrant women, 234
of enslaved African-American women, 9–11
of free African-American women, 6
of German-speaking immigrant women, 231
of Irish immigrant women, 230
of Jewish immigrant women, 233
of Mexican-American women, 289
of Mormon women, 303
of refugees, 347
of Scandinavian immigrant women, 233
on western frontier, 451
women in workforce, 234
See also agricultural women; business owners;
    government girls; industrial women;
    treasury girls; *specific occupations*
Emporium of Fashions, 59
Endreson, Guri Olsdatter, 455
England, *See* Great Britain
entrepreneurs, *See* businesswomen
erysipelas epidemic, 213
Esmonde, Teresa, 464
Espey, Sarah Rousseau, 367
espionage, *See* spies and espionage
Essex County Anti-Slavery Society, 353
Etheridge, Annie, 62, 63, 151–53, 183
Etheridge, James, 151
Europe
art study in, 29, 270
camp women in, 61
and Catholic nuns in U.S., 74
Clara Barton in, 36
immigration from, 229
Jewish immigration from, 232

kindergarten in, 329
women doctors and, 131
Evans, Augusta Jane, 154–56, 278, 365
Evans, John, 313
Evergreen Cemetery, Gettysburg, Pennsylvania,
    186
Ewell, Elizabeth "Lizinka" Brown, 65
Ewell, Richard S., 65
Examiner (Richmond, newspaper), 49, 83

F

Fain, Eliza, 163
fairs, 360
See also sanitary fairs
family life, 157–65
of African Americans, 164–65
agriculture and, 12, 158
childrearing, 161–65
of contraband women, 63, 88–89
female income and, 5, 6, 236
of German-speaking immigrants, 232
among immigrants, 231–32
Lilly Martin Spencer's paintings of, 30–31
lost family members, *See* family life,
    reuniting families
of Mexican Americans, 288–90
reproduction and birth control, 158–61
reuniting families, 10–11, 51–53, 91, 164,
    380
size of families, 159
of slaves, 9–11, 50, 164, 354
soldiers' families, 5, 10–11, 49, 56, 282
women-led families, 48
See also courtship and marriage; girlhood and
    adolescence
family planning, *See* reproduction and birth
    control
"Fanny Ford" (Fern), 166
Farragut, David G., 179, 345
Farrington, Samuel P., 166
Female Medical College of Pennsylvania, 132
female seminaries, 146–47
Fern, Fanny (Sara Payson Willis), 165–69, 276,
    278
fertility rate, 159
Fifteenth Amendment, 4, 24, 391, 468
First Amendment, 3

First Baptist Church, Leavenworth, Kansas, 51–52

First Battle of Bull Run (1861), 54, 140, 152, 155, 196, 412, 429, 438

Five Civilized Tribes, 311

"Flag, The" (Larcom), 265

flagbearers, 54–55

Flag of Our Union, The (newspaper), 20

flags, 325, 364
    See also flagbearers

floating hospitals, *See* hospital ships

Florida, 363

Flower Fables (Alcott), 18

Fogg, Isabella, 426

Food
    as business area for women, 56
    riots over, 47–50
    See also nutrition

food shortages
    guerrilla war and, 199
    in hospitals, 333
    among Native Americans, 311, 312
    among refugees, 214
    on Sea Islands, 409
    in Siege of Vicksburg, 441
    slavery and, 374
    in South, 191, 383

Forever Free (Lewis), 270

Forrest, Nathan Bedford, 106

Fort Donelson, Battle of (1862), 39, 68, 221, 280, 439

Forten, Charlotte, 171–73, 410

Fort Henry, Battle of (1862), 68

Fort Monroe, Virginia, 87, 113, 130

Fort Pickering, Tennessee, 39

Fort Snelling, Minnesota, 312

Fort Sumter, 169–71, 364

Foster, Stephen Symonds, 22

Fourteenth Amendment, 4, 24, 391

Fowle, Elida Rumsey, 320

France, 183, 197

Francis Child, Lydia Maria, *See* Child, Lydia Maria

Franco-Prussian War (1873), 36

Fredericksburg, Battle of (1862), 34, 141, 152, 447

freedmen's aid societies, 8, 250, 408, 410, 411

Freedmen's Book, The, 83

Freedmen's Bureau, 8, 90, 217, 378, 408, 410

Freedmen's Hospital, Washington, D.C., 417

Freedmen's Relief Association (Detroit), 214

Freedmen's Village, Arlington Heights, Virginia, 417

Freedom and Fremont Club, 390

freedpeople
    abolitionists and, 2, 3
    Clara Barton and, 35
    colonization by, 67
    and experience of freedom, 379–80
    future of, conflicts over, 90
    Louisa May Alcott and, 20
    marriage among, 101, 164, 380
    relief efforts for, 23, 35, 83, 85–86, 249–51, 417–18
    on Sea Islands, 408–11
    Susan B. Anthony and, 23
    teachers of, *See* teachers of the freedpeople
    in Vicksburg, Mississippi, 120
    See also Contraband Relief Association (CRA); teachers of the freedpeople

Frémaux, Céline, 191

Frémont, Jessie Benton, 3, 30, 65, 173–77, 462–63

Frémont, John Charles, 23, 65, 124, 173–77, 263, 390, 462–63

Frémont Emancipation Proclamation, 175

French, L. Virginia, 365

friendships, among enslaved women, 9

Froebel, Friedrich, 329–30

frontier life, 449–57

Front Royal, Virginia, 46

Fugitive Aid Society of Boston, 86

Fugitive Slave Act (1850), 69, 83, 250, 393

Fugitive Slave Act (California 1852), 338

fugitive slaves
    abolitionists and, 2, 3
    African-American women's support for, 8
    emigration to Canada of, 69–70
    Harriet Tubman and, 419–20
    relief efforts for, 85–86
    and Sea Islands, 375
    writings by, 8
    See also Contraband Relief Association (CRA); contraband women; refugees; Underground Railroad

Fuller, Margaret, 328

fund-raising
    for antislavery societies, 2
    for church, 349
    for freedpeople's education, 411

Harriet Jacobs and, 251
for ironclad gunboat construction, 201
Jessie Benton Fremont and, 176
Louisa May Alcott and, 19
Mary Ann Shadd Cary and, 71
for New England Hospital for Women and
Children, 133
and sanitary fairs, 281–82, 360
for soldiers' aid societies, 381
for United States Sanitary Commission, 431
Furman, Farish Carter, 267
Further Records (Kemble), 259

G

Gage, Frances Dana, 36
Gardner, Elizabeth, 29
Garland, Anne Burwell, 254
Garnet, Henry Highland, 86
Garrison, William Lloyd, 2, 18, 82, 122, 269,
388, 466
Gayeso military hospital, Tennessee, 40
gender roles
in agriculture, 12–13
Albert D. J. Cashier (Jennie Hodgers) and,
72–73
of authors, 156
in domestic fiction, 277
espionage and, 386
in family, 157–58
Hamilton on, 210
Louisa May Alcott and, 19
in marriage, 95–96, 99–100
among Mexican Americans, 288–90
in Mormon church, 302
among Native Americans, 309–10
in politics, 79–80, 175, 209, 284
in South, 300
in writing, 166, 208
General Order No. 28, 37, 179–82
General Order No. 76, 181
Geneva Convention (1882), 36
Geneva Medical College, Geneva, New York,
132
Georgia, 363, 368–69, 383
German-speaking immigrants, 14, 231–32
Gettysburg, Battle of (1863), 152–53, 182–86,
192, 426

"Gettysburg Address, The" (Lincoln), 186
Gettysburg National Cemetery, 186
Gibbons, Abby Hopper, 75–76, 136, 187–88,
447
Gibbons, James Sloan, 187–88
Gibbons, Julia, 136
Gibbons, Lucy, 136
Gibbons, Sarah, 187
Gilbert Slater, Sarah, *See* Slater, Sarah Gilbert
Gillespie, Emily Hawley, 13
Gillmore, Quincy A., 35
Gilson, Helen, 431
girlhood and adolescence, 189–93
See also children
Gist, Malvina Black, 414–15
Gleanings from Southland (Cumming), 104
Glover, Martha, 376
Godey, Louis, 205
Godey's Lady's Book (magazine), 203–6, 274
gold mining, 51–52, 233, 306, 311, 337, 452
gonorrhea, 341
Goodwin, Olive E., 58
Gordon, Alexander George, 218
Gordon, Fannie, 96
Gordon, John, 96
Gould, Jane Holbrook, 454
government, Confederate, *See* Confederate
government
government girls, 34, 194–95, 344
See also treasury girls
Grand Army of the Republic, 406–7
Grant, Julia Dent, 64
Grant, Ulysses S., 35, 38, 39, 64, 68, 153, 281,
341, 435, 436, 440
grapevine, slave, 375
Gray, Martha, 63
*Great American Battle, The; or, The Contest
Between Christianity and Political
Romanism* (Carroll), 66
Great Britain, 183, 197, 250–51, 256, 258, 259
Harriet Beecher Stowe and, 394–95
Sarah Parker Remond in, 353–55
Great Central Sanitary Fair, Philadelphia,
Pennsylvania (1864), 190, 362
Great Famine (Ireland), 230
Greeley, Horace, 124
Green, Abby, 437
Greenhow, Robert, 196
Greenhow, Rose O'Neal, 195–97, 336, 385
Gregory, Samuel, 470

Greyhound (ship), 46
Griffing, Josephine, 416, 417
Grimes, Octavia, 85–86
Grimké, Francis J., 173
Guerin, Elsa Jane, 306
guerrilla war, 41–43, 197–200, 450
gunboat societies, 200–202

H

habeas corpus, 400
Hale, David, 204
Hale, Sarah Josepha, 203–7, 275
Hallock, Augusta, 99
Hamilton, Gail (pseudonym of Mary Abigail
        Dodge), 146, 207–10, 275, 276
Hamlin, Hannibal, 123
Hammond, William A., 130
Hancock, Cornelia, 318
Handkerchiefs, Battle of the, 36–37
hanging of slaves, 376, 377
Hannah, Robert D., 72
"Hannah Binding Shoes" (Larcom), 263
Hardeman, Ann Lewis, 351
Harding, Samuel, 46–47
Harding Davis, Rebecca, *See* Davis, Rebecca
        Harding
Harper, Fenton, 211
Harper, Frances Watkins, 2, 211–12, 420
Harpers Ferry, Virginia, John Brown's raid on, 2
Harris, Emily Lyles, 16, 376
Harris, Georgina, 221
Harrison, Benjamin, 124
Harrison, Constance Cary, *See* Cary (Harrison),
        Constance
Hart, James E., 96
Hartford Female Seminary, Connecticut, 166,
        208, 392
Haskel, Rachel, 451
Haughery, Margaret, 59
Havelock, Henry, 383
havelocks, 383
Haviland, Charles, 213
Haviland, Laura Smith, 213–16
Hawks, Esther Hill, 89, 132, 216–18
Hawks, John Milton, 216–18
Hawthorne, Nathaniel, 328
Hawthorne, Sally, 191

Hayes, Rutherford B., 437
health, *See* alternative medicine; diseases;
        doctors, women; hospitals; nurses;
        nutrition; surgery and surgeons
Hegel, G. W. F., 226
Henderson, Thomas H., 143
Herald (San Francisco, newspaper), 290
Herman, Judith, 245
Herold, David, 400
Hiawatha (Longfellow), 270
Hickey, Mary, 57
Higginson, Thomas Wentworth, 126, 128, 419
higher education
        for African Americans, 92–95, 120
        Maria Mitchell and, 295, 297–98
        medical colleges and women, 131–34, 215,
            470–71
        state-funded universities, 148–49
        women's colleges, 145, 146–47, 149–50, 205
high schools, 146
Hill Hawks, Esther, *See* Hawks, Esther Hill
Hispanic women, *See* Mexican-American women
Hitchcock, Harriet, 452, 454
Hodgers, Jennie, *See* Cashier, Albert D. J.
Hoffman, Lizzie, 294
Hoge, Jane, 281, 360, 430, 432
Holdredge, Margaret Vedder, 350
Hollinger sisters, 199
Holmes, Emma, 169, 170, 327
Holmes, Oliver Wendell, 261
Home and Foreign Missionary Society, 94
Home for Aged Women, 282
Home for Confederate Widows, 413
Home for Destitute Women and Children, 255
Home for the Friendless, Chicago, Illinois, 40
homeopathic medicine, 133
Homer, Winslow, 350
Homespun Clubs, 364
Homestead Act (1862), 40
Hood, John Bell, 183
Hooks, Charles E., 153
Hopkins, Arthur Francis, 218
Hopkins, Juliet Opie, 218–20
Hopper, Isaac Tatem, 187
Hopper Gibbons, Abby, *See* Gibbons, Abby
        Hopper
Hosmer, Harriet, 28–31, 270, 344
Hospital Act (Confederacy 1862), 320
hospital matrons, 103, 320, 332–33
hospitals

Dorothea Dix and, 129–30
field, 39, 74
floating, *See* hospital ships
Juliet Opie Hopkins and administration of, 218–20
Louisa Cheves McCord and, 285
Mary Ashton Rice Livermore and, 281–82
military, 39, 74, 102, 103, 130, 187, 218–20, 273, 281–82, 316, 320, 321, 332–33, 402–3, 412–13, 427, 428–29, 458
in private homes, 320, 412–13
slave, 257
soldiers' aid societies and provision of, 383
tent, 39
for women with venereal diseases, 342
hospital ships, 74, 152, 221–23, 316, 428–29
Hospital Sketches (Alcott), 17, 19, 278
Hospital Transport Service (HTS), 221–23, 316
"House and Home Papers" (Stowe), 396
household duties, 191, 289–90
House of Commons, English, 259
House of Representatives, 121
housing, in western settlements, 450–51
Howard, Oliver O., 266, 286
Howard Athenaeum, Boston, Massachusetts, 354
Howe, Julia Ward, 224–27, 298
Howe, Samuel Gridley, 224, 419
Howell, William, 111
Howell Davis, Varina, *See* Davis, Varina Howell
Howland, Eliza Woolsey, 321, 458
Hoxie, Richard, 345
Hoyt, E. O. Sampson, 467
Hubbard, Jerusha H., 163
Hunter, David, 420

I

Idahoe (ship), 341
Idyl of Work, An (Larcom), 265
Illinois Soldiers' and Sailors' Home, Quincy, Illinois, 73
Illinois Woman Suffrage Association, 282
immigrant women, 229–35
    agricultural labor of, 14
    Cashier, Albert D. J. (Jennie Hodgers), 72–73
    and Catholic sister orders, 75

discrimination against, 75
and draft riots, 134, 136
and food riots, 49
as prostitutes, 340
religions of, 349
Turchin, Nadine Lvova, 422–24
Zakrzewska, Marie, 469–72
See also Chinese immigrants; German-speaking immigrants; Irish immigrants; Jews; Scandinavian immigrants
Imperial (ship), 322
Incidents in the Life of a Slave Girl, Written by Herself (Jacobs), 83, 249
income, working women and family, 5, 6, 236
    See also wages
Independent (newspaper), 208, 394
Indiana Hospital, Washington, D.C., 447
Indian wars, *See* Native American wars
Indian women, *See* Native American women
industrial women, 235–42
    and draft riots, 136
    ordnance workers, 240–42
    Roswell workers exile, 355–57
    seamstresses, 238–40
    and soldiers' returning to work, 241
    in South, 239
    working conditions of, 236
Inez: A Tale of the Alamo (Evans), 154
infection, 320, 383
inflation
    in New York City, 135
    in North, 361, 431
    in South, 50, 326, 347, 374
insanity, *See* mental illness
Institute for Colored Youth, Philadelphia, Pennsylvania, 94
insurrections, slave, *See* slave insurrections
Intelligencer (newspaper), 108
international peace movement, 4, 212
International Red Cross, 36
invasion and occupation, 191–92, 243–48, 350, 355–57
    See also Battle of the Handkerchiefs; General Order No. 28; Sherman's March to the Sea
Ipswich Female Seminary, Massachusetts, 207
"Irish Biddy," *See* Divers, Bridget
Irish immigrants, 75, 135, 137, 230–31
ironclad gunboats, *See* gunboat societies

Isaac T. Hopper Home, 187

J

Jackson, Charlotte Ann, 374
Jackson, Mary, 48
Jackson, Thomas J. "Stonewall," 46, 176
Jacksonville Standard (newspaper), 365
Jacobs, Harriet, 70, 83, 91, 249–51
Jacobs, John, 249
Jacobs, Louisa, 250, 384
Jacobs Free School, 250
James, Henry, 208
James River, Virginia, 201
Jefferson Davis: A Memoir by His Wife (V. Davis),
    113
Jews
    immigrant, 232–33, 349
    Phillips, Eugenia Levy, 335–36
    Solomon, Clara, 116, 179, 181, 193, 246
"John Brown's Body" (song), 225–26, 360
Johnson, Andrew, 113, 344, 399, 400, 403, 446,
    448
Johnston, Joseph E., 325
Jones, Barbara, 290
Jones, Clarissa Fellows, 426
Jones, Elizabeth, 56
Jones, Mary, 377
Jordan, Thomas, 196
journalists, *See* literary women
*Journal of a Residence on a Georgian Plantation
    1838-1839* (Kemble), 256
*Journal of Hospital Life in the Confederate Army of
    Tennessee, A* (Cumming), 104
jubilees, 379
justice system, U.S., 288

K

Kansas City, Missouri, 199
Kansas-Nebraska Act (1854), 263, 394
Kant, Immanuel, 226
Kearny, Philip, 152
Kearny Cross, 63, 152, 184
Keckley, Elizabeth, 85–86, 253–55, 273–74
Keckley, James, 254–55
Kellogg, David, 151

Kemble, Fanny, 256–59
Keokuk (Iowa) Ladies' Soldiers' Aid Society,
    427, 430
Key to Uncle Tom's Cabin, A (Stowe), 394
kindergarten, 329
Kindergarten Messenger (magazine), 330
King, Edward, 406
King, M. E., 162
Kirk, George W., 42
Kirkwood, Samuel, 345
Knickerbocker (ship), 152
Know-Nothing Party, 66
Knox College, Illinois, 148
Krehbiel, Susanna Ruth, 232
kwashiorkor, 374

L

labor organizations, 236, 241
Ladies' Art Association, 31
Ladies' Emancipation Society of London, 259
Ladies' Freedmen and Soldiers' Relief
    Association, *See* Contraband Relief
    Association
Ladies' Gunboat Association (Richmond,
    Virginia), 201
Ladies London Emancipation Society, 354
Ladies' Magazine, 203–4
Ladies' Mite Association (Idaho), 453
Ladies' Volunteer Association, 383
Lady Godiva (Whitney), 30
"Laggard Recruit, The" (Sutherland), 277
land-grant colleges and universities, 149
Lane Theological Seminary, Ohio, 392
Langston, John, 269
language, 288
Larcom, Lucy, 261–66, 275
laundresses, 5–6, 9, 52, 241–42
lawyers, African-American women as, 69, 71
LeConte, Emma, 116, 190, 191, 247, 266–67,
    327
lectures, public, *See* public speaking
Lectures in Training Schools for Kindergartners
    (Peabody), 330
Lee, Rebecca, 133
Lee, Robert E., 25–26, 65, 183, 244, 397
Lee, Stephen D., 170
Legislation

on African-American education, 146
on African-American employment, 7
against African-American gatherings, 379
on African-American property ownership, 8
against African-American worship, 8
aimed at Mexican Americans, 290
anti-abortion, 161
apprentice laws, 165
on free African Americans, 50
on government girls' wages, 195
Mexican-American women's losses through,
    287
prohibiting polygamy, 305
on property rights for women, 22, 388, 402,
    460, 466–67
on prostitution, 341
on women's rights, 22
See also Black Codes; *specific laws*
Le Grand, Julia, 37
Lehmann, Barbara, 232
Leonard, Ellen, 135
Leslie, Frank, 20
Letcher, John, 48, 329
Levy Pember, Phoebe, *See* Pember, Phoebe Levy
Levy Phillips, Eugenia, *See* Phillips, Eugenia
    Levy
Lewis, Edmonia, 268–70
Lewis, Maria, 294
Liberator, The (newspaper), 18, 84, 91, 122, 172,
    212
Liberia, 204
Liberia; or Mr. Peyton's Experiment (Hale), 204
Liberty Party, 388
"Life in the Iron Mills" (R. Davis), 108
Lincoln, Abraham
    abolitionist pressure on, 3, 22
    Anna Dickinson and, 123–24
    Anna Ella Carroll on, 67
    assassination of, 373, 398–401, 439
    constitutionality of actions by, 67
    and Contraband Relief Association, 86
    contribution to Chicago Sanitary Fair of, 361
    Elizabeth Cady Stanton on, 389
    female arsenal workers and, 239
    and Frances Watkins Harper, 211
    at Gettysburg, 186
    Harriet Tubman on, 419
    and John Charles Fremont, 175
    and Mary Todd Lincoln, 271–74
    opposition to election of, 78

and Sojourner Truth, 417
Southern reaction to, 364
and Thanksgiving Day proclamation, 204,
    205
and United States Sanitary Commission, 429
Vinnie Ream's bust of, 344
Vinnie Ream's sculpture of, 343, 344–45
Lincoln, Mary Todd, 85–86, 113, 123, 253–55,
    271–74, 344, 464
Lincoln, Robert, 273
Lincoln, Todd, 344
Lincoln, Willie, 273
Lint Picks, 383
liquor, 333
Lish, Ira, 72
Litchfield Female Academy, Connecticut, 392
literacy, 145, 380
literary societies, 7
literary women, 56, 274–79
    Alcott, Louisa May, 17–21
    and antislavery writing, 2
    and business practices, 277
    Carroll, Anna Ella, 66–68
    Cary, Mary Ann Shadd, 69–71
    characteristics of, 275–76
    Chesnut, Mary Boykin, 77–81
    Child, Lydia Maria, 81–84
    Davis, Rebecca Harding, 107–10
    Dickinson, Anna, 124
    Dickinson, Emily, 125–28
    Evans, Augusta Jane, 154–56
    and female audience, 275
    Fern, Fanny, 165–69
    Forten, Charlotte, 172
    Hale, Sarah Josepha, 203–7
    Hamilton, Gail, 207–10
    Harper, Frances Watkins, 211–12
    Howe, Julia Ward, 224–27
    Jacobs, Harriet, 249–51
    Kemble, Fanny, 256–59
    Ladies' Magazine and, 203–4
    Larcom, Lucy, 261–66
    LeConte, Emma, 266–67
    Livermore, Mary Ashton Rice, 279–82
    male opinions of, 275
    McCord, Louisa Cheves, 284–86
    Morgan, Sarah, 299–301
    and payment for work, 275, 276
    Stowe, Harriet Beecher, 392–97
    Swisshelm, Jane Grey, 401–3

on women and war, 277–78

   See also diaries

Livermore, Daniel Parker, 280

Livermore, Mary Ashton Rice, 170, 279–82, 291, 293, 319, 324, 360, 381, 430, 432

Lloyd, John, 399

loans, whites' refusal to give, 379

Logan Female Anti-Slavery Society, 213

Longfellow, Henry Wadsworth, 261, 270

"Long Walk," 312–13

Lookout Mountain, Battle of (1863), 40

Lord Montagu, Hannah, 241

Loughborough, Mary Ann, 440, 441

Louisiana, 363

Louisiana (ship), 152

Louisville Female Military Prison, Kentucky, 448

Louveste, Mary, 387

Love: or, Woman's Destiny (Hale), 206

love, romantic, 96, 98

Lowell Offering (newspaper), 262

Lozier, Clemence Sophia, 132, 133

Lutheranism, 232

Lynn, Massachusetts, 237

Lyon, Mary, 147

M

Macaria, or Altars of Sacrifice (Evans), 154, 278

Madame Demorest's Mirror of Fashion (magazine), 58–59

magazines

   reports of war in, 190

   women's, 203–7, 274–75

Mahoney, Mary Eliza, 322

malaria, 65, 281

Mallory, Stephen, 201

malnutrition, *See* nutrition

Manassas, *See* Bull Run, First Battle of; Bull Run, Second Battle of

Mangum, Nancy, 326

Manhattan Anti-Slavery Society, 187

Mann, Horace, 30, 329

Mann, Horace, Jr., 330

Mann, Mary Peabody, 329

marauders, 41, 43, 369, 450

Margret Howth (R. Davis), 108

marriage, *See* courtship and marriage

Married Women's Property Law (New York 1860), 22, 388, 460, 467

Martin, Frank, *See* Clalin, Frances

Martin, Isabella, 81

Martin, Sarah, 86

Martin Spencer, Lilly, 30–31

Mary Chesnut's Civil War, 77, 117

mascots, female, *See* daughters of the regiment

Mason, James, 82

Mason, Margaretta, 82–83

Massachusetts Anti-Slavery Society, 353

Massachusetts General Hospital, Boston, 322

Massachusetts Woman Suffrage Association, 226, 282

mathematics, 297

matrons, hospital, *See* hospital matrons

Maxwell, Miss (Georgia woman), 369

May, Abigail (Abby) Williams, 133, 282, 361, 430, 431, 471

May, Samuel Joseph, 18, 23

Mayflower, The (Stowe), 392

Mayo, Caroline, 320

McAllister, Mary, 183

McClatchey, Minerva Rowles, 244

McClellan, George, 25, 122, 124, 141, 222, 390

McCord, David James, 284, 285

McCord, Louisa Cheves, 284–86

McDonald, Cornelia Peake, 115, 118, 318, 346, 351

McDowell, Irvin, 196

McGuire, Judith White, 363, 367

McKay, Charlotte Johnson, 185, 426

McKinney, Emilie Riley, 351

McLure, Kate, 100

McLure, William, 100

McNiven, Thomas, 44

Meade, George Gordon, 182, 435

measles, 281

Medical Bureau, *See* Army Medical Bureau

medical colleges, 131–34, 215, 470–71

medicine, *See* alternative medicine; diseases; doctors, women; hospitals; nurses; surgery and surgeons

Memminger, Christopher, 414

memorials, 327, 364

Memphis, Tennessee, 143, 342

mental illness, 129, 273

   See also depression; trauma of war

mercury poisoning, Louisa May Alcott and, 19

Meredith, Minerva, 48

USS *Merrimac,* 200, 387

Merritt, Susan, 378

Methodist Church, Central City, Colorado, 51–52

Methodists, 349

Metropolitan Sanitary Commission Fair (New York City 1864), 176, 362

Mexican Americans, 454

Mexican-American War, 154, 287–88

Mexican-American women, 287–91
    See also western women

"Michigan Bridget," *See* Divers, Bridget

middle class
    and diaries, 115
    and education, 146–47
    family life among, 157–61
    farm women of, 12, 14
    and food riots, 49–50
    refugees of, 347
    and United States Sanitary Commission, 430
    and woman suffrage, 466
    and women's war role, 209

Midwest, 233

midwifery, 470

military tribunals, 399

military women, 61, 190, 291–94
    African-American, 294
    Blalock, Malinda Pritchard, 41–43
    Cashier, Albert D. J. (Jennie Hodgers), 72–73
    characteristics of, 292
    disguises of, 292, 294
    Edmonds, Sarah Emma, 139–42
    Turchin, Nadine Lvova, 422–24
    unidentified soldier at Gettysburg, 184
    Velazquez, Loreta Janeta, 438–39
    Wakeman, Sarah Rosetta, 443–45
    See also Mountain Charley

Militia Act (1862), 88

militias, volunteer, 364

Miller, Elizabeth Smith, 390

Miller, Stephen Decatur, 78

Milliken's Bend, Louisiana, 281

Mills, Clark, 344

mining, *See* gold mining

mining towns, 452

ministers, women, 350

Minister's Wooing, The (Stowe), 394

Minnesota, 312, 402

missing soldiers, Clara Barton and identification of, 35

missionaries, 94, 120, 350
    See also teachers of the freedpeople

Missionary Ridge, Battle of (1863), 40

Mississippi, 363

Missouri, 175–76, 199

Miss Ritchie's school, Richmond, Virginia, 218

Mitchell, Maria, 295–98

Mobile, Alabama, invasion of, 72

Monett's Ferry, Battle of (1864), 445

USS *Monitor,* 200

Montgomery, James, 420

Monticello Seminary, Illinois, 262

monuments, 327

Moore, Jane Boswell, 184, 186, 426

Moore, Jane C., 426

Moral Culture of Infancy and Kindergarten (Peabody and Mann), 329–30

moral improvement societies, 7

Morgan, John Hunt, 106

Morgan, Sarah, 299–301, 323, 327, 347–48

Mormon women, 302–5, 454

Morrill Land Grant Act (1862), 148–49

Mott, Lucretia Coffin, 2, 132, 467

Mountain Charley, 306–7

Mountain Charley or the Adventures of Mrs. E.J. Guerin (Guerin), 306

Mountain City, Colorado, 51–52

Mountain Department, 176

Mount Hermon Female Seminary, Mississippi, 120

Mount Holyoke Female Seminary, Massachusetts, 120, 125

Mount Vernon, Virginia, 204

mulattos, 7

Mullaney, Kate, 241–42

munitions factories, *See* ordnance workers

Musical World and Times (newspaper), 166

mutual aid societies, 8

My Imprisonment, and the First Year of Abolition Rule at Washington (Greenhow), 197

My Story of the War (Livermore), 281, 291

N

Nashville, Tennessee, 341–42

National Academy of Design, 29

National American Woman Suffrage Association, 24, 468

National Anti-Slavery Standard (newspaper), 2, 82, 84, 212, 258

National Association of Colored Women, 212

National Era (newspaper), 208, 262, 393

National Federation of Afro-American Women, 421

National Freedmen's Relief Association, 417

National Sailors Fair, Boston, Massachusetts, 226

national unity, 204, 205

National Woman's Party, 468

National Woman Suffrage Association, 24, 391, 468

Native American rights movement, 4

Native Americans
    assistance to whites from, 456
    Edmonia Lewis' sculptures of, 270
    education of, 330
    westward emigrants' attitudes toward, 454–56
    whites' treatment of, 455

Native American wars, 311–15, 449, 455–56

Native American women, 309–15, 402

Neblett, Lizzie, 160, 376

Negroes and Anglo-Africans as Freedmen and Soldiers, The (Remond), 354

Nell, William C., 83

"Nelly Bly" (song), 263

Nesmith, James, 344

Nevada Territory, 314

Newby, Dangerfield, 100–101

Newby, Harriet, 100–101

New Covenant (magazine), 280

New England Female Medical College, Massachusetts, 215, 470

New England Freedmen's Aid Society, 250

New England Freedmen's Union Commission, 173

New England Girlhood, A (Larcom), 265

New England Hospital for Women and Children, Boston, Massachusetts, 133, 322, 471–72

New England Offering (newspaper), 262

New England Sanitary Commission, 225

New England Woman's Auxiliary Association, 282, 361, 384

New England Woman Suffrage Association, 226

New England Women's Club, 226

New Hampshire Association of Military Surgeons, 217

New Mexico Territory, 312–13, 449

New Orleans, Louisiana
    Battle of the Handkerchiefs in, 36–37
    gunboat society in, 201
    resistance to Union troops in, 179–82

Newsom Hospital, Chattanooga, Tennessee, 103

Newspapers
    accounts of military women in, 293
    Fanny Fern and, 165–69
    first African-American publisher/editor of, 69, 70
    on food riots, 49
    Gail Hamilton and, 208
    Louisa May Alcott and, 19–20
    and reaction to General Order No. 28, 181
    religious, 55, 208, 263, 394
    reports of war in, 190
    on Roswell exiles, 356
    See also specific newspapers

New York, New York
    draft riots in, 134–37
    Metropolitan Sanitary Commission Fair, 176, 362
    poverty in, 168
    prostitution in, 341
    seamstresses in, 237

New York Central College, 268

New York Diet Kitchen Association, 188

New York Herald (newspaper), 272

New York Infirmary for Women and Children, 459, 470

New York Ledger (newspaper), 165–69, 276, 278

New York Medical College and Hospital for Women, 133

New York Sunday World (newspaper), 113

New York Times (newspaper), 400

New York Tribune (newspaper), 83, 84, 110, 124, 210

Nichols, Clarina Howard, 463

Nightingale, Florence, 18, 102, 130, 317–18

Nineteenth Amendment, 24, 466, 468

"Nineteenth of April, The" (Larcom), 264

"Noble Army of Martyrs, The" (Stowe), 396

normal departments/schools, 148, 149

Norris, Mary, 150

North Beach and Mission Railroad Company, 339

North Carolina

guerrilla warfare in, 199
secession of, 363
Unionism in, 41–43, 199
Northern Paiutes, 314
Northwestern Sanitary Commission (NSC), 39,
    280, 282, 360, 428
Northwood: or, Life North and South (Hale), 204
Notes on Hospitals (Nightingale), 130
Notes on Nursing: What It Is and What It Is Not
    (Nightingale), 130
NSC, *See* Northwestern Sanitary Commission
nuns, Catholic, 73–76, 316
    and hardships of women, 75
    on hospital ships, 221
    and Irish immigrants, 231
    as nurses, 188
Nurse and Spy in the Union Army (Edmonds),
    141, 278
nurses, 315–22
    African-American, 5
    Alcott, Louisa May, 18–19
    Barton, Clara, 26–27, 33–36
    Bickerdyke, Mary Ann, 38–40
    Boyd, Belle, 46
    Brownell, Kady Southwell, 55
    Catholic nuns as, 73–76
    coping mechanisms of, 318–19
    Cumming, Kate, 102–5
    daughters of the regiment as, 62
    diaries of, 117
    disease exposure of, 320
    Dorothea Dix and, 129–30
    duties of, 319
    Edmonds, Sarah Emma, 139–42
    Etheridge, Annie, 151–53
    at Gettysburg, 183–85
    Gibbons, Abby Hopper, 187–88
    Gibbons, Sarah, 187
    on hospital ships, 221–23
    male, 103, 223, 316–17
    McCord, Louisa Cheves, 285
    motivations for becoming, 318
    numbers of, 316–17
    Protestant versus Catholic sister, 75–76, 188
    selection criteria for, 317
    soldier-nurses, 39
    Tompkins, Sally, 412–13
    training of, 316–17
    of United States Sanitary Commission, 428
    wages of, 319, 320

and WCAR training, 458
women doctors and, 133
working conditions of, 320
and working relations with male medical
    officers, 321–22, 333
See also hospital matrons
nursing schools, 322
nutrition
    and disease incidence, 374
    of hospital patients, 321, 330, 427
    on Sea Islands, 409, 410
    of slave families, 10, 193
    of slave industrial workers, 240
    of slaves, 374
    of Southern children, 191
    of Union soldiers, 15
    See also food shortages; special diet kitchens

O

oaths of allegiance, 336
Oberlin College, Ohio, 92–95, 148, 268–70,
    349
O'Brien, Henry, 135
Office of Correspondence with Friends of the
    Missing Men of the U.S. Army, 35–36
officers, wives of, 64
Old Capitol Prison, Washington, D. C., 46, 197
Oliver, Matilda and Eliza, 57
Olmsted, Frederick Law, 27, 222, 429
O'Neal Greenhow, Rose, *See* Greenhow, Rose
    O'Neal
Ontario, Canada, 338
ordnance workers, 240–42
Orpen, Adele "Doaty," 13–14
O'Sullivan, Michael, 57
Our Young Folks (magazine), 265

P

pacifists, 3
    See also peace movement, northern
Palmer, Fanny (Frances Flora Bond), 31
Palmer, Sarah H., 2
Parcher, Sarah, 97
Parcher, Tabor, 97
Parker sisters (businesswomen), 6

parties, political, 462–64
  See also individual parties
Parton, James, 167
Patent Office, U.S., 33–34, 194
Patriarchal Institution, The (Child), 83
patriotism, 323–27
  of children, 189–91
  Gail Hamilton on, 209
  in literature by women, 278
  in Lucy Larcom's poetry, 263–64
  in New Orleans, 179–82
  northern, 167
  sanitary fairs and, 360
  secession and, 363
  southern, 154–56, 265
  Woman's Relief Corps and, 406
Patterson, Mary Jane, 94
Payne, Lewis, 400
Peabody, Elizabeth Palmer, 297, 328–31
peace movement, northern, 209
  See also pacifists
Peale, Charles Willson, 30
Peale, James, 30
Peale, Sarah Miriam, 30
Pearl of Orr's Island, The (Stowe), 396
Pember, Phoebe Levy, 246, 331–34
Pember, Thomas, 331
Pemberton, John, 440, 441
Pemberton Mill, Lawrence, Massachusetts, 236
Pender, William Dorsey, 160
Peninsula Campaign (1862), 140, 222–23
Pennsylvania Academy of Fine Arts, 29
Pennsylvania Anti-Slavery Society, 122
Pennsylvania Freedmen's Relief Association, 172
Perry, Harriet, 97, 160, 351
Perry, Theophilus, 97
Personal Liberty Law (Massachusetts), 83
Peterson's Magazine, 109
Phelps, Elizabeth Stuart, 237
Phifer, George, 15
Phifer, Louisa Jane, 15
Philadelphia, Pennsylvania, Great Central
      Sanitary Fair in, 190, 362
Philbrick, Edward S., 90
Phillips, Cordelia, 464
Phillips, Eugenia Levy, 246, 331, 335–36
Phillips, Phillip, 335
Phillips, Wendell, 22, 82, 86, 176, 390, 466
philosophy, 226, 327
  See also transcendentalism

Phoebe (servant of Eugenia Levy Phillips), 336
photography, 58
physicians, women, *See* doctors, women
Pickett, George E., 65
Pickett, LaSalle Corbell, 65
Pickett's Charge (Battle of Gettysburg), 184
Pierce, Tillie, 192
Pinkerton, Allan, 196
Pittsburgh Daily Commercial (newspaper), 399
Plank, Elizabeth, 183
plantations
  African-American owners of, 7
  domestic slave economy and, 9–10
  white women on, 14, 375
Pleasant, Mary Ellen, 51, 337–39
Pleasant Hall, Battle of (1864), 445
Pleasants, John James, 338
plural marriage, 303–5, 454
Poe, Orlando M., 141
poetry
  Dickinson, Emily, 125–28
  Harper, Frances Watkins, 211–12
  Howe, Julia Ward, 225
  Larcom, Lucy, 261–66
police, and draft riots, 134–37
political parties, 462–64
  See also individual parties
politics
  gender roles in, 79–80, 175, 209, 284
  religion and, 66–67
  See also women and politics
polygamy, 303–5, 454
population
  of African Americans in 1860, 5
  urban-rural distribution of, 12
Porter, Eliza, 40
Portland Advertiser (Maine, newspaper), 212
Port Royal Experiment, 171, 408–9
Post, Amy Kirby, 250
poverty
  camp women from, 64
  and Catholic sister orders, 74
  and draft riots, 134–37
  Fanny Fern on, 168
  and food riots, 47–50
  Mexican Americans and, 289
  Northwestern Sanitary Commission (NSC),
      282
  and prostitution, 340
Powers, Elvira, 318

Powers, Hiram, 345
prayer, 158
Prentiss, Benjamin, 39
Preston, Ann, 132
Preston, Margaret Junkin, 278
price gouging, 90
Prison Association of New York, 187
prisoners
    escaped, 199
    espionage-related, 386
    exchange of, and Battle of the Handkerchiefs,
        37
    Haviland and release of Union, 214–15
    Union, at Andersonville, Georgia, 35–36, 40
    Union officers at Libby Prison, 436–37
prisons, 187, 188
    See also specific prisons
Pritchard Blalock, Malinda, *See* Blalock,
        Malinda Pritchard
private schools, 145, 147
property
    African-American women as owners of, 7, 52
    Confiscation Acts and slaveholders', 67
    Mexican Americans and, 288
    military invasion and destruction of, 243–44
    veterans' claims on, 40
    whites' refusal to sell, 379
    women's rights to, 22, 204, 388, 460,
        466–67
prostitutes, 340–42
    camp life and, 61, 88, 340
    Chinese immigrants as, 233–34
    as entrepreneurs, 58
    former seamstresses turned, 238
    income of, 341
prostitution
    Abby Hopper Gibbons against, 188
    as business, 58
    Chinese tong control of, 234
    General Order No. 28 and, 181
    legalized, 341–42
protective associations, working women's, 239
Protestantism
    draft riots in Boston aimed at, 137
    as majority religion, 349
    Protestant versus Catholic sister nurses,
        75–76, 188
protests, *See* Battle of the Handkerchiefs; bread
        rebellions; draft riots
Provincial Freeman (newspaper), 69–70

public demonstrations, *See* Battle of the
        Handkerchiefs; bread rebellions; draft
        riots
public schools, *See* common schools
public speaking
    by abolitionists, 2–3
    Anthony, Susan B., 22–23
    Barton, Clara, 36
    Cary, Mary Ann Shadd, 69
    at departure ceremonies, 324
    Dickinson, Anna, 121–24
    Harper, Frances Watkins, 211–12
    Howe, Julia Ward, 226
    Remond, Sarah Parker, 353–55
    Stanton, Elizabeth Cady, 389
    Swisshelm, Jane Grey, 401–3
    Tubman, Harriet, 418–21
    women in politics, 464
publishing, 329
Pulitzer Prize, 77, 117
Putnam, Sallie Brock, *See* Brock (Putnam), Sallie

Q

Quaker Negro College, 44
Quakers, 75, 121, 132, 213, 295
    and abolitionism, 3
    and education, 94, 148
    Gibbons, Abby Hopper, 187–88
    Susan B. Anthony and, 22
Quartermaster General's Office, 194

R

racial discrimination
    in army hospitals, 187
    in Canada, 70
    in Massachusetts, 353–54
    against Mexican Americans, 290
    in Midwest, 71
    in Philadelphia, 94
    Susan B. Anthony on northern, 23
    on transportation, 8, 94, 338, 417–18, 420
    on western frontier, 454
    in workplace, 7
Radical Democratic Party, 176, 464
Radical Republicans, 403

railroad travel, 347

Raisin Institute, 213

Randolph, George W., 331

rape, *See* sexual assault

rats, 333

Raymond, John Howard, 149–50, 297

Ready, Alice, 98

real estate, *See* property

realism, in literature, 278

Ream, Vinnie, 343–46

Reconstruction, 80, 123, 177, 212, 352, 408

Reconstructionist (newspaper), 403

Records of a Girlhood (Kemble), 259

Records of Later Life (Kemble), 259

recruitment, of African American soldiers, 69, 71, 251

Red Cross, *See* American Red Cross; International Red Cross

Red River Campaign (1864), 72

USS *Red Rover*, 221

Reed, John, 57

Reed, Lida Lord, 440

"Re-enlisted" (Larcom), 265

reform movements, 2, 3

refugees, 346–48

    attitudes toward, 347

    children as, 158

    Harriet Jacobs and, 249–51

    in Kansas, 215

    Native American, 311

    Roswell women, 355–57

    United States Sanitary Commission and, 429

    See also contraband women; fugitive slaves

regiments, all-black, *See* all-black regiments

religion, 349–52

    and abolitionism, 225

    African-American women and, 7

    Catholic sister versus Protestant nurses, 75–76, 188

    church benevolent groups, 5

    in family, 96, 158, 161

    of freedpeople's teachers, 409

    among German-speaking immigrants, 232

    God's intervention in war, 170, 226, 264, 329, 350

    growth of, 349

    in hospitals, 75, 213, 413

    Laura Smith Haviland and, 213

    and politics, 66–67

    religious newspapers, 167, 208, 263, 394

    Sarah Dickey and, 119–20

    United States Christian Commission and, 425–27

    on western frontier, 452–53

    women ministers, 350

    See also African Methodist Episcopal Church; Catholicism; Church of the United Brethren in Christ; Lutheranism; Methodists; Protestantism; Quakers; Unitarianism; Universalism; Wesleyan Methodist Church

Reminiscences (Howe), 225

Remond, Charles Lenox, 353

Remond, Sarah Parker, 270, 353–55

"Reply" (Stowe), 395–96

Reply to the Speech of Honorable John C. Breckinridge (pamphlet), 67

reproduction and birth control, 158–61

Republican Party, 122, 174, 462–64

revenge

    guerrilla warfare and, 41

    for invasion and occupation, 246

    Mountain Charley and, 306

Revere, Paul Joseph, 437

Revolutionary War, American, 61–62, 74, 265

Reynolds, Arabella "Belle" Macomber, 62

Rhode Island State Normal School, 93

Rice, Lucy, 437

Rice Livermore, Mary Ashton, *See* Livermore, Mary Ashton Rice

Richmond, Virginia

    bread rebellions in, 47–50

    Chimborazo Hospital in, 332–33

    as Confederate capital, 78, 112

    Elizabeth Van Lew and spy ring in, 435–37

    flag-raising in, 325

    gunboat society in, 201

    hospitals for Alabama soldiers in, 218–19

    munitions factory explosion, 240

    Robertson Hospital in, 412–13

    ruins of, 244

    secession convention in, 366

Right Way, The (Child), 83

Riley, Lucy Ann, 13

riots, *See* Battle of the Handkerchiefs; bread rebellions; draft riots

Robertson, John, 412

Robertson Hospital, 412–13

Robinson, Imogene, 29

Rochester, New York, 418

Romance of the Great Rebellion, The (Cushman), 105
romantic love, 96, 98
Romeo and Juliet (Shakespeare), 256
Rooney, Rose Quinn, 184
Roosevelt, Franklin Delano, 206
Ropes, Hannah, 320
Rose, Ernestine Potowski, 467
Rose Clark (Fern), 166
"Rose Enthroned, The" (Larcom), 264
Ross, Kristie, 318
Roswell, Georgia, 355–57
Roswell women, 355–57
Roulette, Margaret and William, 26
rumors, surrounding invasion, 243
rural areas, population of, 12
Ruth Hall (Fern), 166
Ryan, Mary, 241

S

Salem Female Anti-Slavery Society, 2, 8, 353
Salem Normal School, Massachusetts, 172
Salt Lake City, Utah, 302–5, 312, 449
Sanborn, Frank, 419
Sand Creek Massacre, 313–14
San Francisco Athenaeum Institute, 338
Sanger, William, 238
sanitary fairs, 282, 359–62
    Chicago Sanitary Fair, 282, 361
    children and, 190
    Great Central Sanitary Fair, 190, 362
    Metropolitan Sanitary Commission Fair, 176, 362
    problems caused by, 361–62
    and United States Sanitary Commission, 432
    Western Sanitary Fair, 361
Santa Fe Trail, 313
Saturday Visiter (newspaper), 401
Saxton, Rufus, 420
Scandinavian immigrants, 14, 233
School of Design, Worcester, Massachusetts, 29
Schurz, Margarethe, 329
Schuyler, Louisa Lee, 281, 317, 430, 431, 459
scientists, 295–98
scorched earth policy, 244, 313
Scott, Thomas A., 67
scouts, 5, 143, 420

scouts (vigilantes), 378
scrofula, 265
scurvy, 215, 281, 410
Sea Islands, 375, 408–10
seamstresses, 6, 56, 234, 236, 238–40
    See also dressmaking
secession, 363–67
    of Alabama, 154
    crisis of 1860–1861, 196
    debate over, 363
    Eugenia Levy Phillips and, 336
    Rose O'Neal Greenhow and, 195–97
    of South Carolina, 170
    women's political participation in, 466
secession conventions, 366
Second Annual Report of the Maryland Committee of the Christian Commission, 426
Second Battle of Bull Run (1862), 26, 34, 152
Second Confiscation Act (1862), 88
"second shift," of enslaved women, 9
Seddon, James A., 372
Sedgwick, Elizabeth, 257
Seelye, Linus H., 141
seminaries, female, 146–47
Seneca Falls, New York, 388
Seneca Falls Convention (1848), 388, 465–66
Sequoyah, 345
servants, *See* domestic servants
Seven Days' Battle (1862), 140
Seven Pines, Battle of (1862), 140, 219, 223
Severance, Caroline, 133, 471
Sewall, Samuel Edmond, 133, 471
Seward, William H., 206, 390, 400
sewing and knitting associations, 58, 79
Sewing Women's Protective and Benevolent Union, 239
Sewing Women's Protective Association of Detroit, 239
sexual assault
    of contraband women, 11, 89, 193
    by invading soldiers, 254
    of Native Americans, 311, 312, 314
    of slaves, 245, 354
sexuality, 98, 158, 250
sex workers, *See* prostitutes
Shadd, Abraham, 69
Shadd, Amelia Freeman, 70
Shadd, Isaac, 69–70
Shadd Cary, Mary Ann, *See* Cary, Mary Ann Shadd

Shaftesbury, Lord, 395

Shannon, Julia, 58

Sharp, Helen Maria, 16

Sharpe, George H., 435

Sharpsburg, *See* Antietam (Sharpsburg), Battle
of

Shaw, Robert Gould, 269, 420

Sherman, Ellen Ewing, 65

Sherman, William Tecumseh, 38, 40, 65, 80,
104, 116, 190, 266, 355–57, 448
See also Sherman's March to the Sea

Sherman, Willy, 65

Sherman's March to the Sea, 244, 246, 285,
368–71

Shields, James, 46

Shiloh, Battle of (1862), 39, 103, 439

Ship Island, 214, 336

shoe factories, 237

Shoshoni Tribe, 312

sieges, *See* battles and campaigns

Similitudes, from the Ocean and Prairie (Larcom),
262–63

Simkins, Eldred, 96

"Sinking of the Merrimack, The" (Larcom), 265

Sinnotte, Ruth Helena, 322

Sioux Uprising of 1862, 311–12, 402, 449, 455

Sisters of Charity of Saint Vincent de Paul, 185

Sisters of Notre Dame de Namur, 231

skin infections, 320

Slater, Rowan, 372

Slater, Sarah Gilbert, 372–73

slave codes, 379
See also Black Codes

slave insurrections, 364, 377
See also Brown, John

slave narratives, 249–51

slavery and emancipation, 373–80
African-American women and, 9–11
Anne Whitney's sculpture, *Africa,* 30
antislavery attitudes of Southerners, 79–80
colonization as solution to, 67
effect of slavery on whites, 296
and female slaveholders, 375–77
Frémont Emancipation Proclamation, 175
Harriet Beecher Stowe and, 392–97
Louisa Cheves McCord's defense of slavery,
284–85
Mary Boykin Chesnut on, 79–80
Mary Todd Lincoln's role in, 273
pro-slavery arguments, 284–85, 296

Uncle Tom's Cabin and, 276
in West Indies, 83
See also abolitionists; Emancipation
Proclamation; freedpeople

slaves
abuse of, 375–76
courtship and marriage among, 99, 100
end-of-war disorder and, 377
family life among, 9–11, 50, 164, 354
female, 9–11
as industrial workers, 239
insurrections of, *See* slave insurrections
literacy among, 145
living conditions of, 257
nutrition of, 374
opinions about, 3, 79–80, 90, 204–5
resistance of, 375, 377
and Sherman's March to the Sea, 369–70
and violence against slaveholders, 377
See also fugitive slaves

smallpox, 39, 318, 409

Smith, Ambrose, 51

Smith, Evelyn, 246

Smith, Gerrit, 388

Smith, Lucy Meserve, 303

Smith Haviland, Laura, *See* Haviland, Laura
Smith

smugglers, 143, 386

Snyder, Catherine, 57

social issues, 168, 277

Society for the Dissemination of Radical
Principles, 471

Society of Colorado Pioneers, 53

sodalities, 310

soldiers
African-American, 5, 64, 88, 123, 163–64,
269, 282
departure ceremonies for, 323–24
deserting, 326
guerrilla, 41–43
identification by Clara Barton of dead, 35
immigrant, 229–30
Mexican-American, 287
Native American, 312
recruitment by women of, 69, 71, 251
serving in both armies, 41
slaves impressed as, 375
veterans' claims, 40
wives accompanying, 41–43, 54–55, 62, 64,
152, 164, 292, 422–24

See also all-black regiments; military women
soldiers' aid societies, 380–85
    abolitionists and, 3, 5
    in Alabama, 219
    benevolent associations and, 233
    children's contributions to, 190
    Clara Barton and, 34
    in early years, 381–82
    farm women and, 14
    formation of, 364
    Gail Hamilton on, 209
    Louisa May Alcott and, 17
    males in, 381
    and Northwestern Sanitary Commission,
        280
    patriotism and, 323, 325
    United States Sanitary Commission and,
        428–33
    on western frontier, 453
    and Woman's Central Association of Relief,
        458
    women's role in, 201, 362, 381
Soldiers' Clothing Association, Columbia, South
        Carolina, 285
Soldiers' Relief Association, Columbia, South
        Carolina, 285
Soldier's Relief Fund Fair, 269
Soldiers' Rest, Springfield, Massachusetts, 128
Solomon, Clara, 116, 179, 181, 193, 246
Sorosis, 169
Souder, Emily Bliss, 426
South Carolina
    against African Americans in politics, 466
    antebellum politics of, 78
    contraband women and, 87, 89
    Fort Sumter, 169–71
    secession of, 170, 363
    and Sherman's March to the Sea, 371
    soldiers' aid societies in, 383
    See also Sea Islands
Southern Woman's Story, A (Pember), 332
Southwest, 287–91
Southworth, E.D.E.N., 275, 276
Spalding, George, 341
Spanish-American War (1898), 36
special diet kitchens, 427
spies and espionage, 385–87
    African-American women as, 5
    Bowser, Mary Elizabeth, 44
    Boyd, Belle, 46

Cushman, Pauline, 105–6
    Edmonds, Sarah Emma, 140
    Edmondson, Belle, 142–44
    and embellishment of accounts, 385
    gender roles in, 386
    Greenhow, Rose O'Neal, 195–97
    Phillips, Eugenia Levy, 336
    prison sentences for, 386
    Slater, Sarah Gilbert, 372–73
    Tubman, Harriet, 420
    Van Lew, Elizabeth, 435–37
    Velazquez, Loreta Janeta, 438–39
Spinner, Francis Elias, 194
Spinoza, Baruch, 226
spiritualism, 4
Spotsylvania Court House, Battle of (1864), 35,
        152
Sprague, Catherine "Kate" Chase, 464
Sprague, William, 54
Springfield Musket (newspaper), 128
Springfield Republican (newspaper), 126, 128
St. Albans, Vermont, 372
St. Anthony's Fire (disease), 213
St. Cloud Democrat (newspaper), 402, 403
St. Cloud Visiter (newspaper), 402
St. Elizabeth's Hospital, 231
St. Elmo (Evans), 156
St. Leger, Harriet, 259
St. Pierre Ruffin, Josephine, 71
Stanley, Sara G., 407
Stanton, Edwin, 89, 222, 238, 254–55, 402
Stanton, Elizabeth Cady, 22, 24, 136, 176,
        387–91, 460–61, 464, 466–67
Stanton, Ellen Hutchison, 254–55
Stanton, Henry Brewster, 389
starvation, *See* food shortages
State Hospital for the Insane, Danville,
        Pennsylvania, 124
states' rights, 364–66
Stearns, George, 419
Stebbins, Emma, 29–30, 270
Stephens, Alexander, 156
Stevens, Aaron, 329
Stevens, Thaddeus, 344–45
Still, William, 211
Stone, Kate, 367
Stone, Lucy, 133, 282, 298, 467, 471
Story of Janet Strong, The (Townsend), 278
Story of the Guard, The (Frémont), 176
Stowe, Calvin Ellis, 393

Stowe, Harriet Beecher, 146, 204, 261, 275, 276, 285, 392–97
strikes, labor, 238–39, 239, 241
Strong, George Templeton, 429
subcontractors, and sewing trades, 238, 239
substitutes, for draft, 167
suffrage, woman, *See* woman suffrage
Sumner, Charles, 79, 82, 460–61
"Sunday Law," 290
Superintendent of Female Nurses, 129
Surgeon General, 76, 130
surgery and surgeons
    at Antietam, 26–27
    and Catholic sister versus lay nurses, 76
    Dorothea Dix and, 130–31
    hospital conditions, 223
    incompetence of, 187
    Kate Cummings and, 102
    pre-war status of, 317
    surgeons' working relations with nurses, 321–22, 333
    Walker, Mary Edwards, 446–48
    women surgeons, 133
    See also amputations
Surratt, John, Jr., 398, 400
Surratt, John Harrison, 372–73, 398
Surratt, Mary, 373, 398–401
surveying, 295
Sutherland, Kate, 277
Swarthmore College, Pennsylvania, 148
Swedenborg, Emanuel, 226
Swisshelm, Jane Grey, 75, 273, 345, 399, 401–3, 456, 464
syphilis, 341
Syracuse Medical College, New York, 446

T

Taylor, Russell, 406
Taylor, Susie Baker King, 63, 90, 193, 405–7
teachers
    African-American, 92–95, 171–73, 250
    Hamilton, Gail, 208
    Larcom, Lucy, 261–66
    Taylor, Susie Baker King, 405–7
    teacher preparation, 146, 148–49, 213, 329
    wages of, 411
    women, 145–46, 205, 297

teachers of the freedpeople, 146, 193, 408–11
    abolitionists as, 2
    in contraband camps, 90–91
    Coppin, Fanny Jackson, 93
    Dickey, Sarah, 119–20
    Forten, Charlotte, 171–73
    Hawks, Esther Hill, 217
    Jacobs Free School, 250
    middle class African-American women as, 8
telegraph, 449
temperance movement, 4, 8, 22
Tennessee
    guerrilla warfare in, 199
    secession of, 363
    Union supporters in, 42–43, 105–6
Tennessee Plan, 66, 68
"Tenth of January, The" (Phelps), 237
Tepe, Marie "French Mary," 63, 183–84
Terry, Mary M. Stockton, 386
Testimony Bill (California 1863), 339
Texas, 363
textile manufacturing, 236–37, 262, 356, 383
Thanksgiving Day, 204, 205–6
Thayer, Esther, 163
theater, 256, 258
Third Alabama Hospital, 219
Thirteenth Amendment, 23, 251, 330, 390, 460–61
Thomas, George H., 356, 447
Thompson, Franklin, *See* Edmonds, Sarah Emma
Thompson, Mary Harris, 133
Thoreau, Henry David, 328
Thorn, Elizabeth Masser, 186
Three Weeks at Gettysburg (Woolsey), 185
Thrilling Adventures of Pauline Cushman, The (Cushman), 105
Todd, Mabel Loomis, 128
Todd Lincoln, Mary, *See* Lincoln, Mary Todd
Tompkins, Sally, 218, 320, 412–13
torture, 199
Towne, Laura, 409, 411
Townsend, Virginia, 278
trade unions, *See* labor organizations
training, medical, 131–34
transcendentalism, 17, 328, 330
transient population, 347
trauma of war
    girlhood and adolescence, 191–92
    guerrilla warfare, 199

military invasion, 243–45
military occupation, 247
and Sherman's March to the Sea, 368–71
Siege of Vicksburg, 441
travel, 347
Treasury Department, 194–95
treasury girls, 414–15
Treaty of Guadalupe Hidalgo, 288
Troy, New York, 241–42
Troy Collar Laundry Union, 241
Troy Female Seminary, New York, 388
Truesdail, William, 106
True Womanhood, ideal of, 400
Truth, Sojourner, 215, 416–18
Tubman, Harriet, 386, 418–21
Turchin, John Basil (Ivan Vasilivetch
    Turcheninov), 422–24
Turchin, Nadine Lvova, 64, 422–23
typhoid fever, 223, 447
typhoid pneumonia, 320

U

Uncle Tom's Cabin (Stowe), 204, 276, 285,
    392–94
Uncommon Soldier, An (Wakeman), 444
Underground Railroad, 8, 109, 211, 213, 338,
    420
Union Hotel Hospital, Washington, D.C., 18,
    20
Unionists
    Blalock, Malinda Pritchard, 41–43
    Carroll, Anna Ella, 66–68
    Cushman, Pauline, 105–6
    and guerrilla warfare, 199
    Union troops welcomed by, 247
Unitarianism, 17, 225
United Confederate Veterans, 105, 413
United Daughters of the Confederacy, 105
United States Christian Commission (USCC),
    316, 425–27
    abolitionists and, 3
    at Gettysburg, 184
    Sarah Emma Edmonds and, 141
    soldiers' aid societies and, 384
    versus United States Sanitary Commission,
        426–27, 430–31, 432

United States Sanitary Commission (USSC),
    316, 428–33, 453, 458–59
    abolitionists and, 3
    and Alcott, Louisa May, 19
    at Antietam, 27
    and Bickerdyke, Mary Ann, 39, 41
    children's contributions to, 190
    corruption in, 432
    and Dickinson, Emily, 127
    and Dix, Dorothea, 130
    and Edmonds, Sarah Emma, 141
    and Etheridge, Annie, 152
    and Frémont, Jessie Benton, 174, 176
    at Gettysburg, 184–85
    and hospital ships, 221–22
    and Livermore, Mary Ashton Rice, 279–82
    sanitary fairs and, 359–62
    soldiers' aid societies and, 384
    success of, 35
    versus United States Christian Commission,
        426–27, 430–31, 432
unity, national, 204, 205
Universalism, 281, 350
universities, *See* higher education
University of Iowa, 148
University of Wisconsin, 148, 149
Unsexed; or, The Female Soldier (Edmonds), 141,
    278
upper class
    charitable activity of, 383
    and diaries, 115
    and education, 147
    and female resistance in New Orleans, 181
    and food riots, 49–50
    refugees of, 347
    Sarah Morgan as member of, 300
    and secession, 363
    Southern women as cause of war, 367
    treasury girls, 414–15
    and United States Sanitary Commission, 430
urban areas, population of, 12
U.S. Mint, 121–22
USSC, *See* United States Sanitary Commission

V

Vance, Zebulon, 199, 326
Van Dorn, Earl, 325

Van Lew, Elizabeth, 44, 366, 386, 435–37
Vassall, Sally Barton, 34
Vassar, Matthew, 149, 206, 297
Vassar College, New York, 149, 206, 295, 297–98
Velazquez, Loreta Janeta, 292–93, 293, 438–39
venereal disease, 341
Venereal Disease Hospital, Blackwell's Island, New York, 340
veterans, *See under* soldiers
Vicksburg, Siege of (1863), 40, 65, 72, 120, 182, 351, 440–42
vigilantes, 377
Virginia, 363, 366
CSS *Virginia,* 200, 387
CSS *Virginia II,* 201
vivandière, 63
Voice from Harpers Ferry, A (Anderson), 70

W

Wade, Mary Virginia "Jenny," 183
wages
    of Confederate government workers, 414–15
    disputes over, 90, 238–42
    of government girls, 194–95
    of Mexican Americans, 288
    of nurses, 319, 320
    of prostitutes, 341
    of soldiers, 5, 270
    of teachers, 411
    withholding of blacks', 379
    women's versus men's, 194–95, 236, 237
    of women teachers, 146
    of women writers, 275, 276
"Waiting for News" (Larcom), 265
Waiting for the Verdict (R. Davis), 110
Wakeman, Sarah Rosetta (a.k.a. Lyons Wakeman), 292, 443–45
Walker, Mary Edwards, 133, 446–48
Ward, Lester, 99
Ward, Lizzie, 99
war dead, Clara Barton and identification of, 35
War Department, 194, 402, 403
Ward Howe, Julia, *See* Howe, Julia Ward
War of 1812, nuns as nurses in, 74
War Spirit at Home, The (Martin Spencer), 31
Washington, D.C.

contraband camps around, 87, 249–51, 375
    prostitution in, 341
Washington, George, 204, 205
Washington Female Seminary, Pennsylvania, 108
Washington (Greenhow), 196
Watertown State Hospital for the Insane, Illinois, 73
Watson, Agnes, 56
Webb, Emma, 464
Weichmann, Louis, 399
Weld, Angelina Grimké, 467
Welles, Cornelius, 26
Welles, Gideon, 387
Wesleyan Methodist Church, 213
West, George, 306
Western Female Seminary, Ohio, 392
Western Monthly Magazine, 392
Western Reserve College, Ohio, 470
Western Sanitary Commission, 130, 174, 221, 280, 316, 428, 429
Western Sanitary Fair (Cincinnati 1863), 361
western women, 449–57
    agricultural labor of, 14
    as businesswomen, 58
    and education, 453
    living conditions of, 450–51
    and religion, 452–53
    social life of, 452
    See also Mexican-American women; Mormon women; Mountain Charley
West Gulf Blockading Squadron, 179
West Indies, 83
Westport, Battle of (1864), 306
westward emigration, 449–57
Wheaton Seminary, Massachusetts, 263–64
Wheeler, Joseph, 370
Wheeling, West Virginia, 108–9
Whetten, Harriet, 223
Whig Party, 125, 462
whiskey, 333
White House, redecoration of, 272
Whitney, Anne, 30, 269
Whitney, Mary W., 298
Whittier, John Greenleaf, 30, 172, 261–62
"Wide-Awakes," 463
Wilberforce University, 255
Wilderness Battle of the (1864), 153
Willard, Emma Hart, 147, 388
Williamsburg, Battle of (1862), 140, 152

Willis, Cornelia Grinnel, 250
Willis, Nathaniel, 166
Willis, Sara Payson, *See* Fern, Fanny
wills, 288
Wilson, Edmund, 77
Wilson, James H., 220
Wilson, Lorenzo Madison, 156
Wise, Henry A., 82
Wister, Sarah Butler, 258
Witherow, Mary and Sally, 183
Wittenmyer, Annie Turner, 427, 430
wives
    of officers, 64
    of soldiers, *See* soldiers
Woman in Battle, The (Velazquez), 438
Woman Order, *See* General Order No. 28
Woman's Central Association of Relief
        (WCAR), 130, 132, 281–82, 317, 321,
        361, 429, 457–59
Woman's Hospital, Pennsylvania, 132
Woman's Journal, The (newspaper), 282
Woman's National Loyal League (WNLL), 2,
        23, 251, 388–89, 389–90, 460–61,
        463, 467
Woman's Relief Corps, 406
woman suffrage
    abolitionists and, 4, 391
    and Anna Ella Carroll, 68
    Frances Watkins Harper and, 212
    Harriet Tubman and, 421
    Julia Ward Howe and, 226
    Mary Ann Shadd Cary and, 71
    Mary Ashton Rice Livermore and, 282
    national associations established, 466
    in nineteenth century, 466
    Sarah Josepha Hale's opposition to, 206
    Seneca Falls Convention, 465–66
    and universal suffrage, 468
    in Utah, 305
Woman's Union Missionary Society of America
        for Heathen Lands, 350
women and politics, 462–65
    Anthony, Susan B., 24
    Carroll, Anna Ella, 66–68
    Chesnut, Mary Boykin, 77–81
    Davis, Varina Howell, 111–14
    Dickinson, Anna, 121–24
    Evans, Augusta Jane, 154–56
    Frémont, Jessie Benton, 173–77
    gender roles, 79–80

Greenhow, Rose O'Neal, 195–97
Lincoln, Mary Todd, 271–74
literature by women, 278
McCord, Louisa Cheves, 284–86
Phillips, Eugenia Levy, 335–36
and secession, 363–67
soldiers' aid societies and, 382
southern, 284
Stanton, Elizabeth Cady, 389–91
Woman's National Loyal League, 251,
        460–61
Women's Aid Society of Manchester, New
        Hampshire, 216
women's clubs, 169, 226
women's magazines, 203–7, 274–75
Women's Medical College of Pennsylvania, 132
women's rights movement, 465–68
    Anna Dickinson and, 121
    Augusta Jane Evans and, 156
    conventions for, 465–66
    Elizabeth Cady Stanton and, 387–91
    Fanny Fern on, 166, 168–69
    Gail Hamilton on, 210
    Mary Ann Shadd Cary and, 71
    men in, 466
    and New England Hospital for Women and
        Children, 133
    Susan B. Anthony and, 22, 24
    and Vinnie Ream's Congressional
        commission, 345
Wong Ah So, 234
Woodward, C. Vann, 77, 117
Woolsey, Abby, 321
Woolsey, Georgeanna, 185, 321, 322, 458
Woolsey, Jane Eliza Newton, 185
working class
    camp women from, 64
    and Catholic sister orders, 74
    and draft riots, 134–37
Working Women's Protective Union, 239
Working Women's Relief Association of
        Philadelphia, 238
Working Women's Union of New York City, 239
Works Progress Administration (WPA)
        interviews with former slaves, 9
work stoppages and slowdowns, 240
Wormeley, Katharine Prescott, 223
Wright, Martha Coffin, 391

Y

Yellin, Jean Fagan, 83
yeomanry, 12, 14
Young, Betsy, 221
Young, Brigham, 302–3, 304, 454
Young Men's Christian Association (YMCA),
    425

Z

Zakrzewska, Marie, 132–33, 133, 317, 469–72
Zenobia (Hosmer), 30
Zouaves, 63